BECOMING
JOHN DEWEY

BECOMING
JOHN DEWEY

*Dilemmas of a
Philosopher and Naturalist*

Thomas C. Dalton

INDIANA
University Press
Bloomington & Indianapolis

This book is a publication of

INDIANA UNIVERSITY PRESS
601 North Morton Street
Bloomington, IN 47404-3797 USA

http://iupress.indiana.edu

Telephone orders   800-842-6796
Fax orders   812-855-7931
Orders by e-mail   iuporder@indiana.edu

Manufactured in the United States of America

Library of Congress Cataloging-in-Publication Data

Dalton, Thomas Carlyle.
Becoming John Dewey : dilemmas of a philosopher and naturalist / Thomas C. Dalton.
p.   cm.
Includes bibliographical references and index.
ISBN 0-253-34082-9 (cloth : alk. paper)
1. Dewey, John, 1859–1952. I. Title.
B945.D44 D33 2002
191—dc21
2001006738

1 2 3 4 5   07 06 05 04 03 02

FOR LINDA DALTON
AND IN LOVING MEMORY OF
ARTHUR M. DALTON
AND
CARTER DEWEY WERTHEIM

CONTENTS

ACKNOWLEDGMENTS

ix

INTRODUCTION: ORIGINALITY IN SOCIAL CONTEXT

I

Part One: Sublime Reason and the Comforts of Doubt

ONE

From Calvinism to Evolutionism

23

TWO

Healing an "Inward Laceration"

41

THREE

Experimentalist in the Making

62

Part Two: Rendezvous with the New York Avant-Garde

FOUR

Contrasting Strategies for Educational Innovation

85

FIVE

Cultural Disillusionment

104

SIX

The Evolution of Mind in Nature

125

Part Three: The Transformational Potential of Consciousness
in Art, Politics, and Science

SEVEN

*Post-impressionism, Quantum Mechanics, and the Triumph of
Phenomenal Experience*

149

EIGHT

Communities of Intelligence and the Politics of Spirit

175

NINE

The Function of Judgment in Inquiry

199

TEN

Locomotion as a Metaphor for Mind

230

Part Four: Naturalism Lost and Found

ELEVEN

Cultural Pragmatism and the Disappearance of Dewey's Naturalism

255

CONCLUSION: THE REVIVAL OF DEWEY'S NATURALISM

278

NOTES

293

BIBLIOGRAPHY

345

INDEX

365

ACKNOWLEDGMENTS

There is a large and growing body of scholarship on John Dewey involving philosophers, historians, psychologists, and other disciplinary orientations. The Center for Dewey Studies at Southern Illinois University continually catalogues and updates this scholarly literature on their web site, and also hosts visiting researchers. The Center has completed the publication of the collected works (which are also available on compact disc) and is now in the process of completing forthcoming volumes of Dewey's correspondence. I have conducted research at the Center on three different occasions in the past seven years. During these visits, I have consulted the enormous archive of unpublished manuscripts and correspondence that is housed in the Special Collections of Morris Library at Southern Illinois University at Carbondale. I owe a large debt to Center director Larry Hickman and his staff for making these visits exciting and intellectually rewarding. A complete listing of archive sources is found in the bibliography.

I would also like to express my gratitude to several other persons who provided information that proved to be enormously useful in reconstructing Dewey's activities and relationships with the Neurological Institute of New York, Babies Hospital, and the College of Physicians and Surgeons of Presbyterian Hospital, Columbia University. Dr. Lewis P. Rowland, former director of the Neurological Institute, furnished important personal contacts with persons affiliated with the institute in the 1930s. Dr. Lawrence Pool shared with me his published history of the Neurological Institute and also made it possible for me to contact other colleagues who worked at the Neurological Institute several decades ago. Michael Meyer, Director of the Records and Archives of Presbyterian Hospital, generously assisted me in obtaining minutes and correspondence pertaining to the Neurological Institute. Dr. William Damrosch shared his recollections of Babies Hospital during the 1930s and loaned me a rare published history of the professional accomplishments of the hospital medical staff. Dr. Ronald Oppenheim, a neurobiologist at Wake Forest Medical School, furnished me copies of letters he exchanged with Myrtle McGraw in the 1970s and 1980s that were crucial in establishing Dewey's personal relationship with scientists who worked with McGraw in her experimental infant studies.

In addition, Melissa Smith, an archivist with the Rockefeller Archive Center in Tarrytown, New York, and Patricia Haynes, of the Carnegie Corporation of New York, each helped me locate an impressive number of files from their respective archives. These records contained reports and correspondence relating to grants that supported infant studies conducted by many pioneering researchers, including McGraw and her colleagues. I would also like to express my thanks to Alexandra Mason, former curator of the Spencer Research Library at the University of Kansas, who provided valuable assistance in finding useful information in their neurology collection regarding John Dewey's relationship to C. J. Herrick and other neurologists. Janice Stone and her staff with the Interlibrary Loan Division of Kennedy Library at Cal Poly State University helped me obtain many rare books and articles that were indispensable to me in the course of my research. It is fitting that my book will be published during Cal Poly's centennial celebration, as the university has been guided by Dewey's "learn by doing" philosophy ever since its founding. Special thanks are owed to Dan Howard-Green, executive assistant to the president, for his support and intellectual companionship.

Special thanks are also due to David Ment, Director of Special Collections of Millbank Memorial Library, Teachers College, whose archive containing the records of Lucy Sprague Mitchell and the Bank Street School proved to be enormously helpful in tracing Dewey's involvement in experimental education during his years at Columbia University. Bernard Crystal, Curator of Rare Books and Manuscripts, and his staff at Butler Library, Columbia University, provided valuable assistance in locating information regarding Randolph Bourne and other Dewey acquaintances in New York. Peter Hirtle, former curator of the History of Medicines Division of the National Library of Medicine, helped me obtain documents from Milton Senn and Lawrence K. Frank, papers that revealed Dewey's broad influence among psychologists. Frank's wife, Mary Perry, also provided useful information. Father Omer Kline of St. Vincents College generously assisted me in reviewing the records of Fr. Eric McCormack that shed much-needed light on Dewey's relationship with F. M. Alexander. Special thanks are also due to the late pioneering psychologists Lois Murphy and Tao Abel for their recollections and broad historical perspective.

Completing a project of this magnitude would have been difficult without the support and kindness of many friends and colleagues. I am grateful for their help. I am particularly indebted to Mitzi Wertheim, Myrtle McGraw's daughter, and Victor Bergenn, McGraw's colleague during her later years at Briarcliff College in the late 1960s and early 1970s. They graciously provided access to McGraw's correspondence and other papers, which illuminate her remarkable relationship and collaboration with John Dewey and the extensive network of scientists who knew Dewey and were involved in McGraw's research. Victor has subsequently co-authored with me several journal articles and a book that documents Dewey's role as McGraw's mentor and collaborator. I admire Victor's intellectual integrity and greatly value his advice and friendship. I would also like to thank Brown University psychologist Lewis Lipsitt, who was McGraw's close friend and colleague in her later years, for his fascinating recollection of their relationship. Lew helped McGraw to publish her memoirs, which led to a revival of interest in her work among contemporary developmental psychologists.

Acknowledgments

I am forever grateful to Gerard Piel, founding publisher of *Scientific American*, for recounting for me his fascinating friendship with Myrtle McGraw. Piel's first assignment as a science reporter with *Life* magazine in 1939 was an interview with McGraw, whom he acknowledged as having inspired him to invent a magazine that would make scientific knowledge accessible and comprehensible to the public.

I have accumulated many intellectual debts during the course of writing this book. I have benefited greatly from the many stimulating conversations I have had with my close friend and colleague Gilbert Gottlieb. He read the entire manuscript, provided numerous suggestions, and gave me the benefit of his wisdom as a pioneering scientist, respected developmental theorist, and consummate historian. Sheldon White commented on previous journal articles and read earlier drafts of this book. He contributed important insights about Dewey's influence in the field of developmental psychology and beyond. As a fellow scholar of pragmatist thought, George Cotkin has had a continuous and formidable intellectual presence throughout my endeavor. I am very lucky to have had the benefit of his counsel. Bernard Baars enabled me to better understand the similarities and crucial differences between Williams James's and Dewey's conceptions of mind. Ernest Sternglass read and commented helpfully on chapters in which I discussed Dewey's perspectives on Maxwell, Boltzmann, and the debate over quantum mechanics. Finally, I am very grateful to Gerald Edelman for his generous invitation to do research as a visiting fellow at The Neurosciences Institute, research that had a bearing on this intellectual biography. Not only has he created an exceptional organization for scientific inquiry, but he has also fostered an environment that encourages reflection about the history of the science and the philosophy of mind.

I experienced difficulty in trying to publish in academic journals the results of my preliminary research on Dewey's extensive connections in the scientific community. However, I persisted, gathered additional evidence, and was finally able to persuade Nicholas Jardine, editor of *Studies in History and Philosophy of Science*, a Cambridge University journal, of the merit of my work. I would also like to thank Keith Sutherland and Anthony Freeman of the *Journal of Consciousness Studies* for publishing a recent article in which I argue for the pertinence of Dewey and McGraw's emergent conception of consciousness to the contemporary sciences of mind.

I had the very good fortune of working with Dee Mortensen, sponsoring editor for Indiana University Press. Dee is a superb editor with a gift for envisioning a work in its entirety. She patiently worked with me to ensure that I found ways to best characterize and express the conclusions that can be drawn from this study of Dewey's personal and intellectual development. This has been a delightful and rewarding experience.

I dedicate this book to my wife Linda, whose courage in times of adversity and boundless support throughout my many years spent on this project continue to inspire me and deepen my respect and affection for her.

BECOMING
JOHN DEWEY

Introduction
Originality in Social Context

RECONSTRUCTING DEWEY'S FORMATIVE EXPERIENCES

Over the past decade there has been a resurgence of interest in American pragmatism and the works of its principal founders Charles Peirce, William James,
and John Dewey. Dewey is best known among the general public for his experiential approach to education expressed by the motto "learn by doing." But the
philosophical and scientific roots of his theories about mind and inquiry remain shrouded in mystery. The interdisciplinary character of Dewey's ideas
has attracted commentators from several academic fields who bring different
perspectives to bear on Dewey's works. While this burgeoning scholarship has
produced many new insights, rarely do we learn something previously unknown about Dewey's life that puts his ideas in a new light.

Historians and philosophers interested in Dewey's intellectual development
have not given sufficient weight to Dewey's assertion in his 1930 autobiographical statement that "upon the whole, the forces that have influenced me have
come from persons and from situations more than from books."[1] The scholarship on Dewey is replete with detailed analyses that trace his philosophical
ideas from one book to the next. However, we rarely learn how Dewey's personal acquaintances contributed to the further elaboration of themes central to
his conceptions of mind and experience and the role of science in society. This
intellectual biography describes the details of these formative experiences and
pieces together the network of Dewey's acquaintances that provided the scientific methods and aesthetic perspectives with which Dewey undertook his
pragmatist project of reconstructing the processes of inquiry.[2]

Writing an intellectual biography that attempts to account for the genius,
originality, or other unique attributes of any great thinker without the slightest
acknowledgment of the environment in which these talents were nurtured and
developed would be unthinkable. As George Cotkin, William James's intellec-

tual biographer, points out, while James acknowledged that "the environment did not create the individual of genius," James admitted that the environment did play a substantial role "in determining whether the individual of genius would thrive or perish."[3] Genius probably has more to do with the persistence, resilience, and adaptability of a body of ideas than with their origination. In his penetrating psychological studies of some of the world's most influential historical thinkers in the arts, science, and politics, Howard Gardner singles out several recurring social factors beyond individual control which support creativity, such as a supportive family, strong mentors, helpful collaborators, and other favorable social or collegial conditions.[4]

That is why this intellectual biography is concerned not merely with singling out those unique gifts of mind and character that account for that person's originality. Such a task also involves explaining how novel ideas are developed, circulated, appropriated, defended, and sometimes misinterpreted through interpersonal and institutional processes of intellectual exchange. This requires reconstructing the social and professional domains and the experiential and communicative processes that favor originality and that ensure the continuity of a body of ideas over time. Individuals intent on making truly important breakthroughs must be willing to challenge conventional ideas, cross domains, and be prepared to endure a sometimes prolonged status as a pariah figure at the margins of a chosen field of knowledge or practice. In this sense, original minds have much in common with political reformers. Intellectual pioneers attract adherents who zealously embrace their new way of thinking but whose allegiance falters when key theoretical premises are disputed. That is why I have chosen in this book to put John Dewey's life and work within a longer time period that enables a clearer understanding of how central themes in his work have evolved, attracted criticism, and undergone revision over time.

Despite his public recognition as a celebrated figure in American thought and culture, Dewey remains an enigma. Dewey's career as a public philosopher who zealously advocated and supported reforms of political, economic, and educational institutions is well-documented. Yet the processes through which Dewey brought science to bear on these issues remain shrouded in mystery. One important goal of this book is to show that Dewey derived many of his ideas about learning and the development of mind and consciousness from personal experiences, involving scientific research and aesthetic analyses, that have gone unreported in other Dewey biographies. Dewey's ideas were not immaculately conceived but emerged from a collaborative exchange of ideas and interpersonal experiences that he synthesized into a systematic theory of mind saturated with insight.

In the 1930s, Dewey had advised and worked with infant experimentalist Myrtle McGraw in her studies of motor development. This significant episode revealed Dewey's acquaintance with numerous scientists whose ideas played a significant role in his thinking about the relation between mind, brain, and behavior. These scientists, who were also involved in McGraw's research, helped Dewey to fathom the origins and functions of mind and judgment in ontogeny, a problem of fundamental importance to Dewey's *Logic: The Theory of Inquiry,* published in 1938.

Dewey had numerous other intellectual acquaintances throughout his career that have gone undocumented in the Dewey scholarship. For example, F. M. Alexander, an iconoclastic evolutionary theorist and physical therapist, provided Dewey with insights about the states of consciousness underlying his own intellectually significant experiences. Dewey's acquaintance with art patron Albert Barnes enabled Dewey to gain personal access to the thoughts and experiences of Henri Matisse, one of the foremost exponents of post-impressionism, whose ideas about aesthetics found their way into Dewey's book *Art as Experience* in 1934. Dewey's close association with Rockefeller Foundation officer Lawrence Frank bears close scrutiny because Frank created a university- and community-based network of child study institutes that embodied the relationship Dewey conceived between the practice of science and democratic communities.

The Dewey archive of unpublished manuscripts, correspondence, and interviews has been consulted sparingly by scholars, leaving untouched an enormous resource that provides significant new details about Dewey's scientific acquaintances and experiences. This book rectifies this oversight by drawing from original documents obtained from numerous university and foundation archives that possess information about Dewey, his colleagues and acquaintances. Through correspondence and interviews, diaries, unpublished manuscripts, and other documents, this new information about how Dewey used science and his knowledge of politics and the arts to understand the role of consciousness in human judgment and inquiry was pieced together.[5]

Another key objective of this book is to challenge the widespread but mistaken belief among Dewey scholars and psychologists that Dewey largely abandoned his interest in psychology after the turn of the twentieth century. It is often forgotten that Dewey was elected president of the American Psychological Association (1899) *before* his election to the presidency of the American Philosophical Association in 1905. Dewey's involvement in child development research did not end at the Laboratory School at the University of Chicago. He had two other opportunities to become personally involved in experimental research involving infants and young children long after he moved to Columbia University in 1904. These poorly understood episodes indicate that Dewey continued to gather and interpret scientific evidence that had a direct bearing on the validity of hypotheses supporting his theories of mind and inquiry. This research led Dewey to reformulate his conception of inquiry in *Logic* to better reflect the facts about how infants and children develop their powers of judgment.

The conventional wisdom that Dewey's early infatuation with Hegel ended by the turn of the century has discouraged an important line of inquiry.[6] Dewey's Hegelianism was not a temporary sojourn, as some philosophers have argued, but formed an essential core of Dewey's lifelong endeavor to reformulate, in metaphysical and scientific terms, the idealistic premises of nineteenth-century *Naturphilosophie*.[7] Dewey shared Hegel's concern that splitting apart the fields of philosophy, natural science, and psychology at the turn of the twentieth century had been mistaken.[8] Dewey believed that Hegel illuminated the pathway through which these fields could be reunited. I rectify this underestimation of Hegel's continuing influence by drawing on unpublished manuscripts and lecture notes which indicate that early on, Dewey simply transformed the Hegelian dialectics of being and becoming into psychological terms involving the relationship between human growth and the development of judgment through inquiry. He subsequently collaborated with Myrtle McGraw in the 1930s in her experimental studies to test his theory about the integrated nature of inquiry.

Becoming John Dewey attempts to strike a balance between presenting useful personal details and addressing larger philosophical and scientific issues pertinent to a proper appreciation of Dewey's contribution to American thought and culture. Consequently, a series of books and articles by Dewey that represent important milestones in his intellectual development has been assembled, as has been done by other biographers. The scientific origins of Dewey's conceptions of mind and consciousness have been brought into sharper relief to better illuminate their underlying naturalism. These writings have also been located in the broader historical and intellectual currents and experiential contexts in which they emerged. Dewey's ideas were appropriated to become the common possession of American culture *long before* he had completed his thinking on key issues. His ideas have in this book been disentangled from their many appropriations, and the intellectual and experiential pathways that led to the subsequent refinement of his ideas in his mature writings have been traced.

Becoming John Dewey also will appeal to students and scholars who are interested in the history of American political thought. Recent intellectual biographies by Robert Westbrook and Alan Ryan, for example, focus on Dewey's pre-eminence as a political philosopher. They examine the ideas and episodes that highlight Dewey's contribution to the politics of democratic reform, humanism, and liberalism.[9] These authors thoughtfully use Dewey's highly visible profile as a public philosopher and reformer as a lens through which to focus the disparate elements of Dewey's philosophical ideas into an integrated and coherent whole. Some recent commentators, however, such as John Diggins in *The Promise of Pragmatism: Modernism and the Crisis of Knowledge and Authority*, have underscored the shortcomings of pragmatist philosophy and politics. Diggins contends that because Dewey furnished no reason to believe in the certainty of our judgments or ideas, he failed to overcome the rift between knowledge and authority wrought by politics in modernity. But Dewey believed that the justification of political authority in a democratic state has less to do with the possession of certain knowledge than with how well the resources of intelligence are distributed and whether there are opportunities for the exercise of independent judgment and the accumulation of experience. The child study movement that Dewey inspired pursued these aims in the attempt to engage parents and communities in the development of effective child-rearing strategies. This analysis supports a more positive assessment of the democratic aims and accomplishments of these initiatives than that offered by Diggins or Hamilton Cravens in his book *Before Head Start: The Iowa Welfare Research Station and America's Children* (1994).

This book also traces the interpretive fault lines along which Dewey's students and a second generation of scholars have become divided about his conceptions of science and naturalism. I discuss why they have become preoccupied with discursive and epistemological issues at the periphery of pragmatism's central concerns. This analysis will be of interest to philosophers and scholars in the humanities who have closely followed the debates about postmodernism centered on Richard Rorty's controversial views about Dewey's pragmatism found in *The Consequences of Pragmatism* and more recent collections of his works. The last chapter delves into this debate in some detail, challenging Rorty's wayward notion that Dewey's interests in science and logic were mistaken and should not be viewed as indispensable to the future of pragmatism.

FORGING COALITIONS OF MINDS THROUGH COLLABORATION

Dewey's intellectual leadership of American pragmatism was made possible by his willingness to learn from his predecessors and to let go of his ideas when they needed further development. Dewey continually prospected in history for forgotten but intellectually precious ideas with which to comprehend the present and anticipate future events. He reached out to make new acquaintances and hear new ideas, while finding intellectual renewal in predecessors whose ideas had withstood the ravages of time and disfavor. He was generous in dispensing advice and lending his unassuming but enormous intellect to his students and colleagues in the form of provocative suggestions that enlarged their imaginations and minds. Dewey's students redeemed his investment in their minds by finding a currency in which Dewey's best insights could be exchanged and converted into personal experiences and social experiments of incalculably greater purchase and value. He was a consummate collaborator who adopted a multidisciplinary perspective that acknowledged no disciplinary or professional boundaries to knowledge. He sought new experiences when his ideas ran up against the limits of science, but he also strove to reconcile opposing ways of interpreting an existing body of ideas.

Dewey disavowed that he ever attempted to attract disciples, although he had a considerable following among his former graduate students. Dewey naturally attracted like-minded people, but he was equally adept at mediating between those who held opposing positions in an attempt to find common ground.

As Sidney Hook, one of Dewey's students and close friends, recalled, Dewey really never attempted to dominate his student's thinking. In fact, Morris Cohen, a University of Chicago professor, once complained to Hook that Dewey's fault was that he "contributed to the intellectual delinquency of his students."[10] An unfortunate consequence of Dewey's laissez-faire attitude toward creative thinking, Hook observed, was that Dewey tended to "rely on other thinkers to interpret his work," which sometimes served him well, but also caused him considerable disappointment and, sometimes, personal grief.[11]

Dewey had the uncanny ability to circulate his ideas through the minds of numerous acquaintances before retrieving and reassembling them in a more nuanced form than they would have taken if they had remained in his own mind. Dewey believed, like Hegel, that self-consciousness about methods of inquiry increases scientists' ability to anticipate the unexpected and make new discoveries about nature. Dewey learned how to use his own consciousness and his knowledge of other minds as instruments of inquiry, reaching with occasional success for the highest chords that resonated beyond the limitations of personal bias.

Dewey's apparent indifference to the boundaries of professional roles and institutional structures, which stood in the way of his boundless quest to use science to reconstruct society, was one of his greatest strengths as well as one of his liabilities. Like an actor improvising his lines to convey more simply his character's true nature and aspirations, Dewey started as a philosopher conversant in the esoteric discourse of Hegelian dialectics, but he soon became a celebrated leader of a national movement for educational reform whose simple motto was "learn by doing." When Dewey realized that further progress on this front was impeded by the lack of reliable information about how learning is affected by development, he became personally involved in the conduct of scientific inquiries performed to reveal the hidden drama of biological growth. Dewey also played a philanthropic role as a trustee of a foundation, which contributed to the funding of an international network of child study institutes patterned from the script he wrote for a democratic polity.

In these significant respects, then, Dewey was a bookish academic who seemed equally adept at writing dense philosophical tomes, overseeing laboratory studies, swaying the consciences of corporate elites, and being a public intellectual speaking out for social values, which occupied the center stage of American culture. Through these roles Dewey engaged in a continual process of *becoming* someone whose horizons never ended, whose ideas were forever undergoing further development and dispersal, and whose impact on American thought and culture endures without end.

DEWEY'S DILEMMAS WITH SCIENCE IN MODERNITY

Dewey faced extraordinary dilemmas, however, in his ambitious quest to bring science and personal experience to bear on his metaphysics of mind and nature.

He sought to demonstrate that mind and human experience are not idiosyncratic and subjective but objective phenomena that can be understood scientifically. This was a daunting task during an era in which introspective psychology was discredited and the behaviorist revolution had dismissed consciousness as an uninteresting epiphenomenon of human experience. Dewey believed that scientists and philosophers were forever losing sight of the fact that humans possess brains and minds whose structures and functions have evolved over thousands of years, and that human intelligence is the product of countless historical developmental experiences. Dewey stubbornly resisted the modern trends toward materialism and reductionism in science and logical formalism and epistemological realism in philosophy, which threatened to erase human awareness of the naturalistic origins of mind.

Dewey sought to avoid the methodological dilemmas of mind-body dualism and reductionism that caused William James to vacillate between mentalism and physicalism—between viewing all psychological processes as forms of conscious experience and reducing consciousness to the orchestration of neural processes. As Baars observes, these incompatible claims prevented James from laying "a clear and simple foundation for psychological science."[12] Dewey conceived of mind not only as involving the interaction of brain and behavior within one individual but as a process of mutual engagement or reflection among individuals involved in common experiences. He believed that the phenomenon of consciousness could be better understood by focusing on experiences involving uncertain judgments about values and consequences that implicated more than just one person and one mind. These circumstances favored the suspension of belief, shared perceptions, and mutual problem solving. This captured the essentially interpersonal basis of knowing and the known.

To succeed in his endeavor to render the mind intelligible through nature, Dewey had to demonstrate how propositional knowledge (i.e., warranted assertable truths) involving inference and generalization is governed by experiential conditions and methods generated in the act of inquiry. By pursuing this ambitious quest, he assumed an unenviable burden of convincing his skeptical colleagues that their search for timeless truths and logical first principles was futile, and that the advancement of society and civilization depended less on the accumulation of knowledge than on the enlargement of experience. Dewey's closest students were divided about how to retain a central place for his naturalism and experimentalism within a discipline undergoing a positivist and analytical purge of metaphysics. Subsequent efforts by a second and third generation of philosophers to rescue Dewey's politics and ethics from the clutches of post-modern relativism and nihilism remain inconclusive because they have failed to acknowledge the fundamental importance of Dewey's naturalism in reconstituting the relationship between science and American culture.

Dewey was confronted with difficult dilemmas in his attempt to distance himself intellectually from the zeitgeist of an era bent on specialization and the compartmentalization of knowledge. He was engaging as a participant in the institutional and political forces that would profoundly alter how science is conducted and how American society and culture would undergo the pressures of modernity. He believed that the future of the natural and social sciences could be best secured if their practitioners adopted an interdisciplinary perspective, employed experimental methods of inquiry, and anticipated the potential applications and public consequences of their discoveries. He never wavered in his belief that science was a public possession whose methods could and should be enlisted in the service of human judgment and well-being. Straddling the uncertain territory between discovery and invention, between application and advocacy, Dewey struggled to attain the psychological distance needed to perceive a situation from different perspectives, as a participant and as an observer, to better understand how separate factors, only dimly comprehended in their immediacy, interacted to contribute to a general understanding of a phenomenon as a whole. But Dewey's high-wire act of striking an effective balance on the psychological tightrope between engagement and detachment sometimes brought him down in a free fall of personal grief and political torment.

RECONSIDERING DEWEY'S HEGELIANISM

Dewey recalled in his autobiography that Hegel "left a permanent deposit" in his thinking, and noted that when Hegel's ideas were "taken out of their mechanical dialectical setting," they possessed an "extraordinary depth" and an "extraordinary acuteness."[13] Dewey acknowledged that Hegel's method healed an "inward laceration" by helping him overcome the "sense of divisions and separations" inculcated by his evangelical New England upbringing, between mind and body, nature and spirit, that contributed to the growing gulf between philosophy and science.[14] Dewey's youthful soul-searching gave way to a concerted effort to understand how the behavioral and emotional antecedents of a self-conscious and a morally reflective life could be acquired without having to undergo the torturous Calvinist confession of sin in exchange for redemption. Hegel appeared to offer a way out of this morass by connecting mind and spirit through nature. Dewey's doctoral studies with Charles Morris at Johns Hopkins University, whose influence continued during his years at the University of Michigan, reinforced Dewey's enchantment with Hegel. But Dewey's Hegelian-inspired textbook *Psychology* failed to gain the approval and admiration that Dewey anxiously sought from his pragmatist co-inventors Charles Peirce and James.

Hegel furnished Dewey the key that he sought to unravel the mysteries of mind and spirit, and to show how they contributed to the integrity and continuity of human experience. Hegel envisioned an underlying unity in science, morals, and artistic expression that Dewey believed he could demonstrate through concrete experience. Nevertheless, Dewey doubted whether Hegel's belief that nature and mind are predicated on indisputable truths revealed by

Spirit was realistic. Dewey undertook a critical deconstruction of Hegelian dialectics, during which time he discarded Hegel's idealism and absolutism while finding a way to retain his insights about logic by grounding them in contemporary scientific theories. Dewey's deconstruction of Hegel was dedicated to the propositions that science, aesthetics, and ethics involve essentially the same processes of exercising human judgment under conditions of uncertainty, and that quantitative and qualitative values are intertwined in every act of moral commitment, aesthetic expression, and scientific generalization.

THE METAPHYSICS OF SCIENTIFIC NATURALISM

A distinctive feature of Dewey's pragmatism is its evolutionary naturalism.[15] While Dewey's familiarity with Darwin and Huxley's views is evident, until now little was known about Dewey's continuing interest in *Naturphilosophie* beyond its most conspicuous nineteenth-century exponents such as Schelling, Schopenhauer, Fichte, and Hegel. Yet Dewey explicitly cited the works of several other scientists and theorists such as Herbert Spencer who, he believed, were "reinstating a philosophy of nature in connection with the idea of evolution, rather than spirit."[16] Dewey was familiar with the classical origins of naturalism in which nature was personified as the force or power possessed by gods or deities. Aristotle recast nature in teleological terms, contending that matter was infused with purpose whose final form and function emerged through development. Kant reduced mind and nature to a limited number of constitutive principles about force, space, time, judgment, and human identity. Hegel took a significant step in opposition to Kant by attempting to eliminate the break between mind and experience and show that nature furnishes the field in which Spirit is realized through the development of self-consciousness.[17]

In *American Philosophical Naturalism in the Twentieth Century,* John Ryder makes the case that American naturalism has common roots in Spinoza, Descartes, and Darwinian evolution. But by failing to mention Hegel and German *Naturphilosophie,* Ryder leaves out an important antecedent to American philosophical naturalism that included W. T. Harris and the St. Louis Hegelians, who strongly influenced Dewey and many others. Ryder argues instead that Dewey had stronger intellectual ties with the naturalism expounded by his Columbia colleagues that included Frederick Woodbridge and Ernest Nagel and Harvard philosopher George Santayana. Ryder contends that American philosophers shared several assumptions about naturalism that made it a distinctive school of thought. My impression is that Dewey would take exception to just about all of them, such as the idea that there is an "objective reality," that "science is a model for all inquiry," and that naturalists need not be concerned with the role of reflective self-consciousness in guiding inquiry.[18]

Dewey clearly repudiated epistemological realism, although he saw a need for science to strive for objectivity. But Dewey's notion of inquiry was not patterned exclusively after science. Dewey's experimentalism embodied the kind of practical judgments that need to be made about the contingencies of order, sequence, proportionality, comparison, and measurement that are required to draw inferences or to establish connections between phenomena regardless of the domain in which they occur. So it would be mistaken to equate Dewey's experimentalism with science or even with scientific method. In fact, Dewey dedicated his life to changing how science was practiced, which explains why he was not comfortable with those who accused his naturalism of being "materialistic" and who condemned his experimentalism for being "scientistic."

Dewey clearly took strong exception to the view that *self-consciousness* must be excluded as an object of inquiry. To the contrary, the methodological point of departure for Dewey's psychological naturalism requires an accurate assessment, at the outset, of attitudes and perspectives that tend to bias or push inquiry in one direction rather than another. Dewey adhered throughout his career to the Hegelian-inspired idea that inquiry is propelled forward by the desire to understand the origins and functions of human thought and consciousness, long after Dewey's philosophical contemporaries discarded this as outmoded introspectionism. Nowhere is this more evident than in Dewey's skirmishes with Santayana. Santayana contended that Dewey was a "presentist" who was only concerned with the "foreground" of perception and consciousness in experience.[19] However, Dewey also gave equal weight to the "background" (i.e., the larger field of events in which mind is situated). These differences will be brought out more clearly in the later chapters.

Hegel's idealism and *Naturphilosophie* fell into disfavor by the turn of the century. Undaunted, Dewey continued to follow the work of scientists who he believed were committed to a non-teleological and non-reductionist naturalism, and who continued to view human biological development within a holistic and interactionist perspective. Among this group Dewey included British paleontologists Thomas Huxley, John Fisk, and Edward Cope, and several German scientists that included psychophysiologists Hermann Lotze, Gustave Fechner, and Wilhem Wundt, biochemist Wilhelm Ostwald, and physicist Ernst Mach.[20] Importantly, Huxley's unflinching support of Darwinian evolution but his doubts about natural selection strengthened Dewey's resolve that an alternative to Darwin's environmental theory of adaptation could be advanced if evidence could be provided for the reciprocal modification of structures and functions in early development. Dewey found very informative the highly publicized and rancorous debates about evolution among Darwin, Huxley, and Samuel Butler. Their provocative but inconclusive arguments inspired Dewey to propose highly original but poorly understood alternative principles to the mechanisms of competition and scarcity to account for how species undergo biologically adapted change.

Dewey also closely followed and cleverly synthesized studies by leading experimental psychologists and physicists who were interested in the neural or energetic basis of perception. Wundt's studies furnished Dewey with important insights about the fundamental role of neural inhibition in human behavior, while Mach made crucial connections between sensorimotor control and perception. Ostwald and his successors rejected the materialist trend in physics and biology, focusing instead on the energetic processes in which matter and life undergo continuous transformation. Michael Faraday's discovery of the field properties of force and Maxwell's demonstration that force is converted into alternative forms of potential and kinetic energy contributed to fundamental breakthroughs in Dewey's thinking. Their work enabled Dewey to conceive of mind and consciousness and the processes of inquiry in terms of common energetic processes whereby human thought and behavior were essentially intertwined through experience.

RECONSTRUCTION IN PHILOSOPHY AND EDUCATION

Dewey cultivated professional acquaintances early in his career at the University of Chicago, and later at Columbia University, with scientists in the newly emerging life sciences, many of whom shared his interest in reformulating and carrying forward the aims of *Naturphilosophie*. Dewey knew personally several prominent leaders of the so-called "American School" of neurology, that included the psychiatrist Adolf Meyer, naturalists and neurologists C. L. Herrick and his brother C. J. Herrick. Other colleagues included physiologist C. M. Child, experimental biologist Jacques Loeb, neurobiologist Henry Donaldson, neuroanatomist George Coghill, and paleoneurologist Frederick Tilney. Dewey dedicated his brief years at Chicago to absorbing and synthesizing available knowledge about the nervous system and attempting to put this knowledge to work in a Laboratory School he headed. He wanted to demonstrate how the principles of early growth and psychological development can be incorporated into learning processes. Unfortunately for Dewey, the battle lines about how mind and emotion evolved were already well-drawn before *Studies in Logical Theory* was published in 1903. Dewey dedicated much of his intellectual energy to writing highly original essays that challenged his contemporaries' thinking about evolution. But in *Studies*, Dewey introduced wholly new ideas about the relation between the sequence of development and pattern of inquiry whose connection to his previous observational studies was left unspecified.

Given his growing stature as a pre-eminent American philosopher and educational innovator, it did not take Dewey long to obtain a new academic appointment at Columbia University in 1904, where he resumed his involvement in experimental studies of early growth and development. Dewey's involvement, including that of his daughter Evelyn and several of his Columbia colleagues, in Lucy and Wesley Mitchell's educational innovations invites closer inspection because this furnished Dewey a second but little-known opportunity to examine the scientific relationship between learning and development. During this time, Dewey, the Mitchells, and many of their colleagues became acquainted with Frederick Matthias Alexander, an Australian actor. He boasted of having perfected a method of breaking subconscious habits by rendering within conscious control the inhibitory mechanisms controlling neuromuscular processes. Alexander's subsequent entanglement in Lucy and Wesley Mitchell's educational experiments, his precarious management of a burgeoning number of Dewey colleagues seeking treatment and training in his techniques, his deepening intellectual involvement with Dewey, and the growing pressures to submit his methods to scientific study contributed to Dewey's woes.

FREUDIANISM AND THE CULTURAL CRITIQUE OF DEWEY'S PRAGMATISM

Dewey's dilemmas in endorsing ideas and schemes hatched by close friends like Alexander threatened to compromise his personal and intellectual integrity. Dewey's informal apprenticeship with Albert Barnes, a physician, chemical industry magnate, and controversial post-impressionist art collector, posed similar tensions. Barnes leaned heavily on Dewey to support and to rescue his private museum from public condemnation and castigation by art critics for its unusually elitist approach to art education. Dewey's nemesis Randolph Bourne seized upon Dewey's seemingly uncritical endorsement of Alexander's ideas, among other alleged pragmatist blind spots and sins of omission such as Dewey's support for American involvement in World War I, to discredit Dewey and offer a more radical Nietzschean vision for social change. Dewey's condemnation by some of his former disciples cost him dearly and forced him to publicly defend his own integrity and to refute claims that his philosophical ideas were morally incoherent.

Much of Dewey's intellectual capital and energy was depleted during the latter part of his second decade at Columbia University. Dewey attempted to persuade his colleagues and avant-garde followers that human experience was shaped not only by culture and technology but by natural, biological phenomena that could be understood scientifically. By this time, of course, Freudian ideas had already gained a strong foothold in American consciousness. In 1922 Dewey published an inspirational but polemical book, *Human Nature and Conduct,* in an attempt to persuade educators and psychologists that biology was not destiny and that our development was open-ended and not a predestined tragedy. This was easily the most agonizing and frustrating period of his career, one which challenged Dewey to summon the inner resources needed to move forward against the rising tide of events rapidly reshaping American thought and culture. Dewey responded by seeking safe refuge in the protected harbor of science, where he could anchor his naturalism and social psychology in the metaphysics of mind.

The striking advances Dewey witnessed in the biological sciences and their contribution to knowledge about the evolution and functions of the brain stirred Dewey to attempt one of his most ambitious works in *Experience and*

Nature in 1925. Alexander's extended discussions of the evolution of consciousness and his criticisms of the failures of modern science to improve human well-being also contributed to Dewey's sense of urgency that human progress was not a foregone conclusion.[21] He worried that therapeutic psychologies such as Freudian psychoanalysis had mistakenly reduced human motivation to basic instinctual impulses, denying that humans possessed the control over their minds needed to consciously adopt moral and cultural values. Dewey's tacit but critical dialogue with Freud reflects their very different views about the value of science and ethics as tools to investigate the mind. Their differences are all the more extraordinary given that they pursued their scientific interest in the nervous system and brain along parallel pathways. Their professional interaction with shared acquaintances diverged when Freud abruptly dropped further attempts to establish solid neuroscientific evidence to support his theory of the unconscious mind.

THE METAPHYSICS OF MIND IN NATURE

Experience and Nature constitutes Dewey's most ambitious attempt to explain how human experience is grounded in nature. This work reflects Dewey's complete absorption with mind and consciousness in nature, and it significantly parallels the themes Hegel presents in the *Phenomenology of Spirit*. Dewey acknowledged in *Experience and Nature* that it may never be possible to recover the meaning of the terms "soul" and "spirit" in science, but he says the "realities are there by whatever names they are called." He added that "Spirit quickens; it is not only alive, but spirit gives life. Soul is form, spirit informs. It is the moving function of that of which souls is the substance."[22] However, Dewey pursued a different approach than Hegel. He did not try to show how consciousness realizes Spirit by comprehending and reconciling the contingencies of nature through ideas. Instead, he speculated about how mind and consciousness evolved from and find ultimate expression in nature by the continuous conversion of natural and social contingencies of life into new possibilities for intelligent action. Spirit is not an end state or absolute, but it mediates or brings about the integral but continuously evolving relationship between mind and nature.

In advancing these arguments, Dewey introduced the term "generic traits" to denote universal attributes or powers of nature that are shared by all life forms governed by biological processes of growth and development. Generic traits contributed, through their interaction and embodiment in our mind and behavior, toward the production of values, which, over time, bias and reshape human neurobiological structures. Examples of such traits include those involved in physical phenomena (e.g., force, gravity, energy, motion, space, and time); bodies (e.g., sentience, gesture, and behavior); and mind (e.g., communication, meaning, memory, and significance). Dewey's conception of "generic traits" has become one of the most misunderstood and controversial elements of his metaphysics of mind in the scholarly literature on Dewey. He deserves some of the blame for not making his conception clear. But it is apparent that he continued to seek evidence from ethics, aesthetics, and science that would demonstrate that these attributes of living things have assumed different forms in the course of evolution. These traits invest human experience with its peculiar phenomenal qualities that contribute to the uniqueness of individual perception and identity, while also making possible a shared existence.

THE PHENOMENOLOGY OF EXPERIENCE

Dewey believed he could demonstrate through art that the same underlying processes that energize perception and give form and function to inanimate matter are operative in scientific inquiry, and in any realm in which judgment is required for human understanding. Dewey had unusual opportunities in the late 1920s and early 1930s to glimpse firsthand how perception furnishes the pathways through which mind and nature interpenetrate through bodies and behavior to produce our phenomenal experience and knowledge of the world. He argued that immediately given things in nature are comprehended as independent factors only after we have attempted to combine them to form new traits.

Art epitomized for Dewey this process of reconstruction whereby the qualitative elements of an aesthetic creation, such as color, line, form, depth, and symmetry, exist as abstract potentialities. These aesthetic qualities acquire meaning and significance only after the artist employs them to express his memories, feelings, or experiences. A brief but rewarding informal tutorial with Henri Matisse enabled Dewey to carefully observe how post-impressionist techniques transformed the seemingly random and discordant energies of each stroke of the brush into a scene on canvas that possessed a rhythmic order and variation. In doing so, Dewey asserted that not only have mind and body come together to make the measured release of energy possible (i.e., through scale, perspective, balance, and so forth), but that the possible range of human experience is extended indefinitely.

During this period of changing aesthetic perspectives and styles, the world of theoretical physics was undergoing a similar period of upheaval and reconstruction. The clockwork predictability of the Newtonian universe was profoundly challenged by the probabilistic world of Maxwell's molecules and Einstein's theory of relativity, who suggested the possibility of a new theoretical unification. But quantum mechanics soon threatened Einstein's dream of a unified field theory. Dewey's daughter Jane worked as a post-graduate fellow with Niels Bohr and Werner Heisenberg while the principles of quantum mechanics were formulated and debated, giving Dewey an intimate look at how physicists interpreted the phenomenon of uncertainty. Unlike Einstein, Dewey did not consider this development to have undermined the possibility of unification. Dewey believed that the essential indeterminacy of matter that Heisenberg proposed, and that post-impressionists like Matisse expressed through their paintings, supported his supposition that mind and nature were integrated through experience. The *phenomenal* properties of matter and energy could be known experientially, Dewey contended, even though their exact *physical* embodiment in space is indeterminate and undergoing a continuous process of displacement and transformation over time. The actual world in which we live, the world which extends continuously in space and time enabling us to possess a sense of self and identity, Dewey believed, hosted many other possible worlds of human experience, whose realization depends, in part, on the ingenuity of our minds and the efficacy of our consciousnesses.

BUILDING BRIDGES BETWEEN SCIENCE AND POLITICS

Dewey's passion for the world of art was overshadowed, however, by his public persona as a social reformer and democratic theorist. Instead of focusing on Dewey as a political philosopher, it is important to understand how Dewey's social and political theories were grounded in a science of psychology that called into question the premises of liberal democratic theory. Dewey believed that the utilitarian and Freudian conceptions of human motivation underpinning liberalism entailed moral conceptions that were at odds with human intelligence and freedom. This led Dewey to challenge the scientific grounds and viability of cultural values about childhood that had wide appeal, even among Dewey's most ardent followers.

Support for a participatory democracy is strongest in those societies whose members have a well-developed sense of community identity and spirit and who seek cooperation with other communities to address common problems whose resolution has important consequences for public life. Dewey saw the strategic importance of child-rearing and educational practices in securing support for his conception of democracy. Lawrence K. Frank shared Dewey's vision for strengthening the relationship between developmental science and democratic politics. Frank believed that child development should be a growth-centered science. His stewardship of an international network of community-based child study institutes reflected Dewey's intentions that scientists, parents, educators, and the public should cooperate in a joint endeavor to bring science to bear on child-rearing and schooling and to continuously assess programs to find out what succeeds, why it succeeds, and what values are reflected in the long-term developmental consequences. By focusing on Frank's initiatives begun at the Rockefeller Foundation in the mid-1920s to construct a child development network patterned after Dewey's conception of democracy propounded in *The Public and Its Problems* in 1927, we have a unique opportunity to re-examine and reassess Dewey's conception of a democratic society based on his notion of communities of intelligence.

THE DEVELOPMENTAL ORIGINS OF
DEWEY'S THEORY OF INQUIRY

Dewey's little-known close personal and intellectual relationship with infant experimentalist Myrtle McGraw, with whom Dewey collaborated in the 1930s, helped him to develop and test hypotheses regarding the origin of the brain and mind and the role of human judgment in inquiry.[23] McGraw repaid the debt she incurred from being intellectually nurtured and mentored by Dewey through her undergraduate and graduate studies in psychology at Columbia by conducting pioneering experimental studies of infant motor development. Dewey remained undecided about how to conceive of judgment in naturalistic terms that were scientifically supportable until McGraw provided the crucial insights that enabled him to do so. McGraw's discoveries also vindicated Dewey's Hegelianism by demonstrating that brain and behavior develop through dialectical processes of growth. She demonstrated, drawing on Maxwellian physics, that brain and behavior interact through energetic processes in which consciousness plays a crucial role in rendering judgments explicit about the consequences of alternative ideas and action. Her studies also showed that the order of development is not fixed, but is subject to the contingencies of human experience. Finally, McGraw furnished evidence for how generic traits of human judgment contribute to the organization and transformation of behavior through processes of human learning and inquiry.

Dewey's excursions in the world of art and philanthropic politics and his unusual opportunity to participate in experimental studies of infant development provided invaluable insights Dewey used to formulate a theory about the integral nature of human inquiry. Dewey boldly argued in *Logic: The Theory of Inquiry* in 1938 that the structure of aesthetic, scientific, and social inquiries is foreshadowed in the biological processes of growth in which brain and behavior develop and interact to produce consciousness and judgment. Dewey claimed that the force and momentum that propositional thought acquires by pursuing linkages between different lines of related evidence parallels the processes in which energy is released by growth and learning, bringing about the integration of brain and behavior needed to form judgments based on experience.

He introduced the distinction between propositions, which affirm beliefs that have adequate grounds, and judgments, which assert something about the outcome of inquiry, to support his contention that affirmative propositions have nothing to do the with the truth or falsity of the conclusions reached.[24] Propositions based on empirical evidence collected from contrasting perspectives that involve different but overlapping methods gain cumulative, indicative force as they intersect and converge toward common conclusions carrying signifying force. Scientific inquiries that succeed, Dewey claimed, are those which enlist mind and behavior in a reciprocal process. Propositions that affirm beliefs about natural or social phenomena draw on the generic elements of human experience, which furnish the means by which warranted assertions are grounded.

Dewey felt impelled to revise and rewrite his major works almost as soon as they were published. He used each succeeding book as an opportunity to advance new ideas as well as to reweave the threads of previous arguments and experiences into a richer and more integrated tapestry of ideas. Dewey's sense of urgency for revision was no more strongly felt than with *Experience and Nature*, where he believed that by using the terms "experience and nature," he had failed to convey the phenomenological continuity between what is natural and characteristically human. He believed that if "culture" were substituted for "experience" he could better capture the psychological unity of experience. Culture designated "both what is experienced (i.e., by humans living in one and the same natural world) and the ways (i.e., the various cultural and technological forms of expressing and embodying human relationship in nature and social institutions) of experiencing it."[25]

Unfortunately for Dewey, his remarks were interpreted by many observers as an acknowledgment of his failure to do justice to the important and independent influence of culture. Dewey vigorously opposed setting culture apart from nature, but he was unable to prevent his pragmatism from taking first a positivist, scientistic turn at the hands of Dewey's own contemporaries, and then veering in a linguistic direction under the leadership of philosopher Richard Rorty.[26] Pragmatism became the object of opposing philosophical and political interpretations and this contributed to the demise of Dewey's naturalism.

Recent interpretive conflicts over pragmatist morality and politics were foreshadowed at the turn of the twentieth century when social progressives seized the emancipatory themes embodied in Dewey's ideas about growth, development, and learning to advance numerous social and political reforms. Nevertheless, the unfounded suspicions among a few of Dewey's strongest supporters that Dewey's enthusiasm for science betrayed an undemocratic vein threatening the heart of pragmatist culture led some contemporaries to sever this pathway of inquiry as if it were a diseased and disposable element of pragmatist thought. This unfortunate episode gave way to attempts by some of Dewey's students in the 1940s and 1950s to stay true to his naturalism. They sought a safe haven for Dewey's views about logic and science in the philosophical movement of logical positivism. Dewey realized sooner than these well-meaning but sometimes misguided students that the members of the charmed Vienna Circle of logical empiricists were advancing a verificationist theory of knowledge and truth which was profoundly at odds with his own conception of inquiry.

Dewey's baton was unwittingly passed to pragmatist torchbearers such as

Sidney Hook, who believed that pragmatism conceived as scientific method signaled the "end of ideology," and rendered likely the possibility that America would succeed in attaining democratic hegemony against a growing communist menace.[27] Not until the publication of Richard Bernstein's influential book, eight years after Dewey's death in 1952, was interest in pragmatism renewed among a second generation of philosophers who attempted to reclaim Dewey's metaphysics and democratic theory from the clutches of the positivists and Cold War intellectuals.[28] Unfortunately, with rare exceptions, this resurgence of Dewey scholarship has either sidestepped Dewey's views about science or has been ridiculed by Rorty, who claims that Dewey's views about science and his conceptions of mind and nature do not merit serious consideration and re-examination.[29] Moreover, the current preoccupation with the cultural and political implications of Dewey's pragmatism has frustrated attempts to achieve an integrated understanding of the relation between Dewey's philosophical notions about experience, nature, and aesthetics and his science and politics.

Dewey's naturalism has all but disappeared in the works of his successors, especially those who have gotten sidetracked into endless debates with Richard Rorty about whether or not pragmatism can sustain its claim to be an American *public* philosophy. Rorty's provocative works merit close attention because he has made the strongest case against Dewey's naturalism, arguing that Dewey's notion of generic traits and his emphasis on method are dispensable and inconsequential to the survival of pragmatism. Rorty contends that Dewey "deabsolutized" Hegel, offering instead "a relativist and materialist version of teleology rather than an absolutist and idealist one."[30] Rorty advances the strongest argument—one tacitly accepted by many of Rorty's critics—that Dewey's commitment to science was naive and that the major problems facing America are cultural and discursive rather than heuristic and methodological. I challenge Rorty's argument against Dewey's naturalism and science at several key junctures. Rorty's nominalism and Freudianism discourage the adoption of a conception of embodied minds whereby experience and communication play vital roles in self-discovery and social change. I also indicate why Dewey's ideas remain pertinent to contemporary neuroscientists and philosophers of mind who seek to understand the neurobiological basis of human experience.

Becoming John Dewey traces the remarkable personal and intellectual pathways through which Dewey withdrew from Calvinism, embraced evolutionary naturalism, was swept into Hegelianism, and then sought a way to reconcile the disparate worlds of art, science, and politics by formulating an integrated theory about mind and inquiry. This book documents Dewey's personal and intellectual struggle to find philosophical coherence and spiritual significance in a nation undergoing the relentless pressures of secularization and modernization. Dewey brilliantly conceived a way to transform the Hegelian phenomenology of being and becoming into a psychology of human experience that could be grounded in science. He also demonstrated that spiritual renewal is possible only in those nation-states that invest ultimate authority in citizens dedicated to democratic participation in communities of intelligent action.

Dewey faced many dilemmas, described in the ensuing chapters, in his attempt to straddle the uncertain territory between invention and advocacy, science and politics. Dewey believed that our ideas are always in the process of undergoing further development, of becoming something more than the possession of any single mind. Dewey struggled to attain the psychological distance needed to visualize the mind and human experience from different perspectives in order to understand how human judgment could be enlisted to promote human intelligence and individual freedom. He took enormous strides toward the attainment of his goals as a founder of a philosophical theory that became an intellectual and social movement. But the sometimes discordant roles Dewey adopted to sustain his intellectual leadership created fundamental conflicts between the engagement and advocacy of a social reformer and the objectivity and detachment of a scientist. This book will examine how Dewey's intellectual and scientific quests and his political strategies for educational and social reform became intertwined, creating exhilarating opportunities while posing uncertain personal consequences.

Part One

Sublime Reason and the Comforts of Doubt

ONE

From Calvinism to Evolutionism

John Dewey's life as a public philosopher and reformer is probably one of the more thoroughly documented careers of any American intellectual in this century. Yet remarkably little is known about Dewey's childhood and his early professional life prior to undertaking his academic career as a philosopher. Dewey is partly to blame for this gap because he wrote almost nothing about these lost years, and he preferred to begin his own autobiography, published in 1930 when Dewey was seventy, by describing his intellectual interests as an undergraduate at the University of Vermont.[1] Perhaps Dewey didn't think there was much worth reporting before that time, and by all accounts Dewey seemed to have had an unexceptional childhood.

Dewey's daughter Jane tried to correct this deficiency in her biography in 1939 by persuading her father to furnish more details about his early years. Jane Dewey succeeded in completing a family history with personal anecdotes and occasional insights about Dewey's early development that propelled him toward philosophical pursuits.[2] Several of Dewey's former students and colleagues also contributed their recollections of their personal association with Dewey in articles and unpublished interviews, but their commentaries largely focus on his later years at Columbia University.[3] Max Eastman, a former Dewey student, had more success than other close Dewey friends in getting him to reveal more details about his childhood and youth. Eastman, who had an amiable relationship with Dewey, probed Dewey's early years with a disarming wit that brings Dewey's persona alive.[4] Not until 1977, however, when George Dykhuizen published his biography, which involved extensive research in the Dewey archives and correspondence, including interviews with Dewey family members, did a more coherent picture emerge.[5]

LIVING BY THE CREED OF REDEMPTION

Dewey was born in 1859 into a middle-class Vermont family whose self-educated father, Archibald, traced his lineage to descendants who fled Flanders to escape religious persecution. They eventually settled in a farming colony in western Connecticut. Archibald gave up on farming in his mid-forties to run a grocery business. To the dismay of some prohibition-minded neighbors, he possessed the only license to dispense liquor for medicinal purposes. Archibald took time out in 1860 to serve as quartermaster of a Vermont cavalry unit for four years during the Civil War before resuming his business. The young Dewey and his two surviving brothers, Davis and Charles (John Archibald died in an accident at home at two and a half years old), got reacquainted with their father after the war. He was personable, had a dry sense of humor, and forgave more debts than was financially advisable. Archibald had a surprisingly wide-ranging though intellectually superficial interest in literary figures that included Shakespeare, Milton, Emerson, and Hawthorne and political philosophers William Thackeray and Thomas Carlyle. Dewey's father was fond of quoting from these writers' works, delivering his recitations with an entertaining oratorical flourish. Dewey's father also had an uncanny ability to recall (or so he claimed) exactly what he was doing when he was his sons' ages. This striking gift for recollection through mental association may have stimulated John's curiosity in psychological processes.[6]

Dewey's mother, Lucina Rich, came from a well-to-do, better-educated, and politically active family whose grandfather was a congressman and whose father served as a "lay" judge in a county court. Lucina took pride in her family upbringing and the fact that both her brothers were first-generation college graduates, a goal she ardently sought for her own sons, two of whom, John and Davis, obtained Ph.D.'s. She was a devoted mother, spendthrift, and disciplinarian who made sure her sons had plenty of books to read and lots of chores to complete. When he was old enough, John delivered papers after school until he got a summer job at fourteen, "tallying" in a lumberyard.[7]

Lucina was a devout Congregationalist who expected her sons to adopt the Calvinist creed in word and deed. Her strong religious convictions reflected the conflicting currents of religious belief characteristic of the Reconstruction era. She was a member of the Universalist sect who occupied the liberal wing of Calvinism. Universalists rejected as elitist the doctrine of the elect, believing instead that God would forgive anyone who confessed their sins. This democratic conception of redemption was appealing because it was never too late, as Saint Augustine declared, to rectify one's sins. However, after attending a religious revival sponsored by an evangelical "New Divinity" movement, Lucina had a change of heart and decided to join the "Partialists" who adopted a strict construction of redemption, including the orthodox belief in predestination. Although it was impossible to predict who would be elected for redemption, Partialists believed that good acts could increase the probability of being chosen. In any event, grace could not be purchased with down payments of temporary righteousness, but only through cumulative acts of sacrifice and renunciation.[8]

SECTARIAN SKIRMISHES

The fundamental differences in Calvinist orthodoxy between Unitarians and their New Divinity, or Partialist, rivals merit further elaboration because their creedal conflicts involving free will versus determinism posed dilemmas for the young Dewey that were not easily reconciled.[9] Unitarians challenged the orthodoxy that all mankind was depraved, believing that this robbed persons of their capacity to recognize and choose between good and evil—a choice that each individual ultimately must make to have any hope of attaining God's grace. It was surely more logical to presuppose that mankind had free will or moral agency than to hold that a person's fate was sealed regardless of his or her conduct. Harvard theologians such as Andrew Norton contended that Christ's sacrifice was an affirmation of human freedom and the belief that human beings were capable of recognizing and pursuing the right path to moral righteousness. The scriptures did not require absolute repentance or atonement but only demanded evidence that an individual had sincerely undertaken the effort to reform his or her conduct and character.

The shrill disputes raging between these religious factions were eventually replaced by the moderating voices of reason that wanted to find a place for benevolence in divine governance and to reconcile the rift between spiritual and natural worlds. The "New Divinity" movement led by Jonathan Edwards emerged to defend Calvinism against Unitarian charges of incoherence.[10] Edwards and his followers drew on Baconian and Newtonian science to suggest how the duality of spiritual and natural worlds could be reconciled through a conception of causality that acknowledged human free will while upholding divine intervention. The Baconian conception of science insisted that only natural phenomena are explicable in causal terms. Isaac Newton's theory of universal gravitation supported this dualistic or deistic worldview. Physical laws governing matter and motion could be stated in causal terms that need not specify the ultimate origins of force underpinning these natural phenomena.

Edwards proposed two levels of causation based on these postulates. God, whose divine powers are not susceptible to human comprehension, constituted a sole or sufficient cause of human existence. God's will operated in unseen ways, like Newtonian gravitation, acting at a distance to effect changes beyond human control. A second level of causality was operative in human affairs. Human behavior was subject to natural or social contingencies whose causes and effects could be identified through scientific inquiry.

This cosmology was deployed to reconcile the co-existence of good and evil. In his benevolence, God gave mankind psychological freedom to choose between good or evil. Thus God did not directly cause humans to be evil or sinful, but gave them the power to make their own decisions and to take individual responsibility for their moral conduct. Nathaniel Emmons, an adherent of Edwards's New Divinity, was a popular exponent of the "taste" or "exercise" evangelical movement that swept rural New England during Dewey's mother Lucina's youth. According to Emmons, a taste was a potentiality or disposition to act for good or evil that could only become manifest through "exercise." An exercise was not an overt act but what the heart willed or intended. The tastes codified a certain structure or sequence of good conduct in which heart, soul, mind, and body could function in synchrony. Prayer was indispensable to good behavior because it was directed at the heart and mind where the propensity for wrongdoing could be controlled through an act of will.[11]

Dewey apparently accepted and internalized during his childhood this New Divinity psychological formula for redemption. It hardly could have been otherwise. Lucina was relentless in her solicitude, as a surrogate conscience, watchfully steering her children away from forbidden behavior while reminding them of their obligations to God. Steven Rockefeller reported in his biography that Dewey recalled Lucina's tedious interrogations, which she sometimes conducted in the presence of friends. "Are you right with Jesus? Have you prayed to God for forgiveness?"[12] Temperamentally shy and reticent, Dewey admitted to biographer Max Eastman that his religious upbringing only exacerbated his social anxieties. He recalled:

> I was unduly bashful and self-conscious, always putting myself over against other people. Perhaps that was it. Or perhaps an overemphasis on evangelical morals had given me a feeling of alienation from the world. I can't recover it. If I could, I would write something about adolescence that really would be interesting.[13]

Lucina's piety seems to have sunk into Dewey's psyche. Dewey told another correspondent in the 1920s that as a youngster he was "hypersensitive, morbidly to thinking of others' alleged opinions of me, which I really knew were mostly imaginary anyway, as they weren't bothering to think of me at all."[14] Dewey's mother had so set him apart from other children in terms of expected conduct that Dewey may have feared that befriending those guided by lesser standards would be tantamount to falling from grace, or at least putting him at risk of losing his mother's love. Moreover, his doubts were symptomatic of a spiritual conflict within, one that centered on whether he possessed the necessary will, knowledge, and judgment to think and strive toward a virtuous life.

The New Divinity evangelicals retained a belief in predestination, but left unexplained how election for God's grace could occur solely on the basis of a psychological predisposition. The possibility that just thinking a bad thought was tantamount to doing it must have been inhibiting to the young Dewey. That the fear of moral backsliding was a real one for Dewey was no better expressed, as Eastman reports anecdotally, than when "in the midst of prayer, the question rose up into his [Dewey's] mind: 'Isn't this, after all, just a routine performance?'" Eastman said that "[t]hat question bothered him a good deal for a long time."[15] Dewey continued to struggle with the problem of sin in relation to free will while teaching at the University of Michigan. There he argued that "to sin morally is a moral defect," which originates in an "attitude of one's will and desires."[16] The paradox of original sin was how anyone could knowingly do anything wrong while unaware of the good. If this were true, then mere mortals escape completely the moral responsibility for their actions.

Dewey did not openly question or challenge his mother's relentless appeals to think and behave well in the eyes of God. He preferred instead to interrogate his own heart and mind to find evidence for his emerging belief that the soul is more likely to find release through the expression rather than continuous suppression of one's feelings. He wondered why emotions should be considered suspect, when Darwin was saying that they evolved to enable humans to express and to communicate their feelings more completely and accurately. Moreover, the spiritual and emotional signs of personal revelation seemed ambiguous to Dewey. Continuous prayer did not seem to increase enlightenment or bring about a closer relationship with God.

Apparently, Dewey became increasingly distraught over this issue until his first bout with Hegelianism after graduating from college enabled him to heal this "inward laceration." Perhaps he glimpsed a fatal ontological error in the logic of redemption that rendered faith by introspection incapable of bringing about the spiritual reunification of mind and body. Dewey opined a few years later that "[r]eligious feeling is unhealthy when it is watched and analyzed to see if it exists, if it is right, if it is growing. It is fatal to be forever observing our own religious moods and experiences, as it is to pull up a seed from the ground to see if it is growing."[17]

The fatal flaw Dewey found in fundamentalism and later in psychological introspectionism was the belief that we can comprehend our own divinity simply by praying or thinking about it. The attempt to objectify the soul, he believed, detached it from the natural processes of human growth and experience in which it emerges. To be certain, Lucina's faith was not restricted to creedal admonitions. She engaged in many philanthropic activities benefiting the poor. But her brand of idealism, according to one close friend, "was always reaching to something beyond, something, which might be done for those who needed help in body and soul. She was always looking forward from things as they are, to what they ought to be, and might be."[18] Dewey found through Hegel a way to transform his mother's spiritual idealism into a novel philosophy of social reconstruction.

BELIEF AND PROBABILITY

Joseph Butler's writings were the perfect antidote for someone like Dewey, who was frustrated by ambiguous and inconsistent religious doctrine and uncertain about what constituted moral conduct. Dewey recalled that Butler's "cold logic and acute analysis" contributed to his "developing skepticism."[19] Butler was a sophisticated apologist for Christianity during the eighteenth century, when philosophers such as David Hume were attacking as incoherent the doctrine of free will. The brilliant, argumentative Butler defended the principle of free will by exploiting the probabilistic principles underpinning Hume's idea of contingency to support the rationality of religious faith. Hume is well-known for contending that cause and effect are merely contingently related. But he also argued against the supposition that natural or human phenomena whose origins or causes are unknown or unexplainable can therefore be attributed to divine intervention. Butler cleverly turned Hume's empiricism on its head. Nature furnishes innumerable analogies that life bears only a contingent relationship to death, and that to presuppose otherwise is to introduce a premise that all known life forms will never assume any alternative existences with which we are now familiar.[20]

Butler found a logical parallelism between statements of probability about the outcomes of natural phenomena whose ultimate origins or causes are unknown, and spiritual phenomena whose ultimate ends are unknowable. Uncertainty about just what kind of person we are going to turn out to be justifies our apprehension that what we do in our earliest years (including even the most trivial and minor acts) may significantly affect what we are likely to become or achieve in our later lives. Likewise, Butler contended that no matter how improbable the existence of an afterlife, given the absence of verifiable evidence, the belief in such a supernatural existence is nevertheless justified from a natural point of view. From a probabilistic point of view, Butler reasoned, those beliefs or actions considered only incidental to our development may turn out to be crucial to our future existence.[21] The probability that an afterlife would possess attributes that are analogous to those found in human existence, Butler argued, made it non-frivolous and prudent to live this life as though it were true.

Butler's argument from natural analogy appealed to Dewey, helping him overcome doubts that Calvinism had planted in his mind about whether he could ever exercise his natural capacities morally to increase the likelihood of redemption. Butler dissented from the conventional wisdom of his day that the human body had been corrupted by sin. He believed that God equipped humans with physical functions whose exercise were naturally beneficial and incorrigible. Those functions, such as seeing, hearing, thinking, and so forth, although intended to fulfill specific needs, possessed potential uses or powers that could never be completely anticipated or exhausted by their current uses. We find this probabilistic conception of function surfacing in Dewey's first essays on ethics in the 1890s, where he asserted, "A large part of our moral discipline consists precisely in learning how to estimate probabilities—to distinguish between relatively necessary and relatively accidental results and to mediate the impulse accordingly."[22]

SCIENCE, SATIRE, AND NATURAL SELECTION

The route that Butler charted to the soul through nature and spirit required an appreciation of science that Dewey acquired only late in his college years. Dewey entered college at age fifteen, enrolling in the University of Vermont in 1875. One of the university's first distinguished professors and president, James Marsh, brought attention to the European roots of American transcendentalists Emerson and Thoreau by introducing the works of German philosophers such as Kant, Schelling, and Hegel. Nevertheless, Marsh and other faculty members reflected the same Congregational bias with which Dewey by then was quite familiar.

Dewey was an intellectually restless undergraduate whose mind seemed to be elsewhere. He was indulging his curiosity about science and politics by reading liberal, popular, scholarly journals that delved into the social and moral implications of materialism and evolution, such as the *Fortnightly Review,* the *Nineteenth Century,* and *Contemporary Review,* among many other periodicals.[23] These journals were invaluable to Dewey. Here he could read first-hand about intellectual controversies involving creation, development, and evolution swirling among Christian theologians, philosophers, and scientists. The primary lines of cleavage that formed between those espousing materialistic, non-materialistic, and developmental conceptions of evolution are worth retracing because they provide early glimpses of themes and issues that would continue to occupy Dewey's attention throughout the remainder of his philosophical career.

Prominent among the contributors to these journal debates were Samuel Butler, a satirist and contemporary critic of Darwinian evolution, and Thomas H. Huxley, a zoologist who acquired international fame as Darwin's "bulldog" for his spirited defense of Darwinian evolution. Butler was a talented literary figure of enormous imagination, and his entrance into the scientific debate about evolution was quite unexpected and unwelcome. The iconoclastic Butler first attracted public attention when he published a pamphlet in 1865, and later a book titled *The Fair Haven* in 1873, which challenged the Gospels' account of the resurrection. He claimed in these works that Christ never actually died during the crucifixion and that his subsequent reappearance was mistaken as a miracle.[24]

This affront to Christian dignity was followed by *Erewhon,* a satirical account of a society governed by beliefs that reverse our customary views about morality and the continuity of human experience and personal identity.[25] In this book the protagonist is thrust into an imaginary society that is completely contrary to known experience. Butler's Erewhonians ironically regard the doctrine of predestination and the belief in immortality as immoral because these beliefs render life of secondary importance. Instead, they subscribe to a mythology of pre-existence, which holds that it is the pestering by the unborn that causes parents to conceive babies. Conceived against the will of their parents, children acknowledge guilt for being brought into the world, they accept the penalties for exercising free will, and they face with equanimity the finality of death. Butler deploys these and other examples of unreason to suggest that society could still logically function even if the supposedly rational foundations of beliefs about birth, life, and death were suddenly turned upside down.

Butler's talent for posing contrary-to-fact thought experiments was not confined to the satirical evisceration of the Calvinist dogma about predestination. In a more serious and scholarly way, he also sought to perform major intellectual surgery on Darwinian evolution by exposing its weakly supported underlying premises. In his book *Evolution, Old and New,* Butler asserted that Darwin's theory of natural selection was logically deficient and unpersuasive in explaining the mechanisms of variation. Darwin focused on *environmental* factors contributing to variation within species but this did not adequately explain, in Butler's opinion, the *biological* processes through which these variations occurred. While Darwin contended that those species survived which best adapted to new contingencies, this did not explain the mechanisms or processes through which such advantages were conferred individually or distributed within species.

Moreover, Butler sensed that survival of the fittest was as good as no explanation at all if it did not allow for the constructive power of mind and learning in human behavior. The questions that Butler believed were salient to an evolutionary explanation had to do with how species recognize threats to their existence, how behavioral strategies are selected which eliminate these threats, and how these strategies are retained as habits to promote long-term survival. In fact, Butler believed that evolution would be a more coherent theory if the causal relationship between adaptation and survival was reversed. He asserted, "Our modern evolutionists should allow that animals are modified not because they subsequently survive, but because they have done this or that which led to their modification, and hence to their surviving."[26]

Butler was advancing an argument first made by St. George Mivart, a protégé of Huxley. Mivart took Darwin to task for failing to adequately explain how natural selection causes variations to occur that do not appear to be random or accidental, but rather are the product of developmental processes and constraints. Mivart was not challenging Darwin's contention that advantages can accumulate for species who adopt successful modifications, but he was asserting that natural selection favors animals that already possess the adaptive trait (or "are born fit," as Mivart expressed it). Mutations or parental hereditary peculiarities may produce adaptations that prove to be useful that are then favored by the environment. Butler acknowledged being strongly persuaded by Mivart's arguments made in his book *On the Genesis of Species,* published in 1871. Importantly, when Butler subsequently published *Life and Habit* in 1878, he devoted a chapter to Mivart's alternative explanation of the origin of variation that he considered to be "fatal" to Darwin's argument that novel behaviors arise through mimicry.[27]

Butler showed that Darwinian theory was vulnerable to the same arguments he deployed with such rhetorical style and satirical wit in describing the origins of the imaginary society of *Erewhon*. Erewhon, where events in ontogeny shaped the experience of future progeny, was not as fantastic as it seemed, Butler believed, because it expressed in exaggerated form two essential truths about human evolution: first, that the chain of experience is connected through memory to the habits of previous generations, and second, that novel changes in human form and function occur at the onset of development. These principles formed Butler's mnemonic theory of development to explain how species undergo variation and change and still maintain continuity of identity from one generation to the next.[28]

Butler drew on available evidence from embryological studies by his contemporaries Ewald Hering and Eduard von Hartmann to support his notion that each stage of early development is a reminder of the experiences and functional modifications of previous generations that must be remastered, albeit in an abbreviated sequence. According to Butler, each generation will compress or shorten the period in which the energetic force of phylogenetic memory is operative, allowing greater freedom to exploit the contingencies of experience to produce novel behaviors. This introduces slight changes in the sequence of developmental processes, which eventually result in significant modifications in species. Butler touted a highly original theory whose embryological imagery persisted in Dewey's writings. Traces of Butler's influence are evident in *Art as Experience*, where Dewey described how memories are "compressed" through the force and weight of experience to yield new forms of artistic expression (see chapter 7). Moreover, Myrtle McGraw and Dewey attempted to simulate the production of novel behaviors by creating challenges that accelerated and altered the sequence in which infants attained motor control.

Butler found it exceedingly difficult to shed his image as a satirist and have his scientific ideas taken seriously. The academic press gave faint praise for his speculative insights in *Life and Habit* while dismissing it as "whimsical" science. Alfred Wallace, co-inventor with Darwin of the principle of survival of the fittest, offered a more charitable review when he stated, "Though we can at present only consider the work as a most ingenious paradoxical speculation, it may yet afford a clue to some of the deepest mysteries of the organic world."[29] In contrast, George Romanes viciously attacked *Unconscious Memory* in the British journal *Nature* as a "sorry exhibition" and called Butler "an upstart ignoramus."[30] But Butler's primary target, Darwin, remained annoyingly silent. Not surprisingly, the scientific establishment closed ranks with the exception of Darwin's less-renowned competitor Alfred Wallace and jeered Butler for unfairly undermining Darwin's scientific contributions. Darwin's supporters among the British scientific establishment bluntly advised Butler to return to writing fiction.[31]

The conflict between Butler, Darwin, and the rest of the scientific establishment vividly illustrated to Dewey the disastrous consequences of privileging science by cordoning it from public scrutiny and debate. Science could not be restricted to a quasi-priestly class of practitioners and remain viable, Dewey believed, precisely because human intelligence observed no such boundaries. Huxley's own vigorous and successful attempts to popularize science belied but did not excuse his occasional reproaches against those willing to challenge Darwin's authority or integrity. Huxley's enthusiasm for science and evolution led some theologians to conclude that Huxley was, in fact, proposing a materialist substitute for spiritual salvation—a kind of revivalist scientism shorn of the mysteries of divine intervention. Huxley cleverly coined the term "agnostic" to distinguish between atheists, who deny the existence of God, and people such as Huxley, who thought it simply futile to burden science with metaphysical questions about God and spirit that exceeded the boundaries of inquiry.[32]

HUXLEY'S SECULAR SCIENTIFIC CREED

Dewey's intellectual encounter with Huxley's ideas during his junior year in high school contributed to a sense of urgency about the direction of his future studies. While taking a course in laboratory methods, Dewey was required to read Huxley's text in physiology, which undoubtedly inspired Dewey to later read other books and essays by Huxley.[33] Dewey was mesmerized. Huxley's majestic portrayal of the human body as an exquisitely crafted equilibrium of anatomically distinct but functionally integrated processes was a revelation for Dewey. Savoring the personal and intellectual consequences of this encounter, Dewey recalled

> It is difficult to speak with exactitude about what happened to me intellectually so many years ago, but I have an impression that there was derived from that study a sense of interdependence and interrelated unity that gave form to intellectual stirrings that had been previously inchoate, and created a kind of type or model of a view of things to which material in any field ought to conform. Subconsciously, at least, I was led to desire a world and a life that would have the same properties as had the human organism in the picture of it derived from Huxley's treatment . . . I date from this time the awakening of a distinctive philosophic interest.[34]

Huxley helped Dewey wrestle free from the grips of a Calvinist world populated by souls unable to escape completely from imprisonment in their morally suspect mental and physical embodiment. Huxley described vividly how human physiological processes are perfected by the continuous modification through the evolution of structures and functions that enhance rather than detract from human judgment and intelligence.

Huxley, like Dewey, was spiritually nurtured by the precepts of Calvinism, but unlike Dewey, he experienced little dissonance in his breakaway from religious conventions. Huxley was raised in a working-class family with an unwavering commitment to the Unitarians' equalitarian belief that every individual's soul was salvageable no matter what their station in society, and that each person deserved an opportunity for self-improvement.[35] Huxley preferred to approach the issue of faith from a medical perspective. His training in the new science of physiology (and his tinkering with electromagnetism) led him to conclude that physical and chemical laws are inscribed in our bodies through nature not through divine intervention. Huxley believed that general physical laws governing all natural phenomena could ultimately explain biological processes. "Living bodies," according to Huxley, "were nothing but extremely complex bundles of forces held in a mass of matter, as the complex forces of a magnet are held in the steel by its complex forces."[36]

Huxley's probing naturalism, his public defense and popularization of science, and his quest for public educational reform each furnished windows through which Dewey glimpsed his own future as a naturalist, philosopher, and social reformer. Huxley dominated the public discourse on science and education during Dewey's formative years in high school and college. Huxley advanced a vision of science grounded in experimental physiology and comparative methods of investigation. He considered physiology to be the "experimental science par excellence," arguing that it "affords the greatest field for the exercise of those faculties which characterize the experimental philosopher."[37] The comparative method provided a way to rule out spurious causal relationships by finding similarities and differences between species that existed in different eras. Such classifications, Huxley urged, should also be based on dynamic relationships rather than derived from static categories involving untested distinctions between groups or classes of things.

The celebrated Huxley trumpeted his views about science and evolution to an adoring American audience in a lecture tour in 1876, which occurred during Dewey's freshman year in college. American scientists welcomed Huxley and hoped that his appearance would calm evangelical fears about Darwinian evolution and reduce uncertainty about science in modernity.[38] Huxley's American audiences admired his democratic sentiments that were best expressed by his heroic efforts to implement legislation mandating in Britain a comprehensive system of public elementary schools. He recommended that education become a universal right. He introduced innovative proposals to modernize curriculum, to increase experimentation and to professionalize teaching. Many of Huxley's proposals were adopted by the school board but changes in the science curriculum fell short of his experimental aims.[39] Dewey championed similar educational reforms in America, described in chapter 4, during a period in which educators and industrialists were at odds as to how best to respond to competing demands for technological competence and cultural diversity.

PALEONTOLOGICAL ANCESTORS AND
EMBRYOLOGICAL PRECURSORS

Though an avid defender of Darwin, Huxley considerably extended the range of natural phenomena accounted for solely by evolutionary theory through paleontology and morphological analyses of developmental processes. Huxley followed in Darwin's footsteps in his famous voyages on the *Beagle* in the 1830s by embarking on his own field expeditions in 1846 on the HMS *Rattlesnake*. He searched for clues in embryology and from the fossil record to determine the sequence in which living things grow, develop specific structures, and undergo functional modification.

Ironically, Huxley's views about evolution and development were more closely akin to Samuel Butler's than he was willing to acknowledge. Huxley and Butler had a common interest in embryology that Huxley pursued with a keen eye to finding archetypes that would reveal hidden developmental linkages between apparently unrelated species. Huxley rejected as too simplistic German embryologist Ernst Haeckel's theory that embryos recapitulated phylogeny by repeating the sequence of changes that led from lower to higher life forms. Haeckel's thesis entailed teleological implications that Huxley could not accept. Instead, he chose to pursue the paleontological implications of Kurt von Baer's principles of development. Von Baer rejected the notion that higher life forms pass through the stages of lower forms, proposing instead that more general characteristics shared by related species appear only in the earliest stages of embryonic development. In subsequent stages special attributes become differentiated to form more complex features characteristic of each species. This made it possible for different species to share certain structural characteristics, such as spinal cords, and yet differ profoundly in functional, physiological terms.[40]

Huxley's interpretation did not sit well with Darwin. Darwin's principle of natural selection proposed that adaptive modifications sometimes involved adding new features or appendages that are not derived from pre-existing structures. Their dispute highlights a crucial issue about the relation between evolution and development—one with which Dewey would grapple in advancing his functionalist psychology.[41]

Huxley suspected that Darwin had confused differentiation with functional specification. The order in which a trait first appears and is differentiated from others does not necessarily determine when this trait becomes fully functional. This challenged Darwin's assumption that the processes commencing the production of complex biological structures and organs should necessarily appear earlier in development than those subserving less complex functions. By this reckoning Darwin easily could have confused the difference between potential functional capabilities of a phenotype that require experience for their complete expression and those which involve irreversible genetic modifications that are not subject to further functional modification.

Huxley's theory that antecedent morphological traits do not account for consequent physiological functions furnished Dewey with an important insight that antecedent and consequent do not imply cause and effect. Dewey would refine this seminal idea in ensuing decades through his detailed studies of developmental processes that culminated in his extraordinary collaboration with McGraw in the 1930s. Her experimental studies showed that behavioral sequences are not preset at birth and that novel behaviors can be constructed from movements that appear at different stages of development.

A HUMAN MIND IN AN APE'S BRAIN?

Scientific speculation abounded at the turn of the twentieth century about the possible ape ancestry of the human brain and mind, attracting the rapt attention of scientists and the public. The alternative evolutionary pathways open to neurobehavioral development, Huxley believed, contributed to fundamental differences in species-specific functional traits. Anticipating objections that his theory provided no meaningful way to explain the vast differences between apes and humans who appeared to be anatomically similar, Huxley insisted that structures and functions become dissociated during evolution. Accordingly, the emergence of species-specific traits does not depend on genetic factors alone, but depends also on how these traits developed in relation to other structures and functions of the body as a whole. Huxley argued that the acquisition of human language illustrated this process of divergence whereby the seemingly tangential development of a larynx for speech and mental capacity for symbol use, then widely thought to be located in the hippocampus minor, coalesced, enabling the use of language.[42]

Darwin was not willing, however, to allow his principle of natural selection to be undermined by speculative developmental theories. Huxley was introducing uncertainty about species modification and descent that Darwin found intolerable. Darwin insisted that natural selection operates, as does artificial selection, to produce new attributes by accentuating certain existing traits better adapted to fit new contingencies. By contrast, Huxley was content to use embryology and comparative anatomy, as proposed by the French zoologist Cuvier, arguing that this would "throw the facts of structure into the fewest possible general propositions."[43] The persistence of structural similarities need not be indicative of common descent but may simply represent common solutions adopted by different species.

Huxley was convinced that the descent of species could be explained through paleontology and comparative anatomy without drawing the flawed inference that shared anatomical features associated with common ancestry also involve functional equivalence. Huxley's brilliant interpretation of the fossil record in his widely read book *Man's Place in Nature*, published in 1863, showed that species diverged through a non-linear specialization of structures and functions. Each species appeared to diverge from a generalized body plan through more rapid growth of some structures in relation to others. During this process some structures are suppressed, contributing to behavioral changes, while others coalesce, giving rise to entirely new functional attributes.

Consequently, Huxley argued, those species that occupy an intermediate position between two groups but fail to appear in the fossil record may have disappeared not because they failed to adapt, but because their body plans became dysfunctional or obsolete. These aborted species run into a developmental cul-de-sac that renders them incapable of fully exploiting their own potential and the resources of their niche. Here we find Huxley clearly echoing his antagonist Samuel Butler's sentiments that the supposed causal nexus between environment and development, embodied in the principle of natural selection, could be reversed to provide an equally plausible explanation of evolution.

While the evolutionary principles of descent might account for why humans and apes possess many common traits, Huxley argued, they could not explain their enormous differences in intelligence. Huxley's rigorous materialism, however, did not allow him to take a leap of faith needed to posit a mind, soul, or consciousness to account for this difference. He saw mind as a physiological function of the brain; consciousness simply was a biological epiphenomenon. Huxley maintained a rigorous dualism. He contended that the cosmic process of the struggle for existence "has no sort of relation to moral ends," and that the "ethical progress of society depends, not on imitating the cosmic process, still less in running away from it, but in combating it."[44] That is why Huxley believed that the human capacity for moral judgment could not be accounted for in strictly naturalistic terms.

Huxley's ideas were exhilaratingly provocative but disappointingly incomplete. They led Dewey to the threshold of scientific emancipation from materialism and reductive evolution only to abruptly abandon the possibility that mind or soul could play any serious role in explaining human moral development. Dewey found persuasive Huxley's attempt to substitute a naturalistic explanation of human behavior for a theistic one. But this was not sufficient to satisfy his single-minded objective of reconciling knowledge about human development with moral precepts about human conduct. Hegel ultimately illuminated the intellectual pathway that Dewey would take to challenge theological orthodoxy while preserving a legitimate role for philosophical speculation about the human spirit.

REWEAVING SCIENCE AND SPIRIT

Dewey's undergraduate years of intellectual serenity ended the fall of 1879, when he was jolted back into the reality of having to make a living. Dewey's cousin Affia Wilson, who was principal of a high school in Oil City, Pennsylvania, offered Dewey a teaching job. He taught there for two years from 1879 to 1881. Oil City was a noisy boomtown of wealthy investors, which seemingly was buried much of the year underneath a thick film of Allegheny River mud. Dewey passed on the opportunity to invest in oil shares, which would have made him millions, preferring to read borrowed books by the light of an oil lamp. His teaching duties were undemanding, giving him ample time to read Kant, Hegel, and Leibniz, among other philosophers, and to formulate intellectual positions on evolution. Dewey also read scholarly journals such as *Journal of Speculative Philosophy,* the first American journal in philosophy founded by the Hegelian William Torrey Harris in 1867. The journal provided an early forum for pioneering pragmatists such as Charles Peirce and William James, and was a sounding board for Hegelians that included George Morris and George Howison.[45]

Dewey accepted another brief teaching assignment with the Lake View Seminary in Charlotte, Vermont, during the winter term of 1881–1882. Dewey spent his free months in a tutorial with H. A. P. (Hap) Torrey, who was one of Dewey's undergraduate philosophy professors at the University of Vermont. Torrey furnished Dewey invaluable insights about how to put the controversies swirling in his mind about evolution, materialism, and development in proper philosophical perspective. No one seemed better equipped than Torrey to help Dewey reweave the threads of mind and spirit that were unraveling from the modern tapestry of science. Torrey was grounded in the Scottish school of intuitionism or common-sense realism. He rejected Lockean epistemology and Hume's extreme skepticism. His greatest gift to Dewey was his introduction to Kant and Hegel, whose contrasting views about knowledge and experience created a passion for metaphysics. Torrey succeeded Marsh as chair of the philosophy department and continued to propound his conservative intuitionist account of transcendentalism. But he also mounted a Kantian critique of Darwin, arguing that natural selection accounted only for general patterns of change in species, but did not furnish an explanation for why evolution occurred.

It was largely on the strength of Torrey's letter of reference stating that Dewey "had a marked predilection for metaphysics" that Johns Hopkins accepted Dewey in the Ph.D. program in philosophy in 1884.[46] While Dewey wrote that he admired Torrey for his "sensitive and cultivated mind," Dewey considered Torrey to be "constitutionally timid, and never let his mind go."[47] Dewey recalled his astonishment when he heard Torrey exclaim in one of his few unguarded moments that "[u]ndoubtedly pantheism is the most satisfactory form of metaphysics intellectually, but it goes counter to religious faith."[48] Dewey's personal observations of Torrey are ironic because he had yet to work through his own personal crisis of faith and his lingering doubts that philosophy truly promised a personal and intellectual salvation.

W. T. HARRIS AND THE ST. LOUIS HEGELIANS

During this period of intense reading and study, Dewey became aware of an intellectual movement led by W. T. Harris that promoted Hegelian ideas and sponsored *The Journal of Speculative Philosophy.* Harris and Henry Brokemeyer, a German émigré, founded the St. Louis philosophical movement in 1858. Significantly, the society was composed of Christian lay persons, not professional academic philosophers, who sought to reconcile the divergent streams of naturalism and idealism in American culture. Begun as a small study group intent upon deciphering Hegel's *Science of Logic,* the "St. Louis Hegelians" soon embarked on a critique of larger social and cultural repercussions incurred by the advance of science and the secularization of society.[49] Hegel's dialectical method was seized by the members of the St. Louis society as a useful tool in making sense of the co-existent but contradictory religious, cultural, and economic currents in a society undergoing convulsive industrial and urban transformation. They believed that the challenge to moral certitude and faith posed by the scientific revolution could be effectively countered by revealing through rigorous logical analyses the spiritually flawed epistemological and ontological premises of materialism and evolutionism. Harris contended that Hegelianism complemented the American traits of individualism and spiritual communalism. He believed that the socially divisive consequences of secularization and industrialization could be countered by the expansion of a public educational system dedicated to strengthening the ties between the family, civil society, and the nation-state.

Harris left St. Louis in the 1880s to propagate Hegelian metaphysics at the Concord School in New England. There he received a more critical reaction from academic philosophers such as William James, who found little to applaud in the Hegelian Absolute. While James acknowledged that he was "a Hegelian in so far as the transcendency of the immediate and the principle of totality go," he admitted that, "I can't follow Hegel in any of his applications of detail, and his manner is pure literary deformity."[50] James taunted his colleagues who took Hegel seriously by characterizing his notions of negation, the infinite, and Absolute Idea as products of an unbridled ontological imagination.[51] Hegelianism already was in decline and idealism was on the defensive well before the turn of the twentieth century.

JOINING THE DEBATE ABOUT MIND AND EVOLUTION

This general disenchantment with Hegel did not deter Dewey from his strong desire to get his Hegelian-inspired writings published in *The Journal of Speculative Philosophy.* Throughout its brief existence, the journal tended to focus on the philosophical and religious implications of evolution. Dewey excitedly submitted to the journal three articles between 1881 and 1882, during which time he became a graduate student at Johns Hopkins University. Two essays—one titled "The Metaphysical Assumptions of Materialism" and the other "The Pantheism of Spinoza,"—dealt with philosophical criticisms of evolution that Dewey first read about in the pages of the *Fortnightly Review* and *Contemporary Review.* A third essay, "Knowledge and the Relativity of Feeling," involved a sophisticated attempt by Dewey to resolve the problems of subjectivity and relativism posed by a materialist reading of evolution. He did so by reformulating the psychological terms used to understand the functional role of feeling in human thought and behavior.[52] Through this work we glimpse Dewey's first attempt to define consciousness.

Dewey's analysis in his first published article reflected his dissatisfaction with how the terms of the debate about materialism had been formulated. Those committed to a reductionist position seemed to Dewey to have unwittingly acknowledged that mind exists independently of the body—a position that undermined the validity of materialism. The assertion that every phenomenon must have a material basis, according to Dewey, implies that matter possesses universal attributes that can be demonstrated to exist independently of the phenomena they constitute or cause to occur. But such knowledge necessarily involves a thinking subject who is capable of distinguishing between the merely subjective impressions associated with individual thought and experience and objective events that have real material causes and effects beyond individual control. Accordingly, a strict monistic materialism cannot logically be sustained, Dewey argued, because the phenomenon of thought is itself trapped in materialist premises that deny the possibility of knowledge of self and of other minds.

The issue of pantheism posed a related but perhaps more insoluble problem of dualism. Pantheists believed that the universe was governed by physical laws created by God. Consequently, they believed that the behavior of all finite things could be shown to occur as a result of God's will or intervention. This was an extreme position that reform Calvinists avoided. A pantheistic account of knowledge had to be reformulated in a way that rendered logically consistent the relationship between infinite and finite being. The philosopher Spinoza struggled valiantly to resolve this paradoxical contradiction between the infinite wholeness of the universe and the infinite separateness of worldly existence. Dewey detected that Spinoza cleverly but unsuccessfully traded on the ambiguity between these two different conceptions of infinity—one involving an infinite substance with no separate attributes and another positing infinite attributes with no unitary or common substance. Well-versed in the logical peccadilloes tormenting the Calvinist mind, Dewey saw the absurdity of Spinoza's maneuver, which he glibly caricatured in the following terms:

> In truth, Spinoza is a juggler who keeps in stock two Gods—one the perfect infinite and absolute being, the other the mere sum of the universe with all the defects as they appear to us.[53]

While Dewey's first two published articles give the impression of a schoolboyish display of analytical virtuosity, Dewey's next argument reveals greater personal insight regarding the psychological fallacies that beset materialist epistemology. The ideas for this essay occurred to Dewey in the last few months of his brief sojourn teaching in Oil City High School. He recalled that he was undergoing "a trying personal crisis," that involved coming to grips with the challenge that evolution posed for the moral autonomy of individual conduct.[54]

As noted earlier, proponents of the "New Divinity" movement contended that dispositions or tastes are cultivated to serve as incorrigible guides to right conduct. But these feelings represented subjective inner states that defied unambiguous behavioral expression. Evolutionary theorists such as Herbert Spencer reinforced this subjectivist view of emotions by claiming that human feelings are peripheral rather than formative in human phylogenetic development. Dewey disagreed and believed instead that human feelings were embodied in functionally useful behaviors.

Dewey rejected as implausible the idea that feelings are only contingently or accidentally related to behaviors involved in their expression. Such a position would rule out the possibility that human attitudes and feelings are instrumental in facilitating awareness of the functional advantages of novel behaviors. Without consciousness, Dewey reasoned, our knowledge would never go beyond the immediacy of present sensations. But without feeling we would be unable to determine the difference that any particular occurrence or event makes in our existence.

Dewey's avowed intellectual mentors, including the tough-minded Huxley, conceded that human intelligence was unique. Nevertheless they did not believe that these cognitive powers were likely to be explained by science alone. Yet Dewey wanted to close the growing chasm between soul and body—a divide that Huxley considered unbridgeable—that stood in the way of understanding how mind and consciousness are enlisted to enormously expand human intelligence and judgment. Dewey did not take long to wield the sharp scalpel of Hegelian dialectics to dissect the anatomy of mind and soul, which Calvinists believed indecipherable in natural terms.

TWO

Healing an "Inward Laceration"

Dewey recalled that Hegel's method healed an "inward laceration" by helping him overcome the "sense of divisions and separations," inculcated by his evangelical New England upbringing, between mind and body and between nature and spirit that contributed to the growing gulf between philosophy and science.[1] Hegel fulfilled an "inner demand," Dewey felt, for an "intellectual technique that would be consistent and yet capable of flexible adaptation to the concrete diversity of experienced things."[2] What Dewey admired most about Hegel was his capacity to maintain silence in the presence of nature. Dewey credited him with the realization that "suppression of belief is the fundamental principle of thinking."[3] Hegel demonstrated the extraordinary power that thought acquires when belief is suspended and the impulse for immediate knowledge is inhibited until the tensions and oppositions of ideas play themselves out in experience.

This was wonderful advice about how to philosophize about nature. But Dewey lacked the experience and scientific training possessed by all great naturalists and philosophers, including Hegel, to bring to bear his insights about mind on nature. Darwin, Huxley, and physicists Michael Faraday and James Clerk Maxwell excelled as pioneering nineteenth-century scientists because of their incomparable talent in the field or in the laboratory. While Dewey admired from a distance their scientific rigor and capacity for synthesis, he never had a scientific mentor who stimulated his interest in acquiring expertise in observational and methodological techniques. Although cognizant of his weakness in science, Dewey still felt the alluring pull of philosophy and logic. Dewey could not be more decisive about pursuing his interests in science, he recalled, because he "was controlled largely by a struggle between a native inclination toward the schematic and formally logical, and incidents of personal experience."[4]

Nevertheless, this was a crucial period during which Dewey not only thoroughly assimilated Hegelian dialectics but also acquired an astonishingly sophisticated understanding of ongoing developments in physics. Dewey read Hegel with a critical eye toward bringing his work up to date scientifically by squaring it with the latest theories about force and energy that occupied the minds of Michael Faraday and James Clerk Maxwell. He also brought a Hegelian perspective to bear on Darwinian evolution in the hopes of advancing a developmental theoretical alternative to natural selection. Johns Hopkins University provided a nearly ideal setting to pursue his converging interests in philosophy and science.

THE LURE OF GEORGE SYLVESTER MORRIS AT JOHNS HOPKINS

Enrolling in a Ph.D. program in philosophy at Johns Hopkins University in 1882 did not seem initially to be a particularly auspicious or promising way for Dewey to understand nature through experience. Inaugurated with the intellectual blessings of Huxley, who spoke at the opening ceremonies in 1876, Johns Hopkins under Daniel Gilman's presidency set out to become a first-rate university in the sciences. He attracted G. Stanley Hall from Harvard, who immediately established an experimental laboratory in psychology. Although Gilman cared little for philosophy, he did attract the pioneering pragmatist Charles Sanders Peirce and Hegelian metaphysician George Sylvester Morris.

The iconoclastic Peirce had a formidable reputation in logic, but Dewey was disappointed that Peirce focused in his class primarily on mathematical theory. Dewey expressed his disappointment when he confided in Torrey, saying, "By Logic, Mr. Peirce means only an account of the methods of physical sciences, put in mathematical form as far as possible. It's more of a scientific than philosophical course."[5] Widening his complaint, Dewey added that "Mr. Peirce doesn't think there is any Philosophy outside the generalizations of physical science."[6] Peirce was never supportive of Dewey's work and ended up having to compete with Dewey unsuccessfully for an academic appointment at the University of Chicago in 1896.

Not surprisingly, Dewey's estimation of Morris was completely different. Morris had a special gift for putting philosophical ideas in a historical context that Dewey found extremely helpful. Morris showed how presuppositions about knowledge and existence are continually reformulated to yield new solutions to old problems. In Morris's seminar "The Science of Knowledge," students were required to trace the intellectual lineage of a disputed issue or theme, showing how the fulcrum of the debate was shifted over time to support different interpretations. Morris's predilection for idealism was obvious. According to Morris, there were essentially two points of departure in philosophical inquiry: a science of knowing and a science of being. A science of knowing championed by Locke and other British empiricists posited subject and object in a mechanical relationship and focused on the impact of the object on subject's sense impressions.

1. G. Stanley Hall, about 1910, shortly after Freud's visit to Clark University. Clark University Archives, Worcester, Massachusetts.

A science of being is best exemplified by Hegelian idealism—one that Morris stressed sees subject and object in an organic relation such that "being is *within* consciousness."[7] Already a Hegelian convert, Dewey found Morris's criticisms of transcendental theories of knowledge persuasive, Dewey observed, because "[h]e came to Kant through Hegel instead of to Hegel by way of Kant, so that his attitude towards Kant was the critical one expressed by Hegel."[8] Morris found in Dewey a kindred Hegelian spirit. He helped Dewey secure his first academic appointment at the University of Michigan in 1884 where Morris had been appointed to head the philosophy department.

G. STANLEY HALL AND GERMAN PSYCHOLOGY

Dewey's rapture with Hegel may be hard to fathom, Max Eastman wrote. "Unless you understand how exciting it is to fall in love with Hegel—and what hard work—there is very little Dewey can tell you about those years at Johns Hopkins. It was a full-time romance."[9] Although amusing, Eastman's account of Dewey's preoccupation with Hegel is a bit exaggerated, because Dewey was exposed by Hall to the fledgling field of psychology. Hall provided a fairly sophisticated introduction to experimental methods and the theoretical literature on human growth. Embracing Hegel in his youth, Hall later jettisoned Hegelian dialectics, which he considered "valueless as a method."[10]

Hall considered Dewey's single-minded pursuit of Hegelian thought to be seriously misadvised. Hall's impatience with Dewey's Hegelianism stemmed from his own disillusionment with German idealism and Harris's cliquish followers in St. Louis. Hall advised President Gilman early on that he had "doubts about Dewey's ability as a philosopher," but recommended that Dewey's fellowship be continued his second year, despite his reservations about Dewey's Hegelian misadventures.[11] Any promise that Dewey showed in experimental psychology unfortunately went unacknowledged by Hall, who invited Dewey's fellow graduate students James Cattell and Joseph Jastrow to collaborate in laboratory experiments that measured the relation between sensation and perception.[12]

Hall was eminently suited for his professorship in psychology, a discipline which best expressed the turn-of-the-century modernist impulses to drop metaphysics and embrace science. Trained for the ministry at the Union Theological Seminary, Hall forsook the black frock of Puritan piety in 1869 to enter the bold world of German idealism and science. He took an extended tutorial on Hegel with Friedrich Trendelenburg, but also studied physiology and anthropology under Emil du Bois-Reymond and Rudolf Virchow.[13] Following his graduate studies back in America with William James in 1878, Hall returned to Europe and acquired extensive post-doctoral training from the German psychologist Wilhelm Wundt.

At the forefront of research on the brain, Wundt challenged the conventional stimulus-response theory that sensorimotor functions could be explained solely by the firing of neurons in response to external stimulation. He argued instead that the unity and integrity of mind and body—thought and action—could be better explained by mechanisms of excitation and inhibition.[14] Wundt closely observed and dissected the extensive fiber connections between neurons, now known as axons and dendrites, to determine their role in the central nervous system. These interneuronal connections appeared to mediate the discharge of energy through the antagonistic processes of excitation and inhibition, making possible the coordination of separate functions. Wundt's ideas strongly influenced Dewey's thinking about brain function, which Dewey would later characterize as involving a reciprocal interaction between stimulus and response.

Hall did not pursue brain research at Johns Hopkins, preferring to study how growth processes affect motor and perceptual development.[15] Hall eventually published in 1904 a remarkable theoretical synthesis of studies of biological growth processes in *Adolescence*.[16] In this book Hall contended that children mature through several stages of motor, cognitive, and emotional development. He believed that evidence, which showed that the cerebellum and older regions of the brain mature before the cortex and prefrontal areas, supported the theory that children recapitulate through their development the evolution of the human species. Dewey did not accept this literal construal of the relation between ontogeny and phylogeny. Not until his collaboration in McGraw's studies of neurobehavioral development in the 1930s, however, was Dewey able to formulate what he believed to be a more scientifically credible alternative. Nevertheless, Hall introduced Dewey to the writings of biologists such as William Preyer and C. S. Minot, whose pioneering discoveries about growth processes provided Dewey a scientific point of departure for his own subsequent observational studies of children begun in the 1890s at the University of Chicago.

EXPERIMENTING WITH CONSCIOUSNESS

Hall's charismatic style and provocative speculations about the natural rhythms underpinning neuromuscular and perceptual development reinforced in Dewey's mind the essential truths of Hegelianism. Consciousness was indeed a developmental phenomenon whose pathways of emergence were imperceptibly etched in the processes of human thought. Dewey had only one opportunity in Hall's class on physiological and experimental psychology to study consciousness experimentally. Dewey still believed at this time that Samuel Butler's theory of development that we retain memories of ancestral behaviors had a kernel of truth. Moreover, the New Divinity sectarians had already argued that much of our mental thoughts and moral dispositions appear influenced by psychical activities that never come into consciousness. Dewey suspected that these two phenomena could be demonstrated to be related experimentally by showing that attention operates through mechanisms of association and dissociation, which determine how memory and perception become integrated in thought.

Dewey informed his undergraduate mentor William Torrey about his plans to conduct experimental studies. Dewey complained to Torrey that prevailing theories were misleading because they presented one-sided and mistaken conceptions of how consciousness functions. Dewey described the basis of his misgivings by saying that:

> It seems to the commonest defect of the theories of consciousness is that it [is] looked at or on *affection* of subject, as something going over its surface, and lighting up now a portion here, and now there, or else that as in Hume, Mill, etc., it is something which belongs to the 'perception' or object entirely—the result being in either case that we know nothing but phenomena, while as it seems to me, any state of consciousness contains in itself both subject and object. In short, consciousness is neither presentation *to* something or *of* something beyond it or behind it. An unconscious psychical activity means one that has lost its own existence and has been taken up into the mind, i.e., has become one of the functions whereby the mind apperceives.[17]

Closing his letter in a self-deprecating but serious tone, Dewey announced that he intended to pursue the problem further, saying "Well, I didn't mean to bore you with this, which I could hardly make clear anyway, but I have been very much interested in the subject myself. I intend now taking it for a thesis subject when I come up for the Ph.D. degree."[18]

Although no copy has ever been found of his dissertation, Dewey is likely to have presented a Hegelian critique of Kant's notion of self-consciousness, drawing on the literature in experimental psychology to support his critique. We get a glimpse of what he may have been up to in his thesis by examining what he said in an article about Kant published during the year he completed his dissertation. Dewey speculated in that essay that if Kant had viewed thought as a psychological process "at once synthetic and analytic, differentiating and integrating in its own nature," then he would have demonstrated the Hegelian thesis that "permanent, identical, self-consciousness" consists in "differentiating itself into successive states of consciousness."[19] Clearly, for Dewey, consciousness is involved in the act of assigning boundaries between one's own sentient states and that of another, while making possible the sharing of ideas between two minds.

Although Dewey provided only fragmentary descriptions of his own psychological experiments in his correspondence with Torrey, his methods were clearly grounded in psychological theories advanced by Wundt and Theodule Ribot. Dewey indicated to Torrey that in one experiment he tried "to determine, if possible, what effect fixing attention upon one thing very strongly has upon a 'remainder' in consciousness."[20] No evidence remains as to precisely how Dewey structured these experiments. Dewey provides some clues in his text *Psychology* as to what underlying processes he expected to find. There he predicted that the longer an individual focuses on the same object or repeated event, the more likely that the object or event will become detached from its momentary signs and re-represented to include connections or meanings beyond that suggested at the outset.[21]

The capacity to dissociate or detach elements from the sequence in which they are experienced, Dewey believed, made it possible for individuals to anticipate novel or unexpected events.[22] This was consistent with how Wundt and Ribot used the term "dissociation," to describe how subconscious feelings rooted in memory play an important role in shifting the focus of conscious attention.[23] In other words, the human capacity to anticipate and represent novel events in familiar terms was constantly undergoing expansion through subconscious processes involving what Dewey called "idealization," or the transformation of sensations into useable forms of knowledge.

Dewey described another experiment that he conducted to determine the "effect attention has in producing involuntary muscular movements—something after the mind reading fashion."[24] It is likely that here Dewey is alluding to situations involving behaviors that did not involve explicit consciousness. Psychologists noticed that when individuals were placed under hypnosis, they could be ordered to move and do things without their awareness nor subsequent memory of doing so. In this instance, it was claimed that thought could be completely separated from action or ends to which it was related. Boris Sidis contended that the fixation of attention, when combined with the inhibition of voluntary movements, contributes to a "disaggregation of consciousness" and the "formation of dissociations which constitute the soil of all psychopathic diseases based on fear."[25]

In contrast, Dewey wanted to show that the inhibition of motor response does not necessarily involve the dissociation of thought from deed. He wanted to distinguish between those instances in which the suspension of action enlarges the meaningfulness of the situation and those in which an individual does something without knowing the reason for doing it. While Dewey conceded that it may be possible to get someone to do something contrary to his or her will or intentions, or to express an unreasonable fear, to do so successfully requires that the subject submit to a temporary limitation of his or her field of vision and range of motor response. This is precisely the opposite way of employing suggestion, as Dewey understood the phenomenon. In his view a suggestive idea is seen to have wider meaning or intellectual and emotional implications than initially perceived.

HEGELIAN EVANGELISM AT THE UNIVERSITY OF MICHIGAN

Morris admired Dewey's spirited advocacy of a Hegelian worldview because most of Morris's contemporaries at Johns Hopkins did not think Hegel had anything important to contribute to science. Morris made sure that he had Dewey in tow on his return to the University of Michigan in 1884 by getting him a teaching appointment in the department of philosophy. Dewey's first five years at Michigan revealed his strong predilection for evangelism and only occasional interest in science. Dewey's limited excursions into the biology laboratory resulted one time in an embarrassing incident. Dewey started a small fire while varnishing human brain specimens.[26]

Under Morris's leadership, outsiders easily could have mistaken the philosophy department for a monastery for the scholastic worship of Hegelian principles of Christian thought. The trustees were delighted because the students' minds and their religious faith were "as safe under Morris and Dewey as [they] had been under clergymen" who preceded them.[27] The curriculum was weighed down with courses on the history of philosophy, the philosophy of science, and history of ethics, as viewed from Hegel's lofty perch, with only a smattering of attention to Spencer, John Stuart Mill, and the British Utilitarians.

Dewey devoted a great deal of his time away from the classroom on the Michigan campus discussing issues about faith and Christian ethics with students. Dewey was a regularly scheduled speaker at the Student Christian Association and taught a Bible class, which focused on the life of Christ. He published several of these lay sermons in the Association's *Monthly Bulletin*.[28]

Dewey also attended the First Congregational Church in Ann Arbor, where he taught a Sunday school class and attended business meetings. Dewey's tireless devotion to these duties was an impressive testament to the depth of his Calvinist upbringing and indicative of his increased sense of confidence in social situations.

Dewey became acquainted with his future wife Alice Chipman when she was an undergraduate majoring in philosophy. She was active in the department's Philosophical Society, presenting a paper at one the first meetings. A graduate of a Baptist seminary in a nearby town, Alice possessed an independent mind, tempestuous spirit, and strong principles that led her to question the authority of formal institutions, including the church. In this respect, she was a lot like Dewey's mother. But Alice's belief that "ecclesiastic institutions had benumbed rather than promoted" a critical attitude and intolerance of social injustice gradually eased Dewey out of active participation in church-sponsored activities and launched him into community activism.[29]

John and Alice started a family that would eventually include seven children, one of whom, Evelyn (b. 1889), would become a collaborator in Dewey's educational experimentation and reform activities in the 1920s and 1930s. They had three sons that included Frederick (b. 1887), Morris (b. 1893), and Gordon (b. 1895). Morris, an intellectually precocious boy, tragically died of diphtheria in 1895. Gordon died of typhoid fever in 1904 while visiting Italy with his family. Shortly after Gordon's death, John and Alice adopted Sabino, an eight-year-old Italian orphan. In addition, they had two other daughters, Lucy (b. 1897) and Jane (b. 1900). Jane attained a Ph.D. in physics in the 1920s and obtained a coveted fellowship to study with Niels Bohr in Copenhagen.

The few years at Michigan spent with Morris provided Dewey a unique opportunity to intensely scrutinize the boundaries that purportedly distinguished the metaphysical from the psychological study of the mind. Morris's courses on Hegel's logic augmented Dewey's endeavor by furnishing tools with which to probe the interstices of mind and thought which make possible consciousness and experience. The classroom provided a convenient stage for Dewey to rehearse many of the ideas that would eventually appear in his text *Psychology,* published in 1887. But his lectures were not easy to follow because he was introducing ideas that were contrary to the accepted logic of how people think. The British empiricists who dominated American scholarship argued that thinking involves a cognitive process whereby sensations produce representations and associations that are linked through ideas to furnish thoughts and statements about the identity of things. Dewey advanced a contrary notion that thought commences in non-cognitive experiences involving the attempt to render conscious and explicit the context in which specific feelings and sensations become meaningful. Thought progressed, according to Dewey, not through a cumulative addition of separate sensations or associations into one idea, but through a process involving the continuous differentiation of a feeling into alternative states of mind.

CREATING A COALITION OF IDEALISTS

The nurturing academic environment under Morris at Michigan allowed Dewey to take significant, although at times faltering, strides toward his goal of developing a theory of mind grounded in psychology. But the president of the fledgling University of Minnesota got wind of Dewey and made a compelling offer in 1888 to chair the philosophy department. The appointment included an advance in rank to professor and a substantial increase in salary to support his growing family. Beyond these inducements, his reasons for leaving Michigan were not self-evident. Dewey mentioned finding attractive the challenge of building up the program in a new university, but it also represented the opportunity to break free from Morris's tutelage and scholarly expectations. He naturally wanted the opportunity to be tested on his own and to see if he had the ability to exercise leadership.

However, Morris's unexpected death on a camping trip just six months into the academic year and an offer to return the next year to Michigan to chair the philosophy department cut short Dewey's stay at his new post. Dewey's triumphant return to the University of Michigan in 1889 as the head of the philosophy department was hailed by the board of regents, who observed with some trepidation that "Dewey may not be as ripe and complete a scholar as his predecessor, but he has already shown a degree of ability that has compelled recognition all over the country, and which must remove all doubt and misgivings as to the future of the Philosophical department."[30] Indeed, Dewey's soaring reputation in philosophy made it possible for him to attract other scholars who showed promise in making distinguished contributions to the field. Not surprisingly, the department would continue to serve as a secular chapel for the worship of Hegelian ideas. Dewey surrounded himself with men who had Congregationalist backgrounds and a particular bent for Hegel. But the new faculty members brought with them a strong appreciation for functional psychology and evolutionary biology that Dewey believed would reveal the scientific underpinnings of Hegel's metaphysics.

For example, James Tufts, son of a Congregationalist minister and graduate of Yale Divinity School, took over Dewey courses in psychology and ethics, and he eventually co-authored with Dewey a book on ethics. In addition, Dewey got from Harvard two outstanding pupils of William James and Josiah Royce, both of whom received additional training in psychology from German universities. One was Alfred Lloyd, who contributed courses in logic and the history of philosophy. Lloyd later published his treatise in applied Hegelianism called *Dynamic Idealism*, in which he argued that consciousness develops in interaction with the environment.

The other Harvard graduate was George Herbert Mead. Mead was a brilliant and original philosopher who forged a close relationship with Dewey that would have lasting intellectual consequences. Mead found through Hegel a

2. Formal portrait made when Dewey
was department head at the University of
Michigan, 1893. Original copy owned by
Dr. Philip Smith.
Special Collections, Morris Library, Southern Illinois University, Carbondale, Illinois.

pathway that would lead to important insights about the psychological and social processes involved in the construction of the "self." Mead's greatest insight
was that consciousness presupposed the knowledge and existence of other
minds capable of sharing ideas and experiences. Thinking did not occur in a
solipsistic vacuum but involved intentionality and the imputation of feelings
and ideas to other persons. Mead saw mind as a medium for communication
and intersubjective understanding. He argued that our conception of self or
personal identity emerges from initially undifferentiated social situations. Only
later on in development does a sense of self emerge in which beliefs and interests are claimed as individual possessions. Dewey found Mead's theory compelling because it underscored the idea that knowledge was a product of social
interaction and shared experience.[31]

METAPHYSICS OR PSYCHOLOGICAL SCIENCE?

Dewey still had a long way to go to fulfill the goal of comprehending the
mind—a goal he shared with Mead, Tufts, and his other colleagues at Michigan. The young Dewey struggled to clear a philosophical pathway through the
underbrush of formal logic that obscured how mind and consciousness functioned through experience. Kant erred, Dewey supposed, because he deduced
consciousness from *a priori* principles about mind that were posited to exist
wholly apart from human experience. Yet Dewey believed that consciousness is
a fact of experience and self-consciousness is a trait possessed by minds capable

of self-knowledge through psychological experience. Dewey accepted Hegel's view that the mind through which consciousness emerges dwells *in* the process of thought and not *beyond* it. While Dewey insisted that his conception of mind was naturalistic and empirically defensible, critics still found "illusory" Dewey's contention that consciousness provided a universal standpoint of knowledge and self-understanding. The objection was that even if Dewey could demonstrate that consciousness exists as a property of all human minds, this does nothing to render objectively knowable the contents of consciousness or the essentially subjective nature of human experience.[32]

Dewey's *Psychology* was an ambitious attempt to define the premises of a new psychology that was supported by scientific evidence. Although not possessing the encyclopedic command of the experimental literature that James persuasively marshaled with such literary skill in his *Principles of Psychology*, Dewey based his ideas on controversial studies by scientists who were making pathbreaking discoveries about the brain and nervous system. Unfortunately, few readers acknowledged Dewey's scrupulousness, because he was not always explicit about the science underpinning his ideas. Dewey naively expected reviewers to take a metaphysical leap of faith in endorsing the Hegelian ideas that they considered scientifically unsubstantiated. Dewey's barely disguised Hegelian attempt to show how consciousness acquires universality through the stages of knowledge, feeling, and will did not generate rave reviews.

Dewey's former teacher from Johns Hopkins, G. Stanley Hall, exuded sarcasm by saying: "That the absolute idealism of Hegel could be so cleverly adapted to be 'read into' such a range of facts, new and old, is indeed a surprise as great as when geology and zoology are ingeniously subjected to the rubrics of the six days of creation."[33] William James wrote that he "felt quite enthused at the first glance, hoping for something really fresh; but I am sorely disappointed when I come to read [it]." James added that his enthusiasm waned when he saw Dewey "taking the edge off definiteness" by "trying to mediate between the bare miraculous self and the concrete particulars of individual mental lives."[34] These were not encouraging words coming from two of America's most respected psychologists.

LEAPING THROUGH THE HEGELIAN ABSOLUTE

It is not surprising that Dewey dropped explicit reference to Hegel by the 1890s. Hegel was like an albatross blocking the acceptance of his ideas. Any further working through of Hegel's method would have to be done in the privacy of his own mind, or at least within the confines of the classroom. The difficulty Dewey was having with Hegel was that he furnished no psychological principle or mechanism to explain why the process of becoming should involve the negation of being by its other. In other words, Dewey wanted to understand the process through which a particular form of an idea, a thing, or an activity gets reconstituted through experience to reveal its actual existence. Dewey's own statements provide a striking metaphorical allusion to the challenge he faced in attempting to rectify Hegel's errors. He recalled that:

> I jumped through Hegel, I should say, not just out of him. I took some of the hoop (continuity, anti-hard-and-fast separations) with me, and also carried away considerable of the paper the hoop was filled with. He did me one service—he saved me from the Kantian bug, which was all the vogue—and, in fact, more than once.[35]

During the course of this long leap, Dewey turned to neurophysiologists to find the stable scientific ground on which to secure a smooth landing. Wilhelm Wundt, the German experimentalist, and C. L. Herrick, founder of the "American School" of neurology (see chapter 3), seemed eminently qualified to help put Hegelian consciousness in scientific perspective. Wundt challenged the view favored among introspectionists and associationists of his era that complex images are constructed through the accumulation of stimuli through individual nerve fibers. Neural processes were not as straightforward as this. He found that stimuli travel through a complex and convoluted series of connections between fibers and cells, involving a cumulative process of excitation and inhibition. Each successive cell reacts with the previous one until a unified image is constructed.

Clarence Herrick, a self-designated "psychobiologist," contended that the unity of conscious perception is made possible by an act of attending to those features of a situation that are of interest. Consequently, we are able to continuously distinguish between images at the "focal" point or foreground of consciousness and "marginal" features in the background.[36] This led Dewey to conclude that whatever is actual or here and now in consciousness depends on active attention and limitation rather than on a passive acceptance.[37]

Wundt's and Herrick's theories were highly suggestive about how human thought and action can be understood as a continuous neurobehavioral event that Dewey described in his famous article on the "Reflex Arc Concept in Psychology" in 1896.[38] These and other studies helped Dewey find a way to ground Hegel's dialectic in psychology. Dewey confidently proclaimed in his seminars on Hegel's logic at the University of Chicago during the 1890s that "[p]sychologically, the dialectic means that all inhibition is also stimulus and thereby contributes to a new coordination."[39] Thinking begins, Dewey asserts, "only when there is a tendency to doubt, and in doubt there is an is not."[40] Dewey contended that this insight gave a whole new meaning to Hegel's use of the terms "being" and "non-being." For "if we interpret being, not being, and becoming in terms of focus and background," Dewey argues, "then Hegel's statement that everything becomes another means that attention changes sensation."[41] Non-being simply involves "thinking of nothing in particular," according to Dewey, "involving a sort of general acquiescence."[42] That everything simultaneously is and is not simply means that something could become one thing or another through attention and action, involving the expansion and contraction of the field of vision and motor response. "Becoming produces something definite at every step in the process of growth," Dewey says, "but you get something determinate and limited only when you interrupt that process to reflect upon it."[43]

Dewey also spent a lot of time in the classroom spelling out how revolutionary advances in physics enabled philosophers to move the debate about the ontology of consciousness beyond the boundaries of immanent and transcendent theories of knowledge. Dewey was intrigued by Leibniz's ontology because the principles of force he advanced to explain natural and spiritual phenomena challenged Newtonian mechanics. In his quarrel with Newton, Leibniz believed that the gravitational principle of attractive and repulsive force depicted a discontinuous universe contrary to the belief in the omniscience and continuity of a divine spirit, and one that was at odds with the law of conservation of energy. That is why Leibniz insisted that force is self-sufficient because the same quantity of energy is always preserved in the motion of matter (i.e., monads) wherever they are found in the universe. Leibniz preferred to think of the universe in organic rather than mechanistic terms. In this universe change occurred in infinitesimal degrees rather than in discontinuous leaps and bounds that is characteristic of our modern conception of an exploding and expanding universe.

Dewey was not unsympathetic to Leibniz's organicism and his notion of continuity, but he believed that only Hegel truly grasped the constructive force of dialectic oppositions in furnishing the soul the energy it needed to escape bondage to the material manifestations of human existence. By asserting that all monads are self-identical, Leibniz was unable to fully account for why it is possible or even necessary for monads to exist in a separate form. There actually is no need for monads to come together, for if they are self-subsisting but identical substances, Dewey concluded, they already are in a de facto state of harmonious unity. From his Hegelian perch, Dewey sensed that Leibniz's holism was spurious. Only a *relational* conception of matter and spirit—one that entails a dynamic harmony of opposites—could lay claim to being holistic.[44]

Dewey was unable to fully exploit the naturalistic and developmental implications of Hegelian dialectics, however, until he enlisted the help of physicists Michael Faraday and later James Clerk Maxwell. They showed how to overcome the metaphysical conundrums about the origin of force and elusive relationship between matter and motion over which Newton and his rivals had become deadlocked.[45] Faraday did not limit his criticisms of Newtonian mechanics to their theoretical differences about force. He was calling into question the adequacy of using deductive mathematical methods to disclose the underlying phenomenal attributes of force, which only could be truly revealed through experience. Faraday's insistence that experience should discipline thought led to his becoming one of the most publicly renowned and admired experimentalists in the nineteenth century. He possessed a great gift, shared with Huxley, of being able to perform his experiments so effortlessly and convincingly that the phenomena he demonstrated appeared to occur naturally without even a trace of human ingenuity or artifice.

Faraday's admonishment of scientists to suspend disbelief and show humility in the presence of nature unwittingly echoed Hegel's sentiments that resonated in Dewey's attentive mind. As David Gooding put it aptly, Faraday was performing "in nature's school," which sometimes required that he personally become a part of the experiment to discover and then replicate the effects of these discoveries for an awestruck audience. This experiential basis of Faraday's approach to science was no better illustrated than by his sitting inside an iron cage charged with high voltage to determine whether the charge penetrated the cage or remained contained within a field on the outside of the cage (which it did, fortunately for Faraday).[46]

ENTROPY AND THE UNIVERSAL CONVERTIBILITY OF ENERGY

A brief digression into nineteenth-century physics will help put in sharper historical focus the controversy regarding force and matter into which Dewey plunged. This will make sense of why Dewey introduced technical terms from physics regarding force and energy in his earliest writings to support his conceptions of brain function and mind. Newtonian physics set in motion in the seventeenth century a revolution in our understanding of gravitation and the mechanics of force and energy, the implications of which took more than two centuries to fully comprehend. One of the most pressing problems preoccupying scientists was how to measure force and render this universal phenomenon comprehensible in quantitative terms. A significant breakthrough in resolving the mystery of force posed by Newtonian mechanics came when the German physiologist and psychologist Hermann von Hemholtz proposed in 1847 the second law of thermodynamics or the law of conservation of energy.

Hemholtz brilliantly synthesized the work of his contemporaries by proposing that energy can neither be created nor destroyed but remains constant despite undergoing transformations in form. Hemholtz proposed this law to show how the Newtonian central forces governing the relationship between inorganic physical bodies in space also applied to living bodies, because both involved essentially the same mechanisms through which energy is converted into heat to do work. Hemholtz was in fact proposing not only a principle of conservation but a mechanism of conversion that would account for how energy can undergo transformation from one form to another.[47]

In proposing the principle of conservation, Hemholtz was simply synthesizing the work of numerous other nineteenth-century scientists such as Joule, Carnot, Holtzmann and Faraday. Each of these scientists had successfully converted through experimental laboratory processes known sources of energy, such as motion, light, heat, electricity, magnetism, into alternative forms.

While few disputed the idea that energy is conserved, not everyone shared Hemholtz's belief that the processes in which force is converted into alternative forms of energy could be convincingly explained by Newtonian gravitational mechanics of attraction and repulsion.[48]

Faraday was not satisfied with Newton's theory of central gravitational forces because it failed to explain how force could act at a distance between objects. Faraday believed that he had found a provisional solution to the problem of action at a distance. Newton held that matter consisted of indivisible and impenetrable atoms that were surrounded by gravitational forces of attraction and repulsion. Newton considered matter to be passive and held that it must be acted upon by external forces to overcome its inertia. Newton believed that the ultimate origin of matter was better regarded as a question of faith than of scientific judgment.

Faraday disagreed with Newton's opinion that matter was not susceptible to scientific scrutiny. Faraday saw matter differently as contiguous particles that are extended continuously throughout space and are mutually penetrable by force. Faraday contended that the exchange of charge between magnetic poles was affected by the *medium* through which electricity was transmitted. Faraday's experiments with electromagnetism showed that magnetic poles are connected by invisible lines of force through which a charge is transmitted and that the curve or configuration of these lines would vary according to the medium (i.e., metal, chemical substance, etc.,) in which they are introduced. In essence, Faraday was proposing that *interactions of matter* essentially involve interactions between particles that possess internal "centers of force." This discovery led to the extraordinarily momentous idea that matter possessed potential energy that could be converted through interaction of charged particles into kinetic energy needed to do work. Faraday's attempt to show that matter and energy are interrelated reflected his strong opposition to materialism and reductionism, but he was never able to persuade his colleagues that diamagnetism (i.e., the interdependence of magnetic lines of force and polarized light) was a *new* force of nature.[49]

James Clerk Maxwell brilliantly developed a theoretical framework within which Faraday's discoveries could be given a mathematical foundation. Maxwell demonstrated that the form of any material system derives from the interaction of the potential energy of its configuration and kinetic energy of its motion. These interactions bring about a continuous displacement of mass of individual particles whose force and position is relative to the velocity of the whole system. This phenomenon of displacement is best visualized by imagining a school of fish whose shape and contours are constantly undergoing change due to frequent shifts in direction and speed of the school as a whole. Maxwell derived from these basic relationships between energy, matter, and motion a probabilistic theory that could be used to define the behavioral properties or parameters of molecular and other dynamic phenomena. This was a stunning achievement. Maxwell took Faraday's discoveries and developed them into a full-blown field theory that paved the way for Dewey to further develop the neurobiological implications of this seminal interactionist conception of human experience involving the interchange of energies.[50]

These important advances in nineteenth-century physics were, of course, well beyond Hegel's paradigm. Hegel remained within the Newtonian framework, whose influence is evident in Hegel's philosophy of nature. He found Newton's theories of gravitation useful because they helped explain how *form* and *content* of matter could be separated and recombined through the forces of attraction and repulsion. Hegel was aware that matter possessed a specific gravity that could be quantified. But he was unable to explain how this factor operated in conjunction with motion and gravity to effectuate the separation of the form from matter needed for spirit and consciousness to be fully expressed in nature. Hegel likened the projection of feeling beyond its embodiment in a specific form to a falling body the center of gravity of which is posited externally, enabling it to assume an ideal form before being reconstituted through the force of gravity to assume a final concrete form. Dewey saw in Faraday's interactionism and Maxwell's energetics of matter and motion a way to complete Hegel's dialectical equation for the release of the mind and soul from matter by showing how this occurred through the reciprocal exchange of energy between brain and behavior.

Faraday and like-minded colleagues sensed that a more fundamental principle of equivalence was at work than was implicit in the law of conservation of energy. This was the idea that the powers or forces of nature are essentially interchangeable. Faraday and William Grove collaborated with other colleagues in popularizing the idea of the universal convertibility of energy in a book on the *Correlation and Conservation of Forces*, published in 1846.[51] Grove acknowledged that the thesis of universal convertibility had not been proven. This required demonstrating that conversion leads to results that are *reversible*. Consequently, according to Grove, "it ought to follow, that when we collect the dissipated and changed forces, and reconvert them, the initial motion, affecting the same amount of matter with the same velocity, should be reproduced, and so of the change of matter produced by the other forces."[52] They believed that someday a common denominator could be found that would establish the equivalence of the forces of nature, and this continues to be an elusive goal of twenty-first-century physics.[53]

Undaunted, the contributors speculatively examined the ramifications of the thesis of the convertibility of force for the theoretical unification of the natural sciences. For example, both Grove and William Carpenter boldly contended that a universal energy constant would make it possible to understand the neural processes that connect brain to mind and consciousness.[54] Dewey's earliest writings about the brain indicate that he considered the physics of energy to hold great promise in unlocking the secrets of the brain and mind.

Dewey also took this notion of universal convertibility one step further by reasoning from analogy that art and inquiry involve a similar transformation of force into equivalent forms of aesthetic and intellectual energy. Dewey saw inquiry as involving the continuous substitution of factors known to produce specific consequences by those that alter the sequence of interacting forces to produce a different outcome. Dewey believed that this same process was at work in aesthetics. The feelings evoked by a work of art undergo transformation as our vision is redirected by the curvature of lines, the contours of forms, and shading of colors to reveal previously unseen but unmistakable underlying patterns. Not until he wrote *Art as Experience* was Dewey able to describe metaphorically the underlying unity of forces that make possible the integration of perception and behavior that constitute human experience.

This nineteenth-century notion of *universal convertibility,* as Thomas Kuhn points out, however, was based on the untested presumption "that since any power can produce any other and be produced by it, the equality of cause and effect demands a uniform quantitative equivalence between each pair of powers."[55] Kuhn argues that the mental leaps of bad judgment that led Faraday, Grove, Hemholtz, and many others to embrace the idea of the universal convertibility of force was due to a predisposition "to see a single indestructible force at the root of all natural phenomena."[56] This predisposition was shared by German naturalists such as Friedrich Schelling, who advanced an organic theory based on the unity of the forces of nature, a theory that strongly influenced the thinking of some of the proponents of universal convertibility.[57]

Unfortunately, a major obstacle stood in the way of the goal of subsuming the physics of matter by a theory of energetics. Proof of the first law of thermodynamics, that energy can neither be created nor destroyed, presupposes the validity of the second law of thermodynamics, that the conversion of work to heat is *irreversible* and that all mechanical systems characteristically exhibit increased entropy or dissipation of energy over time. Dewey saw the central nervous system as an ingenious system for partially circumventing the energetic limitations of entropy by spreading out the effects of stimulation to ensure a coordinated response. Dewey observed that the buildup of excitation in one area is usually directed away to other structures or functions. While denying "that there is anywhere a violation of the law of conservation of energy," Dewey insisted nevertheless that "the nervous system is a mechanism for using up that quantity of force in indirect ways so that the final outcome will be redirected in quite a different direction."[58] Consciousness reflected this tension or imbalance between the concentration of nervous energy in one part of the organism and the other activities of the organism as a whole.

THE PHYSICAL EQUIVALENTS OF THOUGHT

That Dewey was bringing these latest developments in physics to bear in his analysis of neurophysiology is evident in his essay "Soul and Body." Dewey believed that Wundt's conceptualization of the nervous system "as a contemporaneous process of stimulation and reaction or inhibition" best expressed how energy is conserved through the reciprocal conversion of potential and kinetic energy. Dewey noted that:

> Any excitation tends to set up such chemical change as will reduce it to relatively simpler and more stable compounds. There is thus set free an amount of energy equivalent to the amount which would be required to lift this lower compound up to its higher state again. The potential energy of the unstable compound has, in short, become kinetic. The first element in nervous action is, therefore, the excitatory or stimulating, which has the setting free of nervous energy for its result. But if this were all, the energy of the nervous system would be soon used up. . . .

To prevent this from happening, Dewey contends that some energy must be stored in another form:

> There must be opposed to the exciting activity one which resists, and thereby prevents the whole force at hand, the whole unstable compound, from being used, and which also restores it as it is expended. And so it is found that there is a complementary process. Not only is energy being constantly put forth, but energy is being constantly stored up or rendered latent. Not all the force which comes to a nervous element is employed in breaking down the unstable compounds and thereby losing energy; part—in some cases much the greater part—is used in building up these unstable compounds, thereby forming a reservoir of energy for future use, while the process itself acts as a restraint upon, a control over, the excitatory factor. Every nervous action is, therefore, a reciprocal function of stimulation, excitation and inhibition; control through repression.

Dewey denied that his account was materialistic and reductionist. To the contrary, the fact that not all energy is used up in involuntary reflex action but is conserved as potential energy to support higher cerebral functions meant, according to Dewey, "that the psychical is immanent in the physical." The soul is not embodied in the localization of function, Dewey argued, but is expressed in the distribution of energy and coordination of activities that must take place for an organism to achieve its higher ends.[59] According to Dewey, the soul emerged through the nervous system that posited objectives or purposes that are beyond immediate satisfaction and that require a deliberate and coordinated response. This deflection of impulse and measured use of energy constituted, for Dewey, the essence of moral conduct. The process through which energy is deferred through postponement of impulse was functionally equivalent, in Dewey's opinion, to right conduct, because moral conduct taps latent energy made available only through reflection.[60]

Dewey's functionalist account admittedly traded on the inability of neurologists of his era to explain higher cortical processes solely in terms of local reflex action. Consequently, speculation about how higher and lower functions were integrated abounded, even though Dewey's account did not specify the neural mechanisms involved. Nor did Dewey demonstrate in satisfactory scientific terms how brain and behavior undergo transformation through the purported Maxwellian processes without violating entropy and the laws of conservation of energy. This burden of demonstrating that biological phenomena involve transformational processes that are not constrained by entropy characteristic of all physical systems required far more sophisticated methods than were available to Dewey and his contemporaries.

Significantly, these early writings clearly foreshadow and explain why Dewey rejected as inadequate the reflex arc conception of psychology in 1896.[61] In a famous essay Dewey contended that stimulus and response could not be treated as if they were two separate events that are causally related. Instead, a stimulus acquires meaning and significance only when it is further elaborated by the motor acts undertaken to bring it under control. Only then does human perception become fully engaged in an act of conscious attention. Importantly, he surmised that this process of coordination of perception and action not only facilitated the exchange of physical energy between the individual and environment, but also brought about the redistribution of nervous energy from higher states of concentration to ones that are more evenly distributed. His predictions were confirmed and soon acquired scientific warrant.

Just a little more than a decade following the publication of Dewey's critique of the reflex arc theory, neurobiologist C. J. Herrick furnished evidence that strongly supported Dewey's contention that inhibition plays a fundamental role in redistributing energy and sustaining consciousness. Herrick argued that inhibition of immediate discharge contributes to the delay or pause between the anticipation and the consummation of an act that is needed to sustain the coordination between peripheral and central brain processes. This allows the brain to process information simultaneously from both input and output to effect proper motor coordination. "From both standpoints," Herrick declared, "Dewey's conception of the unitary nature of the organic circuit, as contrasted with the classical reflex arc concept, receives strong support."[62] Herrick concluded that the distinctive feeling of exercising free will that accompanies conscious action was not due to some feature of the stimulus or object itself, but resulted from "the backstroke or reverberation of a neural discharge from the periphery back to the cortex."[63] Intelligent action is made possible by the feedback that our brain receives indicating that we have accurately gauged the energy requirements for effective action.[64]

CHALLENGING DARWINIAN EVOLUTION

Dewey also persuasively deployed the principles of conservation of force and convertibility of energy to theorize about evolution. In classroom lectures at the University of Chicago near the turn of the twentieth century Dewey presented a brilliant critique of Darwinian evolution that proposed a highly original alternative explanation for variation and modification of species. As noted before, Dewey shared Samuel Butler's and Huxley's misgivings that natural selection did not really explain how species are modified through evolutionary processes. Environment is an agent of natural selection that favors certain random variations, but this does not explain how these variations are originated. This left the door wide open to almost any factor influencing the behavior of a species.

Dewey believed that processes in which traits are selected for fitness operated in a more indirect mediated fashion. He reasoned that behavioral adaptability depends, in part, on the functional capacities and needs of the organism, and its ability to handle uncertainty or respond to novelty. The challenges posed by an environment are not just external and behavioral but internal and physiological.[65] Every biological variation, Dewey contended, is a "mediation of a function already in existence."[66] But each variation is nevertheless, he cautioned, tentative and indeterminate with respect to the future course of development. The true test of the value of any biological modification then, he claimed, is not only whether it perpetuates immediate existence or confers adaptive advantage, but whether it also can be integrated into other ongoing functional processes.

Dewey warned that the problem of functional integrity should not be confused with the issue of genetic heritability or the intergenerational transmission of new traits. Heritability is a subsequent stage of phenotypic transformation, according to Dewey, in which modifications adopted by some individuals within a species are retained to become a general feature possessed by all subsequent generations of their offspring. This was the position put forward by neo-Lamarckians who supported the belief in the inheritance of acquired characteristics. Dewey saw the long-term viability of any slight individual variation in behavioral or physiological function depending in the first instance on whether it enhances the functional integration and needs of each individual within a species, whereas Darwin would have emphasized adaptation to the species' environment.

Dewey's theory put a different spin on evolution. Darwin held that similar species essentially competed for the same scarce resources. Consequently, only those individuals survive who best exploited and adapted to the changing availability of these resources. But Dewey added that each successful variation also potentially reduces competition between individuals within the same species rather than exacerbating it. Moreover, there is enough physiological variability (i.e., in metabolism and other systemic processes) between individuals within the same species to enable them to satisfy their biological needs by using slightly different strategies of coping with the environment. Consequently, he reasoned, "every specific variation must mean the constitution of a new environment that relieves the conflict previously going on between organisms that are homogeneous in their life habits."[67]

Dewey's attempt to furnish the evidence from physics and evolution to support his naturalistic conception of mind was ingenious. He was bringing Hegel up to date by wedding post-Newtonian conceptions of energy to psychological conceptions of nervous processes and to biological theories of evolution. The thesis of the universal convertibility of energy seemed to offer a promising way to avoid reductionism. The discovery that energy was not bound to specific material manifestations seemingly vindicated Hegel's view that soul was immanent in nature, striving to fulfill its ultimate moral purpose through developmental processes of reconstruction.

Dewey saw more clearly than his contemporaries that the mechanisms and functions that biologists described embodied Hegel's notion of mediated knowledge in that these life processes make possible the interaction between organism and environment. While Dewey used the term "interaction" to signify that hereditary and environmental factors were interrelated during the course of development, his contemporaries construed this to mean that individuals acquired experience by interacting with their environment. They incorrectly assumed that Dewey had adopted a neo-Lamarckian position that new habits can be transmitted from one generation to the next.[68] In fact, Dewey believed that hereditary and environmental factors did not interact *directly* with each other but were *mediated* by the ongoing interaction between structure and function, altering the timing and sequence of developmental processes. Concealed within the relatively similar outward appearance of human anatomy and reflexes, he contended, is a far greater potential for variation and psychological change through growth processes than is imagined possible through either genetic alteration or environmental influences.

Contemporary pragmatist Richard Rorty best expresses the lingering suspicion shared by many Dewey scholars today that Dewey failed at this point in his intellectual development to purge his naturalism of an implicit teleology. Consequently, Rorty claims that Dewey "deabsolutized Hegel," offering instead "a relativist and materialist version of teleology rather than an absolutist one."[69] Contrary to Rorty, I think Dewey was well on the way to overcoming the materialist and relativist traps that snared prominent nineteenth-century naturalists and philosophers. To succeed in that endeavor would require that Dewey find an equivalent for Spirit in the mind and the processes in which consciousness gives full expression to the nearly infinite possibilities lodged within human development. He turned increasingly to science to uncover these resources for transformation that lay dormant in the phenotype.

By the early 1890s, Dewey was already showing signs of having intellectually outgrown the department of philosophy at the University of Michigan. He focused increasingly on the experimental ramifications and developmental implications of his theory of mind that required more sophisticated tools of scientific investigation. By surrounding himself with colleagues who saw the world in similar terms, Dewey had only halfheartedly subjected his Hegelian premises to more intense critical and scientific scrutiny. He needed to converse with those who were more competent than he was in the sciences of growth and neurophysiology to see if his theory of mind could explain how learning occurs in early development. The University of Chicago furnished him an ideal place to develop a stronger scientific and pedagogical footing for his fledgling theory of mind.

THREE

Experimentalist in the Making

Dewey was appointed in 1894 to head the department of philosophy at the University of Chicago that included programs in psychology and pedagogy. This was a critical turning point in his career. Here Dewey emerged from an insulated academic life to confront the social upheaval wrought by industrialization and urbanization and to champion the cause of educational reform. Indeed, within two years of their arrival, Dewey and his wife Alice organized a laboratory school dedicated to innovative approaches to primary education that attracted national attention among educators. But a largely unknown story remains to be told about Dewey's acquaintances during this time, scientists who provided important insights about the brain and behavior that would strongly influence Dewey's educational experimentation and have a lasting impact on his philosophy of mind and theory of inquiry.

While Dewey may have been ahead of his philosophical colleagues in advancing a novel perspective about how we think, he was woefully deficient in scientific evidence to support his theories. Luckily for Dewey, his relative isolation from mainstream science was forever ended when he joined the faculty at the University of Chicago. Dewey was entering a new environment where experimentation rather than phenomenology was viewed as an indispensable tool for the conduct of inquiry. Dewey would no longer be preaching exclusively to faithful Hegelians, but would be trying to convince skeptical scientists that life could be explained in other than materialistic terms. His professional life became richly textured with collegial and community collaborations that would constitute the trademarks of his career as a public philosopher. Dewey and his colleagues adopted an interdisciplinary perspective to understand developmental phenomena that defied a reductionist explanation. These intellectual collaborations loosened but did not break Hegel's hold on Dewey's thinking. Instead, he cleverly deployed the knowledge he acquired from his scientific colleagues to ground Hegelian ideas in science by converting the phenomenology of being and becoming into psychological and ontological terms that could be tested scientifically. Dewey embarked on an ambitious undertaking that would require more than just the energy and concentration of one highly motivated but scientifically untrained philosopher.

The ongoing debate among scientists about human origins was increasingly focused on the issue of how the nervous system and brain evolved and whether humans are endowed with a unique intelligence. Dewey's emergent theory of mind became the focal point of intense scientific scrutiny among his colleagues, who adopted different positions about how to interpret the evidence of brain evolution and function, and how to assess the implications for human intellectual and emotional development. This intellectual ferment was reflected in Dewey's seminal writings of the period, as well as in his observational studies of how infants and young children learn through experience. Dewey also searched for ways that community-based schools could connect to the social settlement movement in advancing an agenda for urban reform.

Dewey's intellectual energies continued to be focused on a critical reformulation of Darwin's theory of evolution. Darwin put forward the first systematic theory to explain the evolutionary origins and function of the expression of emotions in animals and humans. His ingenious theory, however, was burdened with popular misconceptions about human phylogenetic heritage and bore the philosophical and theoretical deficiencies of the brain science of his era that his successors strove to overcome. In their attempts to rectify Darwin's errors, William James, James Mark Baldwin, and John Dewey each made important contributions to a theory of emotion that attempted to put it on a more secure philosophical and scientific footing. Dewey believed that Darwin and his successor's attempts to trace the origins of human consciousness and emotional experience back to a remote phylogenetic past, although scientifically alluring, were deeply flawed. Dewey succeeded where his contemporaries failed. He pointed the way out of the morass of recapitulationism and showed how a developmental theory of consciousness, mind, and emotion could be formulated that avoided the epistemological and ontological pitfalls of Darwin's theory.

LAYING THE FOUNDATIONS OF SCIENCE AT THE UNIVERSITY OF CHICAGO

Dewey carried forward his ambitious project to use Hegel's pioneering methods to reconstruct the logic of scientific inquiry. *Studies in Logical Theory*, published in 1903, marked the culmination of his project. In sentences so long they would have given William Faulkner pause, Dewey confidently asserted in this book that psychology provided the medium through which logic may be reconstructed. He said:

> Psychology as the natural history of various attitudes and structures through which experiencing passes, as an account of the conditions under which this or that attitude emerges, and of the way in which it influences, by stimulation or

inhibition, production of other states or conformations of reflection, is indispensable to logical evaluation, the moment we treat logical theory as an account of thinking as a response to its own generating conditions, and consequently judge its validity by reference to its efficiency in meeting its problems. The historical point of view describes the sequence; the normative follows the history to its conclusion, and then turns back and judges each historical step by viewing it in reference to its own outcome.[1]

This attempt to trace the origins of mind back through the experiential conditions that first engaged human thought in deliberate problem solving was an ambitious project. It also required that the processes by which intelligent action acquires value and worth be somehow experimentally reconstructed. To accomplish this objective, Dewey needed to mobilize the minds and talents of many scientists and persuade them to rededicate their efforts toward a common goal of determining how the brain evolved. Dewey also needed to show how human minds acquire judgment, and to explain how humans attain the uncanny capacity to use their experience as a tool to reflect back on their own history and generate values or constants by which they measure their own progress. Although only in the incipient stages of formation as a major research university, the University of Chicago seemed to Dewey to be in an excellent position to support an interdisciplinary approach to the life sciences. Indeed, President William Harper showed early signs of vigorously pursuing this goal by recruiting Dewey to an interdepartmental post and by attempting to consolidate biology-based disciplines into a unified core curriculum.

Established through a generous endowment by John D. Rockefeller in 1890, the University of Chicago sought to attract faculty who would boost the prestige of the institution as quickly as possible. Dewey was ranked third on a short list that included Harvard philosopher George Palmer and logician Charles Peirce. Ironically, Dewey was offered the appointment only after Palmer refused and then strongly recommended against hiring Peirce. The embittered Peirce later would cast aspersions on Dewey's Chicago brand of pragmatism by claiming that Dewey and his students were guilty of hypocrisy "by being greatly given over to what seems to me a debauched or loose reasoning." Peirce added sardonically that "Chicago hasn't the reputation of being a moral place, but I should think that the effect of living there upon a man like you to feel all the more the necessity of making didactic distinctions between right and wrong, truth and falsity."[2]

Peirce's misguided piousness came a little too late to derail Dewey's career. Dewey moved rapidly to build close ties with faculty members in the sciences, many of whom strongly supported Dewey's pragmatic conception of inquiry and who shared his commitment to a democratic society. Dewey's appointment was endorsed by James Tufts, who had joined the Chicago philosophy department the previous year. Dewey subsequently obtained faculty positions for James Angell, a former graduate student, and George Herbert Mead from the University of Michigan.

President Harper adopted an aggressive recruitment strategy to hire talented faculty members and research scientists. Instead of hiring professors in conventional scientific disciplines, he attracted young faculty members who pioneered new disciplines such as biology, embryology, and neurophysiology. Harper's first choice to provide leadership in the yet undefined program in the life sciences was Clarence Luther Herrick. A superbly gifted naturalist, philosopher, and comparative anatomist, Herrick was an American equivalent of the great German *Naturphilosophers* of the eighteenth and nineteenth centuries such as Schelling, Hemholtz, and Wundt. Herrick put his early training in geology to use by compiling a natural history field survey of flora and fauna in the state of Minnesota.

During his graduate studies in zoology in Leipzig, Herrick attended lectures by Hermann Lotze, a German philosopher who developed a theory of human reasoning based on available evidence about brain functions. Captivated by Lotze's speculative insights about the uncanny parallels between neural structures and logical thought processes, Herrick arranged to publish an English translation of his *Outlines of Psychology*. He contributed an afterword on the "Structure of the Brain," marshaling evidence from neuroanatomy that supported Lotze's propositions about mind and consciousness. Significantly, Lotze's work became the critical focal point of Dewey's *Studies in Logical Theory* in 1903.[3]

C. L. HERRICK AND THE "AMERICAN SCHOOL" OF NEUROLOGY

C. L. Herrick acquired an astonishing grasp of knowledge about the brain through experimental studies. He advanced bold theories about the nervous system and the role of consciousness in maintaining the equilibrium of mind and body that Dewey read and assigned to his classes. His pathbreaking theory that consciousness was a form of energy helped Dewey formulate a biologically sophisticated conception of mind. Scientists were unable to find any convincing evidence for the material basis of consciousness, nor had anyone been able to formulate a neurophysiological or psychological basis for the continuity of human experience. Herrick proposed to avoid these quandaries by arguing that consciousness maintains the balanced distribution of energy needed by the brain to regulate sensorimotor processes. He hypothesized that consciousness registers the discordance associated with indecision until an effective motor action is chosen.[4] Herrick also contended that the multiple pathways through which nervous energy is distributed contribute to the integration of the entire organism.[5] Thus Herrick anticipated the subsequent scientific discovery that cerebral metabolic processes play a fundamental role in neuromuscular growth and development.

Herrick was the titular founder of the so-called "American school" of neurology, whose adherents adopted a psychobiological perspective about the relation between brain and behavior. They were seeking to understand the mind from an evolutionary and developmental perspective and were critical of attempts to reduce mind to reflex. Leaders in this movement included psychiatrists Adolf Meyer and Harry Stack Sullivan and Columbia University neurologists Frederick Tilney and Henry Riley. Herrick's seminal research came to Dewey's attention when Dewey served as an associate editor of the *Psychological Review*. Herrick published several articles in the journal that summarized the psychological implications of his neuroanatomical and comparative studies of the brain. President Harper believed that the deeply religious Herrick could provide leadership in the biological sciences without alienating the university's Baptist sponsors. Herrick's reputation in scientific circles was considerable, and his founding editorship of the *Journal of Comparative Neurology and Psychology* at the University of Cincinnati provided additional incentive for Harper to bring him to Chicago.

Herrick strongly urged Harper to consider consolidating the different fields of physiology, psychology, and neurology into one department. Harper seemed amenable to this idea and encouraged Herrick to draw up a plan and recommend other scientists for faculty appointments. Unfortunately for Herrick, Harper lost confidence in Herrick's plan. Not surprisingly, Herrick withdrew his name from consideration in 1891, despite Harper's willingness to appoint Herrick to head a combined program of physiological psychology and comparative anatomy.[6] Instead, Harper appointed Charles O. Whitman, a rising star in biology at Clark University, to head the program in the biological sciences.

Deeply disillusioned, Herrick dissuaded Adolf Meyer from accepting a tenured professorship in neurology the following year, saying, "I would not advise you to associate yourself with Chicago University as long as Harper is president. . . . The paternalism of the institution is enough to prevent a self-respecting man from working in it."[7] Herrick eventually assumed the presidency of the University of New Mexico. Although Dewey's intellectual rendezvous with C. L. Herrick never materialized (forfeiting a potential collaboration of incalculable benefit to both men), C. J. Herrick carried forward his brother's legacy at Chicago a few years later, dedicating his research in part to finding empirical support for Dewey's ideas. C. L. Herrick's influence on Dewey's thinking also persisted through Herrick's student George E. Coghill, who would assume a significant role as a scientific advisor to Dewey and Myrtle McGraw in their collaboration in the 1930s to understand the ontogeny of consciousness and judgment described in chapter 9.

WHITMAN AND PROGRESSIVE EVOLUTION

The successful recruitment of evolutionary biologist Charles O. Whitman from Clark University in 1892 represented an important foundation stone in the edifice of science that Harper sought to build at Chicago. Whitman, the

3. Clarence Luther Herrick, in the 1890s. Courtesy of Denison University Archives, Granville, Ohio.

first director of the Marine Biological Laboratory at Woods Hole, Massachusetts, in 1888, had been appointed to head the first graduate program in biology at Clark University just after G. Stanley Hall had became the school's founding president.

Once at Chicago and facing demands to quickly find other faculty members, Whitman persuaded fifteen other colleagues in the natural sciences at Clark University to join him at Chicago. With the wholesale dismembering of the young faculty at Clark University completed—one that Hall had so painstakingly recruited—Whitman could arguably claim that the University of Chicago was now among the leading institutions in science.[8]

Whitman possessed a deep intellectual commitment to the principles of progressive evolution. Whitman and most of his colleagues saw no distinction between biology and culture. Civilization and cultural achievement represented more refined expressions of mankind's capability to adapt to and remake nature to serve its ends. Whitman saw human evolution as an orthogenetic process whereby biological functions undergo progressive adaptation and improvement. This was compatible with neo-Lamarckian views of Chicago sociologists and Dewey colleagues such as Albion Small and William Thomas. The belief that habits acquired through experience could be gradually internalized and transmitted through heredity was appealing to social scientists because it provided the explanatory bridge between human biology and culture. Although there are superficial resemblances between Lamarckianism and Dewey's early ideas about experience, Dewey sought to distance himself from theories that had little scientific backing. Moreover, after the turn of the century few social scientists invoked Lamarckianism explicitly and preferred to let anthropologists like Franz Boaz wrestle with the issues of cultural variation, persistence, and decline.[9]

Whitman showed he was deserving of Harper's trust by appointing faculty members who were likely to make fundamental discoveries about nature. This was particularly true in the cases of experimental zoologist C. M. Child and physiologist Jacques Loeb. They strongly rejected vitalism or the doctrine that organisms were animated by unknown life forces. Instead, they preferred to pursue studies likely to reveal the mechanisms governing life and the processes of growth. Child, who had studied physiology with Wundt, attracted Whitman's attention in 1895 with his regeneration research at the Zoological Station at Naples, Italy. Child believed that life processes could not be explained solely in morphological terms, but must include the dynamic way in which they interacted with their environment. This was compatible with Whitman's orthogenetic conception of evolution. Child was also advancing a theory consistent with Dewey's notion that structure and function are indissociably connected through the exchange of energy through growth, and that an explanation of individuality must account for the natural forces which make possible the unity between organisms and their environments.[10]

Child proposed a theory strongly rooted in the nineteenth-century embryological evidence with which Dewey was familiar. He contended that biological growth and development reflect the changing metabolic needs of the whole organism. The fastest-growing areas, such as the head, constitute centers of growth transmitting behavioral cues that trigger subsequent growth and differentiation at the periphery. These gradients are not fixed, Child argued, but evolve to reflect the changing demands of energy consumption induced by environmental contingencies. For example, a shift from a terrestrial to a marine environment made new forms of locomotion necessary that altered the anatomical patterns of energy distribution and consumption.

Child's axial gradient theory included four main assumptions that underscored the importance of both natural and experiential influences in early development. He believed that all protoplasm contains energy and that energy is released only by being stimulated or excited by heat, light, electricity, or chemical substances. He also argued that stimulation through these energy sources is required for growth and functional specialization. Finally, Child believed that experience was important in determining the proportionality of functional attributes.

Child's theory was unusual in contending that metabolic processes are functionally equivalent to neural processes and that therefore the nervous system is not an entirely new function, but the further structural elaboration of an existing function.[11] Child's theory was supported by Henry Donaldson's research that suggested that brain growth is governed by metabolic processes which are themselves highly sensitive to experience. Donaldson also contended in his 1895 book *The Growth of the Brain: A Study of the Nervous System in Relation to Education* that mental development was correlated with increasing brain size, and speculated that education constitutes a form of exercise that stimulates neural growth and increases intelligence.

A DISSENTING VIEW: LOEB AND
THE ENGINEERING OF LIFE

Jacques Loeb did not share Child's perspective nor did he approve of Donaldson's theories, which he considered to be blatantly teleological by imputing life with purposeful intelligence. Nor was he comfortable with the progressive evolutionary paradigm that dominated the scholarship at the University of Chicago. Loeb was educated in German laboratories in Berlin at the University of Strasbourg, where he was exposed to the latest advances in brain science by neurologists who were cautious about ascribing intelligence to brain functions.[12] The faculty in physiology included Friedrich Goltz, Loeb's mentor, and Edward Pfluger, who both made important contributions to the study of the brain and neural processes. A student of Hemholtz, Goltz later rejected Hemholtz's reductionist analyses of reflexes in favor of a holistic conception that better expressed the integrative nature of brain function.

Goltz and Pfluger became embroiled in a decade-long scientific debate in the 1870s with their rival David Ferrier as to whether or not physical and mental functions could be localized in the cerebral cortex.[13] Goltz, who disparagingly characterized his rivals as the new phrenologists, claimed that the removal of the parietal and occipital lobes does not impair movement. This suggested that motor behavior is governed by non-cortical areas. In contrast, Ferrier claimed to have caused movement of limbs by stimulating certain regions of a dog's premotor cortex, and to have demonstrated that, when this region of the brain is removed, these same movements are impaired. As it turned out, Ferrier prevailed by showing that the parietal and occipital areas actually govern vision, not movement. When damage is sustained in these areas, attention is impaired but movement remains unaffected as long as the premotor area remains intact. Ferrier's discovery of the motor cortex and other brain functions made possible extraordinary advances in brain science that Dewey and McGraw would exploit in their experimental studies in the 1930s.

At the turn of the twentieth century, Loeb revived this debate about cerebral control by showing that lowly species, such as sea urchins that have rudimentary nervous systems, are perfectly capable of voluntary movements, even though they do not possess cerebral cortexes. Loeb showed that these animals, because of an acute sensitivity to gravitational forces and thermodynamic changes in their environments, are able to respond predictably to forces impinging on them from their immediate environment. These remarkable creatures convert external light and other sources of energy directly into movements that sustain their physiological and nervous equilibrium. Loeb's highly original studies attracted the attention of William James, who considered Loeb "to possess a broader view than anyone on the relation between brain and behavior."[14]

Loeb's research provided the most compelling demonstration that Dewey had witnessed thus far of how natural forces are converted into forms of energy that make intelligent behavior possible. Through his general theory of tropisms, Loeb was able to demonstrate how life could be engineered and manipulated by controlling light, heat, energy, gravity, and other environmental factors affecting growth, development, and behavior. Loeb also became famous for experiments that duplicated in the laboratory the reproductive process of parthenogenesis that occurs in sea urchins. The American news media touted this as the first successful attempt to create life and erroneously predicted that this feat would result in the artificial creation of human life.[15]

According to his biographer Philip Pauley, "Loeb was the single most important live model for Dewey's image of the scientific inquirer in the 1890s."[16] Loeb's stunning achievement was to demonstrate that the mystery of life was revealed in the sequence in which it unfolded. He showed that development could be significantly altered by changing the timing in which factors interact during embryogenesis and after birth to produce species-specific traits. Loeb's brother Leo served as a consulting physician in Dewey's Laboratory School and Jacques sent his son to the school. Loeb provided Dewey a sophisticated understanding of the intricate interrelationships between environmental influences, biological processes of growth, and learning. Loeb's studies suggested to Dewey that given appropriate stimulation during early development, each child could best employ the resources of his or her environment to fulfill that child's individual potential for learning and creativity.

Despite their close personal friendship, Dewey was exasperated by Loeb's indifference, if not hostility, to conceiving of the brain and behavior as purposeful systems for the expression of the human soul. Loeb maintained an uncompromising position against privileging the brain as a primary determinant of behavior or moral conduct, as argued by Dewey and his colleagues Herrick and Child. This forced Dewey to continue to search over the next three decades for evidence that would demonstrate that neural growth processes strongly influence behavioral potentials at the onset of human development.

Dewey faced a monumental task—one that he would pursue for the next several decades—to show how brain and mind harbored the energy of human consciousness that was expressed in forms of human judgment that had aesthetic and moral value. Perhaps the greatest immediate challenge that Dewey faced was to explain how values or standards arise that govern human conduct. Having ruled out the possibility of the existence of universal *a priori* principles of knowledge and morality, Dewey needed to demonstrate that humans naturally possessed from infancy onward the judgment to create and assign value to behaviors that had adaptive significance. Dewey again turned to scientists for answers to these intriguing but elusive questions about the mind.

GROWING UP BY THE NUMBERS

Dewey's biographers have rarely paid much attention to his early attempts to understand how the methods that infants and young children employ to count and keep track of things enlarges their judgment. Nevertheless, he spent considerable time observing his own and other children to uncover the motor and cognitive processes that enable children to accurately gauge and measure the number and relationship between objects they encounter in their world. His observations are worth describing because they reveal that Dewey was attempting to find a new way to resolve Hegel's quandary in his *Science of Logic* about how qualitative thought and quantitative measurement can be reconciled by appealing to naturalistic principles of human judgment.

In *The Psychology of Number*, Dewey and James McLellan, a Canadian educator and collaborator, argued that human judgment is governed by the same demand for economy of thought and effort that constrains the functioning of the nervous system.[17] They reasoned that if our aims could be fulfilled the moment we desired or conceived them, without any delay or postponement, then measurement would not be necessary. More typically, planning and foresight must occur before distant goals are likely to be attained. That is why Dewey believed that the human brain evolved mechanisms of inhibition to furnish the delay that is needed to insure that energy is not wasted, and that the amount of thought put into pursuing a goal is proportionate to the complexity of steps involved in its attainment.

Dewey engaged in the systematic observation of infants and young children at his Laboratory School at the University of Chicago during the 1890s to find out if judgment, as he conceived it, played a functional role in development. Dewey's lecture notes from his class on Hegel's *Logic*, which he taught frequently during the 1890s, reveal that Dewey was preoccupied with the problem of the relation between quality and quantity in human judgment. Hegel's maxim that to know a limit is already to go beyond it led Dewey to make some interesting observations about how infants translate their awareness of their own changing sentient states into a rudimentary recognition of limits and boundaries between things. Through this process children are able to perform simple mathematical calculations. Dewey also concluded from these studies that challenges in overcoming physical limits to movement are indispensable to the development of quantitative and qualitative judgment.

Dewey and McLellan found that infants and young children are initially absorbed by the suggestiveness of an overall situation. For example, an infant's first impressions consist in noticing that the weather is hot or cold, dry or wet, that a room is bare or furnished, or that they are hungry or tired, and so forth. There is an inclination to see things in twos or as opposites of either/or. Being able to count beyond two represents an enormous advance in consciousness, according to Dewey and McLellan, because it leads to the comprehension of succession and series. Counting enables children to convert something possessing a qualitative magnitude of size or shape into so many parts that when recombined yields the whole thing.

They argued that grasping the concept of proportion marks the transition from counting how much to establishing equivalence between qualitatively unlike or incommensurate things. Young children distinguish objects according to shared attributes, such as size or shape. This makes it easier for them to arrange things in a series and to use them to understand simple arithmetical processes involving addition, subtraction, and division.[18] Only later, when infants are able to resist their attraction to immediate qualities, are they able, by isolating and comparing different attributes, to identify what makes one situation different from another. By employing these operations, children are eventually able to "neglect" certain features in order to see the importance of others. Dewey considered this ability to focus attention to be "the essence of abstraction."[19] Their studies demonstrated that consciousness of differences in size or features and the recognition of the contingency of order in which things can be grouped introduce the need for comparison that makes measurement possible.

Nevertheless, *The Psychology of Number* fell short of successfully resolving the problem of the developmental relationship between judgment and measurement posed by Hegel in his *Science of Logic*. In his philosophical discussion of measurement, Hegel proposed that it is completely arbitrary how we divide space up into intervals of time. Whatever magnitude a particular point has will depend on its position in a series and all series can be continued indefinitely. Hegel reasoned that if matter is in continuous motion, as Newton contended, then the form that matter assumes is *indeterminate* and merely expresses the unity of direction that emerges from opposing gravitational forces. Only through the processes of qualitative differentiation and synthesis do objects gain their separate identities by exhibiting a unified form and direction.[20] Hegel contended that the law of falling bodies that Galileo proposed best exemplified what he was driving at, namely, that identification of the actual form and functional attributes of a moving object depends initially on quantitative estimates of its velocity, but whose actual (qualitative) existence can be verified only after movement ceases and the separate moments of its trajectory are unified.

Hegel indicated that a crucial problem remained that had not been resolved by the law of falling bodies. Although Galileo, Newton, and Kepler brilliantly demonstrated that gravity is a universal force governing quantitative relationships between moving objects, they had not explained how gravity functions as an *internal* force providing qualitative shape to formless substance. Hegel complained in his *Science of Logic* that

> The laws they discovered they have proved in this sense that they have shown the whole compass of the particulars of observation to correspond to them. But yet a

still higher proof is required for these laws; nothing else, that is than that their quantitative relations be known from the qualities or specific Notions of time and space that are correlated. Of this kind of proof there is still no trace in the principles of natural philosophy"[21]

Hegel acknowledged that gravity is a force of nature that influences the relation between all known things in the universe. But he contended that scientists still were unable to show precisely how gravity influenced the way that humans experienced their world. Dewey concurred with Hegel that this limitation represented a fundamental obstacle to a naturalistic explanation of human development when he conceded that "[w]e do not get the full statement of the law of gravitation, for instance, until we get it stated in terms of social life."[22] Dewey added, "If we had a good genetic psychology, we could define weight, mass and measure, etc., from a psychological point of view, from the relation they bear to the experience of the human race."[23] Dewey responded initially to this challenging question of how natural forces are reflected or embodied in human sentience by observing how young children use their feelings as indicators of qualitative states that possess quantitative, behavioral significance. He then attempted to see if attitudes and emotions play a functionally significant role in human consciousness by rendering explicit the natural basis of judgments that possess biological, social, and moral values and consequences.

By observing an infant's first movements, Dewey found evidence that counting and movement are intrinsically related. Dewey saw counting as a tool in which internal rhythms and feelings can be used to differentiate the qualitative attributes of situations into quantitatively distinct elements. Dewey wondered if the tendency of infants to wave their arms or kick their legs in a repetitive and seemingly opposing fashion is not merely a form of exercise, but is a playful way of translating movement into some rhythmic order or series. It is only when these movements are coordinated into the act of reaching or walking that an appropriate or proportionate number of steps are consciously taken to approach and grasp objects.

Dewey believed that infants' freedom of movement is governed by whether they can gauge distance and anticipate more remote consequences of their behavior. He considered sitting up as singularly significant because it requires an awareness of the need to balance separate functions, such as holding the head erect, keeping arms equally extended, and so on. Dewey observed that babies will typically expend an inordinate amount of energy in their first attempts to roll over, to sit up, to reach, and to crawl. This is so because infants' attempts to master these maneuvers are typically impeded by gravity and by the inability to connect separate movements in an appropriate sequence.

Dewey argued in *Studies* that attitudes furnish the temporary stability or support humans need to judge the adequacy and appropriateness of their response to dynamic situations. He said:

In the course of changing experiences we keep our balance in moving from situations of an affectional quality to those which are practical or appreciative or reflective, because we bear constantly in mind the context in which any particular distinction presents itself . . . We keep our footing as we move from one attitude to another, because of the position occupied in the whole movement by the particular function in which we are engaged . . . We keep our paths straight because we do not confuse the sequential and functional relationship of types of experience with the contemporaneous and structural distinctions of elements within a given function.[24]

Dewey suspected but could not prove that the development of judgment *parallels* the different phases involved in overcoming the challenge of balance posed by gravity in the attainment of erect locomotion. Dewey formulated the future study of this problem (one that he did not undertake until the 1930s) in his essay on the "Principles of Mental Development." There he indicated that "[i]t is necessary to discover some single continuous function undergoing development in order to bring scientific relevancy and order into various facts of child psychology, and in order to give them practical and pedagogical usefulness."[25] Only decades later did Myrtle McGraw find scientific evidence and mathematical proof that more advanced forms of movement involving the remastery of balance, such as walking, jumping, and climbing, require more complex judgments about proportionate relationships between height, weight, distance, pace, and other factors.

THE EVOLUTION OF INHIBITION

Infants gradually attain control over their moods and motor behaviors through processes that Dewey observed to coincide with the increased capacity to inhibit impulsiveness and prolong inquisitiveness. Dewey supposed that this was indicative of an evolutionary adaptation that enabled early humans to suppress immediate emotional reactions to surprising or unfamiliar events and to mount a coordinated response. He adopted the Darwinian argument that primitive human activity and attention was likely to have been undivided, with coordination occurring effectively with little emotional conflict.[26] Only when human physical and mental capacities increased and the repertoire of behavior grew more complex did emotional tension become a constraining factor, necessitating suspension of an immediate response in order to enable a coordinated response. The mechanism of inhibition was simply viewed as a product of human neurophysiological development geared to the expanding scope of potential response. Dewey clearly rejected the Freudian idea that inhibition is a negative emotional force constraining behavior, believing instead that uncertainty was just as likely to evoke curiosity and approach as it was to trigger fear, anxiety, and withdrawal.

Dewey hypothesized that neural mechanisms of inhibition furnished the de-

4. Dewey in formal academic attire at the University of Chicago, 1902. Photograph by Eva Watson Schutze.
Special Collections, Morris Library, Southern Illinois University, Carbondale, Illinois.

lay necessary for the tension between feeling and perception to be worked out through the coordination of thought and action. Immediate, impulsive actions are temporarily suspended until they fit within a larger unified pattern of behavior. James Mark Baldwin and other psychologists, however, viewed inhibition in nearly opposite terms as a temporary emotional disability of childhood indicative of the bashfulness or fearfulness that they exhibit around strangers or in reaction to the unfamiliar. Baldwin speculated that "bashfulness arose as a special utility-reaction on occasions of fear of persons."[27]

Dewey suspected that inhibition had more universal neuropsychological significance. Inhibition evolved to endow emotions with moral significance. He acknowledged to Alice as having derived from Hegel this insight about the constitutive nature of inhibition in moral development. He candidly indicated, "I can see that I have always been interpreting the dialectic wrong end up—the unity as the reconciliation of opposites, instead of the opposites as the unity in its growth, and thus translated physical tension into a moral thing."[28] This led Dewey to hypothesize that emotions furnish the energy through which attitudes closely tied to physical action are enlarged through development and transformed into behaviors that possess aesthetic, moral, or other significance. For example, children tend to react to verbal abuse or criticism as if it were a physical assault. Indeed, offensive gestures or tactless remarks can precipitate anger in adults, but this anger is usually justified on moral grounds, unless there is some mitigating circumstance such as being unaware of individual's sensitivity, or not knowing that a remark was intended as a joke. Anger may give way to embarrassment, disappointment, or wariness, when the perception of the incident is altered and a different intention or meaning is suggested by the context.

SUGGESTION AS A TOOL FOR LEARNING

Dewey believed that there is a significant connection between inhibition and suggestion that has important implications for learning as well as for emotional development. Ever since conducting his first and only controlled experiments in the psychology of suggestion at Johns Hopkins, Dewey had been searching for a technique that showed promise of directly influencing brain growth. He wanted to encourage creativity without unduly restricting the thoughts, behavior, or freedom of individuals, enabling them to learn through their own experiences. He again turned to scientists for answers.

Francis Warner, a British neuroanatomist and keen observer of infant development, furnished some important insights that Dewey acknowledged.[29] Warner observed that no stimulus, idea, or action is processed immediately by any single pathway in the nervous system, but each involves the combination or concatenation of several nerve centers. This observation complemented and supported C. L. Herrick's contention that brain processes involve interneuronal functional integration. Warner's theory also is remarkably modern in anticipating the growing consensus among neuroscientists and psychologists that information is globally processed in the brain, involving overlapping re-entrant connections.[30]

Warner believed that neural processes of inhibition were indispensable to brain development because they facilitated the sequential union and dissolution of nerve centers that supported different attributes of intelligence, such as memory, perception, and communication. He conducted experiments that showed that children's attention could be temporarily diverted from some ongoing activity that actually increased their mastery of that activity when the activity was resumed. During this interruption the energy of sustained concentration is released, decoupling nerve centers. When the activity is resumed new associations may be formed that alter the way in which the activity is conducted.[31]

Dewey's contemporaries, such as psychologist James Mark Baldwin, who also studied the phenomenon of suggestion, drew different conclusions about the underlying brain functions involved.[32] Baldwin argued that no matter what form of suggestion was used, the process invariably works through *conscious imitation* in which adult judgment and authority is likely to prevail. According to Baldwin, suggestion initiates "a motor process which tends to reproduce the stimulus and, through it, the motor process again."[33] "If children don't succeed in their first attempt to reproduce an image or copy," he asserted, "they will persist in their efforts at imitating an act until an approximately similar result is achieved."[34] But this notion of suggestion was completely contrary to how

Dewey conceived it. The suggestiveness of an action does not necessarily trigger imitation to obtain the same results, Dewey argued, but rather involves the modification or expansion of the motor process to get better or different results.

The teachers in Dewey's Laboratory School clearly attempted to implement his conception of suggestion. Katherine Edwards and Anna Mayhew, former teachers of the Laboratory School, recalled that they were aware of the difference between the imitative approach to learning and one based on the discovery of new or unforeseen connections between familiar things. They said:

> It was understood that the psychological function of both suggestion and imitation is to reinforce and help out, not to initiate. Both must serve as added stimuli to bring forth more adequately what the child is already blindly striving to do. It was accordingly adopted as a general principle that no activity should be originated by imitation. The start must come from the child through suggestion; help may then be supplied in order to assist him to realize more definitely what it is he wants. This help was not given in the form of a model to copy in action, but through the medium of suggestions to improve and express what he was doing . . . Mr. Dewey points out in this connection that the process of learning, under such conditions, conforms to psychological conditions, in so far as it is *indirect*. Attention is not upon the *idea of learning*, but upon the accomplishing of a real and intrinsic purpose—the expression of an idea.[35]

Dewey saw suggestion as a tool for enabling young children to forge connections between motor and cognitive processes that are particularly sensitive to early stimulation. That is why Dewey believed that suggestive ideas or experiences do not deprive children of independent thinking but complement the natural processes involved in the coordination of mind and behavior. In the absence of a well-developed cortex, Dewey observed, "[f]or all practical purposes the new-born baby is like an animal deprived of his cerebral hemispheres. It is virtually a reflex machine."[36] With Warner's studies in mind, Dewey added, "Physiological research has shown that when the sensory motor brain centers of touching, seeing, hearing, develop in the first month, there are no functional cross-paths of communication."[37] "Only when there is a translation from the terms of one activity to another," he reasoned, "when what is heard means something for what can be seen, and what is seen means something for reaching and handling, there is significance."[38] Dewey was convinced that these facts of development strongly supported his contention that suggestive ideas promote "cross-reference, this mutuality of excitation and direction, which constitutes the essence of intelligence wherever found."[39]

THE DEVELOPMENTAL ROOTS OF EMOTIONAL EXPERIENCE

These studies by Warner hinted at the possibility that humans are able to enlarge the scope of emotional experience and moral conduct through the same brain and behavioral interactions involved in learning. Dewey viewed as critical the establishment of a dynamic role for emotions in human consciousness and development, while physiologists, including Huxley, considered the mind to be subordinated to more fundamental emotional drives and instincts. Darwin established the modern terms with which to understand how human emotions evolved, but by doing so, he relegated mind to a secondary status. Darwin believed that humans and their closest primate cousins show striking similarities in bodily gestures and facial expressions involved in communicating feelings and emotions. In his 1872 book *The Expression of Emotions in Animal and Man,* Darwin seized on these apparent similarities in emotional gestures across species and across cultures to contend that there are *universal* emotional expressions, which perform vital survival-related functions, but whose adaptive roles have changed considerably during evolution.

Darwin formulated the principle of *serviceable associated habits* to handle this cross-species leap of logic. This notion enabled Darwin to dispose of the messy problem of discontinuity in evolutionary processes by arguing that seemingly unrelated, even arbitrary behavioral elements that are exhibited in emotional expression originally served some functionally necessary purpose. At some point in evolution, according to Darwin, human gestures lost their primary function and came to serve related but secondary purposes. Unfortunately, he equivocated about the exact mechanism through which this transformation occurred. He seemed to vacillate between treating emotions as instinctual, inherited traits and viewing them as acquired characteristics within the Lamarckian perspective, whereby novel behavioral changes adopted by earlier generations gradually become a part of the genetic inheritance of subsequent generations.

Darwin was a keen observer of human behavior. He noticed that preverbal infants appear to understand language, to correctly interpret facial emotional gestures, and to express their own moods and needs. Nevertheless, he ruled out the possibility that this evidence suggested that infants possess minds. Darwin acknowledged that he "felt much difficulty about the proper application of the terms will, consciousness and intention."[40] Perhaps that is why he searched for postural and facial signs of reflexive emotions, such as fear, anger, surprise, and joy, emotions that are expressed spontaneously without reflection. Moreover, Darwin betrayed his commitment to embryologist Ernst Haeckel's theory that ontogeny strictly recapitulates phylogeny by arguing that the fears young children express are "quite independent of experience," and may be the "inherited effects of real dangers and abject superstitions during ancient savage times."[41] Darwin's collaborator George Romanes concluded that the sequence in which infant emotions unfold represents the historical epochs in which these feelings are first experienced. For example, he suggested that fear and surprise first emerge at three weeks, in keeping with its apparent primacy in the animal world, and that sexual emotions become evident at seven weeks—an assertion that Freud made the centerpiece of psychoanalysis.[42]

While Darwin's ideas were highly original, he still was very much a captive of the science of his day. Darwin proposed that animal emotions bear an antithetical relation of opposition to one another, suggesting an underlying reflexive antagonism. This second principle of emotional development was derived from a neuropsychological theory that held that human emotions associated with pleasure are expressed in motor behaviors involving extension, outreach, and approach. Similarly, motor behaviors that involved flexion or contraction and withdrawal signified emotions associated with pain. This lent credence to the dubious proposition that Baldwin and Freud enthroned that all human emotions reflect the underlying, desire-driven dynamics of pain and pleasure.

William James tried to steer clear of disputes about the meaning of emotions that Darwin had engendered. He adopted the position that emotions are the consequences rather than the causes of physical feelings with which they are associated. Only after experiencing the visceral and physiological effects of crying, James argued for example, do humans then feel and express sorrow or grief.[43] He believed that humans possessed a special kinesthetic sense whose muscular coordinates made possible the recurring association of an affect with humans' appropriate habitual forms of expression. Dewey disputed James's theory, denying that the problematic origin and ambiguity of emotional states are resolved simply by reducing these expressions to pure affective states. Dewey found it difficult to see how the subtle differences between wariness, caution, concern, and fear could be distinguished simply by physical criteria alone. There was too much behavioral similarity in their overt expression.

Baldwin approached the development of emotion from a different angle of vision. Each generation finds new value in recurring stimuli, according to Baldwin, through processes of habit and accommodation to new elements. He believed that neurobehavioral integration was a circular process whereby a stimulus and motor response tend to reproduce one another to form habits. But this circularity is not redundant, Baldwin argued, because some new feeling arises that introduces slight changes in behavior that benefits the whole organism. Infants learn how to reinstate but attach new meaning to the recurring stimuli through *conscious imitation* to produce behavior that has adaptive value. Infants do so by channeling the excess energy of nervous discharge into new motor coordinations, expanding their skills beyond those of their predecessors. Baldwin was vague about how this reinstatement occurred neurophysiologically.[44] Nevertheless, he was confident that he had solved the problem of how it is possible for ancient affective states to persist that are based on pain and pleasure, thus upholding recapitulationism, and yet find new adaptive value in behaviors that express a more complex range of attitudes and emotions.

Dewey rejected Baldwin's imitative realism as implausible. Dewey did not dispute the value of studying consciousness from both ontogenetic and phylogenetic perspectives. But Dewey wondered that, if children learn by imitating their elders' behaviors, then how could they possibly acquire feelings different from the attitudes they observe in conjunction with those behaviors? It is more likely that what they learn first are the predispositions, tendencies, or habits of character that lead adults to react in a particular way to a specific situation.[45]

This probably accounts for why children can predict their parents' reactions to their own misdeeds with such a high degree of accuracy. If evolution indeed favored imitation and redundancy of response, then, Dewey contended, humans would not have acquired the complex feelings that they now possess. Impulsiveness predisposes individuals to act upon visceral feelings that constrain the range of possible behavior. That is why Dewey believed that uncertainty necessitates the suspension of an immediate habitual response in order to enable a coordinated response to new and unusual situations.

Dewey had good reasons to think it erroneous to expect to find an emotion that expresses a single organic or physiological state of arousal, such as pleasure or pain. Dewey was disputing the conventional view that human thought is embodied in relatively changeless neuroanatomical structures and that human behavior is governed by emotional states that are widely shared among species. In his seminal essay "The Evolutionary Method as Applied to Morality," Dewey insisted that there was no such common structure, and that the proper focus of a science of human origins should be "concerned with a common and continuous process and this can determined only historically."[46] Comparative anatomical studies by Huxley had proven, Dewey added, that "external similarity is no guarantee of identity of function . . . and that like functions may be exercised through modes of structure which externally are characterized by the most profound and extensive differences."[47]

Emotions signify the success or failure (i.e., appropriateness) of employing alternative behaviors to attain specific ends that may or may not have distinctive physiological correlates. Some actions better reflect our intentions than others in securing our ends and their appropriateness will depend on the context. Indeed, the expression of regret signifies that one could have done otherwise to avoid causing harm or unhappiness. Emotions, such as anger, grief, and sorrow, involve a sense of loss, violation, or incompleteness that is sometimes accompanied by feelings of divisiveness or precariousness. When these emotions are experienced, the perception of the world is altered and the capacity to complete or finish activities is diminished or partially suspended or inhibited. Consequently, during these episodes physical and mental effort is dedicated primarily to restoring the unity of perception and action and regaining an emotional balance. Similarly, the feelings of joy or pride do not simply express a specific feeling or behavioral state, but are indicative of the restoration of a sense of consummation or completion.[48]

FROM SCHOOLS TO DEMOCRATIC COMMUNITIES

Not surprisingly, Dewey's thinking about the evolution of emotion and its role on human mental development was reflected in the Laboratory School. Dewey strove to attain a "harmonious development of all the powers—emotional, intellectual, moral—of the individual." Individual learning was conceived as a social enterprise in which children recreated the processes of invention that brought about evolutionary changes in human civilization.[49] This demonstration program was guided by the untested assumption that group interaction contributed to the acquisition of individual skills that were novel in an ontogenetic sense. This fueled a recurring criticism of the Laboratory School that by re-enacting the history of occupations children were simply learning how to acquire vocational skills and adopt habits and attitudes already well-established in the workforce. Dewey strongly denied that his school's objectives had anything to do with the doctrine of social adjustment. He declared that he was resolutely opposed to this doctrine "if by adjustment is meant the preparation to fit into present social arrangements and conditions."[50] He was trying to cultivate inquisitiveness and critical attitudes that would lead to new ideas rather than passive acceptance of the status quo.

Dewey was striving to attain more than just educational reform through his Laboratory School. He wanted schools to become centers for technological and social invention where immigrants and other displaced people could regain control over their lives by reclaiming their cultural identity, learning new skills, and participating more fully in the political culture of their cities and states. Sounding like a post-Reagan Democrat nearly a century before his time, Dewey considered state intervention ineffective, asserting that our "most pressing political problems cannot be solved by special measures of legislation or executive activity, but only by the promotion of common sympathies and common understanding."[51]

The settlement house movement led by Jane Addams and her Chicago Hull House associates furnished Dewey the model for his community-centered school. Addams molded her Christian social ethics into a secular discourse for social reform that was enormously appealing to working-class families. The Hull House offered a living laboratory for Chicago sociologists W. I. Thomas, Albion Small, and Robert Parke to conduct field studies that would redefine the responsibilities of municipalities, states, and the nation for the provision of public services and policies affecting the urban poor. Addams contributed to the birth of the profession of social work, whose practitioners became intermediaries between citizen and government in the provision of social services. Addams thus helped to define a profession that embodied the roles and values Dewey considered indicative of emerging professions dedicated to human welfare and social reconstruction.[52]

Dewey's halcyon years at the University of Chicago were cut short unexpectedly by a controversy over administration of the Laboratory School. Dewey was the first director of the school when it was created within his department in 1896, which included the disciplines of philosophy, psychology, and pedagogy. The University Elementary School, as it was formally known, grew rapidly from 13 children and three staff members to 140 children and 23 teachers in 1902. A primary factor contributing to this growth was the merger of the Chicago Institute with the university. The Institute was a private school run by Colonel Francis W. Parker, who was an innovative and progressive educator. At first the Dewey and Parker schools were kept separate until Parker died, creating the possibility of consolidation in 1903. Dewey insisted that his wife Alice be appointed principal even though she did not possess any teaching credentials and despite the opposition of many faculty members, who disliked Alice's abrasive style and precipitous dismissal of staff members she considered incompetent. President Harper reluctantly acceded to Dewey's wishes, but apparently had no intention of giving her a permanent appointment. The ill will and resentment among disgruntled faculty members persisted until Harper felt he had no choice but to tell Dewey that Alice's appointment would terminate at year's end. Disgusted with Harper's duplicitousness and badgered by a proud but humiliated wife, Dewey submitted his resignation before the end of the term in 1904.[53]

The decade of the 1890s at the University of Chicago was for Dewey surely an exhilarating as well as exhausting period in his intellectual development and academic career. His informal introduction to the experimental life sciences and exposure to the contending views among his scientific colleagues whetted his appetite for experimentation and sharpened his arguments for a developmental conception of human evolution. By grounding his theories of mind in the latest scientific evidence about the nervous system, Dewey probed the interstices between brain and behavior to reveal possible mechanisms governing motor and cognitive development. Throughout these endeavors Dewey obtained crucial insights into possible neuropsychological equivalents for the Hegelian phenomenology of consciousness. Dewey would continue for the next three decades to ground and extend his theory of mind in the science of human development. While Dewey seemed poised and self-confident that he would succeed in these ambitious undertakings, he underestimated the extraordinary difficulties he faced in attempting to thread the separate strands of mind and nature and of feeling and morality together in a seamless theory about the structure of human inquiry.

Part Two

Rendezvous with the New York
Avant-Garde

FOUR

Contrasting Strategies for Educational Innovation

By the turn of the twentieth century Dewey had become a revered leader and mentor to student disciples who ardently sought to interpret and apply the experiential principles of pragmatism to social life. The reform of public education stood at the fulcrum of competing societal interests seeking leverage over the agenda for national reconstruction. Corporate elites, labor unions, school administrators, and parents perceived schooling as an important strategic tool to promote their respective economic interests, occupational status, and cultural values. The leaders of these groups and their constituencies viewed the educational system as the crucial battleground in which the fight for their cherished values would be won or lost.

The settlement movement and pragmatism spawned a generation of progressive social reformers who seized upon education to advance their democratic and communitarian conceptions of freedom and individual self-worth. Suspicious of the politics of cultural conformity that the business community espoused, social progressives wanted education to emancipate children and youth from lives of regimentation and routinization by facilitating creativity, freedom of expression, and fulfillment of their civic responsibilities in community life and national governance. Dewey's proposals for educational innovation seemed eminently capable of fulfilling the promise of pragmatism in reconstructing American society. Dewey did not anticipate that he would be pushed by his own disciples into the cauldron of a tragically divisive cultural debate, heightened by the agony of American intervention in World War I, regarding how best to protect individual freedom against the negative consequences of nationalism and war.

THE PUBLIC APPEAL OF EDUCATIONAL REFORM

Public interest in educational reform preceded by several decades the scientific study of childhood that did not get underway until the early 1920s. In the absence of systematic information about growth and developmental processes, parents and educators relied on anecdotal collective wisdom handed down from one generation to the next about effective methods of child rearing and training. The conventional wisdom held that childhood behavior was dictated by emotional rather than rational considerations. Children were believed to possess only limited consciousness and memory. The pedagogical techniques considered most effective in developing the mind were those that involved physical immobility, undivided attention, repetition, rote memorization, and discipline. Dewey's stroke of genius was to show how cognitive and non-cognitive behaviors complement one another when enlisted together in learning processes. That is why his books *How We Think* and *Democracy and Education* were received so enthusiastically by progressive educators. Dewey challenged the dichotomies between emotion and cognition, thought and experience, and freedom and obedience that stood in the way of understanding and exploiting the connections between development, learning, and experience.

Dewey succeeded brilliantly in adopting an unusually accessible prose style in *How We Think* that reached a wide audience of parents, educators, and school administrators in 1909. In the introduction, he acknowledged that the book marked the culmination of ideas generated during the years in which he directed the Laboratory School at the University of Chicago. This gave his book credibility as a practical guide about learning and education. In arguments bearing a remarkable similarity to Huxley's nineteenth-century plea for the introduction of experimental science in British education, Dewey's message in *How We Think* was that experiential education cultivated "experimental attitudes of mind"—attitudes that were essential to scientific discovery and social invention.[1] Dewey succeeded in distilling the ideas and accomplishments of his Laboratory School into an accessible, non-technical prose that a reviewer for the *New York Times* called "commendable for its simplicity, lucidity and directness."[2]

Several other scholarly education journals brought the book to the attention of teachers who would have been unlikely to read Dewey's philosophical works but were eager to learn firsthand about Dewey's ideas. For example, *School Review* characterized *How We Think* as a "rare kind of book in which simplicity is the outcome of seasoned scholarship in diverse fields. . . . Teachers of all kinds will find this book a source of stimulus and enlightenment, and they will doubtless give to it the cordial welcome it so eminently deserves."[3] *Democracy and Education*, published six years later, was also hailed by a reviewer for the *Dial* as comparable to Plato's *Republic* and Rousseau's *Emile* in addressing the role of education in a democratic society.[4]

Despite this well-deserved praise, strikingly absent from these books are any references by Dewey to his extensive studies of brain functions and their possible role in supporting human judgment. This omission is surprising since Dewey seemed to be on the verge of formulating a significant new theory that would demonstrate how judgment plays a vital role in enabling the transition from motor to cognitive development. Clearly, however, his observational studies were tentative and incomplete and he needed additional opportunities to explore these scientific issues in more detail. That Dewey chose to formulate judgment as an act of cognition is perhaps indicative of his indecisiveness on this matter. In *How We Think* Dewey discusses judgment as primarily having to do with stating propositions about events and assigning meanings to terms. In a subsequent essay, "The Logic of Judgments of Practice," Dewey shows how judgment establishes qualitative limits to thought and measurement that he had examined in the *Psychology of Number*.[5] But Dewey does not refer to brain functions underlying the integration of motor, perceptual, and cognitive processes that are involved in the exercise of judgment.

ASSESSING DIFFERENT EDUCATIONAL EXPERIMENTS

Dewey readily accepted the challenge of promoting his developmental conception of education in a democratic society despite the risk of criticism from different political quarters. He endorsed countless educational innovations that he believed, rightly or wrongly, supported his ideas. Embittered about her rejection at the University of Chicago and still suffering the emotional loss of her son Gordon, Alice Dewey apparently had passed the baton to her daughter Evelyn to be Dewey's soul mate in educational reform. Evelyn relished the opportunity. She plunged into the research for *Schools for Tomorrow*, a book she co-authored with her father in 1915, traveling extensively and conducting interviews, compiling notes from her observations, and writing the manuscript. Evelyn probably deserves most of the credit for the book's success as a popular guide to educational reform.

Evelyn's travels from 1913 to 1915 included trips to Illinois, Indiana, Missouri, Alabama, and Italy, where she viewed firsthand Maria Montessori's experimental schools in Rome. John and Evelyn singled out Rousseau as being the first educational theorist to have acknowledged the relationship between education and development. Rousseau believed that children possessed natural instincts to learn and that the best strategy was to maximize their freedom to explore and learn on their own. The imposition of strict disciplinary control only served to undermine childhood innocence and take the joy out of discovery.

While finding Rousseau's emphasis on the child's own interests salutary, John and Evelyn considered Rousseau's ideas to be devoid of any methodological guidance. The task of developing a curriculum that embodied Rousseau's insights in concrete practices was left to Froebel and Pestalozzi and their modern day adherents, who seemed to strike a better balance between freedom and social responsibility.[6] A few of the experimental schools, described in their book, succeeded more than others in achieving an acceptable balance between freedom and discipline and between individual activities and group projects because they devised practical methods of learning that facilitated individual growth and social development.

The Fairhope School in Alabama and the preschool programs directed by Maria Montessori represented one end of the continuum that favored Rousseau's child-centered emphasis on individual development. The Gary Schools, by contrast, adopted the principles of group cooperation and teamwork that were the primary hallmarks of Dewey's educational philosophy. In Fairhope, children were grouped not according to age but put in "Life Classes" composed of children with similar interests. Instructional materials were introduced, such as mathematics, when it seemed likely that this would increase individual understanding of the principles involved. Class assignments were voluntary and grading was avoided so as not to undermine the self-confidence of slower learners.

Montessori's schools adopted individual liberty as a guiding principle of learning. She believed that the process of learning was best expressed in the sequence through which children attain sensorimotor control. Accordingly, she cleverly devised an increasingly more challenging series of physical tasks that children could attempt to master in their efforts to increase their powers of coordination. Games, puzzles, and other learning devices were introduced at appropriate ages that linked cognitive skills with motor coordination. While acknowledging Montessori's important insights about the relation between motor control and cognitive development, John and Evelyn found her methods too individualized and deficient in the cultivation of social skills. They singled out the Play School in New York City as striking a more effective balance between individual and group tasks by creating problem-solving situations which accommodated individual differences in cognitive development without sacrificing the rich social stimulation afforded by group interaction. After having observed Montessori's schools firsthand, Evelyn sensed that students enjoyed too much freedom. She wrote to Randolph Bourne in 1913 and observed that "[t]he chief thing that struck me was the pathetically washed out and tired air of the poor teachers. The children were sweet only like all other Italian kids, they needed their little asses whipped."[7]

Dewey did not fully comprehend the experimental significance of Montessori's methods until two decades later, when Myrtle McGraw employed ramps, pedestals, and other similar mechanical devices to uncover the sequence of neuromuscular development. Her discoveries challenged the widespread assumption, which Montessori accepted, that learning is dictated by *maturational* processes. But at the time, the Deweys were evaluating schools largely from a perspective of balancing individual and social interests. From this perspective Montessori's pupils were seen as having too much individual freedom and not enough opportunities to collectively pursue common ends.[8]

Education succeeded best when it fulfilled individual aspirations while meeting the social and productive needs of the society as a whole. Dewey wanted to change the one-sided relationship of power and subordination between teacher and student that had become the norm of public education. Instead of treating students as passive receptacles of knowledge, Dewey wanted to forge a communicative and experiential interaction between teacher and student that would advance learning through a process of reciprocal understanding. Experimental methods fulfilled this objective nicely by engaging teachers and students in the shared experience of discovery of how natural laws and social principles are functionally interdependent.

It is important to understand how Dewey distinguished natural, individual functions from social or organizational structures. *Democracy and Education,* published in 1916, is frequently interpreted as having viewed self-disciplined experiential learning as a subtle form of "socialization" or social control.[9] The distinction Dewey made between structure and function came from organic analogies having to do with growth and morphology. Biological functions consisted of natural capacities that individuals possessed, such as feeling, perceiving, walking, talking, thinking, learning, and so forth. Dewey likened these functional attributes to tools that an individual possesses to organize one's energies, to develop skills, to communicate, and to form judgments essential to participation in social life.

As noted before, Dewey did not view these human functions as fixed, hereditary instincts, but as potentialities or powers whose complete expressions are shaped by the contingencies of developmental processes and experiences. Dewey considered the categories used to classify individuals and treat them differently, such as hereditary or physical characteristics, age, sex, race, social class, economic status, and so forth, to be formal and artificial criteria, based on structurally or culturally contingent bases of comparison. Dewey believed that educational institutions played a particularly crucial role in human development because teachers perform a formative role in enabling individuals to fully develop their individual functional capacities into occupational skills needed to compete successfully in the national economy. For these reasons Dewey considered any attempt to interfere with these developmental processes through learning strategies that sorted children according to physical, intellectual, or emotional characteristics to be a shortsighted, if not illegitimate, form of social control.

Dewey contended that society generally imposes broad organizational and technological limits or boundaries to individual movement, conduct, and communication. Such structural constraints primarily govern how individual energies are channeled and distributed in various occupational roles by controlling the access to and the possession, utilization, and accumulation of skill, expertise, wealth, and other values. To be certain, Dewey was an outspoken critic of the concentration and abuse of economic and political power, and he participated in endless political campaigns against social injustice and the abuse of civil liberties. Dewey wanted schools to emulate the processes of social governance "in which interests are interpenetrating," and where a "[d]emocracy is more than a form of government; it is primarily a mode of associated living, of conjoint communicated experience."[10]

THE GARY PLAN: THE SCHOOL AS COMMUNITY

Not surprisingly, *Schools for Tomorrow* reported favorably on those schools that came closest to approximating the aims of the Laboratory School in Chicago. The Gary Schools in Indiana were singled out by the Deweys as exemplifying the goals of expanding education into the larger community and culture. William Wirt, a former Dewey student from the University of Chicago, was hired by the Gary school board in 1907 and began to redesign the local school system from the ground up in an attempt to implement what he conceived as Dewey's pedagogy. Wirt successfully proposed keeping Gary schools open eight hours a day, twelve months a year. City administrators found this scheme appealing because Wirt's so-called "platoon system" of staggered classroom use promised greater efficiency for the teaching staff and the school physical plant.[11] Adults were allowed to take extended education classes and use the school facilities for community events. Teachers introduced innovative laboratory-based methods of instruction and provided extracurricular activities that offered opportunities for students to gain meaningful experience in business, the arts, and government.

The Gary Plan attracted a great deal of national attention because it was perceived as an alternative to traditional vocational education that limited instruction to narrow job-related skills. Dewey was so enthralled with the Gary Plan that he persuaded the editors of the *New Republic* to dispatch their newly hired staff writer, Randolph Bourne, a former Dewey student at Columbia University, to visit Gary in 1915 and do a series of articles about it in the journal. The editors couldn't have chosen a more partisan writer for the assignment. Bourne, who characterized himself as an "ironist" critic of puritan culture, idolized Dewey, calling him a "revolutionist," who abhorred propaganda.[12] Dewey threw his support to every conceivable democratic cause, Bourne observed in 1913, yet he refused to "preach." Nevertheless, Bourne added:

> Yet his philosophy is a great sermon, challenging in every line, in spite of his discrete style, our mechanical habits of thought, our mechanical habits of education, our mechanical morality. A prophet dressed in the clothes of a professor of logic, he seems almost to feel shame that he has seen the implications of democracy more clearly than anybody else in the great would-be democratic society about him, and so been forced into the unwelcome task of teaching it.[13]

Bourne was sharply critical of American public education. Public schools had "become as autocratic and military as the industrial" sector, Bourne claimed, by burdening students with a doctrinaire and uninspiring curriculum.[14] He was persuaded that the Gary Schools constituted "the first consistent and wholehearted attempt to apply Dewey's educational philosophy."[15] Bourne was particularly impressed that the schools were intended to be a "clearinghouse for community life," in which the jolting transition from school to work, and from classroom to culture, was eased considerably.[16] Bourne also praised Wirt for respecting the students' freedom to sample different vocations and allow them sufficient time to experience the types of situations involving the application of specific skills.

The Gary Plan became a reform plank in the platform of New York City mayoral candidate John Mitchell, who wanted to modernize the city's public school system. The Tammany machine and its allies in business and education put forward an alternative proposal in 1917 called the Eddinger Plan that essentially called for a two-track system that clearly classified students according to skill and aptitude. The Eddinger proposal attempted to reconcile the growing gap between the supply and demand for a skilled workforce by letting employers decide which skills were needed. Bourne was wary of the Eddinger Plan because business interests were likely to place a higher value on those skills that satisfied their narrow labor market or occupational interests.

Bourne was incensed that children would be forced to choose between college and vocational career tracks, and he saw this as a blatant attempt to impose an "undemocratic class division in the public school."[17] This did not square with Bourne's conception of a vocation broadly defined as "a nucleus of any kind of interesting activity by which one earns one's living, and around which whatever else comes to one's experience clusters to enhance its value and interest."[18] The Gary Plan was designed to produce not just skilled workers, Bourne hoped, but "critical citizens, ready, like the energetic professional man, to affect the standards and endeavors of his profession and the community life."[19] From Bourne's Deweyan perspective, the Gary Plan, unlike the Eddinger proposal, viewed the world beyond the school not as a "collection of trades, but as a community, a network of occupations and interests, of interweaving services, intellectual, administrative, manual."[20]

To defuse the controversy, Abraham Flexner of the General Education Board of the Rockefeller Foundation conducted an independent study. The report dispelled many misconceptions about the school curriculum, teaching methods, and student activities. Nevertheless, the report criticized the platoon system for failing to provide a full complement of academic and vocational experiences for every child. In addition, the evaluation showed that many children scored poorly on academic achievement tests, calling into question the merits of experienced-based methods of evaluating student performance. The effects of the Flexner report were devastating. The reform candidate for mayor was defeated decisively by Tammany Hall, and the Gary Plan quickly disappeared from the national scene as a viable instrument for progressive educational reform. Progressive educators increasingly looked to psychologists for child-centered approaches to educational reform that focused primarily on behavioral and personality traits conducive to creativity and self-esteem.[21]

FORESHADOWING AN IMPENDING DOOM

During this period of educational innovation in public schools, Evelyn Dewey and Randolph Bourne developed a close friendship. Evelyn marveled at Bourne's literary abilities, calling him "Mr. Essayist," and she found much personal inspiration from his principled critique of American culture. Evelyn was an admiring and doting friend who expressed feelings of inadequacy in a letter written to Bourne while he was in Europe on a post-graduate scholarship from Columbia. She observed:

> You seem to be that rare and wonderful combination, a person with literary ability and courage and energy to stand up for what you believe in. Of course, I suppose it means personal disappointment and having perfectly nice people decide they don't like you. But those are the few people who really accomplish things and they have an influence that lasts and inspires their friends to do things, while pleasant, lazy people like myself are no use unless they are superlatively ornamental, which excuse is lucky for me. It is nice to have a friend like you, but it makes one think of all the noble things one is not doing.[22]

Working in the shadow of a famous father overwhelmed Evelyn's sense of individual identity. But she had no reason to challenge her father to find her own voice in educational reform because they shared the same goals. Evelyn was more willing than Bourne to accept such compromises. That is why she found Bourne's skepticism appealing, yet deeply disturbing, when she chided him, saying:

> Do Mr. Essayist write me just one letter that shall be without a single glittering generality or tidy little summing up of the general situation and I will forgive you, and think about being in New York next winter. I never imagined there could be such an indefatigable seeker of hidden meanings as you are. Now you should cultivate a sunny indifference to things, just learn to enjoy them as they are; where could you find a better example than this letter.[23]

Evelyn's and Bourne's career paths were inexorably taking them in different directions. Evelyn shared her father's optimism, believing that the door was still open to educational reform, and that new methods and strategies were looming on the horizon that would emancipate children from the chains of tradition. The study of individual behavior promised to yield many insights about developmental processes that could be used to change educational policies and programs. Evelyn believed that intelligence tests could be adapted and used successfully as diagnostic tools to better meet the special education needs of poor children and those with behavior disorders. While Evelyn sat comfortably in the progressive train heading at a moderate speed toward reform, Bourne pushed for an acceleration that risked derailing all prospects for any meaningful change. The failure of the Gary Plan in New York signaled for

Bourne the slamming of the door on education as a tool of democratization and cultural enlightenment.

Bourne worried that the rapidly expanding and uncritical use of standardized tests was promoting a cult of measurement by norms indifferent to individual needs and skills.[24] The "fallacy of educational averages," Bourne argued, was to wrongly equate literacy with intelligence, and to believe that individual skills are comparable despite dramatic differences in culture and class.[25] Bourne saw the school's primary mission to help students define and refine their values and sharpen their minds; acquiring practical skills was of secondary importance. He preferred the approaches taken by Montessori and Caroline Pratt in her Play School because they made "individual expression and selection the basis of life."[26] Bourne's disillusionment with educational reform would eventually grow into a full-scale assault on pragmatism, as described in the next chapter, when Bourne could no longer reconcile Dewey's support for educational reform and his apparent obeisance to technology and nationalism.

GRAVITATING TOWARD THE CENTER
OF CULTURAL INNOVATION

Dewey's opportunity to resume his personal involvement in experimental education came in 1912, when Lucy Sprague Mitchell and her economist husband Wesley moved to New York. He was appointed professor of political economy at Columbia University and she founded the Bureau of Educational Experiments (BEE). Lucy had given up her job as Dean of Women at Berkeley to pursue her newfound interests in the settlement movement. A year before coming to New York, Lucy took an extended leave from her job to conduct what amounted to a voyage of self-discovery to learn more about settlement houses in several cities and how she might fit in. Like many of the settlement leaders she visited, Lucy concluded that many of the social ills and moral vices she witnessed in her travels, such as poverty, disease, prostitution, and broken families, revolved around ignorance about sex and marriage. But once Lucy made New York City her home, renewed her acquaintance with John Dewey, and was exposed to the liberal intellectual and cultural elite of the city, she realized that she had not been thinking in large enough terms. Mitchell recalled, in a statement which became a common refrain among Dewey admirers, that Dewey's greatest contribution was "to stimulate others to think for themselves. Each of us has his own John Dewey formed by what John Dewey made each of us think."[27]

The gregarious Lucy and Wesley Mitchell settled into a modest home in Greenwich Village that soon occupied the crossroads in New York where progressive and bohemian ideas about education, politics, and culture intersected. John and Alice Dewey were among the frequent guests, visiting on a weekly basis. This provided Dewey an opportunity to further expand his acquaintances among the New York avant-garde in the arts and literature. He also rekindled old friendships that included Jacques Loeb, another Mitchell "regular," who had been appointed research professor at the Rockefeller Institute in 1910. Lucy and Wesley occasionally held receptions with fifty or more guests, but more typically they would have intimate, intellectually stimulating dinner parties with three to five persons.

As documented in Wesley's diary, they entertained an astonishing group of dignitaries. Their guests included figures such as Walter Lippmann and Walter Weyl, contributing editors to the *New Republic,* and Max Eastman, one of Dewey's most promising graduate students and founding publisher of the short-lived journal *The Masses,* a magazine with strong communist sentiments. Randolph Bourne, Van Wyck Brooks, and Waldo Frank, outspoken leaders of the left-leaning literary avant-garde and contributors to *Seven Arts* and the *Dial,* were also occasional guests at the Mitchells' home.[28]

Prominent guests from the field of psychology included Ernst Brill, who formed the New York Psychoanalytic Society to spread Freud's ideas among American physicians and psychiatrists. Jungians Smith Ely Jelliffe and Beatrice Hinkle were also frequent guests. Jelliffe was a consulting psychiatrist at the Neurological Institute, and Hinkle was one of the few female analysts to openly challenge the applicability of Freud's theories to women. Wesley's academic colleagues, economists E. R. Seligman and Joseph Schumpeter, also dined occasionally, as did Lucy's acquaintances in settlement work, Lillian Wald and Florence Kelly, and criminologists William Healy and Grace Fernald. Among the artists visiting the Mitchells was Pablo Casals, who would perform after dinner. Frequent topics of conversation included Dewey's writings, Freud and psychoanalysis, education, technocracy, biology and socialism, among other issues. In addition to these special dinners the Mitchells held countless dinner meetings with bureau board members, which included John and Evelyn Dewey, staff members, and other consultants.[29]

Like their Greenwich Village contemporaries, Lucy and Wesley developed a fascination with Freud and Jung, reading many of their books and essays, including secondary accounts by Brill and Ernest Jones, and syntheses by Edwin Holt. Lucy found certain parallels between psychoanalysis and her own thinking about the problems of sexual identity that confront women entering professions dominated by men, but she remained unconvinced that Freud's theory that childhood fantasies strongly influence later development had any scientific validity.

Eastman also had a strong curiosity about psychoanalysis. But Eastman's initial enthusiasm for Freud waned after he underwent disappointing analyses with Jelliffe and then with Brill. It is likely that the affable Eastman would have entertained Dewey with amusing personal anecdotes about his analyses. Eastman was put off by what he characterized as Jelliffe's "wild Freudian jumps" of logic, which traced the origins of Eastman's radicalism to an underlying

Oedipal conflict.[30] When Eastman turned to Brill for a second opinion, Brill merely offered the same diagnostic formula by saying, "People are always repeating some pattern from their childhood. You and I have not talked much, but from what I know of your history and your family, I think you have a strong mother-fixation. Your pattern is that you want to get away from your mother and yet be with her."[31] Eastman granted that even if terms like "mother fixation" characterized real events, he doubted the value of such knowledge. He glibly observed, "As for inducing by conversation a state of consciousness in which they become identified with or converted back into these infantile tropisms and get lost, that would seem to me—from the standpoint of a robust wish to enjoy life—a misfortune."[32]

THE BUREAU OF EDUCATIONAL EXPERIMENTS

Whether through good luck or by an intuitive sense of good character, Dewey frequently succeeded in cultivating relationships with people who subsequently acquired enormous influence in the field of child development and education. Lucy Sprague Mitchell was one of these individuals. She was an extraordinarily energetic and ambitious woman who had an unquenchable thirst for practical knowledge. She wasted no time in soaking up as much as she could learn about educational psychology by attending lectures by Dewey and Edward Thorndike at Columbia. Thorndike was an expert in mental testing and statistical applications. She also consulted with geneticist C. B. Davenport at Cold Spring Harbor, who was undertaking studies of early growth processes. Mitchell wanted to employ knowledge of growth and mental development to bring about successful learning experiences. Dewey recommended that she read his older works such as *Psychology* and *Studies in Logical Theory,* but she found *Democracy and Education* much more stimulating and easy to read. Dewey graciously accommodated Mitchell's insatiable curiosity, providing a tutorial in developmental psychology that strongly influenced the focus of her subsequent educational experiments.

Mitchell lobbied extensively on behalf of the unsuccessful Gary Plan in New York before turning her attention to the special educational needs of socially deprived children with learning difficulties. During an era in which little was known about learning disabilities, children with remedial disorders, such as attention deficits, were sometimes erroneously and unfairly classified as mentally retarded or uneducable. Mitchell organized a psychological clinic to administer educational tests and to conduct surveys of children to increase knowledge of specific learning dysfunctions and their remediation. Frederick Ellis, director of the Social Department of the Neurological Institute of New York, assisted her in that endeavor by arranging consultations with specialists in the field when their expertise was needed.

Evelyn Dewey and Beardsley Ruml, a psychometrician, were hired to conduct a city-wide survey sponsored by Lucy Mitchell. The survey results, pub-

5. Lucy Sprague Mitchell, 1906. The Bancroft Library, University of California at Berkeley.

lished in 1920, indicated that psychological tests and social surveys could be coordinated effectively to properly identify the specific kinds of needs that existed among the school-aged population.[33] Three years later Ruml was appointed to direct the Laura Spelman Rockefeller Foundation, whose generous financial assistance helped create university-based child study institutes throughout the United States and abroad.

Helen Thompson Woolley, a psychologist, Dewey student, and contributor to Dewey's book *Studies in Logical Theory,* was eventually hired by Mitchell to run the clinic and supervise the survey. Woolley had become well-known for her pioneering efforts in Cincinnati to eliminate instructional disparities that contributed to systematic differences in children's test scores.[34] Woolley headed the clinic for only a month before taking an academic post at Teachers College, Columbia University. Importantly, Woolley eventually served as dissertation advisor in the late 1920s to Myrtle McGraw, who provided John Dewey his last, and perhaps, most significant opportunity in the 1930s to be become personally involved in child development research.

An unexpected gift of $500,000 from her cousin Elizabeth Sprague Coolidge made it possible for Lucy to organize a bureau that served as a clearinghouse of information about various experiments in education in the United States and abroad. A governing board of eleven members was quickly constituted in 1916 as the "Working Council," with Lucy as chair. Other members included

Wesley, Evelyn Dewey, Frederick Ellis, Caroline Pratt, who was already direct-
ing the Play School in New York, and Lawrence K. Frank, a former Dewey
student and associate of Wesley Mitchell. Honorary members included William
Wirt (originator of the Gary Plan), Elizabeth Coolidge, and John Dewey, who
also actively served in an advisory capacity. Dewey persuaded some of his colleagues at Columbia University, among them psychologist Robert Woodworth
and anthropologist Franz Boaz, to offer their services.[35]

During the first two years the general aim of the Bureau of Educational
Experiments was to collect information that would enable a better understanding the "whole child." Mitchell and her staff conducted a broad survey of ongoing educational innovations in the hopes of reproducing successful ones on
a larger scale. Several projects were funded, including Pratt's Play School, nu-
trition and sex education classes, rural school programs, and a special laboratory school run by the Neurological Institute. The BEE was organized into
four departments: information dissemination, teaching, physical and mental
experiments, and research, headed by Evelyn Dewey. Intrigued by these initiatives but sensing a lack of focus, Alice Dewey tried to assert her own leadership
in 1917 by urging Lucy Mitchell to adopt a more systematic approach. She recommended that the Bureau staff consult and use her records from the Laboratory School at the University of Chicago for ideas as to how to reorganize and
refocus Bureau activities. But Alice underestimated Lucy's stubborn determination as Lucy abruptly declined. Lucy subsequently recalled this incident, saying that

> Mrs. Dewey, though one of the great women that I have known, was difficult in
> as much as she never questioned that she was right. . . . She kept only records of
> what was presented to the children; there wasn't anything about the children's
> reactions, which is what we were working on. The records were interesting read-
> ing, but they did not give us any direction in the study of children. I think John
> Dewey would have done very different things if we were organizing a Laboratory
> School now. I think he would have seen how inadequate the records were that Mrs.
> Dewey kept.[36]

ADOPTING THE ALEXANDER TECHNIQUE

During this time, John and Alice, Lucy and Wesley, and many other colleagues
became acquainted with and were treated by Frederick Matthias Alexander, a
physiotherapist. He boasted that his technique enabled his patients (or "students," as he called them) to mitigate physiological and mental consequences
of poor posture by tapping the powers of the subconscious mind. An Australian émigré to Britain who traveled to America to escape conscription in World
War I, Alexander developed an impressive reputation among distinguished clients in Britain to whom he administered lessons in the "Alexander Technique."
The lessons consisted of teaching students how to correct subtle postural mal-
adjustments between head, neck, and shoulders that Alexander believed con-

tributed to unnatural modes of thought and behavior. Alexander's perspective sharply contrasted with psychoanalytic premises and methods that stressed that physiological tensions and anxieties are only symptoms of underlying repressed thoughts that can neither be accessed nor controlled directly by conscious intervention. By contrast, Alexander asserted that subconscious mechanisms of inhibition could be accessed and used to eliminate the physical sources of psychological and behavioral tension.

Dewey was intrigued by Alexander's methods for two reasons. First, Alexander appeared to have isolated the neuroanatomical locus of reflex mechanisms governing inhibition that Dewey contended was a primary requisite to conscious, reflective thought. In all of his previous studies Dewey had never conceived of the possibility that neuromuscular mechanisms of inhibition themselves could be tapped and utilized to reactivate vestigial reflexes that lay dormant in the phenotype. If true, this discovery would have enormous implications for a scientific understanding of evolution and ontogeny. Neurologists had long been puzzled by the abbreviated appearance of involuntary reflexive responses, such as grasping, sucking, or a violent convulsion of the whole body in reaction to being startled. Neurologists generally considered these strange modes of infant response to be transient dysfunctions indicative of an underdeveloped brain. Dewey suspected that this was only half the story and that these earliest reflexes were absolutely essential to the subsequent development of more complex movements characteristic of adult behavior.

Second, Alexander contended that the key to postural change was the capacity to consciously and deliberately override inhibitory processes that locked into place habitual modes of response. This was accomplished through a sort of reverse psychology whereby the individual withholds consent or acquiescence to habitual tendencies until the appropriate proprioceptive signals or kinesthetic feelings are detected that govern a natural response. Alexander believed that this process was best illustrated in the sequence of movements involved in rising from a sitting position to a standing posture. Here the demands of gravity must be overcome through a coordinated series of movements of head, shoulders, arms, back, and legs to maintain balance in the transition from one position to the next.

Alexander's insights comported with Dewey's own observations that consciousness first appeared when infants succeeded in holding their heads up when rising to and assuming a balanced sitting position. Alexander assisted his students in attaining a specific "mechanical advantage," or geometric postural configuration between head, neck, and shoulders that seemingly enabled them to rise effortlessly from a sitting to standing position. Mastering this technique and maintaining this posture had, according to Alexander, other benefits besides reducing tension, including increased energy, more self-confidence, and, importantly, greater effectiveness in learning and problem solving.

Alexander developed the evolutionary and practical implications of his technique in a series of books begun in 1910, some of which Dewey helped Alex-

6. John Dewey and Frederick Matthias Alexander.
© 1916. Society of Teachers of the Alexander Technique, London.

ander rewrite and which he enthusiastically endorsed in lengthy introductions. Several other scientists and literary figures of the 1930s such as neurophysiologist Charles Sherrington, the famous author Aldous Huxley, and neuroanatomist George Coghill believed that Alexander's discoveries had merit and deserved scientific scrutiny. But to Dewey's dismay, Alexander refused numerous opportunities to subject his technique to scientific investigation. This did not deter either Dewey or Alexander's other students from attempting to conduct their own investigations. Alexander's extraordinary personal and intellectual influence on Dewey and his colleagues will be described further in subsequent chapters.

BEE board members seemed genuinely curious about the physical and educational merits of Alexander's methods, partly because the Mitchells, Deweys, and other board members were taking lessons from Alexander. In early 1917, the board conceived an impromptu experiment to see if his technique could somehow ease or mitigate motor dysfunctions that contributed to learning difficulties. The board asked Alexander if he would provide lessons to George Jones, a young boy who had an unspecified motor impairment.[37] The boy was in the care of the Neurological Institute that operated a Social Services Department outpatient clinic run by BEE board member Frederick Ellis for children and young adults.[38] After Alexander saw the boy, he discreetly declined to examine him. Alexander's reluctance was well-founded. The BEE board subsequently reported that "the physical condition in which George Jones was found [by Alexander] put lessons out of the question."[39] While Alexander was prone to exaggeration, he also admitted that he was no faith healer who could perform miracles. Nevertheless, Alexander aroused suspicions among board members about his credentials that were quelled only when the Executive Committee could furnish the board with reassuring references from some of his personal clients. Despite these misgivings, the board eventually adopted his principles of postural control, among other BEE agendas that included teaching science and using the Play School methods of learning.[40]

Lucy Mitchell, who had been taking "lessons" from Alexander for more than two years, made an impassioned pitch to the board on behalf of the educational merits of Alexander's methods, saying in part:

> Mr. Alexander is pleading for us as wide an extension of conscious reasoned control over our bodily and mental activities as we are capable of in our present state of development. . . . Such a thesis needs no pleading. . . . Mr. Alexander's pupils learn by experiencing not through imitation or instruction. Through this experiencing they learn control. This method of teaching applied within a classroom would make teaching dynamic and would equip the children to be experimenters. His analysis of the learning process is such as the Bureau could completely subscribe to. . . . Mr. Alexander's attitude towards the bodily functioning is scientific and his method of teaching sound since it is based on a sound analysis of the learning process.[41]

Mitchell also asserted that Alexander's techniques were superior to the Freudian methods she disdained. Mitchell worried that children who are forced to express themselves emotionally before they had control of their behavior inevitably led to "faulty bodily habits that again inevitably bring faulty mental habits."[42] Despite this ringing endorsement, opposition to Alexander remained strong. Evelyn Dewey opposed an alternative proposal that Alexander train one of the teachers at the Play School who could then give lessons to the children. She asserted, to the astonishment of disbelieving board members, that Alexander could not be trusted, exclaiming that Alexander "was in entire disagreement with the Play School program and the theory upon which it is based."[43] Evelyn's opposition may have been prompted by her anxiety about Alexander's growing influence on her father, who was risking his reputation by endorsing a cult figure whose ideas lacked scientific respectability.

For his part, Dewey may have pushed prematurely for a decision on Alexander because he was leaving the country soon for year-long trips to China and Japan. Evelyn also grew increasingly frustrated with the BEE's one-sided emphasis on research, complaining to her father, while he was in China, that "their [BEE board's] idea of education seems to be to observe children. I never heard teaching them anything ever mentioned. I haven't been to meetings, because their discussions make me sick . . . I shall resign soon."[44] Evelyn made good on her promise and resigned from the board the following month.[45] Years later Mitchell confessed that she too found it difficult to work with Alexander, who, she complained, lacked sensitivity to children. Moreover, as the BEE programs evolved, Alexander's ideas were subsumed within a more global perspective about development and the effects of early intervention on learning.

REESTABLISHING A SCIENTIFIC FOCUS

The wrangle among board members about Alexander was symptomatic of their underlying disagreement about whether the BEE should pursue experimental or applied research or both. Mitchell was undecided. Ellis pushed for a strong experimental approach in the tradition of pragmatism's pioneers James and Dewey.[46] Pratt wanted to emphasize demonstration projects, while Evelyn Dewey wanted to combine these two approaches. Failing to reach a consensus, the BEE board decided to at least go forward with plans to recruit a psychologist and resolve the matter of methodology later on.

Mitchell recruited several impressive candidates for the job, including neurophysiologist and animal experimentalist Karl Lashley, criminologist Grace Fernald, and psychologist John Watson, the founder of behaviorism.[47] Lashley was a student of Watson at Johns Hopkins University and wanted to ground behaviorism in a biological perspective. He shared Dewey's interest in approaching the problem of consciousness in terms of the neural and physiological mechanisms involved. Eventually, he would join C. J. Herrick at the University of Chicago in collaborative investigations of the effects of brain lesions on rat and human behavior.[48] Fernald was knowledgeable about developmental and behavioral disorders contributing to delinquency. But neither Lashley nor Fernald were interested in the position. Watson had been fired from Johns Hopkins for having an affair with his graduate student, Rosalie, whom he later married. Watson declined, but he referred the board to his former student and colleague Buford Johnson at Johns Hopkins, a specialist in child development, who accepted a job offer.

The Executive Committee also attempted to recruit a "Science Fellow" who would help the Play School teachers construct and implement a science curriculum. This proposal strongly reflected Huxley's influence on the young Dewey, who was impressed with Huxley's attempts in Britain, before the turn of the twentieth century, to promote science education in the public schools. Jacques Loeb and Columbia University embryologist Thomas Henry Morgan were also nominated, but they declined. Consequently, the BEE had to settle for a relatively unknown junior scientist.[49] During this period of staffing decisions, the committee sought the advice of Columbia University anthropologist Franz Boaz as to how to proceed. He strongly argued that the BEE conduct experiments in "growth periods" to isolate factors that contribute to the "acceleration or retardation" of development.[50] His recommendations resonated strongly in Mitchell's mind because they reinforced Dewey's perspective. The Bureau hired Boaz's student, Ruth Sawtell, in 1926 to do a five-year study published in 1931 under the title of "How Children Grow."

Through these policy-making processes, board members reached a consensus that "the school should not be made a laboratory for the psychologist or doctor, but essentially a laboratory in spirit, being a place for the study of psychological and physical growth of children."[51] The board did not want to sacrifice the opportunity to test new learning methods while undertaking longer-term studies of growth processes. This meant that the research would have to be conducted without control groups or separate treatments. Buford Johnson then proposed that longitudinal studies of growth be conducted to measure physical, postural, and motor processes of growth, glandular-induced changes in affective and emotional states, changes in reaction patterns, and changes in intelligence and cognitive development. She also recommended filming the sequence of behavioral changes, a useful innovation initiated by infant experimentalists John Watson and Arnold Gesell.[52] Perhaps one of the most important findings Johnson reported was the discovery, through motion-picture analysis, that some babies responded to early stimulation by exhibiting "certain [motor] abilities at an earlier age than usually assumed."[53] A little more than a decade later, Myrtle McGraw brilliantly carried forward this method, with Dewey's help, in her studies of the effects of early stimulation and in her quantitative studies of the development of erect locomotion.

BEE research in the next several years generated a virtual avalanche of data that was not easily collated nor interpreted. Ellis assumed responsibility for interrelating, synthesizing, and analyzing all other data collected by the BEE, but he abandoned the project when he discovered many gaps in the data collected. Mitchell attributed Ellis's failure to complete these analyses to his "perfectionism."[54] Nevertheless, a few pearls of wisdom were extracted that were highly suggestive to Dewey regarding promising lines of future inquiry. Numerous periodic measurements were taken of various indicators of growth, such as height, weight, dentition, skeletal growth, caloric intake, blood pressure, and so forth. Schematograms were used to trace changes in body proportions and postural set. Ellis considered these measurements of little scientific interest since he did not believe there was any one "correct posture." Nevertheless, a few years later his views changed. He speculated that posture could very well be the key to unlocking the sequential processes involved in the development of locomotion.[55]

These physical data were intended to generate physiological norms of development and ultimately did yield some limited inferences about patterns of individual growth. IQ tests were also administered at yearly intervals, which indicated that individual scores fluctuate considerably over time. Johnson reported that the "greatest fluctuations occur in the earliest years and indicate the influence of the environment to a greater extent during these years."[56] She also observed that these fluctuations in test scores decreased and leveled off after nine years. Ellis concluded from this data that IQ was a composite of different abilities and experiences, challenging the validity of single norms of intelligence.[57]

Mitchell presented her own assessment of BEE projects in 1923.[58] While expressing frustration at the laborious ways that physiological data on individual growth was being collected, Mitchell believed that these studies showed promise in generating norms of development. These norms would enable schools to make better-informed decisions about effective learning strategies for children with remedial problems. She singled out the studies of postural development to be the best possible source of data with which to study and even predict the proportional effects of growth on developmental behaviors. Mitchell concluded that the growth data the BEE staff collected supported a "segmental theory of growth" whereby "the greatest growth impulse appeared successively in different parts of the body." Mitchell's hypothesis would eventually find support in the longitudinal growth studies conducted in the 1930s by McGraw, who found evidence that development occurred through growth spurts involving overlapping phases of rapid advance and sharp declines throughout early development.

Mitchell's own pet project during this period involved publishing in 1921 a highly successful children's reader *The Here and Now Story Book*. The book was prompted by Mitchell's dissatisfaction with the educational value of traditional fairy tales. She questioned whether they provided a solid developmental basis for acquisition of communication skills and social adjustment. Mitchell rejected the arguments of her Freudian colleagues, such as Margaret Naumberg, who contended that folk tales influence creative expression by making children aware of their unconscious motives and drives. Mitchell's book generated rave reviews from Deweyan progressives like psychiatrist Adolf Meyer, who welcomed it as "good literature and sound scientific pedagogy."[59] Progressive educator Harold Rugg called it "revolutionary," rival psychologist Arnold Gesell praised it for its Whitmanesque quality, and even avant-garde writer Floyd Dell was effusive in his praise.[60] But the book also contributed to the growing cleavage between the science and culture wings of progressivism, the latter charging Mitchell with attempting to deny children the natural exercise of their creative imaginations. During this time of educational ferment, Dewey's one-time cultural allies found a darker side to pragmatism that they believed called into question Dewey's essential commitment to individual freedom in a democratic society.

FIVE

Cultural Disillusionment

Dewey was confronted in the second decade of the twentieth century with perhaps the most intellectually complex and daunting environment he had ever encountered in his career as pioneering philosopher and social reformer. And it promised to get even more perilous, if not emotionally confusing, as the ominous clouds of world war gathered on the horizon. At Columbia University, Dewey attracted an outstanding and diverse group of students that included Randolph Bourne, Max Eastman, William Kilpatrick, and Waldo Frank. These intellectually creative and culturally unbounded youth were Dewey's disciples, spreading the gospel of progressive educational reform among the literary elite of New York, Boston, and Philadelphia.

As one of America's most admired philosophers and respected cultural figures, Dewey wanted to keep the promise of pragmatism alive during a time of growing international turmoil and cultural disenchantment. But to do so would require that Dewey unhappily assume the role of an intellectual pariah defending his agenda for social reconstruction against former disciples who were unable to resist the lure of cultural currents which ran completely counter to Dewey's conceptions of freedom and community. Dewey's national recognition for his intellectual leadership of American pragmatism was unrivaled. Nevertheless, Dewey had to accept the challenge of personally engaging in intellectual skirmishes with the literary New York avant-garde who challenged the relevance in modernity of his conceptions of American cultural identity and democracy.

A FREUDIAN INTERLUDE

Margaret Naumberg, her husband Waldo Frank, Randolph Bourne, Van Wyck Brooks, and their *Seven Arts* colleagues were among those cultural progressives who, although inspired by Dewey's conceptions of education and learning, ultimately found Dewey's notion of culture to be aesthetically narrow-minded and morally bankrupt. Naumberg was an idealistic Dewey student as an undergraduate of Barnard College. She undertook graduate studies with Sidney and Beatrice Webb in London before working with Maria Montessori in Rome. Naumberg briefly taught at a Montessori kindergarten at Wald's Henry Street Settlement in 1914 before growing disenchanted with this approach.

Shortly thereafter, Naumberg opened the Children's School, later renamed the Walden School, with grants from the BEE supporting its first few years of operation. Naumberg's school was at the opposite end of the psychological continuum from Pratt's Play School. Naumberg believed, like Bourne, that the primary aim of learning was the cultivation of individual expression and achievement. Education worked best, according to Naumberg, only if "[t]he reality of the social group evolves from the child's own needs: it must grow from his gradual sacrifice or transference of ego aims in favor of a wider sphere of satisfaction that the school as a social group can offer."[1] In paraphrasing Freud's great injunction in *Civilization and Its Discontents* that social convention exacts a heavy toll on individual identity, Naumberg believed that social norms and values cannot be imposed from the outside but must emerge from inside the individual. "All prohibitions that lead to nerve strain and repression of normal energy," she asserted, "are contrary to the most recent findings of biology, psychology and education."[2] Naumberg argued instead that the vital force of childhood should be directed into creative work. Waldo Frank, who shared this view of education, visited and featured the Fairhope School in Alabama in the articles in the *Seven Arts,* praising it for adopting Rousseau's belief in the unfettered freedom of the child.

Apparently Naumberg was given the opportunity to read Alice Dewey's notes and records of the Laboratory School and came away with the impression that the Deweys had systematically subordinated the "subjective inner life of feeling" to the pressures of social adaptation.[3] Naumberg wanted to make emotional development an educational priority in order to tap the energy of the "collective unconscious" that Carl Jung believed was the conduit of ancestral values and attitudes that insured the survival of the human race. Naumberg undertook a three-year psychoanalysis with Jungian Beatrice Hinkle, perhaps hoping she could bring her own personal discoveries to bear in the classroom. Naumberg and Evelyn Dewey, who were close friends through the early 1920s, rarely agreed on educational philosophy. That is why Naumberg was surprised when Evelyn visited her on a December evening in 1920 in an extremely depressed mood, mentioning the possibility of suicide. Naumberg wrote to Waldo Frank about their strange encounter, saying that Evelyn had "startled" her "with throwing out the idea of her coming in with me at the school." Naumberg noted the irony by adding, "Isn't life curious?"[4]

Evelyn Dewey had recently resigned from the BEE partly over her disagreements with the board about Alexander and because of the Executive Council's indecisiveness in establishing a clearly focused educational policy. Although Naumberg had taken lessons from Alexander, she shared Evelyn's misgivings about Alexander's educational philosophy. No doubt Evelyn was feeling isolated and lonely since her father and mother had yet to return from their lengthy trip to China. Maybe Evelyn felt a need to assert her independence from her famous father. One can only speculate.

In any event, Myrtle McGraw put Naumberg's recollections in perspective years later in an interview with the Center for Dewey Studies. McGraw observed, "I talked about psychoanalysis with Evelyn, because she went through a little bit with some woman friend."[5] It is quite possible then that Naumberg referred Evelyn to Dr. Hinkle, who was a social acquaintance of the Deweys, when they dined at the Mitchells.[6] McGraw remembered that Evelyn's reference to her analysis occurred when they were talking about the frustration that young professional women faced in pursuing a career without sacrificing marriage and raising a family. Evelyn had confided to Bourne in 1913 that she wanted to find a husband with whom she could settle down into a comfortable country farm. So her anxieties about marriage also could have prompted her to undergo therapy.[7] Evelyn may have found Hinkle's advice particularly helpful in resolving how to handle the growing dilemma of career versus marriage that women faced during an era of increased expectations for personal freedom.

Hinkle was highly critical of an underlying bias, as she characterized it, that "[p]sychoanalysis has been developed upon the basis of masculine psychology and the reverse of this model is considered as sufficient for an interpretation of women's psychology." She added, "Many of the concepts which Freud considers most important in support of his theory . . . have absolutely nothing to do with women or girls."[8] Hinkle contended that the most "important psychological problem" a woman faced was not her "biological sexual life" nor the "winning of her sexuality from the reality principle to the pleasure principle . . . but the need for an adequate development of her individual possibilities."[9] In her practice Hinkle helped female clients overcome gender stereotypes they had internalized that reinforced feelings of inferiority, worthlessness, and confusion about their identities. This was a surprisingly enlightened perspective during an era in which Freudian orthodoxy about Oedipal conflicts commanded popular attention.

PRAGMATISM, WAR, AND THE POLITICS OF RECTIFICATION

Evelyn's brooding about her personal and professional life was only one of many family and personal difficulties that Dewey faced as America was drawn inexorably into World War I. Pragmatism and progressivism had given birth to a new generation of reformers who were more apprehensive about the bright future promised by higher education and professionalization. They grew increasingly skeptical that pragmatism could sustain the momentum for cultural and spiritual renewal. Dewey was ill-prepared emotionally and intellectually to respond to the criticism that by supporting U.S. intervention in World War I,

Dewey had surrendered the moral high ground of pragmatism and that he had succumbed to the technological forces and nationalistic imperatives that jeopardized individual freedom and undermined a democratic conception of community life. Dewey found solace from his critics in Lucy and Wesley Mitchell, Jacques Loeb, F. M. Alexander, and Albert Barnes, a wealthy art collector, friend, and occasional student, who were sympathetic to Dewey's position and who shared his skepticism about Freudian psychoanalysis.

Bourne, Frank, and Van Wyck Brooks, who were contributors to the outspoken journal of cultural criticism *Seven Arts* and later *The Dial*, believed that Nietzsche and Freud had stripped away the thin veneer of human rationality, revealing a wondrously impulsive and rebellious creature capable of great creative insight and irony. They were post-modernists before their time, who found almost nothing admirable about a decadent American culture that worshiped money and technology and sought unfettered industrial development. Brooks best expressed how completely at odds their conception of the human mind and culture was with Dewey's notion of intelligence by asking, "does not pragmatism turn the natural order of things inside out when it accepts the intelligence instead of the imagination as the value-creating entity?"[10] Brooks answered in the affirmative.

Dewey did not mount a systematic response to Bourne and Frank's cultural critique of his naturalism until several years after the war in his book *Human Nature and Conduct*. Instead, Dewey adopted the ill-advised strategy of responding principally to Bourne's vicious attacks on his positions in support of American involvement in World War I. This tended to overpersonalize the dispute between them and to deflect attention from the crucial relationship in pragmatism between culture and nature—an issue which lay dormant until Sidney Hook in the 1940s and Richard Bernstein and Richard Rorty in the 1980s revived this discussion. Dewey initially attempted to put the debate about U.S. intervention in the historical context of an inevitable conflict between German and American philosophical traditions and political ideologies. This argument was easily misinterpreted as an appeal to nationalism. But Dewey soon adopted an internationalist stance, contending that U.S. intervention would bring about the creation of the League of Nations, a new mechanism for resolving nation-state conflicts.

It is not surprising that Dewey would initially view the European conflict in historical and philosophical terms. He believed that German imperialism could be traced to the German Hegelian predisposition to equate state and culture. What Dewey found unusual and threatening about German "Kultur," as Hegel conceived it, was that Hegel sincerely believed that Germany was destined to fulfill its world historical role by embodying Absolute Spirit. Kant set the process in motion in which German culture would strive for universality, Dewey contended, when he argued that the demand that individual autonomy be respected presupposed an intellectual and moral obligation to acknowledge the authority of pre-existing principles of truth.[11]

Hegel made it easy for Germans to make the intellectual connection between observing the dictates of reason and obeying the rule of state authority by arguing that the state was the highest expression of consciousness and truth. The German nation-state, according to Hegel, was embarked in peace and in war on a historic, dialectically driven movement to attain individual freedom for its citizens through the struggle for national supremacy. This was not a prescription for democracy, as Dewey conceived it, but a formula for monopolization of power and force by the state. The essence of freedom in a democracy consisted in a civil society that could function relatively independently of state authority. Dewey insisted that civil society, not the state, must determine which beliefs have cultural and civic value and significance.

The differences Dewey saw between German and American educational systems were indicative of the fundamental distinction he saw between an essentially authoritarian and a democratic regime. The German system separated science from culture by reserving to political authorities the power to develop whatever applications of scientific discoveries they deemed in the interests of the state. The unfortunate result of this functional differentiation between knowledge and authority, Dewey believed, robbed the German people of their judgment and increased their intolerance of countries with different cultural values and traditions.[12] But the American "educational ideal in wartime," Dewey reasoned, must avoid the specialization of mind and regimentation of behavior characteristic of the Prussian state.[13]

Jacques Loeb joined Dewey in becoming an outspoken critic of German nationalism and racism for similar reasons. Loeb condemned as senseless and naive the position of German scientists such as Wilhelm Ostwald, that military organization represented a higher stage of culture and that the German people were a morally superior race. Loeb found a similar disturbing tendency by former president Theodore Roosevelt to assert America's moral superiority throughout the world. This was a romantic and dangerously delusional idea that, Loeb believed, had no place in a democratic culture.[14]

Bourne was convinced that he possessed a more radical vision of pragmatism—an "experimental way of life"—that should be embraced by American political and educational leaders. Only then could American society be considered truly democratic. He had good reason to be leery of the ominous tendency among educators of this era to rely increasingly on intelligence tests and other psychological batteries to differentiate children according to disposition, aptitude, and skill. Psychologist Robert Yerkes removed any lingering doubts about what such tests would be used for when he assisted the American military in employing them as a technique to efficiently screen, process, and assign hundreds of thousands of draftees to military specialties. Bourne condemned the use of such tests for conscription or for any other purposes that were contrary to the goals of American education as he saw it.

Bourne also repudiated the belief that education should serve as a laboratory in which students are themselves the subjects of experimentation. He argued

7. Randolph Bourne in the 1910s.
Randolph Bourne Papers, Rare Book and Manuscript Library, Columbia University, New York.

instead that students should be given "a laboratory to work out [their own] experiments in living."[15] However, had he been willing to go beyond his own self-righteous incantations, Bourne would have discovered that this was precisely the dilemma that Lucy Mitchell, Dewey, and their associates were trying to resolve. They believed that students undergoing observation need not be robbed of their creativity and that the goals of science and educational innovation were not incompatible objectives. The staff of the Bureau of Educational Experiments tried to strike a balance between basic and applied research that would generate new knowledge and new skills.

Bourne concluded that Dewey's pragmatism was incapable of nurturing creativity because it denied the "the fundamental fact of our irrationality."[16] Education was designed to systematically inhibit and suppress what he saw in Freudian terms to be mankind's most creative instincts, impulses, and desires. Bourne wanted to "substitute the experimental ideal" for the "rational ideal" in which human conduct is not presupposed to be governed by laws, norms, or ideals, and individuals "are armed only with instincts and wit to deal with inexhaustible experience."[17] Dewey rejected Bourne's vision as completely unrealistic, perhaps nihilistic. Dewey considered the divorce of reason and desire and of science and culture to be flawed strategies doomed to failure. He argued that only education can "bring the light of science and the power of work to the aid of every soul that it may discover its quality." He added that only in a "spiritually democratic society" may every individual "realize distinction."[18]

Bourne, Frank, and the *Seven Arts* critics persisted in their attempts to lay bare the unwelcome cultural consequences of Dewey's bias toward science and technique. Frank searched in vain for any interest among pragmatists in tracing the aesthetic roots of spirit in culture. By focusing on functional activities that had survival value, Dewey's Darwinism led him to neglect precisely those aesthetic elements of culture that, Frank believed, resisted technical application. Moreover, Frank argued that technology was sundering the organic connection between nature and work by eliminating the craftsmanship and the essential aesthetic powers that humans possessed to endow nature with spirit.[19] Consequently, Frank, Bourne, and their disenchanted fellow writers saw Dewey's adaptationist conception of community falling well short of expressing and representing the aspirations and ideals of all citizens.

The *Seven Arts* critics that Casey Blake so eloquently describes saw themselves as cultural pioneers articulating an aesthetic vision for American communities that they believed would restore a sense of purpose in a culture drained of spiritual meaning and significance.[20] America "suffered from a real shortage of spiritual values," Bourne sensed, largely because pragmatism failed to enunciate the "vividest kind of poetic vision" that would prevent the subordination of values to technique.[21] The fatal flaw of pragmatism, Bourne concluded, was its failure to make any "provision for thought or experience getting beyond itself." "You grow," Bourne added, "but your spirit never jumps out of your skin to go on wild adventures."[22]

In advancing these criticisms, Bourne and Frank seemed unaware of the arduous thought processes through which the young Dewey resisted the temptations of idealism to which Bourne and Frank had succumbed in their embrace of romanticism and instead advanced a conception of spirit and mind grounded in nature. Dewey came to the realization decades earlier that spirit is not something beyond nature or human experience, as Hegel and Bourne supposed, but something that dwells within them. Every thought and action involving the release of energy bares the human soul and reveals new potentialities for the growth of spirit.

Dewey did not share his *Seven Arts* critics' anxieties that the absorption of the modern self in technology and consumption created a shortage of meaningful values that was leading to a despiritualized world. Dewey was more alarmed by a growing surplus of meanings and theories about human motivation, as evidenced by psychoanalysis, that were insecurely grounded in nature and evolution and incapable of furnishing a coherent and consistent direction to human inquiry and conduct. From Dewey's vantage point the more fundamental threat to the growth of human experience was not just a despiritualized world but a denaturalized world, a world with a surplus of energy and ideas but a shortage of methods and values with which to enlarge and extend natural intelligence and human judgment.

Bourne dismissed as disingenuous Dewey's apparent appeal to nationalistic slogans to rescue America from the forces of militarization that led Germany to twist Kant's noble conceptions of moral autonomy and rationality into a justification for supreme state authority. Bourne believed that he saw through the arguments framed by Dewey and other "war intellectuals" and saw them as dangerous rationalizations used to justify American intervention. Borrowing from the Freudian lexicon of therapeutic discourse, Bourne accused Dewey and other war intellectuals of regression or reversion, of adopting and legitimizing primitive methods of force to defend the sovereignty of European nation-states against aggressors who essentially shared America's twentieth-century objectives of industrialization and modernization.[23] The expectation that the post-war League of Nations would introduce an era of political internationalism was suspect in Bourne's eyes because it did nothing to alter the economic power and patterns of injustices that prevailed in all modern nation-states.

Dewey was aware that any attempt to nationalize education must necessarily involve the promotion of equality of opportunity and cultural diversity. But he also acknowledged that public education was vulnerable to abuse by zealots who wanted to enlist schools in nationalistic cultural crusades for which the schools were ill-suited. In alluding to Bourne's charge that he was a victim of wishful thinking and rationalization, Dewey found in German nationalism a tragic illustration of the consequences of Bourne's romantic illusions. He reluctantly admitted that the popular notion that "the wish is uniformly the father of thought, may be applicable to those who search for moral justification for idealizations (i.e., rationalizations) that originate in the illusions of the imagination."[24] Dewey singled out Nietzsche as having contributed to German illusions about power. Nietzsche condemned all attempts at moral justification as weaknesses of a will to power. The dangers of an "unchastened imagination," he observed, in his implicit reference to Bourne, lies in an introspective reveling in the emotional accomplishments of such an imagination."[25] By slipping into this world of imagination, Dewey concluded, the romantic spirit evades the hard test of reality. Such evasions, Dewey believed, supported his conclusion that "Romanticism can mean only undisciplined imagination, immaturity of mind."[26]

CONSCIENCE AND A SENSE OF TRAGEDY GONE AWRY

These exchanges seem to have made Dewey even more resentful and determined in his efforts to discredit his critics as simply misguided pacifists. Dewey detected in America's indecisive response to German aggression a "national hesitation" to assume leadership as "a new spirit in the world," unencumbered by its colonial roots and "humanitarian pacifism," and to defend our interest in multicultural democracies around the world.[27] Dewey blamed the proclivity of many Americans to favor neutrality and pacifism on the evangelical Protestant tradition that Dewey had long jettisoned to "locate morals in personal feelings" and to pay obeisance to fixed rules detached from their social context. This put conscience beyond the reach of intelligence and reason.[28] Instead of assuming a position of absolute opposition to violence, Dewey supported "intelligent pacifists," such as Jane Addams, who saw the need for the United States to play an active, forceful role in bringing about the "political reorganization of the world" through the League of Nations.[29] Violence need not be involved in every kind of force, Dewey reasoned, but what force does require to accomplish anything is the organization and discharge of energy in a controlled and uniform direction.

Bourne believed that all nations, including the United States, were impelled to war by the same underlying, violence-prone psychological mechanisms and nationalistic orientations, and thus he did not believe that American cultural values were worth defending. Dewey held a contrasting view that violence was not the only strategy for the application of force and that it was mistaken to characterize nations with different cultures in one-dimensional psychological terms. Nations wage war for different reasons (e.g., honor, liberty, justice, destiny, or divine purpose) and individuals vary in their susceptibility to these appeals. Dewey shared nineteenth-century Prussian military strategist Karl von Clauswitz's dictum that war is the continuation of politics by other means and that violent conflicts are never fully resolved until the force and rule of law is restored.[30]

However, in attacking the efficacy of a recalcitrant conscience, Dewey was snared in the trap set by Bourne, who contended that "wartime creates a justification for the suppression of dissent that undermines the constitutional freedoms that war is purportedly being fought to defend."[31] In setting this trap, Bourne misread the reaction of people whose civil liberties were jeopardized as an expression of cultural resentment rather than as an attempt by workers to rectify the loss of their rights and dignity. Many of the most vociferous dissidents were disaffected labor leaders and communists whose primary concerns had more to do with the economic consequences of war than with cultural freedom.

Bourne's outspokenness in his articles in the *New Republic* attacking Dewey and denouncing the war infuriated Dewey. Bourne ultimately had to pay for his impertinence when Dewey demanded that Herbert Crowley, editor of the *New Republic*, remove Bourne from the editorial staff. Bourne's misfortunes did not end there. The *Seven Arts*, where Bourne next found employment, folded when their financial backing was withdrawn in 1917 because of their opposition to American war policy.[32] When Dewey heard that the publisher of *The Dial* was willing to give Bourne, Frank, and other *Seven Arts* contributors another chance, Dewey gleefully predicted that "[t]he Waldo Frank–Randolph Bourne bunch will soon be to the fore, when their European curio stock runs low. They're precocity seekers, the old *Dial* bunch won't believe that."[33] This was not just idle speculation. Dewey had just been invited by the publisher to write for the *Dial*, and Dewey had agreed on the condition that Martyn Johnson accept his non-negotiable demand that Bourne be fired. Unhappily for Bourne, he was soon given his walking papers.[34] Dewey biographer and friend Max Eastman recalled that these personally motivated attacks were stressful for Dewey, adding that

> The crisis was momentous in Dewey's history as well as theirs [Bourne and the *Seven Arts* critics]. He was not only alienated from them, but somewhat from himself, I think, by his support of the war against Germany. It was not that he felt, or feels that he made a flatly wrong choice. But his philosophy had not contemplated such a choice . . . And he got into a state of tension that in most people would have been an illness.[35]

Tragically, Bourne's career ended abruptly when he died of influenza during the catastrophic worldwide epidemic in the winter of 1918. Alice Dewey, who admired Bourne's talent but despised his political attacks on her husband, diffidently consoled Evelyn after the death of her onetime close friend, writing that Bourne's death

> brings to my mind the same pathetic fact that his talented life illustrated. I mean the fact that he might have been happy where he made others happy, if only his early misfortunes [Bourne was saddled with congenital back deformity] had been related to his life in a different fashion . . . The trouble came when he attempted to deal with the facts of actual life which represented a struggle that he shrunk from and hated. Literature in its academic and esthetic senses should have been his field.[36]

The unmistakable signs soon appeared, to Dewey's dismay, that opposition to the war had become synonymous with disloyalty to America. Appearing first in subtle propaganda and eventuating in harassment, dismissals, arrests, and imprisonment, the assault against dissidents swept up many of Dewey's close friends at Columbia, including his colleague and close friend, psychologist James Cattell, who was dismissed. Dewey conceded that free thought had been conscripted in America in support of patriotic ideas, and that the demands of war did not justify compromising individual freedoms.[37] The faltering attempts to organize the League of Nations also seemed to justify Bourne's cynical appraisal of American involvement. The professed internationalist aims of American intervention to forge a consensus in a new world order failed to materialize, and retributive measures fashioned to punish the Axis powers were implemented instead, measures that flamed old ethnic hatreds.

BARING THE SOUL OF AN INTROVERT

When the war ended, Dewey continued to express his concerns about post-war nation-state politics. The problem of restoring the governments of countries that were occupied by Germany during the war came to a head, for Dewey, when the Poles became divided over which party leaders in exile had the proper authority to constitute a new government. The Polish National Committee headquartered in Paris consisted of supporters of the monarchy who had supported the Allies. Another faction called the Committee of National Defense, which supported Austria and the Axis, wanted to establish a democratic socialist state. Albert Barnes, who had just enrolled in Dewey's seminar in the fall of 1917, offered to fund the class to conduct an inquiry to ensure that this dispute was resolved fairly. Dewey agreed and they were joined by other students, including Anzia Yezierska, with whom Dewey developed a romantic liaison.

When Congress designated the Polish National Committee as the appropriate recipient of foreign aid, Dewey was incensed because his class research indicated that the Tammany machine had compromised the process by which exiled Polish delegates would select a new government. This guaranteed the defeat of the opposition reform group in their special congress held in Detroit. Dewey felt that the war had been fought more than anything else to respect the rights of minorities whose homelands cut across national boundaries but whose citizenship was essentially contested. He personally asked President Wilson to rectify this desperate situation, but Wilson refused to intervene and the Polish monarchy was ushered back into power.[38]

During this time of national crisis, Dewey cultivated contrasting personal relationships with Yezierska, Scudder Klyce, a didactic philosopher, Albert Barnes, F. M. Alexander, and Myrtle McGraw (see chapters 9 and 10), each of whom brought out different sides of Dewey's personality. Dewey's colorful friends and confidants each provide fascinating insights into his character during a time when Dewey's ideas and leadership were under siege. Yezierska exploited her emotionally intense but fleetingly brief and unrequited passion for Dewey by writing fictional accounts of the affair that found their way into Hollywood movie scripts. Barnes's affable companionship and their mutual interest in art (described in more detail in chapter 7) endured for several decades, fortifying Dewey in his quest to discover the common bonds of science and art. Klyce engaged Dewey in a lengthy and personally vitriolic correspondence, forcing Dewey to articulate and defend his motives and ambitions as a philosopher and advocate for science. Dewey pursued his fascination with Alexander's technique in an attempt to establish its efficacy as a therapeutic instrument and tool with which to understand human consciousness. Alexander's controversial evolutionary theory of conscious control encouraged Dewey to mount an assault on Freudian psychology. Alexander's critique of the physical degeneration wrought by civilized culture also prompted Dewey to clarify his premises about naturalism and to re-examine the problematic relationship between nature and culture that had attracted criticism.

McGraw helped ease the emotional tension that Dewey had accumulated during his extended conflicts with his intellectual detractors. Dewey also shared his personal doubts about his family with McGraw, who first wrote to Dewey as an admiring teenager in 1916. McGraw recalled that "[i]n the early letters, when I was a child, he wrote me very often about the family." She remembered "one letter at great length, . . . when Fred [Dewey's son] went into the army in the first world war."[39] She did not elaborate, but this would have provided an occasion for Dewey to ventilate about his war critics, or perhaps to express regret about supporting the war.

McGraw did go on to say that Dewey tried to correct "a lot of the stories that had crept around about them [his family], many of which were utterly unfounded."[40] McGraw recalled that Dewey expressed his concern about the sensitive nature of the letters he wrote to her and suggested that she dispose of them. McGraw remembered that "there was a time or two when he sort of suggested in those early days that I shouldn't keep his letters. I think he probably felt someone would think it was strange of him writing a little girl from the mountains of Alabama, you see. I don't know; anyway I kept them."[41] Unfortunately, McGraw lost these letters a few years later when a suitcase containing them was stolen in New York City.[42]

Dewey met Yezierska during this same period. Yezierska was much older than McGraw and had been previously married. She was a Polish-born Jew with striking auburn hair and an intense yearning to become a successful novelist. She obtained a diploma in domestic science from Columbia University in 1904 and taught high school for several years. Dewey allowed her to audit his class in political philosophy in 1917, during which time she served as a translator for their Polish investigation. According to Yezierska in her autobiography, she and Dewey had a brief love affair that Dewey suddenly broke off.[43] Yezierska, who published her first short story in 1915, sold the movie rights to her book *Hungry Hearts* to Samuel Goldwyn in 1920 and quickly attracted attention for her talent in vividly portraying the lives of immigrants. This book included an unflattering fictionalized reference to her affair with Dewey set against the background of the humiliation that immigrants endured in their dealings with charities and other institutions in their attempts to escape poverty.[44]

Dewey left behind a stylized and figurative record of his attempt to express in literary terms his aspirations and feelings in ninety-eight poems he wrote between 1911 and 1918. At least two of the poems were intended for Yezierska. The poems were discovered in a wastepaper basket and desk drawer shortly after Dewey vacated his office at Columbia University in 1930. Dewey's second wife Roberta obtained the poems in 1957 and kept them until her death in 1970, when they were donated to the Dewey archive in Morris Library at Southern Illinois University. In these poems Dewey expresses a wide range of emotions from joy to grief, but all are centered around themes involving the separation and unification of the actual and possible, mind and body, nature and spirit— themes at the core of his lifelong intellectual conquest of dualism. Dewey adopts a dialectical style to express the contrasting emotions conveyed by metaphors about light and darkness, birth and death, friendship and betrayal, and growth and aging. Some poems express a sense of utter hopelessness and depression, while others capture the simplicity and happiness of childhood.[45] The introverted Dewey found a way through poetry to bare his own soul without having to indulge in the dubious Freudian pastime of dream interpretation or autobiographical introspection.

Dewey's poetry ultimately conceals more about his actual life experiences than it reveals. Alas, true to his Hegelian philosophical training, Dewey's poetry indicates that he was more adept at weighing the possibilities and consequences of different emotions than acting on them in his personal life.[46] We do learn however about the possible alternative emotions Dewey yearned to experience and the other lives he might have lived if things had been otherwise. Yezierska was the vessel into which Dewey poured emotions left unexpressed in his own life in a particularly poignant untitled poem from which Yezierska may have derived the title for her book, *Hungry Hearts*.

> Generations of stifled worlds reaching out
> Through you,
> Aching for utt'trance, dying on lips
> That have died of hunger,
> Hunger not to have, but to be.
>
> Generations as yet unuttered, dumb, smothered,
> Inchoate, unutterable by me and mine,
> In you I see them coming to be,
> Luminous, slow revolving, ordered on rhythm,
> You shall not utter them; you shall be them,
> And from out the pain
> A great song shall fill the world.[47]

In fact, nowhere else do we get a more candid self-analysis from Dewey than in correspondence he exchanged from 1915 to the late 1920s with the idiosyncratic, self-styled sage Scudder Klyce. Klyce was a didactic philosopher who had a penchant for exploring deeply intellectual but largely insoluble problems about human thought, science, and the universe. Klyce wrote to Dewey in 1913 and included a lengthy, rambling manuscript entitled *The Universe* that essentially consisted of a critique of modern philosophy and science and an elaboration of the unacknowledged holistic underpinnings of modern thought.[48] Dewey wrote an introduction and persuaded two of his colleagues, David Starr Jordan and Morris Cooke, to do the same. Klyce's timing was excellent, as Dewey was struggling to clarify in his *Essays in Experimental Logic* why experience was a fundamental element of knowledge and inquiry. Dewey, in a long footnote near the beginning of his first essay, acknowledged Klyce's help in clarifying the term "experience."[49] Dewey expressed his gratitude by agreeing to write an introductory word to Klyce's book that Klyce published privately in 1921.

Klyce subsequently pressed Dewey to circulate among his academic acquaintances for their response another manuscript titled *Sins of Science*. This time around there were few takers. As time wore on Klyce grew increasingly disappointed that his work wasn't being taken seriously and blamed Dewey. His disappointment was reflected in increasingly bitter and personally insulting letters attacking Dewey's character. Just before their correspondence ended, Klyce indicated, to Dewey's dismay, that he planned to publish his own letters, but he agreed not to publish Dewey's letters. The book appeared in 1928 with the strange title *Dewey's Suppressed Psychology*.[50] Klyce's book consisted of a series of *ad hominem* attacks on Dewey that attributed defects in Dewey's thinking to essential weaknesses in his character. Klyce considered Dewey's relational logic to be symptomatic of his indecisiveness, equivocation, and agnosticism. These weaknesses supposedly prevented Dewey from acknowledging the ontological truth of Klyce's neo-Hegelian argument that all differences between things are ephemeral and are subsumed by a universal spirit.

Klyce and Dewey agreed during the course of their correspondence that the fundamental differences between them stemmed primarily from their divergent personalities and temperaments. Dewey freely characterized himself as an introvert, while Klyce proudly adopted the label of extravert. Dewey's use of the terms "introvert" and "extravert" in his own self-analysis is intriguing. The terms "introvert" and "extravert" were popularized by Carl Jung and his adherents, such as Beatrice Hinkle, to describe their contrasting personalities. Jung introduced the terms introvert and extravert to categorize individuals according to their predisposition for shyness or gregariousness. Jung defined introversion as involving the primary movement of libido inward to the ego, while extraversion was characterized as the movement of libido to the periphery or object.[51]

Hinkle expanded the terms introvert and extravert to encompass a larger range of psychological subtypes. For example, she distinguished between "subjective" and "objective" introverts and extraverts to capture the difference between persons who express their psychological tendencies emotionally and those who do so intellectually. "Simple" extraverts tend to reach out, according to Hinkle, to identify with other people. They tend to act before thinking and project their feelings onto others in ways that enable them to define and dominate their interpersonal relationships. "Emotional" introverts, according to Hinkle, are subjective and unable to discriminate between their emotions or control them, resulting in uncertainty, indecision, and a tendency to erratically swing from one emotional extreme to another. "Objective" introverts, Hinkle observed, display the opposite tendency of subordinating emotions to logical deliberation and giving greater credence to facts than to intuition.[52]

Had it not been for Klyce's persistent and overbearing attempt to force Dewey to concede that his judgment was impaired by temperamental weaknesses, it is unlikely that Dewey, whose modesty was legendary, would have ever bothered to define his persona. By Dewey's own account, he seems to have undergone a transition during his life from what Hinkle termed an "emotional" introvert to an "objective" introvert. Dewey's youthful struggle to find emotional meaning in the Calvinist exhortations to seek grace through redemption and his subsequent embrace of the Hegelian Absolute attested to his tendency to seek an intellectual solution that left him emotionally unfulfilled.

In one of his earliest letters to Klyce, Dewey urged him not to let his evident admiration for Dewey interfere with candidness—an invitation that he would later regret. Dewey also drew attention to a personal deficiency that he believed was actually one of his greatest strengths—refusing to claim to be an authority.[53] Nevertheless, Dewey's frequent failure to cite the influence of other scientific authorities also counts as one of Dewey's most egregious errors of intellectual judgment. Dewey's implacable patience eventually gave way to increased annoyance at the tenor of Klyce's provocations, and he abruptly ended the correspondence. It is hard to believe that Dewey would expend so much effort trying to reason with someone who was so utterly contemptuous of him unless Dewey himself was suffering from a failure of nerve after having been put on the defensive by Bourne and his fellow critics.

MIND CURIST OR EVOLUTIONARY THEORIST?

Fortunately for Dewey, Alexander played a positive, constructive role by helping Dewey maintain an emotional centeredness during this period of personal crisis and intellectual transition. Dewey was still searching for a method that would enable him to personally experience how to use consciousness as a tool to change habitual modes of perception and action. Dewey was naturally curious to meet Alexander and was first introduced to him by Margaret Naumberg, who was one of Alexander's students. Dewey wanted to get other people's impressions and estimates of Alexander's technique, believing that Alexander's methods one day would be experimentally verified. But Dewey also believed that if Alexander's theory proved to be scientifically valid, it would discredit Freud by calling into question the neurophysiological underpinnings of psychoanalysis.

Alexander developed an impressive clientele among Dewey's colleagues and their acquaintances during the next few years after his arrival in New York. According to Father Eric McCormack, a Benedictine priest who completed an impressive doctoral thesis on the Dewey-Alexander relationship, not only were the Dewey and Mitchell families all taking lessons, but so were Dewey's colleagues Professors James Harvey Robinson, Richard Morse Hodge, and Horace Kallen.[54] McCormack found some astonishing parallels between Dewey's views about the underlying mechanisms of inhibition governing reflective thought and Alexander's discovery of a practical method to bring these mechanisms under conscious control. McCormack cited evidence from several of Dewey's books and writings to argue that Alexander persuaded Dewey to rethink his understanding of habit.[55] However, there is also good evidence that Dewey helped Alexander to clarify his conception of the subconscious mind and to distinguish his notion from that popularized by mind curists.

Dewey started his lessons in 1916 after reading Alexander's first book *Man's Supreme Inheritance*.[56] Alexander's thesis was that human evolution and the rise of civilization had increasingly rendered humans unfit to use correctly their natural physical powers. Dewey recommended Alexander's book to Barnes, who found it stimulating but indicated that he found little that had not already been said by James, Freud, Jung, Alfred Adler, and Robert McDougall.[57] During his first lesson with Alexander, Barnes complimented him for writing a book that was based "on sound psychology and the common sense of abnormal psychology."[58] Nevertheless, Barnes thought that Alexander would have greater appeal among intellectuals if he would formulate his thesis in commonly accepted scientific terms. Dewey shared Barnes's concerns. Dewey was particularly interested in getting Alexander to clarify his conception of the subconscious and to specify in more detail precisely how his method overrides mechanisms of inhibition that reinforce habit.

Alexander attempted to distance his theory from that of the mind curists, but he employed key terms, such as "subconscious," or "mind-reading," without demurring to their commonly accepted nineteenth-century meaning or connotation. For example, Alexander asserted in the first edition of *Man's Supreme Inheritance* that "all manifestations of what we have called the 'subconscious self' are functions of the vital essence or life force, which functions are passing from automatic or unconscious to reasoning or conscious control."[59] As Dewey well knew, such terminology had grown in disfavor among philosophers and physicists. In the second edition of *Man's Supreme Inheritance* Alexander no longer imputed immaculate powers to the subconscious. He simply asserted what Dewey had long argued, that the mind and body *interact* and that therefore conscious and subconscious processes both play an important role in human behavior.

Dewey and Alexander developed an intellectual relationship that was mutually beneficial. Alexander's technique enabled Dewey to visualize and experience how habits could be reshaped by being dissociated from immediate ends, broken down into a series of separate movements, and reordered to form a new pattern of coordinated behavior. Dewey helped Alexander to clarify his premises about the subconscious, to further elaborate on how his technique worked, and to reformulate his arguments in contemporary scientific and psychological terms. Apparently Dewey commented extensively on the first edition of *Man's Supreme Inheritance* and made numerous recommendations for changes before Alexander released a second edition in 1918.[60] This book was followed by *Constructive Conscious Control of the Individual* in 1923. In this book Alexander provided a more rigorous and detailed exposition of his central concepts and technique. This text also includes extensive footnotes that responded to Barnes's and Dewey's suggestions that Alexander clearly define the commonly misunderstood terms he used to describe the phenomena he observed. For example, Alexander substituted the term "psychophysical," a word familiar to experimentalists, in the place of "psychic" to avoid equating his work with that of parapsychologists and mind curists.

Dewey's personal and intellectual encounter with Alexander helped him crystallize what he believed were compelling arguments that Freudian psycho-analysis involved flawed and spurious assumptions about human psychology and behavior. Dewey was still trying to regain his intellectual and emotional balance after enduring several years of tension and conflict defending pragma-tism from the Freudian-inspired attacks by the New York cultural avant-garde. Dewey graciously contributed special introductions to the second edition of *Man's Supreme Inheritance* and *Constructive Conscious Control of the Individual* that strongly endorsed Alexander's ideas and asserted that his methods far sur-passed psychoanalysis in promoting physical and psychological well-being.[61]

Randolph Bourne could not resist taking one more swipe at Dewey before he was forced to resign from the *New Republic*, so he submitted his own review of Alexander's book, triggering one last heated exchange with Dewey. Bourne claimed that by endorsing the book *Man's Supreme Intelligence*, Dewey had sim-ply lent legitimacy to a technique that, Bourne jested, offered "a kind of re-versed psychoanalysis, unwinding the psychic knots by getting control of the physical end organs."[62] Bourne scoffed at Alexander's carefully cultivated im-age as a genius possessing enormous and unique insights into human evolution. He considered it a "little appalling" that "[i]f the school must wait until every one of its children has learned conscious guidance and control, the next step in evolution will be very long delayed."[63]

In a letter of rebuttal titled "Other Messiahs," Bourne pointed out that since Alexander had never subjected his technique to experimental test, it was per-fectly appropriate to call his method a purely "intuitive skill" rather than a science.[64] Dewey knew all too well that Alexander's stubborn refusal to allow his method to be scientifically scrutinized called into question his integrity and sincerity. Dewey nevertheless argued that Alexander fulfilled the conditions of scientific rigor even though he made his discoveries through a process of self-experimentation.[65] Why Dewey would risk jeopardizing his reputation in de-fense of a character as controversial as Alexander seems inexplicable unless understood in the context of Dewey's equalitarian notion of human intelli-gence. Dewey believed that all human beings, including scientists and philoso-phers, possessed essentially the same attributes of judgment regardless of dif-ferences in training and educational credentials. That Alexander discovered independently essentially the same neurophysiological mechanisms that scien-tists such as Charles Sherrington demonstrated to control posture justified Dewey's belief in the efficacy of human judgment and common sense.

AN INSIGHT ABOUT THE PHENOMENOLOGY
OF CONSCIOUSNESS

Dewey wrote *Human Nature and Conduct* during a time in which he was en-gaged not only in a spirited and exhausting defense of pragmatism, but also while he was trying to master Alexander's techniques of conscious control.

Alexander found Dewey to be a congenial student but complained of difficulties working with him. Dewey was so "drugged with thinking" that he would frequently fall asleep during the lessons.[66] Dewey recalled that after a few lessons he experienced marked improvement in his vision, less labored breathing, and greater intellectual flexibility in changing his ideas in the face of new evidence. He retained the assistance of one of Alexander's trained students, Irene Tasker, who accompanied and provided lessons to Dewey and his wife while on the train to Stanford in 1918, where Dewey presented the lectures for the book *Human Nature and Conduct*.[67] Dewey apparently took a long time to get the knack for the technique, for he continued taking lessons with Alexander and his brother Albert through the early 1940s, until the Alexanders returned to England.[68]

Dewey admitted that from a practical standpoint he was an "inept, awkward and slow pupil."[69] His primary difficulty had to do with controlling his tendency to let customary ways of thinking overwhelm his actions. Consequently, Dewey confessed that "[i]n bringing to bear whatever knowledge I possessed— or thought, I did—and whatever powers of discipline in mental application I had acquired in the pursuit of these studies, I had the most humiliating experience of my life, intellectually speaking."[70] Dewey explained that he was unable to inhibit customary ways of performing even the simplest act, such as sitting down, until he learned how to stop thinking about the immediate result and instead to break the act down into a series of possible or potential steps to complete this action. Dewey claimed that as a result of his "study" of Alexander's technique "the things which I had known—in the sense of theoretical belief—in philosophy and psychology changed into vital experiences which gave a new meaning to knowledge of them."[71]

The Alexander technique gave a whole new meaning to Hegel's idea that the suppression of thought is the fundamental principle of thinking. Up to that point Dewey had interpreted this principle primarily to mean that thought should not be directed toward securing immediate knowledge. Instead, thinking follows indirect processes, giving full vent to feeling and the suggestiveness of situations that may reveal unexpected relationships and new meanings. The Alexander technique showed in practical terms how to use consciousness as a tool to prevent subconscious habitual behavior that is closely associated with the thoughts we are trying to suppress. This paradox of unintended consequences is illustrated clearly by recovering alcoholics. Their every thought of *not* drinking by an act of sheer mental will power is counteracted by a series of subconsciously triggered behaviors, such as continuing to frequent bars or liquor stores, that will inevitably lead to a resumption of drinking. The key to breaking the implicit link between ideas and physical habits, Dewey claimed, is to think of some entirely different end and to adopt a series of actions that makes it impossible to attain the previous end (i.e., resume drinking) as well as the new one.[72]

Although Dewey was never explicit about the Hegelian implications of Alexander's methods, the connection is undeniable. Alexander had demonstrated the possibility of inhibiting behaviors that were themselves the product of neuromuscular inhibition, by changing the order of movements that are performed to attain an end. Alexander believed that the key to altering postural set and related functions, as exemplified in rising from a sitting to a standing position, lay in focusing not on the end of attaining an erect posture, but focusing instead on intermediate phases. He discovered that the relationship between the head and neck involving the cervical area of the spine crucially affected the order, smoothness, and flexibility of subsequent stages in this physical maneuver. Alexander's technique brought about a state of being comparable to what Hegel characterized as that moment of consciousness involving the negation of being. This was the moment, Dewey believed, when the thought of nothing leads to the realization of possibility or the power of using something we do not have (i.e., an end in view). This was clearly the most difficult state of consciousness in Hegel's dialectic to comprehend and to attain —a state of awareness that Dewey understood intellectually but had not yet mastered physically.

THE MORAL FALLACIES OF PSYCHOANALYSIS

These experiments vividly illustrated for Dewey that we are not prisoners of our habits and desires and that we are capable of adopting new perspectives that alter the relationship between mind and body. Freud's mistake was to assume that habits are cordoned off into isolated somatic forms of complexes and compulsions. Dewey did not deny that instances involving the "compartmentalization" of personality may occur, but the effort required to sustain compulsions through the repetition of specific habits involves considerable strain on the whole personality that is apparent in one's character.[73] Moral conduct involves the capacity to judge situations accurately and respond to them appropriately. Persons with neurotic fixations, according to Dewey, bear the "stigmata" resulting from the failure to keep the act of thinking neutral or uncommitted with respect to alternative modes of behavior.[74] An essential feature of moral conduct, he argued, is the ability to think and act consistently, and this can only happen when thoughts and actions attain the highest degree of synchrony or compatibility. "The evil of checking impulses is not that they are checked," he declared, because "without inhibition there is no instigation of imagination, no redirection into more discriminated and comprehensive activities."[75] Instead, in Dewey's opinion, "[t]he evil resides in a refusal of direct attention which forces the impulse into disguise and concealment, until it enacts its own unavowed uneasy private life subject to no inspection and no control."[76]

Dewey did not deny that we are often unaware of our actual desires and real motives and acknowledged that "psychoanalysis has brought home to us so forcibly" the problem of self-deception, "but of which it gives elaborately cumbersome accounts."[77] The assertion that there is an "unavoidable disparity of desire's object and outcome," Dewey argued, converts a transient psychological state into a chronic state of misperception. A more straightforward explanation of self-deception, Dewey asserted, "originates in looking at an outcome in one direction only—as a satisfaction of what has gone before, ignoring the fact that what is attained is a state of habits which will continue in action and which will determine future results. Outcomes of desire are also beginnings of new acts and hence are portentous."[78] Our ambitions may sometimes prove to be more elusive than we surmised, but this does not condemn us to a life of striving after unattainable dreams. We adjust the ends and the means to get a better fit between our aspirations and capabilities.

Dewey believed that Freud's emphasis on guilt and anxiety had mistakenly defined the moral ramifications of human conduct so broadly that no behavior could be excluded. In tracing mankind's anxiety back to some primordial guilt suffered for killing a father figure, Freud erroneously invested every thought with moral consequences potentially perilous to the ego. From Freud's faulty perspective, the human soul and conscious thought are subjected to the unremitting torture of memories of unresolved conflicts whose moral resolution is impossible. Dewey could think of no worse punishment than perhaps to be denied God's grace. Dewey acknowledged that "the most popular forms of clinical psychology, those associated with the founders of psycho-analysis, retain the notion of a separate psychic realm or force."[79]

Dewey cautioned, however, that "[a]ny moral theory that is seriously influenced by current psychological theory is bound to emphasize states of consciousness, an inner private life, at the expense of acts which have public meaning and which incorporate exact social relationships."[80] While every act may have potential moral consequences, not every behavior actually does have these implications. Standards of moral conduct make sense only when there is a distinction between private behaviors that do not necessarily entail moral issues and ones that have social consequences. That is why Dewey asserted that "[r]elief from continuous moral activity—in the conventional sense of moral— is itself a moral necessity."[81]

Human Nature and Conduct stands out as Dewey's most persuasive attempt to address a crucial dilemma of modernity: how to reconcile the increased consciousness of individual freedom and the inevitable conflicts regarding the moral consequences of individual conduct. The next chapter will describe why Freud believed that this conflict between freedom and morality predated antiquity and was a phylogenetic attribute of an age-old anxiety repressed and carried forward through the unconscious. Freud searched for clinical evidence that demonstrated that this ancient affliction of anxiety about identity and responsibility was recapitulated in ontogeny.

Dewey adopted a very different perspective. He speculated that the tension between freedom and morality implicated in the balance that must be struck between thought and feeling created the conditions for the rise of intelligence and judgment. Dewey sought evidence from paleoanthropology and paleo-neurology that the human potential to overcome uncertainty and to anticipate and control the consequences of individual behavior dramatically expanded with the development of the brain. In doing so Dewey was resolute in his conviction that the natural resources for human transformation were to be found in ontogeny.

SIX

The Evolution of Mind in Nature

Ever since he first laid eyes on Hegel's *Phenomenology of Spirit*, Dewey was determined to complete a systematic statement of his own naturalistic theory of mind. *Experience and Nature* was Dewey's most ambitious, but incomplete and sometimes forbiddingly convoluted, attempt to produce a *Naturphilosophie* in which mind, nature, and culture are understood in common metaphysical terms. Astute reviewers quickly penetrated Dewey's dense prose to grasp the essential Hegelian nature of his enterprise. In a Dewey retrospective, James Harvey Robinson celebrated *Experience and Nature* as "the greatest new addition to metaphysical knowledge since . . . Hegel, for all of his insights, is incredible."[1] Robinson observed, correctly in my opinion, that "Dewey took what is living in Hegel, and rejected what is dead, and reconstructed what he took in terms of biological functionalism."[2] Another favorable reviewer called *Experience and Nature* "pluralistic Hegelianism immersed in the concrete."[3]

However, not everyone shared this enthusiasm for Dewey's book. McGraw recalled that she landed the difficult assignment of typing *Experience and Nature*, which she remembered doing cheerfully with almost no comprehension of what he was saying.[4] Dewey subsequently confessed to having confused readers. He said, "Were I to write (or rewrite) *Experience and Nature* today, I would entitle the book *Culture and Nature* and the treatment of specific subject matters would be correspondingly modified."[5] The term "experience" had become so loaded with subjective connotations that Dewey believed that the word "culture" might better express the idea that shared beliefs and values entail shared experiences.

Understanding *Experience and Nature* can prove frustrating because Dewey interweaves several different levels of analysis whose connections are not self-evident. One of Dewey's objectives involved articulating a philosophy of science. Dewey's aim here is to show how the history of human scientific and cultural achievement reflects changing perceptions of the value of human experience. Dewey presented this account in relatively straightforward terms, drawing on arguments that were well-rehearsed in his previous writings. Dewey's second objective was to provide paleobiological and anthropological evidence to show how nature gives birth to mind and consciousness, including the extraordinary human capacity to use language to communicate and learn from experience. This is where the going gets rough and where Dewey loses many reviewers who had followed his argument to this point.

Finally, there is evidence in *Experience and Nature* that Dewey's antagonism toward Freud's conception of mind persisted. Dewey made a number of telling criticisms that demonstrated the adverse biological and cultural consequences of adopting psychoanalytic assumptions about human nature. This contention of mine is controversial and requires justification, as Dewey never explicitly mentions Freud or psychoanalysis in *Experience and Nature* and only refers to Freud three times in his entire collected works. But even these scant references reveal Dewey's skepticism and antagonism toward Freud's theories.[6] Dewey was put on the defensive by the rapid rise and widespread cultural diffusion of psychoanalysis that many of Dewey's closest adherents found intellectually compelling.

In *Human Nature and Conduct* Dewey explicitly singled out psychoanalysis as having adopted flawed premises, described in the last chapter, about human desire and sexuality, the role of self-deception and the nature of human morality. However, the central themes in this book are presented as a manifesto rather than a comprehensive theory. Dewey outlined a natural and social psychology divested of false or misleading assumptions about human instincts, and one that embraces a conception of mind centered in human experience. But Dewey was not content to rest his case at this point. His conception of critical inquiry dictated that he determine whether there was any scientific support for Freud's assertions that mind is a cultural artifact and that consciousness is simply an epiphenomenon of instinctual behavior. That is why I am contending that Dewey's theory of mind can be better understood not only in terms of what it affirmed, but what it rejected as ungrounded.

Dewey's attempt to critically examine Freudian psychology on evolutionary, biological, and cultural grounds proved to be a more formidable task than Dewey had anticipated when he completed *Human Nature and Conduct*. In their attempt to ground their theories of mind in science, Dewey and Freud found that human civilization and culture furnish ambiguous and incomplete evidence with which to explain the origins of mind. The different ways they chose to handle these gaps in the paleontological evidence and historical record help illuminate why they adopted such strikingly contrary perspectives toward the relationship between mind and culture.

Dewey's take on human evolution led him to conclude that nature, not culture, gives birth to mind and spirit. In locating mind in nature, Dewey believed that he could better explain in *Experience and Nature* and other works how humans acquired from nature a cerebral apparatus that contributed to an enormous expansion of mind, consciousness, and human intelligence. The human soul and spirit emerged through the conversion of the resources of nature and biological growth into a structured series of functionally specific and adaptive behaviors that could be continuously changed and modified through experience. Dewey saw culture as an outgrowth of the natural capacities of human minds to communicate through gesture and language, which furnished common meanings needed for shared experiences.

Freud appeared to Dewey to have turned Hegelian dialectics upside-down by arguing that the advance of civilization and human moral compunctions frustrated fulfillment of mankind's natural instinctual drives. Humans were forced to unconsciously repress their true motives and adopt increasingly elaborate mechanisms to defend their ego ideals from unpleasant intrusions from reality. Freud asserted that the unconscious generates an inner reality that obeys its own logic of necessity that is unaffected by the events of conscious experience. The perceptual contents of mental events, Freud contended, need not involve actual experiences but only imagined ones, eliminating the need to confer a separate existence on the objects of consciousness. Freud tried unsuccessfully to develop a convincing metapsychological theory to explain how nervous energy could be diverted into somatic disturbances that were expressed in inexplicable forms of neurotic behavior. Although Freud gave up his *Scientific Project* to establish a functional neurological basis for psychoanalysis, he insisted that there was ample evidence from the interpretation of dreams and phylogeny that human behavior is rooted in instinctive wishes and drives that are expressed unconsciously in individual experience and culture.

By contending that mankind's sensorimotor apparatus has been corrupted by culturally misguided conceptions of correct use, F. M. Alexander unwittingly lent credence to Freud's contention that mental functions are not subject to the same physical and biological principles operative in nature or evolution. Culture did not represent a higher level of human consciousness, intelligence, and spirit, as Hegel contended, but constituted instead for Freud an expression of mankind's impulse for gratification, rationalization, and self-deception. Freud's theory undermined the claim that nature and mind could be comprehended in the same functional terms—a possibility that Dewey believed was essential to sustaining the emancipative role of consciousness in mind and human culture. Thus Dewey carried forward the threads of his discussion of Alexander's ideas begun in *Human Nature and Conduct* to wind them into a tighter noose around the neck of the questionable biological premises on which psychoanalytic theory depended.

Significantly, neither Freud nor Dewey is explicit about the science underpinning their respective theories of mind in the 1920s. This fact invites a closer inspection of their understanding and use of embryological, neurobiological, and paleontological evidence to support their respective theories of how the brain and mind evolved and develops during ontogeny. Dewey and Freud undertook strikingly parallel lines of inquiry early on in their careers. However, as Frank Sulloway points out, after the turn of the century, Freud seemed content to maintain a neo-Lamarckian position, to rely on dated embryological studies, and to adopt an unusual somatic, sexual conception of psychic energy to sustain his developmental theory that Dewey found lacking.[7] Dewey kept informed of the latest developments in biology and research on the brain conducted by scientists with whom he was personally familiar. Dewey sought evidence that supported his belief that neurobehavioral processes of growth are not constrained by entropy and that mind summons the energy of consciousness needed to expand the powers of human intelligence beyond physical and biological limitations.

Freud questioned, as did Dewey, whether biological processes are constrained by entropy, because his conception of regression implied the possibility of reversal of the flow of psychic energy. But he denied that human consciousness was capable of liberating the human spirit from domination by unconscious instinctual, biological, and emotional forces. Unlike Dewey, Freud ultimately concluded that the energetics of the mind are scientifically insoluble and that forces that determine human emotion and personality have ancient origins beyond the realm of human control. Delving further into the evolutionary and neuropsychological issues that Dewey and Freud contested will thus prove helpful in putting their respective theories of mind in a broader scientific as well as philosophical context.

THE NATURAL HISTORY OF
SCIENCE AND EXPERIENCE

Experience and Nature is dedicated to the paleoanthropological proposition that mind emerged from nature and that human consciousness is the primary tool with which humans learn from experience and develop their capacity for judgment and understanding. During the earliest centuries of human existence, Dewey speculated that mankind revered and worshiped nature, attributing supernatural powers to geological landmarks and animals. These spirits governed the seasons, determined the availability of food, and punished humans for transgressions against nature. The religious rites and celebrations organized around these beliefs helped humans to cope with the fundamental uncertainty of daily existence and to courageously face the future without undue hope and expectation. The introduction of language and tools freed primitive humans from the burdens of immediate existence to communicate, conduct trade, and physically and intellectually explore the boundaries of the material and spiritual world.

The reliance by primitive humans on supernatural and anthropomorphic symbols and metaphors to understand nature and human behavior, Dewey speculated, gave way eventually to a mechanistically inspired experimental revolution. Begun in the seventeenth century, the experimental revolution vastly expanded our knowledge of the basic principles of force, motion, space, and time that govern nature and the universe. While these discoveries were based in part on local analogies of motion and locomotion, they profoundly changed our notions about the earth and its place in the universe. The ancient prohibitions against interfering with nature's course, according to Dewey, gave way to the realization that the attempt to mimic, to change, or to mathematically explain and predict natural processes yielded indispensable knowledge about how nature works. The advance of experimental science undoubtedly reflected a new attitude of mind toward the value of experience. The qualitative attributes of nature were no longer equated with spiritual essences but were now seen as forming the primary or generic empirical constituents of human thought and perception.

Galileo embarked on his studies in an era when ecclesiastical views of the universe were sacrosanct and experimentation was considered a mere contrivance that did not represent the natural order of things. Galileo and his successors convinced their contemporaries that they could be deceived by what they immediately sensed, and that the secrets of nature must be teased out with special apparatus, such as telescopes, and witnessed by others who could corroborate the authenticity of these experiences. Success in persuading other minds of the authenticity of experimental discoveries, Dewey argued, turned on the possibility of reproducing the phenomena involved in their initial discoveries. This was an exacting standard that could be approximated only when reliable instruments became available to reproduce and measure the results.

But Dewey contended that something extraordinary happened in the transition from a culture governed by supernaturalisic beliefs to one dominated by philosophical systems of thought, something that threatened to devalue the importance of phenomenal experience. While agreeing that science is limited to gathering evidence directly from nature, Descartes and Kant believed that principles governing the validity of that evidence are based on timeless *a priori* truths. Dewey saw this as an unfortunate turn of events because it led to an epistemological essentialism in which the validity of scientific knowledge depended on the rigorous differentiation between impersonal, objective facts and subjective, experientially biased opinions. Dewey singled out Freudian psychoanalysis as having introduced into psychological discourse a version of this epistemological essentialism that Dewey repudiated. Dewey examined the consequences of this change of attitude toward mind and experience throughout the rest of *Experience and Nature*, where he develops a highly original emergent theory of mind.

DEWEY'S AND FREUD'S INTERSECTING PATHWAYS

It is all the more remarkable given their fundamentally opposed theories that early in their careers Dewey and Freud had strikingly similar interests in evolution, embryology, neuroanatomy, and the functions of the nervous system. They were familiar with much of the same literature in these fields and drew on these studies to understand the role of mind in psychology and human behavior. Freud read closely Darwin's evolutionary theory of human emotion and was familiar with embryologists Wilhelm Roux, Ernst Haeckel, and the psychologist James Mark Baldwin's theories about ontogeny. He also obtained additional insights about early development from his onetime collaborator, Wilhelm Fliess, who advanced a controversial developmental theory of human bisexuality.

Significantly, Bernard Sachs, Dewey's colleague at Columbia University, studied with Freud in Vienna, and Frederick Peterson collaborated with Jung. Sachs worked alongside Freud in Meynert's laboratory in Vienna from 1881 to 1884. He also received post-graduate training in neurology from the famous French neurologist Jean-Martin Charcot in Paris and J. Huglings Jackson in London. Sachs then joined the Neurological Institute as a staff member and expert in childhood neurological diseases in the 1920s and 1930s, and he served twice (in 1894 and 1932) as president of the American Neurological Association. He was appointed with Dewey and other Columbia University colleagues to be an advisory board member, overseeing McGraw's infant studies at Columbia University in the 1930s. Sachs later became an outspoken critic of psychoanalysis and questioned its applicability to medical disorders.[8] Frederick Peterson, Sachs's colleague at the Neurological Institute, also had firsthand knowledge of psychoanalytic ideas. He collaborated with Jung to develop a psychogalvanic reflex variation of the association test that they described in a joint publication.[9]

When Dewey undertook his study of the evolution of mind, zoologists and comparative anatomists were just starting to accumulate detailed knowledge about possible similarities in the development of nervous structures in animals and humans. Freud conducted several laboratory studies in comparative neuroanatomy during his post-graduate training in neurology from 1878 to 1880. Freud adopted Ernst Brucke's theory that all psychological phenomena must ultimately conform to physical-mechanistic principles, including the laws of conservation of energy. Freud subscribed for a short time to this deterministic perspective before giving up this belief as unrealistic.[10]

Freud also witnessed and closely followed Jacques Loeb's early experiments with decebreated dogs in Berlin in 1886, concurring with Loeb's conclusion that motor control was not localized in the cerebral cortex.[11] Freud also cited Loeb's studies of life-sustaining trophic mechanisms to support his conception of instinct as an inherent tendency of organic life "to restore an earlier state of things which the living entity has been obliged to abandon under the pressure of external disturbing forces."[12] Freud exploited the relative paucity of knowledge at the turn of the century about developmental processes to speculate brilliantly about the possible phylogenetic origins of human psychological phenomena. Freud's compelling narratives about the unconscious in human ancestry captured the imagination of a public unaware of the revolution in the biological sciences that included Hans Spemann's groundbreaking discoveries in the 1920s about the earliest processes of cellular differentiation leading to the development of the nervous system and brain.[13]

PSYCHOANALYSIS AND THE ENERGETICS OF MIND

Freud struggled early in his career to complete a convincing scientific account of the origins and energetic functions of the human brain and mind. Freud's intention in writing the *Project for a Scientific Psychology* was "to furnish a psychology that shall be a natural science: that is, to represent [normal] psychical processes as quantitatively determinate states of specifiable particles, thus making those processes perspicuous and free from contradiction."[14] Freud attempted at that time to develop a quantitative conception of neuropsychological phenomena that conformed closely to the laws of energy conservation. But he found it necessary to deviate from this physical law in order to explain secondary functions of the nervous system, such as perception, memory, and consciousness, which appeared to be governed by qualitative rather than quantitative factors. Freud proposed a complex system of specialized neurons to explain how sensory and motor functions governed by conventional energetic processes were integrated with unconscious, perceptual, and mnemonic functions that did not appear to conform to these processes.

Ultimately this scheme proved untenable and could not explain in consistent neurophysiological and energetic terms how it is possible for memories or perceptions to be split off or become dissociated from behaviors or experiences in which they were formed. Freud's enthusiasm waned considerably with the prospect that his scheme was unworkable, confessing to Fliess that, "I no longer understand the state of mind in which I concocted the psychology; I cannot conceive of how I came to inflict it on you . . . it seems to me to have been a kind of aberration."[15] By the time Dewey had completed *Experience and Nature* in the mid-1920s, Freud had already retreated from any further attempts to characterize the structural attributes of the nervous system or the brain.[16]

But Freud insisted nevertheless that the mental phenomena he described represented real events governed by underlying neurological processes.[17] Consequently, whenever Freud employed his notion of cathetic energy to describe the processes in which somatic events were converted into mental symptoms, he considered that energy to be physical-neural and not psychical. But Freud could not explain how somatic kinetic energy passes through each neural system (i.e., perceptual, preconscious, and unconscious) to be increasingly invested with psychic or cathetic energy that is diverted from immediate discharge. Nor did Freud's contention seem plausible from a thermodynamic point of view. Such processes of conversion could not be delayed indefinitely by unconscious processes.[18]

MIND, BODY, AND THE PROBLEM OF ENTROPY

There were some other ingenious attempts, besides Freud's, to reconcile the principles regulating biological and physical systems. Edward J. Kempf, a psychiatrist, advanced a persuasive theory that purported to overcome the physiological deficiencies of Freud's neurodynamic conception of mind. Kempf, a onetime colleague of Adolf Meyer, undertook one of the most original attempts by any of Freud's followers and rivals to strengthen the thermodynamic basis of Freud's conception of psychic energy. Kempf's work was brought to Dewey's attention in the mid-1920s by two of his doctoral students, who critically examined Kempf's work in their attempt to render explicit the psychobiological principles underlying Dewey's pragmatism. Their analyses helped Dewey to work through key issues that he discussed in *Experience and Nature* involving how the mind evolved perceptual mechanisms that enabled the conversion of physical energy into intelligent behavior.

Kempf argued that the autonomic system was the fulcrum through which physiological, neural, and behavioral processes interact and are integrated to form stable personalities.[19] He claimed that molecular structures supporting autonomic processes, such as blood pressure and respiration, possessed special electromagnetic properties that enabled neurons to form reversible bidynamic reaction systems that sustain acquisitive and aversive or avoidance behaviors.[20] This special energy enables the coordination and integration of sensorimotor processes by maintaining postural vigilance and by providing feedback essential to the proper adjustment of neuroreceptors to changing environmental contingencies. Significantly, Kempf contended that the balancing of opposing drives (e.g., wishes and fears) characteristic of Freudian theory could also be explained by the functioning of the autonomic system.[21]

Kempf was certain he had solved the problem that Freud had encountered in explaining how cathetic energy functioned to govern emotional response. He argued that the autonomic system functions primarily to preserve reactions that protect the integrity of the organism as a whole. The origin of many physiological signals of distress, Kempf asserted, could not be directly traced to external stimuli, but emerge furtively from endogenous sources. Conversely, he observed that significant differences in how individuals react to unfamiliar situations—some showing fear or anxiety, while others expressing curiosity or interest—are indicative of underlying differences in autonomic patterns of response. Kempf concluded from these observations that consciousness is simply a reflection of the body's (somatic) representation of a steady stream of endogenous sensations that are "accepted as representative of the whole" state of the organism at any one point in time.[22]

Significantly, Dewey's doctoral students Meredith Smith and Robert Raup dealt explicitly with the neurobiological literature with which Dewey and Kempf were familiar. Both students used the studies of the nervous system by Herrick and Child as their authoritative point of departure in their critical assessment of how Dewey, Kempf, and other scientists explained the processes of neurobehavioral and psychological integration and why they differed. Smith and Raup found Kempf's work useful in delineating how all living organisms cope with and balance the antithetical nature of their attractive and aversive reactions to environmental contingencies. They found many interesting paral-

lels between Dewey's and Kempf's ideas. However, both students strongly repudiated Kempf's apparent view that endogenous processes controlled overt
behavior—a contention that formed the centerpiece of Freud's theory of the
unconscious.

In his published thesis *Education and the Integration of Behavior,* Smith indicated that his analysis was based on an "educational experiment covering a
period of five years" that was inspired by John Dewey.[23] Smith accepted as
given Child's contention that organisms cannot act on their environment without the presence of some external stimulus that triggers an "acceleration of
energy" involving a higher rate of metabolism.[24] This metabolic energy is redistributed among brain regions during the course of development, enabling
the organism to form adaptive responses to respond to increased complexity.
Smith concluded that this physiological evidence was consistent with Dewey's
view that only through direct contact with the environment is it possible for an
organism to make adjustments consistent with its needs.

Raup waded more deeply into the streams of competing assumptions in the
literature on physiology and the nervous system than Smith in order to establish the primacy of postural tonus in bringing about the integration of autonomic and central nervous systems. He believed that the preponderance of
neurophysiological evidence supported the theories of Charles Sherrington
and F. M. Alexander that muscular or postural tonus was governed by habit and
did not embody preset or predetermined emotions such as fear or rage.[25] Habits
and attitudes are subject to transformation only when the internal conditions
of nervous action and external stimuli are thrown out of synchrony, according
to Raup, necessitating the redistribution of energy to reharmonize the relation
between individual and environment.

Significantly, Smith and Raup cited the work of Eugenio Rignano as showing promise in resolving the problem of entropy. Rignano boldly weighed in
on the ongoing debate about heredity and environmental determinism by offering an evolutionary theory of intelligence grounded in embryology and the
principles of *Naturphilosophie.* Rignano contended that all living substances
possess "affective tendencies" that have special mnemonic characteristics that
enable organisms to maintain a state of constancy despite undergoing continuous change. Ontogenetic modifications are made possible, according to Rignano, by the accumulation of potential energy in early development that,
when released in growth processes, produces slight variations in the patterns
of affective response. Each new generation thereby will possess a different level
of energy use, bringing about slight modifications to phylogeny. Rignano's
theory seemed to resolve the problem of ancestral influences without resorting
to recapitulationism.[26]

Nevertheless, Kempf found many supporters among Freud's partisan followers. Kempf's clinical success led him to proclaim that he "was able to do what
Freud, Brill and other orthodox psychoanalysts dogmatically held, from their
failures, could not be done."[27] G. Stanley Hall and psychiatrists William White

8. Sigmund Freud attending a Psychoanalytic Congress in The Hague, 1920. Manuscript Reading Room, Library of Congress, Washington, D.C.

and Smith Ely Jelliffe agreed that Kempf had succeeded in establishing a bold new theory synthesizing psychoanalysis and the physiological theories advanced by Charles Sherrington and Walter Cannon. They hoped that once Freud became familiar with Kempf's work, he would realize that his objections to those who strayed from psychoanalytic orthodoxy were unfounded.

Consequently, Hall contacted Freud in 1923 and urged that he meet with Kempf in Vienna. Freud reluctantly agreed.[28] However, after his visit, Kempf dejectedly reported his failure to convince Freud. When he explained to Freud that "affective reactions" could be traced to the functioning of the autonomic nervous system, Kempf related that "Freud threw up his hands and said that it would not be possible to correlate mental events with physiological events for hundreds of years."[29] Following his meeting with Kempf, Freud reported to Hall that, although he liked Kempf personally, "[m]y appreciation of his scientific studies is marred by the fact that he is not altogether an analyst, but rather has taken the byway of anatomy which, in my judgment, will lead him nowhere."[30]

FROM METAPSYCHOLOGY TO A SCIENCE OF MIND

Freud and Dewey had remarkably similar interests in neurobiology and shared an intense curiosity about the evolutionary origins and functions of the nervous system and brain. Although for many years Freud believed that psycho-analysis must be ultimately grounded in biological science, he preferred to establish this connection indirectly through an evolutionary and metapsycho-logical framework that elaborated his thesis in the broadest possible terms. Freud wanted to explain how childhood memories are repressed and how elaborate defenses are erected, in the form of physical behaviors and phobias, to prevent the reappearance of memories in adult consciousness. He believed that the pathways could be traced through which sexual excitation or libido is first converted from somatic to psychic form or reversed, as was the case with regression. But Freud was never able to explain scientifically how this process of conversion occurred without appealing to questionable neurological prem-ises and suspect phylogenetic theories.[31]

It was precisely Freud's tendency to run physical laws of nature together with developmental and cultural theories of human evolution to make his nar-rative history of the human psyche seem plausible that irked Dewey. He con-curred that an embodied mind which dwells physically in nature "should be mindful of the past and future."[32] But he found dubious the assumption that human nature could be determined by the lingering psychical consequences of our ancestors' experiences of natural phenomena. Their emotional reactions were governed by perceptions and understandings of these events that differed fundamentally with our own. Moreover, Dewey found it arbitrary that Freud's history of the mind excluded from consideration how brain functions evolved from lower life forms to enable humans to acquire the resources of intelligence that set them apart from other species.

Dewey resolved that a naturalistic theory of mind could be formulated that repudiated Freud's spurious psychoanalytic premises. He believed that scientific research would establish the probable sequence in which the nervous system and brain evolved to support human intelligence. This would show that the nervous system evolved a functional capacity to convert perceptions involving qualitative and quantitative judgments into ideas and behaviors that possessed aesthetic or moral value. This evolutionary question had fundamental ontologi-cal implications for Dewey's conception of judgment and theory of value. As noted before, Dewey advanced the Hegelian argument that judgment performs a decisive role in enabling humans to discriminate among immediate qualita-tive differences between things or events and their quantitative extension in space and time. The capacity to convert qualitative attributes into quantitative ones that possess different values constituted, for Dewey, the essence of valua-tion, namely, the capacity to establish equivalence.

Children tend to rely on the efficacy of judgments based on immediate ex-periences largely because of their sensory-motor limitations. Only when their powers of vision and movement extend beyond their immediate grasp are they able to discount the value of first impressions and adopt a wider view of a situation in its entirety. Dewey believed that this capacity to prolong receptivity to more remote influences or contingencies that alter the basis of comparison or valuation was a neurobiological adaptation that humans acquired in their descent from their animal ancestors. That is why it was important for Dewey to determine the likely sequence in which the nervous system evolved and adapted to fulfill the human need for effective judgment.

These studies were also significant for Dewey for another related reason. Freud's psychology was predicated on the assumption that human behavior was motivated by endogenous drives and affective processes. Dewey believed that evidence of how the nervous system and mind evolved would prove this assumption to be invalid and mistaken. The mind evolved, as Freud supposed, not only to enable the increased elaboration of individual feelings and past memories, but also to extend the powers of movement, vision, perception, and memory to include remote or future events beyond individual reach or immediate grasp. If Dewey's evolutionary scenario were true, then human judgment and valuation did not rest exclusively on either individual desire or external possibilities but on their functional integration and transformation.

Although Dewey never explicitly cited their research in *Experience and Nature*, Herrick and Child synthesized available information on the evolution of the brain into a reasonably supported body of data and hypotheses capable of empirical study that Dewey privately acknowledged as having considerable merit.[33] They believed that two essential attributes that any organism must possess to attain a fully developed and integrated nervous system were sentience or excitability and reflex action. Importantly, Child and Herrick stressed that even in the absence of a nervous system, lower life forms with limited mobility respond accurately to external stimuli. Nervous systems evolved, they argued, to respond to the increasing need to coordinate feeling and movement through a mechanism that enabled the coupling of perception and behavior.[34] Herrick and Child theorized that the sequence culminating in human consciousness and cognition could be traced back through a phylogenetic series of structural and functional changes in sentient and locomotor processes.

George Parker, a Harvard zoologist with whom Herrick, Child, and Dewey were acquainted, seemed best able to conduct an analysis to determine how the human nervous system evolved from primitive precursors. After completing his doctorate in 1891, Parker spent a few months in German laboratories before conducting research in Naples with Jacques Loeb. William James encouraged his student Parker to commence in 1895 his study of the evolution of the nervous system.[35] Parker had the occasion in 1916 to first meet Dewey in New York through their mutual friend Lucy Mitchell.[36]

Parker found that the simplest organisms possess nerve nets composed of separate receptor neurons that conduct diffuse impulses throughout the organism. Only more highly evolved species possess effectors with synaptic connections that enable the transmission of impulses in specific directions.[37] Their receptors are metabolically polarized so that they both originate and transmit impulses. Parker reasoned that some receptors must have been differentiated into effectors that subsequently became *functionally interrelated* through some interneuronal mechanism of joint communication. This made it possible for a reflex arc to be constructed that allowed for the independent movement of separate muscles. This adaptation also provided a rudimentary system for calculating value by enabling simple organisms to detect qualitative differences in nutrients and to select those which best sustained processes of growth and development.

Parker noticed an enormous increase in the number of interneuronal connections in animals with more sophisticated locomotor apparatuses. As nervous systems grow more complex, a central adjuster emerges whose primary sensory neurons migrate inward and appropriate cells not originally a part of the system. Thus a system once dominated by afferent receptors sensitive to immediate, internal stimulation is superseded by one driven primarily by efferent neurons and sensory functions (e.g., hearing, sight) increasingly sensitive to indirect, distant, and more subtle sources of stimulation.[38] Parker's research suggested that Freud's belief in the primacy of the nervous system in maintaining endogenous functions was neither justified on evolutionary grounds nor on a functional basis.

Herrick and paleoneurologist Frederick Tilney amplified and extended the evolutionary sequence begun by Parker, describing how the nervous system developed further through reciprocal changes between brain, body, and behavior. These scientists drew from an impressive body of research that indicated that the brain developed primarily in response to demands for *motor coordination* rather than by the need for increased sensitivity to somatic needs. Structures such as the brain stem, cerebellum, and prefrontal and cerebral cortex evolved to unite efferent and afferent systems into widely distributed centers of nervous action subserving movement.[39]

Tilney described how the demands for increased coordination of physiologically complex organisms possessing more advanced methods of locomotion (e.g., walking instead of crawling or swimming) developed neuroanatomical structures to accommodate this change in posture. The cerebellum emerged to fulfill this need by providing a central mechanism with which to use kinesthetic and proprioceptive sensory organs, such as fingers, arms, legs, feet, and so forth, independently and/or in synchrony.[40] Tilney contended that the cerebellar function of maintaining balance and proportionality of movement was crucial to further development of the brain and behavior. For example, the capacity to learn new behaviors was made possible through proprioceptive feedback necessary for adaptive response. The enlargement of the brain, particularly the prefrontal area of the cortex, enabled the progressive incorporation of the tactile and kinesthetic senses into a unified system capable of anticipating and responding to remote or distant objects, even before vision and hearing came to play a dominant role in frontal control.[41]

Parker's, Herrick's, and Tilney's provocative theories about the development of the brain and behavior carried great weight in Dewey's emergent theory of mind. Dewey believed that the evolutionary sequence through which nervous systems evolved to support increasingly independent forms of loco-motion marked a revolutionary advance of mind and judgment. Unlike immo-bile life forms, "an organism with locomotion," Dewey asserts in *Experience and Nature,*

> is vitally connected with the remote as well as with the nearby; when locomotor organs are accompanied by distance receptors, response to the distant in space becomes increasingly prepotent and equivalent in effect to response to the future in time. A response toward what is in the future is in effect a prediction of a later contact.[42]

That is why Dewey challenged the notion that our perceptions consist of intrinsic and immediate qualities of the stimulus. A stimulus is "underdeter-mined," Dewey cautioned, except as it is correlated with a response. Dewey added that there really is no such thing as an "exclusively peripherally initiated nervous event."[43] A great variety of internal physiological conditions inter-vene to give the stimulus a particular feeling or quality. That is why behavior consists of "a whole avalanche of contemporaneously occurring excitations," Dewey explained, that overwhelm the individuality of any one stimulus.[44]

Moreover, complex life forms in which "activators and effectors are allied to distance," Dewey adds, act in such a way as to spread out their response in space and time. What is perceived is not only conditioned by habit and the memory of the consequences of prior activities, but also reflects how the "or-ganism acts with reference to a serial order of events," involving continual adjustments to changing needs and environmental contingencies.[45] Signifi-cantly (and this is perhaps the most important point Dewey wants to drive home), the preparatory meaning of an initial act of contact is *conserved* as an organism mounts further efforts to make contact with more distant things. When attention is focused on distant things immediate contact is inhibited and functions only as a stimulus or motive to overcome that distance. Dewey jubi-lantly declared that this coupling of mind with the energy of motion and self-awareness was a momentous evolutionary event for human intelligence.

> The result is nothing less than revolutionary. Organic activity is liberated from subjection to what is closest at hand in space and time. Man is led or drawn rather than pushed. The immediate is significant in respect to what has occurred and what will occur; the organic basis of memory and expectation is supplied. The subordination of contact-activity is equivalent to possibility of release from sub-mergence in the merely given, namely to abstraction, generalization, inference. It institutes both a difference and a connection between matters that prepare the way for other events and the affairs finally appropriated; it furnishes the material for the relation of thing signifying and thing signified—a relation that is actualized when discourse occurs.

The important point that Dewey makes here is that "whenever a situation has this double function of meaning, namely signification and sense, mind, intellect is definitely present."[46] In other words, Dewey is contending that, when there is a need to convert the sentient reactions of an organism into a capacity for recognition and choice, this is indicative of the presence of a mind. Perhaps then the most important generic difference Dewey found between non-humans and humans is that animals just *have* feelings while humans *know* they have them and use them to their advantage.

CONSCIOUSNESS, MIND, AND MEANING

Dewey was enough of a realist to admit that the world we are thrust into at birth is heavily encumbered by pre-existing cultural beliefs, meanings, and systems of discourse. Consequently, we are not as free as we imagine to completely remold culture to suit our desires. Yet we enter this world as sentient, gesturing beings unencumbered by the chains of meaning that later link our thoughts and words into structures of discourse. He contended that the natural capacity that humans possess at birth to communicate through gestures and signs suggests that mind captures a much wider universe of meanings than those involving cognition and discourse.

Dewey believed that the scientific study of ontogeny would provide insights about the developmental relationship between the expanding field of response made possible by the onset of erect locomotion, and the ability that infants quickly acquire to communicate with others about common expectations and mutual needs.[47] What is so remarkable about the psychology of anticipation is that it creates a behavioral disposition to act as though a possible outcome is an actual one. Anticipatory behavior paves the way for expectancy characteristic of communication whereby individuals share feelings and meanings that enable the attainment of a common understanding.

Language universalizes human sentience, according to Dewey, because it makes it possible for people to communicate about and to share their feelings. Language provides a medium through which the earliest movements and feelings infants express through preverbal gestures can be given wider meanings than before. Without communication, he argues, the ability to anticipate the future and control its consequences is impossible, because only with shared meanings and understandings do we realize that individual behavior usually has wider effects than are expected. Each successive advance in human development, Dewey believed, is made possible by the release of potential energy that gives birth to new powers and values expressed in alternative forms of communication and experience.

Dewey sought to establish a *prima facie* case in *Experience and Nature* that if communication is a generic trait of human behavior shared by all natural life forms, then culture is simply a further functional elaboration through symbols and meanings of this and other natural traits. While he believed that the psychobiological significance of a large part of our natural heritage remains submerged in the subconscious, it nevertheless provides tacit guidance in our judgments about value and significance. Dewey and F. M. Alexander concurred in their assessment that this natural capacity for good judgment had been corrupted by the ills of modern life. But by acknowledging this problem, wasn't Dewey simply conceding ground to Freud? The question looming in *Experience and Nature* but never satisfactorily answered, then, was how Dewey proposed to remedy these human ills and restore the efficacy of human judgment.[48]

Freud claimed to have provided an explanation of how the mind works by penetrating the veils of human anxiety and ambivalence that conceal its inner workings. He wielded most impressively his knowledge of how to overcome human emotional defensiveness to gain access to individual memories and secret desires by getting clients to reveal how they reacted to and felt about their past experiences. Freud believed that these experientially based narratives revealed more basic truths about the phylogeny and ontogeny of the human mind than any other source of information because they represented the remnants or scars of biological and emotional conflicts indelibly imprinted on the psyche.

Dewey's and Freud's perspectives could not have been more sharply at odds on this aspect of human existence. Dewey argued that humans spend a considerable amount of their lives thinking about and anticipating the future, while Freud insisted that humans are forever remembering but desperately trying to extricate themselves from their own emotional past. Dewey saw humans drawing on the resources of past experience to create a new future; Freud viewed this same process as an exercise in self-deception and futility. Dewey believed that each individual possesses a fundamental curiosity about the boundaries and limits of his or her own identity that impels them to be pioneers. "No one discovers a new world without forsaking an old one," Dewey declared, "and no one discovers a new world who exacts guarantee in advance for what it shall be. . . . This is the truth in the exaggeration of subjectivism."[49]

In *Experience and Nature* Dewey needed to distinguish carefully between his own experiential conception of mind and consciousness and that put forward by introspectionism and Freudian psychoanalysis. Dewey's effectiveness in distinguishing these competing conceptions would affect, in turn, the credibility of the functional connections that Dewey wished to establish between nature, body, and the mind. But above all else he needed to demonstrate persuasively how mind and communication become distorted when enlisted in the service of realist epistemologies and cultural narratives about wishes and desires, undermining the experiential connections between mind and body and between consciousness and behavior that he sought to sustain.

Introspectionism and psychoanalysis occupied opposite ends of the continuum of theories of mind. Proponents of introspectionism dating back to Descartes claimed that consciousness furnishes clear and distinct immediate knowledge of the contents and meanings of sense perceptions. This theory was based on the premise that stimuli constitute the objects of sense perception, which possess intrinsic qualities that distinguish them from other elements of conscious thought, such as memories or emotions. Dewey argued that stimuli are instruments of response or a means of further action and thus do not possess intrinsic significance. Visual and auditory perception occurs at an earlier stage in the process in which peripheral and centrally initiated events converge to trigger awareness. These stimuli are subsequently cognitively processed as objects that are recognized as familiar and meaningful or in need of further identification. Dewey concluded that introspectionism mistakenly collapsed sequentially distinct stages of thought by confusing perception with the cognitive processes whereby sensory information acquires meaning and significance.[50]

Psychoanalysis, which Dewey chose to characterize as "revery-consciousness," was guilty of the contrasting error of denying that perception has anything to do with natural sensory phenomena.[51] Dewey clearly believed this was an untenable position and strongly criticized it in *Experience and Nature.*

> Revery consciousness, and the influence upon beliefs of affective wishes of which we are not always aware, are facts crucial for any theory of consciousness. If they support the hypothesis that all consciousness is awareness of meanings, they also seem at first sight to contradict the supposition that the meanings perceived are those of natural events. Since their objects are notoriously "unreal," they seem to support the notion that consciousness is disconnected from physical events, and that any valid connection which may be set up, either in practical conduct or in knowing, is adventitious.[52]

Dewey acknowledged that there is some merit in challenging the "orthodox tradition that makes consciousness architectonic," but he could not accept the "complete separation of existential consciousness from connection with physical things."[53] This position can be maintained, Dewey argued, "only by holding that the connection of consciousness in its varied forms with bodily action is non-natural."[54] Viewing consciousness in this fashion, Dewey asserted, forces us to characterize consciousness as either "infallible spectatorship or as irrelevant to the world." In a tacit reference to Freud's controversial theories about the interpretation of dreams and their emotional significance, Dewey acknowledged that "[w]e dream, but the material of our dream life is the stuff of our waking life. Revery is not first wholly detached from objects of purposeful action and belief, coming later by discipline to acquire reference to them."[55]

Dewey, like Freud, believed that "the greater part of mind is only implicit in any conscious act," and that the field of mind encompasses a whole system of meanings that is "enormously wider than that of consciousness."[56] But this is where their thinking diverges. Freud contended that the preponderance of implicit meanings or symbolizations are stored as unconscious memories or ideas beyond the access of consciousness. Dewey disagreed. He argued that meaningful ideas were rooted in subconscious sensorimotor processes that can be retrieved in the form of sequential memories. Hence consciousness and memory are linked through a contextual field in which ideas or actions that are in the foreground or the focus of consciousness are surrounded by a much larger but dimly perceived background of implicit meanings. Dewey considered it fallacious to reduce mind or meaning to memory because this confuses the difference between the functions of mind and conscious awareness.

The distinction between mind and consciousness was crucial for Dewey. He contended that "[m]ind is contextual and persistent; consciousness is focal and transitive. Mind is, so to speak, structural, substantial; a constant background and foreground; perceptive consciousness is process; a series of heres and nows. Mind is constant luminosity; consciousness intermittent, a series of flashes of varying intensities."[57] Mind denotes, for Dewey, such things as the capacity for organization, order, and coherence. That is why it is semantically correct, Dewey asserts, to characterize the mind as disorganized, confused, disoriented, and so forth. But "there is no sense," Dewey says, "in referring to a particular state of awareness *in its immediacy* as either organized or disturbed. An idea is just what it is when it occurs."[58] But the force of an idea (i.e., its complete ramifications) often takes longer for the mind to grasp or unravel.

Dewey was alert to the possibility that his notion of mind would be interpreted as merely a more sophisticated version of idealistic or materialistic and deterministic theories that he repudiated. He actually was advancing a conception of matter closely akin to that of Ostwald, Mach, and Maxwell, who believed that matter is the transient form that energy assumes in the course of its continuous transformation. Drawing from field theory, Dewey argued that matter does not naturally possess a determinate form but takes shape within a "particular field of forces or interacting events."[59] Dewey believed that mind could be characterized in similar terms as the forms that ideas assume when they are embodied in behavior. Both Dewey and William James before him shared similar conceptions of mind as being energized by consciousness. We see William James's notion of a "stream of consciousness" echoed in Dewey's conception of mind. Dewey's supposition that mind possesses constancy or biases and yet embodies change is most clearly brought out in the following passage.

> If mind is a further process in life, a further process of registration, conservation and use of what is conserved, then it must have the traits it does empirically have: being a moving stream, a constant change which nevertheless has axis and direction, linkages, associations as well as initiations, hesitations and conclusions.[60]

Freud's apparent indifference to the phenomenon of consciousness probably was encouraged by the behaviorist revolution in American psychology. Behaviorists shoved introspectionism and consciousness to the margins of acceptable inquiry. In its place they enthroned the premise that learning and development occur through conditioning processes that require recursive memory but little awareness and judgment. This lent credibility to Freud's view that individual personality is indelibly determined by early experiences. Moreover, attempts to define consciousness as if it were some separate entity inevitably fail, as Dewey pointed out, because consciousness is erroneously viewed as an external agent *causing* an experience to occur in the brain and mind, thus introducing an illicit mind-body dualism. Dewey believed that the difficulty of defining consciousness was implicated in a more fundamental problem of translating first-person phenomenal experience into objective and intersubjectively verifiable terms. Behaviorism and psychoanalysis were simply contemporary variations on an age-old epistemological theme that knowledge, experience, and judgment are things that are acquired externally rather than developed inwardly.

In Dewey's opinion, psychoanalysis fell into this realist epistemological trap by arguing that every person is disposed psychologically to express instinctive wishes whose symbolic meaning and behavioral consequences are invariable. If it were true that human behavior is motivated by unconscious drives, Dewey surmises, we would be unable to distinguish between actions and consequences of our own making and those beyond our control. We would be forever stuck in a dream world, as marionettes whose every motion gives the appearance of intentionality and control without making a difference. In fact, Dewey makes an even stronger assertion that without continuous change in our field of vision, there would be no perception or consciousness. Only when something unusual or different happens do we take notice or pay attention. While familiarity breeds contentment and habitual behavior, uncertainty instigates vigilance and the need to attend to what one is doing. Dewey characteristically was reluctant to use the term "perception," as employed by psychologists and philosophical realists, because it failed to express the transitive nature of consciousness. We observe objects and we experience situations, but the traits or attributes that an object possesses or the feelings we experience, Dewey argued, should not be confused with the processes through which we assign meaning and make sense of them.[61]

THE CONSOLABLE MEMORIES OF THE SUBCONSCIOUS

Dewey's low regard for psychoanalysis undoubtedly contributed to his peculiar aversion in *Experience and Nature* to the term "memory," which had an unfortunate association with the Freudian unconscious. Nevertheless, Dewey's views on this phenomenon, which he published in 1902, provide important insights about how Dewey's conception of consciousness differs profoundly from that of Freud. In an essay on "Memory and Judgment," Dewey argued that there are at least two forms of memory that should be carefully distinguished. "Reminiscence" is a kind of memory that once started, Dewey wryly observed, "unravels yard by yard."[62] Triggered by some idea or incidental circumstance, more attention is paid to dramatic highlights than actual sequences.

The process of "recollecting or remembering," by contrast, involves according to Dewey, a more systematic and orderly process of "membering or joining things together again."[63] Effective recall involves more than just memorization or an association of ideas, Dewey observed, but requires attentive and careful observation of the sequence of events as they are experienced. In doing so, Dewey said, we are actually "cultivating our faculty of judgment."[64] Memory accumulates information, but judgment is required to sort it out and appraise its value. Hence judgment and memory are closely intertwined and work in tandem. Dewey expressed this relationship best when he declared, "Memory is judgment in the process of making and judgment is memory completely defined."[65]

Dewey wanted to show that consciousness involves more than simple passive awareness of something, but the capacity to detect change. Our judgments must be informed not only by change in the meaning of ideas we remember or perceive but by the different form and direction they assume in our behavior. A change of meaning is equivalent to adopting a new attitude. "What follows," Dewey declared, "is that perception or consciousness *is* literally, the difference in the process of *making*."[66] Much of the energy we expend in trying to understand something is put into the effort of attaining an adequate vantage point and position of mental or mechanical advantage with which to gain increased leverage and control. In this process we must be able to juxtapose simultaneously past experiences, present thoughts, and future expectations to form judgments that reduce uncertainty. Accordingly, the potential energy of mind and meaning is transformed through consciousness, Dewey believed, to take shape in the rich repertoire of feelings, attitudes, emotions, and behavior with which we make sense of and render our experiences significant.

Dewey's adept and spirited critique of psychoanalysis and his ingenious arguments for consciousness are compelling. Nevertheless, an unresolved paradox recurs throughout *Experience and Nature* that Dewey does not attempt to reconcile. One the one hand, Dewey makes a persuasive argument that all physical and cultural forms of human behavior and expression can be explained in naturalistic terms. On the other hand, he also asserts with equal vigor that humankind has been prevented from expressing its potential because of defective child-rearing practices and mistaken cultural conceptions of human identity. Dewey only exacerbated this troublesome paradox he was trying to dispel by acknowledging Freud's diagnosis (albeit from an organic perspective) that modern humans are victims of fixations and other habit-reinforcing attitudes that have prevented them from realizing their potential.

Randolph Bourne exposed the infelicity of Dewey's failure to adequately account for this discrepancy between the appearance and reality of individual conduct. By accepting Alexander's account of the debilitating effects of civilized life, Dewey appeared to Bourne to have contradicted his long-held contention that developmental processes harbor the resources for progressive growth and transformation. Dewey's Hegelian argument in *Experience and Nature* to deal with this paradox was simply to say that humanity had not yet attained complete consciousness of how their attitudes affect their perceptions of the world and their ability to act on them correctly. Dewey asserted that:

As long as our own fundamental psycho-physical attitudes in dealing with external things are subconscious, our conscious attention going only to the relations of external things, so long will our perception of the external situations be subject at its root to perversion and vitiation. This state of affairs is the source of that apparent disconnection between consciousness and action, which strikes us when we begin to reflect.

The connecting links between the two are in our own attitudes; while they remain unperceived, consciousness and behavior must appear to be independent of each other. Hence there will be empirical reason for isolating consciousness from natural events.[67]

Dewey sincerely believed that Alexander's technique had enabled him to personally comprehend phenomenal consciousness by experiencing what it is like to gain control over and alter one's own behavior. *Experience and Nature* is dedicated to the proposition that consciousness is not a subjective phenomenon. Given more adequate scientific study of the mechanisms involved, Dewey believed that the energy of consciousness could be channeled more effectively to emancipate humanity from the shackles of habit and tradition. But this optimistic scenario of scientific deliverance proved more daunting, as foreshadowed in the closing chapters of *Experience and Nature*. Dewey acknowledged that a naturalistic conception of consciousness ultimately required a fundamentally different understanding of the role of energy and spirit in human perception, art, and experimental inquiry than previously surmised.

While Dewey granted that minds require brains with physical attributes, this in no way limited how the energetic processes of consciousness are constituted in space and time. Ironically, Freud was advancing a similar argument that unconscious energy was unbound and not subject to physical laws. Precisely how it was possible for the energy involved in nervous processes to be bound and yet unbound defied easy explanation. Unlike Freud, however, Dewey believed that science was capable of furnishing an answer that would eventually yield knowledge about the human spirit.

A properly formulated metaphysics of mind, Dewey believed, could not only benefit science, but would make inquiry possible regarding soul and spirit. The soul was not something that could be localized in the nervous system or the brain, as some phrenologists supposed. The soul exhibited instead sensitivity, energy, buoyancy, or weightlessness and a capacity for transformation that marked the presence of spirit. "When the organization called soul," Dewey observes, "is free, moving and operative, initial as well as terminal, it is spirit. ... Spirit quickens; is not only alive, but spirit gives life. Animals are spirited, but man is a living spirit. He lives in his works and his works do follow him. Soul is form, spirit informs. It is the moving function of that of which the soul is the substance."[68] The distinctiveness of the human spirit, for Dewey, is marked by the capacity and will to overcome the inertia of habit and the contentment of the familiar by summoning the energy needed to enlarge the realm of individual experience.

Dewey's attempt to understand human experience from an aesthetic or spiritual perspective did not signal for Dewey the impossibility of understanding the energetics of mind and consciousness in scientific terms. Instead Dewey saw this as an opportunity to visualize the universal features of the mind through the eyes of those artists and scientists who believed that aesthetics and science involved the same underlying processes of perception and judgment.

Dewey's turn toward aesthetics signaled his dissatisfaction with how he had handled the problematic relation between culture and nature. The term "culture" better captured what the term "experience" failed to convey, namely, that there are many different ways of perceiving and doing things that are meaningful and possess significance. Dewey had not conceded that phenomenal experience was something ineffable and indefinable. He simply believed that the medium of art would render explicit the implicit knowledge humans possess of nature that underpins the processes of judgment. His subsequent immersion in contemporary art, particularly that of the post-impressionists, was of inestimable value in striking out on yet another pathway to understanding the mind and inquiry through the world of art and culture.

Part Three

The Transformational Potential of
Consciousness in Art, Politics, and Science

SEVEN

Post-impressionism, Quantum Mechanics, and the Triumph of Phenomenal Experience

The decade of the 1920s was easily one of Dewey's most frenetic and yet intellectually productive periods of his career. Dewey was increasingly in demand, as his fame as a philosopher and spokesman for progressive educational causes spread around the world. Dewey's enormously popular extended lecture tours in China and Japan, during a period of civil unrest in those countries (1919–1920), were followed by engagements in Turkey in 1924, in Mexico in the summer of 1926, and an unexpected trip in 1928 with a delegation of American educators invited to observe and comment on Soviet schools. While on these trips, Dewey derived many insights regarding politics and culture and the intimate relationship between national attitudes toward democratic values and educational practices.

These trips led to the publication in the *New Republic* of numerous essays that reflected Dewey's increasingly sophisticated understanding of the strategic importance of culture and education in generating demands for democratic reforms. Dewey would observe later, in his essays on *Individualism Old and New*, that political and economic ideologies were less influential in shaping individual perspectives than the values and social attitudes transmitted through its culture. The "mental poverty" that comes from the demand for conformity, Dewey contended, "is more significant than the poverty in material goods."[1]

For a person who found communism abhorrent, Dewey was favorably impressed with the Russian experiment in cooperative education. Significantly, Dewey perceived that the primary revolution occurring in communist Russia was not political or economic but "a revolution of the heart and mind, this liberation of a people to consciousness of themselves as a determining power in the shaping of their ultimate fate."[2] Even the most doctrinaire and dogmatic principles of Marxism seemed less worrisome to Dewey, having observed that the actual effect of this ideology was "to pull the trigger that released suppressed energies."[3] Perhaps Dewey's most rewarding pleasures on his visit to the Soviet Union were his repeated visits to the Hermitage, an art museum in Leningrad. He was so absorbed in viewing European masterpieces of painting and sculpture that his daughter Evelyn complained one day that she "finally dragged Dad away at three having been there since 11—no lunch!"[4]

After having mounted a frustrating defense of pragmatism against attacks leveled by his bitter rivals earlier in the decade, Dewey was now preparing to launch an uncompromisingly naturalistic theory of aesthetics. Consumed by the bitterness and resentment of these culture wars, Dewey wanted to rectify the falsehood that Bourne and his companions had so maliciously perpetrated, that pragmatism was not only logically faulty but culturally inimical. Possessing only a rudimentary knowledge of art, Dewey felt distinctly disadvantaged when it came to matching wits with those claiming to defend artistic expression against the imperatives of pragmatist technology.

Sadly, however, Alice Dewey would not be with John to close out what had surely been a tumultuous decade for Dewey. Alice tended to internalize and brood over her husband's conflicts, and she was still suffering from the tragic, inconsolable loss of her first son, Morris. She was struck by a sudden and unexpected heart attack while accompanying Dewey on his trip to Mexico, forcing them to return to the states in early July 1926. Weakened by the advanced stages of arteriosclerosis, Alice then suffered a series of strokes that ended her life the following year in mid-July. Dewey's son Frederick invited him to spend the rest of the summer in Hubbards Bay, Nova Scotia, which Dewey adopted as his favorite summer home, completing such books as *The Quest for Certainty* and *Logic: The Theory of Inquiry*. Dewey faced his loss stoically; it did not diminish his enthusiasm for the projects that lay ahead. His daughters each took turns for the next several years living with him and helping him to keep up with a considerably demanding schedule, which included, among many other activities, invitations to present the Gifford lectures on the history of science in Edinburgh, Scotland, in 1929 and to lecture on aesthetics at Harvard University in 1931.

With the exception of his daughters, Dewey's closest companions from the late 1920s through the 1930s were Myrtle McGraw and Albert Barnes. Dewey also began an extended correspondence in 1930 with Corinne Chisholm, an independent researcher and writer. Her inquisitiveness and insightful observations about science and art provided a sounding board for Dewey to rehearse and revise ideas central to establishing linkages between aesthetics and scientific inquiry. As stimulating as Chisholm's correspondence would be to Dewey during the next decade, it was no substitute for the numerous occasions in which Dewey could share experiences with Barnes and McGraw, for whom he had an abiding respect and affection. Both of these colleagues and friends provided experiences of inestimable value to Dewey in his attempt to demonstrate the essential unity of art and science. This chapter will focus on Dewey's relationship with Barnes and their mutual interest in art.

Albert Barnes was an inventor, self-made millionaire, and art collector, who was temperamentally predisposed toward theory, argumentation, and criticism of an intellectually combative sort. Barnes created a private museum and foundation to support art education in 1922, and he wrote several books elaborating his aesthetic theory and featuring specific artists. Over the next decade Barnes gave Dewey an informal education in art history and interpretation that included trips to Parisian and Italian museums and galleries, a personal introduction to Henri Matisse, with whom Dewey had extended discussions, and frequent invitations to his Philadelphia home to view Barnes's latest acquisitions.

During this period, Dewey sought to reconcile the seemingly unbridgeable gulf between artistic creation and scientific inquiry. Newtonian physics was profoundly challenged by Einstein's theory of relativity and quantum mechanics. The young Einstein admired Wilhelm Ostwald, the leading exponent of a *Naturphilosopie*, but sought unsuccessfully to study physics under his tutelage.[5] Einstein, however, soon struck out in a revolutionary new direction. He pushed the implications of Maxwellian physics and field theory to the boundaries of the universe itself, propounding his special and general theories of relativity to demonstrate the essential equivalence of energy and matter.

Dewey shared Einstein's vision of a unified field theory. Dewey was convinced that the same underlying processes that energize perception and give form and function to inanimate matter are operative in scientific inquiry, and in any realm in which judgment is required for human understanding. Mind enabled the *phenomenal* properties of matter and energy to be experienced psychobiologically, Dewey held, even though as *physical* properties of nature, matter and energy possessed imperceptible dynamic qualities undergoing continuous change and transformation.

Dewey also learned from his daughter Jane about the breaking developments in quantum mechanics that called into question Einstein's dream of a unified field theory. Jane had an unusual opportunity to conduct post-doctoral research with Niels Bohr, Werner Heisenberg, Erwin Schrödinger, and other physicists in Copenhagen in the late 1920s. She witnessed firsthand the debates that led to the formulation of quantum theory and Bohr's articulation of the principle of complementarity. Dewey believed that Bohr's principle made it theoretically possible to render physical, biological, and cultural forms in commensurate terms that were intersubjectively understood. This important episode in Dewey's intellectual development will be discussed later in this chapter after Dewey's excursions with Barnes in the world of art are examined.

AN APPRENTICESHIP WITH ALBERT BARNES

Barnes found art criticism appealing because he believed, with characteristic immodesty, that only he could furnish the critical tools with which to interpret new forms of artistic expression that emerged during the rise of post-impressionism. Barnes's improbable route into the center of the controversy over modern art is worth describing because he helped popularize many European artists whose works ran counter to American proclivities for realism in nature and the human form. After being trained as a physician at the University of Pennsylvania in 1892, Barnes served his residency in an institution for the insane, where he studied William James and learned the principles of abnormal psychology. In 1894, Barnes undertook doctoral studies in physiological chemistry in Berlin at the University of Heidelberg. He never completed the degree requirements, but he did pick up valuable laboratory experience, and he attended a philosophy seminar in which he studied Leibniz, Fichte, Kant, and Hegel.[6]

Barnes returned to Philadelphia in 1900 to take a job with a chemical company. Barnes showed no particular laboratory acumen, but he soon formed a partnership with a German chemist, who helped him create Argyrol, a silver nitrate compound used to prevent blindness in babies of mothers who are afflicted with syphilis and to treat other viral infections. The widespread sale of this product to physicians was largely due to Barnes's promotional efforts. His business prospered and Barnes eventually bought out his partner. With his manufacturing business secure, Barnes had accumulated enough money by 1910 to pursue his other interest in art.[7]

An aspiring artist in high school, Barnes painted 190 canvasses, but he did not possess any great aptitude or talent. When Barnes finally got the financial wherewithal, he acquired his own collection of art largely for the nonspeculative purpose of increasing his understanding of aesthetics. He undertook several excursions to European salons to purchase as many paintings as he could afford, focusing particularly on works by Cézanne, Renoir, and Matisse. During a buying spree in Europe in 1912, Barnes became acquainted with the Gertrude and Leo Stein, who served as cultural intermediaries, touting the artistic merits of the revolutionary but misunderstood post-impressionist avant-garde. Initially put off by these strangely conceived compositions of indistinct forms and overlapping colors, Barnes subjected them to intense scrutiny until they slowly revealed their creator's intentions and underlying feelings. Barnes eventually published books in the 1930s on each of these leading figures in modern art in the attempt to articulate the underlying principles that informed their work.

By 1920 Barnes was bragging to Dewey that he owned more than a hundred Renoirs (by 1935 Barnes had added another seventy-five Renoirs) and had purchased only the best Matisses and fifty Cézannes at bargain prices.[8] Barnes's art collection grew so rapidly that he found it necessary in 1923 to construct several buildings to house and display them near his home in Merion, a suburb of Philadelphia. Unfortunately for Barnes, neither the press nor art critics welcomed this development. Post-impressionists initially were regarded by mainstream American viewers as having exceeded their artistic license by distorting and contorting human forms in pathologically sensuous postures that one critic labeled "compressionist."[9] These Parisian innovators were the purveyors of "debased art," according to another critic, who protested that "the attempt for

9. John Dewey and Albert Barnes in the Barnes Museum gallery at Merion, Pennsylvania, late 1920s.
Special Collections, Morris Library, Southern Illinois University, Carbondale, Illinois.

a new form of expression results in the degradation of the old formulas, not in the creation of something new."[10] Barnes only exacerbated the ire of his critics by personally expressing his contempt for their opinions.

Despite these protests, Barnes moved forward with his unique plan to create not merely a museum but an educational foundation for the appreciation of art. This unusual concept reflected Barnes's desire to provide the critical tools that he believed necessary to interpret modern art within a broader historical, cultural, and experiential perspective.[11] Dewey lent his prestige to the Barnes Foundation by accepting an invitation to become founding director of education—an honorific, advisory role that carried few responsibilities but many liabilities. Columbia colleague Lawrence Buermeyer and Dewey student Thomas Munro were appointed associate directors. The art galleries were never opened to the public during Barnes's lifetime and only a limited number of artists and students were ever invited to attend lectures given by Barnes or his staff. Barnes later expressed his gratitude for Dewey's support when the Foundation's policies came under attack by making an annual gift of $5,000 upon Dewey's retirement from Columbia in 1930.

Barnes generously financed and led three summer tours to European museums and galleries from 1925 to 1927 accompanied by Dewey, Munro, and their wives. Munro recalled that Dewey listened intently to Barnes's commentary on these trips but had little to say, adding that Dewey admitted "frankly that he didn't know much about the visual arts."[12] Dewey and Barnes got along surprisingly well for two people with such different, almost opposite, personalities. "Barnes was indefatigable, tireless mentally and physically, always prepared to defend his ideas," Munro indicated, adding that while "never argumentative [Dewey] always seemed to be tentative and wanting to think more about a problem before committing himself on a very controversial line."[13] "Dewey's own approach," Munro remembered, "was quiet, considerate, polite but frank in disagreement, when he felt he was right."[14] He noted that Dewey and Barnes had one important thing in common that created an indelible bond of friendship. They each felt that their respective views on education and art had been badly misinterpreted by professionals in the field.[15]

EXPLAINING THE ORIGINS OF MODERN ART

Intimidated by intellectual art critics, Barnes hesitated at first to put his ideas into print, preferring to recruit other more distinguished art critics to assist him in that task. Everyone he approached, including Thomas Hart Benton, politely rejected his request. Barnes persevered and published his own book, *The Art in Painting*. The book received unexpectedly favorable reviews from museum directors and art critics such as Joseph Wood Crutch, who called it "an important contribution," and Ezra Pound, who called it "the right kind of book about painting."[16] Although complimentary, Leo Stein, writing for the *New Republic*, accused Barnes of "defective methods" when it came to ranking artists he preferred.[17]

Barnes believed that aesthetic judgment was informed by objective, universal standards of value or worth. Works of art from different periods could not only be evaluated by the same criteria, but ranked in terms of their aesthetic merit and cultural achievement. Barnes assessed works of art according to whether they satisfied the requirements of "plastic form." This involved the painter's capacity to successfully integrate several related technical elements that contribute to a feeling of harmony and emotional authenticity. A painting is aesthetically pleasing when emotion and perception are united through the rhythms of contrast and balance. According to Barnes's aesthetic standards, paintings by the classical and romantic masters David, Delacroix, Raphael, and Mantegna failed to measure up as great works of art because their subject matter was presented in an overly dramatic, theatrical, histrionic, and sentimental fashion. "One searches in vain in these artists' works for poignancy, pathos and tragedy," Barnes observed, because "their portrayal of them is essentially a caricature."[18]

Dewey hesitated to make such snap judgments about historical figures to whom modern artists were indebted. Dewey believed that there are no universal aesthetic standards. Works of art must be evaluated primarily according to their capacity to enlarge and enrich the experience of the beholder. The true measure of an artist's contribution cannot be based on retrospective judgments based on contemporary tastes or values. Dewey acknowledged that "I have no right to say a good picture must have a certain form or style." Delacroix may have been a painter "who was unduly romantic," Dewey granted, but "what he said of painters of his day applies to inferior artists generally."[19] Dewey argued that Delacroix avoided the unwitting realist bias that led his contemporaries to use color to "represent" objects, "instead of making them out of color."[20] Delacroix's insight was to see color itself as the medium of expression and not its end, thus contributing to a new way of approaching the subject matter of art that led to impressionism.

Dewey and Barnes's aesthetic perspectives reflected fundamental differences in their interpretations of the history of painting. Barnes did not think of the transition from romanticism to modernism as a departure from realism or literalism, but simply a purer expression of the underlying natural and emotional realities involved. Through their emphasis on form and design, Renoir and Cézanne brought modernism to a climax in impressionism—an aesthetic perspective, Barnes asserted, that only Matisse and a handful of other post-impressionists sustained in their works. Picasso and Braque, on the other hand, offended Barnes's realist sensibilities. He said their "idea of abstract form divorced from a clue, however vague, of its representative equivalent in the real world is sheer nonsense."[21] "Consequently," Barnes added," the very great majority of cubist paintings have no more aesthetic significance than an Oriental rug."[22]

Barnes cited approvingly Dewey's own statements in *Experience and Nature* that aesthetic form must go beyond a scientific or technically correct depiction of some object or scene to capture its emotional essence as supporting a hard-and-fast rule for separating good art from bad art. Dewey, however, was proposing no such rule of comparison. Instead, good science and good art succeed, Dewey argued, when they enlarge and enrich perception and enable the suspension of immediate and visceral reactions to see something in an entirely new light. Dewey wanted to plunge much more deeply than Barnes into the artist's mind and soul to discover the sources of energy that breathed life and beauty into formless, inert matter. Dewey believed that artistic vision fully blossomed in human civilization only when artists acquired the psychological distance needed to express metaphorically their own sense of identity and behavior in the works of art they created.

Only after an important transition occurred in the history of painting, involving a shift from realism and formalism to naturalism, Dewey observed, did psychological distance and a sense of reflective self-consciousness become prominent elements of artistic vision. This transition was made possible in part by secularism. Artists released from bondage to official or church sponsorship were free to pursue new subject matter that reflected their own experiences and attitudes. Naturalism represented not just a rejection of the aristocratic authority but expressed a budding awareness of individual freedom. Stylistically, of course, even classical and romantic painters injected a personal element into their works. But profound change occurred in nineteenth-century artistic sensibilities, according to Dewey, when "consciousness of the rightful place of a strictly personal factor became commonplace."[23] "Genuine naturalism" emerged, Dewey observed, "when the unfixity of human features under the influence of emotions was perceived; when their own variety of rhythm was reacted to."[24]

MATISSE AND THE BIRTH AND TRAGEDY OF ART

Among all the post-impressionists with whom he was familiar, Barnes considered Matisse to have possessed an extraordinary talent and an unrivaled insight about art. During Matisse's first exhibition in America in 1930, Barnes invited him to Merion, where he offered Matisse a commission to create a mural. Although initially resistant to Barnes's incessant pleas, on a return trip a few months later Matisse reluctantly acceded. He accepted Barnes's commission to create an enormous mural (eleven feet high by fifty-seven feet long) *The Dance* to adorn a doorway arch in Barnes's museum. This commission proved to be one of the most exhilarating and frustrating assignments Matisse had ever accepted.

Barnes frequently interrupted Matisse's work to gather personal information for a book he was writing about the artist. The increasing divergence between Barnes and Dewey in their respective views about art would become most apparent during this time. The determination and single-mindedness with which Barnes pursued his acquisitive thirst for art spilled over into a desire to possess the creative mind and soul of the artist whose work he coveted. Unlike Dewey, Barnes's quest was concerned more with control than understanding. Barnes ultimately wanted to use an artist's creativity to express and achieve his own unrealized aesthetic ambitions, long since sidelined by pecuniary preoccupations.

Matisse was extremely anxious to prevent Barnes from learning about a novel cutout technique he devised to refine his color schemes before rendering them in final form. (This turned out to be an important innovation, resulting in Matisse's adoption of a new style.) Matisse feared that if Barnes discovered he had completed but abandoned several preliminary cutout versions of *The Dance*, Barnes would renege on his commission. When Matisse discovered, after finally completing his first final version of *The Dance*, that he had gotten the measurements wrong and would have to start over, Barnes came close to withdrawing his commission.[25]

By the time Matisse completed the Barnes project he was a nervous wreck, suffering a mild heart attack at the Barnes Museum while attempting to frame the mural. Shortly after the mural was installed, Matisse confessed to an art critic that the work he had completed for Barnes took on an entirely different

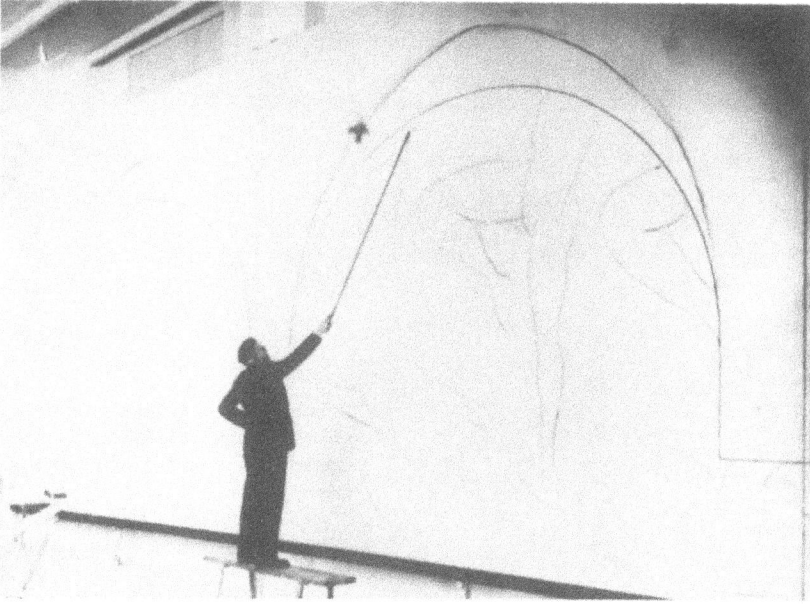

10. Henri Matisse drawing with a bamboo stick on the mural "The Dance," commissioned by Albert Barnes. 1931.
Photograph © reproduced with the permission of The Barnes Foundation™, Merion, Pennsylvania, all rights reserved.

meaning. He said "it became a rigid thing, heavy as stone."[26] Matisse suffered further insult when the presumptuous Barnes, in his book on Matisse, ranked him lower than all the old masters, including Titian, Giotto, and Renoir. Moreover, he characterized Matisse's style (in an insensitive implicit reference to Matisse's law degree) as exhibiting the "calculation and sobriety of a judge or banker," more interested in the "decorative design" than emotional depth.[27]

In rendering these harsh judgments Barnes was hastening the end of their relationship. Nevertheless, Matisse profited artistically from these unfortunate episodes. He glimpsed the possibilities of adopting a new medium of art based on his use of cutouts to guide the painting of the Barnes mural. This constituted a textbook example of Dewey's pragmatism. When Matisse discovered that the cutout method possessed intrinsic aesthetic value, he had simply converted something that was instrumental to the completion of the Barnes mural into an object aesthetic in its own right.

Dewey first met Matisse under less stressful circumstances when he greeted him in New York in December 1930 and accompanied him to Merion.[28] Their first encounter was brief largely because Barnes consumed most of Matisse's time with discussions about details regarding the mural. Before returning to France, however, Matisse asked Dewey to pose for a few sketches in his hotel.

11. *John Dewey*, by Henri Matisse. 1930. Charcoal on paper. The Museum of Modern Art, New York. Gift of Pierre Matisse.
© 2001 The Museum of Modern Art and Succession H. Matisse, Paris/Artists Rights Society (ARS), New York.

These were preliminary studies for a lithograph that Matisse may never have completed.[29] Matisse sketched two different charcoal versions of Dewey. The first version was more realistic. The second version presented a more stylized profile of Dewey's face, with fewer but more sweeping lines, less distinct anatomical detail, and greater accentuation of eyebrows, nose, and mustache.[30]

During a brief return visit with Dewey in New York before leaving for Paris, Matisse shared with Dewey his anxiety about working for Barnes. He shared three sketches of the mural. Dewey subsequently related to Barnes that Matisse told him that he promised "to do his very best for you, and I guess he is right."[31] What Dewey found interesting about the sketches was the "growth" apparent in each successive version. In a prophetic reference to his own book in progress, Dewey wrote to Barnes, saying that:

> If anyone ever writes the actual psychology of the artist's processes in creation, it will be through access to waste paper baskets, and discarded sketches, etc. It was interesting to see Matisse's hands move in the rhythm of his forms when he shows the sketches, a complete refutation of Prall's denial of time and rhythm to paintings.[32]

Dewey had two other occasions to see Matisse in 1931 to gain additional insights from him about painting and aesthetics. Dewey wrote to Chisholm that he had "the pleasure of considerable contact with the French painter, Henri Matisse, first in Paris and then the last ten days in New York."[33] In characterizing his latest visit in New York, Dewey remarked, "I have got a great deal from him. He is a combination of simplicity, humor, directness, balance and insight that is very rare—the most completely coordinated human being I have ever met, I think."[34] Upon his return to Nice, Matisse thanked Dewey for "the delightful moments I have spent in your company," and declared that he, like Dewey, "felt in perfect harmony with everyone."[35] Nevertheless, Matisse did not conceal his continuing anxiety about the Barnes mural and hoped that Dewey could be a friendly intermediary, "whose precious help," Matisse prayed, would make it "possible to conclude this study."[36] It is difficult to see how Dewey could have been of any help to Matisse in preventing the headstrong Barnes from devouring the artist as voraciously as he had consumed his art.

Although there are no direct accounts of Dewey's acquaintance with Matisse, his influence is evident throughout *Art as Experience*. Dewey singled out Matisse as having employed his extraordinary powers of perception to create works of art that grasped the essential rhythms of human emotions. Luckily for Dewey, Matisse was one of the few post-impressionists to write extensively about his techniques and share his views about aesthetics in recorded interviews. In *Art as Experience* Dewey cited Matisse's early seminal essay on aesthetics and included quotes from some of Matisse's interviews.

We can gain a sense of what Dewey and Matisse might have discussed in their brief but intense encounters by noting that Dewey could not have found an artist whose aesthetic theory was more congenial and harmonious. Matisse abided by one overriding principle comparable in simplicity to the principle of silence that Dewey learned through Hegel's example, that an aspiring painter should render himself "incapable of speech" by "cutting out one's tongue."[37] In so doing, Matisse believed, an artist renounces his right to express himself in any other way but on the canvas. Matisse followed this rule up to a point by not characterizing the themes of his works. Matisse regretted, however, breaking his rule when he discussed with Barnes a prototype of the mural *The Dance*. Ironically, the theme for the Barnes mural was suggested to Matisse by a famous passage in Nietzsche's *The Birth of Tragedy* in which the medium of dancing enabled humans to express themselves as if they were members of an otherworldly community.[38]

Inspiration came naturally to Matisse because he relied on his tremendous powers of self-reflection to develop new techniques, trying to articulate the implicit feelings that infused his art. Matisse appeared to Dewey to have gained access to his subconscious powers of suggestion to find new modes of artistic expression. Matisse likened painting to giving birth to a new form whose conception can neither be completely planned nor anticipated. He attempted to circumvent the distorting bias of fixed preconceptions by looking at something as if seeing it for the first time through the eyes of a child.

Matisse helped Dewey penetrate the individual contrivances of style to see the underlying rhythms and forms they embodied. Form was concerned not with objects or matter but with energetic forces that bring about unity and consummation. Consequently, Dewey defined aesthetic form "as the operation of forces that carry the experience . . . to its own integral fulfillment," to suggest how the artist expresses his feelings by capturing their energy in the composi-

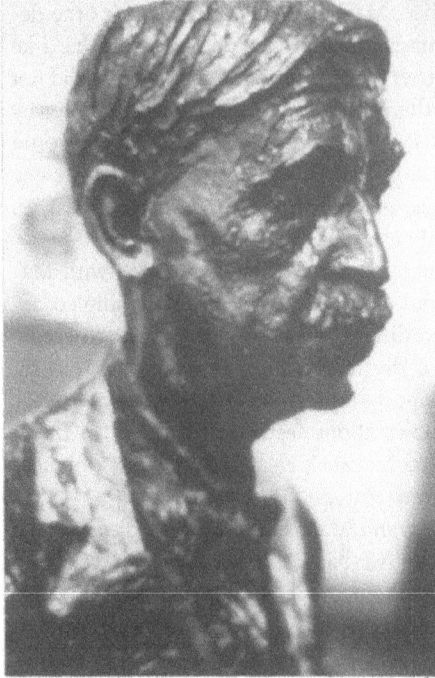

12. Bust of John Dewey by Sir Jacob Epstein, 1929.
Special Collections, Millbank Memorial Library, Teachers College, Columbia University, New York.

tion as a whole.[39] An act of "aesthetic perception" gives shape to the forces of energy by rendering them into rhythmical relationship whereby masses are balanced, colors are harmonized, and planes intersected.[40]

Dewey was at his best on the subject of science or aesthetics, as his acquaintance with Matisse attests, when he became personally involved with practitioners in these fields. In commemoration of Dewey's seventieth birthday (the year Dewey became emeritus at Columbia) a group of his former students and colleagues commissioned a bust by Jacob Epstein. The real gift they gave Dewey was the opportunity to assume the twin perspectives involved in "having" *and* "undergoing" an experience simultaneously, as the subject of an artist's skillful craft and as an observer of his artistic techniques. When Dewey viewed the bust from the point of view of the artist's attempt to express his unique character and identity, he was perplexed with how Epstein captured "rather more forces than my face has I think."[41] He related to Barnes that the bust appeared multifaceted in which "the front view is reflective, a melancholy philosopher; the right side view grim, and the left with a suspicion of a smile, and yet all views hang together, anyway, that is my impression."[42]

By adopting the perspective of an artist, Dewey gained even more insight about how contrasting natural forces contributed to an overall facial expression and attitude. The different emotions that he may have felt during each sitting were harmonized through the skillful organization of the underlying energies of the forces involved in their expression. "What is most characteristic of his work," Dewey observed in commenting on Epstein's bust, "is that he builds it with light and shade. This seems absurd since he works in the solid—but instead of using the planes and letting light and shade result, he subordinates his treatment of surface to get the light and shade. I think this is the source of the peculiarly refractory quality of his work."[43] Dewey discovered that psychologically distancing oneself from one's own beliefs and identity by temporarily assuming an external perspective summoned the energy that carried the entire experience (i.e., the having and the undergoing) forward to consummation.

Dewey clearly was less judgmental and more generous than Barnes in his appraisals of the great classical and contemporary artists. Art revealed the diverse ways that the energy of form and force of motion could be organized and aesthetically appreciated. The reader of *Art as Experience* can hardly find a harsh word about any artist from Dewey, who found something authentic and timeless in the works of almost every artist he discussed. The great masters were historians of the human mind and archeologists of the soul. Their paintings and other works of art excavated the latent energy compressed in the deep recesses of past experience, releasing it to assume newer and sometimes startling forms. "What is retained from the past is embedded within what is now perceived and so embedded that by its compression there," Dewey noted, "it forces the mind to stretch forward to what is coming. The more there is compressed from the continuous series of prior perceptions, the richer the present perception and the more intense the forward impulsion."[44]

THE PHENOMENOLOGY OF PERCEPTION

Dewey continued to search for evidence that would bridge the realms of scientific and artistic judgment and show that both domains of thought essentially involve the common problem of transforming energy into ideas. Dewey appears to have gotten some important insights about the underlying unity of art and science while pondering the perplexing ideas of the writings of Eugenio Rignano in 1926. An Italian theoretical biologist, Rignano advanced a bold theory regarding the biological and developmental origins of intellectual and "affective thought" that was highly suggestive about how human feelings support judgment. Rignano suggested how "affective" energies are released in thought processes that leave traces or residues in human psychobiological processes.[45]

But Dewey also found Rignano's arguments troublesome. Although Rignano may have captured the essence of the creative rhythms underlying biological growth and aesthetic expression, Dewey wasn't certain whether Rignano, who stressed the recurrent aspects of developmental processes, had really formulated a theory that was capable of explaining the origins of novel experiences. Both Meredith Smith and Robert Raup, Dewey's doctoral candidates (see the previous chapter), were persuaded that Rignano had succeeded. However, there was another whole realm of physics that Rignano's theories left untouched. Aesthetic perception entails judgments about the geometry of perception and movement of objects in space and time that involve complex relationships between matter and energy. The physicists Ernst Mach, Ludwig Boltzmann, and James Clerk Maxwell seemed better equipped than Rignano and other biologists to resolve the paradox of recurrence, since they possessed mathematical theories more capable of dealing with this phenomenon.

Dewey's aim in *Art as Experience* was to demonstrate that aesthetic appreciation involves more than just passively viewing works of art. Experiencing art requires active perceptual engagement to discover the specific techniques of composition and form artists employ that evoke an overall impression and feeling for a work. Dewey wanted to "show how conscious experience, as the perceived relation between 'doing' and 'undergoing,'" explains how "art as production and perception and appreciation as enjoyment sustain each other."[46] Dewey set an unusually rigorous standard for the aesthetic appreciation by requiring that the viewer undertake the recreation of the technical and perceptual processes through which a work is created. This act of recreation involved, for Dewey, not a literal reconstruction but "relations comparable to those which the original producer underwent."[47] Why Dewey thought that this act of recreation was essential to the exercise of aesthetic judgment can be better understood by returning to the roots of his naturalism and phenomenalism.

Dewey was familiar with the work of Ernst Mach, a nineteenth-century physicist and experimentalist, who argued that human perception was unique because our psychophysical makeup makes us keenly sensitive to gravity and the underlying geometrical properties of natural phenomena.[48] He contended that the bilateral symmetry of human anatomy makes us extremely sensitive to gravity, direction, distance, motion, and form. The human preference for straight lines, right angles, and median and symmetrical planes satisfies the psychobiological demands for uniformity of depth perception, economy of vision, and predictability of expectation.[49] Accordingly, we rarely have any difficulty distinguishing between up and down, above and below, front and back, right and left. Nor do we often fail to detect movement or confuse the direction in which something moves. We also readily distinguish between different shapes, sizes, locations, colors, and composition of things.

Mach's naturalistic analysis of sensations suggested to Dewey a way to repudiate the subjectivist argument that works of art possess ineffable qualities that can be enjoyed even though the reasons why they affect us in the way they do cannot be articulated. Dewey recognized, of course, that objects and scenes in nature rarely conform to rigid geometric shapes, but appear in a multiplicity of shapes and boundaries that curve, weave, and interpenetrate in ways that increase the range of expressiveness of the objects they frame. Nevertheless, Dewey wanted to underscore the fundamental Machian point that human perception is shaped by our expectations about how things should conform to gravitational forces and geometrical limits. He asserted:

The habitual properties of lines cannot be got rid of even in an experiment that endeavors to isolate the experience of lines from everything else. The properties of objects that lines define and of movements they relate are too deeply embedded. . . . Different lines and different relations of lines have become subconsciously charged with all the values that result from what they have done in our experience in our every contact with the world about us. The expressiveness of lines and space relations in paintings cannot be understood upon any other basis.[50]

While these human perceptual biases reflect the unique neuroanatomical and physiological characteristics of bipedal creatures with stereoscopic vision, Dewey did not think that these modes of seeing are invariable or changeless traits. They could be altered by experience.

Art essentially reflects the perceptual freedom humans experience as physically embodied creatures who are able to select what they see and how they feel it, rejecting what is irrelevant and compressing and intensifying what is significant. In doing so, humans are able to control the proportionality between the field of vision and the relative size, shape, weight, and motion of the bodies with which we interact within that field.[51] Our experience of gravity provides a basis of comparison with which to judge qualities of art that we admire, such as the feeling of weightlessness or timelessness that is expressed in great works of art.

THE NATURAL RHYTHMS OF AESTHETIC EXPRESSION

Dewey insisted that a theory of art could be formulated only if "based upon an understanding of the central role of energy within and without" the human organism.[52] An aesthetic experience sets in motion an "interaction of energies," Dewey indicated, that enables the accumulated potential energy of suspense and opposition involved in the creative process to be conserved in the form of a new unified perception. The attempt to conceptualize aesthetic perception in terms of the reciprocal play of energetic rhythms reflected Dewey's lifelong interest in finding a place for mind in nature and experience. This objective included his ongoing efforts to reconcile the increasingly divergent mechanistic and probabilistic perspectives that physicists adopted to explain natural phenomena. Once it is realized that aesthetics and science are grounded in natural human capacities, Dewey reasoned, it can be seen that the two fields are essentially alternative methods of studying or characterizing the same underlying phenomena. This should not be confused with epistemological realism, materialistic reductionism, or relativism. Dewey wanted to explain that the postures and perspectives we adopt allow us to represent, express, and experience similar phenomena differently because we continually find new facets that possess cognitive, emotional, and/or moral significance.

The recurring debate engaging physicists during the last two decades of the nineteenth century about whether force and energy are universally convertible and whether physical processes are reversible seemed to Dewey to have an important bearing on his endeavor to find a common ontological ground for science and art. Although a number of distinguished scientists, among them mathematician Henri Poincaré and physicists William Thompson and Max Planck, grappled with the problem of convertibility and the paradox of reversibility, the dialogue between physicists Ludwig Boltzmann and James Clerk Maxwell decisively contributed to the eventual consensus.[53]

For handling the uncertainty of molecular actions, Boltzmann developed a probabilistic theoretical approach that retained a commitment to mechanism and determinism. Boltzmann argued that any solution to the paradox of uncertainty must assume that the universe as a whole began in an initial state of disordered motion and then evolved into a more ordered or uniform state of motion. Dewey might have found Boltzmann's thesis attractive if it weren't for the implausible implication of his theory, that over the long run, the universe must periodically return to an initial state of energy distribution, thus reinstating the idea of recurrence.[54]

Maxwell disagreed with Boltzmann that logical consistency dictated that an explanation of the behavior of dynamic systems involving matter in motion must not violate the law of entropy. He ingeniously visualized how each configuration of energy and matter occupying a phase-space could function independently and yet be connected through a shared underlying motion or rhythm. This model helped Maxwell achieve fundamental breakthroughs in explaining how it was possible for a system as a whole to undergo transformation through the interaction of its parts *without* violating entropy and irreversibility.[55]

Maxwell succeeded in this endeavor by showing that a change in the configuration or relative position of molecules or particles in a system results in a change in their velocity or momentum, increasing the potential energy of the system as a whole, *without* altering the total available kinetic energy. Maxwell's calculations demonstrated that *order* persists no matter how *chaotic* a collection of molecules may appear. Moreover, Maxwell speculated that there is a virtually infinite number of configurations of matter and energy in the universe.[56] This was a remarkable achievement that confirmed the underlying constancy of gravitation, yet affirmed the variable configuration and velocity of matter and energy—discoveries that paved the way for relativity theory and quantum mechanics.

Although Dewey never weighed in explicitly regarding this debate among physicists about matter, energy, and entropy, it is evident that Dewey preferred Maxwell's account of these natural phenomena. Dewey believed that these same principles regarding matter in motion applied to human perception. Human perception involves a dynamic and continuous reconfiguration of how our bodies are situated in space and time, such that energy is constantly being redistributed to support new perspectives, while retaining in memory the feeling of what it was like to have experienced the world from these different vantage points.

Dewey believed that the principle of "ordered variation" that Maxwell had proposed to understand molecular phenomena was strikingly evident in Matisse's painting style and techniques. Matisse explicitly construed the act of painting as "a coordination of controlled rhythm."[57] He claimed to "work without theory" and to embrace the fundamental freedom and indeterminacy of aesthetic expression. Matisse best expressed this conviction when he declared, "I am conscious only of the forces I use, and I am driven by an idea that I really only grasp as it grows with the picture."[58] Matisse also remarked that "colors and lines are forces, and the secret of creation lies in the play and balance of those forces."[59] Dewey's encounter with Matisse brought him closer than ever before to actually experiencing the phenomena of perception and aesthetic creation through the eyes, ideas, and gestures of a working artist. Matisse's work vividly illustrated the unbreakable phenomenal bond between mind and experience that had been characterized so brilliantly but abstractly by Dewey and his nineteenth-century predecessors.

Moreover, Matisse and Maxwell furnished Dewey the evidence he sought to sustain the logical and phenomenological connections between art and science. Their influence is undeniably reflected in Dewey's conception of rhythm, which he defines as "the ordered variation of change."[60] He goes on to say:

> There is no rhythm of any kind . . . where variation of pulse and rest do not occur. . . . They serve to define variations in number, in extent, in velocity, and in intrinsic qualitative differences, as of hue, tone, etc. . . . Variations of intensity are relative to the subject matter directly experienced. . . . It is not a variation in a single feature but a modulation of the entire pervasive and unifying qualitative substratum.[61]

The process of aesthetic perception embodies the dialectical phases through which opposing energies are balanced and ordered, Dewey asserted, "involving resistance, accumulation, compression, conservation, expansion, release and transformation." The effort put into comprehending and appreciating a work of art acquires momentum through resistance, according to Dewey, by visualizing how opposing energies are accumulated and compressed until they find release in the sensation of occupying a new space, whose volume and contours evoke an entirely different sense of time and motion than before.[62]

Energy is both conserved and transformed, Dewey explained, "at the moment of reversal, an interval, a pause, a rest, by which the interaction of opposed energies is defined and rendered perceptible. The pause is a balance of antagonistic forces."[63] During this phase of inhibition, when judgment is withheld, the mind gathers up the resources of memory and selects those images, observations, and experiences that best capture the emotional tone evoked by perception. Through this recursive process of emotional clarification, a "cumulative conservation" of energy is released that propels us forward to consummation while preserving the potential energy of the experience just had for responding to future possible contingencies.[64]

RESOLVING THE PARADOX OF RECURRENCE

Dewey rejected the possibility that the evident recursive nature of aesthetic perception involves a *literal* return to the physical or emotional point of origin. The curving lines and overlapping colors of post-impressionist paintings did not seem to Dewey to force perception into any one dominant direction. Yet Freud contended that art provoked primitive reactions that affirmed the compulsive and repetitive nature of human psychological experience. Rignano advanced a powerful alternative to Freud's metapsychological theory of human development that singled out the positive, constructive function performed by "affective tendencies." Nevertheless, Rignano contended that human growth and development are punctuated by *phases* of physiological equilibrium that necessarily involve a periodic return to previous states of physical existence.

This presented a dilemma for Dewey. While recurrence was an essential element of aesthetic rhythm, Dewey denied that this involved literal repetition and the unwarranted implication that the potential energy of past experience was not conserved to free behavior from the bonds of habit. Dewey acknowledged in correspondence with Chisholm during this time that he was uncertain about how best to characterize the problem of recurrence and seemed on the verge of conceding that Rignano's position was correct.[65]

To resolve this dilemma, Dewey turned once again to Maxwell for a solution. In his debate with Maxwell, Boltzmann stated that random molecular action conforms to mechanical laws involving increased entropy. Boltzmann assumed that atomic particles exhibit a stationary pattern of behavior that also conforms to mechanical laws. Boltzmann turned out to be mistaken. Neils Bohr showed that electrons circle the nucleus in an elliptical orbit that is *not* stationary and thus not reducible to mechanics. Maxwell anticipated this discovery by brilliantly showing that all that need be demonstrated is that molecules interact at predictable distances and that interacting molecules pass through every phase-space, thus conserving energy without increasing entropy. For even if ensembles of molecules possess identical energies, Maxwell reasoned, their conditions and consequences of interaction (which are governed by their velocity) are never repeated because they can *interact* in an infinite number of ways. With this achievement, Maxwell believed he had successfully divorced system dynamics from the problem of determinism.

Dewey acknowledged in *Art as Experience* that there is no rhythm without recurrence. He did so in language that closely parallels Maxwell's debate with Boltzmann. Dewey suggested that because perceptual processes are dynamic, not redundant, it won't work to try to resolve the problem of entropy by adopting a mechanistic perspective. Dewey asserted:

> But the reflective analysis of physical science is substituted for the experience of art when recurrence is interpreted as literal repetition, whether of material or ex-

act interval. Mechanical recurrence is that of material units. Esthetic recurrence is that of *relationships* that sum up and carry forward. . . . Recurring relationships serve to define and delimit parts, giving them individuality of their own. . . . Esthetic recurrence in short is vital, physiological, functional. Relationships rather than elements recur, and they recur in differing contexts and with different consequences so that each recurrence is novel as well as a reminder. In satisfying an aroused expectancy, it also institutes a new longing, incites a fresh curiosity, establishes a changed suspense.[66]

When viewed in this way, aesthetic rhythms can be understood as dynamic, relational processes involving the transformation of energy that bring about new experiences. Dewey surmised (in a tacit reference to Maxwellian physics) that "[e]ven the equations of mathematicians are evidence that variation is desired in the midst of maximum repetition, since they express equivalences not exact identities."[67] Dewey offered as evidence for the proof of this assertion an anecdote about Maxwell, who Dewey says, "once introduced a symbol in order to make a physical equation symmetrical, and that it was only later that experimental results gave the symbol its meaning."[68]

CERTAINTY IN AN INDETERMINATE WORLD

Dewey could not have had better timing in accepting the invitation to present the Gifford Lectures in Natural Theology at the University of Edinburgh in Scotland in 1929. The sponsors interpreted the topic of natural theology broadly to include any discussion of the consequences of knowledge and experience for the human spirit. Dewey, like his predecessor William James, who gave the Gifford Lectures thirty years earlier, was quite capable of addressing at least the secular dimensions of this topic with great erudition. The unflappable Dewey was not distracted by an amusing incident when his lecture notes were suddenly blown off the podium by a large fan and scattered all over the stage. After his sponsors retrieved them and handed them to Dewey, they anxiously advised him that they weren't sure the pages were in the correct order, as they were not numbered. Dewey is reported to have said, "Oh that won't make any difference."[69]

The world of science with which James was familiar had undergone a stunning series of theoretical advances culminating in Einstein's theory of relativity and quantum physics. These developments created tremendous uncertainty about nature and the foundations of human experience. This was exactly the kind of environment in which Dewey had thrived throughout his career. His ongoing study of the energetics of perception and phenomenal consciousness, and his daughter Jane's unusual participation in the quantum controversies in Copenhagen, would prove to be extraordinarily useful.

Dewey's argument in *Quest for Certainty* could be stated most concisely in the following way. The most significant achievements in the history of physics have had more to do with advances in experimental methods, measurement, and the changing consciousness and attitudes of the minds of the men and women involved than with the nature of the discoveries they brought about. The ancient Greek and medieval beliefs in a world infused with purpose and finality that Dewey described in his lectures gave way gradually to a Galilean and Newtonian world of force and motion, largely because of the power and persuasiveness of experimentalism.

However, the belief in the immutability of the natural phenomena of space, time, mass, and motion did not disappear but re-emerged in Newtonian theory. Newton's eventual embrace of a deductive, mathematical, and mechanistic conception of the universe betrayed his willingness to adopt a static conception of natural phenomena in which mathematical formalization took precedence over experience. Only near the turn of the twentieth century, Dewey argued, were physicists able to perceive the truly *relational* basis of the natural phenomena, and to do away with the supposition that mass, matter, force, motion, gravity, or other constituents of nature could be reduced to some more elemental property of the universe.

Bohr, Heisenberg, and their colleagues in Copenhagen called into question whether any reliable methods could ever be devised to measure quantum events that defied accurate observation and measurement. It is at this point in the history of science that things got really interesting for Dewey, because he bore witness to the events he was documenting in his Gifford Lectures. Although not a direct participant in these debates, Dewey's daughter Jane's personal involvement in the events that led to the development of quantum theory provides a window through which Dewey glimpsed the illimitability of consciousness and mind in scientific inquiry.

WITNESS AT COPENHAGEN

After graduating from Barnard College in 1922 and earning a Ph.D. in chemistry from MIT in 1925, Jane was a recipient of an International Fellow award from Columbia University that supported her research from 1926 through 1927 at the Institute for Theoretical Physics in Copenhagen, directed by Niels Bohr. This was a prestigious assignment that put Jane in the center of the controversy swirling around the structure and behavior of the atom.

Jane kept her father apprised of her research and shared with him in correspondence her impressions of Bohr and his colleagues. She had little personal contact with Bohr during the initial months of her stay. He was intensely preoccupied with resolving the paradoxical nature of matter and energy that perplexed him and his colleagues. She did report that she got a lot out of the few conversations they had "in the way of ideas and inspiration."[70] As she settled into her experimental work, she reported having "good theoretical discussions with staff about the internal workings of atoms."[71] She described the laboratory as cramped with instruments and portrayed her colleagues "as a strange bunch of birds of all nationalities."[72] By the end of her fellowship, Bohr had

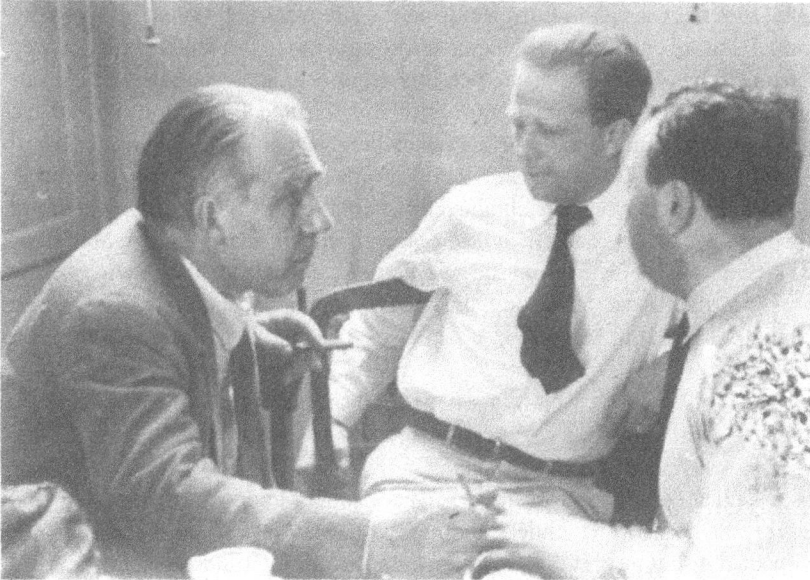

13. Niels Bohr talking with Werner Heisenberg and Wolfgang Pauli, 1936.
Courtesy of the Niels Bohr Archive, Copenhagen.

become more "chatty" and personable, giving her a sense of increased confidence, which she exuded to her father, saying, "I don't know how much I have learned but I have had a good time. I have almost persuaded myself that I am a good scientist, or am going to be some day. Bohr seems to think I know a lot, so maybe I do."[73]

In Ernest Nagel's opinion, Dewey possessed only a shallow knowledge of physics and was not as persuasive in writing about developments in this field as in psychology or biology. Nagel recalled that Dewey got help from his daughter Jane to compensate for this weakness while writing *Quest for Certainty*, observing in a 1966 interview that:

> Dewey's physics and even mathematics was at best second-hand, and he relied very heavily for his information on what are essentially popularizations. He based important parts of his argument in the *Quest for Certainty* upon expositions of modern physics presented in a popular book by the late Sir Arthur Eddington, though he apparently also got some help from his daughter Jane who was a physicist. I confess I never felt entirely at ease when Dewey talked about physical theory (even though his comments were often full of insight), for he didn't exhibit a mastery over this material that comes only from a first-hand knowledge of the subject.[74]

Nagel apparently was unaware that Jane had worked with Niels Bohr and that she was actually in a strategic position to feed Dewey firsthand information about breaking developments in quantum mechanics. Dewey was a frequent summer traveler to Europe during the late 1920s and visited his daughter at the Institute on at least one occasion in August 1926.[75] It is likely that Dewey personally met Bohr on this and possibly other occasions. Jane showed considerable knowledge of foundation politics and solicited Bohr's and her father's help in successfully obtaining a Rockefeller National Fellows Grant (1927–1929) to continue her studies in America two years following her fellowship in Copenhagen. After that she obtained a research fellowship at the University of Rochester (1929–1931) and then held academic appointments at Bryn Mawr and MIT until 1949. For most of the rest of her career, from 1949 to 1970, Jane worked at the Research Lab on Ballistics and Atomic Weapons at the Aberdeen Proving Grounds in Maryland.[76]

RESOLVING THE SCIENTIFIC DEBATE
BETWEEN BOHR AND HEISENBERG

As a dedicated adherent of *Naturphilosophie*, Dewey was not surprised that significant headway in understanding the natural world had been achieved without the slightest bit of scientific consensus on the fundamental properties of force and matter. From his perspective such epistemologically mistaken analyses of immutable material essences had in the past terminated inquiry rather than advancing it. Nevertheless, for most physicists, including Einstein, resolving the question of how electrons bind to and transfer from the nucleus of one atom to another to form the elements in the periodic table was considered crucial to a more complete understanding of the relation between energy and matter. Bohr was determined to get to the bottom of matter experimentally without adopting epistemological assumptions that would prejudge the phenomenon under inquiry. Bohr shared Dewey's predisposition to favor experience over arbitrary conceptualizations, and he strongly desired to preserve the essentially dialectical relationship between thought and observation.[77]

Bohr's compelling quest in Copenhagen lured the brightest physicists of the twentieth century to undertake a collaboration to penetrate the mysteries of the atom. This task proved much more difficult and personally stressful than any of the participants had ever imagined. Arguments were frequent, tempers flared, and constructive discussion ended, on more than one occasion, in bitter disengagement and deafening silence. Bohr's breakthrough in establishing a new theoretical basis for understanding the periodic table set the stage for the subsequent debate about the phenomenon of indeterminacy. Before Bohr's discoveries, chemists believed that the periodic series could be explained solely by the number of electrons occupying stationary positions around the atom. Bohr challenged this view, arguing instead that electrons appeared to circulate around the nucleus of atoms in an *elliptical* orbit. Each successive element would add an additional electron through the *interpenetration* of electron orbits, yielding a new configuration and charge.[78] Bohr was awarded the Nobel Prize for this important discovery of the interactive and unstable nature of particle behavior.

Noteworthy in this regard was Dewey's speculation that consciousness might be explained in similar terms. He envisioned consciousness instigating a transformational process in which tension (i.e., rhythm) or potential energy acquires force through perception, volition, and intentionality. Dewey shared his thoughts in a letter to Chisholm by suggesting the following scenario:

> In all matter there is interpenetration, and hence periodic time. Taking lead as the most inert, say a ball attracting another ball of lead, it extends in the gravitational and electrical field into the other thing, so there is interpenetration, or a measurable periodic time. Presumably, as you go through the elements, there is increase of interpenetration and a more complex time. In living matter this is more marked, and in consciousness there is greater interpenetration and hence tension; varying from the relaxed states to that of intense perception and volition; extension becomes increasingly intension.[79]

Dewey's characterization of the physics of consciousness could not have provided a more apt description of the strikingly parallel processes in which Bohr and his colleagues attempted to penetrate the mysteries of matter by plunging into the furthest recesses of their own minds. Bohr and his distinguished colleagues soon realized that it was one thing to predict paradoxical phenomena and quite another to explain them. The task of resolving the paradox of uncertainty would stretch their minds and emotions to the limits of consciousness.

Bohr's elation was soon replaced by a more somber mood when Heisenberg contended that attempts to experimentally measure quantum events with perfect precision are doomed to failure because the very act of intervention changes either the position or momentum of the particles under examination. The debate about how to control the paradoxical behavior of electrons under observation stemmed, in part, from two different perspectives about how science should be conducted. Bohr, inspired by Faraday's methods of inquiry, strongly favored taking an experimental approach, while Heisenberg, Bohr's primary theoretical antagonist, just as strongly insisted on the elegance and rigor of a mathematical approach. Bohr insisted that a physical interpretation relying on experimental evidence should be pursued as long as the meaning of key terms, such as "position" and "momentum," are set by the operations through which these qualities are measured.[80]

Ultimately Heisenberg agreed with Bohr that spectroscopic experiments should be conducted. These experiments would determine if the Stark effect of the dispersion of light intensities for helium could be better predicted by the correspondence principle or by an equation developed by Heisenberg and his associates to predict the displacement and intensities of spectra emitted by helium. This is where Jane Dewey enters the picture. She was one of several other foundation fellows and Bohr colleagues who undertook several experiments to adjudicate between these competing theories. Jane's first experiment devised to test Bohr's correspondence principle indicated a high level of agreement between the predicted and measured values of the amplitudes and intensities of the helium spectra.[81] However, when she tested Heisenberg's equations, they gave only approximate values for intensity, providing qualitative but not quantitative agreement between theory and experiment.[82] This outcome no doubt was disappointing for Dewey since it failed to establish the equivalence of qualitative and quantitative values that Hegel had led Dewey to expect to be confirmed when human judgment itself was the object of measurement.

Heisenberg's famous explanation for this and other failures to find experimental proof of this mathematical theory was "that nature allowed only experimental situations to occur which could be described within the framework of the formalism of quantum mechanics."[83] In other words, his theory could very well be correct even though no test ever could be devised that did not alter the phenomena as a result of experimental intervention. Heisenberg stubbornly clung to his mathematical models, while Bohr just as defiantly insisted that paradoxes in nature would eventually be explained by employing experimental methods.

Bohr took a more conciliatory tone when he realized that the real issue between Heisenberg and himself was not the elusive ontology of matter or the explanation of its paradoxes, but the need to render the objects of shared consciousness intelligible and communicable. That competing theories involve some illimitable degree of mutual restrictiveness, according to Bohr, should not defeat inquiry but actually advance it, especially when dealing with phenomena in which the viewing subject and phenomenal object are essentially entangled. "The working of our consciousness" in the quantum world, Bohr observed, "implies a demand of objectivity of its content, and yet the thought of the subject, or our own self, is part of the content of our consciousness."[84] Bohr's principle of *complementarity* proposed that seemingly incompatible partial theoretical descriptions of phenomena can be reconciled and integrated to form more complete mathematical descriptions as long as these theories are derived from shared experimental observations. Bohr insisted that only through shared experience do we negotiate the uncertainty involved in characterizing phenomena in which the observers themselves are problematically implicated.

COMPLEMENTARY WAYS OF KNOWING

When he wrote *Quest for Certainty*, these developments in theoretical physics were very much on Dewey's mind. Nowhere is this more evident than in the uncanny similarity of how Dewey approached the problem of mutual restrictiveness sketched by Bohr. Dewey chose the awkward term "compossibility" to describe situations that Bohr characterized as involving "complementarity." This wasn't the same thing as consistency or uniformity, Dewey cautioned, but rather that "all developments are welcome as long as they do not conflict with one another."[85] Dewey called this principle a "canon of liberation rather than restriction." He added, "It may be compared with natural selection, which is a principle of elimination but not one controlling positive developments."[86]

Similarly, Dewey considered the principle of indeterminacy to be "the final step in the dislodgment of the old spectator theory of knowledge," and acknowledged that we now have to accept the fact that there are different ways of knowing.[87] Perhaps the most important consequence of this revolution in knowing, Dewey believed, was to change our conception of natural laws. The deductive model that individual cases can be known (i.e., validated or subsumed by) only through universal laws was now repealed. Instead, Dewey declared, "[t]he individually observed case becomes the measure of knowledge."[88] Quantum mechanics had demonstrated through the uncertainty principle that generalizations about the material world are dependent on subatomic particles whose relationships are unstable and of limited predictability. Dewey welcomed the prospect of dropping misleading deterministic metaphors used to characterize physical events. Instead, he embraced a language of probability and transformation that retained the possibility that phenomena undergoing change can still be intersubjectively authenticated and are generalizable to other similar situations.

Dewey's bold and tantalizing conception of an experientially based transformational conception of science in *Quest for Certainty,* although lacking the prosaic grace of *Art as Experience,* seemed incredibly naive to some of his contemporaries. For them, Dewey's *Quest for Certainty* was a step backward toward a subjectivist conception of knowledge discarded in the Middle Ages. While critics praised Dewey for wanting science to live up to its unfulfilled promise of providing more individually meaningful and useful information, they thought it neither necessary nor advisable that scientists suspend their commitment to certainty and truth.[89] Dewey countered that by disposing of the outmoded demand for secure foundations science actually would be strengthened rather than undermined. Science was at its best, Dewey insisted, when it approximated aesthetic standards of judgment whereby creativity is synonymous with discovery. Dewey portrayed the artistry of science best when he declared that "[a] well conducted scientific inquiry, discovers as it tests, and proves as it explores; it does so in virtue of a method which combines both functions."[90] Dewey conceived of inquiry as an ordered process that sums up preceding experiences in the form of articulable knowledge and then predicts the likelihood of gaining new experiences by applying that knowledge.

Dewey did not believe, however, that science alone could sustain the level of consciousness necessary to promote individual growth, freedom, and community development. Adopting a scientific attitude of experimentalism was an important first step toward disencumbering the mind of preconceptions that block the realization of new modes of perception and action. When science pushes to the limits of knowledge, the boundary is crossed between discovery and creation, freeing us from the limitations of familiar forms to see things differently. Dewey knew very well from his previous attempts that the only way he was going to establish the credibility of his conception of science was to put it into practice. But a secure foundation of philanthropic support and scientific interest had to be laid before the scaffolding for a long-term experimental study could be erected. Consequently, Dewey helped draft a blueprint for democratic reconstruction that involved changing the relationship between state power, science, and community governance processes.

EIGHT

Communities of Intelligence and the Politics of Spirit

Dewey's ambitious quest to scientifically test his ideas about human judgment and inquiry in the 1930s would not have been feasible without the extensive network of scientists that Dewey and his close associates cultivated throughout the first two decades of the twentieth century. Dewey admired the intellect and valued the opinions of his scientific colleagues because they shared Dewey's naturalism and the quest to understand the role of mind in inquiry. Dewey and his colleagues also shared a common morally inspired vision that the social ills afflicting society involving malnutrition, disease, ignorance, and unemployment could be addressed scientifically and mitigated through policies formulated by private and public institutions dedicated to the common good.

The scientists with whom Dewey was acquainted viewed the relationship between their research and society in organic terms. For example, Herrick and Child found perhaps too literal an analogy between cortical control, social stability, and governance processes. They found parallels between the structure and function of the brain and the organization of society and governmental institutions. The processes through which a balance is struck between mental and physical systems supporting human biological development were equivalent to those that reconciled conflict in the social and political sphere. Cortical inhibition was an essential precondition to self-control and a primary requisite to the tolerance, restraint, and compromise needed to reconcile and harmonize the diverse interests of social groups.[1]

This belief that biological and social mechanisms of control should be conceived as complementary modes for the discipline of human desire has its origins in nineteenth-century medicine and psychology. German neurophysiologists sought ways to engineer social systems so that they would replicate the natural mechanisms of neural inhibition that afforded a balance between individual need and social responsibility. Their schemes ultimately betrayed a Hegelian and Prussian proclivity for state supremacy and social regimentation.[2]

Herrick and Child adopted a more democratic perspective. For example, Child reasoned that the national institutions of American governance furnished an executive control equivalent to that provided by the cerebral cortex. The autonomy of widely distributed branches of government (i.e., national and state executive, legislative, and judicial branches) is protected and balanced, while linked together in a federal constitutional system—"a sort of physiological parliament" of the mind.[3]

Early in his career Dewey subscribed to some aspects of the governance analogy proposed by Herrick and Child. The Laboratory School was established to demonstrate the soundness of implementing educational policies that attempted to harmonize individual mental and social development. Nevertheless, Dewey grew increasingly doubtful about the validity of assuming that brain processes involve inalterable executive structures or that the mind embodies universal and unchanging modes of moral reasoning. Frederick Tilney adopted a more realistic paleoanthropological perspective that Dewey found congenial. He was less sanguine than his colleagues about whether human biological functions favored human progress. Increased human intelligence and compassion were not foreordained by the ascendancy of cortical structures. The brain and mind were still evolving and the nascent human capacity for social cooperation would grow stronger only if nurtured by science and social policy.[4]

These visionary men of science were following in the footsteps of Huxley, Faraday, and Maxwell by adopting the attitude that science involved a high public calling. The conduct of basic scientific research was justified only if the fruits of discovery were shared with the larger society. As Huxley demonstrated with such flair and dedication, the potential intellectual implications, practical applications, benefits, and risks of every advance in scientific understanding must be publicly aired and debated. Only when science is subjected to public discussion and debate is it worthy of being deemed in the common good.

Dewey had the good fortune and remarkable timing of meeting people who shared his vision of science in public life and who became senior officers of the Rockefeller and other foundations that were created shortly after the turn of the twentieth century. George Vincent, a sociologist and Dewey colleague at the University of Chicago, was president of the Rockefeller Foundation from 1917 through 1929. Beardsley Ruml, a University of Chicago–trained psychologist and acquaintance of Evelyn Dewey, headed the Laura Spelman Rockefeller Memorial from 1922 to 1929. Lawrence K. Frank, one of Dewey's own brightest students, helped Ruml organize and fund an international network of child study institutes that included Columbia University and Teachers College.

Like a Maxwellian "demon" invisibly influencing molecular interactions, Dewey occupied the interstices of private and public power where he could broker knowledge and influence the direction and amount of intellectual energy expended on scientific projects fundamentally important to American policies for social development. This was an extraordinary achievement for a scholar who elected to retire from teaching at Columbia University in 1930. But Frank and McGraw, two of Dewey's best students, made it possible for him to pursue a scientific investigation of ideas that had important implications for education and human development. Frank brilliantly assimilated and synthesized Dewey's conceptions of science and community, employing them as blueprints with which to erect the scaffolding of an intricately crafted child study network. McGraw seized Dewey's conception of growth and theory of mind and converted them into an experimental program, described in chapters 9 and 10, yielding extraordinary insights about infant development. Together Dewey, Frank, and McGraw challenged the fundamentally deterministic premises of the debate about nature versus nurture and suggested a new direction and strategy for child development policies in America.

My contention in this chapter is that a close examination of how Dewey conceived the parallel scientific study of human development and the construction of communities grounded in intelligent action enables a better understanding of those practices and values Dewey believed to be essential to a viable democracy. This analysis sheds light on why Dewey distanced himself from the Hegelian Absolute by placing greater weight on the community to sustain a sense of public spirit. Dewey was dissatisfied with Hegel's political logic, sensing a flaw in Hegel's reasoning that would account for the paradox of why a perspective based on a radical theory of contingency could lead to a political theory that saw the state as the embodiment of Spirit and truth. Dewey sought to conceive the terms of the dialectic differently to capture the truly transformational potential of communities of intelligence in a democratic polity. Dewey grounded Hegel's method in a science of human psychology and politics of moral contextualism that did not invoke transcendent principles, reduce life to a crude materialism, nor assume that human development fulfilled some immanent purpose or end.

Focusing on how Dewey and his protégé Lawrence Frank conceived the relationship between individual development and community participation and understanding why their conceptions ultimately diverged promises to illuminate the apparent lacuna between Dewey's early ideas about human psychology and his later social and political theories. This uncertainty about the connection between Dewey's theory of mind and his theory about politics may explain why Dewey disappoints many contemporary political theorists. He does not seem to be interested in questions of legitimacy and the issues of sovereignty, rights, and consent that preoccupy those concerned with the juridical basis of authority in modernity.[5] Dewey was not indifferent to the problems of individual rights and regime support. He simply believed that the long-term survival of a democracy required that citizens must acquire the capacity to exercise better political judgment before electoral and other mechanisms can be perfected for enabling participation and support.

REFORMULATING THE POLITICS OF
HEGELIAN ABSOLUTISM

Dewey completed his manuscript on "Hegel's Philosophy of Spirit" in the 1890s at a time when he became increasingly disenchanted with the disparity between Hegel's insights about mind and consciousness and his views about freedom and authority in modernity. Dewey recounted why he believed that Hegel failed to explain why the unifying feelings of Christian love, sacrifice, and redemption had lost their hold on an increasingly secularized society. Hegel rejected Kant's solution to the dilemma of faith in the Enlightenment. Kant mistakenly replaced the infinite being of Spirit with the eternal truth of *a priori* principles, relegating human knowledge to the realm of finite experience. Hegel believed that this subordination of the individual to universal standards of reason and freedom was simply one stage in human consciousness. The presumption of universality of reason and freedom at one stage is contradicted by the separation or alienation of the individual from nature and experience at another. Dewey surmised that this created a tension between knowledge and authority—a rift that he believed could be reconciled only by showing how citizens overcome this contradiction to reclaim their spirit by putting judgment to work in their own communities.

In his critical reading of Hegel's *Phenomenology of Spirit*, Dewey registered his dissatisfaction with Hegel's justification of state authority, calling it "the most artificial and least satisfactory portion of his political philosophy."[6] Dewey criticized Hegel for suggesting that the constitutionalization of the German monarchy represented Spirit in its highest form, when in fact Spirit lies in the people themselves. A constitution does not command immediate respect and compliance, but gets its justification, Dewey says, as a "nation becomes aware of the inner rationality of its own existence."[7]

To be certain, Hegel did see community as a necessary stage in the development of citizens' consciousness of their rights and duties in a juridical order, but this did not represent the expression of Absolute Spirit.[8] Hegel believed that collective actions undertaken by communities to advance their common interests signified that they shared a universal conception of freedom that only the state could secure. In contrast, Dewey argued in 1927 in the *Public and Its Problems* that "the local is the ultimate universal, and as near an absolute as exists."[9] Dewey considered communities that were capable of forming a public to be a universal expression of spirit in politics, because this achievement reflects a conscious agreement to take collective responsibility for the consequences of individual behavior.

Dewey was never completely at ease with the forces of secularization that ushered in utilitarian, Freudian, and other psychologies of individual identity. These secular psychologies denied that a sense of community spirit was essential to public life. Dewey feared that the eighteenth- and nineteenth-century political theories predicated on utility and individualism Hegel condemned left a far more devastating legacy for public life than Hegel had imagined. Dewey believed that laissez-faire liberalism had three important consequences for private and public life. First, it converted the conditions of Christian redemption into a Puritan formula for personal security for those who worked hard, saved, and sacrificed. Second, psychology's privatization of soul relegated judgment to the domain of personal preference, enabling a distinction to be drawn between personal conduct, for which one could be held morally accountable, and the social consequences of collective behavior, which fell outside the realm of individual intention and responsibility.

Finally, Dewey believed that nineteenth-century liberal theorists arbitrarily reversed the sequence through which public life is likely to have emerged. They equated political development with the progressive emancipation of citizens from state interference or regulation. This was tantamount to saying that citizens seek disengagement from any community ties that oblige them to take responsibility for consequences beyond their personal control. How Dewey chose to overcome the political legacies of nineteenth-century liberalism is the subject of this chapter.

Dewey's social and political theory found concrete expression in his attempt in *The Public and Its Problems* and other essays to spell out how science could be enlisted in the service of democracy and the public interest. Dewey considered the capacity of individuals and societies to organize and form associations to be a generic trait of human experience. The bonds forged between families through blood and kinship are naturally extended to include social relationships involving "conjoint activity."[10] These latter forms of interaction produce collective consequences that implicate a much larger public and therefore require more elaborate and remote mechanisms of communication and governance processes than those available to families or communities. Dewey believed that processes of communication and participation in modern democratic states had become seriously compromised and that this threatened the capacity of citizens to make informed judgments and decisions concerning policies affecting the health, education, and welfare of their families and children.

Dewey advanced a position closely akin to that of founding father James Madison that too much emphasis was placed on national electoral processes of majority rule, detracting from the important role of minorities and communities in articulating and defining the problems that merit national attention. Dewey asserted that "all valuable as well as new ideas begin with minorities, perhaps a minority of one. The important consideration is that opportunity be given that idea to spread and to become the possession of the multitude."[11]

An urgent problem facing Western states was how to effectively engage the public in the inquiry about and the dissemination and debate of scientific information regarding child development. Dewey anticipated in his Laboratory School, before the turn of the twentieth century, the organizational implications and social challenges that this objective would pose in engaging parents, children, educators, scientists, and elected officials in a common process of understanding the relationships between development and learning and citizenship and democratic politics. Dewey correctly surmised that this would involve a considerable amount of collaboration, coordination, and reconciliation between individuals and groups with different aims and expectations. He envisioned a parallel process of reconstruction to achieve these aims that involved "a continuous re-distribution of social integrations on the one hand and of capacities and energies of individuals on the other."[12]

Significantly, Dewey's conception of democratic states as communities of intelligence began to take shape with Lucy and Wesley Mitchell's Bureau of Educational Experiments (see chapter 4). This conception was considerably enlarged through Lawrence Frank's initiatives to address issues of public consequence. The university-based child study network funded by the Rockefeller Foundation included an alliance between parent groups and researchers to widely disseminate knowledge about child development, and to attempt to arouse public support for more innovative approaches to learning and child rearing.[13] Dewey hoped that increasing communication between scientists would make it more likely that local communities would communicate more effectively with one another about competing interests and make adjustments commensurate with needs. Dewey's social and political theories and the controversies they engendered can be best understood by tracing how they influenced the development of the child study network that emerged in the 1920s.

ROCKEFELLER PHILANTHROPY AND SOCIAL SCIENCE

The Rockefeller Trust was formed to be chartered by the United States Congress. But attempts to pass legislation in 1910, 1911, and 1912 were rebuffed by a Congress wary of the wealth and power of the Rockefeller family. The foundation's mandate to "cure evils at their source" seemed a draconian form of intervention for a federal government that lacked experience in such an endeavor.[14] In actuality, the Rockefeller Foundation sponsored a forward-looking ambitious agenda which supported sanitation and disease-prevention projects around the world. Rockefeller grants helped build hospitals, clinics, and public health schools throughout Latin America and Eastern Europe. These projects were intended to reduce infant mortality and increase life expectancy. The foundation eventually got involved in social and behavioral research when the Laura Spelman Rockefeller Memorial (LSRM) was established in 1918 and given $74 million to respond to the special needs of women and children.

Beardsley Ruml, a Dartmouth graduate who earned a Ph.D. in psychology from the University of Chicago in 1917, knew his way around foundations, having been an assistant of James Angell, a psychologist who was president of the Carnegie Foundation. When Angell left Carnegie to assume the presidency of Yale University, he recommended that Ruml head the LSRM. The twenty-seven-year-old Ruml enjoyed a reputation, according to Roosevelt appointee

Louis Brownlow, as having "one of the most complex and comprehensive minds in modern times."[15] Ruml adopted a multiyear plan that awarded block grants to academic institutions to sustain longitudinal studies of issues involving social welfare and child care. Ruml prevented Rockefeller corporate executives from interfering in the research and insisted on neutrality about any findings.

Ruml attracted youthful but intelligent assistants that included Lawrence Frank, a business manager of the New School for Social Research and Wesley Mitchell's collaborator in the analysis of American business cycles. Frank was a member of the working council (executive board) of the Bureau of Educational Experiments, whose organizational innovations strongly influenced the strategy that he adopted at the LSRM.[16] Frank could not have been better prepared to carry out this challenging assignment. Frank was a Dewey disciple who glimpsed in Dewey's pragmatism how to move the social sciences away from a preoccupation with the past.[17] Frank contended that the social sciences remained in the grip of philosophical preconceptions about human freedom and autonomy that overshadowed important questions about the developmental sequences and social processes that affected human intelligence. He believed that if social scientists embraced experimentalism, they would truly gain control over events that seemed least susceptible to human intervention and control.[18]

Ruml directed Frank to survey and evaluate the research capabilities of graduate schools in the social sciences at universities that seemed promising recipients of Rockefeller funds. Frank did so and found them deplorable. This deficiency could be overcome, in Frank's estimation, by creating doctoral and post-doctoral fellowships for candidates who possessed quantitative and experimental skills. Ruml realized that intellectual independence and professional interdependence were the lifeblood of scientific inquiry, and consequently he wanted Frank to form a loose network of institutes whose faculty would undertake separate studies with different methods, but who would have opportunities to review and comment on each other's work at conferences and through refereed journals. Ruml also wanted Frank to develop mechanisms for disseminating the results of the child development research to policy makers and parents who could use that information to promote change in public education.

CONSTRUCTING A POLITICAL NETWORK

Frank's extraordinary leadership in child development research lay in his ability to catalyze the seemingly unrelated ideas of different researchers, precipitating them into innovative methodological solutions that led to fundamental scientific discoveries. As beneficiaries of Frank's leadership attested, he expanded their consciousness by encouraging them to think about problems from an interdisciplinary perspective. In 1965 Frank was honored on his seventy-fifth birthday by his colleagues, seventy-one of whom wrote personal letters paying tribute to his intellect and enviable ability to persuade them to pursue an interdisciplinary exchange of methods and ideas. While their interesting recollections and observations are too numerous to cite here, Margaret Mead's succinct statement is representative of the views of her other colleagues.

> More than any other human being, Larry Frank has created the hope, the possibility, the style of genuine interdisciplinary work, grounded in biology, embracing all the human sciences, using analogies and clues from every field, and receptive to the arts and to philosophy. The monument which he has built is, as he would have it, only the barest foundation of what some day—if he has his way—it may become.[19]

Frank's organizational genius and Dewey connections served him well, enabling him to cleverly maneuver fledgling local voluntary child study associations into highly visible national organizations, lobbying for new state policies for childhood and family education. This is well-illustrated by Frank's attempts to persuade the New York–based Federation of Child Study, begun in 1888, to enlarge its efforts to promote parent education and to undertake the national dissemination of information about child development generated by the Rockefeller-funded child study institutes. Dewey was one of a group of several prominent professors from Columbia University and Teachers College that also included Edward Thorndike, Lois Meek, and Helen Woolley. This group continued to serve on the advisory board after the Federation adopted a new name, the Child Study Association of America, that reflected its national constituency. The Child Study Association, among other groups, spearheaded the organization of the first White House Conference on Children in 1930 that made children's mental health a national priority and brought into national prominence the research of child development researchers.[20]

Frank also succeeded in persuading social scientists to form professional societies that promoted interdisciplinary research. In 1920 the National Research Council's (NRC) division on anthropology and psychology created a new committee on child welfare. Robert Woodworth persuaded his NRC colleagues to adopt the model of child development and education that the Bureau of Educational Experiments had implemented under Lucy Sprague Mitchell's leadership.[21] The LSRM then funded a fellowship and conference program administered by the NRC. This program was officially constituted in 1933 as the Society for Research in Child Development (SRCD). Frank also persuaded the Rockefeller Foundation to subsidize *Parent* magazine, which gave researchers an opportunity to reach a popular audience.[22] The SRCD continues to flourish today under leaders and members who occupy strategic positions in government agencies and commissions.

In 1930 Dewey was appointed a founding member of the board of trustees of the Josiah Macy, Jr. Foundation—a fact that has inexplicably eluded researchers until now. This was the first foundation to support psychobiological studies of growth and development, and continues today to support pediatric

14. Lawrence K. Frank celebrating his
75th birthday, 1965.
Courtesy of Kevin Frank.

programs and medical education in developing countries. Dewey probably persuaded the foundation's first president, Ludwig Kast, a cardiologist and professor of medicine at Columbia University, to hire Frank, who served as vice
president from 1936 to 1941. His foundation ties provided Dewey an unusual
opportunity to influence the scope of McGraw's studies as well as to participate
in the selection of many other collateral research projects funded during the
same period.[23] Frank's official role enabled him to continue to provide intellectual leadership and financial support to research institutes that he helped establish a decade earlier with Rockefeller funds. The details of Dewey's and Frank's
involvement in the Josiah Macy, Jr. Foundation and their roles in McGraw's
research will be described in the next two chapters. Before this child study
network can be understood, it is important to understand the larger theoretical
debates among psychologists that influenced parental practices and national
policies for child development.

NATURE, NURTURE, AND THE NORMS OF DEVELOPMENT

The professionalization of psychology after the turn of the twentieth century
occurred in overlapping phases involving different theoretical orientations and
methods. During the 1920s, John Watson's theory of behaviorism and conditioning and Edward Thorndike's conception of learning by reinforcement
weaned young parents from an uncritical acceptance of intergenerationally

transmitted folklore about child rearing. Behaviorism and reinforcement theories generated interest among educators and parents seeking more discipline, control, and predictable outcomes involved in raising and educating their children. Watson's behaviorism was appealing to parents because it promised to give them the psychological tools to mold their children into emotionally stable and professionally successful individuals. Thorndike experienced similar success persuading parents and teachers to adopt his techniques of reinforcement. He believed that his experiments, which rewarded successful behavior (appropriate responses) and punished unsuccessful behavior (inappropriate responses), demonstrated the "law of effect," that positive experiences are more likely to be remembered and repeated.

Freudian psychoanalysis burst dramatically on the American scene soon after the end of the first decade of the twentieth century. Freud's theories exerted an unexpectedly strong and enduring influence on psychological discourse as well as on American culture. The evident environmental strains in psychoanalysis reinforced an American predisposition to support social equality and to reject hereditary influences in favor of environmental explanations of individual behavior.[24] At first stubbornly resisted for offending Victorian sensibilities, Freudian theory about the sexual basis of human identity furnished a discourse about development that completely redefined the role of early childhood experience in the formation of individual identity.

Ironically, Freudian psychology renewed, from a secular point of view, an American preoccupation with childhood sin, temptation, and redemption that Freud had repudiated. Freud's narrative about guilt and the etiology of anxiety provided a secular substitute for the Calvinist story about sin and redemption. The Calvinist belief in original sin ruled out the possibility of childhood innocence and parental culpability. By tracing the source of moral dilemmas to underlying oedipal conflicts within family life, Freud contended that the discourse about original sin was misplaced. He reasoned that parents with doubts and anxieties about their own childhood identity and guilt had simply used their children as convenient pawns to relive the past in the hopes of overcoming their own insecurities and gaining psychological redemption.

By the late 1930s, Arnold Gesell's maturationist theory of development had become a significant competitor to Watson's environmentalism. Gesell, a Yale physician and infant experimentalist, challenged Watson's exaggerated claims about conditioning by showing that the sequence of infant sensorimotor development and maturation is genetically determined and invariable. Consequently, Gesell believed that any attempt to commence learning processes before cognitive capacities are well-developed and the child is emotionally ready may not only be useless, but may be positively harmful. Gesell revived anxieties in parents that Watson had temporally quelled, arguing that overstimulation in childhood could indeed have lasting consequences, as Freud predicted.

Importantly, psychoanalysis and maturationism shifted the terms of the discourse about childhood from nurturing to that of *normality*—a perspective toward developmental phenomena that enlarged the authority of scientific experts.[25] Dewey saw a way around this conundrum of normal development by making growth rather than maturation the focus of analysis. Dewey believed that once society rejected mechanistic and deterministic perspectives about development, the moral dilemmas posed by the dichotomy between heredity and environment would largely disappear. He also hoped that a coalition could be forged between scientists and parents that would increase support for new strategies of child development and national policies to implement them.

COMMUNITIES OF APPLIED INTELLIGENCE

Frank's successful organization of an international and interdisciplinary network of academically based researchers demonstrated a foresight unparalleled today. Frank sought to create through this network of academic institutes at Columbia, Iowa, Berkeley, Minnesota, Yale, and other universities an alliance between parent groups and researchers that would widely disseminate knowledge about child development, arousing public support for more innovative approaches to learning and child rearing.[26] In constructing this network, Frank pursued a holistic Deweyan conception involving the reconstruction of the relationship between science and society.

Frank drafted a proposal for the LSRM board in 1924 that specified how these objectives would be achieved. He stressed that the child study and parent training programs should be set up within the framework of existing programs and structures. He recommended that the LSRM funds be used to strengthen the collaboration between and coordination among national research organizations and child development advocates and their counterparts at the state and local level. He indicated how university-based researchers, child care providers, teachers, and parent organizations could cooperate in the dissemination of research and the provision of training.[27] Frank also recommended the creation of a "laboratory nursery school" that essentially fulfilled the aims first envisioned by Dewey in 1896. It would provide an observational laboratory for researchers, a training school for teachers and child-care workers, and a demonstration center for parents. Frank advised that the program of parent education be based on the Deweyan philosophy of "learn by doing, where the working out of a project empirically is emphasized rather than the study of principles and where observation of actual procedure looms more important than study from books."[28] Teacher's College was the first recipient of a grant from LSRM to establish a laboratory nursery school.

Rockefeller researchers were unaware that Frank's vision for an integrated system for the production and dissemination of developmental science reflected Dewey's thinking. Nor were Dewey and Frank's close professional and organizational ties apparent to most researchers at that time. Dewey succeeded in carefully concealing his foundation ties and close working relationship with Frank and McGraw. For example, Frank's second wife, Mary Perry, was not even aware that Dewey served on the board of the Josiah Macy, Jr. Foundation during the time that Frank served as vice president, saying that Dewey's name just never came up.[29] While acknowledging that most Rockefeller researchers were sympathetic to Dewey's perspective, pediatrician Milton Senn reflected the general impression among experimentalists that Dewey had soured on contemporary psychological research and no longer followed it closely. Even close friends of Dewey, like Lois Murphy, a psychologist and recipient of grants from the Josiah Macy, Jr. Foundation, were unaware of his role in the foundation or his close ties to Frank. Yet Murphy recalled seeing Dewey and McGraw dining frequently for lunch at the Columbia faculty club and thinking that he must still be interested in what was going on.[30] Nevertheless, Dewey's ideas and indirect involvement are apparent from the very beginning of the development of the Rockefeller research network.

The Welfare Research Station at the University of Iowa was the second university institute sponsored in the mid-1920s by the LSRM. Here Frank attempted to fully implement his strategic and collaborative model for child study. Iowa station director Bird Baldwin proposed a highly centralized plan in which the research station would control the distribution of LSRM funds to all other subgrantees in the state, including that requested by other universities.[31] Frank thought better of this idea and made a counterproposal for a decentralized system that maintained a balance or symmetry in the relationship between the parts and system as a whole. Under this scheme each of the organizational entities involved in the research, dissemination, and educational components of the child study program would have latitude to develop specific areas of expertise, and yet be interrelated and interact to coordinate information and services.

Frank's holistic model that ultimately prevailed was based on an analogy to growth enunciated by Dewey. The university-based child study institutes were allowed to pursue different research strategies and given flexibility to decide which specific programs should be implemented, as long as they focused on common developmental problems and issues. Flexible relationships or partnerships could be forged between institutes and parent-run community programs that facilitated the reciprocal flow of information. In practical terms, this interactionist model enabled initiative and innovation to emerge from almost any part of the system without altering the overall focus and direction. For example, parent groups might provide special experiential insights that could lead researchers to refine their studies; or teachers might provide valuable feedback regarding successes or failures in adapting their methods to accommodate new knowledge. Clearly, no one element was intended to dominate the others, but all were to engage in a collaborative and constructive interaction, blending knowledge and experience into effective educational strategies.[32]

Frank's decentralized but transformational model for parent education served as the prototype for state-based collaborative child development research and dissemination projects funded by the LSRM during the 1920s. Not every state project achieved the high degree of integration that Iowa attained among academics, parent-teacher groups, educators, child-care associations, state agencies, and legislative leaders, but there were notable successes in specific research projects or local educational programs. Parent education served as the focal point of projects designed to increase communication and collaboration between state and local groups and to forge partnerships between public and private organizations dedicated to child care and education. A remarkably broad and sophisticated network of programs was formed that facilitated the testing of different organizational approaches and methods involving the support of parent study groups and the dissemination of their findings about successful child-rearing practices. These initiatives were documented in a voluminous report presented at the White House Conference on Child Health and Protection that included histories and case studies of the numerous projects undertaken by national and state associations and organizations and their local counterparts.[33]

A SCIENCE OF CHILDHOOD

Possessing a sophisticated theoretical grasp of developmental biology and psychology, Frank contributed important articles and books to the field of child study.[34] He contended that the fundamental problem of child development is to determine how the "oscillations and fluctuations in the structure and functions or processes of the growing child are interrelated."[35] He believed that it was theoretically possible to correlate biological structures and functions undergoing different rates of growth in the human organism and to determine the effects of changes or perturbations of any single part on development as a whole. Tracking the uneven course of growth was no more challenging, Frank believed, than recording the cyclical changes in the American economy. The real difficulty had to do with interpreting the kinds of organic changes that structures and functions were undergoing during these fluctuating intervals of growth.

Unlike some recent commentators, Frank insisted that the problem of "normal" child development be approached "not as the establishment of statistical norms for chronological age or fixed dimensions that all children should attain at any year or incident of time, but rather as the delineation of the structures and functions calculated from each individual child from the data he yields."[36] Frank believed that a method could be devised to estimate the "relative rates of change appropriate to each structure and function" and to generate "dynamic norms" which yield a profile of an individual child's "coordinations" and "discrepancies" within an overall trend.[37]

Importantly, the university institutes undertook distinctive but complementary studies that contributed to a detailed and comprehensive profile of growth and developmental processes that would not have been obtainable from individual projects. Frank, by exerting his intellectual influence and skilled leadership as an intermediary keeping researchers apprised of each other's work, was largely responsible for this outcome. He also succeeded in getting key individuals to adopt modifications in design or methods that enhanced the comparability and generalizability of the findings.

Frank wasted little time in getting research projects funded and underway. Through Frank's prodding, Iowa was first off the mark in the attempt to become a national leader in child development research. Iowa researchers undertook comprehensive studies of growth processes, but their approach consisted of producing a large but diffuse set of measurements of anatomical, physiological, and other functional processes, much as the BEE had done, that did not lend themselves readily to synthesis and interpretation. Nancy Bayley's longitudinal studies at Berkeley and John Anderson's research at Minnesota came much closer to the mark set by Frank. Bayley and her colleague, Jean MacFarlane, contributed remarkable longitudinal studies of motor development and emotional control that continue to be cited by contemporary researchers. Anderson, the founding president of the Division of Developmental Psychology of the American Psychological Association in 1946, adopted a broad naturalistic and community-based view of child development, which supported Dewey's interdisciplinary conception of inquiry.[38]

Iowa's fortunes were considerably enhanced when George Stoddard, a Columbia-trained Dewey disciple, took over the helm at the Iowa station after Baldwin's sudden death in 1928. Stoddard was well-versed in educational testing, having studied with Theodore Simon, Alfred Binet's collaborator, but he lacked a strong interest in growth processes. An admirer of Dewey's equalitarian philosophy of education, he preferred to conduct research that would challenge the group bias of intelligence testing. The assumption was that IQ tests merely reflected the uneven distribution of inherited intelligence in society and that differences in human intelligence remained relatively constant across family generations, by race, by ethnicity, and by other bases of group membership.

Stoddard challenged this assumption. He and his assistant, Beth Wellman, conducted some highly original controlled longitudinal experiments to determine whether experience and learning-enriched preschools could enhance individual IQ scores. Indeed, they found that individual IQ scores were subject to significant variations that were obscured by group averages. Children transferring into these preschools who initially had the lowest scores showed the largest increases in IQ, but these gains declined sharply after they departed. Children continuously attending these programs showed only negligible, but long-term, improvement in scores. Stoddard and Wellman engaged in a strenuous national debate with other child study institutes, insisting that early experience mattered, but the disappointing long-term performance of these children did little to challenge the widespread belief that IQ was a matter of nature and not nurture.

Thus the focal point of the debate over heredity versus environment, involving the relation between experience and intelligence, was sidetracked into an interminable and unwinnable methodological debate as to how to compare individual and group scores. Decades later, when the IQ debate was revived with Head Start in the 1960s, the same erroneous conclusions that experience did not make a difference in intelligence were initially drawn. Only when researchers discovered that children in poverty-stricken families experienced difficulty learning did the racial and cultural limitations of IQ tests become evident.[39]

Child development researchers at other universities focused on factors that contributed to differences in individual behavior and personality. Laboratory experiments were devised to test and compare the reactions of experimental subjects to a wide variety of situations involving children and parents. Individual behavior that was measured included temperament, patience, caution, resistance, independence, self-assertiveness, persistence, possessiveness, sociability, cooperation, and other behaviors. Institute investigators found that children's emotional reactions were more variable and less fixed in the first four or five years among infants and children than in later childhood. Consequently, their attitudes were more susceptible to modification through changes in the social environment. This research help popularize the construct of "emotional set" or readiness of individuals to react to new situations in either positive or negative ways.[40]

Psychologists also found strong statistical relationships between parental attitudes, their disciplinary techniques, and children's reaction patterns. For example, children of overprotective mothers tended to be timid and submissive, while children who were ignored tended to be aggressive and uncooperative. Parent-child interactions were also compared according to socioeconomic class. Children of working-class families were likely to experience higher levels of interpersonal conflict and physical punishment than their middle-class cohorts. Working-class children were also more likely to pose disciplinary problems in the classroom and to become involved in juvenile delinquency.[41]

Ultimately, each institute formulated a research program that played to their strengths in expertise and methodological skills. Their differences in emphasis contributed to a much richer understanding of childhood than they would have gotten had they been in a lockstep mode. Nevertheless, these researchers adopted an uncompromisingly experimental and critical approach to the problems they investigated. Some researchers, such as Robert Sears at Iowa and Lester Sontag at Antioch, adopted Freudian perspectives, while others, such as Harold Jones and his wife Mary Cover Jones, drew on behaviorist theories of infant development. Sontag showed that contrary to psychoanalytic theory, parent-child interactions vary throughout childhood, a fact that downplayed the importance of events occurring during the earliest years. Sears and collaborator Kurt Lewin, a German émigré, obtained important insights about the relation between frustration and aggression in socialization processes. And importantly, Gesell's research regarding the norms of early development did not go unchallenged, as both Bayley and McGraw were encouraged by Frank to experimentally test opposing hypotheses.

DEMOCRACY BY DESIGN?

Although a rich archive of research reports and documents recording the activities of parent-education groups has been accumulated in the Rockefeller Archive Center and other repositories, until recently few scholars have examined and studied these materials in detail. Scholarly interest has centered primarily on the theoretical and possible ideological leanings of Rockefeller-supported researchers.[42] Some contemporary scholars have questioned Frank's use of research fellowships to channel female scientists into applied rather than basic research, contending that this reinforced gender stereotypes.[43] Frank's attempt to disseminate research widely among potential child development constituencies is even viewed by some social historians as actually a calculated effort to create a mass market for the propagation and consumption of highly prescriptive views about childhood favored by corporate elites and their academic allies.[44]

However, a far more complex picture of social reform processes involving child development has emerged from recent studies of the Rockefeller archives. These studies suggest that a higher degree of critical intellectual give and take occurred than was previously surmised between parent-education groups, university researchers, and state organizations. Historians and social theorists adopting a "social control" perspective appear to have oversimplified the historical processes that gave birth to contemporary views about child development. Parent-teacher organizations and maternal associations existed at the local and state levels long before the Rockefeller initiative. American mothers, the clergy, and schoolteachers, among others, have had a long-standing interest in child-rearing practices. While the advice parents received about child rearing in the nineteenth century largely was morally prescriptive, mothers were unlikely to adopt child-rearing practices that violated common sense or were contrary to their own experiences. This same experiential basis of judgment appears to have been carried forward by parents in their reception of the twentieth-century literature on childhood.[45]

The Rockefeller initiative tapped into a growing secular demand at the turn of the twentieth century among parents and educators to obtain morally nonprescriptive and reliable scientific evidence with which to inform their child-rearing practices. Child-rearing advice was assimilated within the backdrop of individual experiences and expectations. Consequently, as Julia Grant noted, mothers believed that they possessed "useful knowledge that might be juxtaposed or combined with the more socially legitimated knowledge of experts."[46] That is why the heavily prescriptive approach adopted by the federal Children's Bureau and its state-supported agencies was not received with much enthusiasm. Leaders of parent groups frequently rebuffed advocates of national policies, preferring to obtain information from those psychologists who demonstrated that parents could use this knowledge to solve real problems.

Interestingly, parent group discussions about hereditary and environmental influences did not easily fit within the conceptual contours of the nature-versus-nurture dichotomy framed by the experts. The national and state child study associations adopted a strong environmental stance, taking the view that parents and educators could strongly influence their children's behavior and level of achievement. They feared that parents who accepted hereditary explanations of behavior would reject expert advice and attribute any personal failures in child rearing to factors beyond their control. However, parents took a more relaxed and realistic point of view that temperament and character were not quite as malleable as the behaviorists claimed.[47]

The secularization and popularization of child-rearing advice, professionalization, and the feminization of child development research went hand in hand. The rising demand for effective knowledge about child rearing provided professional employment opportunities for women, who sought academic careers in psychology, home economics, or education. Frank facilitated these gains in social status for women by awarding nearly half of all fellowships to women. These women, including McGraw and many other women psychologists and psychiatrists, eventually attained significant research or academic positions. Female pioneers in child development sponsored by the Rockefeller Foundation, the Carnegie Corporation, and the Commonwealth Fund helped educate a second generation of psychologists who would have an enormous influence on national public policies involving children in the 1960s and 1970s.[48]

However, a subtle but unmistakable shift in the interests and focus of discussion among parent-education groups began to appear in the early 1930s. The Depression created economic pressures on the family that destabilized parental roles and intensified feelings of personal insecurity. Delinquency and crime were on the rise, and psychiatrists and clinicians began to assert their professional prerogative to play a more significant role in child development policy. During this period, Freudian theory gained significant footholds in pediatric medicine and psychiatry. The psychoanalytic perspective drew increasing attention to parent-centered issues of identity and the emotional equilibrium of the family unit as a whole. By adopting a clinical orientation to child rearing, child study intermediaries unwittingly undermined the supportive atmosphere of parent discussion groups by encouraging parents to find individualized solutions to their problems. A new emphasis was placed on the importance of maternal attitudes and values in producing well-adjusted, strongly attached, and individually motivated children.[49] Lewin even suggested that Freudian theory was complementary rather than antithetical to democracy. He contended that individual insecurity was mitigated by strong group attachments. His research indicated that group members who selected autocratic leaders tended to be more aggressive and frustrated than those members who chose leaders that reflected laissez-faire and democratic attitudes.

The Transformational Potential of Consciousness in Art, Politics, and Science

PRAGMATISM AND THE POLITICS OF LIBERAL REFORM

Frank found persuasive Lewin's attempt to use field theory to demonstrate the essentially democratic implications of Freudian psychology. Frank carefully concealed from Dewey his growing interest in and fascination with Freudian psychoanalysis, knowing that Dewey found Freud's ideas neither appealing nor valid. But like it or not, Freud's ideas deeply penetrated the thinking of child researchers. Some individuals, like MacFarlane, a Berkeley psychologist, stubbornly declared her independence from psychoanalytic theories, complaining that "sound research in the clinical field has been retarded by the past practice of training to verify theories [like the Oedipus complex] that are abortive or premature through lack of a factual nature."[50] But University of Iowa researcher Harold Anderson conceded that Freud's ideas were so pervasive that "we hardly knew what was Freud in our thinking and what was someone else's ideas."[51] Mary Cover Jones, a former Berkeley Institute experimental psychologist, echoed this sentiment, saying, "I think maybe we [child development researchers] were not as aware of the tremendous influence Freud was going to have. . . . Perhaps that was one of our blind spots."[52]

Frank's intellectual transition from adherence to a strong Deweyan psychological point of view to one that blended pragmatist and neo-Freudian psychoanalytic perspectives was a gradual one. His mature views became evident in a series of journal articles written in the 1930s and 1940s that were subsequently published as *Society as the Patient* in 1949. Frank's Freudian views first emerged in a seminal article in 1928 where Frank asserted that educational and cultural institutions are failing to help children manage the tensions they felt in attempting to strike an effective balance between pressures for conformity and opportunities for independence and creativity.

In his essay "The Management of Tensions," Frank outlined a psychobiological theory of personality development that strayed from Dewey's perspective. He skillfully attempted to push the ramifications of Dewey's energetic theory of growth beyond the limits that Dewey found acceptable. Frank suggested how learning occurred through the functional resolution of a series of physiological and emotional tensions involving the distribution, release, and conservation of energy. Frank viewed growth as "a process of changing dimensions," while development consisted of the "molding and patterning of that growth into specific structures, functions, and activities" through learning processes.[53] Learning essentially consisted, according to Frank, of the substitution of stimuli and tensional adjustment whereby children master and replace infantile sequences of behaviors and attitudes with more mature ones. These tensions, arising initially from physiological reaction patterns, Frank argued, assume an emotional tone that is carried from one experience to the next, giving a definite direction and trend to individual reaction patterns. Accordingly, children must learn through parental assistance the delicate art of knowing when and how long to inhibit the release of tensions accumulated in their attempts to bring their behavior under deliberate and instrumental control.

Frank was keenly sensitive to the need to strike an appropriate balance in socialization processes between unthinking obedience and conformity and undisciplined and aimless behavior. That is why Frank believed that the mechanisms of inhibition that Dewey considered crucial to reflective thought could be therapeutically manipulated, as Freud advocated, to prevent uncontrolled and exaggerated forms of behavior. He acknowledged that all societies prohibit certain forms of behavior and hold as inviolate specific cultural values, such as the possession of private property and the sanctity of the individual. While some degree of external restraint is required to bring about socially prescribed conduct, Frank much preferred mechanisms of self-restraint than methods of social control that were unduly coercive and destructive of personal identity.

Frank was no different than many of his contemporaries who believed that Freudian psychoanalysis and pragmatism could be synthesized without betraying the principles of intelligent behavior that underpinned Dewey's theory of mind. Frank considered Freud's theory that early experiences exert a profound influence on subsequent development to be self-evident. Frank was convinced that the crisis of authority in modern politics was directly rooted in the early frustration of physiological functions, unresolved conflicts, and compulsions carried forward from childhood and manifested in attitudes of resentment and hostility toward institutions and their leaders. One way out of this unfortunate situation was to have better-educated parents capable of taking a more sophisticated and self-conscious look at their own motives and the kinds of attitudes they often carelessly imparted to their children. Toward this end, the LSRM funded a survey to obtain nationwide statistics from a stratified sample of income groups on child-rearing practices such as breastfeeding, weaning, bowel and bladder control, and other practices.[54]

Frank found a strong emancipative theme in Freudian psychoanalysis that Dewey rejected as entirely spurious. Dewey rejected the premise that children are fated to unwittingly serve a life sentence of anxiety and insecurity because of some unknown emotional trauma. Dewey bitterly characterized his surprise and disappointment in learning years later that Frank had adopted a thoroughgoing Freudian perspective when he related uncharitably and inaccurately to Frank Jones, "I think I spoke of Lawrence Frank—but I found on looking into things that he was one of the psychologists [Frank was an economist by training] who are led by psychoanalysts to believe that human destiny is settled in infancy by how the feeding and excretory eliminations are treated by adults."[55] From Dewey's perspective, Freud (and Frank) had selectively and illegitimately converted certain undeniable natural physiological processes into the first principles of human identity and motivation. Dewey's tempestuous dismissal of Frank's sophisticated theory was indicative of his unwillingness to entertain Freudianism, even if a case was made by a close associate who shared Dewey's philosophy and respect for science.

Despite Dewey's protestations, national political commentators such as Walter Lippmann deployed Freudian arguments with consummate rhetorical wit and skill. A regular contributor to the *New Republic*, Lippmann was skeptical of liberal pretensions to attain a participatory democracy in America. He challenged Dewey's premise that the American public would avail itself of scientific knowledge to form intelligent and rational opinions about public policies. Lippmann shared Freud's view of human rationality as limited and shared his low estimation of the value of individual participation in political processes. The demand for self-government was a convenient fiction, Lippmann asserted, because national political parties are controlled by a tiny group of elites whose public appeal and legitimacy is predicated on deception and manipulation of public opinion through the popular press.

Dewey concurred with Lippmann that the political system was organized to deter and thwart knowledge and participation, but he dissented from Lippmann's elitist sentiments that the survival of democracy depends on leadership rather than on a more enlightened public. Lippmann brilliantly illustrated the episodic and inconsistent ways Americans expressed their views about national policies in his books *Public Opinion* (1922) and *Phantom Public* (1925). But Dewey believed that these flaws in reasoning could be rectified if communities were better informed about the effects and consequences of national policies on their daily lives. Moreover, there were many realms of government inaction that citizens could address with new policies if they possessed some control over the political processes where they could express and act on their preferences.[56]

Significantly, Frank's child study network demonstrated that democratic processes of participation flourish if knowledge salient to elected officials and their constituent's interests is made available. This network enabled parents to become self-conscious about their child-rearing practices by gaining access to scientific research, by exercising their judgment to evaluate and weigh it against their own experiences, and by using that knowledge to influence educational practices subject to state and national policies. The child study institutes sponsored by the Rockefeller and other foundations generated new knowledge that led many parents to change how they raised their children. American proclivities to view individuals as products of their environment seemed to give way over time to a more balanced view of nature and nurture. This research challenged and eventually altered some strongly held public beliefs and attitudes about educational methods considered natural yet contrary to observed processes of development. But this formative era of theory building also showed that foundation officials and researchers alike are no less susceptible than parents to the alluring appeal of developmental theories that marginalize their own judgment and responsibility.

The eclipse of the public as an active participant in the formulation and implementation of national policy that Lippmann claimed to be witnessing in the 1920s could be averted, Dewey thought. Communities engaged in national policy-making processes must suspend disbelief and re-examine the limits of possible and permissible behavior.[57] Dewey sensed that the diversion of science into mass production and the overspecialization and narrowing of skills could result in "the monopolization of the spiritual capital," Dewey warned, that "may in the end be more harmful than [the monopolization] of material capital."[58] "A culture which permits science to destroy values but which distrusts its power to create new ones," Dewey warned, "is a culture which is destroying itself."[59]

CONTEXTUALIZING MORALITY

Freudian psychology spawned political realists in the 1920s and 1930s like Lippmann and Reinhold Niebuhr, who occupied different ends of the ideological continuum. Niebuhr, who became an articulate exponent of a radical psychological realism in American politics, began to stalk Dewey in the 1930s. A brilliant graduate of the Union Theological Seminary of New York, Niebuhr admired Dewey and participated with him in many of the same social and political causes in the 1930s and 1940s. Niebuhr's political philosophy consisted of a peculiar mixture of economic radicalism, political realism, and religious fatalism. He had much in common with socialists and communists of his day who demanded social justice and a radical redistribution of wealth and income. But he also considered himself a realist in believing that the struggle for political power necessarily involved conflict and violence. These beliefs were counterbalanced by his unshakable Augustinian conviction (a sort of reversed Freudianism) that the original human sins were egotism and self-love. Not surprisingly, Niebuhr considered Dewey's belief in the human capacity for intelligent action to be unfounded, and he found incredibly naive Dewey's optimism that communities of intelligence could secure a democratic society.[60]

Dewey found it distasteful to respond to personal criticisms made by fellow advocates of social reform. Nevertheless, Niebuhr's provocations pushed Dewey into an unwelcome public conflict. Dewey found Neibuhr's position fraught with inconsistency. On the one hand, Niebuhr insisted that no community or class would ever willingly give up its power, according to Dewey, because of a "collective egoism and the natural depravity of nature."[61] On the other hand, Dewey observed, Niebuhr saw no alternative to violence to achieve "social righteousness."[62] Perplexed by this paradoxical juxtaposition of means and ends, Dewey complained, "I can understand thoroughgoing pacifism, and I can understand the Communistic version of a violent struggle ending in the victory of the proletariat. But Dr. Niebuhr's position escapes me."[63]

Niebuhr protested that Dewey had missed the point that there was no such thing as a politically detached intelligence. "All intelligence is *interested* intelligence," Niebuhr asserted, "and any historical retrospect that sees the past as a matter of *disinterested* ignorance in contrast to an ostensibly enlightened present is patently foolish."[64] While Dewey did not deny the connection between intelligence and power, he rejected Niebuhr's exaggerated conception of political power as a lopsided concentration of force rather than as a continuous struggle between multiple, competing forces. "Intelligence becomes a power," Dewey argued, "only when it is brought into the operation of other forces than itself."[65] Dewey was trying, somewhat ineptly, to argue that power did not involve a zero-sum game, but was situated in a field of conflict, competition, and the ebb and flow of force and dominance between different groups. Niebuhr's Marxism prevented him from ever conceiving of power in terms other than those of class warfare.

Freud put a different spin on liberal individualism than Niebuhr by reformulating the discourse about guilt and redemption into a narrative about how to recover from our tragic sense of loss of individual identity. Freud, unlike Niebuhr, believed that the recovery of individual security in the form of self-love was not sinful but biologically unavoidable. He contended that the state could only exacerbate the pain suffered for the advance of civilization through the renunciation of desire, and that guilt, reinforced through group ties, carries intolerable if not tragic consequences for the ego.[66] Freud argued that a social conscience was born from a persistent and beguiling guilt and that cruelty begins as a self-inflicted wound of the psyche. Recovery of identity then required relocating the source of guilt in family life and cultural institutions.

Dewey rejected the idea that conscience concealed latent guilt, relegating piety and worship to the private sphere. Nor could he accept Niebuhr's genetic view that guilt was something we inherited by virtue of our progenitors' loss of God's grace. Instead, he argued that secularization and the withdrawal of reverence and respect for nature and community narrowed conscience and the quest for salvation to individual happiness rather than societal well-being. The eclipse of community did not come about because of a ritual killing of a worldly or heavenly father figure, condemning us to a life of anxiety and fear of retribution, but occurred because we no longer felt responsible for or capable of controlling the social consequences of our behavior.[67] These purported undemocratic consequences of Freudian psychology are well-illustrated by the evidence from the changing focus of parent education initiatives. Viewed initially as an important asset to science and social reform, parents' attitudes and experiences were increasingly discounted and devalued from a Freudian perspective that implicated their desires for their children's success and well-being in a larger web of self-deception and betrayal.

Niebuhr and Freud were simply repeating the mistakes made by their predecessors among political theorists whom Dewey criticized. They refused to accept the indeterminacy of feelings and attitudes that underlie moral conduct and political conflict. Political philosophers as diverse as Augustine and Aquinas, Rousseau and Hobbes, Burke and Marx, concertedly attempted to trace the origins of politically contentious social problems, such as inequality and injustice, power and oppression, alienation and revolution, to some primordial instinct. Augustine attributed the lust for power or greed to original sin,

while Marx saw these same attitudes rooted in economic inequality and alienation. Rousseau traced social injustice to envy, while Burke believed that revolutions were rooted in resentment and vengeance.

But Dewey argued that political beliefs cannot be reduced to any single attitude or emotion because they are themselves variable and subject to the contingencies of experience. Clearly researchers in child development, with the exception of Freud's and Watson's followers, never reached a consensus as to the
dominance in childhood of any one overriding trait or predisposition that
would account for political attitudes. The political object of attitudes, such as
resentment, is not easily distinguished from envy or suspicion, because each of
these attitudes may be expressed in situations that differ considerably in context. That is why Dewey considered ideologies like communism abhorrent and
psychologies like psychoanalysis deleterious to human freedom. Their adherents reduced complex human sentiments to simplistic, unidimensional motives
that were thought to be easily dominated by appeals to nationalistic slogans,
demagoguery, or therapeutic manipulation.

Dewey asserted that no single principle of behavior or moral conduct could
ever be devised to exhaust completely the range, variety, nuance, and force of
feelings and attitudes that humans are capable of expressing in experience. Uncertainty makes community inevitable, he argued, because doubt drives people
together to solve problems no one can escape alone. Moreover, the full force
and meaning of an idea or particular feeling cannot be known until the individual possessing it expresses it in some overt act that implicates other persons.
Drawing others into one's own affairs creates a potential for mutual understanding and a potential for conflict or violence, but does not inevitably lead to
either outcome because intentions are judged by actions and consequences.

Dewey asserted that the "function of moral judgment is to detect this un-
likeness," or the subtle but decisive difference between feelings expressed in
overtly similar behavior.[68] This is better characterized as a *contextualist* rather
than a relativist conception of moral conduct. Decisions made with the best of
intentions can go awry if the actions (or inaction) taken to sustain them dissipate the feelings of good will they were expected to attain. That is why Dewey
believed that moral dilemmas are not resolved merely by thinking differently
but by adopting new attitudes, trying new approaches, and changing the pathways in which the energy of human feeling is expressed and channeled in human conduct.

Sidney Hook wasted his time trying to convince Dewey that there was a
difference between a communist and a Marxist, and that the early writings of
Karl Marx exhibited a strong humanism that was betrayed by the ideological
slogans of party officials. Stalinism quickly dispelled any doubts about where
communism was headed in its single-minded and brutal attempt to rid Soviet
society of class differences. When Stalin's purges swept his rival Leon Trotsky
into the dragnet of reprisals, Dewey came to his defense in Mexico in 1937,
where Trotsky was in exile, by leading an impartial inquiry of the charges of

treason against him.[69] This was indicative of Dewey's equanimity despite fundamental intellectual differences with his rivals that so distinguished him from his contemporaries. Dewey's defense of Trotsky's human rights was all the more remarkable given that he graciously interrupted work on the final pages of his magnum opus, *Logic: The Theory of Inquiry*, to conduct it. The fascinating events which led to the completion of this lifelong project are worth describing next because at no other time during Dewey's prodigious career did his personal and professional lives converge so resolutely and magnificently, enabling him to focus on scientific problems of utmost importance to his theory of mind.

NINE

The Function of Judgment in Inquiry

Dewey urgently sought to renew his personal involvement in scientific studies after a lapse of several decades following his direct involvement in the Laboratory School at the University of Chicago. During these intervening years research in child development increased enormously. Although much new information had been acquired about child behavior from experimental studies with which he was familiar, including the Bureau of Educational Experiments, many conventional attitudes persisted about human development. In Dewey's estimation, the scientific evidence about normal development was mistakenly intertwined with ideas about moral development. Freud led parents to believe that any interference with a child's natural physiological processes had delayed repercussions that presented moral predicaments in adult life. From Dewey's perspective, however, the natural processes of growth had little to do with cultural beliefs. Growth processes affected the human potential for learning and the capacity to exercise judgment. He wanted to demonstrate that judgment was not primarily concerned with praise or blame, but had to do with the natural capacity to maintain balance and perspective—traits essential to scientific inquiry and aesthetic appreciation, as well as moral conduct.

Dewey's philosophical ideas about growth and learning and the role of the brain, consciousness, and judgment in intelligent behavior posed methodological difficulties that did not lend themselves to conventional psychological analyses. The reflex paradigm popularized by the behaviorist John Watson suggested that learning developed incrementally through stimulus and response and that complex human behaviors were acquired through a process of conditioning. Dewey rejected these notions, arguing instead that intelligence developed from the interaction of mind and body in response to uncertain situations that demanded ingenuity, resourcefulness, and sense of balance. However, Dewey had furnished no direct evidence to support his contention that the brain and mind evolved to meet the demands for coordinated action under conditions of uncertainty. As noted earlier, before the turn of the twentieth century Dewey and

McLellan had speculated that the capabilities of comparison, measurement, inference, and generalization were traits that emerged with the development of consciousness. Consequently, Dewey sought to identify the circumstances that contributed to the need for judgment in the course of development, to isolate generic traits involved, and to show how they helped form the pattern of inquiry.

Nor had Dewey demonstrated convincingly why ideas do not depend on the association of stimulus and response but originate indirectly from feelings rooted in organic processes of suggestion that prolong judgment and control over the direction of inquiry. *Art as Experience* marked the brilliant culmination of Dewey's attempts to capture the evanescent but tangible role of suggestion in human aesthetic experience. Aesthetic perception is always reaching beyond nature, Dewey argued, to find new ways to depict the world and express human feeling. But Dewey had yet to advance a parallel argument that effective inquiry does not depend, as scientific convention supposed, merely on the accumulation of confirming evidence through the repetition of existing operations. Instead, inquiry brings about the conscious modification of our attitudes and methods through developmental learning experiences that expands the scope of human judgment and understanding.

Dewey also sought to justify his long-standing belief, first articulated in *Studies in Logical Theory*, that scientific progress did not depend on conformity to canons of logical validity, but on whether science contributed to the continuous transformation of theories and methods of inquiry. He speculated that our capacity to transform nature and ourselves began with erect locomotion, in which stride and pace furnished rudimentary methods of measurement. However, he required more evidence to defend this assertion by demonstrating that, if judgment is intrinsic to the processes of both human development and science, then the value of the methods and constants we adopt will hinge on whether scientific knowledge produces equivalent advances in human consciousness and understanding.

Most Dewey scholars contend that his conception of inquiry underwent few changes before the publication of his mature work in 1938.[1] Yet Dewey disclaimed that he could ever "write an account of [his] intellectual development without giving it a semblance of continuity it does not in fact own."[2] Moreover, Ernest Nagel, a former student who would have had an opportunity to question Dewey and get him to clarify his arguments, admitted years later that central themes and conceptions in *Logic: The Theory of Inquiry* remain "puzzling" and "essentially obscure."[3] Consequently, little headway has been made until recently in rendering the themes in Dewey's *Logic* intelligible simply by asserting that it is merely a refinement or more explicit elaboration of themes first presented in *Studies*.

Dewey's perturbing lack of explicitness regarding the scientific sources of his ideas about the development of the brain and behavior, and his failure to explicitly acknowledge personal experiences crucial to his theory of mind are shortcomings that previous chapters have attempted to rectify. His sins of omission are not unlike those committed by most other original thinkers, such as Freud, who also frequently failed to acknowledge his intellectual debts.[4] Dewey's arguments in *Logic* remain elusive because they were based on a neuroembryological model of growth and development advanced by scientists with whom he became acquainted in the late 1920s. Before that time, Dewey's seminal analyses of human experience, culminating in *Human Nature and Conduct* in 1922, were guided by a neurodynamic model that construed thought and behavior in terms of *processes of coordination*. Dewey swam against the tide of general opinion that behavior was formed through the channeling of nervous energy through fixed pathways. Nervous energy did not seek immediate discharge through lines of least resistance, according to Dewey, but was delayed or inhibited, forming sensorimotor connections involving the greatest probable effectiveness.[5]

However, Dewey could not rely solely on this mechanistic model to support his argument in *Logic* that "biological functions and structures prepare the way for deliberate inquiry" and "foreshadow its pattern."[6] *Experience and Nature* tried to make scientifically plausible the metaphysical theory that generic traits of mind originate in nature. But there simply were no experimental studies of biological processes that Dewey could point to that supported his notion that these traits give birth to inquiry.

Dewey attempted to overcome weaknesses in his neurobehavioral model of mind by seeing if the principles and methods of neuroembryology could elucidate the *processes of growth* involved in the *integration of behavior*. A neuroembryological perspective does not explain development in terms of the patterns of circulation of nervous energy—a neurodynamic model that Freud employed before abandoning his *Scientific Project*—but explains how early metabolic processes of neuromuscular growth contribute to the differentiation and integration of behavior. Dewey also probably considered the mechanistic neurodynamic and the growth-centered neuroembryological perspectives essentially compatible, and thus was confident that the essential differences in their locus of explanation of behavior could be reconciled.

That is why Dewey continued his active involvement in experimental studies of child development with Myrtle McGraw. Dewey was unable to fully elaborate a conception of inquiry from a neurodynamic perspective alone, leading to his adoption of a neuroembryological model. McGraw's studies helped Dewey fathom the efficacy of this latter perspective in elucidating the pattern of inquiry. Dewey's personal collaboration with McGraw and other participants in her Normal Child Development Study (NCDS) at Columbia University during the 1930s not only provided the experimental techniques to ground his premises about development in available evidence, but it helped Dewey crystallize principles central to *Logic*.

Dewey faced many challenges in his efforts in the 1930s to bring science and personal experience to bear on issues of utmost importance to his theory of inquiry. Dewey attempted to carry forward the ideas and concepts of *Natur-philosophers*, whose conceptions of mind and energy had fallen into disrepute with the emergence of modern physics. Dewey sought to carry forward this theoretical perspective by uniting biology and physics in the study of consciousness at a time when philosophical issues about the relation between mind and body no longer concerned nor held the attention of most mainstream psychologists. Dewey's attempt to find a philosophical discourse grounded in science while still embodying the richness of human experience was obscured by process terms such as "interaction" that failed to convey their underlying biological and psychological significance. Even Dewey's most ardent followers were never quite certain precisely which domains of knowledge Dewey was attempting to interrelate in any one book or article.

I am not contending that Dewey could not have completed *Logic* without McGraw's research. Instead, *Logic* represents the culmination of Dewey's lifelong preoccupation with the intrinsic relationship between human development and inquiry—a connection that Dewey believed could be fully comprehended only while personally engaged in the *process* of inquiry. Indeed, Dewey's numerous references to generic traits of development and integrative functions of the nervous system in *Logic* seem inexplicable elements of inquiry, unless understood in the context of McGraw's experimental studies of neuromuscular development. Dewey's collaboration with McGraw and her associates provided interpersonal interaction that he considered essential to the genesis, testing, and elaboration of ideas in methods that yielded knowledge about the pattern of inquiry. Dewey's interest in interdisciplinary experimentation was not only a characteristic trait but a methodological predisposition, as his experiences prior to the 1930s attest.

CHALLENGING GESELL'S MATURATIONISM

Dewey's previous opportunities to explore the relationship between mind, brain, and learning at the University of Chicago Laboratory School (1896–1903) and through his involvement with the Bureau of Educational Experiments (1916–1920) fell far short of his ambitious goals. These studies were largely *demonstrations* rather than *controlled experiments*. For example, the Laboratory School staff at the University of Chicago tried to understand how structured learning situations produce balanced physical, mental, and social development. The emphasis on group work projects was an innovation in social reconstruction, but it did not provide any direct evidence for how the brain evolves or contributes to functionally adaptive behavior.[7]

Nevertheless, Dewey showed a surprising acuity in identifying sequential stages of sensorimotor development. He hypothesized that attention and awareness come into play when infants attempted to attain balance in a sitting position preparatory to prone locomotion. And the capacity for recognition and comparison seemed to Dewey to accompany crawling and creeping.[8] Dewey concluded from his research that an experimental program must be devised "to discover some single continuous function undergoing development in order to bring scientific relevancy and order into various facts of child psychology, and in order to give them practical or pedagogical usefulness."[9] McGraw ultimately devised such a program, described in this chapter, in her studies of the development of infant locomotion.

The Bureau of Educational Experiments, begun by Lucy Sprague Mitchell and her husband Wesley in 1916, involved an exploratory but not experimentally controlled attempt over a four-year period to measure the effects of stimulation on rate of growth according to age, intelligence, and behavior.[10] Although suggestive, the results were inconclusive. Bureau staff members lacked the skills necessary to obtain a detailed record of the sequence of individual development and found it increasingly difficult to compete for foundation support with psychologist Arnold Gesell, whose motion picture studies of the genesis of infant behavior were already underway at Yale.

Having established his credentials as a leading educational reformer long before Gesell entered the field, Dewey believed that McGraw's research would support his previously untested theories about the role of judgment in learning and behavior development. By the late 1920s, Gesell had become well-known for his theory that the sequence of neuromuscular development is invariable. He contended that learning readiness and aptitude are governed largely by genetically controlled developmental processes and that early stimulation does not appreciably accelerate growth nor enhance ultimate performance.[11] McGraw, who tried unsuccessfully to work with Gesell, challenged this view. She hypothesized that early stimulation may lead to significant variations in the timing and sequence in which infants master motor processes, and also may influence the quality and effectiveness of judgment in learning situations.

Dewey seems to have shared McGraw's growing sense of rivalry with Gesell. Dewey reported to McGraw what he characterized as a "disgusting and amusing incident" involving Gesell while they were on board a ship traveling to an educational conference in South Africa. Dewey, who considered modesty a virtue, typically shunned the posturing and affectation associated with celebrity. Apparently Gesell and Dewey were recognized by a maitre d' who asked Gesell if Dewey was "as celebrated as Gesell." The maitre d' subsequently related to Dewey that Gesell replied by saying, "Oh much more so."[12] During the conference Dewey wrote McGraw boasting, "If I had any sense I would have stolen a march on you by stealing your Johnny and Jimmy films, hired someone who could run a projector, and lectured on the psychology of development with about four illustrated lectures. Wouldn't I have been the hit of the show. However, by not doing so, I've left an opening for you next time."[13]

Dewey was McGraw's protagonist in her uphill battle against hereditary and environmental determinism and her efforts to make a unique contribution to a field already well-colonized by behaviorism and Freudian psychoanalysis. This daunting task was compounded by a public anxious to know the limits of na-

15. Arnold Gesell in the 1930s.
Yale University, Harvey Cushing/John
Hay Whitney Medical Library.

ture and nurture on learning and personality development. The debate over whether behavior was influenced more by environment or heredity, fueled by the rivalry between behaviorist John Watson and maturationist Arnold Gesell, aroused a palpable sense of expectancy among the public that McGraw's research would decisively resolve the issue.[14] Consequently, Dewey and McGraw had to challenge scientific conventions, ignore professional boundaries, and adopt conflicting roles to pursue their conviction that development and inquiry are intrinsically related.

AN ALABAMA SCHOOLGIRL'S DREAM COME TRUE

Perhaps we will never know in any definitive way why Dewey and McGraw were so strongly attracted to one another. But it is evident that they shared a sense of common destiny almost from the very first time they corresponded. McGraw recalled that their extraordinarily close personal and intellectual relationship first began when she wrote to Dewey as an admiring teenager after reading about him in an article in the *Independent* in 1916.[15] This was a profoundly unhappy time for Dewey. He was in the midst of an intellectually combative and personally demeaning exchange with Bourne and his phalanx of culture critics who were challenging the political coherence of pragmatism. Dewey may have found a soul mate in McGraw with whom he shared his doubts about his family life and the unfair criticism he received for his support of American intervention in the First World War. In befriending McGraw, Dewey was able to regain the psychological distance from his immediate personal worries that threatened to engulf him and prevent him from fulfilling his most ambitious remaining scientific agenda.

They continued to correspond frequently until Dewey left for China in late 1918. She received only one touching gift from him during his extended stay there. He sent her a pressed flower with a short note saying it was from the Great Wall of China. When he returned to the United States, McGraw was enrolled in Ohio Wesleyan, where she was pursuing a career in the ministry. Their correspondence picked up again and McGraw soon visited Dewey in New York. Dewey had just opened her telegram that she had sent him weeks before and was surprised by her visit. He graciously took her to a Chinese restaurant for lunch. The lunch left McGraw short for fare for her departure on the subway but she could not bring herself to ask for Dewey's help. Years later, when McGraw related the incident, Dewey was profoundly hurt that McGraw was ashamed to ask him for help. Dewey paid a visit to McGraw at Ohio Wesleyan her senior year. McGraw was ecstatic and her fellow students were quite impressed that a world-famous philosopher would visit a schoolgirl from Alabama. But Dewey continued to take a strong interest in her future and persuaded her to drop her plans to enter the ministry and enroll instead in the Ph.D. program in psychology at Columbia University and Teachers College. Dewey eventually served as a non-departmental member of her dissertation committee.[16]

Not everything went as smoothly for McGraw after she began work on her dissertation. Helen Woolley, director of the child welfare research and McGraw's thesis advisor, suggested that she conduct a comparative study of the early motor development of white and African American babies. Woolley was critical of Gesell's developmental norms and thought that such a biracial study might reveal weaknesses in Gesell's scheme. She suggested that McGraw also employ a test developed by an Austrian psychologist, Charlotte Buhler. McGraw landed a teaching position at the Florida State College for Women, where she immediately began her research. Two obvious challenges first had to be solved: where to do the studies and how to find the babies. McGraw solved the first problem by getting permission from her roommate to use their apartment. She cleverly overcame the second problem by driving around different districts of town looking for diapers on clotheslines. She would simply identify the nature of her study and ask mothers if she could "borrow" their baby for short while. Most mothers cooperated without demur.

Unfortunately, when it came time for McGraw to submit her thesis for approval, Lois Meek had replaced Woolley because of Woolley's ill health. Meek, a Gesell admirer, was not eager to accept McGraw's thesis and postponed an oral defense numerous times. McGraw found evidence that African American babies exceeded their white counterparts in some motor skills, but were slower than white babies to acquire language skills.[17] When the judgment day finally arrived and Meek expressed her objections, McGraw recalled that committee member Harold Pinter saved the day. He defiantly asserted that "any student who goes out searching for diapers on the clothesline to get subjects for an experiment has the potential for becoming a good scientist." Consequently, McGraw said, "The thesis was then accepted."[18]

McGraw also had a stormy relationship with the Institute for Child Guidance, where she served as an intern toward the end of her graduate training. The institute director, David Levy, was a psychoanalytically trained psychiatrist. He expected his staff to conscientiously administer to every child a seemingly endless battery of clinical tests. Staff members were also expected to participate in case discussions. McGraw recalled one staff case discussion that had been particularly amusing. Dr. Levy offered a Freudian explanation for a young patient's chronic enuresis, arguing that the boy did so as a symbolic act of drowning his sister because he resented having to sleep in the same bed with her. McGraw then "impudently" asked whether he could not think of some other explanation.[19] Indeed, after conducting her own research on the subject, McGraw offered a different explanation for why children experience an occasional loss of bladder control. Young children are simply exhibiting the inconsistency and confusion attendant to the demand to integrate new forms of discipline, she explained, while still attempting to perfect an existing repertoire of behavior, such as walking or talking.[20]

Dewey and McGraw were nearly constant companions after Alice's untimely death in 1927 until McGraw was married in 1936. During that time McGraw accompanied Dewey to Scotland for his Gifford Lectures in Edinburgh. She traveled with Dewey on several of his summer voyages to Vienna, where he visited his daughter Lucy and her husband. She also spent many summers with Dewey and his daughters in Nova Scotia in the early 1930s, where Dewey completed his opus, *Logic*, in 1938. Scores of letters they exchanged during this time help document their remarkable personal and professional relationship. McGraw characterized her association with Dewey as "a very devoted sort of daughter-father relationship" in which she was considered a part of the family.[21] McGraw acknowledged in her later years that Dewey, whom she called her "intellectual godfather," was intimately involved in almost every detail of her studies and that many of the ideas and methods she developed were derived from suggestions Dewey made in the course of their continuous interaction.[22]

McGraw's self-effacing attitude was not unusual for women of that era, but she also reflected the sentiments of an admiring student and daughter surrogate, deferring to the fatherly advice of a towering intellect. There was something deeply spiritual about their relationship that defies precise description. They were able to communicate and understand one another's thoughts almost without putting their ideas and feelings into words. This implicit sense of a shared consciousness is vividly illustrated in an interview with pediatrician Milton Senn, who attempted to sort out Dewey's and McGraw's respective roles by ironically asking McGraw

16. Myrtle McGraw and John Dewey, who presided at her wedding in 1936.
Courtesy of Mitzi Wertheim.

Q: Did John Dewey learn enough from you to apply some of your theories and some of your experience into his concept of education?
A: Well, I think I learned the concepts in a way from him, without knowing it. Every now and then I wake up to the fact that some idea that I think was my own, if I happen to pick up something he wrote long ago, he was saying it. My connection with him was just learning by living and by talking, and certainly I discussed everything I did with him.[23]

Dewey's extensive involvement in McGraw's studies was not simply motivated by his evident deep and abiding respect and affection for McGraw, but by the compelling need to ensure that both he and McGraw had sufficient time and resources to address scientific issues that would help resolve questions he had about the relation between development and the structure of inquiry. Dewey publicly acknowledged the importance of McGraw's studies on only two occasions, both in 1935. In an interview with the *New York Times*, Dewey stated that he considered her discoveries comparable in significance to those of his scientific hero Michael Faraday, whose discovery of the principles of electromagnetic induction anticipated field theory and quantum mechanics.[24]

Dewey also praised her work in the introduction to her book documenting her co-twin study, writing that McGraw had tentatively established the general principles of child growth and development.[25] Privately, however, Dewey effusively praised McGraw's work but modestly disclaimed the importance of his own contribution, saying, "You've given me too much credit but I'm proud and happy to be associated with your work."[26] Dewey, in correspondence with Arthur Bentley, acknowledged McGraw's significant influence, saying that:

> It happens that in the last few weeks I have had the occasion to write an introduction to [Myrtle B.] McGraw's report on the development of infants [*Growth: A Study of Johnny and Jimmy*], a study incidentally that ought to revolutionize work in that field. In it I had occasion to criticize the whole child method on the grounds that an individual child could not be investigated until general principles of development had been determined. If I had this point in mind when I wrote the article ["Conduct and Experience"], I might not have reached a satisfactory conclusion, but I think I would have avoided the particular break you have indicated.[27]

Apparently Bentley thought it inconsistent for Dewey to attack behaviorism as reductionist and then to argue that human experience can be explained in terms of underlying behavioral relationships. But Dewey was unprepared in 1930 to clearly specify how such a method could be devised.

PUTTING THE BRAIN AND BEHAVIOR TOGETHER AT THE NEUROLOGICAL INSTITUTE

McGraw initiated her Normal Child Development Study (NCDS) in 1930 after completing graduate studies begun in 1925 in psychology and neuroanatomy. McGraw conducted her research under Dr. Tilney's direction at the Neurological Institute of New York in affiliation with Babies Hospital of the College of Physicians and Surgeons at Columbia University. As noted before, Tilney was closely associated with adherents of the so-called "American school" of psychobiology that included the Herrick brothers, C. M. Child and Adolf Meyer. Tilney taught courses in neuroembryology when the field was in its infancy and directed research before becoming head of the institute in 1935.[28] He was also at the forefront of research on the relation between the brain and behavior before his untimely death in 1938.[29] Tilney sought Dewey's help to coordinate the NCDS with other research projects recommended by the Carnegie Corporation, so that human development could be studied from the broadest possible perspective.[30]

Tilney's extensive comparative studies of the evolution of the brain, described in chapter 6, supported Dewey's contention, stated most explicitly in *Experience and Nature*, that the mastery of erect locomotion marked a decisive event in human history because it gave birth to inquiry.[31] Tilney contended that the human brain developed in response to a series of anatomical and behavioral

17. Frederick Tilney in the 1930s.
Courtesy of The Neurological Institute
and Columbia-Presbyterian Medical Center, New York.

adaptations that culminated in our exquisitely refined motor coordination and
sensory discrimination. For example, Tilney speculated that the development
of hands from paws and the ability to grasp led to changes in posture, hand-eye
coordination, and locomotion which stimulated the growth of the cerebral cortex, eventuating in an enormous enlargement of human intelligence.[32] Tilney
and his colleagues Herrick, Parker, and Child believed that the phases involved
in the progressive advance of the human species could be reconstructed by
identifying the timing and role that the cortex and phylogenetically older cerebellum play in early infant development.[33] Research of this kind provided
Dewey an irresistible and timely opportunity. He could examine in depth
whether the biological sequence through which the nervous system and brain
acquire the powers of thought and judgment foreshadowed the pattern of inquiry.

Dewey surprised his philosophical colleagues by opting for retirement from
Columbia University in 1930. His retirement provided the additional time
he needed to become actively involved in the NCDS throughout the decade.
Dewey was appointed to an advisory council, chaired by Tilney, composed
of scientists reflecting diverse perspectives. Members included Dewey's col-

leagues, psychologists Robert S. Woodworth and Edward L. Thorndike, and faculty members from the College of Physicians and Surgeons such as Willard Rappleye (dean), Rustin McIntosh (head of Babies Hospital), and Ludwig Kast. Charles B. Davenport of the Carnegie Institution of Washington also served as a council member while conducting special research for the NCDS. In addition, Bernard Sachs, who had been Freud's benchmate in Meynert's laboratory, was on the committee, as well as Samuel Orton, a neurologist interested in the growth of the brain. Finally, John B. Watson, the noted behaviorist, and George Coghill, a neuroanatomist with the Wistar Institute in Philadelphia, served as *ad hoc* members, but Coghill was more actively involved providing advice and consultation.[34]

The advisory council of the NCDS met regularly throughout the 1930s to discuss presentations and interim progress reports by McGraw and other staff members, including briefings or talks by members of the advisory council such as Tilney, McIntosh, and Dewey. One of McGraw's associates, Katherine Agate Heyl, who worked in the NCDS and lived with McGraw from 1933 to 1936, recalled that Dewey had an office at Babies Hospital and visited the project on a daily basis.[35] McGraw and Dewey also took part in informal discussions on Thursday evenings with advisory council members, sometimes attracting other interested persons such as Margaret Mead, Arthur Burns, and others.[36]

Grant support that Tilney obtained in 1933 from the Rockefeller General Education Board (GEB) and the Josiah Macy, Jr. Foundation proved to be especially important for two reasons. First, Lawrence Frank, who had assisted Beardsley Ruml at the Laura Spelman Rockefeller Fund, continued to monitor the progress of child development studies for the GEB. Frank defended the need for McGraw's research even though the foundation was already supporting Gesell's ongoing studies of infant development at Yale University. He argued, "Her intent is not establishing age norms as in Gesell's program but is to delineate the sequence through which the child passes and to discover how far that sequence is modifiable by training."[37]

As a founding member of the board of the Josiah Macy, Jr. Foundation under Ludwig Kast, president from 1930 to 1941, and Frank, who served as vice president from 1936 to 1941, Dewey had an unusual opportunity to influence the scope of McGraw's studies. For example, Dewey's daughter Evelyn Dewey was commissioned by the Macy foundation in 1933 to prepare "a more systematic review of existing knowledge, especially with respect to fetal and infant development." She wrote that Tilney and McGraw's research was likely to increase knowledge of the relation between brain and behavior.[38]

Dewey exerted his influence in several other ways beyond acting in an advisory capacity. For example, he participated in preliminary meetings McGraw held with Frank and Tilney to devise a research plan for McGraw's advanced studies,[39] obtained the participation and advice of outside consultants,[40] advised McGraw on negotiating her role and research focus,[41] read and commented on several of McGraw's publications, and urged McGraw not to compromise over her differences with foundation officials who wanted McGraw to investigate behavioral and clinical aspects of brain damage, which eventually led to the termination of her research.[42]

DEWEY'S STAKE IN MCGRAW'S RESEARCH

It was no coincidence that Dewey had attempted to express in aesthetic terms in *Art as Experience* the rhythms of growth that McGraw was trying to conceptualize in quantitative terms in her studies. They both suspected that nature's signature on the mind would be revealed by the pulsating but distinct phases through which the brain and behavior attain synchrony. Dewey expressed aesthetically what he had yet to demonstrate experimentally, that all human experience involves the coalescence of quantitatively variable growth processes (i.e., involving skeletal and neuromuscular structures) and qualitatively variable functional processes, such as walking, communicating, expressing emotions, and so forth, that form the unique behavior and personality of each individual. Dewey was awed by Matisse's ability to evoke entirely different emotions by making only slight alterations in the colors and postures of the human figures he painted, a skill that is well-illustrated in different versions of the Barnes mural *The Dance*.

This aesthetic phenomenon was much akin to the surprising variety of alternative energetic states Maxwell predicted would occur in a molecular system, as a whole, with only slight changes in the position or the momentum of its elements. Both men were successful in their endeavors because they understood how the underlying rhythms that bind complex forces of mass and energy together yield phenomenally distinct events or experiences. Dewey believed that these same natural forces and rhythms of nature were tapped during infancy to convert a wriggling mass of protoplasm into an exquisitely coordinated child who possessed a brain and mind of incalculable power and imagination.

As Dewey's correspondence with Corinne Chisholm indicates, he was still struggling to find a way to resolve the thorny problems of recurrence and entropy posed by Rignano's theory of the energetics of development. Dewey wanted to figure out how it is possible for an organism to reap the resources of past experience to respond more resourcefully and intelligently to future contingencies without exceeding the energy budgeted by entropy to maintain it in a state of equilibrium. Chisholm, a thoughtful philosopher unaffiliated with academic institutions, initiated the correspondence in 1930 by sending Dewey a manuscript titled "The Duality of Experience." Her provocative thesis was that human consciousness dwells in two worlds: a world in which our ideas and energy are embodied in material existence, and an "other world" of fleeting thoughts and possible existences which influence the breadth and depth of the experiences we have. Chisholm posed an argument that bore a striking similarity to that advanced by Hegel and Dewey. She contended that the source of positive action is the negative feeling of absence or incompleteness originating in the "other world" of possibility.[43]

This sounded much like Dewey's premise that potentiality has to do with the power of something that is yet to be possessed. But Chisholm also argued that our intentions and behavior are influenced more strongly by the desire to re-trieve a sense of completeness or wholeness by returning to a prior state of balance or integration than by the desire to be propelled forward by the lure of new but uncertain possibilities. Of course, Dewey had seen this argument ad-vanced before by Rignano, who equated recurrence with *repetition*. The novelty of her argument involved the contention that an organism in a state of ener-getic tension is naturally propelled *backward* rather than forward. An organism that is seemingly propelled forward by its own volition in actuality is simply reacting or adjusting to having already been displaced by a change in its envi-ronment. Chisholm believed that an organism reacting to change in an envi-ronment is essentially restoring a state of equilibrium or the same stable pat-tern of interactions that occurred prior to the disruption. Hence energy is conserved without an increase in entropy.

Dewey was clearly intrigued with her argument. He wrote to her, speculat-ing about the possible implications of her thesis for understanding evolution in non-classical physical terms, saying:

> There is something wrong with the theory of entropy—the fact that difference of temperature during molecular bombardment tends toward a homogeneous state and is a running down of the energies directly involved seems to be experimen-tally established as far as the immediate situation is concerned. But there is some-thing wrong about the absolute generalization of this as a one-way process, the extension of it to the energy of the universe. . . . [a point that Boltzmann had made before] Is it true that the co-presence of these processes (i.e., equilibrium and entropy) indicates there is no evolution as a whole since at times, the changes are all two ways, and that special evolutions occur in nature? Taking the whole, it seems as if the same balances had to be maintained at all times with the tensions and developments inside, so to speak.[44]

Chisholm, like Boltzmann, believed that tension entailed disorder and dis-organization. In this state of existence, the parts of the system are just as likely to revert to a prior state of equilibrium as to dissipate into a higher state of entropy. Nevertheless, Dewey could not agree with the assumption that tension is equivalent to disorder. Disorder implies a break in *serial order*, or the state of transition. Tension implies the possibility of *release* from the temporary oppo-sition of negation and assertion. Hence, a break in serial order meant, for Dewey, that new factors are substituted that carry the momentum from their energetic interaction forward, as a whole, to assume a new state of equilibrium. Dewey was unable to say how energy was conserved to attain this higher level of integration, but he suspected that it had something to do with when the sequence or *serial order* in which structures and functions interact is altered to produce an outcome that is different than before. Since Chisholm's plausible argument possessed some merit and could not simply be dismissed, Dewey urged her to get C. J. Herrick's reaction. Not surprisingly, the like-minded Herrick questioned her contention that nothing really *new* happens in nature or experience. He observed that:

> It seems to me that nature faces forward as well as backward. What you say about tension, backward etc., is all true, but it is not the whole story. Nature is never exactly repetitive. Restoration of equilibrium is not usually a return to the old equilibrium, but very often the establishment of a new pattern of equilibrium. This gives satisfaction and often a keener satisfaction than would a return to previously experienced patterns. Nature and experience run in cycles, it is true, but each cycle runs in its course, not a repetition of the old one. The pattern is spiral, not repetitive. There is a natural motive force to *recover*, but there is just as truly a natural instinctive force to *discover*.[45]

Dewey resumed work on *Logic* in 1934 after dropping initial work on it in 1928, but several crucial issues involving the origin, structure, and function of judgment in development remained unresolved. Dewey told Chisholm he was grappling unsuccessfully with the problem of discrimination and comparison in judgment—a methodological issue of great importance to McGraw's study of normal growth.[46] Dewey proposed, in his emergent theory of mind, that learning occurred not merely through the repetition or application of previous experience but through experiments designed to acquire new experiences. Dewey believed that infants must somehow be able to exercise rudimentary forms of judgment to progress through the not previously experienced stages of locomotion in order to master walking erect. McGraw's co-twin studies from 1930 to 1935 and advanced quantitative studies conducted from 1936 to 1941 addressed these issues experimentally.[47] As Dewey's correspondence with Chisholm attests, he was preoccupied with the dilemma posed by recurrence and frequently vacillated on a satisfactory solution until the year that he published *Logic*.[48]

ADAPTING EMBRYOLOGICAL METHODS FOR BEHAVIORAL STUDIES

George Coghill's involvement as a consultant to the NCDS deserves further comment because of his enormous influence on McGraw's studies and the importance of his ideas to Dewey's theory of inquiry. Herrick's older brother Clarence launched Coghill on his career in neuroanatomy and psychology. Coghill got his Ph.D. in zoology at Brown University in 1902, where he took several courses from the psychologist E. B. Delabarre. Coghill taught at the University of Kansas, among other schools, before taking a position at the Wistar Institute in Philadelphia from 1925 to 1936.[49] Coghill promised Clarence

18. George E. Coghill in the 1930s.
Courtesy of Dr. Robert M. Williamson.

Herrick that he would "study the nervous system as an approach to psychology and philosophy, if that way were ever opened to me." Coghill redeemed his promise. He found Dewey's criticisms of stimulus-response theory and conditioning persuasive and explicitly acknowledged his intellectual debt to Dewey on several occasions.[50] Coghill and C. J. Herrick assisted Dewey in his attempt to find evidence, through McGraw's studies, to support his contention in *Logic* that human intelligence evolved from a long series of ontogenetic adaptations involving the continuous reintegration of the structural and functional traits of human existence.

Coghill challenged the conventional wisdom, as Dewey had done decades earlier, that complex behavior is constructed from chains of simple reflexes. He argued that the "individuation of partial (i.e., reflexive) behavior patterns emerges through the progressive restriction of a previously integrated total pattern."[51] This conception was based on his discovery that "local segmental responses" (a term Coghill used instead of reflexes) occur not as a result of stimulation but by virtue of being released through the *suspension* of inhibition sustaining an integrated response.[52] In other words, the diffuse writhing and wiggling of the whole body occurring in the early stages of growth must be brought under control or inhibited in order for arms, legs, or fingers to be exercised first independently of one another. Only subsequently is it possible to coordinate these separate movements into complex behaviors.

Coghill was inspired by Bohr's injunction that life processes, although more complex, could be understood in (but not reduced to) complementary physical terms.[53] He believed that his research corroborated Dewey's Maxwellian view of development as a continuous transformation of "matter *in* motion" by showing that neural structures provide the substrata for behavioral and functional change throughout development.[54] Coghill seemed to offer a provisional solution to the conundrum of recurrence posed by Chisholm. McGraw would eventually find evidence that supported Coghill's theory in her subsequent studies of locomotion. The displacement in space is not the most salient feature of organisms undergoing environmental pressures of change. Rather it is the release from inhibitory forces that allows an organism to maintain its separate functions in a stable state of integration. The potential energy that is conserved during these moments of temporary equilibrium is released to enable slight modifications in the order in which separate functions are combined and subsequently reintegrated. This is why Dewey believed, contrary to Chisholm, that the release from tension constitutes an act of reconstruction of behavior rather than a recurrence or return to a prior pattern.

Coghill also found evidence that neural growth anticipates the acquisition of function, as some movements associated with walking, such as stepping, can be performed before independent locomotion is possible. Coghill considered this phenomenon of "forward reference," as he termed it, to constitute an example of learning because these precocious movements contribute later to their proper positioning in a sequence of action.[55] This idea was controversial, especially for those psychologists who believed that local reflexes must be well-developed *before* infants engage in more complex behaviors. Gesell interpreted Coghill's term "forward reference" to mean that neural maturation is genetically predetermined and that behavioral development cannot be hastened by stimulation or exercise. Yet Coghill used the term to call attention to the fact that complex motor behaviors, foreshadowed by advanced neural development, cannot be fully integrated to form stable patterns until consolidated through practice or exercise.

Nevertheless, Coghill's studies drew criticism from his own student, E. A. Swenson, and Swenson's colleague W. F. Windle, whose studies supported the competing theory that local reflexes emerge prior to total patterns.[56] Gilbert Gottlieb astutely observed that arguments about whether a specific kind of response is due to the nature of the stimulation or determined by the state of the nervous system has a chicken-or-egg character. This fallacy can be easily avoided, according to Gottlieb, by allowing that "the observed behavior is a joint function of the kind of stimulation employed and the developmental state of the nervous system at the time of stimulation."[57] In commenting on this debate, Gottlieb perceptively noted that no one raised the obvious question "why behavioral development should inevitably follow either the total pattern or the additive course." Only when the possibility is conceived of a "bidirectional relation between structure and function, so that function can determine structure as well as the reverse, Gottlieb argued, "that it becomes an investigative question to ask why behavioral development takes the course(s) it does."[58]

Coghill never took an explicit position on the maturation vs. learning debate during the 1930s, as Oppenheim points out, thus inviting different interpretations.[59] Nevertheless, Coghill closely followed Gesell's and McGraw's infant studies because of their ramifications for his work. Coghill visited Gesell's laboratory at Yale on at least one occasion in 1933, combining the visit with his first visit with McGraw at Babies Hospital.[60] Gesell's experimental studies were nearly finished by the time he met Coghill, while McGraw was just getting her studies underway and could incorporate Coghill's suggestions into the experimental design.

McGraw readily adopted Coghill's methods in her infant studies, contending that "it is the experimental embryologists, not psychologists who deserve credit for formulating the most adequate theory of behavior development."[61] McGraw acknowledged Coghill's extensive influence by saying that "Coghill visited my laboratory many, many, many times—sometimes with Tilney, sometimes not. We talked and exchanged ideas. It was he, John Dewey, and the babies that got me thinking of process, not end result, or achievement."[62] Indeed, McGraw found evidence that infant behavior develops through the unraveling of general movements similar to those Coghill observed in the larval development of salamanders. McGraw stressed also that collaboration among them was essential to the success of the project, saying "[h]ad he [Tilney] lived longer, Tilney, Coghill and Dewey and I (let me say the babies) might have arrived at a synthesis of the meaning of structure and function."[63]

GENERIC TRAITS OF HUMAN EXPERIENCE

Dewey argued in *Experience and Nature* that generic traits of human behavior and development did not consist of isolated capacities but potentialities that are only fully realized through the serial processes of growth.[64] He also contended that consciousness plays a fundamental role in prolonging the doubt and reflection necessary to transform human behavior.[65] Nevertheless, Dewey encountered great difficulty in rendering his conceptions of consciousness and generic traits of experience intelligible to his colleagues, failing to persuade them that these psychological attributes constituted the nucleus of logic and inquiry.[66] Sidney Hook interpreted Dewey's generic traits, incorrectly in my opinion, to be changeless, ultimate and irreducible traits of nature.[67] Dewey, however, believed that generic traits undergo transformation by being combined to form new ones.

Dewey's use of the term "generic" was unfortunate, for the term had certain evolutionary connotations involving the lineage of species, including the notion that humans and apes evolved or descended from a common ancestor.

But he used the term "generic" in the epigenetic sense to characterize the evolution of ontogenetic processes (i.e., early development) which do not necessarily entail natural selection nor common descent. Similar difficulties attended
Dewey's notion of consciousness that critics thought he used to designate an
attribute of mind, such as the capacity for reflection or introspection. But
Dewey saw consciousness as a force intrinsic to judgment that rendered indeterminate ideas and behavior into determinate forms. That is why Dewey and
McGraw believed that far more information was needed to specify the process
of becoming than the resulting state of being.

McGraw explicitly stated that a primary objective of her co-twin study was
to see whether the principles of embryological growth applied to developmental processes during infancy.[68] The distinctive feature of initial embryological
growth is indeterminacy. Experimentalists discovered that the course of development could be altered during this critical period of indeterminacy by trans-
planting cellular tissue in another region, thereby changing the cell's destiny.
McGraw hypothesized that early infancy is governed by these same principles
of growth. McGraw considered behavioral development to consist of "a process of interchange of energies within an organism and energies with its environment."[69] She and Dewey also believed that development could be modified
by "altering the energy relationship between organism and environment," and
by confronting infants with situations involving uncertainty and doubt.[70] Consequently, they considered it possible to change the course of development by
stimulating and recombining behaviors in a different order. McGraw simply
grafted together movements associated with different behaviors, just as embryologists transplant cells and tissues from one region to another, to see what
form they would assume within the parameters of a new situation or different
environment.

McGraw saw behavior playing a key role in the coalescence of neural substrata into centers of action capable of sustaining integrated forms of action.
According to McGraw, neurobehavioral development consists of a series of
neuroanatomical reconstructions that enable a more economical and integrated
repertoire of movements. McGraw hypothesized that the initial energy of neural growth exceeds the capacity of existing muscular structures to channel this
energy effectively, resulting in excessive and diffuse forms of behavior. She
believed that the opposing flexor and extensor movements characteristic of
many forms of locomotion are integrated through rhythmic processes that facilitate the completion of neural circuitry required for integrated forms of
action.

Most neurologists believed that primitive reactions (i.e., older phyletic traits)
that babies exhibit shortly after birth, such as the Moro reflex, or diffuse reaction to surprise, soon disappear and thus are unlikely to influence the course of
subsequent behavior. Coghill and McGraw challenged this conventional understanding. They contended that early behavior is highly integrated and only

subsequently gets differentiated through experience into individual forms, as proposed by Coghill. McGraw reasoned that diffuse reactions exhibited at birth are not dysfunctional but instrumental in the development of subsequent behavior. She suspected that the Moro reflex, the diffuse reaction to surprise, and other behaviors, such as reflexive stepping and grasping, would persist if stimulated, and could be enlisted to perform later ontogenetic behaviors such as roller skating.

THE CONTINGENCY OF ORDER IN DEVELOPMENT

McGraw demonstrated the fruitfulness of these hypotheses by discovering that phylogenetic traits previously considered useless when taken in isolation from other behaviors proved instrumental in hastening the emergence and enhancing the quality of its ontogenetic counterpart when combined with other behaviors. For example, the seemingly disorganized swaying of the torso and alternating movements of legs and arms appearing in the early stages of prone locomotion enabled an infant to swim before being able to crawl.[71] McGraw's discovery that Johnny (the twin receiving special exercise) could skate before he could walk smoothly also demonstrated that the rhythmic stepping movements involved in skating could be stimulated to hasten the attainment of erect locomotion.[72]

Finally, she showed that the introduction of a new movement in a sequence of behavior results in the elimination of more laborious methods. This was demonstrated by Johnny, who was able to dismount a stool by eliminating several intervening steps when placed in a standing rather than sitting position and after suggesting that he try grasping the sides to lower himself down. In discovering that babies could accomplish feats considered impossible at their age, McGraw was challenging the mistaken belief that early stimulation was harmful or that precocious performances or complex behaviors were unnatural. Through her innovative experiments, McGraw was attempting to demonstrate that infants could actually benefit from early stimulation and that this would enhance their capacity to learn.

McGraw's studies also directly challenged Gesell's contention that motor development cannot be accelerated or altered by stimulation. McGraw observed that early experience produced subtle differences in attitude and awareness among infants that contributed to variations in the rate and course of their behavioral development. She also found behavioral evidence that the increased coordination afforded by the development of the prefrontal control and inhibition operates selectively by alternating between upper and lower regions of the body, interacting with the cerebellum to gradually alter the extent and range of movement in each region. She considered this evidence that some behaviors could be performed before complete growth and maturation of underlying neural structures. The introduction of these novel challenges in ontogeny,

The Function of Judgment in Inquiry

19. Myrtle McGraw assisting Johnny Woods on a steep slide in 1932, when he was 22 months old.
Courtesy of Mitzi Wertheim.

McGraw argued, enable infants to tap the potential energy of growth that lies dormant in the phenotype. McGraw considered the maturationist thesis mistaken. She found instead that neuromuscular functions believed inessential to development contribute to "fundamental processes of learning."[73]

McGraw's analyses of the neuromuscular dynamics of development helped Dewey to formulate more precisely an alternative to the traditional rules of logical inference and validity. The validity of the maturationist doctrine that human development occurs through some fixed, irreversible stages depended on whether the traits or factors purported to be involved are actually connected through some underlying sequence or process. Hypotheses regarding the existence of such relationships can be confirmed, according to Dewey, only by experimentation, as McGraw demonstrated, to see if such connections persist by changing the sequence or pattern in which they appear.

Dewey insisted that generic traits are neither irreducible natural phenomena nor fixed hereditary attributes of human behavior. The capacity to walk, to communicate, or to express emotions emerges only when the underlying natural, biological, and behavioral forces involving gravity, movement, sentience, and gesture are fully integrated. Accordingly, Dewey used "generic propositions" to describe the quantitative (i.e., instrumental) and qualitative (i.e., expressive) traits of a situation or event that are hypothesized to be connected in some way, as suggested by an underlying meaningful pattern of behavior. Infants vary considerably in how they respond to the gravitational and perceptual challenges involved in rolling over, sitting up, crawling, creeping, walking, and other generic kinds of human locomotion.[74] For this reason, it is not always easy to classify the behavior that is being exhibited or to identify the goal that is being sought.

That is why "universal propositions" must specify a set of operations to be instituted, Dewey argued, that elicit a trait that is only one of kind, as illustrated by an infant's reflexive attempt to right itself when placed in an inverted position. Universal propositions also must support inferences about the relationship between kinds, as McGraw demonstrated, by showing that similar movements are combined differently in swimming, crawling, and creeping.[75] Dewey concluded, therefore, that productive generic propositions yield discoveries about how contingencies of order affect and redefine our habits or methods of inquiry, altering our expectations about conceivable and attainable forms of human existence.[76] Dewey was acknowledging that propositional discourse can never completely exhaust the totality of phenomenal experiences possible in nature because the occasions for and content of those experiences are themselves subject to *natural* contingencies beyond any one individual's control.

THE COMMON PATTERN OF DEVELOPMENT AND INQUIRY

Perhaps McGraw's most important but least understood contribution to knowledge about infant growth was her conception of the *bidirectional* nature of early development. She proposed that neural structures and behavioral functions interact throughout early development. She likened this process to the interweaving of separate threads to form an integrated tapestry or repertoire of motor and cognitive skills. It is noteworthy that she first employed this metaphor in *Growth*, which was published four years *before* Gesell advanced his own theory of the "spiral organization of reciprocal interweaving" to explain infant development.[77] McGraw and Gesell advanced extraordinarily powerful and elegant explanations of the complex dynamics of neuromuscular development that, in many respects, complement one another. The metaphors Gesell and McGraw employ to explain development are highly suggestive. However, there are several crucial differences in their respective theories that explain why they adopted fundamentally different perspectives about the effects of early experience on development and learning and the importance of brain-behavior interaction for neuromuscular integration.

Gesell contended that behavior emerges from the inside out; that is, specific traits initially reside in the genetic substratum and manifest themselves only after passing through successive stages of latency. Gesell held that older traits are never directly expressed in manifest behavior but subsumed and reformed through recombinant processes. McGraw did not accept this principle of genetic latency. She believed that all traits must be expressed in behavior, no matter how briefly, for extensive remodeling and eventual neuromuscular integration to occur.

Gesell employed the spiral metaphor to suggest how some traits temporarily split off and diverge from one another as they come within the field of influence of other traits, before recombining to form a more complex pattern. Traits that become separated through divergence look like they are "retreating," according to Gesell, but are actually "more mature" because they do not continue on the same trajectory but spiral upward to a "higher level."[78] For example, the pincer or plucking movement represents a higher form of prehension than the more oblique scissors closure represented. Gesell believed that this process by which behavioral traits attain greater complexity occurs solely through mechanisms of reciprocal innervation and inhibition at the subcortical level. There is no cortical involvement and thus these attainments do not entail deliberate or purposeful control. Gesell also saw only a limited role for environmental stimulation, individual experience, and learning in the attainment of developmental outcomes.

Unlike Gesell, McGraw attempted to find out whether cortex is involved in early development. She found evidence that cortical inhibition is not only essential to voluntary action, but is indispensable to the formation of neuronal connections necessary for the coordination of feeling, movement, thought, and action. McGraw believed that cortical inhibition spreads selectively by alternating between upper and lower regions of the body, enabling infants and toddlers to gradually gain increased control over the amount, sequence, and direction of their movement. As cortical functions spread, new behaviors emerge, creating new centers of dominance and the exaggerated or excessive exercise associated with the acquisition of a new capability. The cross-pressures from these competitive processes frequently result in the regression toward more rudimentary and involuntary forms of behavior.

McGraw indicated that the point of intersection of accelerating and decelerating behaviors constituted a critical juncture in integration of behavior, involving two related events illustrated in Figure 21 (see p. 241). Each new trait in a behavior complex (e.g., 1, 2, 3, etc.) contributing to prone locomotion, for example, assumes the leading position in the sequence, subsequently displacing prior traits to the end of the series, where their influence is curtailed (i.e., traits d–g) and/or eventually eliminated (traits a–c). Consequently, excess activity governed by the subcortex (traits a–c) is inhibited with the onset of cortical control in the transition from phase 3 to 4, enabling a temporary, stable pattern to form, before the locus of behavior shifts to new centers of (cortical) control. This checks the regression or further diminution of previously attained capabilities until a new integration is attained by recombination through substitution and displacement.

Thus development proceeds through growth phases involving exaggerated and inhibited movements, the elimination of excess motion, and the consolidation and integration of complex behaviors.[79] This pattern is illustrated in the development of erect locomotion by the alternation between a wobbling and rigid gait, the adoption of wide and narrow stances, the raising and lowering of arms for balance, and so forth. This alternating sequence involving frequent reversions to more rudimentary behavior seems paradoxical because individual variations in the timing, composition, and direction of movements occur without altering the general pattern of progressive development. Nevertheless, with each backward swing, older traits and emergent capabilities are actually recombined and reintegrated in slightly different ways, according to McGraw, to alter the form or configuration of a total pattern. Infants and toddlers contribute to their own development by controlling how much conscious effort they put into practicing or rehearsing movements and having experiences that contribute to the integration of their behavior.

The importance of McGraw's principles of development in Dewey's analysis of judgment in *Logic* cannot be overstated. The distinctive pattern of development McGraw discovered furnished analogies that Dewey used to advance novel arguments about the structure of judgment and function of inference in inquiry. These principles led Dewey to argue that reasoning did not conform to the absolute and non-reversible rules of identity and contradiction, but followed an indirect course, involving the formulation of functionally specific responses to contingencies in human development.[80] Dewey rejected the view that we reason from particular to universal, gradually accumulating knowledge from one inference to the next. Dewey contended instead that inquiry commences with suggestive generalizations about how separate factors are related according to their position in a sequence of interaction. Only after observing how these factors interact over time are we able to specify whether one thing precedes another or know that one thing or event is related to or identical to another.

Dewey believed that the alternating phases McGraw identified, through which development progresses, demonstrated that judgment emerges through overlapping stages of comparison through contrast, reorientation, and redirection that increasingly delineate the scope of effective thought and action. The pattern of inquiry Dewey proposes is also striking in its recapitulation of the stages through which Hegel's dialectic of consciousness realizes its self-identity or "being-for-self." Hegel showed how understanding is attained through the synthesis of different states of consciousness involving a process of affirmation, negation, and reintegration of the subject and objects of human thought. Accordingly, uncertainty instigates a process of "requalification" through "groping," as Dewey calls it in *Logic*, involving the identification of the limits or boundaries of an indeterminate situation.[81] This is comparable to the diffuse writhing and wriggling movements that McGraw found infants making in their initial attempt to explore the limits of their immediate environments. Infants respond to these limits with a general attitude of acquiescence. Similarly, Dewey characterized this initial stage of the dialectic of inquiry as involving an attitude of "bare acquiescence" or assent to the limits of a situation.[82] According to Dewey, doubt arises the moment that acquiescence is suspended, commencing the process of judgment. Significantly, Dewey considered each step in the process of judgment to be mediated by an attitude as evidenced by the shift of mood in verb tenses from the indicative "is" to opative "may be" to the imperative "must be."

The next stage of judgment involves the effort to differentiate specific characteristics and kinds against the background of more general phenomena. Generic propositions are invoked at this point, according to Dewey, to distinguish traits according to whether they belong to one kind or another.[83] McGraw's infants illustrated this stage in their deliberate efforts to attain balance by controlling the frequency and direction of their movements, contributing to one form of locomotion rather than another. Infants are able to unravel, as it were, sweeping, unfocused movements into discrete and controllable parts or segments which can be recombined into different sequences of behavior.

Finally a point is reached, after experimental operations have been performed as specified by "universal propositions," when extraneous elements (i.e., hypotheses proven incorrect or movements deemed inessential) are eliminated. When remaining traits are sufficiently integrated (as exemplified by a stable pattern of walking, involving the seamless integration of stance, stride, and gait), then final warranted judgments can be embodied in propositional form. Dewey characterized this stage of inquiry as a "reaction from some into all," when phenomena sharing the same qualitative attributes as one kind are integrated to form generalizations applying to all such kinds.[84] This is a moment when self-consciousness is recognized as a tool to expand the boundaries of what is known by removing that which is already known from blocking our perception of what lies beyond.

WHY DOUBT IS INTRINSIC TO DEVELOPMENT

The enormous challenges Dewey faced in making his theory of inquiry understandable to philosophers was no more surprising than McGraw's failure to make headway in getting psychologists to appreciate the novelty of her experimental studies. In their rush to embrace modern science, many philosophers and psychologists purged their discourse of so-called metaphysical terms, such as "mind" and "consciousness," in favor of "stimulus," "response," "association," "perception," and "conditioning." These were terms that squared with conventional logic. Learning progressed one stimulus at a time just as reasoning occurred through incremental fact-gathering processes involving one inference at a time. Great leaps of imagination or unanticipated discoveries were believed to be largely restricted to a few geniuses whose thought processes defied logical explanation. Although Freud acknowledged the importance of environmental factors in learning, he believed that the mechanisms governing thought were not open to logical analysis but were concealed in the unconscious. Despite some theoretical differences, behaviorists and Freudians were in agreement that human experience is accumulated through memories of associations governed primarily by fear, pain, and pleasure.

Dewey's conception of human psychology differed fundamentally from these other theories. Dewey clearly rejected the behaviorist and psychoanalytic assertion that fearful or anxious reactions to the unknown have been preserved in human evolution because these conservative responses have survival value. In Dewey's view, uncertainty was just as likely to evoke curiosity as fear and withdrawal. Moreover, Dewey argued that more typically, individuals must make complex judgments about values that do not directly affect human survival. Dewey also contended, contrary to Gesell, that learning occurred during the earliest stages of development. Dewey argued that the emergence of consciousness and the suppression of immediate, impulsive reactions made learning possible. And, as described before, Dewey viewed inhibition as a positive rather than negative force in reflective behavior.

Dewey wanted McGraw to determine how an attitude of doubt affects learning and reasoning processes. Dewey considered this issue fundamental to supporting his contention that inquiry is grounded in preverbal, psychobiological processes.[85] He believed that "doubt as a relationship of two minds preceded the relationship between two ideas in one mind."[86] Rules for reasoning arose, according to Dewey, to resolve doubt in specific situations. Dewey argued in *Experience and Nature* that communication (a generic trait) involves a process of mutual accommodation and adjustment. Common meanings are derived from shared feelings and methods are adopted through which participants cooperate in identifying factors that lead to both anticipated and unexpected events.[87] The experimental twin Johnny was not learning in a vacuum, but he was converting the stimulation McGraw provided into ideas that inspired novel behavior. McGraw had to develop effective means of communicating with and interpreting infants' preverbal signs and gestures so as not to interfere with or limit the development and exercise of their own judgment.

Similarly, Dewey and McGraw considered effective communication to be crucial to their collaboration. Dewey believed, like Hegel, that the full implications of ideas become apparent when ideas are stripped from individual ownership and set free to circulate, grow, and be developed among many minds. McGraw benefited from Dewey's non-proprietary attitude toward his ideas. She recalled years later, "He [Dewey] was marvelous. He would never once say, 'You are right or. You are wrong.' Instead, in his own quiet way, either by question or suggestion he would ask if I had considered some other angle."[88] Dewey was simply repeating Hegel's injunction that she remain silent in the presence of nature. That is why McGraw spent a good deal of time initially just observing the movements and behaviors of newborns. McGraw was uncertain about these exploratory methods, and she admitted years later that she told Dewey she was "not literally following the recommendations of her graduate professors as to the scientific methodology." McGraw observed that she "must have mentioned it to Dewey at least once too often," because Dewey looked her straight in the eye and said, "I've told you many times that your methods are sound!"[89]

Dewey contended that the neurological and psychological foundations of learning processes could be better understood if infants were given the freedom to devise their own motor strategies to respond to unfamiliar situations. McGraw interpreted this experimentally to mean that if infants were confronted with uncertain situations involving multiple sources of stimulation and alternative motor options, they would be likely to suppress or inhibit an immediate, reflexive response and to mount a coordinated response. Thus, when confronted with uncertainty, she thought infants were likely to suppress an immediate response until they got a feeling for the situation as a whole. Consequently, McGraw challenged infants, through non-verbal gestures, to extend their proficiency beyond those conditions already under their control. She placed them in situations that required problem solving through inventive motor responses, such as that involved in climbing off a stool, roller skating, or riding a tricycle. These innovative techniques of suggestive stimulation revealed how infants learn by adopting different physical postures and attitudes, and by drawing out and elaborating the physical movements involved.

McGraw observed that infants demonstrate their inventiveness by using their motor skills to obtain the psychological distance and judgment needed to gain leverage over a situation. Johnny and other experimental subjects appeared better able than controls to size up a situation by shifting their focus of attention between foreground and background features of a situation. Johnny resisted the urge that Jimmy exhibited to jump to reach a lure dangling beyond his reach, or to grab the closest box and jump from it to get the lure. Instead, he patiently rounded up boxes and stacked them in decreasing order of size, creating a platform sufficiently stable to reach the lure. Jimmy took a much longer time to master the same task because he lacked experience in attaining psychological distance needed to assess situations due to his more limited opportunities for exercising his motor judgment.

McGraw's research also rubbed against the grain of behaviorist orthodoxy that reduced consciousness to a minor epiphenomenon of behavior. Behaviorists ruled out attitudes or emotions as reliable indicators of consciousness, as they were thought to be either hereditary expressions of temperament or instinctual (or defensive) reactions triggered by fear or uncertainty. However, she found evidence that infants afforded early stimulation confront challenging situations with greater comprehension and self-confidence. Johnny's early opportunity to attain a sense of equilibrium or balance through roller skating, for example, seemed to increase his awareness, poise, and self-confidence. He tended to pause and gauge the demands of a problematic situation, unlike Jimmy, and he devised a more effective sequence of actions to overcome challenges. He showed a greater ability to estimate distances, to compare sizes and shapes of objects, and to employ tools more effectively to solve problems. Johnny also demonstrated more persistence and was less temperamental.

Jimmy was more direct but less deliberate. He succumbed to frustration and returned to more rudimentary and laborious methods when more complex behaviors proved elusive. In contrast, Johnny's "acquiescent" attitude, as Mc-Graw characterized it, best exemplified Hegel's notion and Dewey's contention that the postponement of an immediate response prolongs inquisitiveness and increases openness to the suggestiveness of the situation. Consequently, Johnny was better able to comprehend the requirements of the situation in its entirety, thus increasing his ability to convert an indeterminate situation into one that yielded more readily to his direction and control.

McGraw concluded from these experiments that the challenges of early motor development are instrumental to increasing awareness and facilitating judgment. Infants advance in motor development by adopting postures and perspectives that enable them to sense limitations to balance, locomotion, and perception differently in order to overcome them. According to McGraw, judgment is derived from somatic feelings and attitudes rooted in the subconscious. Consciousness emerges in conjunction with inhibition to furnish the delay needed to render these feelings explicit. Judgment then can be employed as a tool of memory and cognition to gauge and combine different movements and gestures into coherent, replicable, and transformable behavioral repertoires.

McGraw's insightful studies showed how quantitative and qualitative elements of human experience become integrated. These same judgments regarding balance, synchrony, and proportionality involved in physical movement are later enlisted by infants to personally experience and meaningfully express complex and sometimes conflicting emotional states. Just as infants must experience more than one form of movement to master different postures and forms of locomotion, so too must they be able to undergo and endure different moods and states in order to experience how emotions place different demands on their physical and mental energy. Emotions give shape to a field of energy relationships among neural, metabolic, and physiological streams, which enables infants to eventually acquire a sense of self. Transient emotional experiences provide a temporary readout of the state of the whole organism.

Judgment performs an accounting function by enabling infants to detect discrepancies, based on force, movement, contrast, and balance, to distinguish between a currently experienced state and a preferred one and to know what needs to be done to get to the preferred one. Consciousness performs critical roles in determining where the *difference* lies between precariousness and balance, between asymmetry and synchrony, and between disparity and proportionality. Consciousness and judgment work in tandem with emotions to enable us to determine whether what one does makes a difference that has value.

NATURALIZING QUANTITATIVE JUDGMENT

McGraw's experimental research supported Dewey's fundamental conviction that the human capacity for inquiry is formed through natural processes whereby individual bodies, brains, and behavior are structurally and functionally integrated. This is no better illustrated than in two penultimate chapters in *Logic* where Dewey advances key arguments about how propositions ordered in sets and series attain signifying force in inquiry, as foreshadowed in processes of human growth and development. Each of these arguments is grounded in evidence from McGraw's co-twin studies of growth and development.

Hegel's analyses of quantity and the role of comparison and measurement in propositional reasoning helped Dewey formulate crucial arguments about the role of judgment in inquiry. Hegel saw mathematics as a powerful tool in logic and scientific inquiry. He believed that quantitative calculations are completely indifferent to qualitative differences found in nature. Natural phenomena can be counted and re-represented in innumerable abstract ways that, according to Hegel, do not depend on the way they appear to us in sensation or perception. However, Dewey continued to have doubts in his chapter in *Logic* on "Propositions of Quantity in Judgment" about whether this accurately characterized the "operational" function of propositions about quantity. Counting conceivably can go on endlessly as long as obstacles or limits are not encountered in doing so.

McGraw's babies learned quickly that there is a big difference between kicking or stepping in place and attempting to reach something by moving toward it in a consistent direction. The limits to reaching something are not established solely by how many steps it takes to get there. Another important consideration is the proportionate amount of effort that must be expended through a series of intermediate challenges to overcome (e.g., moving around furniture, negotiating slippery tile surfaces, and so forth), and by the capacity to adopt and hold an appropriate attitude of determination until the object is grasped. These latter challenges are qualitative, not quantitative; they establish the actual limits the baby must overcome to attain any one specific objective. Importantly, McGraw argued that the likelihood is extremely small that any individual baby ever fully exhausts the complete range or universe of alternative maneuvers that could be employed in reaching something because their range of possible opportunities to do so are themselves limited. That is why Dewey believed that the limits that humans encounter in thought and behavior are always provisional rather than absolute.

Dewey contended that these same considerations about measurement, force, and the contingencies of order apply to propositional judgments about quantity. The possible range that phenomena may vary qualitatively, according to Dewey, extends beyond and is never fully exhausted by or reduced to deductive propositions based on discrete quantitative measurements. This indeterminacy of propositional logic arises for three essential reasons. First, Dewey argues in reverting to arguments he first made in *Art as Experience,* measurement always extrapolates from ongoing events that possess endurance and spread. Phenomena that occur over time may be experienced differently as new elements are noticed and come into focus and as others recede into the background. Quantitative propositions enable inquiry to go forward because they allow us to hold constant the force of the evidence derived from initial experiences. This is illustrated when a baby crawls for the first time. It believes it will reach its rattle with enough effort, even though it gets only occasional glimpses and actually may be veering badly off-course.

Consequently, a baby's success in reaching a rattle will depend on whether other relevant conditions affecting the outcome, such as moving around furniture obstructing the pathway, can be brought under control. If such contingencies do arise, then they become additional limiting conditions that further weaken the force (i.e., generality) or constancy of the initial proposition. These contingencies affect the order in which propositions are stated involving the relationship between assertions with the broadest generality to those with the most specific applicability. For example, a baby will either lower its expectations and cry, or it will try to adjust its approach by devising strategies designed to remove constraints to attaining an overall objective and to circumvent the unexpected obstacles that it encounters. Similarly, the assertion that all babies crawl before they walk is not universal and invariant, but is subject to intervening factors or experiences that result in some infants mastering walking without ever having crawled. Dewey insisted that propositions within a series must be reciprocally related such that each successive proposition specifies the conditions that will result in the transformation from one kind of thing or event into another with a wider or narrower field of applicability, depending on the direction of the argument.

Finally, Dewey argued that quantitative judgment is subject to the physical or perceptual limitations of access that make a shared point of reference and comparison difficult but essential to establish. McGraw's babies responded to this challenge with considerable ease because, unlike adults, they are more accustomed to having to continually adjust to their own rapidly changing bodily proportions by adopting postures that permit new vantage points or bases of comparison. Not every change of perspective has value that moves inquiry forward—a contingency that babies experience when they try to use objects ill-suited to perform a particular task. Functionality can be better determined by observing the consequences of using an object to perform several different tasks involving contrasting purposes.

Galileo and other seventeenth-century scientists were confronted with similar technical difficulties that babies encounter in trying to accurately gauge a new situation without a reliable point of reference. This problem was solved when scientists realized that accurate measurement required only that they adopt standard units of measure. This disposed of the mistaken realist assumption that devices used to record change literally represent and exhaust the range of circumstances in which the phenomena can vary. Advances in measurement came about by adopting a *relational* view of knowledge whereby change is construed in terms of how things may *co-vary*. This change is progressive in the sense that a wider range of variables can be substituted or interchanged with one another without changing their basis of comparison.

Dewey asserted that if judgment is understood in these functional terms, then its fundamental role in "ordered" propositional discourse can be better appreciated. In his chapter on "Propositions Ordered in Sets and Series," Dewey introduces a key distinction from Maxwellian physics by arguing that the order of propositions must be "rigorous and productive."[90] In saying that inferences about order must be rigorous, Dewey does not mean that one proposition must follow from another in a *temporal* sense. This would reinstate the primacy of a linear view of the world whereby the future is determined by the past. Instead, Dewey argues that a proposition must be "equivalent in logical force to that which preceded it; otherwise it follows *after* not *from*."[91] McGraw perfectly illustrated how complex behaviors that appear later than more primitive ones in a series, such as swimming, actually followed "from" these earlier counterparts.

For example, the Moro reflex to surprise that is enlisted by infants in swimming seemingly has already been functionally specified at a prior stage in the series. Yet the reconstructive force of the Moro reflex is conserved as potential energy that may be tapped, when combined with other movements, to produce functionally determinate behavior. This is exactly what Maxwell showed to be happening when changes in the position or configuration of molecules increase their velocity without incurring any change in kinetic energy or entropy. This is what Dewey had in mind when he argued that propositions acquire "signifying force," when they are found to apply to a wider series of existential situations than previously anticipated or predicted.

Dewey was not content to reach the threshold of understanding the human mind and not walk through the door, opened by McGraw's research, to comprehend the fundamental neurobehavioral processes involved. Dewey had spent most of his professional life merely speculating about possible brain mechanisms that contributed to the extraordinary powers of mind and human intelligence. As we shall see next, McGraw and her team of researchers provided Dewey one last significant opportunity to apply the very best techniques and methods available to see if he could unravel the mysteries of mind concealed in the human brain.

TEN

Locomotion as a Metaphor for Mind

By the mid-1930s, McGraw and Dewey had completed a remarkable series of studies that laid a solid foundation for understanding how developmental processes give birth to judgment and inquiry. But three important questions remained unresolved: How do specific phases in locomotor development become organized? Through what specific neuromuscular processes do these different behaviors become integrated? And by what neural mechanisms is energy allocated and redistributed to bring about fundamental changes in human behavioral capabilities and cognitive powers? Dewey considered the third problem to be particularly important because it bore directly on the issue of whether evolution sustained a progressive enlargement in human consciousness and intelligence.

McGraw, Dewey, and Lawrence Frank met in Florida in January 1935 to discuss how they could address these problems in future research. To McGraw's surprise, Frank indicated that the General Education Board (GEB) of the Rockefeller Foundation was willing to give away some of its principal to support a larger, longer-term interdisciplinary research project.[1] Frank subsequently persuaded the GEB in 1936 to make a generous multiyear award to McGraw and her colleagues to conduct a broad array of interrelated studies. With the support of Tilney, Dewey, and Frank, McGraw put together an interdisciplinary group of ten researchers and eight technicians that included a neurophysiologist, a physiologist, a biochemist, two pediatricians, three psychologists, and two nurse-lab technicians. The complete scope of this project, documented in more than fifty journal articles, has yet to be fully appreciated.

This ambitious undertaking, that Dewey could only dream of before, proposed to analyze all major structural and functional elements of growth including anatomical, physiological, and psychological developmental processes. McGraw outlined the work program in some detail, proposing to gather and correlate quantitative data about neuromuscular processes with other developmental processes involving the brain, respiratory, circulatory, autonomic, and

metabolic systems. In addition, she proposed behavioral studies of infant gesture, vocalization, development of emotion, and concept formation. Among
these latter proposals, only the study of concept formation was completed and
documented in journal articles discussed later.[2]

BRAIN WAVES, BALANCE, AND CENTERED INQUIRY

Dewey sought more evidence for his long-standing presumption, stated most
explicitly in *Human Nature and Conduct,* that human behavior is governed by
mechanisms that make possible the unity of mind and body in coordinated
action.[3] Dewey believed that biological mechanisms embodied in living organisms are strongly influenced or biased by the natural forces of nature that included gravity, energy, and movement. Hegel's naturalism appealed to Dewey
because it construed thought in terms of how lofty ideas are affected by gravitational forces that ground thought in human experience. Hegel contended that
the complete grasp or comprehension of our own capabilities is attained only
after experiencing the limits of action against gravitational forces that pull us
back to earth. Hegel argued that the time during which a body falls freely back
to earth is highly significant. This moment marks the period of fluidity in
which the self-shaping forces of being come to fruition in Spirit, integrating
form and content into a unified whole. Hegel believed that the universal forces
shaping matter evoked a specific tonality, which he described metaphorically as
"music of the spheres," to designate the equilibrium attained between opposing forces.[4]

Hegel's belief that gravity and balance possess not only scientific importance
for nature but have philosophical significance for thought was given added
credibility by C. J. Herrick in 1924. He argued that behavior is coordinated by
cerebral "mechanisms of correlation" that effectively balance the discharge of
nervous energy by synchronizing metabolic rates governing different physiological functions. Adaptive responses to environmental changes are made possible by the relocation of the center of gravity of neurobiological functions that
create new neural pathways through which excitation can be channeled and
discharged. However, Herrick admitted that little was known about the exact
nature of the nervous mechanism or energetic processes involved.[5]

Rignano believed that he had resolved these issues. He argued that a mnemonic mechanism furnishes the exact amount of nervous energy needed to
bring about neuroanatomical change and then restores the organism to a prior
state of physiological equilibrium.[6] Rignano stated his argument in sketchy
terms that alluded to the possibility that gravity plays a fundamental role in this
balancing process. He speculated that "[a] total potential energy would form as
it were a force of gravitation toward the environment of those conditions,
which allows for the maintenance or restoration of the whole physiological system."[7]

Dewey was not persuaded that Rignano's theory was sound. He considered

20. C. J. Herrick in the 1940s.
Courtesy of Denison University Archives,
Granville, Ohio.

it implausible that potential energy could be siphoned into mnemonic pigeon-holes that subsequently restore an organism to an earlier state. Dewey believed this would entail *reversing* the growth process, which was contrary to known biological processes. The achievement of erect locomotion, for example, occurred as a result of a functional adaptation that necessitated reciprocal adjustments among neuroanatomical structures and behavioral and physiological processes. The reconstructive power of neural growth, therefore, did not derive from its energy content or quantity *per se*, but by virtue of the role it played in some more complex neurobehavioral process. It seemed more plausible to Dewey that a new synthesis of neurobehavioral capabilities and physiological processes was required to support the energetic demands and cognitive capabilities of humans who were able to walk erect. Consequently, Dewey resumed his focus on neurodynamic processes to see if they shed additional light on this phenomenon of reconstruction. Evelyn Dewey subsequently recommended in her monograph, commissioned by the Josiah Macy, Jr. Foundation, that developmental research focus on neural mechanisms governing behavior (a line of inquiry McGraw pursued) because, she asserted, that "would obviously throw light upon the processes by which growth takes place."[8]

McGraw and her associates attempted to identify potential mechanisms governing the succession and transformation of neuromuscular states in her advanced studies from 1936 to 1941. For example, McGraw further investigated why Johnny and other experimental babies developed a precocious ability to defy gravity by fearlessly leaping off stools and pedestals, suggesting an earlier integration of neural functions. Their movements seemed guided by a special "body sense" to adjust to the displacement of mass in the transition between behavioral postures.[9] The movement of head and neck essential to equilibrium also seemed governed by older structures in the mid-brain (i.e., cerebellum) and brain stem. McGraw and her associates conducted additional research to find out whether the capacity to maintain equilibrium in the absence of complete sensorimotor development could be traced to an underlying neural mechanism.

To be certain, Dewey had a long-standing interest in this phenomenon. Alexander had already piqued his curiosity about the fundamental mechanics of postural set. He seemed to have tapped in some unknown way the neural mechanisms governing posture. In his budding collaboration with McGraw, Dewey felt a renewed sense of urgency to conduct parallel investigations of this so-called "body sense." One track would involve testing the effects of Alexander's techniques on infants to see if this somehow stimulated and altered the pattern of early development. The other, more sophisticated approach would entail the use of electroencephalographic (EEG) techniques to trace the possible origin and function of brain waves in early motor development.

Dewey used his newly gained influence on the Josiah Macy, Jr. Foundation to persuade the then president, Ludwig Kast, and Frank to provide funds to Alexander and his brother "A. R." to subject their technique to scientific investigation. Such an experiment was compelling for Dewey because it would provide an opportunity to obtain independent corroboration of Alexander's reports of his own phenomenal experience. The attempt to persuade F. M. Alexander and his brother to cooperate proved to be exasperatingly frustrating and ultimately futile. Alexander would have no part of a scientific establishment whose motives were questionable and whose findings could prove to be potentially perilous to his hard-won reputation among his clients.

Moreover, Alexander preferred to bask in the glow of the numerous endorsements he had accumulated from admiring scientists, such as Sherrington and Coghill, and literary figures that included Aldous Huxley. Dewey suffered no bigger disappointment than to be rebuffed by a pioneer whose achievements he admired and who had been a close personal friend. Fortunately for Dewey, McGraw and Frank's associates conducted some preliminary studies of the Alexander technique. In addition, after McGraw completed her studies in the early 1940s, Dewey became acquainted with Frank Jones, a psychologist from Tufts University, who had been trained by Alexander. Jones would eventually conduct the first series of sophisticated experiments in the 1950s and 1960s to test the efficacy of Alexander's technique.[10]

McGraw acknowledged having taken a few lessons from Alexander's brother A. R., but she confessed that she never mastered the technique and did not attempt to apply it in an experimental context.[11] In one of her very first experiments, McGraw attempted to discern how and why babies differ in the timing in which they are able to walk erect. A fundamental factor that McGraw believed accounted for observed differences in attaining erect locomotion appeared to be how babies handled the challenge of balance differently in the phases of locomotion that preceded walking, such a sitting up and rising to a standing position. She concluded from her studies of assisted and unassisted forms of walking that "an infant's inability to walk at birth is due more to an undeveloped equilibratory apparatus than to the absence of a walking mechanism."[12] This was not a direct test of Alexander's techniques, but it certainly supported his theory.

Another experimental study was conducted several years later by Alma Frank, a student of Alexander, who had been a recipient of a Rockefeller fellowship in child study. Frank claimed to have used the Alexander technique to stimulate in children the spinal mechanism, which Coghill contended controlled the capacity for total integration. Frank furnished silhouetted photographs comparing the posture of children who had received the technique with those who had not. Although there were striking differences between experimental subjects and controls, the experiment did not institute sufficient controls to rule out other contributing or confounding factors. Nevertheless, she believed that her research corroborated Alexander's postural theory of conscious control.

Dewey had bigger ambitions for McGraw than simply corroborating Alexander's ideas. Dewey and Lawrence Frank urged McGraw and her associates to probe deeper to uncover the structural and functional mechanisms governing the patterns of neurobehavioral development. Frank best articulated what he and Dewey envisioned when he recommended that researchers

> eliminate the simple notion of conduction of impulses, as often viewed in nervous tissue, in favor of the notion of space-time alterations of the whole configuration, thus bringing the problem of nervous impulse in line with the problem of light transmission and other energy transformations, wherein a wave of energy transformation passes along or through a sequence of space-time configurations with interacting fields . . . each of which exhibits a space-time alteration and energy transformation in accordance with the pattern of structure-function.[13]

The pursuit of this Maxwellian and Lewinian conception of biological processes was a tall order given the rudimentary tools and techniques available to researchers of that era. Dewey sought the advice of colleagues, such as C. J. Herrick and Lawrence Frank, about possible experts they could bring on board who were knowledgeable and experienced in these new methods. However, McGraw turned out to be her own best advisor on the issue of staffing. McGraw conducted her own search interviews at nearby universities and landed Roy Smith, a promising post-doctoral neurophysiologist from Harvard. While working with McGraw, Smith pioneered the measurement of delta or slow waves and the so-called Berger rhythms which are emitted from the brain during infancy, and he was the first scientist to "relate behavioral development to the ontogeny of the EEG."[14]

Smith contended that synchronous slow-delta-wave brain activity detected in the somatic motor area in neonates seemed to anticipate the acquisition of sensory functions, supporting Coghill's theory.[15] Smith also speculated that this indicated the waning influence of a phylogenetically older pacemaker in the cerebellum governing equilibrium before the onset of cortical control.[16] Smith eventually identified a central occipital rhythm between three and four months that he believed signaled the loss of Babinski and Moro reflexes and the emergence of reaching, which he considered to be indicative of the onset of cortical control.[17] Smith detected a curious dramatic increase in the number, amplitude, and frequency within the first three months of these somatic motor waves, particularly in the post-central area. When he increased the distance of the electrodes, the rhythmic waves rarely registered simultaneously, suggesting that the locus of brain waves shifted subtly from one site to another in the premotor cortex. Smith's studies suggested the possibility that in the absence of a well developed cortex, cerebral rhythms provide the balance infants need in early development to exercise judgment despite undergoing continuously de-stabilizing growth and change.[18]

A. C. Weinbach, a biochemist involved in McGraw's studies, attempted to identify possible mechanisms controlling the rate, succession, and transformation of neuromuscular processes. Weinbach argued that the growth of the brain weight relative to body weight and the frequency of alpha waves studied by Smith followed a similar trajectory, indicating that they were closely correlated. Accordingly, the fact that both brain weight and the magnitude of brain waves exhibit the same rate of increase led Weinbach to propose that brain weight may directly account for, or be proportional to, electrical frequency.[19] This relationship seemed plausible to Weinbach because inhibitory cells seemed to exhibit the largest increase in size and weight in the first three months in the area of the motor cortex from which alpha rhythms originated. Consequently, he reasoned that the duration of the Moro reflex, for example, is directly proportional to the mass of the neural tissue involved and thus would account for the relatively brief appearance and rapid decline of the Moro reflex after birth.[20]

These experimental studies by McGraw and her associates were of considerable value to Dewey because they allowed him to test his premises about inquiry. That is why Dewey contended in *Logic* that he was advancing a set of "hypotheses to be tested" rather than the last word on the subject.[21] For example, before completing *Logic*, Dewey consistently held that "interaction is the primary fact" constituting the structure for behavior that makes continuity of experience possible.[22] However, this premise undergoes a change in *Logic* when Dewey declared that continuity is preserved not by returning to a previous state of existence but by instituting a new integrated relation. Rignano's theory of recurrence was mistaken, as the locus of neural rhythms did not remain constant but shifted from one site of the brain to another. What is "reinstated" then, according to Dewey, "is the form of prior relationships, of the interaction, not the identical conditions" or point or origin.[23] Dewey explained in *Logic* that integration is brought about by a dynamic "mechanism" that maintains balance between the organism and its environment, adding, "This whole system of accurately timed interchanges is regulated by changes in the nervous system."[24]

Dewey adopted this mechanistic view of brain functions, which allowed him to argue that the form and integrity of inquiry, like the equilibrium of the organism, is maintained despite the ever-changing dimensions of the problem under study. Consequently, the indeterminacy of a series of seemingly separate and distinct events or occurrences can be overcome by showing that they are connected through some more basic underlying rhythm or pattern. By assigning interaction this functional role in inquiry, Dewey demonstrated how facts become interrelated or correlated through the positions they occupy within a whole series of propositions, giving inquiry a "cumulative force," converging toward a unified conclusion.[25] Thus successful inquiry, as the locomotion metaphor suggests, is demonstrated by whether the momentum from the measured steps taken to understand and overcome a problem carries us forward to face new uncertainties without losing our footing or breaking stride. This was consistent with Coghill's theory and McGraw's findings that specific behavior patterns, no matter how varied in their sequence of construction or timing of appearance, emerged from and eventuated in a state of neurobehavioral integration.[26]

TRANSFORMATIONAL CONSTANTS AND INTERCHANGEABLE ROLES

Dewey's contention that successful inquiry turns on its functional capacity to bring about the continuous transformation of the objects of perception into the tools of inquiry depended crucially on demonstrating that seemingly incommensurate phenomena can be compared through experiments that render them qualitatively equivalent. Dewey saw in Bohr's struggle to overcome the problematic entanglement between observer and the observed an opportunity to unravel the series of events that first enabled humans to form judgments from phenomenal experience. Dewey speculated that the occasion for the creation of the first units of measure probably involved marking off distances of bodies extended in space. He reasoned that the span of the hand or pace of walking may have been the first units to have evolved, providing primitive humans a convenient way to measure intervals of activity undergoing continuous change.[27] Therefore, Dewey concluded, measurement first arose under dynamic conditions and rudimentary measures of equivalence increased human adaptability to new and unforeseen situations.

Dewey also concurred with Alexander's assessment that in their long ascent toward increased cognitive intelligence, modern humans had grown to distrust or become oblivious to the natural powers of their own judgment. McGraw attempted to demonstrate that infants tap these natural powers to gauge and control their movements. Dewey considered her research essential to his attempt in *Logic* to successfully reconstruct the conditions in which natural modes of measurement first constituted the basis of propositional knowledge.

Significantly, however, Dewey and Lawrence Frank were not in complete agreement on how to proceed. There were growing theoretical differences between them about how to conceptualize the structural and functional elements of developmental processes. Dewey's attempt to work around these differences by persuading McGraw to adopt his approach before commencing her investigations illustrates why Dewey considered the completion of her studies, as he conceived them, crucial to the completion of *Logic*. This was a difficult and crucial period (1936–1938). Dewey was attempting (unsuccessfully) to formulate key arguments about equivalence and the role of qualitative judgments in inquiry with further progress hinging in part on the outcome of quantitative studies by McGraw and her associates.

Dewey told McGraw that he postponed finishing several chapters on mathematics and quantitative judgment because he "considered them the hardest in the whole book."[28] The preliminary results of NCDS studies were available to Dewey through interim progress reports *before* he completed *Logic* in September 1938. These studies suggested to Dewey that he could refute the assumption that psychological and biological phenomena are incommensurable by showing that judgment enables the seamless transformation of the seemingly separate processes of thought and behavior into equivalent terms. Dewey was careful throughout this time to conceal from Frank and other foundation officials his concerns and interests that might compromise the continuation of the project.

Dewey was also anxious to counter misinterpretations of his key concepts when they jeopardized his research agenda. For example, Dewey believed that hereditary and environmental factors did not directly interact with each other in individual development but *mediated* the ongoing interaction between structure and function, altering the timing and sequence of neurobehavioral development. The relatively similar outward appearance of human anatomy and reflexes conceals, according to Dewey, a far greater potential for variation and psychological change through growth processes than is imagined possible through either genetic alteration or environmental influences.

Frank's treatment of neuroanatomical structures and physiological functions as interchangeable variables reflected just this kind of misinterpretation.[29] Frank saw structure as representing the persistence of function over time while function simply constituted a series of changing structures characterized by varying levels and rates of energy use. Frank contended that the growth and functional differentiation of an organism consists essentially of "structural deformations" governed by separate "energy complexes."[30] He believed that growth imbalances can produce functional abnormalities, as Freud argued, that are capable of warping or distorting personality development. Thus normal development was conceived by Frank in terms of the formation of a stable, mature personality.[31]

As an outspoken critic of Freudian psychoanalysis, Dewey resisted any attempt, no matter how subtle, to get McGraw to test Freud's theories of early childhood. Dewey told McGraw that he took exception to Frank's using "process and function as names for the same thing, and yet insist[ing] that structure-function is one thing, which may be studied from two aspects."[32] This essentially collapsed structure into function, obviating their interaction and making it impossible to account for the persistence of adaptive functions and elimination of others. Dewey argued instead that structure and function are "aspects of a process" and that "[f]unction is that which a set of connected processes *do* . . . the net outcome of a system of interrelated processes, such as locomotion.[33] Nor, Dewey believed, is energy partitioned into separate complexes, as Rignano and Freud argued, but is concentrated in thought and action.

Moreover, McGraw had already demonstrated (albeit qualitatively) that erect locomotion involved the successive recombination, not the deformation, of a series of movements and found no evidence that temporary regressions in growth processes had any adverse effects on emotional development, as Freud supposed. Freud's theory of repression directed clinical attention toward the compulsive and repetitive dimensions of human experience. McGraw sought instead to record the processes involved (as Dewey would argue later in *Logic*) in the "transformation" rather than the "recurrence" or "static repetition" of a behavior pattern.[34] These conceptual differences had a direct bearing on whether McGraw's advanced studies could be organized to address problems central to Dewey's analysis of quantitative and qualitative judgments in inquiry. Although initially promising to study functional abnormalities and outlining her proposed research and that of her associates in terms more acceptable to Frank and hospital clinicians, she ultimately focused on philosophical problems of primary interest to Dewey.[35]

THE RECIPROCAL INTERACTION OF
MIND, BRAIN, AND BEHAVIOR

McGraw's attempt to identify neural correlates of developmental phenomena by extrapolating from histological studies by Tilney and Harvard neuroanatomist J. LeRoy Conel, although crude by contemporary standards, did provide useful insights about the neurobehavioral phenomena involved in the development of consciousness. McGraw saw behavior playing a key role in the coalescence of neural substrata into centers of action capable of sustaining integrated forms of action. Accordingly, neurobehavioral development consisted, in her view, of a series of neuroanatomical reconstructions that support a more economical, progressively reintegrated repertoire of movements. She hypothesized that the initial energy of neural growth enervates behavioral reflexes whose motion exceeds the capacity of existing neural structures to channel this energy effectively, resulting in the excessive and diffuse forms of behavior. She believed that the opposing flexor and extensor movements characteristic of most forms of locomotion are integrated through rhythmic processes, which facilitate the completion of neural circuitry required for integrated forms of action.

The Moro or startle reflex illustrates this rhythm-induced reorganization in the apparent flooding or overactivation of all motor groups in the mid-brain that Coghill first reported in his studies of salamanders. Only a few of these tracts become functional, suggesting to McGraw that a common neural pathway was being forged for fluctuating motor behaviors emanating from two different regions of the spine. This convergence of neuronal pathways made possible the reduction of a diffuse extensor response to a more abbreviated and localized flexion. In addition, the locus of this reflex activity appeared eventually to move upward from the brain stem to the cerebellum and mid-brain. Importantly, she contended that the eventual inclusion of the motor cortex in the pathway between stimulus and response furnished the delay necessary for infants to exercise increased judgment. This period of delay enabled mind to capture the energy needed to move the body in the intended direction.

McGraw gathered a significant amount of evidence that indicated that the locus of behavioral control shifted among different brain regions during early development and that functions associated with perception and thought, such as vision, are supported initially by neural motor processes. For example, she found that the somesthetic area of the precentral gyrus supports more complex movements such as reaching and prehensile behavior and rising to a sitting and standing position.[36] Most neurologists of that era believed that reaching in infancy is governed by the occipital lobe. But J. LeRoy Conel, with whom McGraw collaborated in the late 1930s, determined that reaching is supported initially in the precentral gyrus and somesthetic afferent area of the postcentral gyrus, which are more advanced at birth than the striate area of the occipital lobe.[37] McGraw observed that infants do not show good eye conjugation, fixation, and behavioral consistency in their guided reaching until about five months. At that time, she believed, the post-central gyrus and occipital lobe become coupled or coordinated. This led McGraw to conclude that prehension is mastered only after the act of moving the head and shoulders is coordinated, and the infant is able to look away and still reach and grasp.[38]

The adoption of a sitting posture presented the most enigmatic example of an indeterminate behavior that could be performed without apparent reflex organization at the spinal level. McGraw considered this evidence that sitting was of recent phylogenetic origin, and was therefore closely connected with the challenge of balance posed by erect locomotion. Her analysis revealed that sitting up involves the dual behavioral challenge of opposing gravitational forces in sitting up, and then resisting these forces by using head, arms, and hips to keep from falling over. McGraw contended that these behavioral challenges provided the strongest support for Tilney's theory that the parietal portion of the brain governing somatic sense took precedence over other senses such as vision and hearing. McGraw found it entirely plausible that this body sense constituted one of the "cornerstones of conscious action" because "the first manifestation of neuromuscular control would be educed in the anti-gravitational mechanisms, involving the early adjustment to body displacement in space."[39]

McGraw's analysis of crawling and creeping best illustrates how brain and behavior become interwoven through differential processes of growth. She undertook this study when Conel was just starting his two-decade-long, eight-volume research project to trace the development of the newborn brain to the age of six. Conel and his successors continued to find evidence to support McGraw's theories about neuromuscular development long after the completion of her studies.[40] Conel's criteria for measuring brain development included the width of cortical layers, the number, size, and length of nerve cells and processes, the quantity of exogenous fibers, and the extent of myelination (i.e., when axons are wrapped in a protective sheath to become functionally permanent). McGraw determined that at birth the rhythmic flexion and occasional spinal extension commences the process of prone locomotion. The most active reflexes are found in the hips and lower extremities. Conel determined that at this point Betz cells were more numerous and showed extensive myelination in the middle third of the posterior wall of the anterior central gyrus.

McGraw observed that by about three months, movement in the upper trunk, shoulder, and arms is more pronounced, as rhythmic activity in the lower body diminishes and becomes quiescent. Conel's studies indicated a correlative development in the brain as the posterior central gyrus supporting these movements was in the most advanced stage of development.[41] However, by six months, areas of the premotor cortex that Conel examined, involving the regions of the lower trunk, hands, and feet, assumed a dominant role while movements in the upper body were inhibited.[42] This was consistent with McGraw's findings that infants tend to push with their feet and pull with their hands at this stage of prone progression.[43] Conel subsequently determined that by fifteen months these separate movements become well-integrated in the hippocampus.[44]

The behavioral sequence involved in the attainment of crawling and creeping (see Figure 21) illustrates well how one phase overlaps with the next, involving shifting centers of neural control, to produce an integrated form of prone locomotion. Such a pattern is also exhibited in the development of erect locomotion by the alternation between a wobbling and rigid gait, the adoption of wide and narrow stances, the raising and lowering of arms for balance, and so forth. As noted before, McGraw contended that these opposing phases indicated the selective emergence of cortical inhibition, which alternated between upper and lower body regions, enabling a gradual integration of different

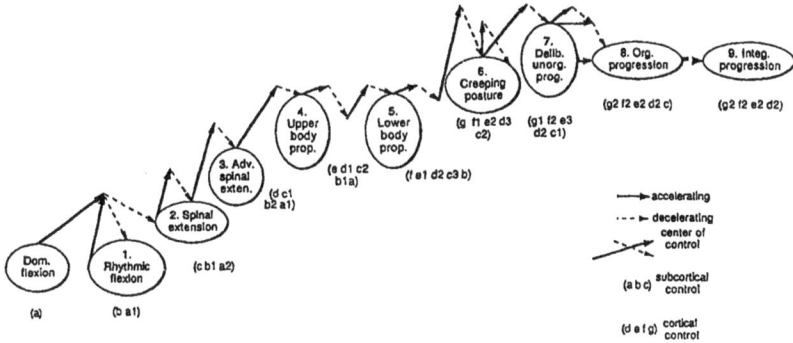

21. The Development of Prone Locomotion
McGraw argued that the phases through which crawling and creeping emerge reflect the differential effects of neural growth processes. She hypothesized that the point at which accelerating and decelerating behaviors intersect constitutes a critical period involving two related events, depicted above. Each new trait in a behavior complex (e.g., 1, 2, 3) contributing to prone locomotion assumes a leading position in the sequence, subsequently displacing prior dominant traits to the end of the series, where their influence is curtailed or eliminated. Consequently, excess activity governed by subcortical regions (traits a–c) is inhibited with the onset of cortical control. How long this process takes for individual children will vary according to the rate of physical growth in size and weight (elements affecting the center of gravity), the timing of the synchronization of propulsion and balance, and the level of awareness exhibited in recognizing and overcoming limits to forward progression.

movements. Although cautioning that such data did not explain the processes of functional specification, Conel believed that his research lent support to McGraw's contention that the pace and sequence of neuromuscular development and integration depends as much on behaviorally mediated neuroanatomical processes as it does on the structural inhibition of efferent behavior.[45]

McGraw insightfully observed that "there is a period of comparative inactivity in those parts of the body representing the areas in which the neural transition is occurring."[46] She believed that this indicated that cortical control emerged gradually and selectively, involving the sequential formation of linkages between premotor functions. Esther Thelen, a contemporary infant experimentalist, has seized upon McGraw's assertion that infant behavior does not become fully integrated until after the onset of cortical control as irrefutable evidence that she was a maturationist. Thelen claims that McGraw was saying that the "immediate causes of new forms of behavior . . . were reorganizations in the nervous system as it matured and in a systematic and predictable fashion," and that therefore, according to Thelen, McGraw believed that "function emerged from structure and not the reverse."[47] Thelen also claimed that McGraw was unable to reconcile the "tension" between her maturationist and experientialist points of view.[48]

This interpretation is incorrect. McGraw was never divided on the relation between structure and function and always considered them to be reciprocally related. McGraw never argued that the cortex "caused" or "determined" motor development, nor did she posit a one-to-one relationship between brain structures and behavior.[49] McGraw explicitly acknowledged that "[t]he problem of developmental or maturational relations between structure and function is more complex than the question of localization of function."[50]

While McGraw believed that development involved an increase in cortical control, she did not believe that this was a unilinear or structurally predetermined process. McGraw proposed instead a *bidirectional* theory of structure and function, contending that consciousness emerges through behaviorally and biologically mediated neuroanatomical and neuromuscular processes of reorganization that support the transition from minimal consciousness to self-consciousness. Developmental theorist Gilbert Gottlieb also has taken exception to Thelen's interpretation of McGraw's work. He argues that McGraw can take credit for having first formulated a tentative *bidirectional* theory of structure and function. Gottlieb has subsequently constructed a probabilistic, epigenetic bidirectional theory based on McGraw's and his own studies which demonstrates the fundamental reciprocal role of experience and endogenous processes in shaping phenotypic behavior.[51] McGraw's conception, represented in the reconstruction in Figure 22, expresses McGraw's notion that there is no one-to-one correspondence between a neural structure and a behavioral trait. Instead, there are a plurality of neural structures sustaining behavior, each of which overlap at different periods of motor development. Needless to say, McGraw's findings strongly supported Dewey's contentions that human experience involves the interactions between body, brain, and mind.

McGraw observed also that there is considerable interplay of antecedent and emerging brain functions and behaviors. No behavioral pattern is achieved until after the occurrence of temporary setbacks that involve reversion to more rudimentary methods of balance and locomotion supported by subcortical structures. Nevertheless, older traits and emergent capabilities are actually recombined and reintegrated in slightly different ways during ontogeny, altering the form or configuration of a behavior pattern in its entirety. Thus, erect locomotion never presents exactly the same problem for each individual, McGraw observed, because toddlers must re-solve the problem of balance encountered during previous stages of neuromuscular development, the experiential circumstances of which vary considerably between children. According to this scheme, minimal consciousness is attained when an infant is able to sit up, a behavior that Dewey observed in his own studies in the late nineteenth century that led him to posit consciousness in infants at three months. Object consciousness or the awareness of the difference between self and other occurs with the act of reaching and pointing. Self-consciousness emerges sometime after the mastery of erect locomotion, when there is an explicit recognition of a causal relationship between self-initiated movement and the movement or manipulation of objects.

Locomotion as a Metaphor for Mind

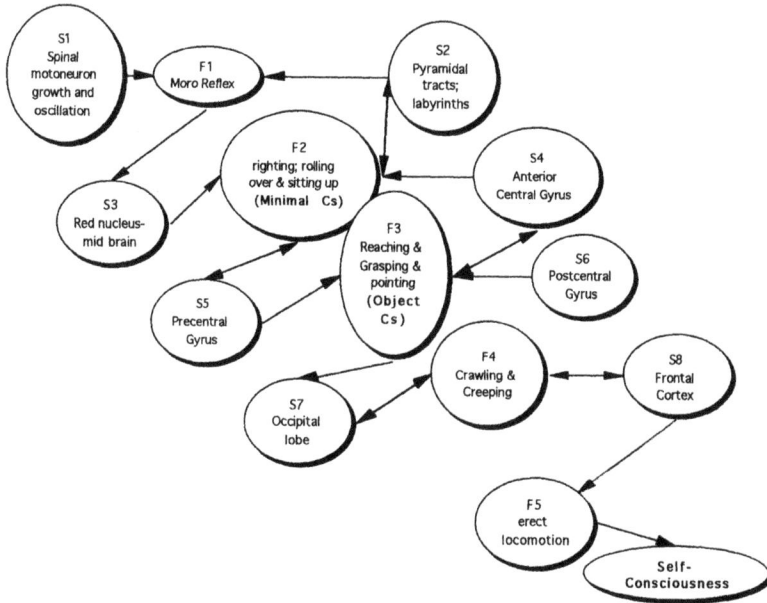

22. McGraw's Neurobehavioral Theory of the Development of Consciousness
Motoneuron growth and oscillation along the spinal column commences a sequence of behaviorally mediated neuroanatomical and neuromuscular reorganizations that sustain successive forms of continuous activity, culminating in erect locomotion and self-consciousness. Each functional pattern (F) constitutes the center of gravity of neural structures (S) undergoing differential growth (i.e., axons and dendritic connections), as illustrated by the neural complex S2–S5 encircling F2. Reciprocal interactions occurring, for example, between F4 (crawling and creeping), and neuroanatomical structures S4 and S7 enable antecedent structures to influence subsequent patterns. Consequently, erect locomotion at F5 entails re-solving the problem of balance by drawing on the energy of consciousness generated by antecedent stages of neuromuscular development occurring previously.

THE ENERGETICS OF GROWTH

McGraw and her colleagues were intrigued by the seemingly inexplicable steep rates of energy consumption and growth in early development. They were also puzzled by their inability to account for how this energy is distributed, suggesting that the developing neurobehavioral system does not completely conform to the law of entropy. Because biologists had demonstrated that cells exhibited self-generating or self-multiplying powers, Weinbach considered it plausible that neural cells possessed an "impulse to grow." He proposed that if a conception of "effective weight" were used as a primary index of growth, then the rate of growth in weight of an embryo should be treated as "proportional to the weight already there plus some inherent (intangible) growth stimulating factor."[52]

Weinbach cited analyses by Norman Wetzel to support his conception of growth. Wetzel adopted a naturalistic perspective, arguing that growth was a form of motion that exhibits mechanical attributes of mass, resistance, and elasticity and also displays electrical properties, such as inductance and capacitance.[53] Dewey was personally acquainted with Wetzel, having attended a conference on growth and education sponsored by Wetzel at Case Western Reserve University in 1936.[54] Wetzel was a pediatrician with sophisticated mathematical skills. He first observed a peculiar trend in a child's first three years of an initial steep increase of basal metabolism at birth that is followed by a rapid decline in metabolism and weight. This appeared to defy entropy and the law of conservation of energy.

Wetzel speculated that growth must possess other thermodynamic properties that enable energy to be transformed to sustain an organism in different structural and functional states of existence. He proposed a Maxwellian equation stating that growth consists of three interacting fields that include the kinetic energy of cellular motion, a potential energy of position and structural and functional configuration, and the composite heat output of dissipation and synthesis. Importantly, Wetzel argued that fluctuations in the rate of growth depend in part on the displacement of structural and functional interactions from a position of equilibrium, allowing the potential energy of growth to be released to assume new forms.[55] This transitional shift in the locus of neurobiological structures appeared to offer a plausible explanation for how excess metabolic energy is channeled into the processes of reconstruction.

Weinbach applied Wetzel's formulas in a series of investigations to predict the velocity and trajectory of behavioral development throughout the life span. Weinbach contended that the human growth curve through age fourteen exhibited the characteristic four-stage alternating sequence of accelerating and decelerating phases of neurobehavioral reconstruction first observed by McGraw. During each phase, changes in body weight appeared to be associated with proportionate changes in brain size and weight. Both of these variables, in turn, seemed strongly correlated with the changes in the overall velocity and direction of behavioral development during each phase.[56]

Nevertheless, McGraw's colleagues could not reach a consensus on precisely how to characterize the nature of the energetic phenomena involved. Advisory board member C. B. Davenport's analysis of a small sample of infants suggested more complex individual patterns of skeletal growth than reflected in Weinbach's growth curves. Davenport concluded that hormonal and metabolic factors affecting early growth processes are largely governed by genetically programmed cell growth factors that relegate behavior to only a marginal role.[57] McGraw's associates H. R. Benjamin and A. A. Weech also challenged Wetzel's findings, although differing in their methodology. They did not find a significant relationship between metabolism and weight among infants from six to twenty months (a much shorter time span than that measured by Wetzel). They also contended that any unaccounted-for heat output could be explained by the changing size and energy consumption of internal organs.[58] Wetzel's theories attracted limited support from several biological theorists. But according to S. L. Zeeger and S. D. Harlow, this promising line of inquiry has not been carried forward.[59]

GROUNDING HEGEL'S SPIRIT: MEASUREMENT AND THE PROBLEM OF EQUIVALENCE

Clearly, the question of whether biological processes constitute an exception to the law of entropy could not be resolved decisively through sophisticated theoretical and mathematical formulations. Bohr and Heisenberg were confronted with a similar conundrum in their arguments about whether quantum uncertainty was more amenable to a mathematical or experimental resolution. McGraw and her colleagues chose to approximate experimentally the neurobehavioral and energetic processes in which mind and matter undergo transformation. Consequently, McGraw's advanced studies made it possible for Dewey to experiment with Hegelian ideas and Maxwellian physics that had long captivated his interest.

In his *Philosophy of Nature,* Hegel advanced an elegant theory to suggest how the forces of motion and gravity that govern the behavior of objects in space and time also explain how Spirit acquires specific form and content through reflective thought. Hegel likened the process in which Spirit is grounded in understanding to the behavior of a projectile in motion. Humans and their ideas are literally thrown into this world with a momentum whose direction and velocity are subject to change by the contingencies of human experience. According to Hegel, the power or theoretical scope of an idea depends on how much intellectual weight and mental determination is put into the initial conceptualization. Hegel reasoned that true consciousness of our intellectual capacities is revealed only after using ideas as levers to catapult ourselves over epistemological limitations, before falling back into a new stage of understanding. Thus the efficacy of an idea, like the shape of Spirit in being, depends on how much energy or force is accumulated from the movement of thought to reveal the complete ramifications of an idea. The form that an idea assumes when it rebounds to earth, Hegel reasoned, reflects the equilibrium attained between inner tension and outer force—between conscious effort and understanding.[60]

As noted before, Hegel furnished Dewey important insights about how measurement functions as a tool of judgment to expand consciousness. Hegel contended in his *Science of Logic* that all being acquires determinant form and content by establishing a "ratio of powers," by fixing the precise balance or proportion between internal demands or needs and external forces.[61] Dewey believed that this capacity for proportionality helps us keep track of separate elements within an ever-changing larger context. Dewey simply naturalized this Hegelian idea by restating it in evolutionary and Maxwellian terms. He wanted to explain how humans who were able to walk fully erect used their newfound capacity to anticipate remote, unforeseen events beyond their immediate reach or grasp, which are subject to variation and impose different levels of energetic response. Dewey argued by analogy that judgment in scientific inquiry depends on whether seemingly incommensurate physical and biological constituents of an experience or event can be rendered in quantitatively equivalent or proportional terms.[62]

McGraw's quantitative analyses of erect locomotion and other behavior patterns provided Dewey a unique opportunity, before completing *Logic,* to see whether the energetic equivalence between thought and behavior could be demonstrated. McGraw tried to ascertain whether the physical form and mental demands of a functionally specific behavior, such as learning to walk or scaling inclines, contribute to neurobiological changes that result in increased awareness and understanding. This also would help decide whether the physical power or mental force needed to perform a task, once it was mastered, was reduced and conserved rather than dissipated.

McGraw and her associates were challenged by whether mental and physical activity can be rendered energetically equivalent. They chose to examine this problem by studying first the neural and behavioral changes involved in the development of erect locomotion. A promising method of analysis came with Weinbach's development of a body volume contour map to measure differential change.[63] This method enabled McGraw and her associates to develop biological and behavioral equivalents for physical and mental processes that could be measured quantitatively. McGraw and Breeze used this technique to plot how changes in volume and surface area of the human form affect the degree of functional integration in erect locomotion.

McGraw showed her genius for improvisation by developing a motion picture apparatus, shown in Figure 23, that allowed changes in balance, stride, gait, and so forth to be recorded as infants progressed in age from assisted to independent walking. McGraw hypothesized that variations in when infants walked independently were due in part to differences in the timing of neural connections formed between the cortex and cerebellum. Significantly, these connections appeared to form more rapidly in infants who more rapidly overcame gravity to master the problem of balance involved in sitting upright and rising to a standing position. By this reckoning, walking is an achievement rather than a genetic inevitability, one that requires effort and skill as well as self-confidence and judgment.

McGraw and Breeze concluded that the development of erect locomotion furnished the best evidence obtainable that the attainment of bilateral symmetry in walking involves a redistribution of energy to accommodate new forms, involving reciprocal adjustments between brain and behavior.[64] They demonstrated through projectile theory the possibility of converting the form and timing of gait into equations that measured the difference in amount of kinetic energy expended from the onset to the attainment of erect locomotion. These analyses showed that the mastery of balance constitutes the greatest

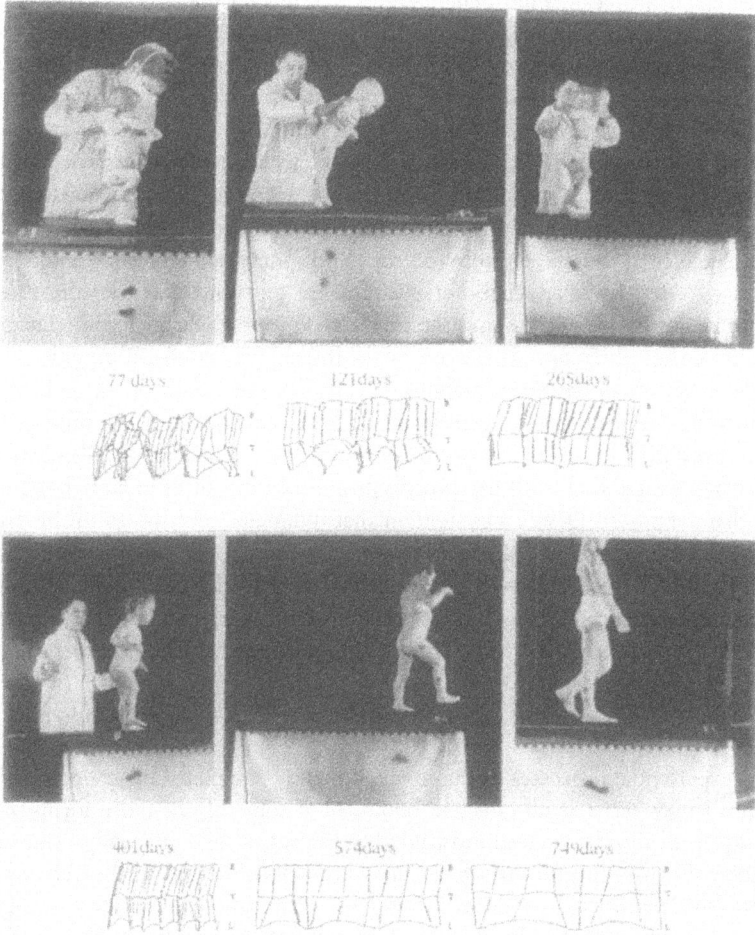

23. The Development of Walking
An apparatus constructed to measure the changing relationship between stride, gait, and center of gravity (i.e., the proportional relationship between upper body "B," thigh "T," and legs "L") consisted of a layer of milk over glass, covered by a rubber mat, and illuminated from behind to reveal footprints. McGraw and Breeze found that at the onset, a baby will spend a disproportionate amount of time and energy by moving with short and frequent steps, as illustrated in the body contour graphs. The gravitational effects on changing body dimensions contribute to the characteristic alternation between wobbling and rigid gaits, the adoption of narrow and wide stances, the raising and lowering of arms for balance, and so forth. However, once anatomical proportionality is reached, which is needed to sustain a stable center of gravity, and leg movements are brought under increased cortical control, a greater amount of time is consumed on the ground stroke, reducing energy input and stabilizing the gait.

challenge, consumes the most energy, and accounts for the largest variation in form among infants in their efforts to achieve a stable gait. This suggested to McGraw that the challenge of overcoming gravity to attain balance heightens consciousness, redirects and focuses energy, and stimulates interneuronal connections crucial to problem solving and adaptation.[65]

Additional studies by McGraw's associates provided further corroboration for her observations and findings. For example, Weinbach also found that an infant's proficiency in climbing a slide increases with age and that power output is adjusted (i.e., decreased) to reflect the child's increased efficiency and competence.[66] McGraw's associate Vera Dammann, a psychologist, demonstrated that changes in proficiency in mastering a slide were associated with changes in attitude and awareness, indicative of the infant's increased self-confidence.[67] Finally, Weinbach devised equations to calculate the effects of physiological growth phenomena involving reciprocal adjustments between the velocity of brain growth (i.e., rate of energy transformation) and behavior.[68] These studies demonstrated that learning involves progressive advances in human behavior that supported Dewey's contention that judgment contributes to the progressive enlargement of human experience by converting energy into a form that facilitates change. Dewey believed that the challenge of inquiry accumulates and concentrates energy rather than dissipating it, compressing, expanding, and remodeling ideas to better reflect our judgments from experience.

DEWEY'S DILEMMA: CONVENTION OR CONVICTION?

The experiential processes through which Dewey completed his conception of inquiry may serve as an effective rejoinder to some of the more formidable critiques of *Logic* advanced most notably by Nagel, who ironically criticized Dewey for reasoning from "second-hand accounts of scientific research rather than from personal experience."[69] Dewey's participation in McGraw's experimental studies gives new meaning to Dewey's own description of his development as a philosopher who said, "Upon the whole, the forces that have influenced me have come from persons and situations more than from books."[70] McGraw's experiments suggested not only how Dewey could re-examine his premises about development from a new perspective, but demonstrated the fruitfulness of collaboration in expanding the scope of judgment in inquiry. Moreover, Dewey found firmer scientific evidence to show why the seminal ideas that Hegel and his intellectual successors in *Naturphilosophie* shared about energy, motion, gravity, balance, and consciousness were fundamental elements of human development and inquiry.

McGraw's regret for failing to formulate a systematic theory of child development is ironic because she contributed to the intellectual development of one of America's greatest philosophers.[71] Had McGraw advanced a distinctive theory, she might have prevented her work from being confused with maturationism and thus being completely overshadowed by Gesell's research. But she assiduously avoided simple prescriptions, holding out for additional break-throughs in knowledge about development. Much of the popular confusion about McGraw's work stemmed from misconceptions by the press, who mistakenly reported her research as a test of effectiveness of behaviorist methods of conditioning. When the experimental twin, Johnny, showed no appreciable increase in his I.Q. score, which was not McGraw's objective, the press falsely concluded that early stimulation makes no difference and thus corroborated Gesell's maturationism. This left the field to Gesell, Freudians, and their followers among physicians and psychiatrists who were eager to give unequivocal advice to their patients and clients. Freud's provocative narrative about the lasting effects of childhood traumas contributed to a crisis of confidence among parents in child rearing. Child care could no longer be left to insensitive, untrained parents, but had to be delegated to professional experts.[72]

It is also possible that the recurring criticisms of the psychological import of Dewey's conception of inquiry could have been handled differently had Dewey been more explicit about the neuroembryological perspective underpinning his mature work. He could have illustrated his argument with references to McGraw's studies of child development in which his theory of inquiry was grounded. But this tactic also risked diverting discussion into the nature-versus-nurture controversy engulfing McGraw's research and challenging the validity of generalizing from personal experience biological or psychological processes whose scientific basis was unresolved.[73] But her farsighted studies furnished evidence neither easily comprehended nor assimilated within the discourse familiar to Dewey's philosophical colleagues. The behaviorist terms of psychological discourse were so well-entrenched in conventional logic that any contrary perspective was bound to produce cognitive dissonance.

Moreover, the terminology in physics, biology, and neurology had become so esoteric, like the Hegelian discourse long discarded, that Dewey only compounded his difficulties in using it to expound the psychobiological import of inquiry for his philosophical colleagues.[74] Ultimately, Dewey's scientific colleagues provided a more receptive audience, repaying their intellectual debts by helping Dewey use science to understand inquiry. They helped him demonstrate that human judgment is a tool for continuously reshaping human experience; that attitudes exert an enormous although indirect influence on consciousness and ideas by providing energy and direction to inquiry; that inquiry enlists doubt in an affirmative act of reconstruction and reintegration; and, most importantly, that we create the constants by which we measure our own progress.

But perhaps an explanation for Dewey's silence about his involvement in McGraw's studies, including his foundation role and network of scientific acquaintances, lies elsewhere. The dilemma Dewey faced in bringing science to bear on philosophic issues of utmost personal interest was the near impossibility of successfully accommodating the expectations and norms governing conduct associated with different roles without bringing them into conflict.

Freud, in gaining scientific acceptance of his controversial ideas about child development, faced similar difficulties that put psychoanalytic orthodoxy in jeopardy.[75] Dewey attempted to fill diverse roles as an academic philosopher, a foundation official, a mentor, a scientific collaborator, and a reformer. Dewey realized that the scientific merit of his philosophical premises about inquiry could not be fully explored without adequate financial support and colleagues who could collaboratively address the interdisciplinary implications of his theories. Yet Dewey's efforts to control the focus and direction of McGraw's research as a foundation trustee and research advisor could not be accomplished without defending her work as an advocate. Dewey's intervention was necessary to prevent McGraw's research from being diverted into clinical investigations and thus risked compromising the confidentiality and trust expected of foundation officials.

While important, Dewey's stewardship of the NCDS was no substitute for the opportunity for personal involvement, especially with someone like McGraw, with whom Dewey was very close, whom he trusted, and who would be receptive to his suggestions. However, by undertaking a collaboration with a former student, Dewey risked compromising the distance and reserve of a mentor and the objectivity of a scientist. Perhaps Dewey saw no need to explicitly acknowledge McGraw's contribution to his work, because they collaborated to test *his* ideas. Had Dewey allowed his involvement to become publicly visible, it is quite possible that this would have led the public to focus on Dewey's celebrity and desire to leave a legacy and discount McGraw's independence. What they gained from their relationship was something of more incalculable value than acknowledgment or recognition. Through the shared experience and joy of discovery, they came to possess each other's soul and spirit.

Dewey's ideas about judgment were not immaculately conceived, but were developed through a process of inquiry. The aims of inquiry, as Dewey defined it, would have been defeated unless it entailed a concerted and cooperative effort to pursue the complete ramifications of ideas no matter who originated or suggested them. Their curiosity was satisfied and their doubts about developmental processes overcome only after McGraw devised methods that enabled Johnny and many other experimental subjects to fully express their capabilities under challenging situations. McGraw and her associates launched several parallel lines of inquiry from different perspectives with different methods, involving key phenomena of infant development. The different paths they took toward a common problem converged to yield knowledge that corroborated or further extended many of Dewey's speculative hypotheses about the role of inquiry in human development.

Dewey refused to allow McGraw's research agenda to be compromised in his ambitious quest because of the impossibility of devising effective methods without the cooperation of technically competent scientists. Dewey cultivated an intellectual, emotional, and experiential kinship with McGraw, and he formed a network of scientists and foundation officials representing diverse perspectives who he believed could bring about integrated solutions to problems affecting the course of human development. Dewey's colleagues possessed many of the same dispositions and perspectives that distinguished Dewey from his contemporaries. They believed in the progressive evolution of man and society. They adopted a philosophical approach toward scientific issues and a holistic, organic perspective. They possessed a commitment to an interdisciplinary, collaborative approach to research and problem solving, and they shared the conviction that scientists could provide practical and moral leadership to bring about social transformation.

Neither Dewey nor his colleagues believed that scientists could or should consider themselves to be a kind of "quasi-priestly" class Richard Rorty abhors, but educators who attempted to increase public knowledge of the discoveries and new methods which could be adopted to improve individual lives.[76] But the holistic perspective and public outlook of Dewey and his colleagues were already being eclipsed by a science establishment demanding specialization and detachment. Scientists were expected to withhold judgment about the social implications of complex phenomena until the laborious and repetitive process of corroboration was completed.

Finally, Dewey correctly surmised that the nature-versus-nurture controversy engulfing and fracturing child development research could never be surmounted solely through philosophical debates. The promise of pragmatism lay in the power of people to influence and control the consequences of science for society. But few scientists possessed the broad knowledge of the complex interrelations between individual development and society needed for an integrated approach to social reconstruction. Dewey's decision to address this controversy through experimental research was consistent with his belief that the transformational potential of science in human development could be fully realized only by a concerted, multidisciplinary effort to reconstruct the foundations and methods of scientific inquiry. Thus, deference to scientific and social conventions gave way to Dewey's conviction as a reformer that the credibility of scientific inquiry depended ultimately on whether it contributed to the progressive enlargement of human self-understanding.

Part Four

Naturalism Lost and Found

Cultural Pragmatism and the Disappearance of Dewey's Naturalism

Dewey's concerted efforts through the first three decades of the twentieth century to define the scientific, cultural, and political implications of his conceptions of pragmatism and human intelligence invited critical scrutiny and misinterpretation. Although applauded for its magisterial breadth, the central conceptions and arguments of Dewey's *Logic* continue to elude many of Dewey's philosophical heirs. Some contemporary thinkers like Richard Rorty dismiss Dewey's theory of inquiry as a regrettable but excusable mistake. Dewey's aesthetic theory, although largely unappreciated during his lifetime, has been revived by some scholars who have made room there for Dewey's naturalism. Dewey's social and political theory has also flourished among theorists who argue that Dewey expressed in thought and deed an unwavering commitment to a democratic conception of community life. However, contemporary philosophers' attempts to articulate the moral foundations of Dewey's pragmatism have attracted criticism among adherents of post-modernism, who deny that any such unequivocal principles can be formulated.

Dewey could have been easily exhausted by having to conduct a defense of his ideas on so many fronts had he not had help from intensely loyal if sometimes misguided supporters. But perhaps the greatest challenge Dewey faced, expressed best in the intellectual encounter he had with Arthur Bentley in the last two decades of his life, was sustaining the primacy of phenomenal experience in human growth and scientific inquiry. Bentley's pointed and presumptuous criticisms of Dewey's *Logic* were intended to help Dewey clarify his arguments for inclusion in a 1949 book they co-authored, *Knowing and the Known*. But Bentley did more than anyone else to shake Dewey's confidence in the possibility of retaining his conception of experience as the centerpiece of pragmatism. As noted before, when Dewey prepared a new introduction to a revised version of *Experience and Nature*, he dejectedly declared that he would replace the word "experience" with "culture" because he had lost any hope of making the philosophical significance of the term clear to his critics.

The difficulties Dewey had in sustaining an unambiguous notion of experience and his own concessions to the importance of culture foreshadowed the linguistic turn of pragmatism, not only at the hands of Dewey's own contemporaries, but by a second generation of neo-pragmatists unable to reach a consensus about how to interpret and put Dewey's legacy in contemporary perspective. To be certain, some of Dewey's adherents, such as Joseph Ratner, Morton White, and Sidney Hook, tried to be true to Dewey by confining their interpretations to the context of Dewey's ideas about nature and experience. Ratner and White were reasonably successful in this endeavor because they were willing to accept Dewey's naturalism and evolutionism at face value. In contrast, Ernest Nagel, enthralled by the bold vision of the Vienna Circle of logical positivists for a unified science, believed that pragmatism would not be compromised if it incorporated realist epistemic assumptions inimical to its phenomenalism and naturalism. And while Hook accepted Dewey's naturalism, he unwittingly sundered the connections Dewey wished to sustain between science and metaphysics by making phenomenal experience and generic traits harmless background assumptions that would not jeopardize the scientific respectability of pragmatism.

The cultural-discursive strain in Deweyan pragmatism has attracted many contemporary proponents who have turned away from the phenomenology of experience in favor of sustaining a dialogue among a community of scholars seeking to articulate an ethic for a democratic way of life. While Dewey was strongly committed to free discourse in a democratic society, he never believed that public life consisted solely of a Habermasian cognitive exercise in achieving a rational and ethical consensus. Communities engaged in solving problems of public consequence must be capable of suspending disbelief, forging collaborations, and attempting experimental solutions that defy precise conceptualization and rarely involve unambiguous moral consequences.

This chapter examines why Dewey's naturalism has all but disappeared in the works of many of his philosophical successors who have gotten sidetracked into endless debates with Richard Rorty about whether or not pragmatism can sustain its claim to be an American *public* philosophy. Nevertheless, Rorty's provocative critique of Dewey's metaphysics merits close inspection because he has made the strongest case against Dewey's naturalism, arguing that Dewey's notion of generic traits and his emphasis on method are dispensable and inconsequential to the survival of pragmatism. Rorty contends that Dewey "de-absolutized" Hegel, offering instead "a relativist and materialist version of teleology rather than an absolutist and idealist one."[1]

Rorty believes that the real value of pragmatic thought dwells in its capacity to redescribe human affairs from new perspectives in which we reweave our beliefs about our past into new narratives involving different expectations about the future. Rorty's argument against Deweyan naturalism—one tacitly accepted by many of Rorty's critics—is that Dewey's commitment to science was naive and that the major problems facing America are cultural and discursive rather than heuristic and methodological. The scientific promise of Dewey's pragmatism remains unfulfilled because scholars who wish to defend Dewey's aesthetics or his experiential, democratic conception of community life are unwilling also to include Dewey's experimentalism, developmentalism, and conceptions of inquiry in that endeavor. By tracing the intellectual pathways through which Dewey's metaphysics and naturalism have been reformulated by some of his successors, we can see how his theories have been adapted to fit different preconceptions about the cultural and political ramifications of human experience.

DEWEY'S HEGELIANISM IN DECLINE AND NATURALISM ON THE DEFENSIVE

Dewey attracted some of his most brilliant students at Columbia University long after his exhilarating formative years, leaving few traces for them of how he transformed the Hegelian phenomenology of being and becoming into a theory of mind and judgment. Dewey's graduate students were consequently in a better position to understand Dewey's criticisms of epistemology and his conception of science than to appreciate the intricate intellectual route to naturalism Dewey charted through Hegel and other *Naturphilosophers*, whom he rarely cited or mentioned in class. Dewey's most prominent students and colleagues included Morton White, Joseph Ratner, Ernest Nagel, and Sidney Hook, among others. They wrote extensively about Dewey's philosophy and each made original contributions to philosophy. Their works therefore provide a significant benchmark in understanding how their interpretations of Dewey's Hegelianism and ideas about science, nature, and human intelligence contributed paradoxically, as I shall argue, to the subsequent misdirection of Dewey scholarship into debates about cultural pragmatism.

Perhaps no other attempt to reconstruct Dewey's philosophical roots came closer to ably tilling the Hegelian soil from which Dewey reaped his naturalism than Morton G. White. White began his doctoral studies at Columbia University in 1936, after Dewey had retired, but he and Dewey formed a rocky intellectual relationship that lasted until Dewey's death in 1952. One of Dewey's closest colleagues, Herbert Schneider, was White's thesis advisor. White obtained access to some of Dewey's early notes and papers, read Jane Dewey's biography, and obtained Dewey's cooperation to answer specific questions about his past. He also consulted with Dewey's former colleagues Ernest Nagel, John Randall, and Irwin Edman to obtain their insights.[2] In his eventual book, *The Origins of Dewey's Instrumentalism*, published in 1943, White attempted to retrace the personal and intellectual pathways which led Dewey from idealism to instrumentalism.

Although Dewey had important reservations about White's thesis, discussed below, Dewey related to Bentley that he thought White was "headed in the right direction." He even ventured that Bentley "should cultivate [an] acquaintance with him, intellectually speaking," adding that, "he has more stuff in him—not stuffed in him—than most of the younger men who are writing. He at least has resisted going out into the wilderness after current false idols—not that there are any true ones."[3] Dewey commended White for being "true to form in emphasis on what he [Dewey] was against" by showing that Dewey used Hegel's ideas to avoid falling back on Kantian premises that Dewey says "were all the vogue."[4]

Dewey liked White's intellectual biography of his formative years that culminated in *Studies*. White focused on Dewey's struggle to define a conception of consciousness that withstood the double demand that it be grounded in biological evidence and also support a logically defensible theory of inquiry. White carefully and concisely retraced how George Sylvester Morris and Stanley Hall provided, through their own critical reading of Kant and Hegel, an opening through which Dewey glimpsed a new psychology and a naturalistic logic of experience.

White showed how Morris's Hegelian critique of Kant led Dewey to question the validity of Hegel's transcendental leanings and to dispense with the Absolute. White also shrewdly observed that despite Hall's anti-Hegelianism, Dewey correctly surmised that Darwinian and Hegelian conceptions of development could be reconciled. Dewey cleverly wielded this synthetic conception of development, White contended, to attack empiricist premises about sense data and to criticize formal logic for its irrelevance to human experience. However, as White incisively pointed out, Dewey had simply gotten the sequence wrong by assuming that mind came first. He did so by erroneously inferring from our tendency to impute minds and intentions to our fellow humans a pre-existing universal consciousness. What looked like an emergent theory of mind in Dewey's *Psychology*, White contended, was in actuality something quite different. For by arguing that "all consciousness is self-consciousness," White noted, Dewey was unwittingly conceiving the mind as predetermined rather than emergent.[5]

White found Hegel's shadowy presence always looming over Dewey as he attempted to construct an instrumentalist logic purged of any lingering idealism. White concluded that Dewey was really an "instrumental Hegelian" despite his protestations to the contrary. For during the same period in which he was jettisoning "Hegelian garb" in the 1890s, White observed, he still believed that Hegel was "the quintessence of the scientific spirit."[6] White surmised that Dewey believed that Hegel had simply come too early for modern empirical science that was bent on severing its philosophical roots. Dewey's attempt to find a safe harbor in science to anchor the Hegelian logic of inquiry unfortunately came a decade too late, as the science establishment was by then firmly divorced from metaphysics.

While Dewey generally liked White's book *The Origin of Dewey's Instrumen-*

talism, Dewey told Bentley that it was "good, but [White was] not tackling the fundament[al]."[7] Dewey's criticism seems to have been well-taken by White, who acknowledged years later that he "fully understood what Dewey meant."[8] White explained that he initially planned "a full-scale critical examination of Dewey's logical theory" that included an analysis of Dewey's *Logic*.[9] But he claimed that Nagel's intimidating presence on his dissertation committee dissuaded him from tackling this more ambitious task and caused him to opt instead for a "respectable, modest thesis that they would accept [rather] than possibly an exciting one they might not accept."[10] But in deferring to Nagel's demands, White seemed to have developed an inadequate appreciation for Dewey's *Logic*. When he wrote his popular book on social thought in America, White admitted he did not think "that the details of the *Logic* or the *Essays in Experimental Logic* form part of liberal American social thought."[11] Of course, White was not alone in tearing out the methodological heart of Dewey's strategy for social reconstruction. But the absence of references to Dewey's theory of inquiry in a book critical of Dewey's views on social reconstruction rankled Dewey, who refused to ever comment on or write about White's book.

In one respect, White's analysis of Dewey's intellectually formative years nearly grasped what Dewey considered to be the "fundamental" aspect of his work at that time, which had eluded White. Of all Dewey's early commentators, only White paid much attention to Dewey and McLellan's book *The Psychology of Number*. In it he recognized that Dewey was up to something important in making the argument that counting and measurement perform equivalent functions that have fundamental biological and behavioral significance. White correctly surmised that Dewey believed that these mathematical functions furnish "physical constants" with which scientists and non-scientists form judgments about the world. Had White chosen to include Dewey's *Logic* in his thesis study, it is quite possible that he would have discovered how this Hegelian-inspired conceptualization of human judgment eventually found its way into Dewey's mature philosophical works. Instead, he focused, as did subsequent commentators, on the critical reactions Dewey's novel conception of measurement aroused among educators and philosophers, who insisted that mathematics had nothing to do with human biological or behavioral development.[12]

Many of White's contemporaries who enthusiastically endorsed Dewey's conceptions of science and naturalism were also uncertain as to whether Hegel's ideas are pertinent to understanding Dewey's metaphysics and logic. This uncertainty has led many commentators to treat separately Dewey's Hegelian-inspired views about experience and to argue that Dewey's science and empiricism reflect an underlying realism. Disconcerted by this tendency, Dewey told his commentators in 1939 that "understanding my position would be facilitated if more attention were paid to my naturalism and less to my empiricism."[13] This tendency to situate Dewey within the idealist-realist dichotomy was unfortunately reinforced by the rise of logical positivism in the early

1930s. Rudolf Carnap, Hans Reichenbach and other positivists involved in the charmed "Vienna Circle" emigrated to the United States and were welcomed by many of Dewey's disciples, including Nagel and Hook. Initially seeking common ground regarding the principles of science, positivist adherents soon adopted Bertrand Russell's extreme atomistic epistemology, psychological realism, and a verificationist principle of inquiry that are completely contrary to Dewey's pragmatism.[14]

Joseph Ratner was one of Dewey's students and intellectual disciples who adopted a strict construction of Dewey's holistic naturalism and experimentalism. He refused to be sidetracked into debates about knowledge and verification. Ratner assembled some of the earliest collections of Dewey's essays in books published in 1929 and 1939, and he made an important contribution to the Dewey scholarship in his 1939 book *Intelligence in the Modern World*. There he argued that Dewey provided the philosophical justification for experimentalism that was first introduced in modern science by Galileo and Newton. Nevertheless, Dewey did not share Ratner's rigid insistence on a laboratory-based notion of experimentalism—a prescription that has led later commentators, such as Rorty, to reject as erroneous the Deweyan-inspired idea that science is the only legitimate method of pragmatism. While Dewey demurred in Ratner's quest for methodological uniformity, Dewey saw some value in accepting Ratner's recommendation that "experiencing [be used] as a methodological term," because experience has to do with the different ways that an individual can obtain knowledge about the world.[15]

Ratner cared little for Hegel and was not interested in tracing his influence in Dewey's thought. Hegel's error, Ratner believed, was that he tried "to force the mind to swallow the natural world whole." Instead of satisfying the mind's hunger for knowledge, Ratner added in vivid terms, Hegel's "grotesque act of intellectual outrage gave it convulsive indigestion. And the spasmic regurgitations of Absolute Idealism are splattered over all the pages of subsequent cultural history."[16] Needless to say, Ratner considered futile Dewey's attempt to follow in Hegel's footsteps. Aside from his strong distaste for Dewey's Hegelianism, Ratner was steady in his conviction that Dewey correctly anticipated the need for a "general logic of experience." Ratner believed that Dewey envisioned a new philosophical perspective whereby

> Nature, after all, is not a set of separate locks and human beings the keysmiths. Indeed, in a very important and fundamental sense it may be said that the keys *are* the locks for they *are* Nature in so far as she constructs herself through our reconstructions.[17]

THE LURE OF THE VIENNA CIRCLE

As a logician, Nagel was much less enamored than Ratner with Dewey's naturalism. Nagel was more concerned that Dewey's theory of logic be capable of furnishing standards of empirical validation that were at least as rigorous as those being proposed by the emerging philosophical movement of logical positivism. Led by the logicians Rudolf Carnap and Otto Neurath, logical positivists advocated a philosophy of science that strongly emphasized the principles of verification, deductive explanation, and prediction. Positivists who claimed Ernst Mach for their inspiration wanted to cleanse scientific theories of all unprovable metaphysical terms and limit them to operationally verifiable statements. While it is true that Mach wanted to purge science of metaphysics, he did so because he wanted scientific propositions to be stated in a language about perception that accurately represented *phenomenal* experience. The positivists proposed something very different. They demanded that scientists rid themselves of subjective perceptual terms and their epistemic premises and adopt a language that provided a strictly *physical* account of natural and social phenomena they wished to explain. This positivist physicalist orientation was barely distinguishable from materialism and reductionism—philosophical positions that Mach vigorously opposed.[18]

Nagel, University of Chicago pragmatist Charles Morris, and Sidney Hook met the members of the Vienna Circle in Europe, became admirers of their attempt to reconstruct the logic of inquiry, and urged them to emigrate to the United States. These American pragmatists believed that logical positivists and pragmatists had a lot in common despite their different emphases. They believed that pragmatists and positivists could benefit by joining forces to build a unified language of science. Largely ignorant of American pragmatism, Carnap and many other positivists gladly accepted the invitation and rejoiced at the prospect that they would find a congenial companion in pragmatism. Morris best expressed the sentiments of his colleague Nagel when he declared that pragmatism and logical positivism should adopt a common theory of meaning. He declared that his theory must be "wide enough to include the results of socially cooperative science, and do justice to the logical, biological, and empirical aspects of the symbolic process, and yet be narrow enough to exclude from claims to knowledge those expressions which are meaningless."[19] Morris nevertheless failed to foresee that the positivist's agenda for reconstruction actually involved a purified rather than a unified science—one cleansed of any residue of naturalism and references to phenomenal experience.

Dewey respected Nagel's intellectual integrity, admired his "great natural ability," was impressed with his adeptness in mathematics and logic, and sought his comments on several books, including *Experience and Nature* and *Quest for Certainty*.[20] Nagel held Dewey in high esteem and appreciated his genuine interest in his own intellectual development, even though he was disappointed that Dewey largely ignored and did not take a stronger interest in the field of symbolic logic.[21] For his part, Dewey regretted that such an able student as Nagel "should be taken with logical positivism."[22] Although respectful of Dewey, Nagel had an eye out for vulnerabilities in his naturalism when he challenged the logical coherence of Dewey's contention that generic traits not only exist in nature but enter into and can be known through inquiry. The details of their argument bear repeating because the controversy swirling around Dewey's conception of generic traits has continued unabated ever since in the scholarship on pragmatism.

Dewey seems to have precipitated the controversy by arguing that the so-called law of the excluded middle or if-then conditional statements applied only to propositional discourse and not to the existence of *real* events that occur in the present, future, or past. This was so, Dewey contended, because all natural phenomena, including human experience, are typically in a process of transition from one state to another. Phenomena or events do not become changeless facts that are never re-examined just because they happened in the past, Dewey argued, nor are future events irreversible just because predicted consequences happen to occur. In Dewey's view knowledge about the past remains hypothetical because we are unable to know with certainty what are the necessary and sufficient conditions that make an event unique and non-recurrent.

Nagel accused Dewey of playing fast and loose with the idea of continuity by deploying the closely related but equivocal terms of "determinate" and "indeterminate" to exaggerate the supposed ontological gap between logical discourse and natural phenomena. Nagel confidently believed that he had found the idealist Achilles' heel in Dewey's argument. Nagel rhetorically badgered Dewey by asking how it was possible for him to know that such things as change, contingency, and precariousness are generic traits of existence if he is unable to characterize them unambiguously in logical terms? More pointedly, Nagel asked, "Why does he [Dewey] impute the features presented in human experience to a nature embracing, but containing more than that experience?"[23] Nagel cautioned that if "logical traits are cut off from ontological traits, so that the former have no prototype in the latter, Professor Dewey's belief that the precarious and stable are exhibited, not only in the human foreground, but as outstanding features of nature throughout, is untenable."[24]

Dewey was willing to accept the realist's position that the term "determinate" has a fixed meaning according to the context in which it is used, or that by instituting operations one can show that physical objects have a determinate existence. But Dewey strongly denied the nominalist assumption Nagel defended, that something was logically determinate by virtue of the meanings of the words used to describe it. Dewey deflected Nagel's other, seemingly more devastating criticism about divorcing thought from reality, observing that human thought in general takes place and exists *within* experience. This was consistent with Dewey's anthropology that human judgment and methods of inquiry are reciprocally related in human experience. Nature presents limits and challenges to human ingenuity but it also provides the resources and energy for intelligence and judgment. Logic and discourse are products of linguistic conventions that enable us to reflect on the meaning and significance of those experiences.[25]

McGraw's experiments with prelinguistic and prelogical infants provided the best evidence Dewey could find that mind is shaped and influenced by natural forces that enable the formation of judgments in the absence of concepts. The precarious but natural situations that McGraw posed for Johnny in her experiments contributed to his uncertainty until he successfully translated through his own movements and judgment the forces of motion needed to gain deliberate control over a situation.

Hook also contributed, along with Nagel, to the warm reception accorded logical positivism, and he personally endorsed Hans Reichenbach's probabilistic version of positivism. But Hook nevertheless maintained his strong identification with Dewey's conception of science and naturalism. Hook did not challenge the need for empirical rigor but he took a more relaxed attitude (as has his successor, Richard Rorty) than Nagel and the logical positivists about how to frame the terms of logical discourse involving scientific inquiry. Hook was willing to support Dewey's metaphysics and science as long as "naturalism is not committed to any theory concerning which categorical terms are irreducible or basic in explanation." What all naturalists should agree on, Hook recommended, is "the 'irreducibility' of a certain method by which knowledge is achieved and tested."[26]

Hook wanted to preserve the distinction between metaphysics and science that Dewey's colleague John Randall preferred to dissolve.[27] Hook considered absurd Randall's assertion that metaphysics is just another form of scientific inquiry whose claims can be tested as if they were well-formulated hypotheses. Hook insisted on drawing the line between philosophical discussions that pose unanswerable questions and the ones that sometimes help scientists avoid inconsistency and contradiction. Hook anticipated Rorty's complaint four decades later that it is a waste of time trying to get scientists to become more self-conscious about the metaphysical implications of inquiry. Rorty contended that attempts to clarify terms such as causality, inertia, or energy are not going to get scientists any closer to the underlying realities that the terms are thought to conceal.

THE ONTOLOGICAL ENIGMA OF "GENERIC TRAITS"

Hook believed that attempts to postulate a metaphysics of experience had fallen into disrepute in the 1930s because there was no consensus among philosophers about the meaning of the term "ontology." To remedy this confusion, Hook defined ontological to refer to propositions "which we believe to be cognitively valid, or which assert something that is true or false, and yet which are not found in any particular science, whether of physics, psychology, or sociology, but which are taken for granted by the sciences."[28] According to Hook, Dewey's generic traits are simply "indeterminate commonplaces or truisms" that "nobody bothers to make explicit nor deny."[29] By treating generic traits as global background assumptions, Hook believed that philosophers and scientists could avoid the awkward epistemological problem of positing a theory of mind without "committing us to any specific theory as to how what we know was learned."[30]

Dewey never concurred with Hook's representations of his metaphysics. He agreed with Hook that no one discipline possesses exclusive ownership of the facts, or possesses a theory which convincingly explains all of them. If there were such a discipline, it would obviate the existence of other fields that claim to have alternative ways of knowing those facts. It is for this reason that Dewey favored interdisciplinary research as the hallmark of a mature science. Of course, Dewey knew full well, through his own struggle to makes his ideas clear, that much confusion was wrought by terminological misunderstandings of key ontological and epistemological terms. Dewey's "generic traits" was no exception. But I do not believe that Dewey would have been comfortable with Hook's characterization of generic traits as "irreducible" phenomena. There are two important reasons for this.

First, Dewey insisted that no traits exist in isolation but bear a dialectical relation to one another as implied by motion and rest, balance and precariousness, certainty and uncertainty, determinacy and indeterminacy, and so forth. Only through their interaction and reciprocal play do generic traits acquire form and function. McGraw demonstrated this point effectively by showing how the timing and sequence with which gravity, balance, motion, force, and other natural phenomena are experienced in early development contributed to fundamental differences in Johnny's and Jimmy's behaviors, attitudes, and performances.

Second, from a Deweyan perspective Hook errs in relegating generic traits to the implicit background of conscious experience. Dewey held that generic traits can be operative in the foreground while others remain implicit. As the context changes so do the sequences in which traits are combined to form the foreground and background of conscious experience. This revolving process of substitution or replacement of features in the foreground and background of phenomenal experiences renders our judgments conditional, tentative, and approximate, because the order in which events occur is forever undergoing slight variations which change our basis of comparison. That is why it would be closer in keeping with Dewey's preferences if we characterize generic traits as *possibilities awaiting realization* in alternative forms of thought and action rather than as fundamental and changeless features of the world or of our neurobiological constitution.

Herbert Schneider, a close Dewey colleague who shared with Dewey his excursions into the world of art, seems to have grasped more deftly than anyone else the ontological and energetic basis of Dewey's generic traits. According to Schneider, Dewey's naturalism was not a self-contained process "but a cooperation among processes."[31] In Dewey's philosophy, Schneider says, "[n]ature is neither in things nor external to them, but of them," because "[i]t [nature] is normative."[32] Dewey's conception of nature consists neither of substances nor essences, Schneider argues, but mechanical forces or productive processes.

Forces of nature work well or poorly depending on their "fitness" for working together, Schneider observes, and "[b]y fitting together, things disclose nature."[33]

When Schneider says that nature is a norm, he does not mean this in a statistical, moral, or even a probabilistic sense. Instead, he says that it falls somewhere between the ideal and actual—a possibility that is definitely attainable, but one that is just as likely to be accidental as to occur through design. For example, not every organ or appendage that a species possesses serves that animal equally effectively over time. Changing demands of the environment contribute to the gradual obsolescence of some functions, which are either remodeled, disappear, or are overtaken by other functions. That is why Dewey believed that experimentalism discloses *new* values by revealing unsuspected relationships among familiar things.

Rorty, who closely identifies with Hook, has pushed Hook's interpretation of Dewey's metaphysics to its logical conclusion. Rorty has done so with flair and a sense of irony that prevented Hook (perhaps due to his loyalty and deference to Dewey) from dispensing altogether with terms that Dewey considered fundamental to inquiry. Rorty finds Hook's defense of Dewey's generic traits ironic because the positivists whom Hook admired correctly foresaw the futility of dealing with "pseudo-problems" such as those posed by "generic traits of experience."[34] Wittgenstein occupied a charmed position in British empiricism, Rorty observes, because he sowed the seeds of the destruction of logical positivism by bringing out the self-refuting consequences of language turned inward on itself.

Dewey's mental lapse in embracing Hegel, Rorty argues, led Dewey to erroneously believe that there was a "neutral standpoint from which experience can be seen in terms of some generic traits, which once recognized, will make it impossible for us to describe it" in other than a holistic perspective.[35] Rorty considers Dewey's "naturalistic metaphysics to be a contradiction in terms." Even Hegel showed, according to Rorty, that everyone is already trapped from the start in a dialectical contradiction. Consequently, Rorty says, we are prevented, on logical grounds, from taking the "inclusive integrity of experience as the starting point," as human experience has already been compromised by the impurities of our thoughts and beliefs about it.[36]

Rorty evades the problem of specifying his own philosophical standpoint by assuming an omniscient perspective. He places Dewey in a hypothetical debate with continental philosophers with whom Dewey was barely acquainted and about whose ideas he never wrote one word. Although a silent participant in Rorty's conversation, if Dewey were given a voice, he would probably respond to this issue of "standpoint" by agreeing that we are already in the middle of things when we commence inquiry. Naturally things are muddled and confused, because novel experiences lack unity and integrity. However, we are not neutral or indifferent to what is going on, and that is why it is essential to get one's bearings straight. This requires that an effort be made to reduce uncertainty by physically and perceptually identifying the limits to action. In doing so, we acknowledge that we have biases and preferences and that there are alternative choices that carry with them either complementary or opposing consequences. We recognize that our energy and resources are limited and that we must maintain our balance and center of gravity in responding to opposing forces that pull us in different directions.

Rorty thinks that Dewey mistakenly saw mind in larger metaphysical terms than was needed to support a Darwinian point of view. There is no need to posit a seamless continuity between all life forms just because sentient creatures all happen to possess nervous systems and brains. This is an unfortunate remnant from Dewey's Hegelian past that Rorty says is not needed to scientifically explain how human thought is possible. However, Dewey would be the first to acknowledge that first-person phenomenal perspectives may not be neutral or objective, but first-person states of consciousness may very well be a necessary attribute of an embodied mind. By dispensing with a naturalistic conception of mind and by discounting the role of human experience and judgment in inquiry, Rorty fails to show how the conversations and traditions that he favors can be sustained merely by a "rational agreement" to do so.

BENTLEY'S NOMINALIST DETOUR

None of Dewey's friends and intellectual foes did more to dismantle Dewey's naturalism and his experiential conception of inquiry than Arthur Bentley. This is ironic, for as a Dewey admirer and onetime student at the University of Chicago, Bentley believed he was actually strengthening pragmatism by erasing through terminological changes any unwanted epistemological or ontological props he thought Dewey would favor discarding. Bentley's circuitous route leading to his presumptuous ambition to help Dewey rewrite *Logic* is worth retracing because Bentley marks the first in a series of Dewey's successors, including Rorty, who have found inventive but problematic ways to "renew" pragmatism by gutting its core beliefs.

After two unsuccessful attempts to complete undergraduate studies at York College in Nebraska and the University of Denver, Bentley enrolled at Johns Hopkins in 1890 and studied political economy with Richard Ely.[37] After Bentley obtained his Ph.D., he was appointed a temporary lecturer in sociology at the University of Chicago. He wisely took the opportunity to audit Dewey's courses on the "Theory of Logic" and the "Logic of Ethics." After this, Bentley continued to keep up with Dewey's scholarship, until they began a long correspondence in 1932. Bentley's intellectual interests focused on mind and society. But Bentley considered Baldwin to have succeeded where Dewey had up to that point failed in arguing convincingly that mind is rooted in nature *and* society. Consequently, Bentley wanted Dewey to adopt the even bolder cosmological argument that society and the "world is in the mind."[38]

Bentley dabbled in journalism and various philanthropic activities before writing a series of books over the next three decades, books that ranged over such diverse subjects as politics, linguistics, and mathematics. Only one of the many books Bentley wrote during his lifetime became a memorable classic, *The Process of Government,* published in 1908. Bentley propounded in this book a highly original functional theory of politics. Instead of presenting a conventional account of formal institutional structures and roles, Bentley focused on the informal processes whereby interest groups compete for power and reap the rewards of the political system. After a long lapse, Bentley published *Relativity in Man and Society* in 1926, contending that social scientists must dispense with a Newtonian perspective of space and time that Einstein successfully deposed and embrace a field conception of social phenomena. Bentley published next a difficult but seminal book, the *Linguistic Analysis of Mathematics,* in 1932. Dewey found Bentley's deconstruction of mathematical formalism very useful in formulating his own philosophical views about mathematics in *Logic.*

Their ensuing voluminous correspondence that spanned almost two decades quickly focused on terminological issues in Dewey's *Logic* that Bentley believed contributed to some needless misinterpretations. Bentley's determination to treat separately biological and behavioral phenomena set the tone for the remainder of Dewey's reluctant, defensive, and sometimes quarrelsome collaboration with Bentley to redefine the terms of social inquiry. Their efforts eventuated in the publication in 1949 of *Knowing and the Known.* Bentley politely but self-assuredly argued that there were limitations to Dewey's organic approach that could be strengthened by including Bentley's perspective. Bentley cared little for Dewey's biologically based "naturalistic position" and was convinced that "the language-reasoning-symbolization-concept construction will only get itself efficiently formulated, when it is worked out in a naturalistically social rather than in a naturalistically organic form."[39]

Dewey had always been self-conscious about his terminology largely because he wanted to find words that were not closely identified with philosophical ideas that he rejected. He probably wouldn't have been as responsive to Bentley's urgings had the leaders of the logical positivist movement, such as Rudolf Carnap and Percy Bridgman, not been so critical of the operational slackness in the terms Dewey used to describe the logic of inquiry. Bentley gleefully played the role of devil's advocate, increasing Dewey's doubts about terms like "interaction," "experience," and "inquiry" that he had used for decades. Bentley opposed the emergent view of consciousness that Dewey defended, saying, "Where consciousness enters as a quasi-thing with a definite organic location, alleged to possess and exercise a power-specialization of its own, it carries with it all the old embroilments of solipsism and realism."[40] As Thelma Lavine cogently observes, the biological structures of mind that underpinned Dewey's view of human experience and inquiry "dissolved" under the pressures of Bentley's "structureless cosmology."[41]

Bentley denied that his attempt to construct a hierarchy of meaningful terms for social inquiry was essentially a nominalist project akin to Bertrand Russell's logical atomism. He claimed instead that "at each step logical behavior is an *aspect* of linguistic behavior" and vice versa. Taken together, words and behaviors, according to Bentley, involve conjoint processes of "knowing-known," and thus there is no explanatory gap between what is said and what is done.[42] While Bentley eventually succeeded in getting Dewey to agree to the term "transaction" as the centerpiece of a new typology of behavioral discourse, he underestimated how strongly Dewey would resist dispensing with his belief in the continuity between nature and human experience.

Bentley's intention to replace Dewey's phenomenalism with a linguistic account of human experience is no better illustrated than in correspondence he exchanged with Dewey in 1943. Bentley's motives for doing so were foreshadowed in his 1935 book *Behavior, Knowledge, and Fact*. In this book, read closely by Dewey, Bentley proposed that all human events must be rendered into units of "behavioral space-time" in which observable processes can be assigned meaning and reference. Dewey insisted, however, that communication, as a generic trait of experience, involved more than just exchanging information through language, but involved a physically active process of "grasping" the significance of events.[43] Bentley preferred to distinguish between mere acquaintance and actual knowledge by conceptually differentiating between information exchanges that involve "indirect communicative buildup" and ones that confer "formal communicative status."[44] Nevertheless, Dewey resisted this amendment and for good reason. Bentley was undercutting the inseparable relationship between implicit and explicit knowledge in judgment and undermining the distinction between the having and the undergoing (i.e., being and knowing that) that constituted phenomenal experience.

Dewey readily acknowledged that he was "enough of a naturalist to hold to the continuity of development" and still identify knowledge with statements.[45] And he was willing to drop the term "experience," but he was repulsed by the thought that non-cognitive knowledge would be thereby marginalized. He indignantly asserted:

> Now I am quite willing to modify my terminology, and I wouldn't want to have anything put in our document that in any way suggested the exclusion of the use of knowledge to cover pre-linguistic transactions and, especially, nothing that would militate against treating knowing through designations as the all-inclusive knowledge, in terms of which all the events I called being and having are themselves observed, described, etc.[46]

Unfortunately for Dewey, his interactive conception of experience was ultimately replaced by a less evocative but perhaps more useful operational term, "transaction." To be certain, the word "transaction" seemed better able than "interaction," saddled as it was with a Newtonian imagery of attraction and repulsion, to express the complex reciprocal forces that Dewey and Bentley wanted to explain. Lawrence Frank approved of the use of the term "transaction" precisely because it captured the essential Maxwellian insight that social phenomena occur in a field of social forces involving "dynamic circular pro-cesses."[47] The term "transaction" also implied a transformational relationship between knower and known that was not apparent in the term "interaction."

SELF-CONSCIOUSNESS AND PHENOMENAL EXPERIENCE

None of Dewey's philosophical ideas were received with greater incomprehen-sion and subjected to more criticism than his theory of mind. Dewey's distinc-tion between cognitive and non-cognitive knowledge, the importance he at-tached to doubt and uncertainty in human judgment, and the significant role he believed that consciousness played in enlarging experience and advancing in-quiry were each challenged on logical, empirical and metaphysical grounds. Dewey attracted considerable criticism from realists like Bertrand Russell and positivists like Hans Reichenbach, who rejected as subjectivist and paradoxical Dewey's claims that immediate qualitative knowledge could be known through non-cognitive processes.

They did not recognize as valid Dewey's Jamesean notion that implicit mean-ings can originate from the subconscious "fringe" of explicit thought. Nor did they acknowledge the relevance of accumulating evidence from neurology and psychology that seemed to support Dewey's theories about the constructive and integrative role of inhibition in human judgment. As one of the founders of logical empiricism, Russell was committed to the realist notion that the world consists of atomic facts that can be characterized accurately in proposi-tional terms. He also believed that mind and matter are logical constructions of sense data, which themselves are neither physical nor mental.

Russell, like his successor Rorty, was leery of naturalists like Dewey, who insisted on converting epistemological questions of knowledge and truth into psychological matters of perception and judgment. Russell contended that Dewey had run perception and judgment together, thereby confusing sensory processes manifested in a causal chain of events with reasoning and inferential processes governed by language and logic. By attributing the source of doubt to uncertain situations as well as to individual minds, Dewey seemed to Russell to be confusing the difference between psychological states of mind and those elements properly ascribed to situations. Consequently, Russell argued that Dewey failed to acknowledge that it is individual perceptions that are corrigible, not the sense data, and that the language and reasoning we use to describe the world must furnish judgments independent of the processes through which we perceive them.[48]

Rorty has criticized Dewey for similar reasons. Rorty believes that Dewey is guilty of "running together the vocabularies in which we describe the causal antecedents of knowledge with those in which we offer justifications of our claims of knowledge."[49] Rorty asserts that Dewey could have avoided this con-fusion by dropping a "spectator model of knowledge," and thus eliminated altogether the problem of mind-body dualism.[50] Had Dewey adopted a "therapeutic" perspective instead, Rorty conjectured—one where he merely "re-describes" the problems of traditional philosophy rather than prescribing new ones—then he would have succeeded in refuting the charge that he tacitly subscribed to realism.[51] But what conceptions of mind and self should Dewey have adopted to avoid taking culturally partisan and epistemologically suspect positions that Rorty condemns? Ironically, Rorty finds Freud's conception of mind preferable to Dewey's for precisely the reasons that Dewey resoundingly rejected Freudian psychoanalysis. Rorty's arguments deserve closer scrutiny because the "decentered" Freudian conception of mind and self that he advances fails to reach the threshold of intersubjective consciousness that is needed to sustain the conversation about culture that he endorses.

Rorty argues that before the sixteenth century, philosophers mistakenly thought it appropriate to treat "man as a natural kind," who not only occupied the center of the universe, but possessed a soul which provided a moral center of gravity to human life. This belief in a universal mind was eventually replaced by a mechanistic conception introduced by physicists like Descartes and Newton, who contended that mind was governed by the physical laws of nature. Realistically, of course, scientists were never faced with the overly simplistic choice between mechanical and non-mechanical models, as preformationism, vitalism, and functionalism in biology thrived alongside mechanism from the mid-seventeenth century onward. And, for the most part, nineteenth-century *Naturphilosophers* saw the world in complementary biological and physical terms. Nevertheless, Rorty claims that Freud appropriated this mechanistic conception to persuasively support his novel contention that the mind is a de-centered collection of associative mechanisms. Rorty commends Freud for providing a more realistic conception of ourselves as consisting of a composite of different persons with whom we may silently converse. Each persona we adopt provides a different story or pretext to support the type of person we would most like to be.[52]

Rorty believes that Freud furnished us "new vocabularies of moral reflection" that move us away from questions of personal purity to those involving self-justification. Accordingly, we are told that we should no longer pose questions that imply the possibility of perfection or the preservation of integrity. These concerns would be replaced by self-serving questions such as, "If I do this rather than that now, what story will I tell myself later?"[53] It is hard to fathom how these solipsistic forms of self-interrogation, however, could ever connect to form a conversation about the larger aims of society as a whole. There is indeed little incentive for people to cooperate who have no larger purposes in life than to acknowledge the contingency of their existence and the inevitability of pain.[54]

Rorty is sanguine about the possibility that science may be able to predict and control our desires by understanding scientifically how the brain functions. He contends that this will not "threaten or change our self-image" because "such discoveries do not suggest that we are being shouldered aside by somebody else."[55] Rorty does not seem to have considered the possibility that if scientists succeed in mimicking brain functions or consciousness, humans may forfeit their claim to possess a unique form of intelligence. But if Freud is right, as Rorty seems to think, that "repressions . . . are the products of countless contingencies that never enter experience," then the question of whether our current self-image is of our own choosing seems strangely out of place.[56]

In his eagerness to strip away the moral delusions that stubbornly cling to mind and soul-centered epistemologies, Rorty leaves humans bereft of the tools needed to form judgments about what attributes of their minds and humanity are worth preserving. Whether or not the mind is decentered and whether or not the body and mind actually do function separately or operate in a functionally integrative way are ultimately questions for science to decide, not philosophy or psychoanalysis. Dismissing questions about the human mind that pose moral conflicts or scientific dilemmas is not going to get us any closer to self-understanding.

Conspicuously absent in Rorty's theory of mind is the capacity for *psychological distance*. Normally we look outward rather than inward for examples of character possessed by individuals that we admire and want to emulate. We do so in order to correct for our own biases and habits of mind that predispose us to favor some personas rather than others. This will sometimes require that we distance ourselves physically or emotionally from our own experiences and put ourselves in someone else's shoes. Engagement presupposes detachment. The capacity to distance oneself from immediate feelings and desires, Dewey contends, is essential to discovery and self-assessment. Yet if what Rorty (and Freud before him) claims is true, that all narratives are self-spun webs of desire and deceit, then humans are incapable of the psychological distance needed to have novel experiences. Perhaps that is why Rorty eliminates the "metaphors of discovery" from the narratives of self-justification. The desire to discover something new demands an inquisitive, experimental attitude; self-justification merely requires an ironic stance and sense of futility.[57]

Dewey's own life and career were replete with stunning examples of the severe limitations of self-justification and the enormous advantages of expanded consciousness and political leverage that came from adopting the perspectives of colleagues who occupied different roles and institutions in a society that Dewey wanted to transform. Dewey's bitter personal duels with Randolph Bourne and Scudder Klyce consumed Dewey in strategies of self-defense that were personally distasteful and professionally disgraceful. Dewey displayed far more grace and attained far keener insights when he was able to distance himself from the immediacy of ephemeral events and put them in larger historical or political contexts.

Dewey was challenged to find in these different roles an individual and social center of gravity. He had to balance his single-minded and sometimes lonely philosophical quest to understand the mind and his equally fervent passion to engage others in the shared experiences of scientific discovery and social reform. Dewey succeeded in these endeavors through collaborations with Frank and McGraw, who made it possible for Dewey to project his ideas into institutional domains where their political, scientific, and moral consequences could be more accurately gauged. Through these strategies Dewey's ideas became the common intellectual property of the American public.

Rorty thinks it is mistaken to view the mind as the last refuge of intrinsicality because it makes the realist's and idealist's pretensions of transcending human fallibility and grasping the essence of things appear attainable. But once we drop the idea that the mind and language constitute the objects of perception and simply hold that only beliefs can make other beliefs true, Rorty concludes, then "we have no use for the intentional-real distinction."[58] By eliminating the distinction between the intentional and the real, according to Rorty, we dispose of the Hegelian "idealists claim that all relations are internal, for we will have no use for the external-internal contrast."[59]

It is important to understand why Dewey considered mind to be personal and intentional as well as a socially extrinsic phenomenon of human experience. Dewey considered the practice among epistemologists of isolating cognitive experience from other modes of experiencing to be pernicious because non-cognitive experiences constituted the great bulk of all knowledge. Dewey did not mean by this that most knowledge we acquire is purely private and subjective, but only that much of what we know and learn involves a mixture of attitudes, habits, and beliefs that reflect shared values. Only when we create or encounter novel or discrepant situations do our habits and beliefs fail to be reliable guides. Energy must be summoned to handle uncertainty and consciousness, and this seemed to Dewey to be the catalyst by which perception and memory are brought to bear to make problematic situations resolvable and comprehensible to oneself and others. Consciousness of how the contingencies of order affect differently the perceived limits to an indeterminate situation introduces the need for comparison and the possibility of measurement. Formulating a response to a problem requires that values be made explicit and interpersonally comparable with respect to some intended outcome. The ensuing challenge involving the measured release of mental and physical energy in a consistent direction makes judgment the fulcrum of action in reaching a determinate result.

Dewey believed that consciousness furnishes the leverage of expanded awareness to move from a purely internal, subjective state of mind to one informed by a broader horizon involving awareness of the limits to and opportunities for individual satisfaction and interpersonal interaction. The sensation of pain or the emotion of fear instigates a search for the possible internal or external sources of these feelings and emotions in an effort to control and limit their duration. This is accomplished by getting control over the situation by either increasing the distance between oneself and the source of irritation or preventing it from recurring.

But the interaction of these cognitive and conative processes is not all that

Dewey considered to be involved in phenomenal experience. We may experience all sorts of incidental twinges, pangs, and other qualia in our daily lives that may or may not be intersubjectively understood, but these do not add up to a complete experience as Dewey defined it. A phenomenal experience involves a threefold sense of consummation or fulfillment by connecting what one is undergoing now to what one and others have undergone in the past and to what one expects to achieve or attain in the future. Human experience is consummated by the sense of *personal continuity and connection* that comes from an immediately experienced but indeterminate situation that unfolds into an ordered series of intentional interactions that have social consequences.

One other trait of human behavior that is vital to shared experience is the capacity to communicate. Dewey advanced perhaps his strongest argument, in *Experience and Nature,* that communication is a prelinguistic, generic trait of human interaction that paves the way for the acquisition of language and the development of self-consciousness. Dewey and McGraw found strong evidence to suggest that mastery of prelinguistic communication enables infants to develop a theory of mind. Infants are able to convert their understanding of the meaning of gestured cues and physical feedback provided by adults into a theory of mind that they use to anticipate responses by imputing their own thoughts and intentions to other minds. Significantly, McGraw's toddlers successfully performed experimental tasks considered impossible for their age, not by mastering complex narratives, as Rorty would have us believe, but by converting sentient cues into resources with which to confront *firsthand* the challenges of locomotion. Only later are infants able to put their feelings into words that can be intersubjectively understood.

EXPERIMENTALISM AND THE POLITICS OF METHOD AND TRUTH

Rorty thinks we need to differentiate between a good Dewey worth keeping around and a bad Dewey whose regrettable errors can be safely forgotten. The bad Dewey is the philosopher of science who thinks we can learn something about how mind and consciousness function by examining historical episodes in which scientists confronted with uncertainty and unable to form clear judgments were forced to redesign their methods of inquiry. The good Dewey is the philosopher of language and discourse who "would like to be naturalistic without being scientistic."[60] He is the pragmatist whom Rorty endorses—the one who "wants to hold on to the materialistic world view that typically forms the background of liberal self-consciousness" without claiming to have attained this perspective through any reliable method.[61]

However, Dewey sought the unification of the physical, biological, and social sciences through the adoption of interdisciplinary, experimental methods of inquiry. This was a pluralistic rather than a monolithic vision of science and political culture. Dewey wanted to liberate all forms of natural and social in-

quiry from the shackles placed on them by epistemological realists and nomi-
nalists, logical formalists and positivists, and by political ideologists who construed human motivation in narrow utilitarian terms. He also tried to make his
best case that science advances when the minds engaged in inquiry are not set
apart from naturalistic phenomena in which they are embodied. Discursive
strategies based on all-or-nothing epistemologies maximize the role of belief,
style, and assertion while minimizing the role of perception, judgment, and
experience. These crucial elements of inquiry forming the heart of Dewey's
agenda for the reconstruction of science and society ironically fell into disrepute at the hands of Dewey's most ardent supporters. Their zealous defense of
Dewey's experimentalism became an easy target for those advocating a more
relaxed attitude about questions of method and truth.

As noted before, Joseph Ratner led the way in perpetrating the misconceptions about Dewey's notion of science by proclaiming that "Dewey takes modern science as the exemplar of what knowledge is, and the method of modern
science as standard for the method of knowing."[62] He followed this unfortunate statement with a brilliant although tendentious critical history of the rise
of experimentalism led by Galileo and Newton that, Ratner claims, enthroned
the reign of the laboratory method of the experimental sciences. Ratner apparently thought the physical sciences were paradigmatic of the control that must
be instituted in a laboratory to reproduce the conditions in which phenomena
vary in nature. Dewey and McGraw clearly adopted a different conception of
experimentalism, one that emphasized methodological innovation rather than
replication and that placed greater weight on the spontaneity rather than control of the behavior of their experimental subjects.

Hook shared Ratner's inclination to insist that the conduct of inquiry be
naturalistic while satisfying the standards of scientific rigor. Hook asserted
that "systemization of what is involved in the scientific method is what we
mean by naturalism, and the characteristic doctrines of naturalism like the denial of disembodied spirits generalize the cumulative evidence won by the use
of this method."[63] Hook tended to equate science with epistemological realism
by saying that "there is some common method of determining when a position
is adequate to the facts of experience and when not," adding that "this common
method is continuous with the method which we ordinarily use to hold individuals to responsible utterances about the existence of things in the world."[64]
Adhering to the accepted practices of science was no different than obeying the
law. Hook went so as far as to equate a scientific attitude toward nature with a
democratic temperament. "Democracy needs no cosmic support," Hook argued, "other than the *chance* to make good. That chance it has, because man is
part of nature."[65]

Rorty thinks that Hook was mistaken in wanting to make the scientific
method a universal method for American culture. This made pragmatism seem
more positivistic than it need be and less amenable to the post-positivist and
post-structuralist insights of continental philosophers like Heidegger and Fou-

cault. Rorty traces his disillusionment with Hook's pragmatism-as-method back to Dewey's allegedly mistaken belief in *Logic* that scientific progress occurs through advances in methodology. As far as Rorty is concerned, Dewey wasted his time trying to "discover Galileo and Darwin's methodological secret," which Rorty contended that neither of them actually possessed.[66] By Rorty's reckoning, Thomas Kuhn has shown that "the whole idea of 'analysis of methods' is misconceived," leading Rorty to conclude "that 'logic' as Dewey conceived it, is a subject not worth developing."[67] Rorty claims that Kuhn liberated us from the false belief that science is reducible to nature by showing that science advances through theoretical redescriptions that do not consist of "collections of judgments," nor do they require, as Dewey insisted, that we make judgment "the ultimate subject matter of logic."[68]

Dewey's argument in *The Public and Its Problems* and *Logic* is that the governance of science and the governance of human conduct are inseparable politically but are also *irreducible*.[69] The discoveries and inventions of science must be realizable and justifiable within the communities and society where they have important consequences for human behavior. The judgments or conventions that govern the conduct of science, while not identical with social conventions, overlap in significant ways, as Frank's child study network illustrated, to ensure that research originated in laboratories is viable in nature and in the social order in which it is introduced. There must be some reasonable fit between experimental claims and the actual results that people experience in applying this knowledge to child rearing.

Rorty's insouciant attitude toward Dewey's pragmatism has attracted considerable criticism from Dewey scholars, whose works are too numerous to discuss. Democratic social theorists who hesitate to fully embrace Dewey's empiricism and experimentalism for fear of appearing too scientistic unwittingly make themselves vulnerable to Rorty's critique by using pragmatism as a *discursive* method to enunciate community values that they consider commendable. Richard Bernstein is an American political theorist who made a strong case for upholding experience and community as the core values of Dewey's pragmatism.[70] But Bernstein also thinks that Dewey's pragmatism is well-served by continental European philosophers like Gadamer and Habermas, who seek to discover the rules for structured communication and practical discourse.[71] These theorists are clearly uncomfortable with the inevitable uncertainty that Dewey believed was intrinsic to all judgments. They are also reluctant to engage in unstructured communication without specifying some minimum preconditions of competence (i.e., standards of practical judgment) shared by those who seek a rational consensus. Habermas and his followers are vulnerable to Rorty's criticism that their work constitutes just another mistaken attempt to encapsulate communication and discourse in universal standards of validity that are contrary to what Dewey espoused.[72]

Bernstein believes that the discursive and experiential dimensions of pragmatism are not incompatible and can be reconciled. Bernstein has interpreted

Dewey's insistence that all judgments of fact involve judgments of value to mean that practical judgments about social and community values are no more resistant to interpretation and consensus than other individual goods. This may be so, but Dewey considered mistaken Bernstein's idea that human experience furnishes a universal moral language with which to iron out irreducible differences in perspectives. Dewey argued that no experience ever presents completely unambiguous choices about values. Judgments about value have to do with comparability, not exact equivalence, and individuals differ in their willingness to substitute one value for another. People want to know what the consequences really are going to be before committing themselves to ideas, theories, or principles of action.

Rorty believes that debates about issues involving moral certitude are better handled in the political arena than handled by philosophers of epistemology and metaphysics. Rorty is perfectly comfortable in a world full of inconsistency, incompatible beliefs, and ethnocentric biases. In his semi-autobiographical commentary on American politics and culture since the 1930s, Rorty acknowledged that he was a youthful admirer of Hook's brand of labor reform-liberalism who concentrated his energies in the 1950s on attacking communism through his leadership of the Congress for Cultural Freedom.[73] Rorty indicated that his parents were "fellow-travelers" of the communist party until Stalin's excesses drove them into the willing arms of Hook.

Rorty remains convinced that the Cold War was a necessary response to avert Soviet world domination. He recalled that he truly believed every "anti-Stalinist" word Hook ever published in the *Partisan Review*. Rorty was neither surprised nor appalled when it was revealed recently that Hook's Congress for Cultural Freedom received money from the CIA. Rorty viewed the "cohabitation of bad guys with good guys in the CIA" as a natural by-product of a political system rife with conflicts of interest.[74] Rorty also fondly recalls being reminded by his mother that Dewey and Hook were guests at their Halloween party, which was also attended by such diverse personages as Italian anarchist Carlo Tresca and Whittaker Chambers, a former communist who Rorty says "feared retaliation by Stalin's hitmen."[75]

Rorty's autobiographical remarks are not just sentimental excursions. They bear directly on his argument that the so-called "cultural" liberals of today have forsaken their labor-based political constituencies of the New Deal era. Rorty condemns cultural liberals for pursuing the politics of identity instead of defending the economic interests of the working class. Rorty disapproves of the New Left's agenda for individual dignity involving the rectification of inequities of power, political oppression, sadism, and social cruelty. The defeat of radicalism in the 1960s led cultural liberals to prefer Foucault, Neitzsche, and Freud than Marx, Rorty observed, but by doing so, they see everyone, including themselves, as martyrs sacrificed for their resistance to some ubiquitous but unseen oppressive force.[76] Rorty's criticism of the cultural left is ironic because the politics of individual identity insists that differences be respected, including the kinds of differences in political outlook that Rorty celebrated in his youth.

There are theorists among Dewey scholars whose pragmatist conceptions of culture and politics do not fit the mold into which Rorty has poured the postmodernist cultural left. Robert Westbrook has presented a persuasive argument that Dewey saw democracy as a way of life, of social existence, and not "merely a way of public life."[77] Westbrook contends that the so-called democratic realists Rorty admires ignored Dewey's broader conception of democratic intelligence and pared it down to fit the needs of a garrison state locked into a Cold War mentality. Alan Ryan persuasively argues that Dewey occupied the great liberal middle ground of "intelligent persuasion" between a formal, overly legalistic orientation and one focused on "pure policy."[78] According to this reading, pragmatism is more than just a useful personal creed that provides little practical advice about participation in public life.

Thomas Alexander presents a neo-Hegelian argument that individuality and community need not be at odds and that the politics of identity need not lead to Foucault's self-negating practices of resistance. Alexander's counterpoint to Foucault is that *Art as Experience* showed how "an ecology of self becomes the basis for an ethics of care rather than one of judgment in accordance with formal rules."[79]

Rorty seems not to notice that the ecology of American culture and society has undergone wrenching changes that have redefined the social strategies involved in securing respect and a sense of dignity for all individuals.[80] The indignities of segregation and discrimination involving physical and psychological pain, social indifference, degradation, and humiliation have become objects of public attention because people have actually suffered these experiences. Martin Luther King understood clearly that real change never comes from endless talk, but entails *methods* and *strategies* designed to create empathy for those enduring the agonizing pain and uncertainty of lived experience. Civil rights leaders made a statement more powerful than words could express; they put their beliefs and their bodies in harm's way. Their gesture of refusal helped African Americans to affirm a cultural identity that has been accorded recognition and respect in the mainstream of American law and society.

A sense of common community identity and spirit can be maintained in the midst of diversity, Dewey believed, when the lines of communication are open and leadership is not monopolized by any one group. This conception of association should not be confused with pluralism and the politics of consensus. Although Dewey strongly supported democratic elections and representative processes of government, he felt that individual attitudes about equality, freedom, and social justice were significant determinants of the likelihood that majority rule would include the respect for and vigorous protection of minority rights.

Conclusion

The Revival of Dewey's Naturalism

As this intellectual biography draws to a close, recounting the highlights of Dewey's career as a public philosopher and naturalist enables us to assess and put his contribution in contemporary perspective. Unlike the criticisms leveled against Dewey's pragmatism during its heyday, the rhetorical strategies mounted by some contemporary interpreters *endorse* rather than condemn the cultural implications of pragmatism, even while gutting its scientific core. This has contributed to the neglect of the relationship between logic and science that Dewey considered fundamental to the relationship between mind and inquiry. Fortunately, there have been recent efforts to reinstate Dewey's attempt to naturalize science and technology by showing that the inclination to forge philosophical tools as instruments of inquiry is rooted in human evolution and the demand to make thought productive.[1] This is an encouraging development that enables Dewey scholars to retrieve the missing strands of Dewey's naturalism, his philosophy of mind, and his theory of inquiry and to reweave them to form a more integrated understanding of his work as a whole.

There are several interrelated themes that emerge from previous chapters that invite some concluding remarks. These have to do with how contemporary scholars and scientists have interpreted differently Dewey's analysis of the relationships between spirit, nature, mind, and inquiry. This enables us to assess how recent attempts to carry forward Dewey's attempt to reconstruct the logic of inquiry from a naturalistic perspective have fared. This will also make it possible to situate Dewey in the ongoing debate about instrumental and expressive conceptions of thought and inquiry, and to determine how this debate affects philosophical questions about spirit and scientific conceptions of the brain and mind.

Dewey was a dedicated leader of and critical participant in the processes of secularization and modernization that forever transformed American thought and culture after the turn of the twentieth century. His dissatisfaction as a youngster with the Calvinist formula for redemption and God's grace impelled him to embrace a philosophy that would enable him to better understand and to personally address the social and moral consequences of secularization and modernity for community life. Hegelian idealism initially provided Dewey a congenial platform from which to launch a spirited critique of the materialist theories advanced by Spencer and the transcendental conception of mind proposed by Kant that stood in the way of an experiential and experimental understanding of human development.

While he welcomed the advent of the Darwinian and scientific revolutions, Dewey reformulated the premises of evolution and reconstructed the methods of science to better capture their power to advance human inquiry and understanding. By adopting a naturalistic perspective, Dewey was able to argue that mind is an emergent phenomenon and that intelligence consists in developing and enlarging the powers of human judgment. He reasoned that consciousness and judgment work in tandem with emotions to enable us to determine whether our actions and discoveries make a difference that has aesthetic, moral, scientific, or social value. Dewey encountered resistance among his esteemed fellow pragmatists to his Hegelian-inspired attempt to reconcile mind, nature, and spirit. These criticisms foreshadowed Dewey's subsequent professional and personal dilemmas involved in his strategies to enlist science in the service of educational and social reform.

Dewey's ambitious goal to demonstrate that mind and society are connected through experience placed a premium on the strategic role of education in increasing the resources for intelligent action. He made a seminal contribution to early childhood education through his Laboratory School at the University of Chicago. There he showed that children learn best when given sufficient latitude to define the rules of intellectual engagement and to choose the tools with which they construct communities for learning and participation in civic life.

This agenda for social reconstruction ironically stirred the most enthusiasm and admiration among his students and disciples, such as Randolph Bourne, who believed that educational reform would instigate a *cultural* rather than a scientific revolution. An economy based on the worship of science and technology, they believed, would be routed and replaced with one rooted in a romantic vision of freedom and creativity. Dewey soon realized that control over the agenda for social reform was slipping from his grasp and that Freudian psychoanalysis had become a cultural *fait accompli* before entering the mainstream of science. To sustain the relevance of an argument first proposed by Bourne, Rorty paradoxically has recruited Freud as Dewey's unlikely ally. He has done so in the attempt to show that Dewey's experimentalism is applicable to American culture just as long as it does not put more weight on human rationality, intelligence, and inquisitiveness than the human psyche can bear.[2]

Dewey found it deeply troubling that the New York literary avant-garde would so thoroughly and unconditionally embrace Freudian psychology without bothering to question whether Freud's premises were warranted. Only

Dewey's closest scientific acquaintances shared his extremely critical stance toward psychoanalysis. They believed that Freud's conception of mind impeded rather than advanced scientific understanding of the brain in relation to behavior. As his subsequent forays in the 1920s politics of educational and cultural reform indicate, Dewey was among a minority of intellectuals who challenged psychoanalysis. Moreover, even his closest former student and foundation associate Lawrence K. Frank could not resist the lure of psychoanalysis. Frank found persuasive Freud's theory that the root of individual and civil discontent lay in the structure of family life, which frustrated fulfillment of fundamental drives and desires. This perspective ultimately became the dominant one in the child study network, calling into question the judgment of parents and their capacity to succeed in child rearing without the intervention of experts.

Given these disappointing reversals of his reform agenda, it should not be surprising that Dewey would turn his inquisitive energy inward and seek insights from art about the naturalistic origins of mind and perception. After all, this is where he could challenge his culture critics on their own turf and show that their criticisms that pragmatist technology was inimical to art were misplaced. For similar reasons, Dewey helped Myrtle McGraw mount a multiyear, interdisciplinary experimental study of early motor and cognitive development to show that early brain growth and behavior are not predetermined, but reciprocally interact and develop through experience. Their collaborative studies indicated that the capacities to gesture, walk, talk, remember, and anticipate the future do not entail the mastery of an ancient narrative or a contemporary discourse. Instead these skills involve overcoming the limitations of gravity, accurately expressing needs, developing the capacity for joint attention, effectively communicating and interpreting intentions, and anticipating the actions and needs of others. By making these seminal discoveries, Dewey and McGraw anticipated and paved the way for the resurgence of neuroscientific research in early motor and cognitive development, discussed later, that has revolutionized our understanding of the extraordinary capacities of infants to learn from experience.

A LOGIC FOR INQUIRY

While Dewey's enormous intellectual influence and social advocacy remain undisputed, doubt persists among Dewey's critics about whether a logic or framework for propositional discourse that supports the experimental conduct of inquiry while avoiding epistemological realism can be constructed from naturalistic premises. This is a legitimate issue, as Dewey never succeeded in persuading his contemporaries, especially Bertrand Russell, that propositional statements do not entail assertions of truth or falsity, but express existential relations whose warrant is redeemed by judgments of practice. Moreover, most philosophers are unwilling to give up their reliance on the tools of symbolic and mathematical logic, insisting that the rules which establish the truth or falsity of statements should never be confused with the rules or methods for gathering evidence to support them.

There is a growing body of Dewey scholarship, however, that is revisiting and reassessing the terms and arguments that Dewey advanced in *Logic: The Theory of Inquiry* in 1938. The authors of several of these works deserve praise, in my opinion, for carefully reading the formidable prose in *Logic* and rendering comprehensible the naturalistic ontological foundations that underpin Dewey's theory of logic as an instrument of inquiry. My purpose here is not to challenge their interpretations, with which I largely concur. Rather I suggest how the insertion of a Hegelian and a developmental, neuroscientific perspective into their arguments enables a better grasp of how mind not only directs inquiry, but is *embedded* within neurobehavioral processes that *unfold and expand* the mind during the conduct of inquiry. Consciousness is thereby enlarged beyond the physical limits of one mind to encompass other minds and the interpersonal experiences involved in a situation in its entirety. By taking this tack, I believe that the purported logical and epistemological inconsistencies in Dewey's naturalism and instrumentalism can be repudiated.

Tom Burke is a contemporary philosopher at the University of South Carolina at Columbia who has helped revive an interest in Dewey's *Logic*.[3] He has cleverly done so by reconstructing the lengthy and sometimes rancorous debate about logic between Dewey and Bertrand Russell that consumed them for most of their careers. Burke argues that Russell never clearly understood or bothered to comprehend the crucial difference that Dewey posited between propositions and judgment and the idea that inquiry is broader than logic. Dewey's view that logic should be concerned with justification of warranted assertions of judgment and Russell's perspective that logic deals only with statements involving truth or falsity could not have been further apart. Burke considers Dewey's attempt, toward the end of their long dispute, to propose a correspondence theory of truth to be singularly significant, as this enabled him to adopt an "operation-based theory of meaning" that actions be specified in terms of actual consequences.[4]

Burke contends that the metaphors from cognitive science, such as information processing, better capture Dewey's attempt to translate linguistic expressions into operational statements whose systematic meanings can be connected to social life than does the term "instrumentalism." Burke justifiably cautions that this should not be confused with the operationalism that was advocated by Percy Bridgman and the Vienna Circle. Nevertheless, I think Burke errs in arguing that Dewey was proposing a formal theory of semantics alternative to that advanced by the logical positivists and that this approach could be reconciled with a "Tarskian treatment of truth."[5] Dewey spent a good deal of time, largely due to Arthur Bentley's incessant badgering, grappling with the operational implications of experiential terms that resisted formalization. However, Dewey and Bentley never satisfactorily resolved this problem of the relation between meaning and reference in *Knowing and the Known*, and Dewey clearly distanced himself from Bentley and the aims of the logical positivist movement.

The cognitive sciences have popularized the notion that thought is a form of computing and have encouraged the belief that the neural networks subserving cognition can be replicated to produce artificial intelligence. Burke believes that this computational approach could be modified to demonstrate that a fundamental challenge of intentional agents involves "stabilization" or "the maintenance of balance in a gravitational field." Such a model would show that the ability to anticipate and avoid problems by making postural adjustments is as important as the capacity to solve them. I concur emphatically with this latter suggestion that thought and action are integrated within a gravitational field. Developmental scientists since McGraw's era have accumulated an enormous amount of information about how infants who possess embodied minds respond to such challenges in their motor and cognitive development. Computational and neural network theories considerably enhance but are unlikely to replace ongoing brain imaging and experimental behavioral studies that have revealed how brain and behavior interact throughout development.[6] I believe that Dewey scholars stand to reap greater insights about his theories of mind and inquiry by adopting a developmental perspective than by attempting to understand cognition through the reconstruction of semantics or by the creation of artificial intelligence. I think that philosophers are better advised to take seriously the fundamental advances in the developmental sciences and to mend the rift between philosophy and psychology that has prevented these two complementary fields of inquiry from pursuing problems of mutual interest.

Another noteworthy attempt has been mounted by John Shook, a philosophy professor at Oklahoma State University at Stillwater and the director of the Pragmatism Archive, to anchor Dewey's logical theory in naturalistic premises. Shook adopts an interpretive strategy that complements Burke's analysis by outlining how Dewey's ontology enables him to adopt a conception of logic that differs fundamentally from Russell's realism.[7] Shook argues persuasively that by beginning with the practice of inference, logic can be used as a tool to understand the relationships between generic traits and natural kinds, a tool that need not appeal separately to rules of implication to justify propositions about the meaning or significance of these relationships. Inference is more fundamental than implication, Shook argues, because individuals are existentially *involved* in inquiry. They use their powers of induction to convert evidence involving interactive causal relationships into ones that possess significance that can themselves be transformed into tools for further inquiry.

Shook is right on target in declaring that "the discovery of the inclusion of one kind in another is fundamental" to understanding Dewey's logic, and he adds that this "extends enormously the number of characteristics that are inferable."[8] According to Shook, this enabled Dewey to argue that universal or "generic propositions extend the range of reference, and thus enlarge the grounds of inference, by applying the basic relation of involvement to the relationship of kinds."[9] But it should be evident by now that Dewey was also challenging how biologists and embryologists used the term "kinds" to characterize species in terms of fixed ancestry and lineage. This critique led Dewey to propose that what is real or actual depends on the contingencies of order, and that the relationships that obtain between biological and behavioral growth and development condition our reasoning and judgments about the world.

Dewey was not forced to adopt an "emergent realism" as an alternative to idealism or nominalism.[10] Nor did he intend to use generic propositions in the stronger sense of reference, which prompts Shook to conclude "that it is the ontology of the object that is Dewey's ultimate ground of reference."[11] Contrary to Shook, I believe that Dewey's ontology treats subject and object dialectically—a relationship that makes possible the continuous interpenetration of so-called subjective and objective perspectives (i.e., expressive and instrumental) and their comparative analysis by different disciplines. Dewey does so by showing that judgment exhibits a common pattern across disciplines and that there is a correlative development of mind as new methods of inquiry are adopted.

Dewey's complaint against modern logic, often overlooked, is that it has drained propositional thought of its evolutionary and ontological significance and thus undermined its functional relationship to inquiry. One consequence of this was to remove the existential import and functional role of evidence in inquiry. The use of the terms "affirmation" and "denial" as a means of distinguishing between true and false statements is indicative of this ontological deficit, whereby affirmative and negative propositions no longer serve their primary functions. According to Dewey, affirmative propositions represent cumulative agreement by pointing in the same direction as a similar outcome. Negative propositions play a crucial role in *eliminating* evidence that is irrelevant, enabling the transformation of an indeterminate situation into a determinate one that is subject to further control and testing.

Affirmation and negation bear a *dialectical* relationship to one another such that the evidential relationships among traits and kinds under alternative limiting conditions can be narrowed sufficiently to permit generalizations regarding their role in the phenomenon under inquiry. This is the strategy that McGraw successfully employed in her studies of the overlapping phases in which erect locomotion enlarges the realm of human judgment. She showed that motor and cognitive development is essentially intertwined through experiences involving the act of inquiry.

It is therefore important to understand why Dewey contended in *Logic* that "[n]othing is more important to inquiry than institution of contradictory propositions."[12] This approach to reasoning about natural phenomena allows inquiry to proceed with comparative methods that vary the initial and intervening conditions to produce different outcomes and consequences. Negative propositions specify change to be effected through the elimination of obstacles that obscure the phenomena and thus impede a more clear understanding of the subject matter. That is why Dewey resolutely rejected the law of the excluded middle that A is either B or not-B. Dewey contended that the law of the excluded middle does not rule out the possibility that something exists that actually has the properties of both A and B. It is conceivable that this principle would apply unconditionally only if it applied *exhaustively* to all past and future situations involving the relationship between A and B. However, this would require eliminating all contingencies from past and future events that may show that A and B are related—something that can only be attained through inquiry.

The more profound ontological point that Dewey was making is that mind, brain, and behavior become integrated through the exercise of judgment *in the act* of inquiry. Once this existential connection between mind and inquiry is acknowledged, we can move forward with the project of reconstruction of logic that Dewey so boldly pursued throughout his long career. One philosopher who takes seriously the contention that mind is embedded in inquiry is Larry Hickman, director of the Center for Dewey Studies and professor of philosophy at Southern Illinois University. Hickman grasps Dewey's essentially Darwinian perspective that inquiry is the "means by which reflective organisms seek to achieve stability through adaptation."[13] Instruments of inquiry not only enable control over individual habits. "In the long run," Hickman argues, "they enable us to influence the course of our own evolution."[14]

Hickman's use of Dewey's embryological term that logical forms *accrue* to subject matter through inquiry best characterizes Dewey's instrumental naturalism. This statement expresses exactly how Dewey imagined the pattern of inquiry to be foreshadowed in the serial processes of growth. The initial subject matter of inquiry is indeterminate and without form. The problem takes shape through the accumulation of force and energy sufficient to give it a specific form and direction. By analogy, the physical processes by which neurons attain specificity of function and the mental processes by which thought acquires meaning and significance are strikingly congruent. Only after neurons adhere to the glial substrate and send out axons to other neurons nearby do they attain a functional role in a global system whereby information is distributed and exchanged to sustain higher levels of consciousness. Similarly, only after propositions form sets in a series of increasingly more general statements do they attain warrant and carry inquiry forward to support theories that possess added explanatory force.

As Hickman points out, the mistake among philosophers has been to impose old forms on new subject matter, forcing them into conclusions about thinking and logic that are not borne out by science. Judgment does not consist merely in accepting as given the facts or outcomes of previous deliberation, but in appraising their worth in rendering new situations amenable to analysis. Of course, many of Dewey's contemporaries interpreted Dewey to mean that the point of judgment is primarily to change individual mental states or attitudes.

But Hickman stresses that this captures only part of what Dewey had in mind. The point of judgment for Dewey, according to Hickman, goes beyond subjectivity by making "a difference in the existential conditions which gave rise to the inquiry of which the final judgment is the termination."[15] Judgments of practice have to do with appraising the value of something that was not evident prior to inquiry.

SPIRIT, NATURE, AND MIND

Contemporary philosophers who embrace Dewey's naturalism and his conception of inquiry need not set aside as futile Dewey's attempt to conceive the mind as spiritually significant. Dewey pointed a way out of the conundrums about idealism and materialism that doomed his predecessors to failure. The study of consciousness historically has been motivated by essentially three concerns. First, philosophers since antiquity have tried to explain human reasoning and intelligence by showing that reason is endowed with divine spirit through soul or consciousness. Following in the footsteps of his Greek forebears, Descartes separated the mind from the brain and the body from the soul in a dualism that has had a lasting legacy. Kant ultimately sought a transcendental foundation for his theory of consciousness in *a priori* principles, which placed mind beyond experience.

Second, Hegel rejected this dualism. He wanted science to rejoin knowledge and existence, sundered by Descartes and Kant, into a series of dialectical encounters between mind and nature in which the development of consciousness is measured by its journey toward the realization of Absolute Spirit. Hegel's idealism was tempered by a psychological naturalism which held that mankind was summoned by Spirit through nature to become ever more self-conscious of how the exercise of thought revealed human divinity. Kant and Hegel further elaborated these conceptions of mind to form the transcendental and idealist underpinnings of modern thought.

Third, Darwinian evolution helped reformulate the problem of mind from a different perspective. Darwin wanted to understand the natural circumstances (selective pressures) that give rise to consciousness and to determine the functional advantage this confers on life forms that acquire it. Finally, after the turn of the twentieth century, consciousness once again was reconceptualized to support biological and mechanistic theories of the relationship between mind and brain. The analysis of consciousness today focuses less on its ultimate origins and morphology and more on how it emerges in development and the structural and functional biological mechanisms that make it possible. Importantly, during the last three centuries, the interest in consciousness has shifted from comprehending the divine sources of human awareness to seeking to understand, to reproduce, and to control the conditions in which consciousness arises.

Dewey succeeded in preserving a role for spirit that avoided the pitfalls of Hegel's idealism and absolutism while steering clear of evolutionary determinism. Dewey took Hegel's naturalism and spiritualism seriously while disposing of his idealism and duplicitous absolutism. Consciousness can be understood scientifically, Dewey argued, if the phenomenology of being and becoming is reformulated into psychological terms involving human judgment. But Dewey was enough of a Darwinian to realize that Hegel's dialectical and idealistic notions of mind and consciousness had to be recast into a biological and epigenetic framework in which brain and body and thought and behavior were viewed as essentially intertwined through experience. Darwinian evolution saw the brain and the mind as simply contingent responses to nature's demands to acquire new functions.

Dewey appropriated Darwin's notion of contingency and functionalism while disposing of Darwin's materialism or environmental determinism. Dewey differed from Hegel in positing the human spirit *in* rather than *beyond* nature. Spirit grows from embodied minds that have emerged from nature and which are impelled to find meaning and significance in their thoughts, words, and deeds. Spirit is manifested and expressed in the relationships of joint attention and mutual acknowledgment that obtain when two minds attempt to communicate with one another, as illustrated in Dewey's collaboration with McGraw. Spirit is also evidenced in the recognition that the universe of language and discourse never completely exhausts the universe of human experience. This leaves room for the possibility of discoveries and inventions that are sometimes capable of completely transforming our understanding of life and the relation between humans, nature, and the cosmos. This transformational potential of new discoveries is no better illustrated than by the momentous cultural consequences attending the shift from a geocentric to heliocentric view of our world.

Dewey had no problem with the fact that individually we live in an unpredictable world full of contingencies, because only through shared ideas and experiences do we escape the indeterminate and idiosyncratic nature of individual phenomenal consciousness. Consciousness of difference implies awareness of an "other" whose being sooner or later impinges on our own existence. That is why Dewey (and Hegel before him) believed that social experience makes self-consciousness possible. But few philosophers and neuroscientists are as eager as Dewey once was to revive and squarely address the implications that Hegel's bold ideas posed for human inquiry, ideas that launched Dewey on a lifelong quest.

INSTRUMENTALISM AND EXPRESSIVISM

Charles Taylor's brilliant works on Hegel and the emergence of the mind and self in modernity are important exceptions to the contemporary trend to set mind apart from history and culture and to take a minimalist approach to consciousness.[16] He believes that Hegel's project of tracing the emergence and defining the role of self-consciousness is worth pursuing in an era that is witnessing an increasing divergence between humanist and technological perspectives toward mind. He is critical of computational conceptions of mind and the tendency of some physicists to reduce consciousness to physical processes.[17] Taylor is persuaded that our theories of mind and consciousness must preserve the Diltheyan distinction between *Naturwissenshaften* and *Geisteswissenshaften* and with it the difference between instrumental and expressive perspectives. He supports the attempts by neuroscientists such as Gerald Edelman, whose efforts "to define a new kind of physiological understanding of our embodied mental life," according to Taylor, "cannot but be engaged in the Diltheyan project of defining the difference."[18]

Dewey differed with Charles Taylor on this matter of perspective in one crucial respect. Dewey was not interested in sustaining the dichotomy between nature and spirit that supports the distinction between the empirical and interpretive sciences. He sought instead to reconcile the splits between nature/spirit and instrumental/expressive, believing that neither perspective alone provides a more meaningful account of human experience. He found no methodologically supportable reason why conscious experience should not include the *co-relationship* of expressive and instrumental judgment. Dewey spent most of his life trying to undo this dualism between expressive and instrumental by showing that not only do these two attributes of the human mind interact in every experience, they are also interchangeable.

For example, walking can be understood instrumentally as moving in order to reach an object. But walking is also used as a metaphor to express our innumerable potentialities as inventors and explorers, a meaning best illustrated, perhaps, by Neil Armstrong's famous utterance that his first small and faltering footsteps on the moon represented "a giant leap for mankind." (Incidentally, at the same time he made this declaration, Armstrong was struggling to maintain his balance under weaker gravitational conditions. So one could say that his stepping was an instrumental and meaningful preparatory gesture to his declarative expression.) We possess the power to choose how we will focus and distribute our energy, express our intentions, and attain our goals. These may involve any number or combination of judgments that include a blend of aesthetic, moral, scientific, or other considerations.

Dewey was sensitive to the different contexts in which these perspectives are operative. He argued unequivocally in *Logic* that "[t]he notion of a complete separation of science from the social environment is a fallacy which encourages irresponsibility on the part of scientists regarding the social consequences of their work."[19] Dewey stated in *Logic* that "[a]ll inquiry proceeds within a cultural matrix which is ultimately determined by the nature of social relations."[20] But social contextualism should not be confused with cultural relativism. While Dewey conceded that social inquiry reflects cultural norms and commitments, he believed that social inquiry generates knowledge about neurobiological biases that lead individuals to make different judgments about the material and moral conditions of their existence. In doing so, social scientists explain how instrumental and expressive perspectives can vary between individuals over time and yet yield knowledge of underlying shared patterns of behavior.

THE PRESENCE OF MIND IN ONTOGENY

Recent advances in neuroscience support Dewey's belief that the mind, brain, and behavior are integrated through experience. Enormous strides have been made in identifying brain structures and the neuronal processes that appear to support the formation of attitudes, the capacity to plan, the ability to acquire a concept of self, and to form moral judgments. When the connections that sustain these structural and functional relationships are compromised, these capacities can be become severely impaired.[21] There are key brain structures that furnish the mind information about internal states that are *instrumental* to the formation of higher conscious states. Antonio Damasio's seminal clinical neurological studies indicate that the feeling of being conscious is sustained by a core of tightly convergent and overlapping neural circuits in the mid-brain that provide a continuous non-verbal narrative or imagery of the changing neurobiological state of our sentient being. Without this core, Damasio contends, extended consciousness and the feeling of personal continuity in space and through time are seriously compromised or impaired. With it, we are able to generate an autobiographical consciousness from memories that are grounded in emotional attitudes that guide our perceptual experiences.[22]

There are philosophers of mind today who do not think that increased knowledge of brain states is going to lead to a better understanding of consciousness. David Chalmers thinks that the so-called "hard problem" today is to explain how the *experience* of feeling what it is like to be conscious is possible without reducing consciousness to brain structures and functional mechanisms.[23] Chalmers became one of the founders of the Society for the Scientific Study of Consciousness in 1997 and is a professor and organizer of the University of Arizona's annual conference, "Toward a Science of Consciousness," first hosted in Tucson in 1994. He adopts the strong position that reduction of mind to matter or spirit should be avoided and that consciousness should be treated as fundamentally equivalent to other basic elements of the universe, such as energy, matter, and motion. Dewey would have found Chalmers's view enchanting because he believed that consciousness could be fruitfully understood within a naturalistic perspective. However, Dewey would not agree with Chalmers's *naturalistic dualism* (a throwback to Cartesianism) that consciousness itself should be considered irreducible and supervening to brain function. Consciousness emerges from brain processes and is interrelated with feeling, judgment, and perception.[24]

Dewey saw consciousness as an emergent phenomenon that has assumed different forms and functions throughout the evolution of life. The ascent of human self-consciousness involved not only a series of neurobiological and neurobehavioral transformations, but it depended on the capacity of humans to find interpersonal meaning and significance in their mutually shared lives. Physicists like Roger Penrose, who contends that a new quantum theory of biologically infinitesimal gravity waves may explain consciousness, acknowledges nevertheless that the attempt to distinguish human from artificial intelligence ultimately depends on whether we consider judgment to be a uniquely human possession.[25] Dewey would simply add to this the notion that more than one mind is needed for us to reach the conclusion that judgment is a significant human trait worth preserving. It is difficult to see how those endowed with artificial intelligence could even understand this question, much less reach a consensus on it.

Chalmers is wary of the ever-present danger in modern neuroscience of focusing on the allegedly easier problem of explaining how brain processes work and forgetting the more difficult task of explaining how it is possible for humans to know that they are aware of their own conscious states. He believes that first-person states of awareness should be accorded a privileged status and that any scientific inquiry must first resolve the epistemological problem of knowledge of one's own mind before confronting the more daunting ontological problem of knowledge of other minds. Dewey concurred that one must possess self-consciousness to be aware of one's own experience. However, he did not believe that first-person consciousness should be privileged, as consciousness also presupposes the possibility of communication between persons with minds whose brains possess the same biological structures and functions. The need to attain and sustain joint attention among our hominid forebears probably was a more salient factor than individual awareness of sentient states in giving rise to consciousness. Experimental studies support this hypothesis that Dewey favored by showing that early on, infants must secure their mother's attention to a specific need to obtain the desired method of satisfaction.[26]

Experiencing what it is like to be conscious, although essential to establishing a sense of self and knowledge of other minds, is not crucial to establishing the epistemic validity of the contents of consciousness. Persons afflicted by neglect or other syndromes involving deficits in conscious awareness nevertheless claim to experience things they are actually incapable of perceiving and, therefore, their claims are defeasible. Moreover, a central phenomenological attribute of experience, that Barry Dainton contends is irreducible to the subject or contents of perception, is that it involves "co-consciousness" of a stream of concurrent and overlapping relationships. Most everyday experiences are multimodal, involving the simultaneous combination of sight, sound, and/or taste or other sensory motor properties that contribute to an overall impression of unity. Dainton persuasively demonstrates that experiences involving coconsciousness are neither fully intrinsic nor extrinsic but derive their warrant from co-occurring events that possess holistic relationships among their parts or properties. Each modality has the capacity to evoke an equivalent sense of unity as it is attended to in relation to the experience as a whole.[27]

Theories of mind that privilege the knowledge of those who experience their own states of consciousness assume that there is an unambiguous boundary between the contents of central neural processes and those elements of phenomena which exist "outside" these central processes. Gerald Edelman and Giulio Tononi have demonstrated that experience triggers multiple re-entrant processes involving the sampling and recombination of alternative states that obscure the exact locus of perception in relation to action.[28] Neuroscientific studies of vision also indicate that the instability of perception experienced in binocular rivalry produces extensive changes in neural processing of sensory input that are coordinated with behavioral changes. When subjects are exposed to ambiguous and dissonant scenes, shifts in attention are initiated by eye saccades that reverse the order (i.e., foreground, background, and sequence) of objects in the field of vision. This prevents subjects from being locked in to one epistemically privileged interpretation and allows them to find alternative ways to ground objects or scenes that have multistable phenomenal properties.[29]

These and other studies support Susan Hurley's contention that it may very well be impossible to duplicate a first-person experiential perspective, because that would require that all internal and peripheral phenomena that allegedly make an experience uniquely personal be isolated and then correlated.[30] The conundrum of whether perception takes place inside or outside the brain, Hurley asserts, can be avoided by allowing perception and action to be "constitutively as well as instrumentally interdependent."[31] This interdependent conception of perception and action, according to Hurley, establishes a "point of contact between modern philosophy and some of Hegel's views, for example, on the interdependence of subject and object." While such talk may exude a "whiff of mysticism," Hurley admits, she cogently adds that a "nonnegligible amount of contemporary philosophy seems to consist of the rediscovery of broadly Hegelian positions, even if they are not recognized as such."[32]

The apparent neurobiological and perceptual basis of shared experience is stunningly illustrated in recent studies using functional magnetic resonance imaging. Italian neuroscientists discovered that monkeys who observe the behavior of a conspecific show the same pattern of neural electrical activity as does the one performing the behavior.[33] Examples of anticipatory or prepotent response have also been identified by infant experimentalist Philip Zelazo and his colleagues, who observed that infants who received practice in assisted stepping showed the same firing patterns in anticipation of stepping practice.[34] Vittorio Gallese and Alvin Goldman have concluded from these studies that there is a "cognitive continuity within the domain of intentional-state attribution from non-human primates to humans." They also believe that this ability to detect beliefs and goals in others was a necessary phylogenetic stage leading to the human capacity to read minds.[35]

Moreover, Dewey would reject Chalmers's construal of phenomenal experience as primarily an epistemological problem of self-knowledge. This needlessly reintroduces the problems of subjectivity and validity that Dewey sought to eliminate. He believed that spirit was revealed through the minds of persons engaged in the attempt to communicate and to express authentic and sincere emotions and feelings about one another.

Again, recent evidence from brain imaging studies supports Dewey's contentions. Neuroscientists Chris and Uta Frith found that self-directed deliberation and the attribution of intentions to other minds is nested in a cluster of closely interacting brain regions. These regions include the inferior frontal regions, the superior temporal sulcus, which possesses face-recognition neurons that process actions and goals, and the anterior cingulate and medial frontal regions, which process mental states of the self. They contend that consciousness is made possible by the fact that we use our analysis of someone else's behavior, in conjunction with reference to our own mental states, to make inferences about the intentions of other persons and their emotions. They also assert that our ability to mentalize "evolved largely from the dorsal action system rather than the ventral object identification system."[36]

Only when individuals express themselves within communities, where differences in belief are acknowledged, is it possible for an individual to be released from the solitude of private thoughts and desires to experience what it is like to reflect on the nature of one's own identity as others view it. Childhood marks the passage through which instrumental judgments based on dimly understood physiological states and emotive feelings are transformed into expressive acts that draw upon personal reflection and interpersonal interaction to render explicit the shared values on which these preconscious judgments are based. Knowledge about individual brain states and neural functions underlying behavior provides information that is vital to the attribution of intentions, the expression of emotion, and ascription of responsibility. That is why two-year-olds do not fully understand the moral consequences of their conduct even though they are quite capable of understanding rules and rule-governed behavior. Their prefrontal cortexes are not sufficiently connected to limbic and other brain regions to make such judgments possible. These mitigating considerations apply to children with autism, whose capacity to form and recognize intentions, to express sympathy, and to show empathy are severely impaired because of the absence of or damage to these crucial prefrontal connections.[37]

One of Dewey's lasting legacies to American thought and culture, then, was his attempt to restore confidence in our natural powers of judgment and to let experience be our guide. He believed that the resources of intelligence derive from brains and minds that have evolved and that continue to develop and enlarge in response to the contingencies of experience. He never wavered from his conviction that the true measure of human achievement lies not in the content of our beliefs, but in the value we place on processes and methods by which we experience nature, attain self-understanding, and show compassion for our fellow beings.

The prospect of restoring Dewey's naturalism to its rightful place at the center of pragmatism's concerns is looking brighter than ever before. The revolution in the neuroscientific study of mind and consciousness is rejoining

Conclusion

psychology with philosophy, such as found in the cognitive sciences, as experimental knowledge about the importance of experience in the development of the brain and behavior accumulates.[38] Reductionism in biology and physics is waning as these scientists increasingly embrace an interactionist perspective. In the not-too-distant future, the collaborative interdisciplinary study of human experience, which Dewey and his colleagues pursued with such passion, may become the norm of scientific advancement.

NOTES

INTRODUCTION

1. John Dewey, "From Absolutism to Experimentalism," in *John Dewey: The Later Works*, vol. 5: *1929–1930*, Jo Ann Boydston, ed. (Carbondale: Southern Illinois University Press, 1984), p. 155. Hereafter *EW* (Early Works); *MW* (Middle Works); *LW* (Later Works).

2. Randall Collins adeptly employs the tools of social network analysis, pioneered by Bernard Groffman, in his ambitious and scrupulously researched book *The Sociology of Philosophies: A Global Theory of Intellectual Change* (Cambridge, Mass.: Belknap and Harvard University Press, 1998), p. 7. Collins's provocative thesis (one shared by the author) is that an original and distinctive body of thought is the product of "coalitions in the mind." Individual scholarship reflects the influence of "intellectual communities" and networks that cut across generations and make possible, according to Collins, "a repartitioning of attention space," whereby the focus of interpretive conflicts and innovation is shifted to reflect the ascendancy of one interpretive point of view over others. For a technical discussion of the methods employed by network analysis see Stanley Wasserman and Katherine Faust, *Social Network Analysis: Methods and Applications* (London and New York: Cambridge University Press, 1997).

3. George Cotkin, *Reluctant Modernism: American Thought and Culture 1880–1900* (New York: Twayne, 1992), 40. See also George Cotkin, *William James, Public Philosopher* (Baltimore and London: Johns Hopkins University Press, 1990).

4. Howard Gardner, *Creating Minds: An Anatomy of Creativity Seen through the Lives of Freud, Einstein, Picasso, Stravinsky, Eliot, Graham and Gandhi* (New York: Basic Books, 1993).

5. My research, begun in 1989, has included consultation of numerous archive collections and libraries listed in the bibliography. In addition, I have conducted an extensive number of personal interviews with individuals who were directly acquainted with Dewey or familiar with his colleagues and associates, including Myrtle McGraw. Individuals personally acquainted with Dewey that I interviewed and with whom I corresponded included Lois Murphy and Tao Able, psychologists, Mary Perry, wife of Dewey associate and Rockefeller and Macy Foundation executive Lawrence K. Frank, and Katherine Heyl, former lab assistant to Myrtle McGraw.

Persons familiar with Dewey's scientific associates and acquaintances in the arts whom I consulted included Lawrence J. Pool, a neurosurgeon who worked with Frederick Tilney, director of the Neurological Institute during McGraw's studies; Muriel Coghill, daughter of neuroanatomist George Coghill, a Dewey acquaintance who served as a consultant in McGraw's research; Dr. William Damrosch, a pediatrician at Babies Hospital familiar with McGraw; Dr. Alan Frank, son of Lawrence Frank, who was familiar with his father's colleagues in psychology and psychiatry; Willard C. Rappleye Jr., son of the former director of the Josiah Macy, Jr. Foundation during Dewey's tenure on the board; Yvette Eastman, daughter of Max Eastman, a Dewey student and literary figure;

Dr. Thomas Frank, son of Waldo Frank, a Dewey friend and literary figure; and Maurice Rudiselle, a student and confidant of Fr. Eric MacCormack, who was personally familiar with Dewey's second wife Roberta. In addition, Gerard Piel, founding publisher of *Scientific American* who covered McGraw's research as a science reporter for *Life* magazine, McGraw's daughter Mitzi Wertheim, and Victor Bergenn, McGraw's associate at Briarcliff College, each provided important recollections.

I have also interviewed persons who were acquainted and/or corresponded with Myrtle McGraw and have referred to her in their published works. Among them are the following psychologists: Berry Brazelton, Jerome Bruner, Gilbert Gottlieb, Lewis Lipsitt, and Philip Zelazo. Also included are neurobiologist Ronald Oppenheim and developmental neurologist Bert Touwen.

6. This account is shared by those holding divergent views of pragmatism. For example, Robert Westbrook in *John Dewey and American Democracy* (Ithaca, N.Y.: Cornell University Press, 1991), p. 61, contends that Dewey made the shift from absolute idealism to pragmatic naturalism in the early 1890s after "he stripped his work of the metaphysical method, the transcendental logic of internal relations." While Westbrook is correct in insisting that Dewey dropped Hegel's transcendentalism, it is misleading to say that Dewey no longer expressed an interest in metaphysics or logic. Some of Dewey's most important ideas about judgment and measurement can be traced back to Hegel's *Science of Logic*.

Steven Rockefeller argues in *John Dewey: Religious Faith and Democratic Humanism* (New York: Columbia University Press, 1991), p. 216, that Dewey sought a humanist version of Christian spirit to replace the Hegelian system he discarded. Rockefeller thinks that Dewey's profession of a strong religious faith indicates that he clung to idealism, though there is scant evidence in Dewey's mature works to support this contention.

Alan Ryan contends in his book *John Dewey and the High Tide of American Liberalism* (New York: Norton, 1995), p. 242, that Dewey "repudiated with equal vigor" his Congregationalist faith and Hegel. Nevertheless, Ryan says that Dewey retained "Hegel's passion for finding the truth in the whole rather than the parts and for seeing every phenomena reflected in the other phenomena to which it was related." Ryan is more concerned with showing why Dewey distanced his social and political philosophy from Hegel's absolutism and state-centered nationalism than with delving into any detail about how Dewey extricated his naturalism and theory of mind from Hegel's idealistic premises.

7. See Thomas C. Dalton, "Dewey's Hegelianism Reconsidered: Reclaiming the Lost Soul of Psychology," *New Ideas in Psychology* 15 (1997): 1–15 for my analysis of how Dewey transformed Hegel's phenomenology of being and becoming into scientifically testable ideas about the developmental origins of mind and judgment.

8. Robert J. Sternberg, in "A Propulsion Model of Types of Creative Contributions," *Review of General Psychology* 3 (1999): 83–100, has constructed a useful typology for understanding the creative contributions of individual thinkers to different domains of knowledge. Sternberg's "reconstruction/redirection" model seems applicable to Dewey because of its emphasis on learning from experience and striking out in a new direction.

9. See references to Westbrook's, Rockefeller's, and Ryan's intellectual biographies of John Dewey in note 7. To my knowledge there have been few attempts to critically compare and contrast Dewey's and Freud's conceptions of human experience. Two of

the earliest studies included Morton Leavitt's *Freud and Dewey on the Nature of Man* (New York: Philosophical Library, 1960) and Lewis Feuer's "The Standpoints of Dewey and Freud: A Contrast and Analysis," *Journal of Individual Psychology* 16 (1960): 121–136. More recently, Richard Rorty suggests how pragmatism could profitably view morality from a Freudian point of view in "Freud and Moral Reflection," in *Pragmatism's Freud: The Moral Disposition of Psychoanalysis,* ed. Joseph H. Smith and William Kerrigan (Baltimore and London: Johns Hopkins University Press, 1986), pp. 1–27.

10. Sidney Hook, *Out of Step: An Unquiet Life in the Twentieth Century* (New York: Harper & Row, 1987), p. 62.

11. Ibid., p. 91.

12. Bernard Baars, *A Cognitive Theory of Consciousness* (New York: Cambridge University Press, 1988), p. 6.

13. Ibid., p. 153.

14. Dewey, "From Absolutism," p. 153.

15. For an unusually succinct yet thorough discussion of the function of evolutionary naturalism as a presupposition of psychological theories proposed by James, Dewey, and numerous other pioneers, including Stanley Hall, John Watson, Mark Baldwin, and William McDougall, see Hamilton Cravens and John C. Burnham, "Psychology and Evolutionary Naturalism in American Thought, 1890–1940," *American Quarterly* 23 (1971): 635–657.

16. John Dewey, "Nature," in *MW* 2: 149.

17. George W. F. Hegel, *Phenomenology of Spirit,* trans. A. V. Miller (New York: Oxford University Press, 1977).

18. John Ryder, "Introduction," in *American Philosophic Naturalism in the Twentieth Century* (Amherst, N.Y.: Prometheus Books, 1994), pp. 9–26.

19. George Santayana, "Dewey's Naturalistic Metaphysics," in *LW 3:* 376–377.

20. Dewey, "Nature," 149.

21. Frederick Matthias Alexander, *Man's Supreme Inheritance* (New York: E. P. Dutton and Co., 1918).

22. John Dewey, *Experience and Nature,* in *LW* 1: 224.

23. I discovered Dewey's involvement in McGraw's research in early 1989. Disappointingly, I was unable to interview McGraw, as she died in September 1988. However, she left her papers, from which I have documented their remarkable collaboration in a recent article, co-edited with McGraw colleague Victor Bergenn, titled "John Dewey, Myrtle McGraw and *Logic:* An Unusual Collaboration in the 1930s," *Studies in History and Philosophy of Science* 27 (1996): 69–107.

24. John Dewey, "Propositions, Warranted Assertibility and Truth," in *LW* 14: 175.

25. Dewey, *Experience and Nature,* p. 362.

26. Richard Rorty, *The Consequences of Pragmatism* (Minneapolis: University of Minnesota Press, 1982).

27. See Sidney Hook's *The Quest for Being* (New York: St. Martin's Press, 1961) first published in 1934 for his best collection of essays on Dewey's pragmatism, politics, and the arts.

28. Richard Bernstein, ed., *John Dewey* (New York: Washington Square Press, 1966).

29. See James Kloppenberg, "Pragmatism: An Old Name for Some New Ways of Thinking?" *The Journal of American History* 83, June 1996, pp. 100–138, for an excellent historical analysis of the changing interpretive perspectives taken toward Dewey and William James's pragmatism.

30. Richard Rorty in "Dewey between Hegel and Darwin," in *Rorty and Pragmatism: The Philosopher Responds to His Critics,* ed. H. J. Saatkamp Jr. (Nashville, Tenn.: Vanderbilt University Press, 1995), p. 13.

1. FROM CALVINISM TO EVOLUTIONISM

1. John Dewey, "From Absolutism to Experimentalism," in *LW* 5: 147–160.

2. Jane Dewey, "Biography of John Dewey," in *The Philosophy of John Dewey,* ed. Paul A. Schlipp (New York: Tudor, 1939), pp. 3–45

3. Jo Ann Boydston, former director of the Center for Dewey Studies and the editorial board for the collective works of John Dewey, sponsored a cooperative research project in the 1960s to obtain oral histories from Dewey acquaintances. Kenneth Duckett, a university archivist for the Special Collections at Morris Library, Southern Illinois University, taped and transcribed several interviews in the 1960s with some of Dewey's former students and closest philosophical colleagues at Columbia University. Dewey colleagues who were interviewed included Horace Kallen, Ernest Nagel, Corliss Lamont, Thomas Munro, and Robert Raup. These interviews provide colorful anecdotes about Dewey's mannerisms, personality, teaching style, his interaction with students, his dealings with colleagues, and how he handled conflict and controversy. They also furnish occasional insights about Dewey's unique temperament and habits of mind that set Dewey apart from his contemporaries. Excerpts from these interviews will be cited in this and other chapters.

4. Max Eastman, "The Hero as Teacher: The Life Story of John Dewey," in Max Eastman, *Heroes I Have Known* (New York: Simon and Schuster, 1947).

5. George Dykhuizen, *The Life and Mind of John Dewey* (Carbondale: Southern Illinois University Press, 1973).

6. See Jane Dewey, "Biography of John Dewey," pp. 5–8; Eastman, "The Hero as Teacher," pp. 277–278; and Rockefeller, *John Dewey,* p. 34, for more details about Dewey's family life in Vermont.

7. Jane Dewey, "Biography of John Dewey," p. 6.

8. See Dykhuizen, *The Life and Mind of John Dewey,* p. 35, and Steven C. Rockefeller, *John Dewey,* pp. 35–36, for useful discussions of Lucina Dewey's changing religious loyalties.

9. Joseph Harotunian presents a colorful and detailed account of the issues which contributed to the Unitarian revolt in *Piety versus Moralism: The Passing of the New England Theology* (New York: Henry Holt and Co., 1932), pp. 186–199.

10. Bruce Kuklick's *Churchmen and Philosophers: From Jonathan Edwards to John Dewey* (New Haven, Conn.: Yale University Press, 1985) remains one of the most concise and philosophically penetrating accounts of Calvinist scriptural and sectarian politics.

11. Ibid., pp. 54–57.

12. John Dewey, quoted in Rockefeller, *John Dewey,* p. 37.

13. John Dewey, quoted in Eastman, "The Hero as Teacher," p. 287.

14. John Dewey to Klyce, July 5, 1915, Scudder Klyce Papers, Rare Books and Manuscripts, Library of Congress, Washington, D.C.

15. Eastman, "The Hero as Teacher," p. 281.

16. John Dewey, quoted in Rockefeller, *John Dewey,* p. 65.

17. John Dewey, "The Place of Religious Emotion," in *EW* 1: 91.

18. Quoted in Rockefeller, *John Dewey,* p. 36.

19. John Dewey, "From Absolutism to Experimentalism," in *LW* 5: 149–150.

20. For a brief biography and critical analysis of Butler's work, see Terence Penelhum, *Butler* (London and New York: Routledge and Kegan Paul, 1985), pp. 1–3. Joseph Butler was an Oxford-educated Presbyterian minister who was appointed chaplain and then chosen by Queen Caroline in 1736 to be Clerk of the Closet under George II of England. She regularly invited Bishop to evening gatherings attended by notable intellectuals and philosophers, such as Leibniz, who was a close personal friend of the queen. After her death in 1738, King George appointed Butler Bishop of Durham.

21. Joseph Butler, *Analogy of Religion* (New York: F. Unger Publishers, 1961; orig. pub. 1736).

22. John Dewey, "The Study of Ethics: A Syllabus," in *EW* 4: 238.

23. Jane Dewey indicated in her "Biography of John Dewey," p. 11, that the University of Vermont subscribed to these and other British periodicals during the time when evolution was hotly debated. She noted that these "English periodicals which reflected the new ferment were the chief intellectual stimulus of John Dewey at this time and affected him more deeply than his regular courses in philosophy."

24. Samuel Butler, "The Evidence for the Resurrection of Jesus Christ as given by Four Evangelists," published privately in 1865, and *The Fair Haven* (New York: AMS Press, 1968; orig. pub. London: Trubner, 1873).

25. Samuel Butler, *Erewhon or Over the Range* (New York: AMS Press, 1968; orig. pub. London: Trubner, 1872).

26. Samuel Butler, *Evolution, Old and New* (New York: AMS Press, 1968; orig. pub. London: Hardwicke and Bogue, 1879), p. 266

27. I am grateful to Gilbert Gottlieb for pointing out that Mivart first championed the view that Butler subsequently appropriated and deployed in his critique of Darwin. For an excellent discussion of Mivart's ideas that places them within the context of the history of developmental studies of behavior. See Gilbert Gottlieb, *Individual Development and Evolution: The Genesis of Novel Behavior* (New York: Oxford University Press, 1992), pp. 38–47.

28. Samuel Butler, *Life and Habit* (New York: AMS Press, 1968; orig. pub. London: Trubner, 1878).

29. Samuel Butler, quoted in Lee E. Holt, *Samuel Butler* (New York: Twayne, 1964), p. 71.

30. Ibid., p. 82.

31. Ibid., p. 77.

32. For an interesting account of Huxley's woes with religious leaders in Britain see Adrian J. Desmond's *Huxley: From Devil's Disciple to Evolution's High Priest* (Reading, Mass.: Addison Wesley, 1997), pp. 371–376.

33. Thomas H. Huxley and William J. Youmans, *The Elements of Physiology and Hygiene: A Textbook for Educational Institutions*. rev. ed. (New York: American Book Co., 1873).

34. John Dewey, "From Absolutism to Experimentalism," p. 147.

35. See Desmond, *Huxley*, pp. 8–14.

36. Thomas H. Huxley, *Man's Place in Nature and Other Essays* (New York: Dutton, 1906), p. 307.

37. Huxley, *Man's Place in Nature*, pp. 271–272.

38. Desmond, *Huxley*, p. 474. For other useful accounts of Huxley's public lecture tour and encounters with American scientists see Albert Ashforth, *Thomas Henry Huxley* (New York: Twayne, 1969), pp. 81–84, and Cyril Bibby, *T. H. Huxley: Scientist, Humanist and Educator* (New York: Horizon Press, 1960), pp. 235–239. Cotkin, in *Reluc-*

tant Modernism, pp. 1–26, also provides a cogent analysis of the confrontation between American scientists and theologians over Darwinian evolution.

39. See Bibby, *T. H. Huxley*, pp. 156–159.

40. For a thoughtful commentary on Huxley's interests in embryology and paleontology and how his views about these fields led to disagreements with Darwin, see Mario A. di Gregorio, *T. H. Huxley's Place in Natural Science* (New Haven, Conn.: Yale University Press, 1984), pp. 26–82.

41. Ibid., pp. 56–65. See also Desmond, *Huxley*, pp. 222–224.

42. Huxley in *Man Place in Nature*, pp. 87–100, presented evidence and arguments in support of his theory that the hippocampus subserves language. For two intriguing case studies of the Owens-Huxley debate over the hippocampus minor and its impact on the general acceptance of evolutionary theory, see Charles G. Gross, *Brain, Vision, Memory: Tales in the History of Neuroscience* (Cambridge, Mass.: MIT Press, 1998), pp. 136–178; and Sherrie Lyons, "Convincing Men They are Monkeys," in *Thomas Henry Huxley's Place in Science and Letters, Centenary Essays*, ed. Alan P. Barr (Athens, Ga.: University of Georgia Press, 1997), pp. 95–118.

43. Charles Darwin quoted in di Gregorio, *T. H. Huxley*, p. 112.

44. Thomas Huxley, *Evolution and Ethics and Other Essays* (New York: Appleton and Co., 1896), p. 83.

45. For a thoughtful history with contrasting critical perspectives, see John S. Roberts, ed., *William Torrey Harris: A Critical Study of His Educational and Philosophical Views* (Washington, D.C.: National Education Association, 1924).

46. John Dewey, quoted in Dykhuizen, *The Life and Mind of John Dewey*, p. 26.

47. John Dewey, "From Absolutism to Experimentalism," p. 147.

48. Ibid.

49. William H. Goetzmann, ed., *The American Hegelians: An Intellectual Episode in the History of Western America* (New York: Alfred Knopf, 1973) remains one of the best general discussions of American Hegelianism. It includes some of the original seminal essays written for the journal. For a useful collection of biographical portraits of the leaders of the St. Louis movement and correspondence exchanged among their members, see Charles M. Perry, ed., *The St. Louis Movement in Philosophy: Some Source Materials* (Norman: University of Oklahoma Press, 1930).

50. William James, quoted in Ralph Barton Perry, ed. *The Thought and Character of William James* (Boston: Little Brown, 1935), p. 774.

51. See particularly William James's polemical essay "On Some Hegelians," in James, *The Will to Believe and Other Essays* (New York: Longmans, 1931), pp. 196–221; and "Hegel and His Method," in William James, *The Writings of William James* (Chicago: University of Chicago Press, 1977), pp. 512–528.

52. John Dewey, "The Metaphysical Assumptions of Materialism," in *EW* 1: 3–8; "The Pantheism of Spinoza," in *EW* 1: 9–18; and "Knowledge and Relativity of Feeling," in *EW* 1: 19–33.

53. John Dewey, "The Pantheism of Spinoza," in *EW* 1: 17.

54. John Dewey, "From Absolutism to Experimentalism," p. 153.

2. HEALING AN "INWARD LACERATION"

1. John Dewey, "From Absolutism to Experimentalism," p. 153.

2. Ibid.

3. John Dewey, "Hegel's Philosophy of Spirit," unpublished manuscript, 1897, p. 3. Joseph Ratner Papers and Collection of John Dewey, Collection 142, Series II, Box 49/7, Special Collections, Morris Library, Southern Illinois University, Carbondale, Illinois.

4. John Dewey, "From Absolutism to Experimentalism," p. 150.

5. Quoted in Dykhuizen, *The Life and Mind of John Dewey*, p. 30.

6. Ibid., pp. 30–31.

7. Ibid., p. 33.

8. John Dewey, "From Absolutism to Experimentalism," p. 152.

9. Eastman, "The Hero as Teacher," p. 286.

10. Quoted in Cotkin, *Reluctant Modernism*, p. 47.

11. Hall to Gilman, January 16, 1887. John Dewey Papers, Collection 102, Box 1, Folder 13, Special Collections, Morris Library and Center for Dewey Studies, Southern Illinois University, Carbondale, Illinois.

12. Dorothy Ross, *G. Stanley Hall: The Psychologist as Prophet* (Chicago: University of Chicago Press, 1972), pp. 154–156.

13. See ibid., pp. 37–61 for an account of Hall's early Hegelianism.

14. Wilhelm Wundt, *The Principles of Physiological Psychology*, trans. E. T. Titchner (New York: Krause, 1969; orig. pub. 1874).

15. See Ross, *G. Stanley Hall*, pp. 71–99 for a description of Hall's research focus.

16. G. Stanley Hall, *Adolescence: Its Psychology and Its Relations to Physiology, Anthropology, Sociology, Sex Crime, Religion and Education*, vols. 1 and 2 (New York: Appleton, 1904.)

17. Dewey to Torrey, November 17, 1883. George Dykhuizen Papers, Special Collections, Bailey/Howe Library, University of Vermont, Burlington, Vermont.

18. Ibid. In this letter, Dewey also describes a paper he presented on "The Psychology of Consciousness" at a meeting of the Metaphysical Club at Johns Hopkins on November 13. Although this paper was never published and has never appeared in the *Collected Works*, Dewey described it in his letter in the following way: "I worked up what I had got so far for the last Metaphysical Club, tho' I can't say I have got much light yet. I was directly convinced that of the entire insufficiency of the 'unconscious cerebration theory,' or rather that it was only at most a physiological explanation and what is wanted is a psychological one."

19. John Dewey, "Kant and Philosophic Method," in *EW* 1: 40.

20. John Dewey to Torrey, November 13, 1882. John Dewey Collection, 102, Box 1, Folder 6.

21. John Dewey, *Psychology*, in *EW* 2: 88–90.

22. Ibid., pp. 120–121.

23. Ribot first proposed the possibility that implicit states of awareness could be sustained through "unconscious cerebration." He also reported that simultaneous but competing stimuli lead to the suppression, dissociation, or decoupling of attention and volition. Only after the stimuli have been properly discriminated or distinguished can the direction of response be resolved. See Theodule Ribot, *Diseases of the Will*, trans. by Marwin-Marie Snell (Chicago: Open Court, 1915; orig. pub. 1894).

24. Quoted in Dykhuizen, *The Life and Mind of John Dewey*, p. 31.

25. Boris Sidis, *The Foundations of Normal and Abnormal Psychology* (Boston: Badger, 1914), p. 104.

26. Walter Pillsbury, interview by John Burnham. Personal communication from

John Burnham. Pillsbury indicated in an interview with Burnham that this incident occurred while he was a psychologist at the University of Michigan.

27. Quoted in Dykhuizen, *The Life and Mind of John Dewey*, p. 47.

28. Ibid., 50. Included in Dewey's sermons were essays with titles such as "The Obligation to Knowledge of God," "Faith and Doubt," and "The Place of Religious Emotion."

29. Jane Dewey, "Biography of John Dewey," p. 21.

30. Ibid., p. 63.

31. For a thoughtful discussion of Dewey's intellectual debt to Mead, see Neil Coughlan, *The Young Dewey* (Chicago: University of Chicago Press, 1975). Coughlan argues persuasively that Mead provided Dewey important insights about how to translate Hegelian consciousness into a non-idealistic, social conception of mind.

32. This critique was presented forcefully by Shadworth H. Hodgson in "Illusory Psychology," in *EW* 1: xxx–xxxii.

33. Quoted in Dykhuizen, *The Life and Mind of John Dewey*, p. 55.

34. Ibid., p. 55.

35. Dewey to Bentley, July 9, 1945. Arthur Bentley Papers, Manuscripts Department. Lilly Library, Indiana University, Bloomington, Indiana.

36. C. L. Herrick, "Focal and Marginal Consciousness," *Psychological Review* 3 (1898): 193–194.

37. John Dewey, "Lecture Notes on a Theory of Logic: Autumn Quarter, 1899–1900," p. 113. Joseph Ratner Papers and the Collection of John Dewey, Collection 142, Series II, Box 54/3.

38. John Dewey, "The Reflex Arc Concept in Psychology," in *EW* 5: 96–110.

39. John Dewey, "Commentary on Hegel's Logic," Lecture Notes, 1896, p. 10. Joseph Ratner Papers and the Collection of John Dewey, Collection 142, Series II, Box 55/6.

40. Ibid., p. 11.

41. Ibid., p. 3.

42. Ibid., p. 8.

43. Ibid., p. 12.

44. John Dewey, *Leibniz's New Essays Concerning the Human Understanding*, in *EW* 1: 420–423.

45. See P. M. Harman, *Metaphysics and Natural Philosophy: The Problems of Substance in Classical Physics* (Sussex, Great Britain: Harvester Press, 1982), pp. 44–46. According to Harman, Newton contended that the inability of mechanistic principles to explain the origin of forces acting at a distance through gravity demonstrated that divine intervention is possible and necessary to set events into motion in the natural world. Accordingly, Newton argued that Leibniz's claim that natural forces were self-sufficient actually excluded God from governance of the natural order.

46. For insightful analyses of Faraday's conception of science, see David Gooding, "In 'Nature's School': Faraday as an Experimentalist," and Elsbeth Crawford, "Learning from Experience," both in *Faraday Rediscovered: Essays on the Life and Work of Michael Faraday*, ed. D. Gooding and F. James (London: Stockton Press, 1985).

47. Harman, *Metaphysics and Natural Philosophy*, pp. 41–43.

48. For an interesting account of the changing views about the forces of nature from the Greeks to twentieth-century physics, see Mary B. Hesse, *Forces and Fields: The Concept of Action at a Distance in the History of Physics* (Westport, Conn.: Greenwood Press,

1962). See also P. M. Harman, *Energy, Force and Matter: The Conceptual Development of Nineteenth Century Physics* (Cambridge: Cambridge University Press, 1982) for a thorough but concise discussion of the key issues in the development of thermodynamics, field theory, and energy physics.

49. For an excellent intellectual biography see L. Pearce Williams, *Michael Faraday* (New York: Basic Books, 1965). See especially Chapter 9, "The Correlation of Forces," and Chapter 10, "The Origin of Field Theory," for particularly cogent discussions of the challenges Faraday faced in getting his colleagues to think in unfamiliar non-Newtonian terms.

50. James Clerk Maxwell, *Matter in Motion* (New York: Van Nostrand, 1892). Dewey acknowledged Maxwell's influence years later in a letter to Arthur Bentley January 22, 1946, saying, "Years ago I had a copy of Maxwell's little book, Matter in Motion—I think when I was at Ann Arbor [University of Michigan]. I remember thinking it was the only thing on physical science principles I could understand." Arthur Bentley Papers, Manuscript Department, Lilly Library, Indiana University, Bloomington, Indiana.

51. William R. Grove, ed., *The Correlation and Conservation of Forces: A Series of Expositions* (New York: Appleton and Co., 1865). Grove's book included articles by Faraday, Hemholtz, Robert Mayer (a codiscoverer of the conservation principle), Justus Liebeg, and William Carpenter, a physiologist whom Dewey admired.

52. Quoted in Thomas Kuhn, *The Essential Tension: Selected Studies in Scientific Tradition and Change* (Chicago: University of Chicago Press, 1977), p. 80. Kuhn provides an insightful look at the debate about convertibility of force in Chapter 4, "Energy Conservation as an Example of Simultaneous Discoveries."

53. In *Before the Big Bang: The Origins of the Universe and the Nature of Matter*, 2nd ed. (London: Four Walls Eight Windows, 2001), physicist Ernest Sternglass contends that Faraday was justified in his belief that electromagnetic theory pointed the way toward a unified field theory of matter. Sternglass has outlined how Faraday and Einstein's "dream of a unification of electromagnetism and gravity is realizable" (p. 285). He gathers impressive recent evidence from the Hubble space telescope, among other sources, that appear to confirm many of Einstein's theoretical predictions.

54. See Grove, "Introduction," in Grove, ed., *The Correlation and Conservation of Forces*, pp. 40, 44.

55. Kuhn, *The Essential Tension*, p. 80.

56. Ibid., p. 96.

57. Kuhn noticed the similarity in views about physical processes among *Naturphilosophers* and physicists like Faraday and Hemholtz and observed that "*Naturphilosophie* could, therefore, have provided an appropriate philosophical background for the discovery of energy conservation," ibid., p. 99.

58. John Dewey, "The Psychological Process in Relation to the Biological," in *John Dewey: Lectures in Psychological and Political Ethics, 1898*, ed. Donald F. Koch (New York: Hafner Press, 1976), p. 301.

59. John Dewey, "Soul and Body," pp. 100, 111.

60. Dewey makes this connection between energy consumption and moral conduct in "The Study of Ethics," in *EW* 4: 244–245.

61. John Dewey, "The Reflex Arc Concept in Psychology," pp. 96–111.

62. C. J. Herrick, "Some Reflections on the Origin and Significance of the Cerebral Cortex," *The Journal of Animal Behavior* 3 (1923): 235.

63. C. J. Herrick, "The Evolution of Intelligence and its Origins," *Science* 3 (1910): 16.

64. Ibid., p. 18.

65. These and other critiques of biological, psychological, and ethical theories, including early formulations of Dewey's own views, which are presented with considerable argumentative force in classroom lectures, are found in an invaluable collection introduced by Koch, *John Dewey, Lectures on Psychological and Political Ethics.*

66. Ibid., p. 290.

67. Ibid.

68. The intellectual processes through which Dewey's contemporaries came to view his work in Lamarckian terms is best documented by George W. Stockings, "Lamarckianism in American Social Science, 1890–1915," *Journal of the History of Ideas* 23 (1962): 239–256. See also Cravens and Burnham, "Psychology and Evolutionary Naturalism in American Thought, 1890–1940," 635–657.

69. Richard Rorty, "Dewey between Hegel and Darwin," in *Rorty and Pragmatism: The Philosopher Responds to His Critics,* ed. H. J. Sattkamp Jr. (Nashville, Tenn.: Vanderbilt University Press, 1995), p. 13.

3. EXPERIMENTALIST IN THE MAKING

1. John Dewey, *Studies in Logical Theory,* in *MW* 2: 310.

2. Peirce to John Dewey, April 15, 1905. In *The Collected Papers of Charles S. Peirce,* ed. A. W. Burks (Cambridge, Mass.: Harvard University Press, 1958), p. 181.

3. For four excellent intellectual biographies documenting C. L. Herrick's little-known scientific achievements and early leadership of American neurology see: Adolf Meyer, "The Contemporary Setting of the Pioneer," *Journal of Comparative Neurology* 74 (1941): 1–24; C. J. Herrick, "Clarence Luther Herrick: Pioneer Naturalist, Teacher and Psychobiologist," *Transactions of the American Philosophical Society* 45 (1955): 1–85; William F. Windle, *The Pioneering Role of Clarence Luther Herrick in American Neuroscience* (Hicksville, N.Y.: Exposition Press, 1979). For C. L. Herrick's translation of Lotze, see Hermann Lotze, *Outlines of Psychology* (Minneapolis: S. M. Williams, 1885; reprint, New York: Arno Press, 1973).

4. C. L. Herrick, "Psychological Corollaries of Modern Neurological Discoveries," *Journal of Comparative Neurology* 7 (1896): 155–161.

5. C. L. Herrick, "The Vital Equilibrium and the Nervous System," *Science* 7 (1898): 813–818.

6. For accounts of Herrick's woes at the University of Chicago, see Windle, *The Pioneering Role of C. L. Herrick,* pp. 74, 85; Meyer, "The Contemporary Setting," p. 19; and Gilbert Gottlieb, "A Tribute to Clarence Luther Herrick (1858–1904): Founder of Developmental Psychobiology," *Developmental Psychobiology* 20 (1987): 1–5. Gottlieb includes excerpts from a statement by C. L. Herrick that his brother C. Judson read at an international conference in St. Louis in 1904, shortly before his older brother's death, which describes his philosophical rationale for the unification of the biological and behavioral sciences at the University of Chicago. In a statement that expresses exactly Dewey's own sentiments about the interdisciplinary practice of science, Herrick stated, "If we are dealing with dynamic things, absolute isolation is impossible. When any conscientious worker dips his oar into our common ocean the wave he creates is not lost but he may feel that the universe of thought will never be quite the same thereafter" (p. 4).

7. Windle, *The Pioneering Role of C. L. Herrick,* p. 94.

8. Hall's miserable failure as an administrator to deal effectively with Clark University trustees and deal even-handedly with faculty is examined by Ross, *G. Stanley Hall*, pp. 221–230.

9. See Philip Pauley, *Controlling Life: Jacques Loeb and the Engineering Ideal in Biology* (New York: Oxford University Press, 1987), p. 67, for a description of Whitman's program at the University of Chicago.

10. For an excellent discussion of Child and C. J. Herrick's naturalistic theories of neurobiological processes, see Sharon E. Kingsland, "Toward a Natural History of the Human Psyche: Charles Manning Child, C. Judson Herrick and the Dynamic View of the Individual at the University of Chicago," in *The Expansion of American Biology*, ed. Keith R. Benson, Jane Maienschein, and Ronald Rainger (New Brunswick, N.J.: Rutgers University Press, 1991), pp. 198–230.

11. C. M. Child, *The Origin and Development of the Nervous System* (Chicago: University of Chicago Press, 1921).

12. See Pauley, *Controlling Life* for a definitive intellectual biography. Pauley argues quite convincingly that Loeb's ideas were never understood very well by the public, nor were they completely comprehended by his own colleagues.

13. See Stanley Finger, *Minds Behind the Brain: A History of the Pioneers and Their Discoveries* (New York: Oxford, 2000), pp. 159–166, for a discussion of this remarkable debate.

14. William James, *The Principles of Psychology*, vol. I (Cambridge, Mass.: Harvard University Press, 1981; orig. pub. 1890), p. 46.

15. Pauley, *Controlling Life*, pp. 100–101.

16. Ibid., p. 68.

17. James McLellan and John Dewey, *The Psychology of Number* (New York: Appleton and Co., 1898). This book has not been included in the Collected Works of John Dewey because the former director of the Center for Dewey Studies, Jo Ann Boydston, could not verify whether Dewey actually contributed to the writing of the book. However, Dewey's own daughter Jane indicated in her biography that Dewey worked "[w]ith Professor McLellan of the University of Toronto, who wrote the portions dealing with practical applications, he [Dewey] published two books for teachers in training" (see Jane Dewey, "Biography of John Dewey," p. 27). In my judgment, Dewey is most likely to have written the theoretical chapters 3 and 4 on "The Origin of Number," where paleoanthropological speculations appear in conjunction with a detailed discussion of the role of measurement in early learning processes. In his introduction, W. T. Harris praised Dewey and McLellan for demonstrating the fundamentally qualitative basis of quantitative measurement that Hegel had argued in his *Science of Logic*.

18. For passages pertinent to this discussion, see McLellan and Dewey, *The Psychology of Number*, pp. 25–27, 31, 45–51.

19. Ibid., p. 26.

20. See G. W. F. Hegel, *Science of Logic*, trans. A. V. Miller (Atlantic Highlands, N.J.: Humanities Press International, 1989), p. 185.

21. Ibid., p. 346.

22. John Dewey, Commentary on Hegel's Logic, Lecture Notes, University of Chicago, 1897, Section 160. Joseph Ratner Papers, Center for Dewey Studies, Morris Library, Southern Illinois University, Carbondale, Illinois.

23. Ibid.

24. John Dewey, *Studies in Logical Theory*, in *MW* 2: 310–311.

25. Dewey, "The Principles of Mental Development," in *MW* 1: 191.

26. Dewey, "The Theory of Emotion," in *EW* 4: 152–188.

27. James Baldwin, *The Mental Development in a Child and the Race* (New York: Macmillan, 1895), p. 140.

28. Dewey to Alice Dewey, October 9, 1894. Collection 102, The John Dewey Papers.

29. Dewey, "The Principles of Mental Development," p. 179.

30. For one of the best contemporary expositions of the interdependent global and local features of conscious brain processes, see Bernard Baars, *In the Theater of Consciousness: The Workspace of the Mind* (New York: Oxford University Press, 1997).

31. Francis Warner, *The Nervous System of the Child: Its Growth and Health in Education* (New York: Macmillan, 1900), p. 198.

32. Baldwin was appointed professor of philosophy and psychology at Johns Hopkins after Dewey graduated. He became editor of the *Psychological Review* (a journal founded by G. Stanley Hall), on which Dewey served as an associate editor, and was the founding general editor of the *Handbook of Psychology*. Baldwin shared Dewey's ambition to advance a theory of inquiry derived from the principles of psychology, and he succeeded in publishing his version, *Thought and Things*, 2 vols. (New York: Macmillan, 1906, 1911) just three years after Dewey published *Studies in Logical Theory*. Baldwin's book instigated an intellectual rivalry with Dewey. Baldwin's acclaim was short-lived, however, because an embarrassing disclosure of his consorting with a prostitute led to his humiliating resignation from Johns Hopkins in 1909 and lonely exile in French, Mexican, and Canadian universities.

33. Baldwin, *Mental Development*, p. 126.

34. Ibid.

35. Katherine Mayhew and Anna Edwards, *The Dewey School* (New York: Atherton, 1936; reprint, 1965), pp. 61–62.

36. Dewey, *Psychology*, p. 180.

37. Ibid.

38. Ibid., p. 185.

39. Ibid.

40. Charles Darwin, *The Expression of Emotion in Animals and Man* (London: John Murray, 1872), p. 356.

41. Charles Darwin, "The Biographical Sketch of an Infant," *Mind* 2 (1877): 288.

42. George Romanes, *Mental Evolution in Animals, With a Posthumous essay on Instinct by Charles Darwin* (London: Kegan Paul, 1883).

43. William James, "The Physical Basis of Emotion." *Psychological Review* 1 (1894): 516–529.

44. John Dewey, "Theory of Emotion," pp. 177–179.

45. John Dewey, Review of *Social and Ethical Interpretations in Mental Development*, by James Mark Baldwin, *Philosophical Review*, in *EW* 5: 419–420.

46. John Dewey, "The Evolutionary Method as Applied to Morality," in *MW* 2: 17.

47. Ibid.

48. John Dewey, "The Theory of Emotion," p. 168.

49. Quoted in Mayhew and Edwards, *The Dewey School*, p. 465.

50. Quoted in ibid., p. 466.

51. John Dewey, "The School as a Social Center," in *MW* 2: 83.

52. For three outstanding critical intellectual histories that focus on Dewey's leader-

ship and Addams's influence at the University of Chicago, see Andrew Feffer, *The Chicago Pragmatists and American Progressivism* (Ithaca, N.Y.: Cornell University Press, 1993); Mary Jo Deegan, *Jane Addams and the Men of the Chicago School, 1892–1918* (New Brunswick, N.J.: Transaction Books, 1988); and Charlene Haddock Seigfried, *Pragmatism and Feminism: Reweaving the Social Fabric* (Chicago: University of Chicago Press, 1996).

53. For more details about this unhappy episode in Dewey's career, see George Dykhuizen, *The Life and Mind of John Dewey*, pp. 107–108, 113.

4. CONTRASTING STRATEGIES FOR EDUCATIONAL INNOVATION

1. John Dewey, *How We Think*, in *MW* 6: 301.

2. Quoted in George Dykhuizen, *The Life and Mind of John Dewey*, p. 139.

3. Ibid., p. 140.

4. Ibid., p. 180.

5. John Dewey, "The Logic of Judgment of Practice," in *MW* 8: 46–49.

6. See John Dewey and Evelyn Dewey, *Schools of To-Morrow*, in *MW* 8: 218–219, for their views about Rousseau-inspired educational experiments.

7. Evelyn Dewey to Bourne, November 17, 1913, Rare Books and Manuscripts, Butler Library, Columbia University, New York City.

8. John Dewey and Evelyn Dewey, *Schools of To-Morrow*. They contended that "[a]djustment means not just the ability to control their bodies, but an intellectual adjustment as well, an ability to see the relations between things, to look behind their surface and perceive their meaning not alone to the individual, but to the community as well" (p. 309).

9. For thoughtful arguments against the view that Dewey saw social control as a technique for enabling teachers to manipulate or indoctrinate their students through group-based activities, see Robert Westbrook, *John Dewey and American Democracy*, 177–178. Dewey wanted to keep open the possibility that children's dispositions and interests were not fixed, but susceptible to influence and change as they interacted in group settings. This is consistent with Dewey's view that self-consciousness becomes a tool of self-reflection, when there are other minds with which one can communicate and share ideas or experiences.

10. John Dewey, *Democracy and Education*, in *MW* 9: 92–93.

11. See John Dewey and Evelyn Dewey, *Schools for To-Morrow*, pp. 314–338 for their evaluation of the Gary Schools. See also Lawrence Cremin, *The Transformation of the School* (New York: Knopf, 1961), pp. 155–156. Cremin's book remains one of the best critical histories of educational reforms in the progressive era that brilliantly puts Dewey's ideas about education in a larger social and political context.

12. Randolph Bourne, "The Life of Irony," and "John Dewey's Philosophy," in *Randolph Bourne, The Radical Will: Selected Writings 1911–1918*, ed. Olaf Hansen (New York: Urizen Books, 1977).

13. Bourne, "John Dewey's Philosophy," in *Randolph Bourne, The Radical Will*, ed. Olaf Hansen, p. 154.

14. Bourne, "Schools in Gary," in *The New Republic* (March 27, 1915), p. 199.

15. Ibid.

16. Ibid.

17. Randolph Bourne, "The Issue of Vocational Education," in *The New Republic* (June 26, 1918), p. 192.

18. Ibid., p. 191.

19. Ibid., p. 192.

20. Ibid.

21. See Cremin, *The Transformation of the School*, pp. 156–157, for a detailed account of why the Gary Plan was not easily transferred to other school systems.

22. Evelyn Dewey to Bourne, December 18, 1913.

23. Evelyn Dewey to Bourne, June 28, 1913.

24. Randolph Bourne, "Education in Taste," in *The New Republic* (March 4, 1916), p. 123.

25. Randolph Bourne, "Experimental Education," in *The New Republic* (April 21, 1917), p. 347.

26. Bourne, "Education in Taste," p. 122.

27. Joyce Antler, *Lucy Sprague Mitchell: The Making of a Modern Woman* (New Haven, Conn.: Yale University Press, 1987), p. 208. Antler consulted the personal diaries of Lucy and Wesley Mitchell and drew on the extensive archive collections at Columbia University and many other repositories in the preparation of her excellent book. I am indebted to Antler for her discovery, in these memoirs and archives, that John Dewey and his daughter Evelyn were actively involved in the organization and implementation of the Mitchells' educational experiments. Antler first documented the activities of the Bureau of Educational Experiments in "Progressive Education and the Scientific Study of the Child: An Analysis of the Bureau of Educational Experiments," *Teachers College Record* 83 (1982): 559–591.

28. Wesley Mitchell made extensive daily entries in his diary from 1905 through 1948. His diary constitutes an important but abbreviated source of information and observations about people with whom he and his wife Lucy had frequent professional and social contact throughout their long productive years in New York. Mitchell's diary, correspondence, and other documents can be found in the Rare Books and Manuscripts Division of Butler Library, Columbia University, New York City.

29. See Antler, *Lucy Sprague Mitchell*, p. 205. Lucy Mitchell furnishes numerous details about her educational theories and her extraordinary level of activity during early years in New York in *Two Lives: The Story of Wesley Clair Mitchell and Myself* (New York: Simon and Schuster, 1953).

30. See Max Eastman's autobiography, *The Enjoyment of Living* (New York: Harper Brothers, 1948), p. 492. Apparently Dewey, for whom Eastman worked as a teaching assistant, rescued Eastman from some awkward moments during his comprehensive oral examination for the Ph.D. by asking him a question about the philosopher John Locke that he could easily answer. After furnishing the answer, according to Eastman, "Dewey looked around at the others and said: 'That's the first time any pupil of mine ever answered that question correctly.'" Dewey then quickly adjourned the examination (ibid.).

31. Ibid.

32. Ibid., p. 493.

33. Evelyn Dewey and Beardsley Ruml, *Methods and Results of Testing Children* (New York: Dutton, 1920).

34. Antler, *Lucy Sprague Mitchell*, pp. 215–217. John Dewey attended a two-day conference in January 1915 in which Woolley presented her proposed plan for a psychological survey. See also Katherine S. Milar, "A Coarse and Clumsy Tool: Helen Thompson Woolley and the Cincinnati Vocation Bureau," *History of Psychology* 2 (1999): 219–235, for a more detailed account of Woolley's work in Cincinnati.

35. Antler, *Lucy Sprague Mitchell*, p. 220.

36. Lucy Sprague Mitchell, Oral History, conducted by Joan Blos and Irene Prescott, August 29, 1962, New York City, p. 84. Rare Books and Manuscripts, Butler Library, Columbia University, New York City.

37. Reported in the Minutes of the Executive Committee of the Board, January 16, 1917. Lucy S. Mitchell, Administrative Records, Bureau of Educational Experiments and Bank Street School, Series Group 1 Mitchell, Box 1, Folder 1. Special Collections, Millbank Memorial Library, Teachers College.

38. The relationship between the Neurological Institute of New York and the BEE is recorded in the Minutes of the Board, January 30, 1916, 1–3. Archives of the Neurological Institute of New York, Presbyterian Hospital, Columbia University, New York. See also Charles Elsberg, *The Story of a Hospital: The Neurological Institute of New York, 1900–1938* (New York: Hoeber, 1944), pp. 34–45, for an account of this episode.

39. Minutes of the Board, February 13, 1917, p. 1.

40. A motion was approved to conduct an inquiry into Alexander's former pupils. See Minutes of the Executive Committee of the Bureau of Educational Experiments, February 26, 1917. Lucy Mitchell proposed to the Executive Committee on November 18, 1918, that they adopt "Alexander's system of conscious control" as one of the express objectives of bureau programs. Minutes of the Executive Committee, Series Group 1 Mitchell, Box 1, Folder 2.

41. Lucy Sprague Mitchell, "For Discussion by the Bureau of Educational Experiments," November 18, 1918, pp. 2–3.

42. Ibid., p. 2

43. Minutes of the Executive Committee of the Board of the Bureau of Educational Experiments, November 4, 1918.

44. Evelyn Dewey to John Dewey, December 18, 1918. John Dewey Papers, Collection 102, Box 6, Folder 1.

45. Reported in the Minutes of the Executive Committee of the Board of the Bureau of Educational Experiments, January 28, 1919. Series Group 1 Mitchell, Box 1, Folder 3.

46. Frederick Ellis, "A Bureau of Educational Experimenters," Address delivered to the Working Council, January 23, 1917. Series Group 1 Mitchell, Box 1, Folder 1.

47. Lashley and Fernald were mentioned as possible candidates for the psychologist position in early May. See Minutes of the Executive Board, May 11, 1917. Later in the month, the board considered approaching John Watson. See Minutes, May 29, 1917.

48. Sharon Kingsland, "A Humanistic Science: Charles Judson Herrick and the Struggle for Psychobiology at the University of Chicago," *Perspectives on Science* 1 (1993): 1–33, provides an interesting analysis of Lashley's views. Lashley and Herrick never accepted Watson's radical environmentalist conception of behaviorism, preferring instead to adopt Dewey's interactionism.

49. Minutes of the Executive Board, June 25, 1918, and July 30, 1918.

50. Minutes of the Executive Board, January 23, 1918, and January 30, 1918.

51. Minutes of the Executive Board, February 15, 1919.

52. Minutes of the Executive Board, October 13, 1919.

53. Johnson, "Report of Studies," 2–3. Johnson subsequently published a summary of research conducted by the BEE staff in the book *Mental Growth of Children in Relation to the Rate of Growth in Bodily Development: A Report to the Bureau of Educational Experiments* (New York: Dutton, 1925). See also Charlotte Windsor, ed., *Experimental Schools Revisited: Bulletins of the Bureau of Educational Experiments* (New York:

Schocken Books, 1973). This collection consists of retrospective articles by the directors of various BEE school projects.

54. Quoted in Antler, *Lucy Sprague Mitchell,* p. 290.

55. Frederick Ellis, "A Note on Posture for Staff Meeting, April 27, 1927." Bank Street, Barbara Biber Papers, Series Group II, Box 4, Folder 36.

56. Buford Johnson, "Report of Studies from the Psychological Laboratory," p. 2, presented to the Research Committee, January 20, 1922. Bank Street Record Group I, Board of Trustees, Subgroup I, Series 2, Folder 10.

57. Ibid., pp. 5–6.

58. Lucy Sprague Mitchell, "Chairman's Report of the Bureau of Educational Experiments, 1921–22 and 1922–23," Bank Street, Record Group 1, Board of Trustees, Subgroup 1, Series 2, Folder 10.

59. Quoted in Antler, *Lucy Sprague Mitchell,* p. 251.

60. Ibid.

5. CULTURAL DISILLUSIONMENT

1. Margaret Naumberg and L. C. Deming, "The Children's School," in Windsor, ed., *Experimental Schools,* p. 13.

2. Margaret Naumberg, *The Child and the World* (New York: Harcourt Brace, 1928), p. 14.

3. Quoted in Robert Holmes Beck, "American Progressive Education, 1875–1930" (Ph.D. dissertation, Yale University, 1942), p. 205.

4. Naumberg to Frank, December 4, 1920. Special Collections, Van Pelt Library, University of Pennsylvania, Philadelphia, Pennsylvania.

5. Myrtle McGraw, interview by Kenneth Duckett, Center for Dewey Studies, February 9, 1967, p. 17. John Dewey Papers, Collection 102.

6. For example, Hinkle and Dewey attended a dinner party at the Mitchells' in December 1936 as documented in an entry in Wesley Mitchell's diary, December 7, 1936. Rare Books and Manuscripts, Butler Library, Columbia University, New York City.

7. Evelyn wrote to Bourne telling him she was "crazy about farming and thinking of advertising for a position as a wife of a widower with six children, so as to get the work without loneliness." Letter to Randolph Bourne, June 28, 1913. Special Collections, Butler Library, Columbia University, New York City.

8. Beatrice Hinkle, *The Re-creating of the Individual: A Study of Psychological Types and Their Relation to Psychoanalysis* (New York: Harcourt Brace, 1923), p. 285.

9. Ibid., pp. 328–329.

10. Quoted in Casey Nelson Blake, *Beloved Community: The Cultural Criticism of Randolph Bourne, Van Wyck Brooks, Waldo Frank and Lewis Mumford* (Chapel Hill: University of North Carolina Press, 1990), p. 161.

11. John Dewey, *German Philosophy and Politics,* in *MW* 8: 169–179.

12. Ibid., pp. 181–182.

13. Ibid., p. 182.

14. Pauley, *Controlling Life: Jacques Loeb and the Engineering Ideal,* p. 144.

15. Randolph Bourne, "The Experimental Life," in *Randolph Bourne, The Radical Will,* ed. Hansen, p. 157.

16. Ibid.

17. Ibid., p. 153.

18. John Dewey, "American Education and Culture," in *MW* 10: 200.

19. Waldo Frank, "Towards a National Culture," *Seven Arts* 1 (January 1917): 270–280.

20. See Blake, *Beloved Community*, pp. 122–156. Blake perceptively notes that in attempting to fuse pragmatism and romanticism, these young American prophets ironically justified a retreat from the world with which they were disenchanted and which they despised. They preferred to adopt a self-justifying Weberian pessimism that ran contrary to their communitarian aims.

21. Bourne, "Twilight of Idols," in *Randolph Bourne, The Radical Will*, ed. Hansen, p. 342.

22. Ibid., p. 344.

23. Bourne, "War and the Intellectuals," in *Randolph Bourne, The Radical Will*, ed. Hansen, pp. 312–313.

24. John Dewey, "On Understanding the Mind of Germany," in *MW* 10: 216.

25. Ibid., p. 231.

26. Ibid.

27. John Dewey, "In a Time of National Hesitation," in *MW* 10: 257, 259.

28. Ibid., p. 262.

29. Ibid., pp. 266–267.

30. John Dewey, "Force, Violence and Law," in *MW* 10: 212–213.

31. Bourne, "Twilight of Idols," p. 347.

32. For an interesting account of the difficulties Bourne encountered in his writing career because of his outspokenness against the war and Dewey's pragmatism, see Bruce Clayton, *Forgotten Prophet: The Life of Randolph Bourne* (Baton Rouge: Louisiana State University Press, 1984), pp. 219–234. While Dewey apparently instigated the decision by the editors of the *New Republic* to dump Bourne, according to Clayton, the publisher, Walter Crowley, Walter Lippmann, and most other editorial contributors had endorsed American intervention by early 1917 and thus saw Bourne as a political liability. James Oppenheim attracted Bourne to write for the *Seven Arts* in the belief that this tactic would boost sales in their competition with the *New Republic*. However, this maneuver failed when financial backers withdrew support because of Bourne's outspoken views. See also Blake, *Beloved Community*, pp. 122–123, for a similar account.

33. Dewey to Barnes, October 15, 1920. Joseph Ratner Papers, Collection 142, Box 6, Folder 9.

34. See Clayton, *Forgotten Prophet*, pp. 232–235, for details about Bourne's misfortunes. After being given a few months' advance notice from the publisher, Bourne resigned on December 14, 1918, just eight days before his untimely death.

35. Max Eastman, "The Hero as Teacher," in *Heroes I Have Known*, ed. Eastman, p. 313.

36. Quoted in Westbrook, *John Dewey and American Democracy*, p. 231.

37. Dewey denounced as unconstitutional and inimical to democracy the imprisonment of war dissidents in two articles he wrote for the *New Republic* in late 1917. See John Dewey, "Conscription of Thought," in *MW* 10: 276–280 and "In Explanation of our Lapse," in *MW* 10: 292–295.

38. Westbrook, *John Dewey and American Democracy*, pp. 212–221, provides a thoughtful and detailed description of Dewey's involvement in this divisive Polish conflict.

39. McGraw, interview by Duckett p. 8.

40. Ibid., p. 9.

41. Ibid., p. 4.

42. McGraw's daughter Mitzi Wertheim verified for me in March 1988 that the letters were lost. I also searched McGraw's papers in August 1988, which were possessed at that time by her colleague Victor Bergenn in Leonia, New Jersey. My search was unsuccessful. McGraw's papers are now housed in the Special Collections of Millbank Memorial Library, Teachers College, Columbia University, New York City, and are available to researchers.

43. Anzia Yezierska, *All I Could Never Be* (New York: Brewer, Warren and Putnam, 1932).

44. See Louise Levitas and Jo Ann Boydston, *Anzia Yezierska: A Writer's Life* (New Brunswick, N.J.: Rutgers University Press, 1988).

45. Dewey's poems were published by Jo Ann Boydston, ed., *The Poems of John Dewey* (Carbondale: Southern Illinois University Press, 1977). Boydston describes in detail the history surrounding Dewey's writing of the poetry. She also explains how Southern Illinois University eventually acquired the poetry and provides insightful interpretations. See also Mary V. Dearborn, *Love and the Promised Land: The Story of Anzia Yezierska and John Dewey* (New York: Free Press, 1988). She argues that Dewey is to blame for the affair's demise by exhibiting emotional cowardice and adopting a patronizing attitude, failing to live up to his own principles. While Westbrook does not agree with Dearborn's interpretation, he acknowledges that Dewey may have been inconsistent in his dealings with people, as he was in his response to Bourne's attacks. See Robert Westbrook, "On the Private Life of a Public Philosopher: John Dewey in Love," *Teachers College Record* 96 (1994): 93. Seen within the context of this conflict, Westbrook concedes that "[t]his argument [Dearborn's] is enticing. It would enable us to find Dewey guilty of simultaneously violating his own best insights publicly and privately, for his conduct in the debate with Bourne in these same months was indeed cowardly, contemptible and pathetic. Unfortunately, this is not a persuasive reading of the love affair, for Yezierska was at least as responsible as Dewey for its collapse."

46. In his reading of Dewey's poetry, Westbrook concludes that Dewey's "Hegelian expressionism" was "still very much in evidence." Ibid., p. 185.

47. Quoted in Boydston, ed., *The Poems of John Dewey,* pp. 4–5.

48. Scudder Klyce, *Universe* (Winchester, Mass.: Scudder Klyce, 1921).

49. John Dewey, *Essays in Experimental Logic,* in *MW* 10: 324–325. Dewey acknowledged the difficulty of putting into words the nature of human experience. He argued that the word "experience" is used "to remind the thinker of the need for reversion to precisely something which never can be one of the terms of his reflection but which nevertheless furnishes the existential meaning and status." Dewey added that the term "experience" is an "invitation to note the fact that no plunge is needed, since one's own thinking and explicit knowledge are already constituted by and within something which does not need to be expressed or made explicit." Here Dewey is awkwardly trying to make a contextualist case that whatever we try to put into words is made sense of within a larger field of implicit knowledge. That may be true, but the question can still be raised as to whether the intended meanings of some common term can be the same for two individuals if their underlying experiences are different.

50. Scudder Klyce, *Dewey's Suppressed Psychology: A Psychological Study of John Dewey* (Winchester, Mass.: Scudder Klyce, 1928).

51. See Carl Jung, "A Preliminary Study of Psychological Types," in *The Collected*

Works of Karl Jung, vol. 1, ed. Herbert Read, Michael Fordham, and Gerhard Adler (New York: Pantheon, 1953).

52. Hinkle, *The Re-creating of the Individual,* pp. 169–171.

53. Dewey further elaborated on what he meant in the following intriguing terms:

> As a man I dislike taking responsibility; As a teacher I managed to turn this defect to account and have within reasonable quantitative limits succeeded in converting it into a virtue—a capacity. That is the explanation for my success in avoiding an authoritative or "pedagogical" tone; as matter of fact, I am supposed to have if not make "disciples." Moreover, my "egotism" made me realize very early that I could not grow intellectually except by taking difficulties and objections into account and that it was my interest to call them out . . . it is doubtless true that I have the kind of agnosticism of which you speak. In other words, I haven't wholly converted my deficiency as a man. A student told me this spring that I was supposed to avoid emotional appeal purposely and wish to rely upon "cold intellectual considerations." I replied that that was my defect not my desire—so there is your case proved for you.

Dewey to Klyce, May 29, 1915. Scudder Klyce Papers, Rare Books and Manuscripts, Library of Congress, Washington D.C.

54. For a thoroughly researched account of Dewey's acquaintance with Alexander, drawing on original documents and interviews, see Fr. Eric McCormack, "Frederick Matthias Alexander and John Dewey: A Neglected Influence" (Ph.D. thesis, University of Toronto, 1958). McCormack continued his research and uncovered an extraordinary network of Alexander's students and followers, some of whom had direct contact with Dewey for several years, including Frank Jones, a psychologist at Tufts University. Jones, who provided lessons to Dewey for several years, shared with McCormack copies of his correspondence with Dewey and helped him make important contacts with other Alexander acquaintances. Jones was the first to publicly reveal that Dewey took lessons from Alexander in "The Work of F. M. Alexander as an Introduction to Dewey's Philosophy of Education," *School and Society* 57 (1943): 1–4. Dewey read a draft of Jones's paper and hoped that *School and Society* would publish it. Dewey assured Jones that he "certainly [would] endorse all you say about my work in relation to that of Alexander's (see Dewey to Jones, October 5, 1942. Eric McCormack Papers, St. Vincent's College, Latrobe, Pennsylvania).

Jones subsequently pieced together some of the threads of the story that McCormack tried to complete in his book, *Body Awareness in Action: A Study of the Alexander Technique* (New York: Schocken, 1976). Tragically, McCormack, who suffered from alcoholism, died in 1963 without having found a publisher for his thesis.

55. McCormack, "Frederick Matthias Alexander," pp. 111–112, believes that the strongest evidence that Dewey reformulated his notion that habit is a redundant train of thought into one which stressed habit as a course or sequence of activity rooted in "will" is found in *Human Nature and Conduct.* Here is where Dewey explicitly acknowledges Alexander's influence and attempts to clarify how Alexander's notion of refusing to respond to inhibitory signals which reinforce habitual but incorrect movements actually alters the sequence in which these movements occur. In essence, Alexander helped Dewey better appreciate the practical behavioral implications of enlisting the body to overcome certain afflictions of thought which perpetuate habit.

56. Frederick Matthias Alexander, *Man's Supreme Inheritance,* 2nd ed. (New York:

Dutton, 1918). Alexander's book was first published in 1910 by a London publisher. The second edition in 1918 includes an introduction by John Dewey.

57. Letter to Dewey, March 5, 1918. John Dewey Papers. Special Collections, Morris Library, Southern Illinois University, Carbondale, Illinois.

58. Barnes to Dewey, November 19, 1918. Joseph Ratner Papers, Collection 142, Box 7, Folder 5.

59. See Alexander, *Man's Supreme Inheritance*, p. 43.

60. Roberta Dewey, Dewey's second wife, put McCormack in touch in 1959 with Goddard Binkley, a British instructor in the Alexander technique. Binkley indicated to Eric McCormack that he learned from F. M. Alexander in the early 1950s that "Dewey gave Alexander considerable assistance in the writing of his books, particularly with *Constructive Conscious Control of the Individual* [New York: Dutton, 1923] and *The Use of the Self* [New York: Dutton, 1932]." Binkley added that "Dewey went over these [book manuscripts] very carefully before they ever saw a publisher," saying that, "[o]ne can imagine the long and sometimes torturous discussions the two men must have had together, especially over terminology." See Binkley to McCormack, February 7, 1959, 3. Eric D. McCormack Papers, St. Vincent's College, Latrobe, Pennsylvania. Beaumont Alexander, F. M. Alexander's younger brother, confirmed that Dewey read Alexander's manuscript *The Use of the Self* and commented on it before it was published. See Alexander to McCormack, September 9, 1957. Dewey wrote introductions to both books.

61. John Dewey, "Introduction to F. Matthias Alexander's *Constructive Conscious Control of the Individual*," in *MW* 15: 308.

62. Bourne, "Making Over the Body," *The New Republic* 15 (May 4, 1918): 29. McCormack notified Frank Jones on June 16, 1958, that he had received from Beaumont Alexander a copy of a letter Dewey had sent to an unnamed reviewer of Alexander's book *Man's Supreme Inheritance*. Dewey criticized this unknown reviewer for drawing some unfair and misleading comparisons to Freudian psychoanalysis. McCormack asked Jones's opinion as to whom the letter was directed. Jones speculated, correctly in my opinion, in his response to McCormack's query on June 20 that Dewey's letter, which was dated May 22, 1918, was intended for Randolph Bourne. It seems clear from the context of Dewey's remarks that he had additional criticisms of Bourne's review that he preferred to send directly to Bourne. For example, Dewey asks in his letter that he be "pardoned for repeating that only an almost incredible bias could have led you to write as if the thing you are objecting to had anything to do with Mr. Alexander's theory and practices." Dewey also argued that instead of being what Bourne had asserted was "an inverted psychoanalysis," Dewey protested that "his method [Alexander's technique] is a completed psychoanalysis, completed by having its organic basis placed under a merely floating parallelistic 'psychic,' and by being carried from the negative to the positive." Dewey contended that Alexander's important discovery that "all of the psychic complexes have their basis in organic discoordinations and tensions . . . reduces the present technique of the psychoanalyst to an incidental accompaniment, and cuts out the elaborate ritualistic mummery with which the present psychoanalysts have been obliged to surround their method."

63. Ibid., p. 28.

64. Bourne, "Other Messiahs: A Letter to the Editor," *The New Republic* 15 (May 25, 1918): 117.

65. See John Dewey, Introduction to F. Matthias Alexander's *Constructive Conscious*

Control of the Individual, for one of his more thoughtful interpretations of Alexander's thesis and methods of conscious control.

66. Jones, *Body Awareness in Action,* p. 97.

67. Tasker told McCormack that she first learned about Alexander from Margaret Naumberg while both were visiting Maria Montessori's school in Rome in 1913 (see letter to McCormack, June 28, 1951). Naumberg was with a delegation of Americans which included Evelyn Dewey. Tasker indicated that when Naumberg returned to London she contacted Alexander for lessons and said that Naumberg "urged upon Alexander the importance of his making contact with Dewey, and begged him to come the U.S. to teach." Tasker was hired in 1916 to teach at Naumberg's BEE-funded Walden School in New York. Naumberg denied that she ever mentioned Dewey in asking Alexander to come to the U.S., but simply pointed out the educational significance of his ideas for American schools. Nevertheless, she acknowledged that she got Alexander his first pupils in America, who included the Mitchells and Deweys (see Naumberg to McCormack, December 6, 1957).

During this time, Tasker indicated that she took "a post-graduate course with Dewey at Columbia in Psychological Ethics." Tasker recalled that in the summer of 1918 she "traveled to California in the company of Dr. and Mrs. Dewey." According to Tasker, Dewey "was busy on the train typing out the lectures he was to give at Stanford University, which formed the basis of *Human Nature and Conduct.*"

68. Jones, *Body Awareness in Action,* pp. 103–104.

69. John Dewey, "Introduction" to F. Matthias Alexander's *The Use of the Self,* in *LW* 6: 317.

70. Ibid., p. 318.

71. Ibid.

72. John Dewey, *Human Nature and Conduct,* in *MW* 14: 23–24.

73. Ibid, p. 30.

74. Ibid.

75. Ibid., p. 114.

76. Ibid.

77. Ibid., p. 173.

78. Ibid.

79. Ibid., p. 61.

80. Ibid.

81. Ibid., p. 112.

6. THE EVOLUTION OF MIND IN NATURE

1. John Harvey Robinson, "John Dewey, 1859–1952," *Journal of Philosophy* 1 (1953): 9.

2. Ibid.

3. Quoted in ibid., p. 9.

4. McGraw, interview by Duckett, p. 4.

5. John Dewey, *Experience and Nature,* p. 361.

6. Two of these references to Freud deserve quotation in their entirety, while a third (see John Dewey, "Santayana's Orthodoxy: Review of George Santayana's *Some Turns of Thought in Modern Philosophy,*" in *LW* 9: 243) is too brief and insignificant to mention.

In "A Key to the New World. Review of Bertrand Russell's *Education and the Good Life*," in *LW* 2: 229, Dewey expressed his apparent agreement with Russell's criticisms of Freudianism. Dewey said

"He [Russell] wisely remarks that because Freudians have failed to recognize the instinctive differences in the affection of husband and wife, parents for children, and children for parents, they have been rendered, in a sense, ascetics as regards the relations of parents and children. Certainly as far as most American families are concerned it is the desire for power on the one hand and the desire on the other hand for being recognized as individuals who count for something in their own behalf, which is the ultimate root of most difficulties between them."

Dewey again commented unfavorably on Freud's views about sex and marriage in *Ethics*, in *LW* 7: 449, when he argued, "The school of Freud has magnified the place of sex and has emphasized the dangers of repression of this primitive urge." While Dewey welcomed the attempt to bring sex out into the open, he indicated that "it is not yet apparent" whether doing so "exaggerates by isolation" or "prepares the way for a truer estimate of the significance of sex in its relation to other life interests."

7. Frank Sulloway, *Freud: Biologist of the Mind: Beyond the Psychoanalytic Legend* (New York: Basic Books, 1979).

8. For more details on Sachs, Peterson, and many other pioneering neurologists who worked at Columbia University, see Charles Elsberg, *The Story of a Hospital: The Neurological Institute of New York*. Also see John Burnham, *Psychoanalysis and American Medicine, 1894-1918* (New York: International Universities Press, 1967), for Freud's impact on neurology and psychiatry. Nathan G. Hale, *Freud and the Americans: The Beginnings of Psychoanalysis in the United States, 1876-1917* (New York: Oxford University Press, 1971) and F. H. Matthews, "The Americanization of Sigmund Freud: Adaptations of Psychoanalysis before 1917," *Journal of American Studies* 10 (1967): 39-62, provide excellent analyses of Freud's impact on American medicine and culture.

9. Burnham, *Psychoanalysis and American Medicine*, p. 24.

10. For interesting accounts of Freud's early years in Brucke's laboratory, see Robert R. Holt, "Beyond Vitalism and Mechanism: Freud's Concept of Psychic Energy," in *Historical Roots of Contemporary Psychology*, ed. Benjamin B. Wolman (New York: Harper and Row, 1968), pp. 203-207, and Lucille B. Ritvo's chapter "Freud's Research in Brucke's Institute of Physiology and Meynert's Institute of Cerebral Anatomy," in Lucille Ritvo, *Darwin's Influence on Freud* (New Haven, Conn.: Yale University Press, 1990), pp. 161-169.

11. This was reported by Pauley in *Controlling Life*, p. 206.

12. Sigmund Freud, "Beyond the Pleasure Principle," in *The Standard Edition of the Complete Psychological Works of Sigmund Freud*, ed. James Strachey [hereafter *SE*], vol. 18 (London: Hogarth Press, 1953), p. 47.

13. For a historical account of Hans Spemann's contribution to neuroembryology that puts his work in contemporary perspective, see Viktor Hamburger, *The Heritage of Experimental Embryology: Hans Spemann and the Organizer* (New York: Oxford University Press, 1988).

14. Sigmund Freud, "Project for a Scientific Psychology," in *SE* 1: 295.

15. Quoted in Marie Bonaparte, Anna Freud, and Ernst Kriss, eds., *The Origins of Psychoanalysis: Letters to Wilhelm Fliess, Drafts and Notes: 1887-1902* (New York: Basic Books, 1954), p. 134.

16. Freud's decision to drop further reference to how neurons function did not re-solve the issue. According to Robert Holt, this "had the paradoxical effect of preserving these assumptions by hiding their original nature, and by transferring the operations of the apparatus into a conceptual realm where they were insulated from correction by progress in neurophysiology and brain anatomy." Holt, "Beyond Vitalism," 208. There is an alternative argument that Freud's energetic assumptions can be justified if two adjustments are made. First, cathetic energy could be understood as a form of potential energy, as described by Maxwell. This would preserve the distinction between kinetic and potential energy that is eliminated in Freud's theory. Second, Bohr's principle of complementarity could be incorporated to allow for the exchange of energy between biological beings and their environments. This would replace Freud's dualism with an interactionist perspective. See Kenneth M. Colby, *Energy and Structure in Psychoanalysis* (New York: Ronald Press, 1955). Colby proposed a "cyclic-circular model of the psychic apparatus" to suggest how energy is transformed as it recirculates through different functional neural processes and is exchanged with the environment.

17. By adopting a topographic view of mental events, Freud asserted that it "has for the present nothing to do with anatomy; it has reference not to anatomical localities, but to regions in the mental apparatus, wherever they may be situated in the body." Sigmund Freud, "The Unconscious," in *SE* 14: 175.

18. For example, Dewey's Columbia University colleague Lawrence Kubie, a neu-rologist and collaborator with Frederick Tilney, attacked Freud's economic conception of energy as being misleading and fallacious. Kubie insisted that psychological phe-nomena "are the results of the interplay of many conflicting intrapsychic forces." Kubie added that Freud's failure to acknowledge the competitive and contrasting nature of hu-man emotions makes "so-called economic formulations a species of ad hoc speculative descriptive allegory." Lawrence Kubie, "The Fallacious use of Quantitative Concepts in Dynamic Psychology," *The Psychoanalytic Quarterly* 16 (1947): 518. Neurophysiologist Karl Lashley was also critical of Freud's energetic assumptions, arguing, "Neural ac-tivity has been sufficiently well explored to rule out such broad assumptions as of the energy of the libido or of the id." Karl Lashley and Kenneth M. Colby, "An Exchange of Views on Psychic Energy and Psychoanalysis," *Behavioral Science* 2 (1957): 238.

19. Edward J. Kempf, *The Autonomic Functions and the Personality* (New York: The Nervous and Mental Disease Publishing Co., 1921).

20. See Edward J. Kempf, "The Holistic Laws of Life," in *Edward J. Kempf: Selected Papers*, ed. Dorothy C. Kempf and John C. Burnham (Bloomington: Indiana University Press, 1974), pp. 309–311.

21. Kempf, *The Autonomic Functions of the Personality*, pp. 148–149.

22. Ibid., p. 131.

23. Meredith Smith, *Education and the Integration of Behavior* (New York: Teachers College, 1927). Smith does not describe this experiment. However, it is possible that he may have been involved as a student researcher in the growth studies sponsored by the Bureau of Educational Experiments.

24. Ibid., p. 5.

25. Robert Bruce Raup, *Complacency: The Foundation of Human Behavior* (New York: Macmillan, 1925), pp. 59–60, 84–85. Raup used the term "complacency" as an equivalent to habit. He believed that the term "complacency" better expressed the mental and physical attributes of unreflective human behavior than did the word "habit."

26. See Eugenio Rignano, *The Psychology of Reasoning* (New York: Harcourt Brace and Company, 1923), and *Biological Memory* (New York: Harcourt Brace and Company, 1926).

27. Edward Kempf, "Autobiographical Fragment," in *Edward J. Kempf*, ed. Kempf and Burnham, p. 8.

28. This fascinating episode was recorded in correspondence exchanged between Hall and Freud, subsequently published by John C. Burnham, "Sigmund Freud and G. Stanley Hall: Exchange of Letters," *Psychoanalytic Quarterly* 29 (1960): 309.

29. Ibid., p. 311.

30. Ibid. Burnham found curious Freud's use of the term "anatomy" to describe Kempf's perspective, because Kempf's theory was distinctly physiological and dynamic in orientation.

31. Sulloway, in *Freud: Biologist of the Mind*, contended that Freud's clinical theories were grounded in discredited nineteenth-century evolutionary theories advanced by Ernst Haeckel.

Disputes about the source of Freud's clinical theories were revived recently with the discovery of his unpublished manuscript "A Phylogenetic Fantasy: Overview of the Transference Neuroses," which Freud had sent to Sandor Ferenczi in 1915. This paper was one of a series of never-published essays on metapsychological topics that included an essay on consciousness. Based on her analysis, Freud scholar Ilse Grubrich-Simitis concluded that Freud wrote it at Ferenczi's prompting and never intended it to be interpreted as other than "a playful fantasy." See Ilse Grubrich-Simitis, *Freud's Phylogenetic Fantasy* (Cambridge, Mass.: Harvard University Press, 1987), p. 83. Nevertheless, Freud made a number of speculative assertions about the phylogeny of neuroses which if proven true would provide a solid evolutionary foundation for psychoanalysis. These ideas subsequently appear as premises underpinning Freud's conception of instincts and the psychological mechanisms Freud uses to explain phenomena central to psychoanalytic theory, such as unconscious memory, fixation, and regression.

32. Ibid., p. 211.

33. Dewey indicated in correspondence with Corinne Chisholm that she "would find help on the nervous system" by reading C. M. Child's *Origin and Development of the Nervous System: From a Physiological Viewpoint* (Chicago: University of Chicago Press, 1921) and C. J. Herrick's *Neurological Foundations of Animal Behavior* (New York: Hafner, 1924). Dewey to Chisholm, February 28, 1930. Rare Books and Manuscripts, Butler Library, Columbia University, New York. Dewey made an intriguing observation about embryogenesis in the same letter referring to works by Herrick and Child when he said, "I have always thought that the evolution of the ectoderm and mesoderm structures has a deep significance, but I have never followed it through."

34. See Sharon E. Kingsland, "Toward a Natural System of the Human Psyche." According to Kingsland, Herrick and Child were collaborators. Although they published separate books in 1924, Herrick drew heavily from Child's ideas about neurogenesis in his book *The Neurological Foundations of Animal Behavior* (New York: Hafner, 1962; orig. pub. 1924).

35. See A. S. Romer, "George H. Parker," in *Biography of National Academy of Sciences* (Washington, D.C.: National Academy of Sciences, 1955), p. 363.

36. Wesley Mitchell reported in his diary that George Parker came by for a letter of introduction to John Dewey on March, 17, 1918. Dewey indicated in correspondence in 1930 that he "remembered reading something years ago pointing out that motility pre-

cedes definite nerve centers in the organism. I think it was by G. H. Parker. His main point as I remember it was that the evolution of sense organs and centers could not be separated from that of responsive acts." Dewey to Chisholm, February 28, 1930. Rare Books and Manuscripts, Butler Library, Columbia University, New York.

37. See George H. Parker, "The Origin, Plan and Operational Modes of the Nervous System," in National Research Council, *The Problem of Mental Disorder* (New York: McGraw Hill, 1934), pp. 184–196 for a concise statement of his previous research.

38. For a complete statement of his theory, see George H. Parker, *The Elementary Nervous System* (Philadelphia: J. B. Lippincott, 1919).

39. Herrick, *Neurological Foundations of Animal Behavior,* p. 236.

40. Frederick Tilney, "The Genesis of Cerebellar Functions," *Archives of Neurology and Psychology* 1 (1923): 167–169.

41. Frederick Tilney and Lawrence Kubie, "Behavior in Its Relationship to the Development of the Brain," *Bulletin of the Neurological Institute of New York* 1 (1931): 299.

42. Dewey, *Experience and Nature,* p. 197.

43. Ibid., p. 213.

44. Ibid., p. 125.

45. Ibid., p. 197.

46. Ibid., p. 200.

47. Ibid., pp. 140–145.

48. Dewey dramatically underscores the importance of this theme throughout *Experience and Nature* by echoing the lament popularized by Alexander during this period that mankind's psychophysical well-being was threatened by "possible destruction" and "catastrophe" (p. 225). Dewey conspicuously cited Alexander's books (in footnotes Dewey normally used sparingly) to support his contention that the human subconscious —a term Dewey used rarely until *Experience and Nature*—consists of a repertoire of feelings and acquired habits "that gives us our sense of rightness and wrongness." Dewey concurred with Alexander's diagnosis that the power of the subconscious mind was corrupted by the substitution of cultural meanings for organic functions, which severed the relationship between mind and body. These effects were exhibited, according to Dewey, in "one-sided, degraded and excessive susceptibilities; creating both dissociations and the rigid fixations in the sensory register." Consequently, Dewey argued that the subconscious had become least reliable with respect to "intimate matters of health, morals and social affairs, involving human conduct and interpersonal interaction." Thought cures and other similar remedies, Dewey believed, simply exacerbated the problem by creating secondary "pseudo-environments," in which "fantasies of consolation," "stereotyped beliefs," "fanaticisms," and "paranoiac systems" could flourish without serious challenge (all quotes from p. 229).

49. Ibid., p. 189.

50. For Dewey's arguments against introspectionism and psychoanalysis, see ibid., pp. 255–260.

51. Ibid., p. 257.

52. Ibid., pp. 257–258.

53. Ibid., p. 258.

54. Ibid.

55. Ibid., p. 259.

56. Ibid., p. 230.

57. Ibid.

58. Ibid.
59. Ibid., p. 201.
60. Ibid., p. 215.
61. For Dewey's argument against what he believed to be the misleading use of psychological terms by Freud and other "realists," see ibid., pp. 242–245.
62. John Dewey, "Memory and Judgment," in *LW* 17: 325.
63. Ibid., p. 325.
64. Ibid.
65. Ibid., p. 334.
66. Dewey, *Experience and Nature*, p. 239.
67. Ibid., p. 240.
68. Ibid., p. 224.

7. POST-IMPRESSIONISM, QUANTUM MECHANICS, AND THE TRIUMPH OF PHENOMENAL EXPERIENCE

1. John Dewey, *Individualism, Old and New*, in *LW* 5: 103.
2. Quoted in George Dykhuizen, *The Life and Mind of John Dewey*, pp. 238–239.
3. John Dewey, "Impressions of Soviet Russia: New Schools for a New Era," in *LW* 3: 239.
4. Quoted in Dykhuizen, *The Life and Mind of John Dewey*, p. 236.
5. See Gerald Holton, "Mach, Einstein and the Search for Reality," in *Ernst Mach, Physicist and Philosopher*, ed. Robert S. Cohen and Raymond J. Seeger (Dordrecht, Holland: Reidel, 1970), pp. 165–166. According to Holton, Einstein felt a kinship to Ostwald because he thought of himself as a "heretic," like Ostwald, by opposing mechanistic accounts of physical phenomena.
6. For a recent biography, see Howard Greenfield, *The Devil and Dr. Barnes: Portrait of an American Art Collector* (New York: Viking, 1987), pp. 10–11. Also useful are William Schack's *Art and Argyrol: The Life and Career of Albert C. Barnes* (New York: T. Yoseloff, 1963) and Henry Hart, *Dr. Barnes of Merion: An Appreciation* (New York: Farrar Straus, 1963).
7. Greenfield, *The Devil and Dr. Barnes*, pp. 15, 20–21.
8. Ibid., p. 68.
9. Quoted in ibid., p. 95.
10. Ibid.
11. For his theory of art as an educational experience, see Albert C. Barnes, "The Roots of Art" and "Method and Design," in *Art and Education*, ed. Albert C. Barnes (Merion, Pa.: The Barnes Foundation, 1929). These essays were reprinted from Albert C. Barnes's *The Art in Painting* (New York: Harcourt Brace, 1925).
12. Thomas Munro, interview by Kenneth Duckett, Center for Dewey Studies, August 21, 1967, Cleveland Ohio. John Dewey Papers, Collection 102.
13. Ibid., p. 9.
14. Ibid., p.12.
15. Ibid., p.13.
16. Quoted in Greenfield, *The Devil and Dr. Barnes*, pp. 109–110.
17. Ibid.
18. Barnes, "Plastic Form," in *Art and Education*, p. 75.

19. John Dewey, *Art as Experience*, in *LW* 10: 204.
20. Ibid.
21. See Barnes, "The Evolution of Contemporary Painting," in *Art and Education*, 157.
22. Ibid.
23. Dewey, *Art as Experience*, p. 256.
24. Ibid.
25. For an excellent historical reconstruction of Matisse's unfortunate encounters with Barnes, which draws on Matisse's correspondence and writings, see Jack Flam, *Matisse: The Dance* (Washington, D.C.: National Gallery of Art, 1993).
26. Quoted from an interview in Jack Flam, ed., *Matisse on Art* (Berkeley: University of California Press, 1995), p. 113. There are several transcripts in Flam's book of interviews recorded with Matisse throughout his long career in which Matisse comments on his relations with Barnes.
27. Quoted in Flam, *Matisse: The Dance*, p. 63.
28. Dewey reported his first meeting with Matisse in a letter to Albert Barnes, December 10, 1930. John Dewey Papers, Collection 102, Box 10, Folder 4, Special Collections, Morris Library, Southern Illinois University, Carbondale, Illinois.
29. See Greenfield, *The Devil*, p. 162.
30. The Center for Dewey Studies possesses copies of these two charcoals. The originals can be found in the New York Museum of Modern Art and in the Special Collections of the Yale University Library in New Haven, Connecticut.
31. Letter to Barnes, December 26, 1930.
32. Ibid. David W. Prall, in *A Study of the Theory of Value* (Berkeley: University of California Press, 1921), adopted the position that aesthetic judgment consists in a non-rational sensorimotor act of "liking" something on the basis of specific attributes of a work of art which one finds pleasing. Consequently, Prall argued that aesthetic judgment is essentially subjective and that standards of artistic worth resist formalization. Dewey and Prall carried on a lively and contentious debate during the 1920s. See, for example, John Dewey, "The Meaning of Value" and "Value, Objective Reference and Criticism," in *LW* 2: 69–97. For one of Prall's rejoinders, see David W. Prall, "Value and Thought Process," in *LW* 2: 393–402.
33. Dewey to Chisholm, January 1, 1931.
34. Ibid.
35. Matisse to Dewey, January 16, 1931. John Dewey Papers, Collection 102, Box 10, Folder 5.
36. Ibid.
37. Flam, *Matisse on Art*, p. 2.
38. For a discussion see Flam, *Matisse: The Dance*, p. 25.
39. Dewey, *Art as Experience*, p. 142.
40. Ibid., p. 141.
41. John Dewey to Barnes, December 23, 1927. John Dewey Papers, Collection 102, Box 8, Folder, 9.
42. Ibid.
43. Ibid.
44. John Dewey, *Art as Experience*, p. 187.
45. Referring to Rignano's *Psychology of Reasoning*, Dewey announced dramatically

that "[r]ecent advances in some fundamental generalizations regarding biological functions in general and those of the nervous system in particular have made possible a definite conception of continuous development from the lower functions to higher . . . There has long been talk about the unity of experience and mental life, to the effect that knowledge, feeling and volition are all manifestations of the same energies, etc.; but there has now been put in our hands the means by which this talk may be made definite and significant." John Dewey, "Affective Thought," in *LW* 2: 104–105. The original essay was entitled "Affective Thought in Logic and Painting," in *Art and Education*, ed. Barnes, pp. 63–72. See Eugenio Rignano, *The Psychology of Reasoning*, trans. Winifred Holl (London: Harcourt Brace, 1923).

46. Dewey, *Art as Experience*, p. 53.

47. Ibid., p. 60.

48. See Floyd Ratliff, "Mach's Contributions to the Analysis of Sensations," in *Mach: Physicist and Philosopher*, ed. Robert Cohen and Robert Seeger (Dordrecht, Holland: Reidel, 1970), pp. 23–41.

49. See Ernst Mach, *The Analysis of Sensations*, trans. C. M. Williams (New York: Dover, 1959). In his introduction to this book, Thomas Szasz found only one significant reference to Mach in Freud's correspondence. Freud related to Wilhelm Fliess in 1900, according to Szasz, that he saw many parallels between Mach's *Analysis of Sensations* and his about to be published *Interpretation of Dreams*. This may have been a gratuitous comparison, Szasz argued, because there is little similarity in their views about mind other than that Freud shared some of Mach's physicalistic views about psychology.

50. Dewey, *Art as Experience*, pp. 106–107.

51. Ibid., p. 211.

52. Ibid., p. 165.

53. For original essays by the participants in this dispute see Stephen G. Brush, ed., *Kinetic Theory*, vol. 2: *Irreversible Processes* (New York: Pergamon, 1966). An illuminating discussion of the convertibility hypothesis and the problem of entropy is also presented by Brush in "The Development of the Kinetic Theory of Gases, VIII: Randomness and Irreversibility," *Archive for the History of the Exact Sciences* 9 (1974): 1–88.

54. See Ludwig Boltzmann, "On Statistical Mechanics," in *Ludwig Boltzmann: Theoretical Physics and Philosophical Problems*, ed. Brian McGuinness (Dordrecht, Holland: Reidel, 1974), pp. 169–172, for his probabilistic theory of energy states of the universe. Also see Brush, "Kinetic Theory," pp. 72–74.

55. James Clerk Maxwell, "The Theory of Electrical Vortices Applied to Electric Currents," in *The Scientific Papers of James Clerk Maxwell*, vol. I, ed. William Niven (New York: Dover, 1952), pp. 468–488. P. M. Harman, *Energy, Force and Matter: The Conceptual Development of Nineteenth Century Physics* (Cambridge: Cambridge University Press, 1982), pp. 84–98, provides an interesting analysis of how Maxwell's vortex model was received by his colleagues. See also the "Introduction" in Stephen G. Brush, Elizabeth Garber, and C. W. F. Everitt, eds., *Maxwell on Heat and Statistics* (Bethlehem, Pa.: Lehigh University Press, 1995), pp. 1–102, for a discussion of Maxwell's debate with Boltzmann.

56. For his most lucid presentation of his theory of force and energy, see James Clerk Maxwell, *Matter and Motion* (New York: Van Nostrand, 1892).

57. Quoted in Flam, *Matisse on Art*, p. 121.

58. Ibid., p. 19.

59. Ibid., p. 219.

60. Dewey, *Art as Experience*, p. 158.

61. Ibid., p. 159.

62. Ibid., pp. 212–213.

63. Ibid., p. 159.

64. Ibid., p. 170.

65. See, for example, the following letters John Dewey wrote to Chisholm. On July 1, 1930, Dewey indicated that "I haven't seen yet just what the connection between the avoidance factor in rhythm and the accumulation—release function, recurrent waves, etc." On January 6, 1932, Dewey admits that Chisholm seems correct in asserting that "tensions seem related to movement backwards rather than forwards. Striving forwards is a mere phase. It is almost impossible that there should be any such thing and that equilibrium would have to be conceived in terms of return."

66. Dewey, *Art as Experience*, pp. 171, 174.

67. Ibid., p. 174.

68. Ibid., pp. 202–203.

69. Personal communication with Prof. Holmes Rolston. Rolston, who presented the Gifford Lectures at the University of Edinburgh in 1997–1998, related to me this anecdote during his visit at California Polytechnic State University, San Luis Obispo, to present a lecture in the Philosophy at Poly Speakers Series, February 22, 2001. Rolston is the author of *Genes, Genesis and God: Values and Their Origins in Natural and Human History* (New York: Cambridge University Press, 1999).

70. Jane Dewey to John Dewey, April 2, 1926. John Dewey Papers, Collection, 102, Box 7, Folder 7.

71. Jane Dewey to John Dewey, August 12, 1926. John Dewey Papers, Collection, 102, Box 7, Folder 8.

72. Ibid.

73. Jane Dewey to John Dewey, November, 12, 1926. John Dewey Papers, Collection, 102, Box 7, Folder 9.

74. Ernest Nagel, interview by Kenneth Duckett, New York City, October 10, 1966, p. 17. John Dewey Papers, Collection 102.

75. Jane Dewey to John Dewey, August 19, 1926.

76. The only professional biographical information I could find about Jane Dewey is found in *American Men of Science* (Lancaster, Pa.: Science Press, 1938).

77. See L. Rosenfeld, "Niels Bohr in the 1930s," in *Niels Bohr: His Life and Work as Seen by his Colleagues*, ed. S. Rozental (New York: Wiley, 1967), pp. 114–146. For historically focused conceptual essays about and by Bohr and quantum mechanics, see A. P. French and P. J. Kennedy, eds., *Niels Bohr: A Centenary Volume* (Cambridge, Mass.: Harvard University Press, 1985).

78. Niels Bohr, "The Structure of the Atom," in, *Niels Bohr*, ed. French and Kennedy, pp. 91–97.

79. John Dewey to Chisholm, April 15, 1930.

80. For an excellent discussion of the theoretical conflicts between Bohr and Werner Heisenberg, see Edward MacKinnon, "Bohr on the Foundations of Quantum Theory," in *Niels Bohr*, ed. French and Kennedy, pp. 101–120. Also see Werner Heisenberg, "Quantum Theory and Its Interpretation," in *Niels Bohr*, ed. Rozental, pp. 101–103, for his own account of his differences with Bohr.

81. Jane Dewey, "Intensities in the Stark Effect of Helium: I," *Physical Review* 28 (1926): 1124. Dewey expressed her thanks to Niels Bohr "for the suggestion of the problem" and thanked "Dr. Heisenberg for valuable assistance in handling the theory."

82. Jane Dewey, "Intensities of the Stark Effect of Helium: II," *Physical Review* 30 (1927): 776.

83. Heisenberg, "Quantum Theory," p. 105.

84. Quoted in John Honner, "The Transcendental Philosophy of Niels Bohr," *Studies in History and Philosophy of Science* 13 (1982): 8.

85. John Dewey, *Quest for Certainty*, in *LW* 4: 128.

86. Ibid.

87. Ibid., p. 163.

88. Ibid., p. 164.

89. See, for example, J. S. Bixler's review, "Professor Dewey Discusses Religion," *Harvard Theological Review* 23 (1930): 213–133.

90. Dewey, *Art as Experience*, p. 174.

8. COMMUNITIES OF INTELLIGENCE AND THE POLITICS OF SPIRIT

1. See C. J. Herrick, *The Neurological Foundations of Animal Behavior*, pp. 305–309.

2. Roger Smith, *Inhibition: History and Meaning in the Sciences of Mind and Brain* (Berkeley: University of California Press, 1992) provides a thorough and thoughtful critical analysis of the physiological presuppositions that informed the social views of nineteenth-century European experimentalists in psychology and neurology. European scientists adopted a hereditary explanation for children and adults who suffered from brain dysfunctions and attendant learning disabilities. Criminologists, such as Lomboroso and Nordau, popularized the view that criminal and other subnormal elements in society were racial degenerates who threatened, through uncontrolled reproduction, to undermine the vitality and well-being of the Caucasian race.

In contrast, American scientists and the public were divided as to the relative importance of hereditary and environmental factors. Some scientists and their public allies faulted poor public sanitation for epidemics, such as tuberculosis, while others cited unsafe sexual practices and syphilis for the decline in human well-being. But unlike their European counterparts, American progressives possessed a strong moralistic fervor, which led them to favor a strong emphasis on re-educational strategies designed to reform individuals who exhibited bad habits. For a similar perspective see John C. Burnham, "Psychiatry, Psychology and the Progressive Movement," *American Quarterly* 12 (1960): 457–465.

3. C. M. Child, *Physiological Foundations of Behavior*, p. 282. For a useful and insightful study of the relation between Herrick's and Child's biological and social perspectives, see Kingsland, "Toward a Natural History of the Human Psyche," pp. 206–216.

4. Frederick Tilney, "Neurology and Education," *Archives of Neurology and Psychiatry* 16 (1926): 539–554; Frederick Tilney, *Master of Destiny* (New York: Hoeber, 1929; reprint, New York: Doubleday, 1968), pp. 330–343.

5. See Diggins, *The Promise of Pragmatism*, pp. 39–49.

6. John Dewey, "Hegel's Philosophy of Spirit," p. 84.

7. Ibid., p. 85.

8. Hegel, *The Phenomenology of Spirit*, pp. 286–294.

9. John Dewey, *The Public and Its Problems*, in *LW* 2: 369.

10. Ibid., p. 250.

11. Ibid., p. 365.

12. Ibid.

13. See Lawrence K. Frank, "The Beginnings of Child Development and Family Life Education in the Twentieth Century," *Merrill-Palmer Quarterly of Behavior and Development* 8 (1962): 207–228.

14. Quoted in Harold Romney, "The Rockefeller Foundation," in *Foundations*, ed. Harold Keele and Joseph Kiger (Westport, Conn.: Greenwood Press, 1984), p. 364.

15. Quoted in Martin Bulmer and Joan Bulmer, "Philanthropy and Social Science in the 1920s: Beardsley Ruml and the Laura Spelman Rockefeller Memorial, 1922–1929," *Minerva* 19 (1981): 358.

16. Lawrence K. Frank, "Parent Training," p. 3. Box 30, Subseries 5, Series 3, Laura Spelman Rockefeller Memorial Archive, Tarrytown, New York.

17. Lawrence K. Frank, "The Locus of Experience," *Journal of Philosophy* 20 (1923): 328–329.

18. Lawrence K. Frank, "The Development of Science," *Journal of Philosophy* 21 (1924): 5–25.

19. Unpublished Folder of Letters to Lawrence K. Frank, December 1965, obtained in December 1989 from Mary Perry, Watertown, Massachusetts. Excerpts from the letters of two other colleagues are worth quoting. Myrtle McGraw said in part, "Larry was always a step ahead of the rest of us. He had a way of synthesizing the bits of information he picked up from one laboratory or another and then visualizing a totally new approach." McGraw to Frank, November 19, 1965. Ronald Lippitt had this to say: "Perhaps most of all I've admired your amazing ability to combine the insights and concepts of very different disciplines into integrated gestalts that can be called genuine interdisciplinary conceptual creations. (Memorandum to Frank, n.d.)

20. See Steven L. Schlossman, "Philanthropy and the Gospel of Child Development," *History of Education Quarterly*, Fall 1981, 285–288. See also Julia Grant, *Raising Baby by the Book: The Education of American Mothers* (New Haven, Conn.: Yale University Press, 1998), pp. 51–54. Grant contended that the Child Study Association never appealed to a broad segment of the population because of its rigorous academic standards and dominance by middle-class, well-educated mothers.

21. Woodworth to Frank, February 18, 1925. Box 30, Folder 320, Laura Spelman Rockefeller Memorial, Rockefeller Archive Center, Tarrytown, New York. See also Alice Smuts, who documents Woodworth's role in securing support for an interdisciplinary approach to child development research in *The National Research Council Committee on Child Development and the Founding of the Society for Research in Child Development, 1925–1933*, Monographs of the Society for Research in Child Development, vol. 50 (serial no. 6) (Chicago: University of Chicago Press, 1986).

22. Smuts, *The National Research Council*. See also Hamilton Cravens, "Child Saving in an Age of Professionalism, 1915–1930" in *American Childhood: A Research Guide and Historical Handbook*, ed. Joseph M. Hawes and N. Ray Hiner (Westport, Conn.: Greenwood Press, 1985), pp. 462–467, and Elizabeth Lomax, "The Laura Spelman Rockefeller Memorial: Some of Its Contributions to Early Research in Child Development," *Journal of the History of the Behavioral Sciences* 13 (1977), p. 285.

23. Dewey is listed as a past founding member of the board of directors in a report by Willard Rappleye, president from 1941 to 1964, titled *The Josiah Macy, Jr. Foundation:*

Twentieth Anniversary Review, 1930–1955 (New York: Josiah Macy, Jr. Foundation, 1955), p. ix. McGraw's research is also described in this report (see p. 25). Ludwig Kast (1930–1941) describes funded research in growth including McGraw's and Coghill's studies in a report titled *A Review by the President of Activities for the Six years Ending December 31, 1936* (New York: Josiah Macy, Jr. Foundation, 1937), pp. 34–37. Frank, a Dewey student at Columbia, served as Vice President of the Josiah Macy, Jr. Foundation from 1936–1941. Dr. Thomas Meikle, executive director of the foundation, indicated to the author that all minutes of trustee meetings and other memoranda concerning grant awards in the foundation's early years, including material documenting Dewey's involvement, had been destroyed due to limited storage space (interview with Meikle, New York City, April 27, 1992).

24. See John C. Burnham, "The New Psychology: From Narcissism to Social Control," in *Change and Continuity in Twentieth Century America: The 1920s*, ed. John Braeman, David Broder, and Robert Brenner (Columbus: Ohio State University Press, 1968), pp. 351–398. Burnham argues that by focusing on the adverse social consequences of unchecked individual desire and ego ideals, American behavioral psychologists legitimated the use of environmental conditioning as a means of obtaining social control.

25. Gesell's contribution to child development has been documented by Louise B. Ames, a former collaborator, in *Arnold Gesell: Themes of his Work* (New York: Human Sciences Press, 1989). Also see Arnold Gesell, *Infant Behavior: Its Genesis and Growth* (New York: McGraw Hill, 1934). Esther Thelen and Karen E. Adolf, in "Arnold L. Gesell: The Paradox of Nature and Nurture," *Developmental Psychology* 28 (1992): 368–380, have leveled several criticisms at Gesell's developmental theory for purporting to present a neurogenetic reductionist account of early motor development. Thelen and Adolf, in my opinion, have incorrectly argued that McGraw applied the same neurogenetic logic as did Gesell. In fact, McGraw considered structure and function—brain and behavior—to interact throughout development. See Thomas C. Dalton, "McGraw's Alternative to Gesell's Maturationist Theory," in *Beyond Heredity and Environment: Myrtle McGraw and the Maturation Controversy*, ed. Thomas C. Dalton and Victor W. Bergenn (Boulder, Colo.: Westview Press, 1995), pp. 127–152.

26. Frank, "The Beginnings of Child Development," pp. 225–228. Frank emphasized the collaborative nature of these early studies but also indicated that there were significant differences among researchers with respect to methods and results. There are several other excellent studies of Ruml and Frank's efforts to create a child study network involving extensive parent involvement and support from state and local elected officials and educators. The first published studies of Rockefeller programs were done by Elizabeth Lomax, "The Laura Spelman Rockefeller Memorial: Some of Its Contributions to Early Research in Child Development," *Journal of the History of the Behavioral Sciences* 13 (1977): 283–293, and by Steven L. Schlossman, "Before Home Start: Notes Towards a History of Parent Education in America, 1897–1929," *Harvard Educational Review* 46 (1976): 436–467. Both Lomax and Schlossman gained access to important documents regarding Rockefeller-sponsored studies when they were first made available at the Rockefeller Archive Center in Tarrytown, New York, in 1976. Lomax also reviewed the Milton Senn and Lawrence K. Frank Collections in the National Library of Medicine, Bethesda, Maryland.

Two other studies soon followed involving extensive archive research by Martin Bulmer and Joan Bulmer, "Philanthropy and Social Science," and by Schlossman, "Philanthropy and the Gospel of Child Development," pp. 275–299. Bulmer and Bulmer credit

Ruml and Frank with successfully building the capacity of universities to do credible experimental research by maintaining the independence and integrity of the researchers funded by Rockefeller. Schlossman concludes that the Rockefeller program succeeded because it provided educated but isolated middle-class women a professional perspective toward child rearing. Perhaps more importantly, Schlossman observes that the parent education programs raised a central issue of whether school-based or family-based interventions would ultimately be more successful. Frank believed that the latter strategy promised to be more successful only if it led to a transformation of the American family as a whole.

27. Lawrence K. Frank, "Memorandum: Child Study and Parent Training," pp. 2–3, May 23, 1924, Box 315, Subseries 5, Series 3, Laura Spelman Rockefeller Memorial, Rockefeller Archive Center, Tarrytown, New York.

28. Ibid.

29. Mary Perry, telephone interview by the author, November 10, 1989.

30. These comments were reported in a summary of unusually rich and detailed oral histories recorded by Milton Senn with more than eighty pioneers in child development in the fields of experimental and clinical psychology, pediatrics, and psychiatry. See Milton J. Senn, *Insights about the Child Development Movement in the United States*, Monograph of the Society for Research in Child Development, vol. 40, nos. 3–4 (Chicago: University of Chicago Press, 1975).

31. Hamilton Cravens, *Before Head Start: The Iowa Welfare Research Station and America's Children* (Chapel Hill: University of North Carolina Press, 1993), pp. 7–17.

32. Cravens in *Before Head Start*, pp. 52–53, contends that Frank's interactive child study network was constructed with the objective of downplaying the political differences of the parents, researchers, and state organizations in order to create a mass constituency and market for child care programs. Yet the available evidence indicates that Frank believed that growth, not groups, formed the first principle of the human sciences and employed it as an organizational metaphor. Frank anticipated that the development of the separate elements of the network would be uneven and that this would be reflected in the changing patterns of influence of each element. Frank was a field theorist, not a group theorist or elitist, who believed that public debate was inimical to scientifically sound policies. Cravens obscures the important differences between the organizational and bureaucratic emphasis of group theory and the transformational orientation of field theory.

33. Sidonie M. Gruenberg, ed., *Parent Education: Report of the Subcommittee on Types of Parent Education, Content and Method* (New York: The Century Co., 1932).

34. See, for example, Lawrence K. Frank, "The Problem of Child Development," *Child Development* 1 (1935): 7–18.

35. Ibid., p. 9.

36. Ibid., p. 12.

37. Ibid., p. 12. See also L. K. Frank, "Structure, Function, and Growth," *Philosophy of Science* 2 (1935): 210–235, for an interesting attempt philosophically to situate growth studies in the biological and physical sciences. Cravens, "Child Saving in an Age of Professionalism," p. 453, adopts the perspective of scholars of critical social history that Frank was simply uncritically accepting and promoting among Rockefeller researchers a culturally laden conception of childhood.

38. For a history of the contributions of these and other pioneers of Division 7, see Thomas C. Dalton, "The History of Division 7 (Developmental Psychology)," in *Unification through Division: Histories of the Divisions of the American Psychological As-*

sociation, vol. 1, ed. Donald A. Dewsbury (Washington, D.C.: American Psychological Association, 1996), pp. 67–100.

39. Cravens, in *Before Head Start*, argues that Stoddard and his Iowa colleagues were blind to the culturally grounded group bias of their studies, which prevented them from gaining significant knowledge about the factors affecting individual development. In my opinion, Cravens focuses too heavily on only one dimension of the Iowa and other institute programs, virtually excluding any meaningful analyses of longitudinal studies of growth and motor development undertaken at Iowa and elsewhere. For a critical review of Cravens's book, see Thomas C. Dalton, "Challenging the Group Bias of American Culture," *Contemporary Psychology* 40 (1995): 201–204. For more recent accounts of Iowa programs since the 1950s by participating researchers, see Joan H. Cantor, *Psychology at Iowa: Centennial Essays* (Hillsdale, N.J.: Erlbaum, 1991).

40. E. Faris, "Attitudes and Behavior," *American Journal of Sociology* 34 (1928): 271–281.

41. See Lomax, "The Laura Spelman Rockefeller Memorial," pp. 283–293, for a sampling of the different approaches.

42. See Christine M. Shea, "The Ideology of Mental Health and the Emergence of the Therapeutic Liberal State: The American Mental Hygiene Movement, 1900–1930" (Ph.D. thesis, University of Illinois at Urbana-Champaign, 1980).

43. Emily Cahan, "Science, Practice and Gender Roles in Early American Child Psychology," in *Contemporary Constructions of the Child: Essays in Honor of William Kessen*, ed. Frank S. Kessel, Marc H. Bornstein, and Arnold J. Sameroff (Hillsdale, N.J.: Erlbaum, 1991), pp. 225–250.

44. Compare Cravens's analysis in *Before Head Start*, where he takes this position, and Grant, *Raising Baby by the Book*, who found significant archival evidence of a widely varied response among parents to advice dispensed by popular baby books, a response that could hardly be characterized as homogeneous and uncritical. For an excellent review and critical appraisal of critical social histories that involve Dewey's educational philosophy, see Westbrook, *John Dewey and American Democracy*, pp. 172; 182–185.

45. See Grant, *Raising Baby by the Book*, pp. 30–33.

46. Ibid., p. 139.

47. Ibid., p. 149.

48. See Agnes N. O'Connell and Nancy F. Russo, *Models of Achievement: Reflections of Eminent Women in Psychology* (New York: Columbia University Press, 1983).

49. Grant, *Raising Baby by the Book*, pp. 172–180.

50. Quoted in Lomax, "The Laura Spelman Rockefeller Memorial," p. 287.

51. Harold Anderson, interview by Milton Senn, New York City, August 17, 1968, p. 39. Milton Senn Papers, Oral Histories of Child Development, Box 9, Folder 5, National Library of Medicine, Bethesda, Maryland.

52. Mary Cover Jones, interview by Milton Senn, Berkeley, California, April 5, 1968, p. 4.

53. Lawrence K. Frank, "The Management of Tensions," in Lawrence Frank, *Society as the Patient* (New Brunswick, N.J.: Rutgers University Press, 1949), p. 115.

54. White House Conference on Child Health and Protection, Report of the Committee on the Infant and Preschool Child; John E. Anderson, *The Young Child in the Home, A Survey of Three Thousand American Families* (New York: D. Appleton-Century Co., 1936).

55. McCormack to Jones, June 13, 1948. Fr. Eric McCormack Papers, St Vincent's College, Latrobe, Pennsylvania.

56. Dewey was involved in numerous voluntary political action groups and third-party movements throughout these years. These groups included Theodore Roosevelt's Progressive Party, the League for Industrial Democracy, the League of Free Nations, and the League for Independent Political Action (LIPA), the latter forming the United People's Party, which ran candidates during the Depression. As the national chairman of the LIPA in 1929, Dewey and his collaborators tried to forge a coalition among labor, farmers, and the middle class for the promotion of national policies involving unemployment insurance, social security, farm credit, and public works programs. Many of these proposals subsequently became a part of Franklin D. Roosevelt's New Deal. The LIPA also proposed programs that went well beyond the New Deal agenda to include the expansion of civil liberties, the creation of consumer and producer cooperatives, the creation of mechanisms for industrial democracy, and income redistribution. While the LIPA fell short of its goals, Dewey never ceased being one of the staunchest critics of the New Deal. See Westbrook, *John Dewey and American Democracy*, pp. 443–452.

57. Dewey advanced these criticisms of American culture in a series of articles published in the *New Republic* in the 1930s and reprinted together in "Individualism, Old and New," *LW* 5: pp. 115–120.

58. Ibid., p. 117.

59. John Dewey, "Freedom and Culture," in *LW* 13: 172.

60. For an intriguing account of Dewey's embattled relationship with Niebuhr, see Daniel Rice, *Reinhold Niebuhr and John Dewey: An American Odyssey* (Albany, N.Y.: SUNY Press, 1993). See also Reinhold Niebuhr, *Moral Man, Immoral Society* (New York: Scribners, 1932), in which he launches a full-scale assault on Dewey's pragmatist premises about intelligence and democratic politics.

61. John Dewey, "Unity and Progress," in *LW* 9: 73.

62. Ibid.

63. Ibid.

64. Niebuhr, *Moral Man, Immoral Society*, p. 81.

65. John Dewey, "Intelligence and Power," in *LW* 9: 109.

66. Sigmund Freud, *Civilization and Its Discontents*. In The Standard Edition of the Complete Psychological Works of Sigmund Freud, vol. 21, Freud considered group affiliations to have only exacerbated the negative demands placed on the ego by society. He said: "This danger is most threatening when the bonds of society are chiefly constituted by the identification of its members with one another, while the individuals of the leader type do not acquire the importance that should fall to them in the formation of the group" (pp. 62–63).

67. John Dewey, *The Public and Its Problems*, pp. 49–50.

68. John Dewey, *Human Nature and Conduct*, p. 174.

69. For an excellent discussion of Dewey's disputes about socialism and communism, see Westbrook, *John Dewey and American Democracy*, pp. 429–496.

9. THE FUNCTION OF JUDGMENT IN INQUIRY

1. Dewey scholars adopting the continuity thesis include Joseph Ratner, *Intelligence in the Modern World* (New York: Modern Library, 1939), p. 155; Joseph Ratner and

Robert Altman, eds., *John Dewey and Arthur Bentley: A Philosophical Correspondence, 1932–1951* (New Brunswick, N.J.: Rutgers University Press, 1964), pp. 36–39; Ernest Nagel, "Introduction," in *LW:* 12, pp. ix–xxvii; and Sidney Hook, "Introduction," in *MW* 2: xvi).

2. John Dewey, "From Absolutism to Experimentalism," p. 152.

3. Nagel, "Introduction," p. xviii.

4. Nagel found this tendency frustrating when he recalled in an interview that "he [Dewey] introduced fundamental questions without preparing his readers for them." Nagel added that "one didn't quite know what the argument was until you had the wit to discover that he was discussing a position related to the one he was advancing." Ernest Nagel, interview by Kenneth Duckett, p. 4. John Dewey Papers, Collection 102.

5. For Dewey's most extensive elaboration of his neurodynamic model, see Donald F. Koch, ed., *John Dewey: Lectures on Psychological and Political Ethics, 1898* (New York: Hafner, 1976), pp. 110–142, 271–323.

6. Dewey, *Logic: The Theory of Inquiry, LW* 12, p. 30.

7. See John Dewey, "Principles of Mental Development as Illustrated in Early Infancy," pp. 175–191, and Mayhew and Edwards, *The Dewey School.* For an intriguing discussion of Dewey's psychology of education within the broader context of educational reforms advanced by turn-of-the-century educators G. Stanley Hall and Edward L Thorndike, see Sheldon H. White, "Three Visions of a Psychology of Education," in *Culture, Schooling and Psychological Development,* ed. L. T. Landsmann (Norwood, N.J.: Ablex, 1991), pp. 1–39.

8. John Dewey, "Principles of Mental Development," pp. 184, 187–188.

9. Ibid., p. 191.

10. See Antler, "Progressive Education and the Scientific Study of the Child," pp. 559–591.

11. Arnold Gesell, *Infant Behavior: Its Genesis and Growth,* pp. 315–332. See also Thelen and Adolf, "Arnold L. Gesell: The Paradox of Nature and Nurture," pp. 368–380.

12. John Dewey to McGraw, July 22, 1934. John Dewey Papers, Collection 102, Box 10, Folder 7.

13. Ibid.

14. See Paul Dennis, "'Johnny's a Gentleman but Jimmy's a Mug': Press Coverage during the 1930's of Myrtle McGraw's Study of Johnny and Jimmy Woods," *Journal of the History of the Behavioral Sciences* 25 (1989): 356–370.

15. Myrtle McGraw, "Memories, Deliberate Recall, and Speculation," *American Psychologist* 45 (1990): 934. For a more detailed account of McGraw's career and contributions to developmental psychology, see Victor W. Bergenn, Thomas C. Dalton, and Lewis P. Lipsitt, "Myrtle McGraw: A Growth Scientist," *Developmental Psychology* 28 (1992): 381–395.

16. For a previously unpublished memoir recounting her relationship with Dewey, see Thomas C. Dalton and Victor W. Bergenn, "Myrtle McGraw: A Pioneer in Neurobehavioral Development," in *Portraits of Pioneers in Psychology,* ed. Gregory Kimble and Michael Wertheimer (Washington, D.C.: American Psychological Association, 1998), pp. 211–228.

17. Myrtle B. McGraw, "A Comparative Study of a Group of Southern White and Negro Infants," *Genetic Psychology Monographs* 10 (1931): 1–105.

18. Ibid., p. 216.

19. Myrtle McGraw, interview by Milton Senn, p. 5.

20. Myrtle McGraw, "Neural Maturation as Exemplified in the Achievement of Bladder Control," *Journal of Pediatrics* 16 (1940): 587.

21. Myrtle McGraw, interview by Kenneth Duckett, p. 6.

22. McGraw, "Memories, Deliberate Recall and Speculations," p. 934.

23. Myrtle McGraw, interview by Milton Senn, p. 32.

24. *New York Times*, December 16, 1935, p. 19. McGraw's research was comparable to Faraday's in the sense that she used physical analogies to characterize the wave-like nature of human growth just as Faraday had done to understand the field properties of electromagnetism.

25. John Dewey, Introduction to Myrtle B. McGraw, *Growth: A Study of Johnny and Jimmy*, in *LW* 11: 510.

26. John Dewey to McGraw, September 15, 1935. John Dewey Papers, Collection 102.

27. John Dewey to A. Bentley, July 26, 1935. Arthur Bentley Papers.

28. See Elsberg, *The Story of a Hospital: The Neurological Institute of New York, 1909–1938*, and Lawrence Pool, *The Neurological Institute of New York, 1909–1974* (Lakeville, Conn.: Pocketknife Press, 1975), for historical studies.

29. Tilney, "Genesis of Cerebellar Functions," pp. 137–169.

30. Tilney to Keppel, March 22, 1933, and Merriam to Keppel, March 15, 1943. The Normal Child Development Project, Carnegie Corporation Papers, Rare Books and Manuscripts, Butler Library, Columbia University, New York.

31. John Dewey, *Experience and Nature*, pp. 197–211.

32. Frederick Tilney, *Master of Destiny* (New York: Hoeber, 1929; reprint, New York: Doubleday, 1968), pp. 281–290.

33. Tilney and Kubie, "Behavior in Its Relation to the Development of the Brain," 233–237.

34. See McGraw, "Memories, Deliberate Recall and Speculations," p. 936.

35. Katherine Agate Heyl, telephone interview by the author, Norwich, Vermont, December 23, 1989. Heyl shared an apartment with McGraw and worked as a laboratory assistant for three years until she married a neurosurgeon from the Institute. Heyl noted that Dewey used to come over for dinner (or take McGraw out to dinner) every Wednesday evening. Heyl was not privy to their conversations but was generally under the impression that Dewey had originated the NCDS study.

36. McGraw, interview by Milton Senn, p. 41.

37. McGraw, memorandum of interview by L. K. Frank, March 13, 1933, at Babies Hospital, Columbia Medical Center, Rockefeller Archive Center, General Education Board, Record Group I., Series 1.3, Box 370, Folder 3858.

38. Evelyn Dewey, *Behavior Development in Infants: A Survey of the Literature on Prenatal and Postnatal Activity, 1920–1924* (New York: Columbia University Press, 1935; reprint, New York: Arno, 1972), pp. 354–356.

39. John Dewey to McGraw, September 15, 1935, and John Dewey to McGraw, November 16, 1936.

40. John Dewey to McGraw, May 31, 1934, and John Dewey to McGraw, September 1, 1935.

41. John Dewey to McGraw, Sat., ca. 1933; John Dewey to McGraw, Wed., ca. 1935; John Dewey to McGraw, July 20, 1935; and John Dewey to McGraw, November 16, 1936.

42. McGraw, interview by Milton Senn, p. 15.

43. I was able to identify Corinne Frost Chisholm as the probable author of a manuscript, "The Duality of Experience," by finding in the text key words and phrases which

appear in Dewey's correspondence to her. Several chapters of the manuscript can be found in Series II, Boxes 76/14, Folder 1; 76/15, Folder 2; and 76/16, Folder 3. John Dewey Papers, Special Collections, Morris Library, Southern Illinois University, Carbondale, Illinois.

44. John Dewey to Chisholm, July 22, 1935.

45. Herrick to Chisholm, January 14, 1934. The Neurology Collection, C. Judson Herrick Papers, Spencer Research Library, University of Kansas, Lawrence, Kansas.

46. John Dewey to Chisholm, July 1, 1930.

47. See Rappleye to Frank, December 2, 1935. Rockefeller Archive Center, General Education Board, Record Group I, Series 1.3, Box 370, Folder 3858.

48. Dewey wrote to Chisholm that he was continuing to struggle with the phenomenon of recurrence. On July 26, 1936, Dewey indicated that he was "still finding difficulties with recurrence even though sure of the fundamental character." On June 25, 1937, Dewey wrote that he was now "focusing on the backward look as well as striving forward in the sense of being a response to new conditions, not consciously, but intentionally in the sense of in-tension."

49. For Coghill's biography, see C. J. Herrick, *George Elliott Coghill: A Naturalist and Philosopher* (Chicago: University of Chicago Press, 1949).

50. George E. Coghill, "The Neuro-Embryologic Study of Behavior: Principles, Perspectives, and Aims," *Science* 78 (1933): 131–136.

51. George E. Coghill, *Anatomy and the Problem of Behavior* (New York: Cambridge University Press, 1929; reprint, New York: Hafner Publishing Co., 1964), p. 38.

52. George E. Coghill, "Individuation versus Integration in the Development of Behavior," *Journal of Genetic Psychology* 3 (1930): 432.

53. Niels Bohr, "Life and Light," *Nature* 131 (1937): 421–423, 457–459.

54. Coghill, "The Neuro-Embryologic Study of Behavior," p. 137.

55. See Coghill, *Anatomy and the Problem of Behavior*, p. 109.

56. Z. Y. Kuo, "Total Pattern or Local Reflexes?" *Psychological Review* 46 (1939): 93–122. Also see W. F. Windle, "Correlation between the Development of Local Reflexes and the Reflex Arcs in the Spinal Cord of Cat Embryos," *Journal of Comparative Neurology* 59 (1934): 487–505.

57. Gilbert Gottlieb, "Conceptions of Prenatal Behavior," in *Development and the Evolution of Behavior*, ed. L. R. Aronson, E. Tolbach, D. S. Lehrman, and J. S. Rosenblatt (San Francisco: Freeman, 1970), p. 120.

58. Ibid., p. 121. For a complete elaboration of his "bidirectional" theory of development, see Gilbert Gottlieb, *Probabilistic Epigenesis and Evolution*, Heinz Werner Lecture Series, vol. XXII (Worcester, Mass.: Clark University Press, 1999).

59. Ronald W. Oppenheim, "G. E. Coghill (1872–1941): Pioneer Neuroembryologist and Developmental Psychobiologist," *Perspectives in Biology and Medicine* 22 (1978): 45–64.

60. Coghill to Herrick, October, 27, 1933. Neurology Collection, Herrick Papers, Spencer Research Library, University of Kansas, Lawrence, Kansas.

61. McGraw, *Growth: A Study of Johnny and Jimmy* (New York: Appleton-Century, 1935; reprint, New York: Arno Press, 1975).

62. McGraw to Oppenheim, December 31, 1979. Myrtle B. McGraw Papers, Special Collections, Millbank Memorial Library, Teachers College, Columbia University, New York.

63. Ibid.

64. Dewey, *Experience and Nature,* pp. 201, 210.

65. Ibid., pp. 226–241.

66. Ernest Nagel, "Can Logic Be Divorced from Ontology?" in *Dewey and His Critics,* ed. Sidney Morgenbesser (New York: Journal of Philosophy, 1977), pp. 507–514.

67. The passages cited by Hook are found in John Dewey, "The Subject Matter of Metaphysical Inquiry," in *MW* 8: 4. They have been taken out of context. Dewey made it clear that by using the terms "ultimate" or "irreducible" traits, he did not mean that these terms referred to origins or causes but pertained to the conditions under which existences assume particular forms and then undergo change. These terms were used by Dewey to express the transformational properties of nature and were not intended to specify some more basic properties from which all others were derived. Interaction was one of these limiting conditions, according to Dewey, because nothing exists in isolation. Traits like "interaction" and "change" possess a constancy without determinacy. For contemporary analyses which rectify this erroneous interpretation, see Raymond Boisvert, *Dewey's Metaphysics* (New York: Fordham University Press, 1988), and Craig Cunningham, "Dewey's Metaphysics of the Self," in *The New Scholarship on John Dewey,* ed. Jim Garrison (Dordrecht, Holland: Kluwer, 1995), pp. 175–192.

68. See McGraw, *Growth: A Study of Johnny and Jimmy,* pp. 22–23.

69. Ibid., p. 16.

70. Ibid.

71. Myrtle B. McGraw, "Swimming Behavior of the Human Infant," *Journal of Pediatrics* 15 (1939): 485–490.

72. See McGraw, *Growth: A Study of Johnny and Jimmy,* pp. 160–164.

73. Myrtle B. McGraw, *The Neuromuscular Maturation of the Human Infant* (New York: Columbia University Press, 1943), p. 123.

74. Ibid., pp. 267–268, 294.

75. Ibid., p. 271.

76. Ibid., p. 277. McGraw associates Livingston Welch and Louis Long (both psychologists) also demonstrated how children rely on suggestive ideas in demarcating the boundaries of generic concepts involving geometric objects. Significantly, the experimental subjects were better able, as Dewey supposed, to accurately identify the shapes at the opposing ends of a scale (i.e., comprehending the limits of the universe of objects) than to properly differentiate shapes toward the middle. Discriminating accurately between these shapes occurred only after the children had sufficient time rearranging the sequence of objects in an order that best highlighted the differences.

These studies by McGraw and her associates provided the ground that Dewey sought for his argument in *Logic.* There he argued that reasoning with concepts is subject to the same alternating forces of expansion and contraction as are the processes of neuromuscular growth and development in that disputes about meaning stem from uncertainty over the boundaries or applicability of terms and hypotheses. Accordingly, Dewey says that the extensiveness or intensiveness (i.e., connotation and denotation) of a term depends ultimately on whether objects designated by terms share the same qualitative attributes.

77. Arnold Gesell, "Reciprocal Interweaving in Neuromotor Development," *The Journal of Comparative Neurology* 10 (1939): 161–180.

78. Ibid., p. 179.

79. McGraw, *Growth: A Study of Johnny and Jimmy,* pp. 306–308.

80. Dewey, *Logic,* pp. 197–199.

81. Ibid., pp. 191–192.

82. Ibid., p. 74. Dewey's scientifically grounded conceptualization of consciousness bears a striking similarity to that advanced by Hegel, as he applied it to *being-for-self*, when he stated in *Phenomenology of Spirit*, "If the genus, as a quiescent unitary being, had within it the differentiated parts, and if, too, its simple negativity as such were at the same time a movement which ran through parts which were equally simple and immediately universal in themselves, parts which here were actual as such moments, then the organic genus would be *consciousness*" (p. 176; italics added).

83. Ibid., pp. 193–194.

84. Ibid., pp. 194–195.

85. Dewey urged McGraw in a letter on June 6, 1934, to devise methods to determine how infants use gestures to communicate their feelings and reason. He wrote, "I have a hunch that the beginning of language is your best problem now. It doesn't seem like the work that has been done gets very far. Your general principles of development ought to be well exemplified in control both of sounds and ideas and it is the best field it seems to me for studying relations of sensory and motor control." Correspondence with Myrtle McGraw, 1934–1942, John Dewey Papers.

86. John Dewey, "Theory of Logic," p. 3. John Dewey Papers.

87. See John Dewey, *Logic*, pp. 132–145.

88. Myrtle B. McGraw, "Growing Up With and Without Psychology," 64. Unpublished manuscript in Myrtle B. McGraw Papers, Millbank Memorial Library, Teachers College, Columbia University.

89. Ibid.

90. John Dewey, *Logic*, p. 313.

91. Ibid.

10. LOCOMOTION AS A METAPHOR FOR MIND

1. McGraw to Frank, December 31, 1934. McGraw, Dewey, and Frank met at the Orange Park Anthropoid Research Station (a predecessor of the Yerkes Primate Center) in Florida, where they observed some demonstrations of chimpanzee intelligence. Rockefeller Archive Center General Education Board, Record Group 1, Series 1.3, Box 370, Folder 3558. Also see Myrtle McGraw, interview by Milton Senn, Hastings-on-Hudson, New York, May 9, 1972, pp. 8–9.

2. See Rappleye to Frank, December 2, 1935. General Education Board.

3. See *Human Nature and Conduct*, p. 51, where Dewey asserts, "All life operates through a mechanism, and the higher the form of life the more complex, sure and flexible the mechanism. This fact alone should save us from opposing life and mechanism, thereby reducing the latter to unintelligent automatism and the former to aimless splurge."

4. Ibid., p. 253. See also H. S. Harris, *Hegel's Development* (Oxford: Clarendon Press, 1983), pp. 238–255, 419–427, for the significance of free-falling bodies in Hegel's philosophy of spirit and understanding.

5. Herrick, *The Neurological Foundations*, pp. 234–235. Dewey's exchange of ideas with Herrick about biological mechanisms governing human development was stimulated by a manuscript they read by Owens (first name unknown) titled "The Principles and Mechanisms of Evolution." Dewey thought Owens's work particularly admirable

because it involved the collaboration between a philosopher and biologist (see Dewey to Herrick, November, 29, 1941. C. J. Herrick Papers, Neurology Collection).

6. E. Rignano, *The Psychology of Reasoning*, p. 4.

7. Ibid., p. 11.

8. Evelyn Dewey, *Behavior Development in Infants*, p. 300.

9. Myrtle B. McGraw, "Neuromotor Maturation of Anti-Gravity Functions as Reflected in the Development of a Sitting Posture," *Journal of Genetic Psychology* 59 (1941): 160, 172.

10. See Jones, *Body Awareness in Action: A Study of the Alexander Technique.*

11. McGraw, interview by Kenneth Duckett, p. 17.

12. Myrtle B. McGraw, "From Reflex to Muscular Control in the Assumption of Erect Posture and Ambulation in the Human Infant," *Child Study* 3 (1932): 292.

13. Frank, "Structure, Function and Growth," pp. 223–224.

14. See McGraw to Frank, June 11, 1935. For Smith's historical contribution to modern techniques of electroencephalography, see M. A. Bell and N. A. Fox, "Brain Development over the First Year of Life: Relations between Electroencephalographic Frequency and Coherence and Cognitive and Affective Behavior," in *Human Behavior and the Developing Brain*, ed. G. Dawson and Kurt W. Fischer (New York: Guilford, 1994), p. 318.

15. J. Roy Smith, "The Electroencephalogram during Normal Infancy and Childhood I: Rhythmic Activities Present in the Neonate and Their Subsequent Development," *Journal of Genetic Psychology* 53 (1938): 431–453.

16. J. Roy Smith, "The Electroencephalogram during Normal Infancy and Childhood II: The Nature of Growth of Alpha Waves," *Journal of Genetic Psychology* 53 (1938): 455–469.

17. J. Roy Smith, "The Frequency Growth of the Human Alpha Rhythms during Normal Infancy and Childhood," *Journal of Psychology* 7 (1941): 177–198.

18. J. Roy Smith, "The Occipital and Pre-Central Alpha Rhythms during the First Two Years," *Journal of Psychology* 7 (1939): 223–227.

19. A. C. Weinbach, "Some Physiological Phenomena Fitted to Growth Equations III: Rate of Growth of Brain Potentials (Alpha Frequency) Compared with Rate of Growth of the Brain," *Growth* 2 (1938): 247–251.

20. A. C. Weinbach, "Some Physiological Phenomena Fitted to Growth Equations I: Moro Reflex," *Growth* 1 (1937): 549–555.

21. John Dewey, *Logic*, p. 12.

22. Ibid., p. 220.

23. Ibid., p. 35.

24. Ibid., pp. 32–33.

25. Ibid., pp. 452–453.

26. Ibid., p. 40. Dewey is explicit about this when he says, "Integration is more fundamental than is the distinction designated by interaction of organism and environment. The latter is indicative of a partial disintegration of a prior integration, but one which is of such a dynamic nature that it moves (as long as life continues) toward redintegration" (p. 40).

27. Ibid., pp. 211–213.

28. Katherine Poulos, "Textual Commentary," in *LW* 12: 540. Dewey also told Sidney Hook in early 1938 that he would further delay revisions on mathematics chapters, thus

giving him more time to reflect on the results of McGraw's quantitative studies. The NCDS annual progress report documenting preliminary findings by McGraw's associates Weinbach, Smith, and Weech was available in June 1938 (see *Report of the Normal Child Development Study*, July 1937–June 1938, General Education Board, Record Group I, Series 1.3, Box 370, Folder 3859). Dewey sent his manuscript to the publisher in early June 1938, after making extensive revisions. In addition, Dewey made additional extensive changes in the galleys in July before sending them back to the publisher in September. See Poulos, "Textual Commentary," p. 543.

29. Lawrence Frank, "Structure, Function and Growth," p. 213

30. Ibid., pp. 215–230.

31. Ibid., p. 220. See also Lawrence Frank, "The Management of Tensions," pp. 140–142.

32. John Dewey to McGraw, October 1935, p. 2 (n.d.), Correspondence with Myrtle McGraw, 1934–1942, John Dewey Collection.

33. Ibid. Dewey stresses that "[l]ocomotion is a function, not a process, the processes are all the changes, muscular, nervous, skeletal, etc., that come together to *do* the walking. Frank argued that the value assigned to any specific structural and functional properties of an organism was relative to the field in which they were situated and that therefore the energetics of each field possessed incommensurate magnitudes" (see Frank to Brody, August 4, 1938, Lawrence K. Frank Papers, MS C, 280b, Box 1, General Correspondence, History of Medicine Division, National Library of Medicine, Bethesda, Maryland).

In contrast, Dewey believed that energy was a form of motion that could be assigned a common value (based on his assumption of the interconvertibility of energy) despite differences in the attributes of energy characteristic of any single organic field. Thus differences in the velocity of the growth of energy complexes were evened out by rhythms issuing from a central neural mechanism. In this regard see Norman C. Wetzel, "On the Motion of Growth, XVII: Theoretical Foundations," *Growth* 1 (1937): 6–59, for a complete elaboration of the principles underpinning Dewey's position.

34. M. B. McGraw and A. C. Weinbach, "Quantitative Measures in Studying Development of Behavior Patterns of Erect Locomotion," *Bulletin of the Neurological Institute of New York* 4 (1936): 553.

35. Several memoranda document differences between McGraw and Frank as to the roles of additional researchers recruited to the NCDS, including a pediatrician, a biochemist, and a neurophysiologist. See for example Frank, memorandum of interview with McGraw and Tilney, May 8, 1935; McGraw to Frank, June 11, 1935; McGraw to Frank, June 12, 1935; and Frank, memorandum of interview with McGraw, August 18, 1935. General Education Board, Record Group I, Series 1.3, Box 370, Folder 3859.

The research that McGraw's associates eventually completed differed significantly from what McGraw proposed to the Advisory Council on May 17, 1935. For example, although designated to assist McGraw in the study of bladder control and enuresis, biochemist A. C. Weinbach derived an acceleration constant with which to calculate the growth curve over the life span. Similarly, although neurophysiologist Ray Smith was assigned to determine how brain waves affect the development of vision and contribute to nystigmus, he actually completed a series of studies differentiating the source and effects of brain waves on sensorimotor development. These diversions of effort did not cost McGraw her job. Rockefeller officials offered to extend her grant if she focused on growth dysfunctions contributing to brain abnormalities. McGraw refused to take this approach because she did not feel that enough was understood yet about early developmental processes of normal children.

36. Myrtle B. McGraw, "Neural Maturation as Exemplified in the Reaching-Prehensile Behavior of the Human Infant," *Journal of Psychology* 11 (1941): 136, and "Neuromotor Maturation of Anti-Gravity Functions as Reflected in the Development of a Sitting Posture," *Journal of Genetic Psychology* 59 (1941): 172.

37. J. LeRoy Conel, *The Postnatal Development of the Human Cerebral Cortex, Volume 1: Cortex of the Newborn* (Cambridge, Mass.: Harvard University Press, 1939), pp. 103–104.

38. Myrtle B. McGraw, "Neural Maturation as Exemplified in the Reaching-Prehensile Behavior of the Human Infant," p. 139, and Myrtle B. McGraw, *The Neuromuscular Maturation of the Human Infant* (New York: Columbia University Press, 1943), pp. 96–97, 101.

39. Myrtle B. McGraw, "Neural Maturation as Exemplified in the Reaching-Prehensile Behavior of the Human Infant," p. 172. Also see Myrtle B. McGraw, "The Maturation of Behavior," in *The Manual of Child Psychology*, ed. Leonard Carmichael (New York: Wiley, 1946), pp. 357–365.

40. William R. Shankle, Romney A. Kimball, Benjamin H. Landing, and Junko Hara, "Developmental Patterns in the Cytoarchitecture of the Human Cerebral Cortex from Birth to 6 Years Examined by Correspondence Analysis," *Proceedings of the National Academy of Sciences* 95 (1998): 4023–4028.

41. J. LeRoy Conel, *The Postnatal Development of the Human Cerebral Cortex, Volume 3: Cortex of the Three Month Infant* (Cambridge, Mass.: Harvard University Press, 1947), p. 147.

42. J. LeRoy Conel, *The Postnatal Development of the Human Cerebral Cortex, Volume 3: Cortex of the Six Month Infant* (Cambridge, Mass.: Harvard University Press, 1951), pp. 175–176.

43. Myrtle B. McGraw, "Development of Neuromuscular Mechanisms as Reflected in the Crawling and Creeping Behavior of the Human Infant," *The Journal of Genetic Psychology* 58 (1941): 83–111.

44. J. LeRoy Conel, *The Postnatal Development of the Human Cerebral Cortex, Volume 5: Cortex of the Fifteen Month Infant* (Cambridge, Mass.: Harvard University Press, 1955).

45. Ibid., 135.

46. McGraw, "The Development of Neuromuscular Maturation as Reflected in Crawling and Creeping," p. 92.

47. Esther Thelen, "The Role of Motor Development in Developmental Psychology: A View of the Past and an Agenda for the Future," in *Contemporary Topics in Developmental Psychology*, ed. Nancy Eisenberg (New York: Wiley, 1987), p. 6.

48. Esther Thelen, "Reply to Dalton," *American Psychologist* 51 (1996): 552–553.

49. Thomas C. Dalton, "Was McGraw a Maturationist?" *American Psychologist* 51 (1996): 551–552.

50. McGraw, *The Neuromuscular Maturation of the Human Infant*, p. 4.

51. See Gilbert Gottlieb, "Myrtle McGraw's Unrecognized Conceptual Contributions to Developmental Psychology," *Developmental Review* 18 (1998): 437–448, and

Gilbert Gottlieb, *Synthesizing Nature and Nurture: The Prenatal Roots of Instinctive Behavior* (Hillsdale, N.J.: Erlbaum, 1997).

52. A. C. Weinbach, "The Human Growth Curve I: Prenatal," *Growth* 5 (1941): 220.

53. Norman C. Wetzel, "On the Motion of Growth XVII: Theoretical Foundations," *Growth* 1 (1937): 18; 25.

54. John Dewey to McGraw, May 4, 1936. John Dewey Papers.

55. Wetzel, "The Motion of Growth," pp. 15–16.

56. See A. C. Weinbach, "The Human Growth Curve I: Prenatal," pp. 232–233; A. C. Weinbach, "The Human Growth Curve II: Birth to Puberty," pp. 254–255.

57. See C. B. Davenport, "Interpretation of Certain Infantile Growth Curves," *Growth* 1 (1937): 279–283, and C. B. Davenport, "Bodily Growth of Babies during the First Postnatal Year," Proceedings of the Carnegie Institution, no. 169: *Contributions to Embryology,* pp. 273–305.

58. H. R. Benjamin and A. A. Weech, "Basal Heat Production in Relation to Growth," *American Journal of Diseases of Children* 65 (1943): 34.

59. For studies that support Wetzel's theories, see Samuel Brody, "Relativity of Physiological Time and Physiological Weight," *Growth* 1 (1937): 60–67; P. Kohn, "Increase in Weight and Growth of Children in the First Year of Life," *Growth* 12 (1948): 149–155; and D. E. Schneider, "The Growth Concept of Nervous Integration, V: The Theoretic Formulations and the Basic Equations of Heat Production, Body Mass, Body Length, Body Area, Brain Weight, Cord Weight and Electroencephalographic Frequency—Basis for an Electroencephalographic Method of Determining Basal Metabolism," *Growth* 8 (1944): 43–51. For a historical survey, see S. L. Zeeger and S. D. Harlow, "Mathematical Models from Laws of Growth to Tools for Biologic Analysis: Fifty Years of Growth," *Growth* 51 (1987): 13–21.

60. See Michael J. Petry, ed., *Hegel's Philosophy of Nature,* Vol. 1 (London: Allen and Unwin, 1970), pp. 242–248. For an analysis of the significance of free-falling bodies in Hegel's philosophy of spirit, see Harris, *Hegel's Development,* pp. 238–255, 419–427.

61. Hegel, *Science of Logic,* pp. 314–325.

62. John Dewey, *Experience and Nature,* pp. 206–207.

63. A. C. Weinbach, "Contour Maps, Center of Gravity, Moment of Inertia and Surface of the Human Body," *Human Biology* 10 (1938): 356–371.

64. M. McGraw and K. Breeze, "Quantitative Studies in the Development of Erect Locomotion," *Child Development* 12 (1941): 295.

65. Although unable to develop a behavior constant, McGraw and Breeze overcame technical difficulties by adapting projectile theory to measure key variables. Maxwell contended that mass constitutes a form of energy regardless of whether it is in motion or at rest. He correctly deduced that the behavior and trajectory of objects could be predicted by determining the magnitude of the difference between potential energy governing internal movements (i.e., center of gravity, vibration, and spin) and external movements (i.e., momentum, velocity, and so forth). They assumed that the stages of erect locomotion were analogous to trajectory taken by a projectile through a viscous medium. The speed of the projectile is slowed as it encounters resistance and its energy is dissipated, causing it to assume a parabolic trajectory. Similarly, McGraw found that at the outset, a baby will spend a disproportionate amount of time and energy in moving with characteristic staccato-like steps, contributing to sudden bursts of forward

movement. Over time, however, as the center of gravity shifts with the lengthening of the legs and movement in the lower body is brought under increased cortical control, a greater amount of time is consumed on the ground stroke, reducing energy input and stabilizing the gait.

66. A. C. Weinbach, "Some Physiological Phenomena Fitted to Growth Equations IV: Time and Power Relations for a Human Infant Climbing Inclines of Various Slopes," *Growth* 4 (1938): 123–134.

67. V. T. Dammann, "Developmental Changes in Attitudes as One Factor Determining Energy Output in a Motor Performance," *Child Development* 12 (1941): 241–246.

68. See also A. C. Weinbach, "Some Physiological Phenomena Fitted to Growth Equations I: Moro Reflex," *Human Biology* 9 (1937): 549–555; "Some Physiological Phenomena Fitted to Growth Equations II: Brain Potentials," *Human Biology* 10 (1938): 145–150; and "Some Physiological Phenomena Fitted to Growth Equations III: Rate of Growth of Brain Potentials (Alpha Frequency) Compared with Rate of Growth of the Brain," *Growth* 2 (1938): 247–251. See also A. C. Weinbach, "The Human Growth Curve, I: Prenatal," *Growth* 5 (1941): 217–233, and "The Human Growth Curve, II: Birth to Puberty," *Growth* 5 (1941): 233–255. Davenport's longitudinal skeletal studies of a sample of babies from the NCDS differed from Weinbach, suggesting that skeletal growth could not be subsumed under a general formula (see C. B. Davenport, "Interpretation of Certain Infantile Growth Curves," *Growth* 1 [1937]: 279–283).

69. Ernest Nagel, "Dewey's Theory of Natural Science," in Ernest Nagel, *Sovereign Reason and Other Studies in the Philosophy of Science* (New York: Free Press, 1954), pp. 110–117.

70. John Dewey, "From Absolutism to Experimentalism," p. 153.

71. Myrtle B. McGraw, "Professional and Personal Blunders in Child Development Research," *Psychological Record* 35 (1985): 170.

72. McGraw also complained that a prejudice against subjective judgments favored established methods that "precluded the evolvement of new techniques which could adequately handle the type of data obtained only through the mental integration of the trained observer." See McGraw, "Appraising Test Responses of Infants and Young Children," *The Journal of Psychology* 14 (1942): 99.

73. It was widely reported in the press that Johnny's special stimulation did not result in any significant differences in ultimate performance, as Jimmy eventually was able to complete the same tasks as Johnny. This belief overshadowed the significant qualitative differences in Johnny's capacity for problem solving (see Dennis, "Johnny's a Gentleman, Jimmy's a Mug," pp. 362–363).

74. Dewey's defense of *Logic* in his "Experience, Knowledge and Value: A Rejoinder," in *LW* 14: 3–90, was consumed largely by responding to challenges posed about the validity of the psychological premises underpinning his theory of knowledge. Dewey's frequent but perfunctory appeal to the "facts" of sensorimotor processes and oblique reference to the term "integration" seemed insufficient gestures to support the psychological validity of theory of inquiry. These rhetorical skirmishes left little opportunity for Dewey to demonstrate the transformational nature of inquiry, or to illustrate in more detail the principles with which he proposed to replace the traditional canons of formal logic.

75. See Sulloway, "The Myth of the Hero in the Psychoanalytic Movement," in Sulloway, *Freud, Biologist of the Mind*, pp. 445–495.

76. Richard Rorty, "Science as Solidarity," in Richard Rorty, *Objectivity, Relativism and Truth: Philosophical Papers, Volume I*, pp. 35–45 (Cambridge: Cambridge University Press, 1991).

11. CULTURAL PRAGMATISM AND THE DISAPPEARANCE OF DEWEY'S NATURALISM

1. Rorty, "Dewey between Hegel and Darwin," p. 13.

2. For an autobiographical account of his relationships with Dewey, Nagel, and their colleagues, see Morton G. White, *A Philosopher's Story* (University Park: Pennsylvania State University Press, 1999), pp. 28–43, 74–83.

3. John Dewey to Bentley, July 9, 1944. Arthur Bentley Papers Special Collections, Lilly Library, Indiana University, Bloomington, Indiana.

4. Ibid.

5. Morton G. White, *The Origins of Dewey's Instrumentalism* (New York: Columbia University Press, 1943), pp. 38–45.

6. Ibid., p. 83.

7. John Dewey to Arthur Bentley, November 6, 1944. Arthur Bentley Papers.

8. White, *A Philosopher's Story*, p. 33.

9. Ibid., p. 32.

10. Ibid., p. 33.

11. Ibid., p. 80. See also Morton White, *Social Thought in America: The Revolt against Formalism* (New York: Viking, 1949).

12. White, *The Origins of Dewey's Instrumentalism*, pp. 130–131.

13. John Dewey, "Experience, Knowledge and Value: A Rejoinder," p. 14.

14. See David Depew, "Introduction," pp. 109–121, and Daniel Wilson, "Fertile Ground: Pragmatism, Science and Logical Positivism," pp. 123–145, among other essays documenting the impact of logical positivism on Dewey's disciples in *Pragmatism: From Progressivism to Postmodernism*, ed. Robert Hollinger and David Depew (Westport, Conn.: Praeger, 1997).

15. John Dewey to Arthur Bentley, October 6, 1942. Arthur Bentley Papers.

16. Joseph Ratner, *Intelligence in the Modern World* (New York: Modern Library, 1939), p. 37.

17. Ibid., p. 73.

18. For commentaries which specifically divorce Mach's views from those held by the leaders of logical positivism, see Philipp Frank, "Ernst Mach and the Unity of Science," pp. 235–244, and Richard Von Mises, "Mach and the Empiricist Conception of Science," pp. 245–270, in *Ernst Mach: Physicist and Philosopher*, ed. Robert Cohen and Ray Seeger (Dordrecht, Holland: Reidel Publishing Co., 1970).

19. Quoted in Wilson, "Fertile Ground: Pragmatism, Science and Logical Positivism," in *Pragmatism*, ed. Hollinger and Depew, p. 136.

20. John Dewey to Arthur Bentley, February 5, 1939. Arthur Bentley Papers.

21. Ernest Nagel, interview by Kenneth Duckett, October 10, 1966, p. 5. John Dewey Papers.

22. John Dewey to Bentley, March 5, 1939. Arthur Bentley Papers.

23. Ernest Nagel, "Can Logic Be Divorced from Ontology," in *LW* 5: 455.

24. Ibid.

25. John Dewey, "The Applicability of Logic to Existence," in *LW* 5: 206–207.

26. Sidney Hook, *Quest for Being* (New York: St. Martin's Press, 1934), p. 164.

27. See John Randall Jr., "John Dewey's Interpretation of the History of Philosophy," in *The Philosophy of John Dewey* 3rd ed., ed. Paul Schlipp (La Salle, Ill.: Open Court, 1989), pp. 75–102.

28. Hook, *Quest for Being*, p. 168.

29. Ibid.

30. Ibid.

31. Herbert Schneider, "The Unnatural," in *Naturalism and the Human Spirit*, ed. Yervant Krikorian (New York: Columbia University Press, 1944), p. 124.

32. Ibid.

33. Ibid., p. 125.

34. Richard Rorty, "Dewey's Metaphysics," in Richard Rorty, *The Consequences of Pragmatism* (Minneapolis: University of Minnesota Press, 1982), p. 75.

35. Ibid., p. 80.

36. Ibid., p. 81.

37. For a useful intellectual biography of Arthur Bentley, see Sidney Ratner, "Introduction," in *John Dewey and Arthur F. Bentley: A Philosophical Correspondence, 1932–1951*, ed. Sidney Ratner and Jules Altman (New Brunswick, N.J.: Rutgers University Press, 1964).

38. Arthur Bentley, "Knowledge and Society," in *Inquiry into Inquiries*, ed. Sidney Ratner (Boston: Beacon Press, 1954), p. 25.

39. Bentley to John Dewey, January 24, 1939. Arthur Bentley Papers.

40. Arthur Bentley, "Situational versus Psychological Theories of Behavior," in *Inquiry into Inquiries*, ed. Ratner, p. 145.

41. Thelma Lavine, "America and the Contestations of Modernity: Bentley, Dewey and Rorty," in *Rorty and Pragmatism*, ed. Saatkamp, pp. 40–41.

42. Arthur Bentley, "Logic and Logical Behavior," in *Inquiry into Inquiries* ed. Ratner, pp. 316–317.

43. John Dewey to Bentley, June 25, 1943. Arthur Bentley Papers.

44. Bentley to John Dewey, June 30, 1943. Arthur Bentley Papers.

45. John Dewey to Bentley, May 12, 1944. Arthur Bentley Papers.

46. John Dewey to Bentley, May 21, 1944.

47. Lawrence K. Frank, "Genetic Psychology and its Prospects," in *Symposium on Genetic Psychology: Sixth Anniversary of Clark University* (Worcester, Mass.: Clark University Press, 1950), p. 516.

48. In his provocative book, Tom Burke contends that Russell's critique of Dewey's logic fell wide of the mark. Russell largely ignored the fact that Dewey's book *Logic: The Theory of Inquiry* was not primarily a study of language or of propositional logic, but was an analysis of the process of scientific inquiry. Thus Russell and Dewey were talking past one another rather than truly engaging and critiquing each other's premises. Tom Burke, *Dewey's New Logic: A Reply to Russell* (Chicago: University of Chicago Press, 1994).

49. Rorty, "Dewey's Metaphysics," in Rorty, *Consequences of Pragmatism*, p. 81.

50. Ibid., p. 84.

51. Ibid., p. 76.

52. Rorty, "Freud and Moral Reflection," in *Pragmatism's Freud*, ed. Smith and Kerrigan, p. 11.

53. Ibid., p. 18.

54. Richard Rorty, *Contingency, Irony and Solidarity* (Cambridge: Cambridge University Press, 1989), p. 40.
55. Rorty, "Freud and Moral Reflection," in *Pragmatism's Freud*, ed. Smith and Kerrigan, p. 3.
56. Rorty, *Contingency, Irony and Solidarity*, p. 31.
57. Ibid, p. 42.
58. Richard Rorty, "Daniel Dennett on Intrinsicality," in Richard Rorty, *Truth and Progress*, Philosophical Papers, vol. 3 (Cambridge: Cambridge University Press, 1998), p. 109.
59. Ibid.
60. Rorty, "Pragmatism Without Method," in Richard Rorty, *Objectivism, Relativism and Truth*, p. 65.
61. Ibid.
62. Ratner, *Intelligence in the Modern World*, p. 57.
63. Sidney Hook, *Quest for Certainty*, pp. 174–175.
64. Ibid., 178.
65. Sidney Hook, "Naturalism and Democracy," in Kirkorian, *Naturalism and the Human Spirit*, p. 64.
66. Richard Rorty, "Comments on Sleeper and Edel," *Transactions of the Charles Peirce Society* 21 (1985): 41.
67. Ibid.
68. Ibid., p. 42.
69. For a particularly insightful analysis of how social constructions of the processes of scientific inquiry form the background for community judgments regarding the significance and merit of new discoveries, see Thomas Nickles, "Justification and Experiment," in *The Uses of Experiment: Studies in the Natural Sciences*, ed. David Gooding, Trevor Pinch, and Simon Schaffer (New York: Cambridge University Press, 1988), pp. 299–333.
70. See Richard Bernstein, ed., *John Dewey* (New York: Washington Square Press, 1966).
71. Richard Bernstein, *Beyond Objectivism and Relativism: Science, Hermeneutics and Praxis* (Philadelphia: University of Pennsylvania Press, 1983).
72. Richard Rorty, "Habermas, Derrida and Philosophy," in Rorty, *Truth and Progress*, p. 318.
73. Richard Rorty, *Achieving Our Country: Leftist Thought in Twentieth Century America* (Cambridge, Mass.: Harvard University Press, 1998).
74. Ibid., p. 63.
75. Ibid., p. 61.
76. Ibid., p. 95.
77. Westbrook, *John Dewey and American Democracy*, p. 541.
78. Alan Ryan, *John Dewey and the High Tide of American Liberalism*, p. 366.
79. Ibid., p. 191.
80. See Rorty, *Contingency, Irony and Solidarity*, pp. 170–171.

CONCLUSION

1. See especially Larry Hickman's recent books *John Dewey's Pragmatic Technology* (Bloomington: Indiana University Press, 1990) and *Philosophical Tools for Technological*

Culture: Putting Pragmatism to Work (Bloomington: Indiana University Press, 2001). Hickman is one of the few philosophers I am aware of who have molded Dewey's ideas into tools with which to systematically address wide-ranging public consequences of American policies involving technology, education, and the arts.

2. See Rorty, "Dewey's Metaphysics," p. 85.

3. Burke, *Dewey's New Logic: A Reply to Russell.*

4. Ibid., p. 247.

5. Ibid.

6. For an excellent, scientifically documented argument that illustrates why neural network modeling supplements but is unlikely to replace live experimentation, see J. L. Elman, E. A. Bates, M. Johnson, A. Karmiloff-Smith, D. Parisi, and K. Plunkett, *Redefining Innateness: A Connectionist Perspective on Development* (Cambridge, Mass.: MIT Press, 1998).

7. John R. Shook, *Dewey's Empirical Theory of Knowledge and Reality* (Nashville, Tenn.: Vanderbilt University Press, 2000).

8. Ibid., p. 148.

9. Ibid.

10. Ralph Sleeper, *The Necessity of Pragmatism* (New Haven, Conn.: Yale University Press, 1986), shares Shook's view that Dewey used his critique of epistemological realism as his point of departure in the reconstruction of logic. Sleeper also perceptively argues that Dewey's naturalism comprised not only an "empirical theory of knowledge, but also a theory of the causal (i.e., biological) origins of the empirical logic of experience" (p. 144). In essence, Dewey's most original contribution in *Logic*, according to Sleeper, "was the reconstruction of the traditional realist doctrine of natural kinds" (ibid.). While I concur that Dewey strongly criticized the realist doctrine, my research suggests that Dewey saw the need first to reconstruct the biological and recapitulationist conception of natural kinds propounded by Haeckel and other embryologists. This would then provide surer footing in the subsequent attempt to reformulate a logic for inquiry.

11. Ibid., p. 161.

12. Dewey, *Logic,* p. 197.

13. Larry Hickman, "Dewey's Theory of Inquiry," in *Reading Dewey: Interpretations for a Postmodern Generation,* ed. L. Hickman (Bloomington: Indiana University Press, 1998), p. 167.

14. Ibid.

15. Ibid., p. 179.

16. See Charles Taylor's *Hegel* (Cambridge: Cambridge University Press, 1975) for an illuminating study of Hegel's monumental works. For an unrivaled analysis of the problems of mind and self in modernity, see Charles Taylor, *Sources of the Self: The Making of the Modern Identity* (Cambridge, Mass.: Harvard University Press, 1989).

17. Charles Taylor's "How Is Mechanism Conceivable," in Charles Taylor, *Human Agency and Language,* pp. 164–186, Philosophical Papers, Vol. 1 (Cambridge: Cambridge University Press, 1985).

18. Charles Taylor, "Reply and Rearticulation," in *Philosophy in an Age of Pluralism: The Philosophy of Charles Taylor in Question,* ed. James Tully (Cambridge: Cambridge University Press, 1994), p. 235.

19. John Dewey, *Logic: The Theory of Inquiry,* p. 483.

20. Ibid., p. 481.

21. There is a large and growing body of scientific evidence that so-called higher cortical functions do not exercise a monopoly over executive functions associated with reasoning, but are mediated by a complex matrix of subcortical processes that influence actions, emotions, perceptions, intentions, and goals. When the interactions between these functions are disrupted completely, as is the case with autism, the capacity to form a conception of self and of other minds is severely impaired. For a good summary of recent scientific studies, see N. Krasnegor, G. Lyon, and P. Goldman-Rakic, eds., *Development of the Prefrontal Cortex: Evolution, Neurobiology and Behavior* (Baltimore: Paul H. Brookes, 1997).

22. Antonio Damasio, *The Feeling of What Happens: Body and Emotion in the Making of Consciousness* (New York: Harcourt Brace, 1999), pp. 264–276. In Damasio's previous book, *Descartes Error: Emotion, Reason and the Human Brain* (New York: Avon Books, 1994), Damasio contended that humans possess a special body sense which enables them to draw on somatic signals in anticipating and responding to contingencies, as if they had already occurred. McGraw proposed a similar capacity for preparatory or anticipatory response, which she believed was located between the parietal and cingulate cortices where Damasio contends that core consciousness is sustained.

23. David Chalmers, "Facing Up to the Problem of Consciousness," *Journal of Consciousness Studies* 2 (1995): 200–219.

24. Dewey and his collaborator Myrtle McGraw were pioneers in advancing an emergent conception of consciousness based on evidence from developmental science. See Thomas C. Dalton, "The Ontogeny of Consciousness: John Dewey and Myrtle McGraw's Contribution to a Science of Mind," *Journal of Consciousness Studies* 6 (1999): 3–26.

25. Roger Penrose, *Shadows of the Mind: A Search for the Missing Science of Consciousness* (New York: Oxford University Press, 1994). For a review of the implications of Penrose's thesis for studies of the ontogeny of consciousness, see Thomas C. Dalton, "The Revival of Consciousness," review of Roger Penrose, *Shadows of the Mind*, *Contemporary Psychology* 41 (1996): 546–547.

26. Charles Stenberg and Joseph Campos, "The Development of Anger Expressions in Infancy," in *Psychological and Biological Approaches to Emotion*, ed. N. L. Stein, B. Leventhal, and T. Trabasso (Hillsdale, N.J.: Erlbaum, 1990), pp. 247–282.

27. Barry Dainton, *Stream of Consciousness: Unity and the Continuity of Conscious Experience* (New York: Routledge, 2000), pp. 215–224.

28. Gerald Edelman and Giulio Tononi, *The Universe of Consciousness: From Mind to Imagination* (New York: Basic Books, 2000), pp. 113–124.

29. Dan Leopold and Nico Logothetis, "Multistable Phenomena: Changing Views on Perception," *Trends in Cognitive Sciences* 3 (1999): 254–263.

30. For an extraordinarily imaginative use of counterfactual thought experiments to challenge the notion that mind involves central, internal-state processes and that behavior involves essentially external ones, see S. L. Hurley, *Consciousness in Action* (Cambridge, Mass.: Harvard University Press, 1998), especially Chapter 8, "Perception, Dynamic Feedback and Externalism," pp. 285–337.

31. Ibid., p. 420.

32. Ibid., p. 426.

33. See Vittorio Gallese and Alvin Goldman, "Mirror Neurons and the Simulation Theory of Mind Reading," *Trends in Cognitive Sciences* 2 (1998): 493–501.

34. Philip R. Zelazo, Phillippe Robaey, and Marthe Bonin, "The Development of

Movement Related Brain Potentials with Exercise of the Neuromotor Stepping Pattern in 14 Week-Old Infants," poster presented at the Society for Research in Child Development, Albuquerque, New Mexico, April 15–18, 1999.

35. Ibid., p. 500. It should be pointed out that Gallese and Goldman find no evidence that the firing of mirror neurons facilitates learning in monkeys.

36. Chris Frith and Uta Frith, "Interacting Minds: A Biological Basis," *Science* 286 (1999): 1694.

37. For an analysis of the neurobiological and neurobehavioral events that contribute to the emergence of consciousness, emotion, intentionality, and moral conduct, see Thomas C. Dalton, "The Developmental Roots of Consciousness and Emotional Experience," *Consciousness and Emotion* 1 (2000): 55–166.

38. Toward this end, see Thomas C. Dalton and Victor W. Bergenn, *Early Experience and the Brain: A Historical and Interdisciplinary Synthesis* (Mahwah, N.J.: Erlbaum, forthcoming).

BIBLIOGRAPHY

ARCHIVE REPOSITORIES

SPECIAL COLLECTIONS, MORRIS LIBRARY, SOUTHERN ILLINOIS UNIVERSITY,
CARBONDALE, ILLINOIS

The John Dewey Papers, 1858–1970. The Joseph Ratner Papers and Collection of John Dewey,
1862–1978. General Correspondence and Unpublished Manuscripts.

SPECIAL COLLECTIONS, MILLBANK MEMORIAL LIBRARY, TEACHERS COLLEGE,
COLUMBIA UNIVERSITY, NEW YORK, NEW YORK

Administrative Records of the Bureau of Educational Experiments, 1916–1925; Bank
Street Archives, 1920–1923; Barbara Biber Papers, 1917–1937; Myrtle B. McGraw Papers, 1930–1988.

RARE BOOKS AND MANUSCRIPTS, BUTLER LIBRARY, COLUMBIA UNIVERSITY,
NEW YORK CITY

The Carnegie Corporation of New York, Archives, 1911–1977. The Lucy Sprague
Mitchell Papers, 1916–1952. Lucy Sprague Mitchell Oral History, 1962. Wesley C.
Mitchell Diaries, 1905–1948. John Dewey's correspondence with Corinne Chisholm
Frost, 1930–1950. John Dewey's Correspondence with Abraham Flexner, 1932. Evelyn
Dewey Correspondence with Randolph Bourne, 1913–1914. Randolph Bourne correspondence with Max Eastman, 1913–1917.

SPECIAL COLLECTIONS, VAN PELT LIBRARY, UNIVERSITY OF PENNSYLVANIA,
PHILADELPHIA, PENNSYLVANIA

Waldo Frank Papers, 1889–1965. Correspondence with John Dewey, 1917–1937; Correspondence with Margaret Naumberg, 1917–1922; Correspondence with F. M. Alexander, 1916–1939.

SPECIAL COLLECTIONS, CLARK UNIVERSITY, WORCESTER, MASSACHUSETTS

The G. Stanley Hall Papers, 1844–1924.

AMERICAN PHILOSOPHICAL SOCIETY, ARCHIVES, PHILADELPHIA, PENNSYLVANIA

C. B. Davenport Papers, correspondence with Myrtle McGraw, 1931–1941.

MUSEUM OF MODERN ART, NEW YORK CITY

Henri Matisse: A Retrospective. A Special Exhibition, September 24, 1992, to January
12, 1993.

NEUROLOGICAL INSTITUTE OF NEW YORK, PRESBYTERIAN HOSPITAL, COLUMBIA
UNIVERSITY, NEW YORK CITY

Minutes of the Board of Trustees, 1915–1931.

Bibliography

JOSIAH MACY, JR. FOUNDATION, NEW YORK CITY

Annual Reports, 1930–1960.

NEW YORK ACADEMY OF MEDICINE, NEW YORK CITY

Correspondence of Herbert Wilcox and Frederick Tilney, 1933–1936.

AMERICAN MUSEUM OF NATURAL HISTORY, NEW YORK CITY

Correspondence of Frederick Tilney, Kingsley Nobel, and Ludwig Kast, 1930–1938.

ROCKEFELLER MEMORIAL ARCHIVE, TARRYTOWN, NEW YORK

Laura Spelman Rockefeller Memorial, Series III, Record Group 5, Child Study and Parent Education, 1923–1944. The General Education Board, Series I, Normal Child Development Study, and Fellowships, Columbia University, 1926–1937. The Commonwealth Fund 1929–1942.

ALAN MASON CHESNEY MEDICAL ARCHIVES, JOHNS HOPKINS MEDICAL
INSTITUTIONS, BALTIMORE, MARYLAND

Adolf E. Meyer Papers, 1866–1950.

RARE BOOKS AND MANUSCRIPTS, NATIONAL LIBRARY OF CONGRESS,
WASHINGTON, D.C.

Arnold Lucius Gesell Papers, 1880–1958.

NATIONAL GALLERY OF ART, WASHINGTON, D.C.

The Great French Paintings from the Barnes Foundation, A Special Exhibiton, May, 1993.

HISTORY OF MEDICINE DIVISION, NATIONAL LIBRARY OF MEDICINE,
BETHESDA, MARYLAND

Milton J. Senn Papers and Oral Histories of Child Development, 1927–1983. Lawrence K. Frank Papers, 1914–1974.

SPECIAL COLLECTIONS, LILLY LIBRARY, INDIANA UNIVERSITY,
BLOOMINGTON, INDIANA

Arthur Bentley Papers. 1870–1953.

SPENCER RESEARCH LIBRARY, UNIVERSITY OF KANSAS, LAWRENCE, KANSAS

Neurology Collection: C. J. Herrick Papers. George E. Coghill Papers, 1926–1937.

ARCHIVES, ST. VINCENT'S COLLEGE, LATROBE, PENNSYLVANIA

Eric McCormack Papers, 1911–1963.

CHRONOLOGICAL LISTING OF WORKS BY JOHN DEWEY

The references listed below are from The Collected Works of John Dewey, 1882–1953, published by Southern Illinois University Press, Carbondale, Illinois. The Collected Works are divided into three series: The Early Works, 1882–1898 (five volumes); The

Middle Works, 1899–1924 (fifteen volumes); and The Later Works, 1925–1953 (seventeen volumes). Hereafter cited as: *EW* (Early Works); *MW* (Middle Works); *LW* (Later Works).

"The Metaphysical Assumptions of Materialism." In *EW* 1: 3–8.
"The Pantheism of Spinoza." In *EW* 1: 9–18.
"Knowledge and Relativity of Feeling." In *EW* 1: 19–33.
"Kant and Philosophic Method." In *EW* 1: 34–47.
"The Place of Religious Emotion." In *EW* 1: 91.
"Soul and Body." In *EW* 1: 93–115.
Leibniz's New Essays Concerning the Human Understanding. In *EW* 1: 420–423.
Psychology. In *EW* 2: 98–90.
"The Study of Ethics: A Syllabus." In *EW* 4: 219–362.
"The Theory of Emotion." In *EW* 4: 152–188.
"The Reflex Arc Concept in Psychology." In *EW* 5: 96–110.
"Review of *Social and Ethical Interpretations in Mental Development,* by James Mark Baldwin, New York: Macmillan, 1987. Philosophical Review." In *EW* 5: 419–420.
"Principles of Mental Development as Illustrated in Early Infancy." In *MW* 1: 175–191.
"The Evolutionary Method as Applied to Morality." In *MW* 2: 3–38.
"The School as a Social Center." In *MW* 2: 80–96.
Studies in Logical Theory. In *MW* 2: 293–368.
"Nature." In *MW* 2: 142–149.
How We Think. In *MW* 6: 177–356.
"The Subject Matter of Metaphysical Inquiry." In *MW* 8: 3–13.
"The Logic of Judgment of Practice." In *MW* 8: 46–49.
German Philosophy and Politics. In *MW* 8: 135–204.
with Dewey, Evelyn. *Schools of To-Morrow.* In *MW* 8: 205–406.
Democracy and Education. In *MW* 9: 3–370.
"American Education and Culture." In *MW* 10: 196–201.
"On Understanding the Mind of Germany." In *MW* 10: 216–233.
"Force, Violence and Law." In *MW* 10: 211–215.
"In a Time of National Hesitation." In *MW* 10: 256–259.
"Conscription of Thought." In *MW* 10: 276–280.
"In Explanation of our Lapse." In *MW* 10: 292–295.
Essays in Experimental Logic. In *MW* 10: 319–396.
Human Nature and Conduct. In *MW* 14: 3–227.
"Introduction to F. Matthias Alexander's *Constructive Conscious Control of the Individual.*" In *MW* 15: 308–315.
Experience and Nature. In *LW* 1: 3–328.
"The Meaning of Value" and "Value, Objective Reference and Criticism." In *LW* 2: 69–97.
"A Key to the New World. Review of Bertrand Russell's *Education and the Good Life.*" In *LW* 2: 226–230.
The Public and Its Problems. In *LW* 2: 275–374.
"Impressions of Soviet Russia: New Schools for a New Era." In *LW* 3: 203–250.
Quest for Certainty. In *LW* 4: 3–250.
Individualism, Old and New. In *LW* 5: 41–124.

"From Absolutism to Experimentalism." In *LW* 5: 147–160.
"The Applicability of Logic to Existence." In *LW* 5: 206–207.
"Introduction to F. Matthias Alexander's *The Use of the Self.*" In *LW* 6: 315–320.
Ethics. In *LW* 7: 3–462.
"Santayana's Orthodoxy: Review of George Santayana's *Some Turns of Thought in Modern Philosophy.*" In *LW* 9: 240–243.
"Unity and Progress." In *LW* 9: 71–75.
"Intelligence and Power." In *LW* 9: 107–111.
Art as Experience. In *LW* 10: 7–397.
"Introduction to Myrtle B. McGraw, *Growth: A Study of Johnny and Jimmy.*" In *LW* 11: 510–514.
Logic: The Theory of Inquiry. In *LW* 12: 3–527.
"Freedom and Culture." In *LW* 13: 63–188.
"Experience, Knowledge and Value: A Rejoinder." In *LW* 14: 3–90.
"Propositions, Warranted Assertibility and Truth." In *LW* 14: 168–188.
"Memory and Judgment." In *LW* 17: 323–325.

SECONDARY SOURCES

Alexander, Frederick Matthias. *Constructive Conscious Control of the Individual.* New York: Dutton, 1923.
———. *Man's Supreme Inheritance.* New York: E. P. Dutton and Co., 1910.
———. *Man's Supreme Inheritance.* 2nd ed. New York: Dutton, 1918.
———. *The Use of the Self.* New York: Dutton, 1932.
Ames, Louise B. *Arnold Gesell: Themes of his Work.* New York: Human Sciences Press, 1989.
Anderson, John E. *The Young Child in the Home: A Survey of Three Thousand American Families.* New York: D. Appleton-Century Co., 1936.
Antler, Joyce. *Lucy Sprague Mitchell: The Making of a Modern Woman.* New Haven, Conn.: Yale University Press, 1987.
———. "Progressive Education and the Scientific Study of the Child: An Analysis of the Bureau of Educational Experiments." *Teachers College Record* (1982), 83: 559–591.
Ashforth, Albert. *Thomas Henry Huxley.* New York: Twayne, 1969.
Baars, Bernard. *A Cognitive Theory of Consciousness.* New York: Cambridge University Press, 1988.
———. *In the Theater of Consciousness: The Workspace of the Mind.* New York: Oxford University Press, 1997.
Baldwin, James Mark. *The Mental Development in a Child and the Race.* New York: Macmillan, 1895.
———. *Thought and Things.* 2 vols. New York: Macmillan, 1906, 1911.
Barnes, Albert C. *The Art in Painting.* New York: Harcourt Brace, 1925.
———. "The Evolution of Contemporary Painting." In *Art and Education,* edited by Albert C. Barnes, pp. 151–159. Merion, Pa.: The Barnes Foundation, 1929.
———. "Method and Design." In *Art and Education,* edited by Albert C. Barnes, pp. 184–190. Merion, Pa.: The Barnes Foundation, 1929.
———. "Plastic Form." In *Art and Education,* edited by Albert C. Barnes, pp. 73–91. Merion, Pa.: The Barnes Foundation, 1929.

———. "The Roots of Art." In *Art and Education,* edited by Albert C. Barnes, pp. 16–20. Merion, Pa.: The Barnes Foundation, 1929.

Beck, Robert Holmes. "American Progressive Education, 1875–1930." Ph.D. dissertation, Yale University, 1942.

Bell, M. A., and N. A. Fox. "Brain Development over the First Year of Life: Relations between Electroencephalographic Frequency and Coherence and Cognitive and Affective Behavior." In *Human Behavior and the Developing Brain,* edited by G. Dawson and Kurt W. Fischer, pp. 314–345. New York: Guilford, 1994.

Benjamin, H. R., and A. A. Weech. "Basal Heat Production in Relation to Growth." *American Journal of Diseases of Children* 65 (1943): 1–35.

Bentley, Arthur. "Logic and Logical Behavior." In *Inquiry into Inquiries,* edited by Sidney Ratner, pp. 286–319. Boston: Beacon Press, 1954.

———. "Situational versus Psychological Theories of Behavior." In *Inquiry into Inquiries,* edited by Sidney Ratner, pp. 141–174. Boston: Beacon Press, 1954.

Bergenn, Victor W., Thomas C. Dalton, and Lewis P. Lipsitt. "Myrtle McGraw: A Growth Scientist." *Developmental Psychology* 28 (1992): 381–395.

Bernstein, Richard. *Beyond Objectivism and Relativism: Science, Hermeneutics and Praxis.* Philadelphia: University of Pennsylvania Press, 1983.

———, ed. *John Dewey.* New York: Washington Square Press, 1966.

Bibby, Cyril. *T. H. Huxley: Scientist, Humanist and Educator.* New York: Horizon Press, 1960.

Bixler, J. S. "Professor Dewey Discusses Religion." *Harvard Theological Review* 23 (1930): 213–133.

Blake, Casey Nelson. *Beloved Community: The Cultural Criticism of Randolph Bourne, Van Wyck Brooks, Waldo Frank and Lewis Mumford.* Chapel Hill: University of North Carolina Press, 1990.

Bohr, Niels. "Life and Light." *Nature* 131 (1937): 421–423, 457–459.

———. "The Structure of the Atom." In *Niels Bohr: A Centenary Volume,* edited by A. P. French and P. J. Kennedy, pp. 91–97. Cambridge, Mass.: Harvard University Press, 1985.

Boisvert, Raymond. *Dewey's Metaphysics.* New York: Fordham University Press, 1988.

Boltzmann, Ludwig. "On Statistical Mechanics." In *Ludwig Boltzmann: Theoretical Physics and Philosophical Problems,* edited by Brian McGuinness, pp. 169–172. Dordrecht, Holland: Reidel, 1974.

Bonaparte, Marie, Anna Freud, and Ernst Kriss, eds. *The Origins of Psychoanalysis: Letters to Wilhelm Fliess, Drafts and Notes—1887–1902.* New York: Basic Books, 1954.

Bourne, Randolph. "Education in Taste." *The New Republic,* March 4, 1916, pp. 122–124.

———. "Experimental Education." *The New Republic,* April 21, 1917, pp. 345–347.

———. "The Experimental Life." In *Randolph Bourne, The Radical Will: Selected Writings 1911–1918,* edited by Olaf Hansen, pp. 149–158. New York: Urizen Books, 1977.

———. "The Issue of Vocational Education." *The New Republic,* June 26, 1915, pp. 191–192.

———. "John Dewey's Philosophy." In *Randolph Bourne, The Radical Will: Selected Writings 1911–1918,* edited by Olaf Hansen, pp. 331–335. New York: Urizen Books, 1977.

———. "The Life of Irony." In *Randolph Bourne, The Radical Will: Selected Writings 1911–1918,* edited by Olaf Hansen, pp. 134–148. New York: Urizen Books, 1977.

———. "Making Over the Body." *The New Republic*, May 4, 1918, p. 28–29.

———. "Other Messiahs, A Letter to the Editor." *The New Republic*, May 25, 1918, p. 117.

———. "Schools in Gary, II." *The New Republic*, March 27, 1915, pp. 198–199.

———. "Twilight of Idols." In *Randolph Bourne, The Radical Will: Selected Writings 1911–1918*, edited by Olaf Hansen, pp. 338–347. New York: Urizen Books, 1977.

———. "The War and the Intellectuals." In *Randolph Bourne, The Radical Will: Selected Writings 1911–1918*, edited by Olaf Hansen, pp. 307–318. New York: Urizen Books, 1977.

Boydston, Jo Ann, ed. *The Poems of John Dewey*. Carbondale: Southern Illinois University Press, 1977.

Brody, Samuel. "Relativity of Physiological Time and Physiological Weight." *Growth* 1 (1937): 60–67.

Brush, Stephen G. "The Development of the Kinetic Theory of Gases, VIII: Randomness and Irreversibility." *Archive for the History of the Exact Sciences* 9 (1974): 1–88.

———, ed. *Kinetic Theory*, vol. 2: *Irreversible Processes*. New York: Pergamon, 1966.

Brush, Stephen G., Elizabeth Garber, and C. W. F. Everitt. "Introduction." In *Maxwell on Heat and Statistics*, edited by Stephen G. Brush, Elizabeth Garber, and C. W. F. Everitt, pp. 1–22. Bethlehem, Pa.: Lehigh University Press, 1995.

Bulmer, Martin, and Joan Bulmer. "Philanthropy and Social Science in the 1920s: Beardsley Ruml and the Laura Spelman Rockefeller Memorial, 1922–1929." *Minerva* 19 (1981): 358.

Burke, Tom. *Dewey's New Logic: A Reply to Russell*. Chicago: University of Chicago Press, 1994.

Burks, A. W., ed. *The Collected Papers of Charles S. Peirce*. Cambridge, Mass.: Harvard University Press, 1958.

Burnham, John C. "The New Psychology: From Narcissism to Social Control." In *Change and Continuity in Twentieth Century America: The 1920s*, edited by John Braeman, David Broder, and Robert Brenner, pp. 351–398. Columbus: Ohio State University Press, 1968.

———. "Psychiatry, Psychology and the Progressive Movement." *American Quarterly* 12 (1960): 457–465.

———. *Psychoanalysis and American Medicine, 1894–1918*. New York: International Universities Press, 1967.

———. "Sigmund Freud and G. Stanley Hall: Exchange of Letters." *Psychoanalytic Quarterly* 29 (1960): 309.

Butler, Joseph. *Analogy of Religion*. New York: F. Unger Publishers, 1961; orig. pub. 1736.

Butler, Samuel. *Erewhon; or, Over the Range*. New York: AMS Press, 1968; orig. pub. London: Trubner, 1872.

———. "The Evidence for the Resurrection of Jesus Christ as given by Four Evangelists." London: published privately, 1865.

———. *Evolution, Old and New*. New York: AMS Press, 1968; orig. pub. London: Hardwicke and Bogue, 1879.

———. *The Fair Haven*. New York: AMS Press, 1968; orig. pub. London: Trubner, 1873.

———. *Life and Habit*. New York: AMS Press, 1968; orig. pub. London: Trubner, 1878.

Cahan, Emily. "Science, Practice and Gender Roles in Early American Child Psychology." In *Contemporary Constructions of the Child: Essays in Honor of William Kes-*

sen, edited by Frank S. Kessel, Marc H. Bornstein, and Arnold J. Sameroff, pp. 225–250. Hillsdale, N.J.: Erlbaum, 1991.

Cantor, Joan H. *Psychology at Iowa: Centennial Essays.* Hillsdale, N.J.: Erlbaum, 1991.

Chalmers, David. "Facing Up to the Problem of Consciousness." *Journal of Consciousness Studies* 2 (1995): 200–219.

Child, C. M. *The Origin and Development of the Nervous System: From a Physiological Viewpoint.* Chicago: University of Chicago Press, 1921.

———. *Physiological Foundations of Behavior.* New York, Hafner 1964; orig. pub. 1924.

Clayton, Bruce. *Forgotten Prophet: The Life of Randolph Bourne.* Baton Rouge: Louisiana State University Press, 1984.

Coghill, George E. *Anatomy and the Problem of Behavior.* New York: Cambridge University Press, 1929; reprint, New York: Hafner Publishing Co., 1964.

———. "Individuation versus Integration in the Development of Behavior." *Journal of Genetic Psychology* 3 (1930): 432.

———. "The Neuro-Embryologic Study of Behavior: Principles, Perspectives, and Aims." *Science* 78 (1933): 131–136.

Colby, Kenneth M. *Energy and Structure in Psychoanalysis.* New York: Ronald Press, 1955.

Collins, Randall. *The Sociology of Philosophies: A Global Theory of Intellectual Change.* Cambridge, Mass.: Belknap and Harvard University Press, 1998.

Conel, J. LeRoy. *The Postnatal Development of the Human Cerebral Cortex, Volume 1: Cortex of the Newborn.* Cambridge, Mass.: Harvard University Press, 1939.

———. *The Postnatal Development of the Human Cerebral Cortex, Volume 2: Cortex of the Three Month Infant.* Cambridge, Mass.: Harvard University Press, 1947.

———. *The Postnatal Development of the Human Cerebral Cortex, Volume 3: Cortex of the Six Month Infant.* Cambridge, Mass.: Harvard University Press, 1951.

———. *The Postnatal Development of the Human Cerebral Cortex, Volume 5: Cortex of the Fifteen Month Infant.* Cambridge, Mass.: Harvard University Press, 1955.

Cotkin, George. *Reluctant Modernism: American Thought and Culture 1880–1900.* New York: Twayne, 1992.

———. *William James, Public Philosopher.* Baltimore and London: Johns Hopkins University Press, 1990.

Coughlan, Neil. *The Young Dewey.* Chicago: University of Chicago Press, 1975.

Cravens, Hamilton. *Before Head Start: The Iowa Welfare Research Station and America's Children.* Chapel Hill: University of North Carolina Press, 1993.

———. "The Professionalization of Child Development." In *American Childhood: A Research Guide and Historical Handbook*, edited by Joseph M. Hawes and N. Ray Hiner, pp. 415–488. Westport, Conn.: Greenwood Press, 1985.

Cravens, Hamilton, and John C. Burnham. "Psychology and Evolutionary Naturalism in American Thought, 1890–1940." *American Quarterly* 23 (1971): 635–657.

Crawford, Elsbeth. "Learning from Experience." In *Faraday Rediscovered: Essays on the Life and Work of Michael Faraday*, edited by D. Gooding and F. James. London: Stockton Press, 1985.

Cremin, Lawrence. *The Transformation of the School.* New York: Knopf, 1961.

Cunningham, Craig. "Dewey's Metaphysics of the Self." In *The New Scholarship on John Dewey*, edited by Jim Garrison, pp. 175–192. Dordrecht, Holland: Kluwer, 1995.

Dainton, Barry. *Stream of Consciousness: Unity and the Continuity of Conscious Experience.* New York: Routledge, 2000.

Dalton, Thomas C. "Arnold Gesell's Maturationism Reconsidered." In *From Past to Future: Clark Papers on the History of Psychology* (forthcoming).

———. "Challenging the Group Bias of American Culture." *Contemporary Psychology* 40 (1995): 201–204.

———. "The Developmental Roots of Consciousness and Emotional Experience." *Consciousness and Emotion* 1 (2000): 55–166.

———. "Dewey's Hegelianism Reconsidered: Reclaiming the Lost Soul of Psychology." *New Ideas in Psychology* 15 (1997): 1–15.

———. "The History of Division 7 (Developmental Psychology)." In *Unification through Division: Histories of the Divisions of the American Psychological Association*, vol. 1, edited by Donald A. Dewsbury, pp. 67–100. Washington, D.C.: American Psychological Association, 1996.

———. "McGraw's Alternative to Gesell's Maturationist Theory." In *Beyond Heredity and Environment: Myrtle McGraw and the Maturation Controversy*, edited by Thomas C. Dalton and Victor W. Bergenn, pp. 127–152. Boulder, Colo.: Westview Press, 1995.

———. "Myrtle McGraw's Neurobehavioral Theory of Development." *Developmental Review* 18 (1998): 472–503.

———. "The Ontogeny of Consciousness: John Dewey and Myrtle McGraw's Contribution to a Science of Mind." *Journal of Consciousness Studies* 6 (1999): 3–26.

———. "Was McGraw a Maturationist?" *American Psychologist* 51 (1996): 551–552.

Dalton, Thomas C., and Victor W. Bergenn. *Early Experience and the Brain: A Historical and Interdisciplinary Synthesis*. Mahwah, N.J.: Erlbaum, forthcoming.

———. "John Dewey, Myrtle McGraw and *Logic:* An Unusual Collaboration in the 1930s." *Studies in History and Philosophy of Science* 27 (1996): 69–107.

———. "Myrtle McGraw: A Pioneer in Neurobehavioral Development." In *Portraits of Pioneers in Psychology*, edited by Gregory Kimble and Michael Wertheimer, pp. 211–228. Washington, D.C.: American Psychological Association, 1998.

Damasio, Antonio. *Descartes Error: Emotion, Reason and the Human Brain*. New York: Avon Books, 1994.

———. *The Feeling of What Happens: Body and Emotion in the Making of Consciousness*. New York: Harcourt Brace, 1999.

Dammann, V. T. "Developmental Changes in Attitudes as one Factor Determining Energy Output in a Motor Performance." *Child Development* 12 (1941): 241–246.

Darwin, Charles. "The Biographical Sketch of an Infant." *Mind* 2 (1877): 288.

———. *The Expression of Emotion in Animals and Man*. London: John Murray, 1872.

Davenport, C. B. "Bodily Growth of Babies during the First Postnatal Year." Proceedings of the Carnegie Institution, no. 169: *Contributions to Embryology* (1938): 273–305.

———. "Interpretation of Certain Infantile Growth Curves." *Growth* 1 (1937): 279–283.

Dearborn, Mary V. *Love and the Promised Land: The Story of Anzia Yezierska and John Dewey*. New York: Free Press, 1988.

Deegan, Mary Jo. *Jane Addams and the Men of the Chicago School, 1892–1918*. New Brunswick, N.J.: Transaction Books, 1988.

Dennis, Paul. "'Johnny's a Gentleman but Jimmy's a Mug': Press Coverage during the 1930s of Myrtle McGraw's Study of Johnny and Jimmy Woods." *Journal of the History of the Behavioral Sciences* 25 (1989): 356–370.

Depew, David. "Introduction." In *Pragmatism: From Progressivism to Postmodernism*, edited by Robert Hollinger and David Depew, pp. 109–121. Westport, Conn.: Praeger, 1997.

Desmond, Adrian J. *Huxley: From Devil's Disciple to Evolution's High Priest.* Reading, Mass.: Addison Wesley, 1997.

Dewey, Evelyn. *Behavior Development in Infants: A Survey of the Literature on Prenatal and Postnatal Activity, 1920–1924.* New York: Columbia University Press, 1935; reprint, New York: Arno, 1972.

Dewey, Evelyn, and Beardsley Ruml. *Methods and Results of Testing Children.* New York: Dutton, 1920.

Dewey, Jane. "Biography of John Dewey." In *The Philosophy of John Dewey,* edited by Paul A. Schlipp, pp. 3–45. New York: Tudor, 1939.

———. "Intensities in the Stark Effect of Helium: I." *Physical Review* 28 (1926): 1108–1124.

———. "Intensities of the Stark Effect of Helium: II." *Physical Review* 30 (1927): 770–780.

Dewey, John. "The Psychological Process in Relation to the Biological." In *John Dewey: Lectures in Psychological and Political Ethics—1898,* edited by Donald F. Koch, p. 301. New York: Hafner Press, 1976.

di Gregorio, Mario A. *T. H. Huxley's Place in Natural Science.* New Haven, Conn.: Yale University Press, 1984.

Diggins, John. *The Promise of Pragmatism: Modernism and the Crisis of Knowledge and Authority.* Chicago: University of Chicago Press, 1994.

Dykhuizen, George. *The Life and Mind of John Dewey.* Carbondale: Southern Illinois University Press, 1973.

Eastman, Max. *The Enjoyment of Living.* New York: Harper Brothers, 1948.

———. "The Hero as Teacher: The Life Story of John Dewey." In *Heroes I Have Known,* edited by Max Eastman, pp. 275–322. New York: Simon and Schuster, 1947.

Edelman, Gerald, and Giulio Tononi. *The Universe of Consciousness: From Mind to Imagination.* New York: Basic Books, 2000.

Elman, J. L., E. A. Bates, M. Johnson, A. Karmiloff-Smith, D. Parisi, and K. Plunkett. *Redefining Innateness: A Connectionist Perspective on Development.* Cambridge, Mass.: MIT Press, 1998.

Elsberg, Charles. *The Story of a Hospital: The Neurological Institute of New York, 1900–1938.* New York: Hoeber, 1944.

Faris, E. "Attitudes and Behavior." *American Journal of Sociology* 34 (1928): 271–281.

Feffer, Andrew. *The Chicago Pragmatists and American Progressivism.* Ithaca, N.Y.: Cornell University Press, 1993.

Feuer, Lewis. "The Standpoints of Dewey and Freud: A Contrast and Analysis." *Journal of Individual Psychology* 16 (1960): 121–136.

Finger, Stanley. *Minds Behind the Brain: A History of the Pioneers and Their Discoveries.* New York: Oxford, 2000.

Flam, Jack. *Matisse: The Dance.* Washington, D.C.: National Gallery of Art, 1993.

———, ed. *Matisse on Art.* Berkeley: University of California Press, 1995.

Frank, Lawrence K. "The Beginnings of Child Development and Family Life Education in the Twentieth Century." *The Merrill-Palmer Quarterly of Behavior and Development* 8 (1962): 207–227.

———. "The Development of Science." *Journal of Philosophy* 21 (1924): 5–25.

———. Folder of Letters on his 70th birthday. December, 1965. Mary Perry, Watertown, Massachusetts.

———. "Genetic Psychology and Its Prospects." In *Symposium on Genetic Psychology:*

Sixth Anniversary of Clark University, p. 516. Worcester, Mass.: Clark University Press, 1950.

——. "The Locus of Experience." *Journal of Philosophy* 20 (1923): 328–329.

——. "The Management of Tensions." In Lawrence Frank, *Society as the Patient*, pp. 115–142. New Brunswick, N.J.: Rutgers University Press, 1949.

——. "The Problem of Child Development." *Child Development* 1 (1935): 7–18.

——. "Structure, Function, and Growth." *Philosophy of Science* 2 (1935): 210–235.

Frank, Philipp. "Ernst Mach and the Unity of Science." In *Ernst Mach: Physicist and Philosopher*, edited by Robert Cohen and Ray Seeger, pp. 235–244. Dordrecht, Holland: Reidel Publishing Co., 1970.

Frank, Waldo. "Towards a National Culture." *Seven Arts* 1 (January 1917): 270–280.

Freud, Sigmund. "Beyond the Pleasure Principle." In *The Standard Edition of the Complete Psychological Works of Sigmund Freud*, vol. 18, edited by James Strachey, pp. 3–64. London: Hogarth Press, 1953.

——. *Civilization and Its Discontents.* In *The Standard Edition of the Complete Psychological Works of Sigmund Freud*, vol. 21, edited by James Strachey, pp. 59–145. London: Hogarth Press, 1953.

——. "Project for a Scientific Psychology." In *The Standard Edition of the Complete Psychological Works of Sigmund Freud*, vol. 1, edited by James Strachey, pp. 1–385. London: Hogarth Press, 1953.

——. "The Unconscious." In *The Standard Edition of the Complete Psychological Works of Sigmund Freud*, vol. 14, edited by James Strachey, pp. 161–204. London: Hogarth Press, 1953.

Frith, Chris, and Uta Frith. "Interacting Minds: A Biological Basis." *Science* 286 (1999): 1692–1695.

Gallese, Vittorio, and Alvin Goldman. "Mirror Neurons and the Simulation Theory of Mind Reading." *Trends in Cognitive Sciences* 2 (1998): 493–501.

Gardner, Howard. *Creating Minds: An Anatomy of Creativity Seen through the Lives of Freud, Einstein, Picasso, Stravinsky, Eliot, Graham and Gandhi.* New York: Basic Books, 1993.

Gesell, Arnold. *Infant Behavior: Its Genesis and Growth.* New York: McGraw Hill, 1934.

——. "Reciprocal Interweaving in Neuromotor Development." *The Journal of Comparative Neurology* 10 (1939): 161–180.

Goetzmann, William H., ed. *The American Hegelians: An Intellectual Episode in the History of Western America.* New York: Alfred Knopf, 1973.

Gooding, David. "In 'Nature's School': Faraday as an Experimentalist." In *Faraday Rediscovered: Essays on the Life and Work of Michael Faraday*, edited by D. Gooding and F. James, pp. 105–136. London: Stockton Press, 1985.

Gottlieb, Gilbert. "Conceptions of Prenatal Behavior." In *Development and the Evolution of Behavior*, edited by L. R. Aronson, E. Tolbach, D. S. Lehrman, and J. S. Rosenblatt, pp. 111–137. San Francisco: Freeman, 1970.

——. *Individual Development and Evolution: The Genesis of Novel Behavior.* New York: Oxford University Press, 1992.

——. "Myrtle McGraw's Unrecognized Conceptual Contributions to Developmental Psychology." *Developmental Review* 18 (1998): 437–448.

——. *Probabilistic Epigenesis and Evolution.* Heinz Werner Lecture Series, vol. XXII. Worcester, Mass.: Clark University Press, 1999.

———. *Synthesizing Nature and Nurture: The Prenatal Roots of Instinctive Behavior.* Hillsdale, N.J.: Erlbaum, 1997.

———. "A Tribute to Clarence Luther Herrick (1858–1904): Founder of Developmental Psychobiology." *Developmental Psychobiology* 20 (1987): 1–5.

Grant, Julia. *Raising Baby by the Book: The Education of American Mothers.* New Haven, Conn.: Yale University Press, 1998.

Greenfield, Howard. *The Devil and Dr. Barnes: Portrait of an American Art Collector.* New York: Viking, 1987.

Gross, Charles G. *Brain, Vision, Memory: Tales in the History of Neuroscience.* Cambridge, Mass.: MIT Press, 1998.

Grove, William R., ed., *The Correlation and Conservation of Forces: A Series of Expositions.* New York: Appleton and Co., 1865.

Grubrich-Simitis, Ilse. *Freud's Phylogenetic Fantasy.* Cambridge, Mass.: Harvard University Press, 1987.

Gruenberg, Sidonie M., ed. *Parent Education: Report of the Subcommittee on Types of Parent Education, Content and Method.* New York: The Century Co., 1932.

Hale, Nathan G. *Freud and the Americans: The Beginnings of Psychoanalysis in the United States, 1876–1917.* New York: Oxford University Press, 1971.

Hall, G. Stanley. *Adolescence: Its Psychology and Its Relations to Physiology, Anthropology, Sociology, Sex Crime, Religion and Education.* Vols. 1 and 2. New York: Appleton, 1904.

Hamburger, Viktor. *The Heritage of Experimental Embryology: Hans Spemann and the Organizer.* New York: Oxford University Press, 1988.

Harman, P. M. *Energy, Force and Matter: The Conceptual Development of Nineteenth Century Physics.* Cambridge: Cambridge University Press, 1982.

———. *Metaphysics and Natural Philosophy: The Problems of Substance in Classical Physics.* Sussex, Great Britain: Harvester Press, 1982.

Harotunian, Joseph. *Piety versus Moralism: The Passing of the New England Theology.* New York: Henry Holt and Co., 1932.

Harris, H. S. *Hegel's Development.* Oxford: Clarendon Press. 1983.

Hart, Henry. *Dr. Barnes of Merion: An Appreciation.* New York: Farrar Straus, 1963.

Hegel, George W. F. *Phenomenology of Spirit.* Trans. A. V. Miller. New York: Oxford University Press, 1977.

———. *Science of Logic.* Trans. A. V. Miller. Atlantic Highlands, N.J.: Humanities Press International, 1989.

Heisenberg, Werner. "Quantum Theory and Its Interpretation." In *Niels Bohr: His Life and Work as Seen by His Colleagues,* edited by S. Rozental, pp. 101–103. New York: Wiley, 1967.

Herrick, C. J. "Clarence Luther Herrick: Pioneer Naturalist, Teacher and Psychobiologist." *Transactions of the American Philosophical Society* 45 (1955): 1–85.

———. "The Evolution of Intelligence and its Origins." *Science* 3 (1910): 7–18.

———. *George Elliott Coghill: A Naturalist and Philosopher.* Chicago: University of Chicago Press, 1949.

———. *The Neurological Foundations of Animal Behavior.* New York: Hafner, 1962; orig. pub., 1924.

———. "Some Reflections on the Origin and Significance of the Cerebral Cortex." *The Journal of Animal Behavior* 3 (1923): 222–236.

Herrick, C. L. "Focal and Marginal Consciousness." *Psychological Review* 3 (1898): 193–194.

———. "Psychological Corollaries of Modern Neurological Discoveries." *Journal of Comparative Neurology* 7 (1896): 155–161.

———. "The Vital Equilibrium and the Nervous System." *Science* 7 (1898): 813–818.

Hesse, Mary B. *Forces and Fields: The Concept of Action at a Distance in the History of Physics.* Westport, Conn.: Greenwood Press, 1962.

Hickman, Larry. *John Dewey's Pragmatic Technology.* Bloomington: Indiana University Press, 1990.

———. "Dewey's Theory of Inquiry." In *Reading Dewey: Interpretations for a Postmodern Generation,* edited by Larry Hickman, pp 166–186. Bloomington: Indiana University Press, 1998.

———. *Philosophical Tools for Technological Culture: Putting Pragmatism to Work.* Bloomington: Indiana University Press, 2001.

Hinkle, Beatrice. *The Re-creating of the Individual: A Study of Psychological Types and Their Relation to Psychoanalysis.* New York: Harcourt Brace, 1923.

Hodgson, Shadworth H. "Illusory Psychology." In *John Dewey: The Middle Works,* vol. 1: *1929–1930,* edited by Jo Ann Boydston, pp. xxv–xli. Carbondale: Southern Illinois University Press, 1969.

Holt, Lee E. *Samuel Butler.* New York: Twayne, 1964.

Holt, Robert R. "Beyond Vitalism and Mechanism: Freud's Concept of Psychic Energy." In Benjamin B. Wolman, ed., *Historical Roots of Contemporary Psychology,* pp. 196–226. New York: Harper and Row, 1968.

Holton, Gerald. "Mach, Einstein and the Search for Reality." In *Ernst Mach, Physicist and Philosopher,* edited by Robert S. Cohen and Raymond J. Seeger, pp. 165–166. Dordrecht, Holland: Reidel, 1970.

Honner, John. "The Transcendental Philosophy of Niels Bohr." *Studies in History and Philosophy of Science* 13 (1982): 1–15.

Hook, Sidney. "Introduction." In *John Dewey: The Middle Works,* vol. 2: *1929–1930,* edited by Jo Ann Boydston, pp. ix–xvi. Carbondale: Southern Illinois University Press, 1984.

———. "Naturalism and Democracy." In Yervant Kirkorian, *Naturalism and the Human Spirit,* pp. 40–64. New York: Columbia University Press, 1944.

———. *Out of Step: An Unquiet Life in the Twentieth Century.* New York: Harper and Row, 1987.

———. *The Quest for Being.* New York: St. Martin's Press, 1961.

Hurley, S. L. *Consciousness in Action.* Cambridge, Mass: Harvard University Press, 1998.

Huxley, Thomas H. *Evolution and Ethics and Other Essays.* New York: Appleton and Co., 1896.

———. *Man's Place in Nature and Other Essays.* New York: Dutton, 1906.

Huxley, Thomas H., and William J. Youmans. *The Elements of Physiology and Hygiene: A Textbook for Educational Institutions.* rev. ed. New York: American Book Co., 1873.

James, William. "Hegel and His Method." In William James, *The Writings of William James,* edited by John McDermott, pp. 512–528. Chicago: University of Chicago Press, 1977.

———. "On Some Hegelians." In *The Will to Believe and Other Essays,* edited by William James. New York: Longmans, 1931.

———. "The Physical Basis of Emotion." *Psychological Review* 1 (1894): 516–529.

———. *The Principles of Psychology.* vol. 1. Cambridge, Mass.: Harvard University Press, 1981; orig. pub., 1890.

Johnson, Buford. *Mental Growth of Children in Relation to the Rate of Growth in Bodily Development: A Report to the Bureau of Educational Experiments.* New York: Dutton, 1925.

Jones, Frank. *Body Awareness in Action: A Study of the Alexander Technique.* New York: Schocken, 1976.

———. "The Work of F. M. Alexander as an Introduction to Dewey's Philosophy of Education." *School and Society* 57 (1943): 1–4.

Jung, Carl. "A Preliminary Study of Psychological Types." In *Collected Works of Karl Jung,* vol. 1, edited by Herbert Read, Michael Fordham, and Gerhard Adler, pp. 287–298. New York: Pantheon, 1953.

Kast, Ludwig. *A Review by the President of Activities for the Six years Ending December 31, 1936.* New York: Josiah Macy, Jr. Foundation, 1937.

Kempf, Dorothy C., and John C. Burnham, eds. *Edward J. Kempf: Selected Papers.* Bloomington: Indiana University Press, 1974.

Kempf, Edward J. *The Autonomic Functions and the Personality.* New York: The Nervous and Mental Disease Publishing Co., 1921.

———. "The Holistic Laws of Life." In *Edward J. Kempf: Selected Papers,* edited by Dorothy C. Kempf and John C. Burnham, pp. 309–311. Bloomington: Indiana University Press, 1974.

Kingsland, Sharon. "A Humanistic Science: Charles Judson Herrick and the Struggle for Psychobiology at the University of Chicago." *Perspectives on Science* 1 (1993): 1–33.

———. "Toward a Natural History of the Human Psyche: Charles Manning Child, Charles Judson Herrick and the Dynamic View of the Individual at the University of Chicago." In *The Expansion of American Biology,* edited by Keith R. Benson, Jane Maienschein, and Ronald Rainger, pp. 195–230. New Brunswick, N.J.: Rutgers University Press, 1991.

Kloppenberg, James. "Pragmatism: An Old Name for Some New Ways of Thinking?" *The Journal of American History* 83 (June 1996): 100–138.

Klyce, Scudder. *Dewey's Suppressed Psychology: A Psychological Study of John Dewey.* Winchester, Mass.: Scudder Klyce, 1928.

———. *Universe.* Winchester, Mass.: Scudder Klyce, 1921.

Koch, Donald F., ed. *John Dewey: Lectures on Psychological and Political Ethics, 1898.* New York: Hafner, 1976.

Kohn, P. "Increase in Weight and Growth of Children in the First Year of Life." *Growth* 12 (1948): 149–155.

Krasnegor, N., G. Lyon, and P. Goldman-Rakic, eds. *Development of the Prefrontal Cortex: Evolution, Neurobiology, and Behavior.* Baltimore: Paul H. Brookes, 1997.

Kubie, Lawrence. "The Fallacious use of Quantitative Concepts in Dynamic Psychology." *The Psychoanalytic Quarterly* 16 (1947): 507–518.

Kuhn, Thomas. *The Essential Tension: Selected Studies in Scientific Tradition and Change.* Chicago: University of Chicago Press, 1977.

Kuklick, Bruce. *Churchmen and Philosophers: From Jonathan Edwards to John Dewey.* New Haven, Conn.: Yale University Press, 1985.

Kuo, Z. Y. "Total Pattern or Local Reflexes?" *Psychological Review* 46 (1939): 93–122.

Lashley, Karl, and Kenneth M. Colby. "An Exchange of Views on Psychic Energy and Psychoanalysis." *Behavioral Science* 2 (1957): 226–238.

Lavine, Thelma. "America and the Contestations of Modernity: Bentley, Dewey and Rorty." In *Rorty and Pragmatism: The Philosopher Responds to His Critics*, edited by H. J. Saatkamp Jr., pp. 37–49. Nashville, Tenn.: Vanderbilt University Press, 1995.

Leavitt, Morton. *Freud and Dewey on the Nature of Man*. New York: Philosophical Library, 1960.

Leopold, Dan, and Nico Logothetis. "Multistable Phenomena: Changing Views on Perception." *Trends in Cognitive Sciences* 3 (1999): 254–263.

Levitas, Louise, and Jo Ann Boydston. *Anzia Yezierska: A Writer's Life*. New Brunswick, N.J.: Rutgers University Press, 1988.

Lomax, Elizabeth. "The Laura Spelman Rockefeller Memorial: Some of Its Contributions to Early Research in Child Development." *Journal of the History of the Behavioral Sciences* 13 (1977): 283–293.

Lotze, Hermann. *Outlines of Psychology*, translated by C. L. Herrick. Minneapolis: S. M. Williams, 1885; reprint, New York: Arno Press, 1973.

Lyons, Sherrie. "Convincing Men They Are Monkeys." In *Thomas Henry Huxley's Place in Science and Letters: Centenary Essays*, edited by Alan P. Barr, pp. 95–118. Athens, Ga.: University of Georgia Press, 1997.

Mach, Ernst. *The Analysis of Sensations*. Trans. C. M. Williams. New York: Dover, 1959.

MacKinnon, Edward. "Bohr on the Foundations of Quantum Theory." In *Niels Bohr: A Centenary Volume*, edited by A. P. French and P. J. Kennedy, pp. 101–120. Cambridge, Mass.: Harvard University Press, 1985.

Matthews, F. H. "The Americanization of Sigmund Freud: Adaptations of Psychoanalysis before 1917." *Journal of American Studies* 10 (1967): 39–62.

Maxwell, James Clerk. *Matter in Motion*. New York: Van Nostrand, 1892.

———. "The Theory of Electrical Vortices Applied to Electric Currents." In *The Scientific Papers of James Clerk Maxwell*, vol. 1, edited by William Niven, pp. 468–488. New York: Dover, 1952.

Mayhew, Katherine, and Anna Edwards. *The Dewey School*. New York: Atherton, 1965; reprint, 1936.

McCormack, Fr. Eric. "Frederick Matthias Alexander and John Dewey: A Neglected Influence." Ph.D. thesis, University of Toronto, 1958.

McGraw, Myrtle B. "Appraising Test Responses of Infants and Young Children." *The Journal of Psychology* 14 (1942): 89–100.

———. "A Comparative Study of a Group of Southern White and Negro Infants." *Genetic Psychology Monographs* 10 (1931): 1–105.

———. "Development of Neuromuscular Mechanisms as Reflected in the Crawling and Creeping Behavior of the Human Infant." *The Journal of Genetic Psychology* 58 (1941): 83–111.

———. "From Reflex to Muscular Control in the Assumption of Erect Posture and Ambulation in the Human Infant." *Child Study* 3 (1932): 292.

———. *Growth: A Study of Johnny and Jimmy*. New York: Appleton-Century, 1935; reprint, New York: Arno Press, 1975.

———. "The Maturation of Behavior." In *The Manual of Child Psychology*, 1st ed., edited by Leonard Carmichael, pp. 331–369. New York: Wiley, 1946.

———. "Memories, Deliberate Recall, and Speculation." *American Psychologist* 45 (1990): 934–937.

———. "Neural Maturation as Exemplified in the Achievement of Bladder Control." *Journal of Pediatrics* 16 (1940): 587.

——. "Neural Maturation as Exemplified in the Reaching-Prehensile Behavior of the Human Infant." *Journal of Psychology* 11 (1941): 127–141.

——. "Neuromotor Maturation of Anti-Gravity Functions as Reflected in the Development of a Sitting Posture." *Journal of Genetic Psychology* 59 (1941): 160, 172.

——. *The Neuromuscular Maturation of the Human Infant.* New York: Columbia University Press, 1943.

——. "Professional and Personal Blunders in Child Development Research." *Psychological Record* 35 (1985): 165–170.

——. "Swimming Behavior of the Human Infant." *Journal of Pediatrics* 15 (1939): 485–490.

McGraw, Myrtle B., and K. Breeze. "Quantitative Studies in the Development of Erect Locomotion." *Child Development* 12 (1941): 267–303.

McGraw, Myrtle B., and A. C. Weinbach. "Quantitative Measures in Studying the Development of Behavior Patterns of Erect Locomotion." *Bulletin of the Neurological Institute of New York* 4 (1936): 553–559.

McLellan, James, and John Dewey. *The Psychology of Number.* New York: Appleton and Co., 1898.

Meyer, Adolf. "The Contemporary Setting of the Pioneer." *Journal of Comparative Neurology* 74 (1941): 1–24.

Milar, Katharine S. "A Coarse and Clumsy Tool: Helen Thompson Woolley and the Cincinnati Vocation Bureau." *History of Psychology* 2 (1999): 219–235.

Mises, Richard Von. "Mach and the Empiricist Conception of Science." In *Ernst Mach: Physicist and Philosopher,* edited by Robert Cohen and Ray Seeger, pp. 245–270. Dordrecht, Holland: Reidel Publishing Co., 1970.

Mitchell, Lucy Sprague. *Two Lives: The Story of Wesley Clair Mitchell and Myself.* New York: Simon and Schuster, 1953.

Nagel, Ernest. "Can Logic Be Divorced from Ontology?" In *John Dewey: The Later Works,* vol. 5: *1929–1930,* edited by Jo Ann Boydston, pp. 453–460. Carbondale: Southern Illinois University Press, 1984.

——. "Dewey's Theory of Natural Science." In *Sovereign Reason and Other Studies in the Philosophy of Science,* edited by Ernest Nagel, pp. 110–117. New York: Free Press, 1954.

——. "Introduction." In *John Dewey: The Later Works,* vol. 12: *1929–1930,* edited by Jo Ann Boydston, pp. ix–xxvii. Carbondale: Southern Illinois University Press, 1984.

Naumberg, Margaret. *The Child and the World.* New York: Harcourt, Brace and Company, 1928.

Naumberg, Margaret, and L. C. Deming. "The Children's School." In *Experimental Schools Revisited: Bulletins of the Bureau of Educational Experiments,* edited by Charlotte Windsor, pp. 41–48. New York: Schocken, 1973.

New York Times, December 16, 1935, p. 19.

Nickles, Thomas. "Justification and Experiment." In *The Uses of Experiment: Studies in the Natural Sciences,* edited by David Gooding, Trevor Pinch, and Simon Schaffer, pp. 299–333. New York: Cambridge University Press, 1988.

Niebuhr, Reinhold. *Moral Man, Immoral Society.* New York: Scribner's, 1932.

O'Connell, Agnes N., and Nancy F. Russo, eds. *Models of Achievement: Reflections of Eminent Women in Psychology.* New York: Columbia University Press, 1983.

Oppenheim, Ronald W. "G. E. Coghill (1872–1941): Pioneer Neuroembryologist and Developmental Psychobiologist." *Perspectives in Biology and Medicine* 22 (1978): 45–64.

Parker, George H. *The Elementary Nervous System*. Philadelphia: J. B. Lippincott, 1919.
———. "The Origin, Plan and Operational Modes of the Nervous System." In National Research Council, *The Problem of Mental Disorder*, pp. 184–196. New York: McGraw Hill, 1934.
Pauley, Philip. *Controlling Life: Jacques Loeb and the Engineering Ideal in Biology*. New York: Oxford University Press, 1987.
Penelhum, Terence. *Butler*. London and New York: Routledge and Kegan Paul, 1985.
Penrose, Roger. *Shadows of the Mind: A Search for the Missing Science of Consciousness*. New York: Oxford University Press, 1994.
Perry, Charles M., ed. *The St. Louis Movement in Philosophy: Some Source Materials*. Norman: University of Oklahoma Press, 1930.
Perry, Ralph Barton, ed. *The Thought and Character of William James*. Boston: Little Brown, 1935.
Petry, Michael J., ed. *Hegel's Philosophy of Nature*. Vol. 1. London: Allen and Unwin, 1970.
Pool, Lawrence. *The Neurological Institute of New York, 1909–1974*. Lakeville, Conn.: Pocketknife Press, 1975.
Poulos, Katherine. "Textual Commentary." In *John Dewey: The Later Works*, vol. 12: *1929–1930*, edited by Jo Ann Boydston, pp. 533–549. Carbondale: Southern Illinois University Press, 1984.
Prall, David W. *A Study of the Theory of Value*. Berkeley: University of California Press, 1921.
———. "Value and Thought Process." In *John Dewey: The Later Works*, vol. 2: *1929–1930*, edited by Jo Ann Boydston, pp. 393–402. Carbondale: Southern Illinois University Press, 1984.
Randall, John Jr. "John Dewey's Interpretation of the History of Philosophy." In *The Philosophy of John Dewey*, 3rd ed., edited by Paul Schlipp, pp. 75–102. La Salle, Ill.: Open Court, 1989.
Rappleye, Willard. *The Josiah Macy, Jr. Foundation: Twentieth Anniversary Review, 1930–1955*. New York: Josiah Macy, Jr. Foundation, 1955.
Ratliff, Floyd. "Mach's Contributions to the Analysis of Sensations." In *Mach: Physicist and Philosopher*, edited by Robert Cohen and Robert Seeger pp. 23–41. Dordrecht, Holland: Reidel, 1970.
Ratner, Joseph. *Intelligence in the Modern World*. New York: Modern Library, 1939.
Ratner, Sidney. "Introduction." In *John Dewey and Arthur F. Bentley: A Philosophical Correspondence, 1932–1951*, edited by Sidney Ratner and Jules Altman, pp. 1–48. New Brunswick, N.J.: Rutgers University Press, 1964.
Raup, Robert Bruce. *Complacency: The Foundation of Human Behavior*. New York: Macmillan, 1925.
Ribot, Theodule. *Diseases of the Will*. Trans. Marwin-Marie Snell. Chicago: Open Court, 1915; orig. pub. 1894.
Rice, Daniel. *Reinhold Niebuhr and John Dewey: An American Odyssey*. Albany, N.Y.: SUNY Press, 1993.
Rignano, Eugenio. *Biological Memory*. New York: Harcourt, Brace and Company, 1926.
———. *The Psychology of Reasoning*. Trans. Winifred Holl. New York: Harcourt, Brace and Company, 1923.
Ritvo, Lucille. *Darwin's Influence on Freud*. New Haven, Conn.: Yale University Press, 1990.

Roberts, John S., ed. *William Torrey Harris: A Critical Study of His Educational and Philosophical Views.* Washington, D.C.: National Education Association, 1924.

Robinson, John Harvey. "John Dewey, 1859–1952." *Journal of Philosophy* 1 (1953): 1–10.

Rockefeller, Steven. *John Dewey: Religious Faith and Democratic Humanism.* New York: Columbia University Press, 1991.

Rolston, Holmes. *Genes, Genesis and God: Values and Their Origins in Natural and Human History.* New York: Cambridge University Press, 1999.

Romanes, George. *Mental Evolution in Animals, With a Posthumous Essay on Instinct by Charles Darwin.* London: Kegan Paul, 1883.

Romer, A. S. "George H. Parker." In *Biography of the National Academy of Sciences,* pp. 128–135. Washington, D.C.: National Academy of Sciences, 1955.

Romney, Harold. "The Rockefeller Foundation." In *Foundations,* edited by Harold Keele and Joseph Kiger p. 364. Westport, Conn.: Greenwood Press, 1984.

Rorty, Richard. *Achieving Our Country: Leftist Thought in Twentieth Century America.* Cambridge, Mass.: Harvard University Press, 1998.

———. "Comments on Sleeper and Edel." *Transactions of the Charles Peirce Society* 21 (1985): 40–48.

———. "Daniel Dennett on Intrinsicality." In Richard Rorty, *Truth and Progress,* pp. 98–121. Philosophical Papers, vol. 3. Cambridge: Cambridge University Press, 1998.

———. "Dewey between Hegel and Darwin." In *Rorty and Pragmatism: The Philosopher Responds to His Critics,* edited by H. J. Saatkamp Jr., pp. 1–15. Nashville, Tenn.: Vanderbilt University Press, 1995.

———. "Dewey's Metaphysics." In Richard Rorty, *The Consequences of Pragmatism,* pp. 72–89. Minneapolis: University of Minnesota Press, 1982.

———. "Freud and Moral Reflection." In *Pragmatism's Freud: The Moral Disposition of Psychoanalysis,* edited by Joseph H. Smith and William Kerrigan, pp. 1–27. Baltimore: Johns Hopkins University Press, 1986.

———. "Habermas, Derrida and Philosophy." In Richard Rorty, *Truth and Progress,* pp. 307–326. Philosophical Papers, vol. 3. Cambridge: Cambridge University Press, 1998.

———. "Pragmatism Without Method." In Richard Rorty, *Objectivism, Relativism and Truth,* p. 65. Philosophical Papers, vol. 1. Cambridge: Cambridge University Press, 1991.

———. "Science as Solidarity." In Richard Rorty, *Objectivity, Relativism and Truth,* pp. 35–45. Philosophical Papers, vol. 1. Cambridge: Cambridge University Press, 1991.

Rosenfield, L. "Niels Bohr in the 1930s." In *Niels Bohr: His Life and Work as Seen by His Colleagues,* edited by S. Rozental, pp. 114–146. New York: Wiley, 1967.

Ross, Dorothy. *G. Stanley Hall: The Psychologist as Prophet.* Chicago: University of Chicago Press, 1972.

Rozental, S., ed. *Niels Bohr: His Life and Work as Seen by His Colleagues.* New York: Wiley, 1967.

Ryan, Alan. *John Dewey and the High Tide of American Liberalism.* New York: Norton, 1995.

Ryder, John. "Introduction." In *American Philosophic Naturalism in the Twentieth Century,* pp. 9–26. Amherst, N.Y.: Prometheus Books, 1994.

Santayana, George. "Dewey's Naturalistic Metaphysics." In *John Dewey: The Later Works,* vol. 3: *1929–1930,* edited by Jo Ann Boydston, pp. 367–384. Carbondale: Southern Illinois University Press, 1981.

Schack, William. *Art and Argyrol: The Life and Career of Albert C. Barnes.* New York: T. Yoseloff, 1963.

Schlossman, Steven L. "Before Home Start: Notes Towards a History of Parent Education in America, 1897–1929." *Harvard Educational Review* 46 (1976): 436–467.

———. "Philanthropy and the Gospel of Child Development." *History of Education Quarterly,* Fall 1981, 285–288.

Schneider, D. E. "The Growth Concept of Nervous Integration, V: The Theoretic Formulations and the Basic Equations of Heat Production, Body Mass, Body Length, Body Area, Brain Weight, Cord Weight and Electroencephalographic Frequency— Basis for an Electroencephalographic Method of Determining Basal Metabolism." *Growth* 8 (1944): 43–51.

Schneider, Herbert. "The Unnatural." In *Naturalism and the Human Spirit,* edited by Yervant Krikorian, pp. 121–132. New York: Columbia University Press, 1944.

Seigfried, Charlene Haddock. *Pragmatism and Feminism: Reweaving the Social Fabric.* Chicago: University of Chicago Press, 1996.

Senn, Milton J. *Insights about the Child Development Movement in the United States.* Monograph of the Society for Research in Child Development, vol. 40, nos. 3–4. Chicago: University of Chicago Press, 1975.

Shankle, William R., Kimball A. Romney, Benjamin H. Landing, and Junko Hara. "Developmental Patterns in the Cytoarchitecture of the Human Cerebral Cortex from Birth to 6 Years Examined by Correspondence Analysis." *Proceedings of the National Academy of Sciences* 95 (1998): 4023–4028.

Shea, Christine M. "The Ideology of Mental Health and the Emergence of the Therapeutic Liberal State: The American Mental Hygiene Movement, 1900–1930." Ph.D. thesis, University of Illinois at Urbana-Champaign, 1980.

Shook, John R. *Dewey's Empirical Theory of Knowledge and Reality.* Nashville, Tenn.: Vanderbilt University Press, 2000.

Sidis, Boris. *The Foundations of Normal and Abnormal Psychology.* Boston: Badger, 1914.

Sleeper, Ralph. *The Necessity of Pragmatism.* New Haven, Conn.: Yale University Press, 1986.

Smith, J. Roy. "The Electroencephalogram during Normal Infancy and Childhood I: Rhythmic Activities Present in the Neonate and Their Subsequent Development." *Journal of Genetic Psychology* 53 (1938): 431–453.

———. "The Electroencephalogram during Normal Infancy and Childhood II: The Nature of Growth of Alpha Waves." *Journal of Genetic Psychology* 53 (1938): 455–469.

———. "The Frequency Growth of the Human Alpha Rhythms during Normal Infancy and Childhood." *Journal of Psychology* 7 (1941): 177–198.

———. "The Occipital and Pre-Central Alpha Rhythms during the First Two Years." *Journal of Psychology* 7 (1939): 223–227.

Smith, Meredith. *Education and the Integration of Behavior.* New York: Teachers College, 1927.

Smith, Roger. *Inhibition: History and Meaning in the Sciences of Mind and Brain.* Berkeley: University of California Press, 1992.

Smuts, Alice. *The National Research Council Committee on Child Development and the Founding of the Society for Research in Child Development, 1925–1933.* Monographs of the Society for Research in Child Development, vol. 50 (serial no. 6). Chicago: University of Chicago Press, 1986.

Stenberg, Charles, and Joseph Campos. "The Development of Anger Expressions in

Infancy." In *Psychological and Biological Approaches to Emotion*, edited by N. L. Stein, B. Leventhal, and T. Trabasso, pp. 247–282. Hillsdale, N.J.: Erlbaum, 1990.

Sternberg, Robert J. "A Propulsion Model of Types of Creative Contributions." *Review of General Psychology* 3 (1999): 83–100.

Sternglass, Ernest. *Before the Big Bang: The Origins of the Universe and the Nature of Matter.* 2nd ed. London: Four Walls Eight Windows, 2001.

Stockings, George W. "Lamarckianism in American Social Science, 1890–1915." *Journal of the History of Ideas* 23 (1962): 239–256.

Sulloway, Frank. *Freud: Biologist of the Mind: Beyond the Psychoanalytic Legend.* New York: Basic Books, 1979.

Taylor, Charles. "How is Mechanism Conceivable." In *Philosophical Papers*, Vol. 1: *Human Agency and Language*, edited by Charles Taylor, pp. 164–186. Cambridge: Cambridge University Press, 1994.

———. "Reply and Rearticulation." In *Philosophy in an Age of Pluralism: The Philosophy of Charles Taylor in Question*, edited by James Tully, pp. 213–257. New York: Cambridge University Press, 1994.

Thelen, Esther. "Reply to Dalton." *American Psychologist* 51 (1996): 552–553.

———. "The Role of Motor Development in Developmental Psychology: A View of the Past and an Agenda for the Future." In *Contemporary Topics in Developmental Psychology*, edited by Nancy Eisenberg, pp. 1–13. New York: Wiley, 1987.

Thelen, Esther, and Karen E. Adolf. "Arnold L. Gesell: The Paradox of Nature and Nurture." *Developmental Psychology* 28 (1992): 368–380.

Tilney, Frederick. "The Genesis of Cerebellar Functions." *Archives of Neurology and Psychology* 1 (1923): 137–169.

———. *Master of Destiny.* New York: Hoeber, 1929; reprint, New York: Doubleday, 1968.

———. "Neurology and Education." *Archives of Neurology and Psychiatry* 16 (1926): 539–554.

Tilney, Frederick, and Lawrence Kubie. "Behavior in Its Relationship to the Development of the Brain." *Bulletin of the Neurological Institute of New York* 1 (1931): 226–313.

Warner, Francis. *The Nervous System of the Child: Its Growth and Health in Education.* New York: Macmillan, 1900.

Wasserman, Stanley, and Katherine Faust. *Social Network Analysis: Methods and Applications.* London and New York: Cambridge University Press, 1997.

Weinbach, A. C. "Contour Maps, Center of Gravity, Moment of Inertia and Surface of the Human Body." *Human Biology* 10 (1938): 356–371.

———. "The Human Growth Curve, I: Prenatal." *Growth* 5 (1941): 217–233.

———. "The Human Growth Curve, II: Birth to Puberty." *Growth* 5 (1941): 233–255.

———. "Some Physiological Phenomena Fitted to Growth Equations I: Moro Reflex." *Human Biology* 1 (1937): 549–555.

———. "Some Physiological Phenomena Fitted to Growth Equations II: Brain Potentials." *Human Biology* 10 (1938): 145–150.

———. "Some Physiological Phenomena Fitted to Growth Equations III: Rate of Growth of Brain Potentials (Alpha Frequency) Compared with Rate of Growth of the Brain." *Growth* 2 (1938): 247–251.

———. "Some Physiological Phenomena Fitted to Growth Equations IV: Time and Power Relations for a Human Infant Climbing Inclines of Various Slopes." *Growth* 4 (1938): 123–134.

Westbrook, Robert. *John Dewey and American Democracy.* Ithaca, N.Y.: Cornell University Press, 1991.

———. "On the Private Life of a Public Philosopher: John Dewey in Love." *Teachers College Record* 96 (1994): 183–197.

Wetzel, Norman C. "On the Motion of Growth, XVII: Theoretical Foundations." *Growth* 1 (1937): 6–59.

White, Morton G. *A Philosopher's Story.* University Park: Pennsylvania State University Press, 1999.

———. *Social Thought in America: The Revolt against Formalism.* New York: Viking, 1949.

———. *The Origins of Dewey's Instrumentalism.* New York: Columbia University Press, 1943.

White, Sheldon H. "Three Visions of a Psychology of Education." In *Culture, Schooling and Psychological Development,* edited by L. T. Landsmann, pp. 1–39. Norwood, N.J.: Ablex, 1991.

Williams, L. Pearce. *Michael Faraday.* New York: Basic Books, 1965.

Wilson, Daniel. "Fertile Ground: Pragmatism, Science and Logical Positivism." In *Pragmatism: From Progressivism to Postmodernism,* edited by Robert Hollinger and David Depew, pp. 123–145. Westport, Conn.: Praeger, 1997.

Windle, W. F. "Correlation between the Development of Local Reflexes and the Reflex Arcs in the Spinal Cord of Cat Embryos." *Journal of Comparative Neurology* 59 (1934): 487–505.

———. *The Pioneering Role of Clarence Luther Herrick in American Neuroscience.* Hicksville, N.Y.: Exposition Press, 1979.

Windsor, Charlotte, ed. *Experimental Schools Revisited: Bulletins of the Bureau of Educational Experiments.* New York: Schocken Books, 1973.

Wundt, Wilhelm. *The Principles of Physiological Psychology.* Trans. E. T. Titchner. New York: Krause, 1969; orig. pub. 1874.

Yezierska, Anzia. *All I Could Never Be.* New York: Brewer, Warren and Putnam, 1932.

Zeeger S. L., and S. D. Harlow. "Mathematical Models from Laws of Growth to Tools for Biologic Analysis: Fifty Years of Growth." *Growth* 51 (1987): 1–21.

Zelazo, Philip R., Phillippe Robaey, and Marthe Bonin. "The Development of Movement Related Brain Potentials with Exercise of the Neuromotor Stepping Pattern in 14 week-old Infants." Poster presented at the Society for Research in Child Development, Albuquerque, N.M., April 15–18, 1999.

INDEX

Page numbers in italic type refer to illustrations.

Absolute Idea, 380
Absolute Spirit. *See* Hegelian Absolute
Addams, Jane, 81, 112
Adler, Alfred, 119
Adolescence (Hall), 44
aesthetic expression, 163–165
aesthetic form, definition of, 159
aesthetic perception, 57, 154, 155, 159–160, 162–
   163, 200, 319n22
affirmative proposition, 16–17, 283
"agnostic," coining of, 32
Alexander, Albert R., 121, 233
Alexander, Frederick M., 3, 12, 13, *99*, 105–
   106, 107, 127, 133, 139–140, 237. *See also*
   Alexander's Technique
Alexander, Thomas, 277
Alexander's Technique, 97–98, 101, 307n40;
   and consciousness, 120–122; Dewey's interest in, 97, 98–99, 114, 118–119, 121–122,
   145, 311n55, 312nn60,62; Hegelian implica-
   tions of, 121–122; lack of scientific investiga-
   tion of, 99, 233; opposition to, 100; test of,
   233–234
American naturalism, 9
American Philosophical Association, 3
*American Philosophical Naturalism in the Twenti-
   eth Century* (Ryder), 9
American Psychological Association, 3
American school of neurology, 11, 52, 65–66
American school of psychobiology, 208
Anderson, Harold, 192
Anderson, John, 188
Angell, James, 64, 180
anticipatory behavior, 139
applied intelligence, 185–187
Aquinas, Thomas, 196
Argyrol, 152
Aristotle, 9
art: Dewey on, 14–15, 57, 154–156, 157–160; at
   Hermitage, 150; impressionistic, 155; mod-
   ern, 154–156; post-impressionistic, 3, 152,
   155, 156–160, 166; relationship to science,
   114, 163–165

Art as Experience (Dewey), 3, 31, 57, 159, 161,
   162–163, 166–167, 173, 200, 211, 227, 277
The Art in Painting (Barnes), 154
artificial intelligence, 282
Augustine (Saint), 196–197
axial gradient theory, 68–69

Baars, Bernard, 7
Babies Hospital, 208, 210, 216
Babinski reflex, 235
Baconian science, 25
Baer, Kurt von, 34
Baldwin, Bird, 186, 188
Baldwin, James Mark, 63, 75, 76, 79, 130,
   304n32
bare acquiescence, 222, 226
Barnes, Albert, *153;* and Alexander's Tech-
   nique, 119; art collection of, 152–153; back-
   ground of, 150–152; and history of art, 154,
   155; and Matisse, 156–157, *157;* relationship
   with Dewey, 3, 12, 107, 114, 153–154, 158
Barnes Foundation, 153
Barnes Museum, 153, 156
bashfulness, 75
Bayley, Nancy, 188, 190
BEE. *See* Bureau of Educational Experiments
*Before Head Start: The Iowa Welfare Research
   Station and America's Children* (Cravens), 5
behavior: anticipatory, 139; development,
   theory of, 214–216; reflexive, 214, *214,*
   217–218
Behavior, Knowledge, and Fact (Bentley), 268
behaviorism, 7, 101, 142, 143, 183–184, 225,
   249, 307n48; behaviorism/conditioning
   theory, 183
belief, and probability, 27–28
Benjamin, H. R., 244–245
Bentley, Arthur, 208, 255, 258, 259, 266–267,
   268, 281–282
Benton, Thomas Hart, 154
Berkeley Institute, 188, 192
Bernstein, Richard, 18, 107, 275–276
Binet, Alfred, 188

The Birth of Tragedy (Nietzsche), 159
bisexuality, 130
Blake, Casey, 110, 309n20
Boaz, Franz, 68, 97, 101
body sense, 233
Bohr, Niels, 166, 236, 245, 315n16; debate with
  Heisenberg, 170–172; and Jane Dewey, 14,
  48, 151, 168–168, *169*, 170
Bois-Reymond, Emil du, 44
Boltzmann, Ludwig, 162, 164, 166, 212
Bourne, Randolph: criticism of Dewey, 12, 104–
  105, 111, 112, 118, 120, 144, 150, 204, 271;
  criticism of education, 90–91, 92–93, 108–
  109, *109;* death of, 113; and *New Republic,*
  309nn32,34; and New York avant-garde, 94;
  relationship with Evelyn Dewey, 92; support
  of Dewey by, 279
Boydston, Jo Ann, 296n3, 303n17, 310n45
brain, 69, 76–77, 145, 291. *See also* develop-
  ment, McGraw's theory of; growth; neuro-
  biology; neuroembryology
Braque, Georges, 155
Breeze, K., 246, 336n65
Bridgman, Percy, 267, 281
Brill, Ernst, 94, 95, 133
British Utilitarians, 47
Brokemeyer, Henry, 37
Brooks, Van Wyck, 94, 104–105, 107
Brownlow, Louis, 181
Brucke, Ernst, 130
Buermeyer, Lawrence, 153
Buhler, Charlotte, 205
Bureau of Educational Experiments (BEE),
  180, 181, 188, 199; and Alexander's Tech-
  nique, 97, 99–101, 307n40; Evelyn Dewey's
  resignation from, 105; founding of, 93, 96–
  97, 203; reestablishing scientific focus at,
  101–103, 109
Burke, Edmund, 196, 197
Burke, Tom, 281
Burns, Arthur, 210
Butler, Joseph, 27–28, 297n20
Butler, Samuel, 10, 29–32, 34, 36, 45, 59

Calvinism, 24, 25–27, 28, 32–33, 39, 184
Cannon, Walter, 134
Carnap, Rudolf, 260, 261, 267
Carnegie Corporation, 191
Carnegie Foundation, 180
Carnegie Institution, 210
Carpenter, William, 56
Casals, Pablo, 94

cathetic energy, 131, 315n16
Cattell, James, 44, 113
Center for Dewey Studies, 106, 284, 296n3,
  303n17
Cézanne, Paul, 152, 155
Chalmers, David, 288, 289
Chambers, Whittaker, 276
Charcot, Jean-Martin, 130
Child, C. M., 11, 68, 70, 133, 175–176, 208, 209
child development: doubt as intrinsic to, 223–
  226; feminization of research on, 190, 191
child development study: heredity vs. environ-
  ment, 188–189; individual behavior/person-
  ality, 189; motor development/emotional
  control, 188; norms of early development,
  187, 189–190; parent-child interaction, 189.
  See also individual researcher
child-rearing: advice, rising demand for, 191;
  practices study, 193
Child Study Association of America, 182,
  323n20
child study movement, 5
Children's Bureau, 190
Children's School. *See* Walden School
China, 149, 205
Chipman, Alice. *See* Dewey, Alice Chipman
Chisholm, Corinne, 150, 158, 166, 171, 211–
  212, 215, 321n65
civil rights, 277
Civilization and Its Discontent (Naumberg), 105
Clark University, 66, 67
Clauswitz, Karl von, 112
Clayton, 309n32
"co-consciousness," 289
Coghill, George E., 11, 235, 236; and Alexan-
  der's Technique, 99; influence on Dewey, 66,
  213; influence on McGraw, 66, 213, 215, 216;
  and NCDS, 210, 213; on reflexive behavior,
  214, 217–218; salamander study of, 239
Cohen, Morris, 6
Cold War, 276, 277
collective unconscious, 105
College of Physicians and Surgeons, 208,
  210, 216
Collins, Randall, 293n2
Columbia University, 3, 11, 12, 93, 96, 104,
  130, 176, 177, 182, 185, 208, 257
common-sense realism, 37
Commonwealth Fund, 191
communication, human, 139, 273; as a generic
  trait, 13, 139
communism, 195, 197

comparative anatomy, 35
complacency vs. habit, 315n25
complementarity, 172–174, 315
compossibility, 172
Concord School, 38
Conel, J. LeRoy, 238, 239
Congregationalist, 24, 29
Congress for Cultural Freedom, 276
consciousness, 281; and Alexander's Technique, 120–122; Bohr on, 172; Damasio on, 342n22; Dewey on, 50–51; Dewey on physics of, 171; difficulty defining, 142–143; distinction between mind and, 142; experiments by Dewey on, 45–47; Hegel on, 222; C. L. Herrick on, 65; and memory, 141–142; neurobehavioral theory of development of, 242–243, *243;* relationship to judgment/emotions, 7, 226, 272, 279; revery, 141; role in transforming human behavior, 216, 217; stream of, 142; traits that emerge with development of, 199–200. *See also* self-consciousness
The Consequences of Pragmatism (Rorty), 5
Constructive Conscious Control of the Individual (Alexander), 119, 120
Contemporary Review, 29, 38
contingency, 286; of order, 218–220
continuity, 53, 262
contradiction, 222
convertibility/reversibility, 56–57, 163
Cooke, Morris, 116
Coolidge, Elizabeth, 96, 97
cooperative education, 149
coordination, processes of, 201
Cope, Edward, 10
Correlation and Conservation of Forces (Grove), 56
Cotkin, George, 1–2
Cravens, Hamilton, 5
cross-reference, 77
Crowley, Herbert, 112
Crowley, Walter, 309n32
Crutch, Joseph Wood, 154
cultural diversity, 111, 277
cultural liberalism, 276–277
culture, 104–105, 107, 127, 146
Cuvier, George, 35

Dainton, Barry, 289
Damasio, Antonio, 288, 342n22
Dammann, Vera, 248
The Dance (mural), 156–157, *157,* 159, 211
Darwin, Charles, 41, 275

Darwinian evolution, 9, 10, 35; Butler attack on, 29, 30–32; and Dewey, 59–61, 63, 74, 110, 279, 285, 286; of human emotion, 130; and Huxley, 29, 33; Mivart critique of, 30; Torrey critique of, 37
Davenport, Charles B., 95, 210, 244
Delacroix, Eugène, 154, 155
Dell, Floyd, 103
democracy, 4–5, 179–180, 194–195, 256, 274, 277
Democracy and Education (Dewey), 86–87, 95
Descartes, René, 9, 129, 140, 270, 285
determinism, 142, 191, 201–204, 286
development, McGraw's theory of, 220–223
developmental theory of human bisexuality, 130
Dewey, Alice Chipman (JD's wife), 48, 62, 75, 82, 87, 97, 105, 113, 121, 150, 206
Dewey, Archibald (JD's father), 23–24
Dewey, Evelyn (JD's daughter), 48, 150, 176; and Alexander's Technique, 99, 100, 313n67; and BEE, 97, 100–101, 105; and Bourne, 113; critique of naturalism of, 107; emotional behavior of, 105, 106, 308n7; evaluation of experimental school by, 87–88; influence of Huxley on, 101; resigns from BEE, 105; on Tilney/McGraw research, 210
Dewey, Frederick (JD's son), 115, 150
Dewey, Jane (JD's daughter): biography by, 23, 257; Dewey visits in Vienna, 206; and quantum theory, 167, 168, 169–170, 171–172; work with Niels Bohr, 48, 151
Dewey, John (JD), *50, 75, 99, 153, 207;* and Alexander's Technique, 97, 98–99, 114, 118–119, 121–122, 145; analysis of intellectually formative years of, 257–260; becomes emeritus, 160; and BEE, 99, 102, 199, 202; bust of, *160,* 160–161; children of, 48, 115, 150 (*see also* Dewey, Evelyn; Dewey, Jane); collaborative nature of, 5–6, 264; college years of, 23, 29, 32, 37, 38; at Columbia University, 3, 11, 12, 104, 177, 182, 209, 257; commonalities with Freud, 129–130, 134–135, 145; criticism of, by Bentley, 255; criticism of, by Nagel, 169, 200, 248, 261–262; defends Trotsky, 117, 197–198; drops Hegel, 51, 52–54; early teaching jobs of, 36–37, 39; equanimity of, 198; evangelical bent at University of Michigan, 47–48; fame/popularity of, 149; family background of, 23–24; formative experiences of, 1, 2–5; influence of Butler on, 27–28, 31; influence of Coghill on, 66, 213; influence of Hall on, 43–45; influence of Hegel on, 8–

9, 16, 43–44, 49; influence of C. L. Herrick on, 66; influence of Huxley on, 32–33, 35, 36; influence of McGraw on, 2–3, 4, 16, 219, 222, 246; influence of Maxwell on, 301n50; influence of Mead on, 300n31; influence of Morris on, 42–43, 47; as introvert, 117–118; at Johns Hopkins, 8, 37, 38, 42–43, 51, 76; at Josiah Macy, Jr. Foundation, 182–183, 186, 210, 233, 324n23; Matisse sketch of, *158;* modesty of, 117, 203, 208; on NCDS advisory council, 209, 210; personal relationship with Barnes, 3, 12, 107, 114, 153–154, 158; personal relationship with McGraw, 114–115, 150, 204–205, 206–207, *207,* 250–251; Ph.D. program of, 8, 37, 38, 42–43, 51, 76; poetry writing of, 115–116, 310n45; presents Gifford Lectures in Natural Theology, 167, 168, 206; publishes writings on mind and evolution, 38–39; relationship with F. M. Alexander, 12, 118; relationship with Nagel, 62, 64, 261–262; religious upbringing of, 26–27, 33, 41, 48, 278–279; rivalry with Gesell, 203; romantic liaisons of, 114, 115; silence on involvement in McGraw's studies, 249–251; on term "experience," 310n49; travels to China, 205; travels to Europe, 169–170; travels to Nova Scotia, 206; travels to Scotland, 167, 168, 206; travels to Vienna, 206; at University of Chicago, 11, 62, 64, 82; at University of Michigan, 47–49; at University of Minnesota, 49; at University of Vermont, 29, 37; and U.S. involvement in World War I, 12, 106–108, 111, 204; weakness in knowledge of science of, 41; wife of, 115 (*see also* Dewey, Alice Chipman)

Dewey, Lucina Rich (JD's mother), 24, 26, 27
Dewey, Morris (JD's son), 150
Dewey, Roberta (JD's second wife), 115
Dewey's Suppressed Psychology (Klyce), 117
Dial (journal), 86, 94, 107, 112–113
diamagnetism, 55
differentiation, 34
Diggins, John, 4, 5
Dilthey, Wilhelm, 287
displacement, 55–56
dissociation, 46
Division of Developmental Psychology (APA), 188
doctrine of the elect, 24
Donaldson, Henry, 11, 68–69
dream interpretation, 127
dualism, 7, 36, 115, 142–143, 269, 288

"The Duality of Experience" (Chisholm), 211–212
Dykhuizen, George, 23

Eastman, Max, 23, 26, 43, 94–95, 104, 113, 306n30
Eddinger Plan, 91
Edelman, Gerald, 287, 290
Edman, Irwin, 257
education: cooperative, 149; criticism of, by Bourne, 90–91, 92–93, 108–109, *109;* parent-education group, 186–187, 191, 324–325n26, 325n27; as social control, 89–90
Education and the Integration of Behavior (Meredith Smith), 133
educational reform: and Dewey, 33 (*see also* Laboratory school [University of Chicago]); Fairhope School, 88, 105; Gary Plan, 88, 90–91, 92–93, 95; Huxley's proposals for, 33, 86; Montessori School, 87, 88, 93, 105, 313n67; Play School, 88, 93, 97, 100, 101, 105; public appeal for, 85–86; in Russia, 149; Walden School, 195, 313n67
educational system, German vs. American, 108
Edwards, Johnathan, 25
Edwards, Katherine, 77
Einstein, Albert, 14, 151, 167, 170, 301n53, 318n5
Ellis, Frederick, 95, 97, 99, 101, 102–103
Ely, Richard, 266
embryogenesis, 316n33
embryology, 34, 35, 78
emergent realism, 283
Emerson, Ralph Waldo, 29
Emmons, Nathaniel, 25–26
emotional: experience, developmental roots of, 77–80; introvert, 117; set, 189
emotions: animal, 78–79; human, 78, 79, 80, 130, 226, 279
Enlightenment, 178
entropy, 57, 58, 128, 133, 164, 166–167, 211, 212–213, 243, 244, 245
environment, effect on genius, 1–2
epistemological realism, in philosophy, 7; Dewey's rejection of, 7
Epstein, Jacob, 160–161
equality of opportunity, 111
erect locomotion: Dewey on, 208–209, 232, 245–246, 334n33; McGraw analysis of, 233–234, 238, 242, 246–248, *247*
Erewhon (Butler), 29–30, 31
Essays in Experimental Logic (Dewey), 116, 259

essentialism, 129

Evolution, Old and New (Butler), 30

"The Evolutionary Method as Applied to Morality" (Dewey), 80

evolutionary theory: of conscious control, 114; of human emotion, 130

evolutionism, 38, 40. *See also* Darwinian evolution

experience, phenomenology of, 14–15

"experience": Dewey on, 310n49

Experience and Nature (Dewey), 12–13, 17, 125–126, 128–129, 131, 132, 139–140, 141, 143, 144–145, 155, 201, 208, 216, 224, 255–256, 261, 273, 317n48

experimental science, 128, 129

experimentalism, 274; of Dewey, 7, 9–10, 116, 173–174, 257, 279; of Faraday, 53–54; German, 52; of Ratner, 260

The Expression of Emotions in Animal and Man (Darwin), 78

expressivism, and instrumentalism, 286–288

extrovert, 117

The Fair Haven (Butler), 29

Fairhope School, 88, 105

Faraday, Michael, 11, 41, 42, 53–54, 55–56, 57, 171, 176, 301n53

Fechner, Gustave, 10

Federation of Child Study. *See* Child Study Association of America

Fernald, Grace, 94, 101, 307n47

Ferrier, David, 69

Fichte, Johann Gottlieb, 9

field theory, 142, 151, 192

Fisk, John, 10

Flexner, Abraham, 91

Fliess, Wilhelm, 130, 131, 320n49

foreground/background, 10, 52, 225, 263–264, 290

Fortnightly Review, 29, 38

forward reference, 215

Foucault, Michel P., 274–275, 277

Frank, Alma, 234

Frank, Lawrence K., 234; child study network of, 3, 15, 176, 177, 275, 325n30; collaborative work of, 324n26; differences with Dewey on developmental processes, 237–238; on energy, 334n33; and Freudian psychoanalysis, 192–193, 280; at Josiah Macy, Jr. Foundation, 182–183, *183*, 185–186, 324n23; monitors child development studies at GEB, 210; parent education model of, 186–187; and

Play School, 97; and science of childhood, 187–190; tests Alexander's Technique, 233; on transaction, as operational term, 268–269; tribute to/admiration of, 181–182, 323n19

Frank, Waldo, 94, 104–105, 107, 110, 112

free will, 25, 28, 30

Freud, Sigmund, 119, 133, *134*, 315nn16,17; acceptance of child development theory of, 250; on childhood trauma, 249; commonalities with Dewey, 129–130, 134–135, 145; gender bias of, 106; on individual identity, 105; on inhibition, 74; on learning, 223; on Mach, 320n49; meeting with Kempf, 134; on natural growth process, 199; and normal/moral development, 199; on pain/pleasure, 79; source of clinical theory, 316n31; theory of mind of, 127–128, 135, 136, 140, 141–142, 270, 271

Freudianism, 15, 18, 184, 195, 315nn16,17; Dewey's critique of, 13, 107, 118, 122–123, 126, 129, 135, 193, 196, 238, 279–280, 314n6; influence/popularity of, 12, 184, 191, 192; McGraw's critique of, 206; moral fallacies of, 122–124. *See also* psychoanalysis

Frith, Chris, 291

Frith, Uta, 291

Froebel, Friedrich W. A., 87

functional specification, 34

functionalism, 34, 228–229, 286

Gadamer, Hans Georg, 275

Galileo, 72, 129, 228, 274, 275

Gallese, Vittorio, 290

Gardner, Howard, 2

Gary Plan, 88, 90–91, 92–93, 95

General Education Board (GEB), 230

generic proposition, 219

generic traits, 13–14, 18; Hook on, 263–264, 265; in human experience/development, 216–218, 219–220; as known through inquiry, 261–262; Rorty on, 265

genetic latency, 220

genius, effect of environment on, 1–2

Germany, 107–108, 111–112, 113

Gesell, Arnold, 102, 103, 189–190, 205; on behavioral traits, 220, 221; on child development, 184–185, 202–204, *204*, 210, 215, 216, 218, 219; McGraw's theoretical differences with, 220, 221, 248, 249, 324n25

Gifford Lectures in Natural Theology, 167, 168, 206

Gilman, Daniel, 42, 44
Goldman, Alvin, 290
Goltz, Friedrich, 69
Gooding, David, 54
Gottlieb, Gilbert, 215–216, 242, 302n6
Grant, Julia, 190, 326n44
Greeks, ancient, 168
Groffman, Bernard, 293n2
Grove, William, 56, 57
growth: embryological, 217; energetics of human, 243–245; of judgment, 71–74; logic of, 289
Growth (McGraw), 220
The Growth of the Brain: A Study of the Nervous System in Relation to Education (Donaldson), 69
guilt, 196; and anxiety, 123; and sin, 184

Habermas, Jürgen, 275
Haeckel, Ernst, 34, 78, 130, 316n31
Hall, G. Stanley, 42, *43*, 43–45, 51, 67, 133–134, 258
Handbook of Psychology (Baldwin), 304n32
Harlow, S. D., 245
Harper, William, 64, 65, 66, 68, 82
Harris, William Torrey, 9, 37–38, 44
Hartmann, Eduard von, 31
Harvard University, 25, 49, 234
Head Start, 189
Healy, William, 94
Hegel, Georg W. F., 6, 13, 18, 29, 41, 47, 248, 294n6; Absolute Spirit of, 110, 178, 245, 285; on consciousness, 222; criticism of, by Ratner, 260; on culture, 127; Dewey distances from, 51, 52–54, 257–260; dialectic of consciousness of, 222; on German world historical role, 107–108; idealism of, 10, 43, 285, 286; influence on Dewey, 8–9, 16, 43–44, 49; naturalism of, 231; and Newton's theory of gravitation, 56; notion of mediated knowledge of, 61. *See also* St. Louis Hegelians
Hegelian Absolute, 9, 51–54, 110, 118, 177, 178–180, 245, 258, 285, 286
Hegelianism: connection with Alexander's Technique, 121–122; decline of, 51, 52–54, 257–260; of Dewey, 3–4, 8–9
"Hegel's Philosophy of Spirit" (Dewey), 178
Heidegger, Johann H., 274–275
Heisenberg, Werner, 14, 15, 151, 168, *169*, 170–172, 245
Hemholtz, Hermann von, 54–55, 57, 65, 69
Henry Street Settlement, 105
The Here and Now Story Book (L. Mitchell), 103

hereditary/environmental determinism, 191, 201–204, 322n2
Hering, Ewald, 31
heritability, 60
Herrick, C. J., 11, 59, 66, 101, 208, 213–214, 231, *232*, 234, 301nn62,63, 302nn3,6, 332n5
Herrick, C. L., 11, 52, 65–66, *67*, 70, 76, 175–176, 208, 209, 302n6, 307n48
Heyl, Katherine Agate, 329n35
Hickman, Larry, 284–285, 340n1
Hinkle, Beatrice, 94, 105, 106, 117–118
Hobbes, Thomas, 196
Hodge, Richard Morse, 118
Holt, Edwin, 94
Holt, Robert, 315n16
Holtzmann, Karl, 54
Hook, Sidney, 6, 18, 107, 197, 216, 256, 257, 260, 261, 263–264, 265, 274, 275
"How Children Grow" (Sawtell study), 102
How We Think (Dewey), 86–87
Howison, George, 37
Hull House, 81
human ancestry, according to Huxley, 35–36
human development, biological mechanism governing, 332–333n5
human intelligence, 32, 138, 176, 199, 209, 237, 279
human language acquisition, 35, 139
Human Nature and Conduct (Dewey), 12, 107, 120, 121, 123, 126, 127, 201, 231
Hume, David, 28
Hungry Hearts (Yezierska), 115, 116
Hurley, Susan, 290
Huxley, Thomas H., 10, 29, 32–36, 40, 41, 42, 54, 59, 78, 99, 101, 176

idealism, 9, 38, 110, 142, 285; German, 44; of Hegel, 10, 43, 285, 286; and Morris, 42–43
idealization, 46
identity, 196, 222
if-then conditional statement, 262
imitative realism, 79–80
immortality, 29
impressionism, 155
indeterminacy, 173, 217
inhibition: and Alexander's Technique, 98; Dewey's theory of neural, 74–76; evolution of, 74–76; and reflex, 214
inquiry, of Dewey, 9, 57, 257; Coghill's influence on, 213; developmental origins of, 16–17; and mechanistic brain function, 235–236; mind as embedded in, 284; role of

self-consciousness in, 10; using science to
understand, 249–250
inquiry, renewed interest in Dewey's theory:
by Burke, 281–282; by Hickman, 284; by
Shook, 282–283
instrumental naturalism, 284
instrumentalism, and expressivism, 286–288
integration, 333n26; of brain and behavior, 201, 221, 223; and interaction,
235–236
intelligence: applied, 185–187; artificial, 282;
human, 32, 176, 199, 209, 237, 279; interested, 195–196
Intelligence in the Modern World (Ratner), 260
intelligence test, 92, 102–103, 188–189
intelligent pacifist, 112
interactionism, 55, 61, 235–236, 238, 307n48.
See also integration
introspection, 140–141
introvert, 117
I.Q. test, 102–103, 188–189
irreversibility, 164

Jackson, J. Huglings, 130
James, William, 1–2, 7, 8, 37, 49, 51, 63, 70, 79,
142, 151, 167
Japan, 149
Jastrow, Joseph, 44
Jellife, Smith Ely, 94, 134
Johns Hopkins University, 8, 37, 38, 42–43, 47,
76, 101, 266
Johnson, Buford, 101, 102
Jones, Ernest, 94
Jones, Frank, 193, 233, 311n14
Jones, George, 99–100
Jones, Harold, 189
Jones, Mary Cover, 189, 192
Jordan, David Starr, 116
Josiah Macy, Jr. Foundation, 182–183, 186,
210, 232, 233, 323–324n23
Joule, James P., 54
*Journal of Comparative Neurology and
Psychology*, 66
The Journal of Speculative Philosophy, 37, 38
judgment, 200; critique of Dewey's views on,
284–285; development of, 71–74, 222–223;
Dewey's theories on role of, 203; as distinct
from proposition, 16; evolution of, 135–136;
and memory, 144; quantitative, 228, 236–
237; relationship to consciousness/emotions,
226, 279; role in cognitive development, 87;
role of inhibition in, 269
Jung, Carl, 94, 105, 117, 119, 130

Kallen, Horace, 118
Kant, Immanuel, 9, 29, 43, 46, 50, 111, 129,
178, 258, 279, 285
Kast, Ludwig, 210, 233. *See also* Josiah Macy,
Jr. Foundation
Kelly, Florence, 94
Kempf, Edward J., 131–134
Kepler, Johannes, 72
Kilpatrick, William, 104
King, Martin Luther, Jr., 277
Klyce, Scudder, 114, 116–117, 271
Knowing and the Known (Dewey & Bentley),
255, 267, 281
Kubie, Lawrence, 315n18
Kuhn, Thomas, 57, 275, 301n57

Laboratory School (University of Chicago), 3,
70, 71, 77, 80–82, 86, 90, 97, 105, 176, 179–
180, 199, 202, 279
Lamarckianism, 68
language, 78, 139
Lashley, Karl, 101, 307nn47,48
Laura Spelman Rockefeller Foundation, 96
Laura Spelman Rockefeller Fund, 210
Laura Spelman Rockefeller Memorial (LSRM),
176, 180, 181, 182, 185, 186, 193
Lavine, Thelma, 267
law of conservation of energy, 54–55, 56, 58–
59, 130, 131, 244
law of effect, 184
law of the excluded middle, 262, 284
League for Independent Political Action
(LIPA), 327n56
League of Nations, 107, 111, 112, 113
Leibniz, Gottfried W., 53, 300n45
Levy, David, 206
Lewin, Kurt, 189, 191, 234
liberalism, 179
Life and Habit (Butler), 30–31
Linguistic Analysis of Mathematics (Bentley), 267
Lippman, Walter, 94, 194, 195, 309n32
Lloyd, Afred, 49
local segmented response, 214
Loeb, Jacques, 11, 68, 69–70, 94, 101, 107,
108, 130
Loeb, Leo, 70
"The Logic of Judgments of Practice"
(Dewey), 87
Logic: The Theory of Inquiry (Dewey), 3, 16,
150, 198, 200, 202, 213, 214, 222, 227, 235–
236, 237, 246, 248, 255, 259, 275, 287
logical atomism, 268
logical empiricism, 269

logical formalism, in philosophy, 7

logical positivism, 256, 259–260, 261, 263, 267, 269, 281–282

Long, Louis, 331n76

Lotze, Rudolf Hermann, 10, 65

LSRM. *See* Laura Spelman Rockefeller Memorial

McCormack, Eric, 118, 311nn54,55, 312nn60,62, 313n67

McDougall, Robert, 119

MacFarlane, Jean, 188, 192

McGraw, Myrtle: and Alexander's Technique, 233–234; analysis of erect locomotion, 233–234, 238, 246–248, *247;* analysis of prone locomotion, 240–241, *241;* analysis of sitting up, 239–240; on anticipatory response, 342n22; bidirectional theory of structure and function of, 241–242; collaboration with Dewey, 2–3, 4, 16, 31, 35, 44–45, 66, 69, 185, 186, 201, 233, 249, 250–251; critique of work of, 249; Dewey on importance of studies of, 207–208; dissertation of, 96, 205–206; on Evelyn Dewey, 106; and feminization of child research, 191; findings on judgment, 74; on genetic latency, 220; human growth studies by, 244–245; infant locomotion studies by, 203, 213, 221–222, 233–234, *241,* 336–337n65; infant study at Columbia, 130; influence of Coghill on, 66, 213, 215, 216; influence of Dewey on, 216, 224, 280; influence of Tilney on, 216; influence on Dewey, 2–3, 4, 16, 219, 222, 246; internship at Institute for Child Guidance, 206; and maturationist theory, 190, 218, *219;* motor ability studies by, 102, 202–203, 205–206; on neurobehavioral development, 217, 234–235, 238–242, *241, 243;* neuromuscular development studies of, 88; Normal Child Development Study of, 201, 208; personal relationship with Dewey, 114–115, 150, 204–205, 206–207, *207,* 250–251; on primitive reactions of infant, 217–218; Thelan's critique of, 241–242; her understanding of *Experience and Nature,* 125

McGraw, Myrtle, co-twin study, 250; benefit of early stimulation, 217, 218–219, *219,* 225; communicating with infant in, 224, 225; integrative neural function, 232–233; motor development in, 225–226; primary objective of, 217

Mach, Ernst, 10, 11, 142, 162, 261, 320n49

McIntosh, Rustin, 210

McLellan, James, 71–72, 200, 259

Madison, James, 179

"The Management of Tensions" (L. K. Frank), 192–193

Man's Place in Nature (Huxley), 35–36

Man's Supreme Inheritance (Alexander), 119, 120

Marsh, James, 29, 37

Marx, Karl, 196, 197

Marxism, 149, 196, 197

The Masses (journal), 94

materialism, 7, 38, 39–40, 142, 261, 285, 286

Matisse, Henri, 3, 14, 15, 151, 152, 155, 156–160, *157,* 165, 211

maturationist theory of development, 184–185, 202–204, 215, 216, 217, 219, 242, 248

Maxwell, James Clerk, 41, 42, 53, 55–56, 142, 162, 164, 165, 166, 167, 176, 301n50, 315, 336n65

Maxwellian physics, 14, 16, 56, 58, 151, 167, 176, 215, 229, 234, 244

Mayhew, Anna, 77

Mead, George Herbert, 49–50, 64, 300n31

Mead, Margaret, 182, 210

mediated knowledge, 61

Meek, Lois, 182, 205

memory, 31, 141–144

"Memory and Judgment" (Dewey), 143

mentalism, 61

"The Metaphysical Assumptions of Materialism" (Dewey), 38

metaphysics, 7

Mexico, 149, 197–198

Meyer, Adolf, 11, 66, 103, 132, 208

Meynert, Theodor, 130, 210

Mill, John Stuart, 47

mind: distinction from consciousness, 142; as spiritually significant, 285–286; universal, 270. *See also* theory of mind; theory of mind, of Dewey

mind in nature, 7, 13–14, 126–127

mind-body dualism, 7, 269

Minot, C. S., 45

Mitchell, John, 91

Mitchell, Lucy S., 11, 93–94, *96,* 107, 306n27. *See also* Bureau of Educational Experiments

Mitchell, Wesley, 11, 93–94, 107, 306nn27–28; and Alexander's Technique, 97, 99. *See also* Bureau of Educational Experiments

Mivart, St. George, 30–31, 297n27

modern art, origins of, 154–156

monads, 53

Montessori, Maria, 87, 88, 93, 105, 313n67

moral conduct, 58, 197

Morgan, Thomas Henry, 101
Moro reflex, 217, 218, 229, 235, 239
Morris, Charles, 8, 261
Morris, George Sylvester, 37, 42–43, 49, 258
motor response, 46–47, 79
Munro, Thomas, 153, 154
Murphy, Lois, 186

Nagel, Ernest, 9, 248, 257, 259, 328n4; and
    Dewey, 62, 64, 169, 200, 248, 261–262; and
    logical positivism, 256, 263
National Research Council (NRC), 182
naturalism, 7, 38; in art, 155–156; critique of
    Dewey's, 107, 341n10; critique of Evelyn
    Dewey, 107; demise of Dewey's, 17–19; of
    Dewey, 114; of Hegel, 231; of Huxley, 33;
    instrumental, 284; roots of American, 9;
    scientific, 9–11
naturalistic dualism, 288
naturalistic theory of aesthetics, 150
nature-versus-nurture, 249, 251
Naturphilosophie, 4, 9, 10, 11, 65, 125, 133, 151,
    170, 202, 248, 257, 270, 301n57
Naumberg, Margaret, 103, 104–106, 118,
    313n67
NCDS. *See* Normal Child Development Study
negative proposition, 283–284
neo-Lamarckianism, 61, 128
neo-pragmatist, 256
Neurath, Otto, 261
neurobehavioral model of mind, 201
neurobehavioral theory of development of con-
    sciousness, 242–243, *243*
neurobiology, 132–133, 134–139
neuroembryology, 201, 249
Neurological Institute of New York, 97, 99,
    130, 208
neuromuscular development, of infant, 203
neurophysiology, 57–58
New Divinity movement, 24, 25–26, 40, 45
New Republic, 90, 94, 112, 120, 154, 194,
    309nn32,34,37
New School for Social Research, 181
New York avant garde. *See* Mitchell, Lucy S.;
    Mitchell, Wesley
New York Psychoanalytic Society, 94
New York Times, 207
Newton, Isaac, 72, 270, 274
Newtonian science, 14, 25, 53, 54, 55, 151, 168,
    300n45
Niebuhr, Reinhold, 195–196
Nietzsche, Friedrich W., 12, 107, 111, 159
nihilism, 7

Nineteenth Century (journal), 29
Nobel Prize, 170–171
nominalism, 283; Rorty's, 18; Bentley's,
    266–268
Normal Child Development Study (NCDS),
    201, 208; advisory council of, 209–210;
    Coghill's work with, 213; Dewey's work
    with, 209–211
Norton, Andrew, 25
NRC. *See* National Research Council

objective introvert, 117
Oil City High School, 39
On the Genesis of Species (Mivart), 30
ontogeny, 124, 130, 139, 140; presence of mind
    in, 288–292
"ontological," definition of term, by Hook, 263
operationalism, 281
Oppenheim, James, 216, 309n32
ordered variation, 165
organicism, 53
original sin, 27, 196
The Origins of Dewey's Instrumentalism
    (White), 257, 258–259
Orton, Samuel, 210
Ostwald, Wilhelm, 10, 108, 142, 151, 318n5
"Other Messiahs" (Bourne), 120
Outlines of Psychology (Herrick), 65

Palmer, George, 64
pantheism, 37, 39
"The Pantheism of Spinoza" (Dewey), 38
Parent (magazine), 182
parent-child interaction, 189
parent-education group, 186–187, 191,
    324nn26,27
Parke, Robert, 81–82
Parker, Francis W., 81–82, 209
Partialists, 24, 25
Partisan Review (journal), 276
Pauley, Philip, 70
Pauli, Wolfgang, *169*
Peirce, Charles Sanders, 1, 8, 37, 42, 64
perception, aesthetic, 57, 154, 155, 162–163, 200,
    319n22
Perry, Mary, 185–186
pessimism, Weberian, 309n20
Pestalozzi, Johann H., 87
Peterson, Frederick, 130
Pfluger, Edward, 69
Phantom Public (Lippmann), 194
phenomenal experience, 272–273
Phenomenology of Spirit (Hegel), 13, 125, 178

Philosophy of Nature (Hegel), 245
philosophy of science, 125–126
phylogenetic traits, 218
phylogeny, 127, 140
physicalism, 7
physiology, 33
Picasso, Pablo, 155
Pinter, Harold, 206
Planck, Max, 164
plastic form, 154
platoon system, of classroom use, 90
Play School, 88, 93, 97, 100, 101, 105
Poincaré, Henri, 164
Poland, 114
Polish National Committee, 114
positivism: logical, 256, 259–260, 261, 263, 267, 269, 281–282; post-, 274–275
post-impressionism, 3, 152, 155, 156–160, 166
post-modern relativism, 7
post-modernism, 255
post-positivism, 274–275
post-structuralism, 274–275
Pound, Ezra, 154
pragmatism, 85, 106–107, 274–276; and liberal reform, 192–195; linguistic turn in, 256; and romanticism, 309n20
pragmatism, of Dewey, 132; cultural critique of, 12–13, 109–110; revival of, 17–18; Rorty critique of, 256–257, 275, 276–277
Prall, David W., 319n22
Pratt, Caroline, 93, 97, 101, 105
predestination, 24, 26–27, 29, 30
Preyer, William, 45
primitive reaction, in infant, 217–218
principles of development, 34; Coghill on, 214–216; McGraw on, 222–223
"Principles of Mental Development" (Dewey), 74
Principles of Psychology (James), 51
probability, and belief, 27–28
The Process of Government (Bentley), 267
progressive evolution, 67–68
progressivism, 85, 92, 103, 104–105, 106, 322n2
Project for a Scientific Psychology (Freud), 127, 131, 201
The Promise of Pragmatism: Modernism and the Crisis of Knowledge and Authority (Diggins), 4
prone locomotion, 221, 240–241, *241*
proposition: affirmative, 16–17, 283; as distinct from judgment, 16; generic, 219; negative, 283–284; universal, 220, 223
propositional knowledge, 7, 237

psychoanalysis, 94–95, 140; Dewey's critique of, 122–124, 126, 135, 141, 143–144, 197. *See also* Freudianism
psychobiology, 52, 65–66, 151, 192–193, 208, 225
psychological distance, 155, 271
psychological experiments, of Dewey, 46–47
Psychological Review, 66, 304n32
psychology, Dewey on, 63–64
Psychology (Dewey), 8, 46, 48, 51, 95, 258
"The Psychology of Consciousness" (Dewey), 299n18
The Psychology of Number (Dewey & McLellan), 71–72, 87, 259, 303n17
psychophysical, 119
The Public and Its Problems (Dewey), 15, 178, 179, 275
Public Opinion (Lippmann), 194

quantitative judgment, 236–237
quantum mechanics, 14, 172, 173
The Quest for Certainty (Dewey), 150, 167–168, 169, 172, 173, 261

Randall, John, 257, 263
Rappleye, Willard, 210
Ratner, Joseph, 256, 257, 260, 274
Raup, Robert, 132–133, 161
realism, 269, 270, 282, 341n10; common-sense, 37; emergent, 283; epistemological, 163; imitative, 79–80; psychological, 195
recollecting/remembering, 143
reconstruction, 11–12, 215; reconstruction/redirection, 284n8
recurrence, 161–162, 164, 166–167, 211, 212, 215, 235–236, 238
reductionism, 7, 163, 261
"Reflex Arc Concept in Psychology" (Dewey), 52
reflex arc theory, 59
reflex theory, 199
reflexive behavior, *214*, 217–218
regression, 111, 128, 238
Reichenbach, Hans, 260, 263, 269
reinforcement theory, 183–184
relativism, 7, 163
Relativity in Man and Society (Bentley), 267
reminiscence, 143
Renoir, Pierre-Auguste, 152, 155
revery consciousness, 141
RGEB. *See* Rockefeller General Education Board
Ribot, Theodule, 46, 299n23

Rignano, Eugenio, 133, 161–162, 166, 211, 212, 231, 235–236
Riley, Henry, 66
Robinson, James Harvey, 118, 125
Rockefeller, Steven, 26, 294n6
Rockefeller Archive Center, 190
Rockefeller Foundation, 91, 176, 191, 194
Rockefeller General Education Board (RGEB), 210
Rockefeller Institute, 94
Rockefeller Trust, 180
Romanes, George, 31, 78
romanticism, 110, 309n20
Roosevelt, Theodore, 108
Rorty, Richard, 17, 107, 263, 295n9; on American politics, 276–277; criticism of Dewey by, 5, 18, 61, 251, 255, 256–257, 265–266, 269–270, 275, 279; on cultural liberalism, 276–277; on Freud, 270–271; theory of mind of, 270–271, 272
Rousseau, Jean-Jacques, 86, 87, 88, 105, 196, 197
Roux, Wilhelm, 130
Royce, Josiah, 49
Rugg, Harold, 103
Ruml, Beardsley, 95, 96, 176, 180–181, 210
Russell, Bertrand, 260, 267–268, 269, 280, 281, 282, 314n6
Ryan, Alan, 4, 277, 294n6
Ryder, John, 9

Sachs, Bernard, 130, 210
St. Louis Hegelians, 9, 37–38, 44
Santayana, George, 9, 10
Sawtell, Ruth, 102
Schelling, Friedrich, 9, 29, 57, 65
schematogram, 102
Schneider, Herbert, 257, 264–265
school, experimental, 87–90
School Review, 86
Schools for Tomorrow (Dewey & Dewey), 87–88, 90
Schopenhauer, Arthur, 9
Schrödinger, Erwin, 151
Schumpeter, Joseph, 94
science: Baconian, 25; and democracy, 179–180, 193–195; experimental, 128, 129; in modernity, 6–8, 33, 179–180; Newtonian, 14, 25, 53, 54, 151, 168, 300n45; philosophy of, 125–126; relationship to art, 114, 163–165
Science of Logic (Hegel), 38, 71, 72–73, 245
scientific naturalism, 9–11
Scottish school of intuitionism, 37

Sears, Robert, 189
segmental theory of growth, 103
self-confidence, 98, 248
self-consciousness, 9, 10, 46, 50–51, 155, 223, 242, 269–273, 288–289, 305n9
self-control, 175
self-deception, 122–123, 140
self-justification, 271
self-reflection, 305n9
Seligman, E. R., 94
Senn, Milton, 186, 206, 325
sensorimotor development, in infant, 202–203, 233
serial order, 212–213
serviceable associated habits, 78
settlement movement, 81, 85, 93
Seven Arts (journal), 94, 104, 105, 107, 110, 112, 309n32
Sherrington, Charles, 99, 120, 133, 134
Shook, John, 282, 283, 341n10
Sidis, Boris, 47
Simon, Theodore, 188
simple extrovert, 117
Sins of Science (Klyce), 117
Sleeper, Ralph, 341n10
slow-delta-wave brain activity, 234–235
Small, Albion, 67, 81
Smith, Meredith, 132–133, 161
Smith, Ray, 334n35
Smith, Roy, 234–235
social control, 89–90, 324n34
social network analysis, 293n2
social progressives, 17, 85
social science philanthropy, 180–181
Society as the Patient (L. K. Frank), 192
Society for Research in Child Development (SRCD), 182
Society for the Scientific Study of Consciousness, 288
Sontag, Lester, 189
soul, 58
"Soul and Body" (Dewey), 57
Southern Illinois University, 284
Soviet Union, 149–150
Spemann, Hans, 130
Spencer, Herbert, 9, 40, 47, 279
Spinoza, Baruch, 9, 39
SRCD. *See* Society for Research in Child Development
Stalinism, 197
standardized test, 93
startle reflex. *See* Moro reflex
Stein, Edith, 152

Stein, Leo, 152, 154
Sternberg, Robert J., 294n8
Sternglass, Ernest, 301n53
stimulus-response theory, 44, 214
Stoddard, George, 188, 326n39
stream of consciousness, 142
Studies in Logical Theory (Dewey), 11, 63, 65, 73–74, 95, 96, 200, 258, 304n32
subconscious, 119, 143–146, 317n48
subjective introvert, 117
subjectivism, 140
suggestion, as learning tool, 76–77
Sullivan, Harry Stack, 66
Sulloway, Frank, 127–128, 316n31
Swenson, E. A., 215
symbolic logic, 261
Szasz, Thomas, 320n49

Tammany Hall, 91, 114
Tasker, Irene, 121, 313n67
taste/exercise evangelical movement, 26
Taylor, Charles, 286–287
Teachers College, Columbia University, 96, 176, 182, 185
tension, 192, 212, 321n65
Thelen, Esther, 241, 242
theory of behavior development, 214–216
theory of emotion, 63, 77–80
theory of gravity, 55, 56, 72–73; Dewey's, 245–246; Hegel's, 245
theory of mind, 63; of Freud, 127–128, 135, 136, 140, 141–142, 270, 271; of Rorty, 270–271, 272
theory of mind, of Dewey, 125–127, 128, 134–136, 137–138, 140, 141–142, 213; criticism of, 270
theory of ontogeny, 78
theory of relativity and quantum physics, 167
theory of unconscious, Freud's, 133
theory of universal gravitation, Newton's, 25
thermodynamics: first law of, 54–55, 57; second law of, 54–55, 56
Thomas, William I., 67, 81, 164
Thoreau, Henry David, 29
Thorndike, Edward L., 95, 182, 183–184, 210
thought, suppression of and thinking, 121
Thoughts and Things (Baldwin), 304n32
Tilney, Frederick, 176, 315n18; and "American School" of neurology, 11, 65; brain evolution studies of, 208–209, 209; histological study of, 238; influence on McGraw, 216; on NCDS advisory council, 210
Tononi, Giulio, 290

Torrey, H. A. P. (Hap), 37, 42
Torrey, William, 45, 46
trait, phylogenetic, 218. *See also* generic traits
"transaction," as operational term, 268–269
transcendentalists, 29
Trendelenburg, Friedrich, 44
Tresca, Carlo, 276
Trotsky, Leon, 197–198
Tufts, James, 49, 50, 64
Tufts University, 233

ultimate/irreducible trait, 264, 331n67
unconscious cerebration, 299n23
Unconscious Memory (Romanes), 31
Union Theological Seminary, 195
Unitarianism, 25, 33
universal convertibility, of energy, 56–57, 59, 60–61
universal mind, 270
universal proposition, 220, 223
Universalist sect, of Calvinism, 24
The Universe (Klyce), 116
University Elementary School. *See* Laboratory School (University of Chicago)
University of Chicago, 11, 42, 52, 61, 62, 64, 66, 67, 81, 82, 266. *See also* Laboratory School
University of Cincinnati, 66
University of Edinburgh, 167
University of Iowa, 186, 188, 192
University of Kansas, 213
University of Michigan, 27, 43, 47, 49
University of Minnesota, 49
University of South Carolina, 281
University of Vermont, 23, 29, 37
utilitarianism, 15

verification theory of knowledge and truth, 17
Vienna Circle, 17, 256, 260, 261, 281
Vincent, George, 176
Virchow, Rudolf, 44

Wald, Lillian, 94
Walden School, 105, 313n67
Wallace, Alfred, 31
war dissidents, Dewey on, 309n37
Warner, Francis, 76, 77
Watson, John B., 101, 102, 183, 184, 199, 204, 210, 307n48
Webb, Beatrice, 105
Webb, Sydney, 105
Weech, A. A., 244–245

Index

Weinbach, A. C., 235, 243–244, 246, 248, 334n34
Welch, Livingston, 331n76
Welfare Research Station, 186
Wellman, Beth, 188
Westbrook, Robert, 4, 277, 294n6, 310n45
Wetzel, Norman, 244–245
Weyl, Walter, 94
White, Morton G., 256, 257–260
White, William, 133–134
White House Conference on Child Health and Protection, 187
White House Conference on Children, 182
Whitman, Charles O., 66–68
Wilson, Affia (JD's cousin), 36
Wilson, Woodrow, 114
Windle, W. F., 215
Wirt, William, 90, 97

Wistar Institute, 210, 213
Wittgenstein, Ludwig, 265
Woodbridge, Frederick, 9
Woods, Jimmy, 225
Woods, Johnny, 218–219, *219*, 225–226
Woodworth, Robert S., 97, 182, 210
Woolley, Helen Thompson, 96, 182, 205, 306n34
Wundt, Wilhelm, 10–11, 44, 46, 52, 57, 65, 68

Yale Divinity School, 49
Yale University, 180, 203, 210, 216
Yerkes, Robert, 108
Yezierska, Anzia, 114, 115, 116, 310n45

Zeeger, S. L., 245
Zelazo, Philip, 290

THOMAS C. DALTON is Senior Assistant to the Provost and Senior Research Associate with the Office of the Dean of the College of Liberal Arts at California Polytechnic State University, San Luis Obispo. He is author of *Early Experience and the Brain: An Historical and Interdisciplinary Synthesis* and co-editor (with Rand Evans) of *The Life Cycle of Psychological Ideas: Understanding Prominence and the Dynamics of Intellectual Change* and (with V. W. Bergenn) of *Beyond Heredity and Environment: Myrtle McGraw and the Maturation Controversy.* His scholarly research interests include historical studies of the developmental sciences, theoretical studies of consciousness, and the philosophy of mind.

www.ingramcontent.com/pod-product-compliance
Lightning Source LLC
Chambersburg PA
CBHW070450100426
42812CB00004B/1256